Technological Innovations in the Food Service Industry

Anshul Garg
Taylor's University, Malaysia

IGI Global
Scientific Publishing
Publishing Tomorrow's Research Today

Published in the United States of America by
IGI Global Scientific Publishing
701 East Chocolate Avenue
Hershey, PA, 17033, USA
Tel: 717-533-8845
Fax: 717-533-8661
E-mail: cust@igi-global.com
Website: https://www.igi-global.com

Library of Congress Cataloging-in-Publication Data

Names: Garg, Anshul, 1976- editor.
Title: Technological innovations in the food service industry / edited by Anshul Garg.
Description: Hershey, PA : IGI Global Scientific Publishing, [2025] | Includes bibliographical references and index. | Summary: "This book serves as a platform for academicians, scholars and practitioners in the food service and hospitality industry to explore the emerging trends and technologies that are expected to shape the future of the food service industry, including operational efficiency, customer experience, and supply chain management"-- Provided by publisher.
Identifiers: LCCN 2024053050 (print) | LCCN 2024053051 (ebook) | ISBN 9798369376836 (hardcover) | ISBN 9798369376843 (paperback) | ISBN 9798369376850 (ebook)
Subjects: LCSH: Food service--Technological innovations. | Food industry and trade--Technological innovations.
Classification: LCC TX943 .T43 2025 (print) | LCC TX943 (ebook) | DDC 664--dc23/eng/20241228
LC record available at https://lccn.loc.gov/2024053050
LC ebook record available at https://lccn.loc.gov/2024053051

British Cataloguing in Publication Data
A Cataloguing in Publication record for this book is available from the British Library.

Table of Contents

Detailed Table of Contents

Demographic shifts in economies across the world, the penetration of the Internet, cheaper data, and the availability of digital payment options have made online grocery services attractive. The pandemic precipitated customer behaviour towards online grocery services due to the convenience offered. Post COVID-19, businesses have switched over to hybrid working adding to the appeal of these services. Attractive discounts and reward points complemented by flexible delivery models have managed to lure a sizeable section of the users. The competition between unorganized, organized, and online grocery retail has now intensified. E-grocers are using technology to accurately forecast and drive demand, manage inventory efficiently and make informed decisions based on an understanding of consumer behaviour. E-grocers are also resorting to personalization to make product recommendations, satisfy customers, and build loyalty. This chapter attempts to map the digital transformation of the grocery sector to understand how the market has evolved over the years and where it is headed.

This chapter explores the evolution of social media's role within the Chinese food industry, emphasizing its profound impact on marketing strategies. The progression of the Internet from Web 1.0's static content to Web 4.0's immersive experiences has significantly influenced prominent local platforms such as WeChat, Weibo, Douyin and Xiaohongshu, which now play a crucial role in China's digital ecosystem. These platforms offer rich, interactive content and leverage big data for precise marketing, thereby enhancing brand engagement and consumer interaction. The chapter examines how social media marketing has transformed the food industry, providing an in-depth analysis of successful case studies. It also identifies key performance indicators and future trends. By delving into these elements, the chapter aims to offer actionable insights for food industry, enabling them to effectively utilize social media for branding and market expansion.

The restaurant world is fast and competitive with advancement in technology. Success in the business world heavily relies on customer happiness. Providing exceptional dining experiences to customers is no longer considered a luxury, but rather a necessity. Fortunately, the advent of AI has brought a wave of transformation in the restaurant industry. AI technology, restaurants can provide unmatched customer satisfaction. From personalized dining experiences to streamlining operations, AI is revolutionizing the industry by introducing innovative solutions in the competitive restaurant industry by enhancing food quality, kitchen efficiency, and customer service. AI ensures consistency, safety, and excellence in dining experiences through advanced algorithms and real-time data analytics. Exploring how AI-powered technologies streamline restaurant operations and elevate hospitality standards is the main focus of this study. Case studies include AI robots manage various services showcasing AI's potential to transform guest interactions and operational accuracy.

This chapter explores the transformative impact of self-service kiosks in the fast food industry in the Philippines. The chapter traces the humble beginnings of kiosks in the early 2000s and examines their evolution as fast-food chains recognized the need to enhance customer satisfaction and operational efficiency. The chapter discusses the practical advantages of kiosks. Despite these hurdles, the positive customer experience and operational benefits have driven the widespread adoption of kiosks in the fast food industry. In response to these challenges, fast food chains have made significant investments in upgrading their kiosk systems, incorporating features such as intuitive interfaces, multilingual support, and seamless payment options. The chapter provides recommendations for further enhancing efficiency and customer satisfaction, including mobile ordering and payment apps, AI integration for personalized recommendations, streamlined drive-thru operations, and improved delivery services.

Social media marketing has revolutionized the way businesses in the food industry engage with consumers, offering unprecedented opportunities alongside distinct challenges. This form of marketing leverages platforms like Facebook, Instagram, Twitter, and TikTok to promote products, engage with customers, and build brand loyalty. For the food industry specifically, social media provides a visual and interactive platform ideal for showcasing food products, sharing recipes, promoting restaurants, and influencing consumer behavior. This essay explores the key opportunities and challenges that social media marketing presents to the food industry, offering insights into how businesses can effectively navigate this dynamic landscape. By crafting visually appealing content that highlights food aesthetics, ingredients, and preparation methods, businesses can attract the attention of potential customers who are browsing for meal inspiration or restaurant recommendations.

While it is encouraging to see the food industry thriving, growing concerns exist about increased demand and reliance on plastic packaging. The convenience of plastic wraps for food and durable plastic containers for drinks, designed to prevent spillage, has led to a significant rise in plastic consumption. This chapter highlights the growing plastic waste associated with food delivery services and explores the potential health risks of plastic materials, including microplastics, in food delivery operations in Malaysia. By analysing existing policies and regulations on plastic use, this chapter highlights the need for enhanced sustainable practices in the food service industry. It aims to provide insights into balancing convenience with environmental responsibility and proposes strategies for mitigating the negative impacts of plastic consumption.

Social media has emerged as a pivotal force inside the food enterprise, basically reworking how manufacturers engage with clients, marketplace merchandise, and power sales. It explores the crucial function of social media advertising in the food enterprise, highlighting its capacity to influence consumer conduct, foster logo loyalty, and facilitate the discovery of recent products and dining reviews. Thru structures like Instagram, TikTok, and facebook, meals brands can connect to a worldwide target market, leveraging visually attractive content, influencer partnerships, and focused marketing to reach and engage clients. The integration of e- trade and food shipping services within these systems in addition streamlines the consumer journey, bearing in mind seamless transitions from discovery to purchase. Additionally, the chapter delves into emerging developments together using AI and data analytics for personalized marketing, and the significance of user-generated content material.

As technological facilities and devices become increasingly popular in restaurants, restaurant consumers are increasingly influenced by technologies. With the increase in consumer health needs, the impact of technology on consumer health has gradually received more attention. This study employs bibliometrics and thematic analysis methods to review and analyse 52 English journal articles from WoS and Scopus from five aspects: research focus, time overlay, methodological characteristics, theoretical framework, and research topics. The results reveal that previous studies have explored the relationship between various types of restaurant technology and consumer health behaviours, health literacy, physical health, mental health, social health, and health literacy from multiple disciplines. In addition, existing studies mainly focus on the impact of health information presented by technology on consumer health. Finally, after a comprehensive review and summary of previous studies, this study puts forward specific suggestions for future research based on the gaps in existing research.

The chapter explores the transformation created by technology driven online sensory marketing in the food sector. The growing competition and prominence of e-commerce in the food industry has made marketers exhibit intangibility elements as equivalent as tangible attributes of their food products in the digital platforms by employing sensory marketing techniques for positive customer evaluation of their brands. It is essential to use all five senses of sensory marketing to create enduring experiences and foster brand loyalty among the target market. This chapter, backed by previous research, investigates how sensory elements such as tactile, gustatory, olfactory, and auditory can be better presented in digital platforms in order to obtain effective appeals in the communications. This chapter also analyzes the evidence of past research on how sensory marketing accelerates online consumers experiences and engagements in e-commerce platforms in various dimensions.

This paper explores the successful adoption of technological innovations in the food service industry, focusing on restaurant automation, mobile ordering and delivery platforms, and the use of AI and data analytics. Through case studies, it highlights how these technologies have transformed operations, enhanced customer experiences, and improved efficiency. Restaurant automation optimizes processes and reduces labor costs with smart kitchen technologies, while mobile platforms like UberEats and DoorDash expand market reach and convenience. AI and data analytics enable businesses to personalize services, optimize supply chains, and enhance decision-making. The paper also addresses challenges such as workforce displacement and data privacy. Looking forward, emerging technologies like augmented reality (AR), virtual reality (VR), blockchain, robotics, and sustainability innovations will further shape the industry. Continuous innovation and adaptability are essential for businesses to remain competitive, with a focus on balancing technology with human interaction.

courts, as this can help to implement smooth and efficient cashless payment systems. By understanding the factors that influence the adoption of cashless payment, stakeholders can address these issues and improve consumers' experiences, leading to more convenience, faster transactions and shorter queues at food courts, which can benefit both consumers and food court operators. Moreover, this research can provide insights that can promote the use of cashless payments and ensure that everyone, regardless of age or technology skills, can participate in a cashless society.

Digital transformation and technology development in Industry Revolution (IR) 4.0 are here to stay. The automation, digitalization, robotizing, and a tsunami of innovations that make up IR 4.0 are making their presence stronger as days go by. Newer technologies, like AI, Big Data, the Internet of Things (IoT), and machine-based algorithms, have given the world various choices of high-speed connectivity through online bookings, online shopping, chats, blogs, and virtual realities. AI and technologies have infused digital transformation and continued to dramatically alter the hospitality industry. This qualitative paper aims to explore what type of digitalization has been incorporated and the challenges faced aftermath. The interview results from eight hospitality managers reveal that all hotels except one have incorporated newer technologies mildly aligned with IR 4.0 within their hotels. All the hotels face trials related to technology, namely budgets, rapid upgrading of digitalization, and insufficient technical employees to oversee the administration of these systems.

This paper attempts to investigate how satisfied customers are with online meal delivery services in the Klang Valley, an industry that is expanding quickly due to changes in consumer behaviour and technological improvements. This study aims to examine the relationship between customer satisfaction and important elements including food quality, sales promotion, and e-service quality, as the demand for efficiency and convenience grows. The study will collect data from purchasers who use online meal delivery services by using an online questionnaire and a quantitative research approach. The results will shed light on consumer preferences and expectations, which is critical for improving the level of services and streamlining business operations in the food delivery industry.

Preface

In today's rapidly evolving food service industry, the integration of technology has become essential for maintaining competitive advantage and meeting the ever-changing demands of consumers. As editors of *Technological Innovations in the Food Service Industry*, we believe that robust research plays a pivotal role in not only understanding these advancements but also in addressing the challenges they present.

Our industry is at a crossroads, where the intersection of technology and food service has opened new avenues for efficiency, customer engagement, and sustainability. However, many food service businesses struggle to keep pace with these innovations. This book aims to bridge that gap by providing a comprehensive examination of the most significant technological trends, underpinned by rigorous research and practical applications.

Research is the cornerstone of informed decision-making. In the chapters that follow, we delve into crucial topics such as the adoption of contactless technologies, the implications of artificial intelligence in menu planning, and the potential of blockchain for enhancing food safety. Each section is backed by empirical studies, case analyses, and industry insights, offering readers not only theoretical knowledge but also practical strategies for implementation.

By highlighting the benefits and challenges associated with these technologies, we provide a roadmap for stakeholders to navigate the complexities of modern food service. Our aim is to empower professionals with the insights needed to leverage technology effectively—whether it's enhancing operational efficiency through automation or improving customer satisfaction via personalized experiences driven by data analytics.

Moreover, this book addresses the critical issue of sustainability in the food service sector. As technological advancements offer solutions to reduce food waste and improve energy efficiency, our research emphasizes how businesses can adopt these practices not only for compliance but as a means of fostering long-term growth and customer loyalty.

We understand that change can be daunting, especially when it involves integrating new technologies into established practices. However, through well-researched strategies and successful case studies, we aim to equip our audience with the tools to face these challenges head-on. The insights presented here will help you identify which innovations are best suited for your operations, ensuring that you can adapt and thrive in this competitive landscape.

In *Technological Innovations in the Food Service Industry*, we present a diverse range of chapters that highlight the critical role of technology in reshaping the food service landscape. Each chapter offers unique insights and practical solutions to the challenges faced by industry stakeholders. Below is a summary of the key themes explored throughout the book:

Chapter 1: Digital Transformation of Grocery Delivery Services in India

This chapter examines the evolution of grocery delivery services in India, highlighting how demographic changes, internet penetration, and the pandemic have accelerated the shift to online grocery shopping. It discusses how e-grocers leverage technology for demand forecasting, inventory management, and personalized customer experiences, ultimately reshaping the market landscape and consumer behavior.

Chapter 2: Harnessing the Power of Social Media Marketing to Transform the Food Industry in China

Focusing on the Chinese food industry, this chapter explores the transformative impact of social media marketing. It details how platforms like WeChat and Douyin have evolved to offer immersive consumer interactions and targeted marketing strategies. Through case studies, it provides actionable insights on maximizing social media's potential for brand engagement and market expansion.

Chapter 3: Optimizing Food Quality and Customer Service in Restaurants through AI-Powered Monitoring Systems

This chapter highlights the revolutionizing effects of AI in restaurants, where customer satisfaction has become paramount. It discusses AI's role in enhancing food quality, operational efficiency, and personalized dining experiences, showcasing how data analytics and advanced algorithms can transform customer interactions and restaurant operations.

Chapter 4: Kiosk Revolution: The Transformation of Fast Food in the Philippines

Here, we trace the journey of self-service kiosks in the fast food sector in the Philippines. This chapter covers their initial introduction, evolution, and the operational benefits they bring, including enhanced customer experience and efficiency. It also offers recommendations for further integration of technology to elevate service quality.

Chapter 5: Social Media Marketing and Its Role in The Food Industry

This chapter examines how social media has transformed engagement strategies in the food industry. It discusses the unique challenges and opportunities presented by various platforms and offers insights on crafting compelling visual content to attract and retain customers.

Chapter 6: Navigating Sustainability: Addressing Plastic Waste and Health Risks in Food Delivery Services in Malaysia

Addressing the urgent issue of plastic waste, this chapter explores the environmental and health risks associated with food delivery services in Malaysia. It emphasizes the need for sustainable practices and offers strategies to mitigate the negative impacts of plastic consumption in the food service industry.

Chapter 7: Role of Social Media Marketing in Food Industry

Expanding on the previous chapter, this exploration of social media's influence delves into how brands can effectively connect with consumers through engaging content and strategic marketing. It highlights the importance of adapting to digital trends and leveraging analytics for optimal outreach.

Chapter 8: The Impact of Evolving Technologies on Restaurant Consumer Health: A Systematic Review

This systematic review analyzes the relationship between restaurant technologies and consumer health outcomes. It identifies gaps in existing research and suggests directions for future studies, emphasizing the importance of understanding health impacts in an increasingly tech-driven dining environment.

Chapter 9: Impact of Content-Driven Online Sensory Marketing on Customers' Food-Buying Intentions

This chapter investigates the role of sensory marketing in e-commerce, highlighting how the integration of sensory elements can enhance customer experiences and drive purchasing intentions. It offers insights into effective marketing strategies that engage all five senses to foster brand loyalty.

Chapter 10: Successful Stories on the Usage of Technologies in Service Industries

Through case studies, this chapter showcases how technological innovations—such as automation and mobile ordering—have transformed the food service industry. It discusses the challenges these innovations present while emphasizing the importance of continuous adaptation and innovation.

Chapter 11: The Role of Social Media Marketing in the Food Industry

Focusing on the tactical aspects of social media marketing, this chapter discusses strategies for leveraging analytics and maintaining authentic customer relationships. It also anticipates future trends in social commerce and the integration of emerging technologies.

Chapter 12: NEXT-GEN EATS: Tech, Trends, And Sustainability

This chapter explores how advanced technologies are redefining the food service sector while promoting sustainability. It examines the role of automation and AI in improving operational efficiency and aligning practices with global sustainability goals.

Chapter 13: The Effective Role of Mobile Apps in Food Service Industry

This chapter discusses the profound impact of mobile applications on the restaurant industry, highlighting how these platforms enhance customer convenience and streamline ordering processes. It explores the growing consumer preference for mobile technology in food service interactions.

Chapter 14: The Future on Your Plate: How Food Technology is Becoming a Driver of Sustainability

Here, we explore the transformative role of food technology in promoting sustainable practices. The chapter highlights how innovations can reduce waste and improve customer satisfaction while presenting the challenges and opportunities in this evolving landscape.

Chapter 15: Augmented Reality (AR) Dining Experiences: Transforming Customer Engagement and Interaction

This chapter investigates how AR technology enhances dining experiences, focusing on its impact on customer satisfaction and engagement. It provides guidelines for effective AR integration, emphasizing the importance of continuous innovation and feedback.

Chapter 16: The Impact of Technology on Payment Methods in the Food Service Sector in Singapore

This exploration of cashless payment systems in Singapore examines consumer acceptance and the factors influencing the transition to cashless transactions in food courts. It highlights the benefits of improved efficiency and consumer experience in this evolving payment landscape.

Chapter 17: Digital Transformation and its Challenges in the Hospitality Industry in Malaysia

This qualitative study reveals the challenges and successes of digital transformation within Malaysia's hospitality sector. It highlights the integration of new technologies and the obstacles that management faces, providing insights for navigating Industry Revolution 4.0.

Chapter 18: Assessment of Customer Satisfaction in Online Food Delivery Within Klang Valley

Focusing on the burgeoning online food delivery sector, this chapter analyzes customer satisfaction metrics in the Klang Valley. It identifies key factors influencing consumer preferences, offering insights for improving service quality and operational efficiency.

Chapter 19: Innovative Solutions for a more Sustainable Food Supply Chain: Role of New Technologies in Food Waste Prevention

This chapter presents a thorough overview of how IoT and blockchain technologies can be harnessed to address food waste in the supply chain. It discusses certification systems and their potential in mitigating food waste while providing actionable insights for the industry.

Through these chapters, we aim to equip readers with a comprehensive understanding of how technology is shaping the future of the food service industry, addressing current challenges while highlighting the opportunities that lie ahead.

In conclusion, this book is more than just a collection of information; it is a vital resource for anyone seeking to navigate the complexities of technology in the food service industry. By grounding our exploration in rigorous research, we aspire to illuminate the path forward, enabling food service professionals to embrace innovation with confidence and foresight.

Chapter 1

Digital Transformation of Grocery Delivery Services in India:
Understanding the Past, Present, and Future

Venkatesh Ganapathy
Presidency University, India

Chithambar Gupta
https://orcid.org/0009-0002-1364-5425
Presidency University, India

Radhika Arora
https://orcid.org/0000-0003-1519-9633
Presidency Business School, India

ABSTRACT

Demographic shifts in economies across the world, the penetration of the Internet, cheaper data, and the availability of digital payment options have made online grocery services attractive. The pandemic precipitated customer behaviour towards online grocery services due to the convenience offered. Post COVID-19, businesses have switched over to hybrid working adding to the appeal of these services. Attractive discounts and reward points complemented by flexible delivery models have managed to lure a sizeable section of the users. The competition between unorganized, organized, and online grocery retail has now intensified. E-grocers are using technology to accurately forecast and drive demand, manage inventory efficiently and make informed decisions based on an understanding of consumer behaviour. E-grocers are also resorting to personalization to make product recommendations, satisfy customers, and build loyalty. This chapter attempts to map the digital transformation of the grocery sector to understand how the market has evolved over the years and where it is headed.

DOI: 10.4018/979-8-3693-7683-6.ch001

INTRODUCTION

The retail sector in India accounts for 11% of GDP. The digital world has made consumers seek convenience in their purchase transactions, leading to a monumental growth in online shopping. Across the globe, consumer expenditure on online business increased from $65 billion in 2019-20 to $100 billion in 2021-21. This is expected to reach $250 billion as per Red Seer Consulting. The grocery sector trailed other e-commerce businesses.

The retail market in India accounts for 10% of the nation's GDP. Additionally, the retail sector provides jobs for 8% of India's population.

The predicted grocery retail spending in India in 2030 is approximately $1.10 trillion. This prediction aligns with a report from the Boston Consulting Group's Retailers Association of India. The total grocery retail sales are predicted to reach INR 85.46 trillion in 2030. This figure considers the growth rates of modern and traditional grocery stores, as well as online grocery sales. India's grocery retail market had a 7.2% CAGR between 2020-2022. India will be the second-largest grocery market globally by 2036 if the current compound annual growth rate (CAGR) persists.

According to a 2021 forecast by The Institute of Grocery Distribution, U.K. (IGD), India ranked as the third-largest grocery retail market in the world as of 2022. In 2022, the market size of India's grocery retail was $656 billion. The supermarket format is the most prevalent in the Indian grocery market. In 2021, supermarkets accounted for an estimated 49% of the Indian grocery market. This is followed by convenience stores at 43% and hypermarkets at 8%. It is predicted that India's online grocery market will increase at an annual compound growth rate of 37.1% between 2021 and 2030. India's "quick commerce" market, which promises grocery delivery in 10-15 minutes, is expected to further boost the growth of online grocery shopping.

The online grocery market is expected to grow at 57% CAGR and reach $18.2 billion by 2024. The market (as per Mintel) will be worth £22.4 billion by 2025. India's online grocery market is expected to grow at a CAGR of 37.1% from 2021 to 2028.

Kirana Stores (Neighbourhood Stores): Dominating the Indian market

90% of India's grocery retail sales happened in neighbourhood Kirana stores. These stores offered fresh produce, free delivery to consumers' homes, informal credit and an understanding of customer needs at a personal level. But things changed during the pandemic.

While modern grocery retail outlets in India numbered more than 8,000 in 2021, this is dwarfed by the estimated 12.8 million traditional grocery retailers, such as Kirana stores and corner shops. However, despite their prevalence, traditional grocery retailers experienced a decline in 2020, dropping from 12.83 million stores in 2018 to 12.64 million in 2020, potentially due to the COVID-19 pandemic. This number rose again in 2021 to 12.79 million stores.

Kirana stores in India will remain significant due to personalized service and proximity. Organized and online formats will drive substantial growth, fueled by factors like urbanization, increasing disposable income, and technological advancements. While traditional "kirana" stores still hold a large market share (around 61% in 2019), organized grocery retail is on the rise. This growth is fueled by factors like foreign direct investment, changing consumer preferences, and urbanization. Large, organized retailers are partnering with local Kirana stores to leverage their strengths, such as proximity to customers and personalized service while expanding their reach and efficiency. E-commerce giants like Flipkart and Amazon are also engaging in similar collaborations.

The Kirana stores that faced competition from organized retail now face the competitive threat from e-grocers. But the Kirana stores in India have continued to sustain. They were able to provide services to customers during the lockdowns imposed by the government to contain the spread of the Covid-19 pandemic. Kirana King is a retail-as-a-service start-up that has enabled Kirana stores in Rajasthan to transform themselves into super stores. Technology has played a major role in this transition. Kirana King has a distinct and unique business model that is starkly different from other online players like D Mart, Zepto, Blink It, Dunzo, Big Basket, Jio Mart etc.

88% of the retail sector in India remains unorganized. However, the growth of the online grocery sector has intensified the competition between the Kirana stores, offline retail stores and e-grocers. Online grocery retail is perceived as convenient by shoppers and the discounts and offers add to the appeal of the services. The inbound marketing efforts of e-grocers have led to increased customer engagement. Customers have been spoilt by choice and becoming more demanding than ever. Customer experience and personalization have become an integral part of the marketing strategies of online grocery retailers. Traditional retailers are increasingly going digital, integrating technology to compete with organized retailers. This includes online ordering, digital payments, and delivery services.

Large, organized retailers are partnering with local Kirana stores for efficient delivery and network expansion. Both organized and unorganized retail have growth potential, with the former leveraging technology and the latter capitalizing on personalized service and community ties. Retailers focusing on personalized experiences through data analytics and customer-centric approaches are likely to thrive. The ability to adapt to changing consumer preferences, integrate technology, and ensure a robust supply chain will be crucial for long-term success.

Drivers of Online Grocery Shopping

Changes in consumer lifestyles, growing urbanization, smartphone penetration, a 24x7 workplace, and growth in disposable incomes are factors that have led to the growth of online grocery shopping. Increased internet penetration, cheaper data and improved digital literacy have stimulated the demand for online grocery services. The pandemic accelerated the adoption of digital technologies in the grocery retail sector, including online ordering, home delivery, and digital payments. This shift forced Kirana stores to adapt, with many going digital to meet consumer demand.

During the pandemic, the share of grocery spending in India rose to an estimated 73.4% in 2020 due to reduced overall spending that prioritized essential items. While this is expected to stabilize to around 65% by 2025, it highlights the pandemic's impact on consumer spending habits. The pandemic forced large retailers to cut costs, leading to the emergence of digital stores and the relocation of physical stores to cheaper locations. This shift was facilitated by technology and data analytics, which helped retailers manage supply chain disruptions and expand their reach by collaborating with local Kirana shops. This period also saw incredible digital adaptation among Kirana stores, with around 1 million going digital to meet consumer demand during lockdowns. This digital transformation, enabling online ordering and delivery, helped 80% of these stores see exponential growth in 2020.

The pandemic accelerated the adoption of home delivery options and digital payment methods like Phone Pe, Google Pay, Paytm, and Bharat Pe. This trend is expected to continue as both retailers, including Kirana stores, and customers have become comfortable with these options. The integration of online and offline retailing has gained momentum, enabling hyperlocal and fast deliveries while reducing the need for large warehouses. This trend led to a rise in "phygital" models, particularly among Kirana stores, combining the convenience of digital technology with the trust and familiarity of physical stores.

While the pandemic caused disruptions in supply chains, it also highlighted the importance of building more resilient and agile systems.

History and Evolution of Online Grocery Retail

Peapod and Net Grocer began experimenting with online grocery delivery services in the early 1990s in the US. Webvan began selling groceries online in the 90s and promised customers attractive discounts and a delivery time window of 30 minutes. However, the model was not sustainable. In 2001, Webvan filed for bankruptcy. Limited internet penetration, concerns about product quality and freshness and logistical challenges were some of the reasons these ventures failed.

The online grocery retail faced failure when the dotcom bubble burst in the late 90's. It was then described as the Bermuda Triangle of Retail. But during those years, the technology was premature and the one or two companies that took the risk of selling groceries online had to face the ignominy of winding up their businesses soon. High operating costs, inefficient delivery logistics and pervasiveness of organized retail formats led to many of the startups struggling to remain profitable.

Online grocery began achieving traction in 2010. Developments in mobile phone technology and the emergence of smartphones made mobile phone shopping a reality. Democratization of data resulted in increased patronage of mobile phones across the globe. Amazon, Tesco and Walmart invested heavily in online grocery platforms offering consumers convenience, attractive offers, competitive pricing and improved delivery options. In 2000, Ocado began selling groceries in the UK in the online mode. Despite several challenges in its operations, Ocado has maintained a grip on the market by investing in efforts to leverage technology and choosing creative ways to earn additional revenues. Ocado's proprietary online platform has been sold to other retailers in the UK. Ocado pioneered the use of automated warehouses and robotics for fulfilment to achieve accuracy in order processing and delivery. Over the years, Ocado has partnered with established supermarket chains and expanded its reach.

In India, the earliest online grocery business was formally launched by Big Basket. This was followed by regional players like Local Banya and Pepper Tap who managed to make a dent in the market, but they had to shut down their business when operations ceased to be profitable and the investment tap became dry. Urbanization, changing consumer lifestyles, increasing internet penetration and a growing Gen Y population were the earliest drivers of this development. Soon, other e-grocery players like Grofers (now Blink It) entered the market. These actors have managed to deal with the complexities in online grocery businesses like complex supply chains, perishability of grocery items and last-mile delivery issues. Now, e-grocers have a multitude of business models to cater to the needs of customers.

The grocery business is unique compared to other sectors. This is the reason why the online grocery business was slow to pick up. Grocery business is a low-margin business that has immense potential for growth in a huge market like India. But in the early days when online grocery shopping business models were available to customers, there were issues related to the freshness of groceries and green groceries available online. There were reports that customers would never patronize online grocery services because they were fastidious about the quality of groceries sold online. Customers were also concerned about making payments in advance through digital modes. The fear of cybercrimes still looms large in the minds of customers.

In the initial days, online grocery services were largely patronized by millennial customers who began valuing the convenience of ordering groceries online and getting them delivered at home.

Then a cataclysmic event that shook the globe changed everything. The Covid-19 pandemic created an atmosphere of fear in communities. Governments declared lockdowns. Many locations were declared containment zones. People were advised to stay indoors and maintain social distancing to protect themselves from contracting the dreaded virus. During such a crisis, the E-commerce businesses sprang into action using the challenges presented by the Covid-19 pandemic as an opportunity to reach out to customers.

The one sector that immensely benefited from such a black swan event was the online grocery business. If customers had any reservations about using these services, they couldn't do anything about it as they were by circumstances beyond their control. The impetus given by the Indian government to popularize digital payment gateways proved beneficial during such a crisis. Gradually, customers began using online grocery services during the pandemic and they also adapted to the practice of making digital payments. Despite critics cautioning that the online grocery business would face a slump once the pandemic abated, what happened in the new normal was unexpected. Despite some teething problems in the initial days of the new normal, e-grocery businesses continued to do business as usual. In the last two years, the growth of digital grocery businesses has been astounding.

The new normal after the COVID-19 pandemic was expected to diminish the prospects of online grocery services. But the sector has flourished in the new normal. The other start-ups that have entered this market have invested in technology, logistics, and last-mile delivery capabilities to meet the diverse needs of Indian consumers. These companies are also becoming more customer-centric so that they succeed in growing a loyal customer base.

Habits once formed are not easy to break. Customers used to the convenience of ordering groceries online during the pandemic continued with this practice. Most businesses resorted to a hybrid mode of working. This made those employees working from home appreciate the convenience of online grocery delivery services even more.

On their part, the e-grocery businesses have pushed the envelope by introducing different business models to cater to customer needs. Interestingly, e-grocery businesses face competition among themselves and also from local mom-and-pop stores and organized retail stores. Fulfilment processes were strengthened to improve their efficiency. Subscription models were introduced. The Click and Collect model where customers could order groceries online and pick the groceries from the store at a time convenient to them was introduced.

In early 2022, a few e-grocery start-ups launched quick commerce services promising customers delivery of groceries within a time window of 10 – 30 minutes. Even though this model attracted criticism from multiple quarters on account of the logistical issues associated, the fact remains that in the next two years, the quick commerce business model has not only stabilized but has also attained immense popularity among customers. The quick commerce model is capital-intensive and needs the setting up of dark stores in local regions to support hyperlocal delivery.

E-grocers have launched several innovations to lure customers to buy from them. They have also made attempts to encourage customers to indulge in repeat purchasing behaviours. The returns policy has been made robust. Product quality has improved. Customers are enticed through offers, reward schemes and loyalty points. Last-mile delivery efficiency has improved. The design of the websites and the apps have been upgraded to make them user-friendly. Information asymmetry between e-grocery businesses and customers has been reduced as e-grocers make it easy for customers to compare prices. Customers are also provided with the relevant information that they need.

Initially, online grocery retailers focused on selling groceries and non-perishable items like canned goods and household essentials. Improvement in technology and logistics led to an increase in the assortment of goods sold. Spurred by developments in the grocery sector, brick-and-mortar grocery chains have embraced an omnichannel approach. The integration of offline and online channels provides customers with greater flexibility and convenience. The sector has been marked by consolidation. Amazon acquired Whole Foods Market to strengthen its presence in the grocery market. In India, the TATAs invested in Big Basket. Zomato, the food delivery company, acquired Blink It. Dunzo was backed by Reliance, though it couldn't sustain its operations in the Indian market successfully.

Automation is being used to improve inventory management and make delivery processes more efficient. Customer data analytics is being deployed to draw unique insights into customer's buying preferences and patterns. These insights have enabled e-grocers to make informed decisions. For example, data analytics has made it easy to personalize customer experiences through appropriate product recommendations.

The Indian grocery retail market has undergone a significant evolution, driven by factors like changing consumer habits, government policies, increasing disposable income, and urbanization. This evolution has led to new business models focused on speed, efficiency, and affordability.

The grocery retail sector in India now consists of a diverse array of formats and business models. Each stage in this evolution is a result of changing consumer preferences, technological advancements, and innovative business strategies. Thus, we have local Kirana stores (Mom-and-Pop Stores) jostling for space with traditional retail formats, such as supermarkets hypermarkets and e-grocers. Going forward, customers' concerns about environmental issues will force e-grocers to reduce waste, opt for eco-friendly packaging, resort to responsible sourcing and promotion of local products.

Review of Literature

Online grocery shopping has been pervasive and disruptive providing services for educated, affluent and technically savvy customers (Dillahunt et al, 2019). Though margins are low, and profitability is modest, the online grocery sector remains an attractive business due to its immense potential. Perishability, variability of product, and frequency of shopping activity – are different characteristics of grocery shopping (Mortimer et al, 2016).

Indian retail has truly evolved from 1980 to 2020. Phygital (physical and digital) platforms have emerged in the last few years paving the path for omni-channel retail. Retail no longer serves merely a utilitarian purpose. Entertainment and social dimensions of retail need consideration while designing a truly omnichannel online shopping experience (Krishnamurthy & Venkitachalam, 2022).

The growth of e-commerce has led to factors conducive to the growth of online grocery retail (Habib & Hamadneh, 2021) with the pandemic driving a massive transformation in consumer behaviour. The convenience of ordering groceries using a smartphone, a user-friendly interface, offers and discounts and home deliveries are driving the growth of online grocery retail. In addition, security, information quality, payment methods, quality of service, quality of products, range of products, customer interface quality, and privacy are some of the variables that affect customer satisfaction in online grocery (Vasic et al, 2019) (Ali & Naushad, 2021) (Ahmad et al, 2017)

Product quality, variety and the availability of grocery items on demand are also factors that will exert a positive influence on a buyer's behaviour. The ability to track orders and superior delivery effectiveness are other factors that can lead to positive customer experience (Prasad & Raghu, 2020). Trust, after-sales service, price promotions and personalized recommendations impacted online grocery buying behaviour.

Advanced browsing, filtering, and search options, along with effective categorization can have a positive impact on customer satisfaction and improve profitability. The use of automation to reduce delivery costs and the use of click-and-collect models can reduce delivery costs. Generation of shopping lists that can be reused can improve e-grocery shopping efficiency (Karkkainen, 2015; Grudzien, 2020; Sodano, 2020).

Despite Americans' preference for in-store grocery shopping, many households have adopted online grocery shopping. Factors influencing behaviour include household income, education, race/ethnicity, age, gender, work status, and residential location. Higher-educated households are more likely to order food online (Saphores & Xu, 2021).

Millennials are attracted to online promotions and side-panel ads, while graphics and competitive pricing also influence their purchasing behaviour (Smith, 2011). Positive attitudes toward online grocery shopping, supported by the Theory of Planned Behavior (Blomqvist et al., 2015), encourage intentions to order groceries online. Ease of price comparison, changes in consumer attitudes, and logistical constraints impact e-grocery purchasing behaviour. The proportion of fresh products ordered online exceeds those purchased offline. Location, device use, and basket editing influence behaviour. This study explores customer behaviour shifts in the online grocery sector, focusing on socio-technical factors driving these changes (Munson et al., 2017).

Perceived usefulness and perceived ease of use influence online grocery shopping behaviour (Fong et al, 2020) in addition to trust and perceived security of the transactions (Ruangkanjanases et al, 2021) (Winnberg & Martensson, 2021). In online grocery retailing, brand relationship quality mediates the effect of online relational bonds on customer loyalty (Alagarsamy et al., 2021). A sense of community, driven by convenience, structural, financial, empathy, and social bonds, is the primary driver of brand loyalty. Efficiency, fulfilment, and privacy impact purchase intention and behavioral loyalty (Goutam et al., 2022). The Online Customer Experience-Attitude-Behavior Context (OCE-ABC) model has been proposed for online grocery retailing, where better customer experience leads to increased loyalty (Anshu et al., 2022). Reliability, responsiveness, and return policies can optimize customer satisfaction and influence repurchase intention (Singh & Rosengren, 2020). Consumers can co-create social values in online food delivery systems (Liu & Lin, 2020). Utilitarian and hedonic values are important in building cognitive and emotional relationships with customers (Al Nawas et al., 2021).

The association between behavioral intention to order groceries online and actual app use is moderated by household size with larger households likely to use e-grocery apps (Chakraborty et al, 2022). Technology readiness and e-service quality shape the intention to buy online (Goutam et al, 2022).

Lead time, order fill rate and delivery-service price were the variables considered for a study in Brazil. Order fill rate is the most important attribute. If the order cannot be properly fulfilled, it can compromise customer satisfaction (Dillahunt et al, 2019) in online grocery shopping.

Post Covid-19 pandemic, grocery shopping is characterized by consumer demand for healthy and nutritive grocery items (Kuijpers et al, 2020). A study found that customer engagement drives loyalty, specifically repurchase intention and positive word-of-mouth. Stores should focus on reducing perceived risk, increasing ease of use, and enhancing e-satisfaction and trust to improve customer engagement (Annisa & Ezni, 2021). Gamification is now being used to manipulate customer behaviour and influence customer experience with brand engagement playing a mediating role (Pour et al., 2021).

Retail giants like Kroger and Walmart have leveraged their traditional retail strengths to innovate in online shopping, offering seamless experiences and effective last-mile delivery (Karkkainen, 2015). The "click-and-collect" model, where customers can order online and pick up in-store, has been successful.

However, challenges like sub-optimal food quality have deterred customers from online grocery shopping. Ocado, a UK retailer, pioneered this space by disintermediating several stages of the supply chain and focusing on order taking, order picking or fulfilment, and order delivery (Mason, 2019).

Mental associations, including functional, relational, and premium store connections, foster positive attitudes and emotional bonds with customers, crucial for loyalty. Grocery retailers should focus on building emotional connections to enhance loyalty (Maggioni, 2016). Convenience and reliability are key factors in grocery delivery services, influencing customer satisfaction and loyalty. Responsiveness has no significant impact. Analyzing delivery service quality is crucial to enhancing customer satisfaction, loyalty, and repurchase intention (Chung et al., 2016). A new loyalty model proposes three conditions: no loyalty, latent loyalty, and true loyalty, influenced by marketing actions and switching costs (Ngobo, 2017). Urban-rural differences in loyalty were found in Lithuania (Pileliene & Zikiene, 2017). Offline-online congruence can positively impact customer loyalty (Ruiz-Molina et al., 2021).

Consumers' self-enrichment, self-gratification, and self-enablement influence emotional attachment, which in turn predicts behavioral loyalty and word-of-mouth (Vlachos et al., 2010). A study found that Dick and Basu's four loyalty typologies exist across all grocery product categories, with significant differences in loyalty proportions between categories. Men exhibit lower loyalty than women. True loyal consumers delay purchases, resist promotions, and reject variety-seeking. The study highlights the importance of building true loyalty for retention in the grocery industry (Moller et al., 2011).

In the initial days, consumers wishing to touch and feel grocery products were hesitant to order groceries online. Some consumers were reluctant to pay the delivery charges (Klepek & Bauerova, 2020). Slow delivery speed, inability to inspect grocery items and lack of trust dissuaded people from indulging in online grocery shopping. Focused efforts to improve product quality and delivery efficiency along with attempts at personalization could tilt the scales in favour of the e-grocers. Price-sensitive consumers in China shopped for groceries online less frequently as they had adverse perceptions about the freshness of food items and their quality (Zheng, Chen, Zhang & Wang, 2020).

An inadequate understanding of the online buying behaviour of consumers resulted in a tepid growth of the online grocery market in Germany (Gusken et al, 2019). Using mobile technologies to understand consumer behaviour and introducing business models catering to the specific needs of customers is important. These business models must also support innovations in grocery retail (Gupta & Nag, 2013). A strong supply chain is also crucial for the success of an online grocery store. Dark stores are e-commerce grocery fulfilment centres to serve the needs of online shoppers (Gibbs, 2016) and are responsible for the successful operation of the quick commerce model.

Offline retailers retaliated in response to the threat from online grocery retailers. Some offline retailers decided to explore online grocery services (Bauerova, 2019) further intensifying the competition in the marketplace.

Digital transformation in retail necessitates understanding the shift in consumer behaviour and addressing evolving consumer needs (Foncillas, 2020). A customer-centric approach to improve last-mile logistics in e-grocery delivery will lead to customer satisfaction (Olsson, 2021).

Sustainability remains a key priority for online retail, offering a competitive advantage. To achieve this, online retailers must align their ESG agenda with stakeholder needs and financial impact. Measuring environmental impacts, such as food waste and emissions, can lead to positive results, with online grocery retail reducing emissions by 8-41% in US cities (Astashkina et al, 2019).

To minimize waste, reduce lost sales, and deliver fresher products to consumers, omnichannel grocery firms should align with both store and online channel requirements, mitigate demand variability, extend product shelf life, and improve item-level shelf-life visibility (Saghiri et al., 2023). Three crucial performance metrics - product waste, lost sales, and freshness - are influenced by channel effect, demand fluctuation, product perishability, and shelf-life visibility (Saghiri et al., 2023). A study in Australia and Switzerland found that e-grocery websites in both countries fall short of meeting customer expectations (Kurnia and Schubert, 2023). As consumer behaviour changes amid technological advancements, it is essential to study the effectiveness of diverse e-tailing strategies on customer satisfaction and loyalty (Altintas et al., 2020). Top US grocery companies are investing heavily in online shopping, store operations, pickup/delivery systems, and advanced analytics to boost customer loyalty and profitability (Abbu et al., 2021).

To stay competitive, e-grocers must optimize logistics networks, inventory management, and fulfilment methods (Saphores & Xu, 2021). Understanding generational differences in consumer perceptions can improve business processes (Bauerova & Klepek, 2018). For instance, Mercadona, a leading Spanish grocer, used ethnographic research to study barriers to retail innovations (Albors-Garrigos, 2020). Subscription-based delivery services can increase customer spending and frequency but also pose profitability challenges (Wagner et al., 2021).

Retail service quality is crucial for customer satisfaction and loyalty, with physical aspects, reliability, personal interaction, problem-solving, and policy all having a positive impact (Reddy & Krishna, 2019). Online retailers should focus on price verification and product display to enhance assortment satisfaction and overall satisfaction, leading to increased customer loyalty and online repurchase intention (Verma & Pant, 2021). The digital grocery landscape is transforming with investments in online shopping experiences, automated picking, delivery, and digital supply chain management (Abbu et al., 2021). This transformation aims to improve customer loyalty, increase revenue, and boost profitability. Brand equity and online customer experience can also enhance e-loyalty (Winnberg & Martensson, 2021).

Grocery retailers should combine “mass” and “targeted” loyalty strategies to optimize customer loyalty. Traditional “mass” factors like product range and price remain important, but “targeted” marketing efforts based on individual customer data are also crucial for sustaining loyalty (Bellini et al., 2011). Retail service quality is a key driver of customer loyalty, with perceived service quality positively influencing customer satisfaction, conative loyalty, and action loyalty (Martinelli & Balboni, 2012). Loyalty program structure affects perceived status differently in exclusive and non-exclusive industries (Arbore & Estes, 2013). Self-checkout systems' service quality also positively influences loyalty through customer satisfaction (Orel & Kara, 2014).

The study investigates the factors influencing customer satisfaction, loyalty, and quality attributes in mobile grocery shopping. The results indicate that trust and commitment play a crucial role in strengthening the relationship between satisfaction and loyalty

(Kim et al, 2018). Product quality, convenience, reasonable prices, and product variety also impact customer satisfaction. To improve customer satisfaction and loyalty, mobile retailers should focus on providing high-quality products, convenient shopping experiences, and competitive prices. Trust is a key factor in service encounters, influencing repurchase intentions (Mittendorf et al., 2019). Additionally, trust, security, and privacy concerns need to be addressed (Fong et al., 2020). A study found that men and women have distinct online shopping preferences. Men have more favourable sentiments towards e-tailers and online purchases, while social factors have a greater impact on women's online buying intentions. Online enterprises must adapt their platforms to cater to different gender groups, taking into account customer browsing and web navigation preferences (Kanwal et al., 2022).

Perceived risk plays a crucial role in shaping online repurchase behaviours, mediating the impact of trust on online repurchase intentions (Mortimer et al., 2016). Higher trust leads to increased online repurchase intention, but only if the perceived risk is low. Customer satisfaction is the foundation of trust, and reducing perceived risk can foster positive repurchase attitudes (Mortimer et al., 2016). Factors such as convenience, product quality, cost, variety, social norms, and website design also influence the intention to shop for groceries online. Offline grocery stores are perceived as having limited product variety and higher prices, making e-grocery services more appealing. To address trust issues in non-tech-savvy demographics, marketing strategies must focus on building trust (Saleem et al., 2018). Consumer perceptions of retailers, including price, risk perception, and services rendered, impact the acceptance of private-label products in both offline and online contexts (Manikandan, 2020).

Following a positive initial experience, consumer reinforcement is critical for loyalty, with trust and commitment playing important roles in the consumption process and mediating loyalty-building (Denison and Knox, 1995). The Diamond of Loyalty is used to divide consumers into loyalty kinds based on satisfaction and behavioral characteristics. Trust and commitment mediate the relationship between satisfaction and loyalty (Boukhobza, 2005). In India, online grocery purchasing behaviour is shaped by convenience, trust, and product variety (Sharma et al., 2014). The cumulative effects of satisfaction, trust, and perceived value provide more explanatory power for customer loyalty intentions than customer delight (Maria et al., 2014). Trust and perceived benefits determine consumer views in e-grocery shopping, with trust influenced by perceived site quality and eWOM (Al-Debei et al., 2015). To foster loyalty, grocery retailers should prioritize customer trust and satisfaction (Filipe et al., 2017).

Drivers of Digital Transformation in Grocery Retail

Consumers today are seeking convenience, variety and personalized experiences when they indulge in online shopping. Data enables electronic retailers to understand consumer preferences so that they can make personalized recommendations. The entry of Amazon, Reliance and Flipkart in the Indian grocery market has intensified the competition comprising players like Zepto, Blink It, Big Basket, D-Mart and Swiggy Instamart.

Innovation has been the hallmark of digital transformation in grocery services. Services like on-demand delivery, subscription schemes, doorstep delivery and click-and-collect have redefined consumer convenience. Digital transformation has also made it easier for e-grocers to access and analyze customer data. Mobile commerce, automation and artificial intelligence have enabled the optimization of supply chains and enhanced the customer experience.

Before the COVID-19 pandemic, e-grocery services were patronized by millennials and Gen Z as they are comfortable with technology and prefer seamless digital experiences. The Covid-19 pandemic became a major disruptor in the grocery market making online grocery services a necessity for consumers. The widespread adoption of smartphones has transformed the way consumers shop for groceries. Consumers can browse products, place orders, and make payments on the go.

User engagement and retention in e-grocery services can result from collaboration design. The various elements in the website and the way they interact with one another to engender a user-friendly experience is what collaboration design is all about (Kumar et al, 2023). Users can search and purchase things, navigate the app, and have an overall seamless and joyful shopping experience. The website design should be such that navigation of the same on a smartphone must be easy. Collaboration design along with innovative promotions strengthens the connection between users and brands. This will motivate users to continue to use the mobile app regularly.

Mobile apps provide users with a seamless shopping experience, offering features such as barcode scanning, digital coupons, and real-time order tracking. E-grocers are using location-based services and push notifications to target customers with relevant promotional offers.

Research in Serbia revealed that cash on delivery was the preferred method for consumers shopping for groceries online. Accurate product descriptions are valued by customers as credible information enables them to make informed decisions. Efficient shipping results in delivering ordered products promptly, securely, and as described. Product and service quality have a positive impact on customer satisfaction. Reasonable prices of grocery products add to the allure of e-grocery services. Competitive prices and low switching costs enable shoppers to scout for the best deals online. The internet's influence on convenience, speed, price, and product information has made vendors redefine value propositions (Vasic et al, 2019). In the Serbian market, consumers prioritize using website information to find lower-priced products and ensure efficient delivery, rather than time savings. Even though in markets like South Africa concerns about fraud and cybercrimes act as a deterrent for online shopping, in Serbia, it was observed that once customers were used to the services their fear and inhibitions regarding the security of the transactions and integrity of their private data were decimated.

Government policies have also supported the growth of e-grocery services. Governments across the globe have supported small and medium business enterprises. High-speed internet connectivity, cloud computing, and data analytics have laid the foundation for the digital transformation in the grocery retail sector.

Data privacy regulations like the General Data Protection Regulation (GDPR) have made it critical for retailers to ensure data protection and integrity. Today, customers expect e-tailers to be transparent about their data handling capacities. Regulations related to food safety, packaging, labelling and traceability have made retailers embrace digital supply chain management solutions. Going forward, e-grocers will feel the need to adopt sustainable business practices.

E-Grocery Business Models

In the subscription model, customers pay a recurring fee in exchange for value-added services like discounts, free delivery, and exclusive deals. This model is aimed at growing a loyal customer base. In the marketplace model, the e-grocery platforms act as intermediaries and connect consumers with multiple sellers offering a wide range of products from various brands and suppliers. Sellers can reach a larger audience and access new markets. Buyers benefit from wider choice and better prices. In the inventory model, e-grocery platforms maintain their warehouses and inventory. This gives them greater control over product selection, quality, and availability to ensure consistent service and timely delivery. The click-and-collect model allows customers to order groceries online and pick them up at designated locations like storefronts, lockers, or drive-through facilities. This model aims to attract customers who prefer to shop on their terms.

Integration of online and offline channels (omni-channel) allows customers to shop for groceries across multiple channels, including websites, mobile apps, physical stores, and third-party platforms, with the option for home delivery, in-store pickup or curbside pickup.

Quick Commerce and Instant Commerce

Quick commerce and Instant Commerce are emerging business models in online grocery retail services that are differentiated from other models due to their delivery mechanisms.

Quick Commerce is a subset of e-commerce that focuses on ultra-fast delivery of goods to customers. Customers are delivered grocery and other items within a short delivery window generally between 10 minutes to 30 minutes. These platforms offer a limited assortment of goods like groceries, milk, household items, and ready-to-cook meals. However, of late, the quick commerce platforms have begun diversifying their portfolio and are earning substantial margins from non-grocery items as well.

Quick commerce deliveries are facilitated by the support of dark stores- neighbourhood fulfilment centres that stock the relevant items and have a pool of employees to sort, pick and deliver the goods. The process of sorting, picking and delivery happens within a specified time frame.

The quick commerce deliveries began getting popular when e-grocers like Zepto and Blink IT began advertising them as an important customer value proposition. But customers had not demanded such quick delivery services. Despite concerns about such a channel choking logistics and causing traffic congestion, the model has picked up momentum in India in the last year. This model has now raised customer expectations and it has forced other e-grocers in the industry to follow suit as they fear loss of competitive advantage.

The quick commerce platforms offer a curated selection of essential items that are in demand. These on-demand services rely on strategically located dark stores to ensure fulfilment and overcome last-mile delivery issues. Technological interventions support real-time order tracking, route optimization, and automated fulfilment systems. This can lead to streamlined operations and maximum customer value.

Instant Commerce delivers goods to consumers instantaneously through a vending machine located in large apartment complexes in metropolitan cities. These carry a limited assortment of items (mostly ready-to-eat items and convenience foods). An app facilitates the placement of the order and use of the vending machine. Micro warehouses and a network of delivery staff ensure rapid replenishment of stock.

Both the quick commerce and instant commerce platforms offer delivery of grocery items at speed. These hyperlocal models are enabling e-grocers to meet the evolving needs of customers. These models are expected to play a greater role in the future growth of online grocery retail.

Digital Automation Tools in Online Grocery Retail

Digital automation tools are assets to enhance operational efficiency and improve customer experience. These tools can streamline inventory management and e-fulfilment processes and help reduce costs. This can enhance the competitive advantage of e-grocers. Digital tools can provide real-time visibility into stock levels, sales trends, and supplier performance.

Data analytics and predictive algorithms can help in demand forecasting and optimization of stock levels. This can minimize stockouts. Automation of replenishment processes and integration of the same with supplier's systems can ensure uninterrupted flow of products end to end.

Robotics and artificial intelligence for automated picking systems can improve fulfilment times and reduce labour costs. Route optimization algorithms can optimize delivery routes based on traffic patterns and delivery timelines. This can improve fill rates and enable a better customer experience.

Chatbots and virtual assistants leverage natural language processing and machine learning to provide instant support and assistance to customers, answering queries, resolving issues, and offering product recommendations in real-time.

CRM systems can centralize customer data so that this can facilitate personalized marketing communications. Intuitive interfaces and seamless check-out processes will add to the appeal of e-grocery shopping. Multiple payment options, one-click ordering, and secure payment gateways are value-added services. This can reduce cart abandonment, drive incremental sales and increase conversion rates.

Pricing optimization algorithms help determination of the optimal price points for products, taking into account factors such as demand elasticity, inventory levels, and seasonal trends.

Use of Analytics in Online Grocery Retail to Understand Consumer Behaviour

Technological advancements and changing consumer preferences are driving the growth of online grocery retail. The extensive use of analytics to understand consumer behaviour renders useful insights. Customer transactions can be used to analyze behaviour and glean information about how often customers visit a website or app or how receptive customers are to product recommendations. Based on the data, the recommendation pages can contain useful content like the nutritional composition of products and information about how to use these products. This can be used to bubble up more product recommendations on the description page with an option called "Add to Cart". E-grocers are refining traditional algorithms to drive business impact. Analytics can thus be used to deliver personalized experiences to customers. Grocery being a repeat business, each customer can act as a wide repository of data. Every single transaction of customers can be a data point. Historical sales data, seasonality trends, and external factors such as weather patterns, can aid demand forecasting and optimization of inventory levels.

Analysis of data from past purchases, browsing behaviour and demographic information can help identify customer preferences. This can help retailers tailor their product offerings, promotions, and marketing strategies to meet the needs of the target segment.

Machine learning algorithms can predict consumer behaviour and this can be used to replenish stock to avoid stock-out situations. Factors like demand, supply and competitor pricing can help adjust prices in real time to maximize revenue and increase profitability. Lower prices on certain products during off-peak hours can stimulate demand.

Data from suppliers, transportation partners, and internal operations can help in identifying bottlenecks to optimize the supply chain. Better segmentation and targeting results from the effective use of data analytics.

Actionable Strategies by E-grocers

Robust analytics tools can empower e-grocers to plan and execute actionable strategies based on insights from data. The customer base can be segmented so that marketing campaigns can be tailored to specific demographics and meet the demands of the particular segment. Product recommendations can be sent to customers based on past purchases or browsing history. This can drive sales and growth. Identification of fast-moving products and adjustment of the assortment in real time can optimize inventory management and improve profitability. New products can be introduced based on emerging trends or customer demands. Targeted promotions and discounts on specific products can stimulate demand. This can help the refinement of pricing and promotional strategies over time. Analysis of customer feedback and support interactions can throw the spotlight on areas of improvement. Chatbots and virtual assistants can offer instant support and reduce response times.

Emerging Trends in Grocery Retail

AI is used for tailoring recommendations and offers that satisfy customers. E-grocery businesses are focusing on meeting customer demands for faster service. They offer 24/7 accessibility, an extensive assortment of grocery products and flexible delivery options.

Omni-channel helps in bridging online and offline experiences. Click-and-collect models, virtual stores and in-store digital kiosks provide customers the convenience and personalization with the immediacy and social aspects of in-store shopping.

Integration of AI technologies like chatbots in e-grocery operations helps automate inventory management. This results in product availability and improvement in customer experience.

Convenience of digital ordering and home delivery of groceries has become an attractive value proposition now.

As Gen Z become more price-sensitive, e-grocers are introducing private labels. In the US, e-grocers are offering subscription services and meal delivery kits. The meal delivery kits are curated to meet the unique needs of customers. They are also revamping their fulfilment strategies and product selections to better meet customer needs. AI, machine learning, and automation are transforming operations, and improving efficiency in customer service, pricing, and promotional strategies. Dynamic pricing algorithms help retailers adjust prices based on competitor data and market conditions, while AI-driven analytics enhance decision-making in inventory allocation and waste reduction.

Cloud technologies are improving the accuracy of demand forecasts so that inventory can be managed better. E-grocers need to design a user-friendly interface with responsive design, good-quality visuals and intuitive navigation. A seamless checkout process with flexible payment options and robust security measures can inspire trust in consumers and foster repeat purchase behaviour. A successful e-grocery platform integrates convenience with variety and competitive pricing, supported by promotions and loyalty rewards. E-grocers can form strategic alliances with brands and sell them online.

Future of Online Grocery Retail

The proliferation of digital media channels in the last decade has played a crucial role in shaping consumer behaviour. Today advances in mobile phone technology have resulted in the services reaching the lowest common denominator in an emerging economy like India. This has also resulted in massive societal changes and changes in the business ecosystem. It is not an exaggeration to say that the rapid growth of the Internet and the availability of cheap data has democratized the usage of mobile devices.

The grocery industry is facing major changes due to changing consumer tastes, rising costs, complicated supply chains, and changing store environments. Digital technologies, especially those that enable online grocery shopping and improved last-mile delivery services, are essential for responding to these shifts and spurring growth. Leveraging technology, logistics, and customer data, a cohesive digital shopping experience is essential to improving retention and operational efficiency.

Using subscription services, marketplace integration, and omnichannel models like BORIS and BOPIS improves consumer engagement and operational flexibility. Micro-fulfilment centres (MFCs) and cybersecurity investments are essential to satisfying changing customer needs while preserving data integrity and transaction security.

Significant changes are occurring in the grocery sector as a result of pressure from competitors, evolving consumer tastes, and technology improvements. Retailers use their supply chains, customer relationships, shop spaces, and strategic collaborations to promote growth. Online grocery retailers are making use of first-party customer data across digital and physical touchpoints by utilizing advanced analytics to improve marketing precision.

Consumer expectations are converging in the retail sector, requiring seamless experiences that include personalized participation via digital platforms and social media, as well as transparency from farm to fork.

Personalized product suggestions through digital marketing methods, loyalty program optimization for client retention, and in-home delivery services are examples of strategic initiatives that improve convenience. Gaining efficiency through supply chain optimization, labour management, and AI-driven demand forecasting is essential for meeting changing market demands and maintaining growth in the face of shifting consumer behaviour and unstable economic conditions.

The global management consulting firm Oliver Wyman has released a study titled "The Future of Online Grocery: Threats and Opportunities." The profitability of grocery stores that operate only online is the main subject of this report's analysis of the feasibility and prospective effects of e-commerce on the grocery market. According to the analysis, traditional brick-and-mortar grocery stores would be severely impacted by online grocery shopping, which might result in store closures and the need for traditional grocers to adjust to the shifting market dynamics. The report's conclusion provides solutions for online and brick-and-mortar merchants to prosper in this changing environment.

Certain concerns remain and these pertain to customer data. Customers are concerned about the protection of their data. This is an area that e-grocers have to pay greater attention to. The perception of risks in online grocery shopping might have reduced over time but these have not been completely obliterated. If these concerns about cyber security and privacy protection are not addressed, this can have serious economic, social and technological consequences for businesses and society.

Customers will expect a seamless and flexible shopping experience across multiple channels. They would want exceptional service from purchase to delivery, availability of stock when they order groceries online and the availability of different payment options. E-grocery operations can be profitable through increased sales, improved margins, reduction of costs and operational upgrades.

E-grocers across the globe will be forced to increase their spending on digital technology budgets. Enhancing digital operational efficiency is no longer an option – it is a necessity. System-wide inventory accuracy is achievable through the use of AI. There are tier-II and tier-III cities in India where the digital divide is narrowing. These geographies present an attractive business opportunity for e-grocery businesses to explore.

Sustainability will remain a core business value in the future. So, when we document the future of the e-grocery business, it is vital to explore how e-grocery businesses can embrace sustainability and ethical ways of doing business. Consumers are also opting for sustainable products and packaging. They are seeking healthier options and expressing their preference for consuming grocery products that are sourced responsibly. Grocers can offer sustainable products like plant-based meats and products having biodegradable packaging. Transparency about product information and proper labelling have become important.

Ensuring that physical and digital channels are integrated through omnichannel models can aid in fulfilling client expectations. E-grocers need to take advantage of insights to develop lucrative business models that satisfy changing consumer demands. E-grocers must adopt a "hands off the wheel" approach by embracing automation and algorithms. This approach will be crucial in handling large amounts of data and making rapid decisions efficiently. Grocers can achieve this through dark stores, and automated fulfilment centres that use robots for picking and packing.

Investing in technology that supports employees, such as omnichannel fulfilment tools, can improve the worker experience and attract talent. For instance, in-store associates can use technology to help digital and physical shoppers. Additionally, gig-work-like scheduling systems can provide the workforce with greater flexibility.

Grocers must navigate a rapidly changing technological landscape to meet diverse consumer demands. While it might be tempting to focus solely on technology, sources highlight the importance of remembering that a successful grocery store prioritizes the consumer and their needs above all else.

The future of grocery retail in India hinges on personalization. Retailers using data analytics and algorithms to offer tailored experiences, simplified checkout processes, and efficient delivery will likely thrive. Future growth in the grocery retail market is expected to come from both semi-urban (Tier 2 and Tier 3 cities) and rural areas, driven by increasing urbanization and rising incomes. Overall, the Indian grocery retail market is becoming increasingly competitive and dynamic. The integration of technology, evolving consumer behaviours, and collaborations between different retail formats are shaping its future.

REFERENCES

Abbu, H., Fleischmann, D., & Gopalakrishna, P. (2021, June). The Case of Digital Transformation in Grocery Business: A Conceptual Model of Digital Grocery Ecosystem. In *2021 IEEE International Conference on Engineering, Technology and Innovation (ICE/ITMC)* (pp. 1-9). IEEE. DOI: 10.1109/ICE/ITMC52061.2021.9570219

Abbu, H. R., Fleischmann, D., & Gopalakrishna, P. (2021). The digital transformation of the grocery business is driven by consumers, powered by technology, and accelerated by the COVID-19 Pandemic. In *Trends and Applications in Information Systems and Technologies: Volume 3 9* (pp. 329-339). Springer International Publishing. DOI: 10.1007/978-3-030-72660-7_32

Ahmad, A., Rahman, O., & Khan, M. N. (2017). Exploring the role of website quality and hedonism in the formation of e-satisfaction and e-loyalty: Evidence from internet users in India. *Journal of Research in Interactive Marketing*, 11(3), 246–267. DOI: 10.1108/JRIM-04-2017-0022

Al-Debei, M. M., Akroush, M. N., & Ashouri, M. I. (2015). Consumer attitudes towards online shopping: The effects of trust, perceived benefits, and perceived web quality. *Internet Research*, 25(5), 707–733. DOI: 10.1108/IntR-05-2014-0146

Al Nawas, I., Altarifi, S., & Ghantous, N. (2021). E-retailer cognitive and emotional relationship quality: Their experiential antecedents and differential impact on brand evangelism. *International Journal of Retail & Distribution Management*, 49(9), 1249–1270. DOI: 10.1108/IJRDM-07-2020-0239

Alagarsamy, S., Mehrolia, S., & Singh, B. (2021). The mediating effect of brand relationship quality on relational bonds and online grocery retailer loyalty. *Journal of Internet Commerce*, 20(2), 246–272. DOI: 10.1080/15332861.2020.1868213

Albors-Garrigos, J. (2020). Barriers and enablers for innovation in the retail sector: Co-innovating with the customer. A case study in grocery retailing. *Journal of Retailing & Consumer Services, 55*, N.PAG. DOI: 10.1016/j.jretconser.2020.102077

Ali, I., & Naushad, M. (2021). Determinants of customer satisfaction in online grocery shopping. *Journal of Retailing and Consumer Services*, 61, 102618.

Altıntaş, M. H., Kılıç, S., & Akhan, C. E. (2020). The transformation of the e-tailing field: A bibliometric analysis. *International Journal of Retail & Distribution Management*, 48(2), 152–168. DOI: 10.1108/IJRDM-10-2018-0232

Annisa Islam, H., & Ezni Balqiah, T. (2021, April). Loyalty and Customer Engagement in Online Grocery Shopping in Indonesia. In *Proceedings of the 5th International Conference on E-Commerce, E-Business and E-Government* (pp. 53-59). DOI: 10.1145/3466029.3466036

Anshu, K., Gaur, L., & Singh, G. (2022). Impact of customer experience on attitude and repurchase intention in online grocery retailing: A moderation mechanism of value Co-creation. *Journal of Retailing and Consumer Services*, 64, 102798. DOI: 10.1016/j.jretconser.2021.102798

Arbore, A., & Estes, Z. (2013). Loyalty program structure and consumers' perceptions of status: Feeling special in a grocery store? *Journal of Retailing and Consumer Services*, 20(5), 439–444. DOI: 10.1016/j.jretconser.2013.03.002

Astashkina, E., Belavina, E., & Marinesi, S. (2019). The environmental impact of the advent of online grocery retailing. *Available atSSRN* 3358664 DOI: 10.2139/ssrn.3358664

Bauerova, R. (2019). Online Grocery Shopping Acceptance: The Impact on the Perception of New Technologies and Loyalty in Retailing. *Central European Business Review*, 8(3), 18–34. DOI: 10.18267/j.cebr.216

Bauerová, R., & Klepek, M. (2018). The Digitalization of Grocery Shopping from a Generation Perspective. *Marketing Identity*, (Part 1), 243–255.

Bellini, S., Cardinali, M. G., & Ziliani, C. (2011). Building customer loyalty in retailing: Not all levers are created equal. *International Review of Retail, Distribution and Consumer Research*, 21(5), 461–481. DOI: 10.1080/09593969.2011.619666

Blomqvist, A., Nyman, L., & Lennartsson, F. (2015). Consumer attitudes towards online grocery shopping: A research conducted on Swedish consumers.

Boukhobza, T. (2005). *An investigation into customer loyalty and relationship marketing: case UK grocery retailing and telecommunication sectors*. University of Salford.

Chakraborty, D., Bhatnagar, S. B., Biswas, W., & Khatua, A. K. (2022). What drives people to adopt grocery apps? The moderating role of household size. *Business Perspectives and Research*, •••, 22785337221091640. DOI: 10.1177/22785337221091640

Chung, J. B., Choi, B. C., Cho, Y. S., & Chung, L. C. (2016). Service quality of online grocery shopping in Korean local regions. *Journal of Distribution Science*, 14(8), 67–75. DOI: 10.15722/jds.14.8.201608.67

de Magalhães, D. J. A. V. (2021). Analysis of critical factors affecting the final decision-making for online grocery shopping. *Research in Transportation Economics*, 87, 101088. DOI: 10.1016/j.retrec.2021.101088

https://www.refrigeratedfrozenfood.com/articles/100885-study-shows-more-americans-embracing-online-grocery-shopping (Dec 24, 2021)

Dillahunt, T. R., Simioni, S., & Xu, X. (2019, May). Online grocery delivery services: An opportunity to address food disparities in transportation-scarce areas. In *Proceedings of the 2019 CHI Conference on Human Factors in Computing Systems* (pp. 1-15). DOI: 10.1145/3290605.3300879

Dillahunt, T. R., Simioni, S., & Xu, X. (2019, May). Online grocery delivery services: An opportunity to address food disparities in transportation-scarce areas. In *Proceedings of the 2019 CHI Conference on Human Factors in Computing Systems* (pp. 1-15). DOI: 10.1145/3290605.3300879

East, R. (2022). Online grocery sales after the pandemic. *International Journal of Market Research*, 64(1), 13–18. DOI: 10.1177/14707853211055047

Filipe, S., Marques, S. H., & de Fátima Salgueiro, M. (2017). Customer's relationship with their grocery store: Direct and moderating effects from store format and loyalty programs. *Journal of Retailing and Consumer Services*, 37, 78–88. DOI: 10.1016/j.jretconser.2017.03.002

Foncillas, B. L. F. (2020). *The future of retail* (Doctoral dissertation, Massachusetts Institute of Technology).

Fong, C. M., Mat Hasan, N. H., Rahmat, S. M., & Abenoh, N. A. (2020). Consumer purchase behaviour towards online grocery in Melaka. *International Journal of Business. Economics and Law*, 23(1), 25–31.

Gibbs, P. (2016). What is a shop? Evolution of the retail store. *Operations Management (1755-1501), 42*(2), 24–26.

Goutam, D., Ganguli, S., & Gopalakrishna, B. V. (2022). Technology readiness and e-service quality–impact on purchase intention and loyalty. *Marketing Intelligence & Planning*, 40(2), 242–255. DOI: 10.1108/MIP-06-2021-0196

Grudzien, P. (2020). Comparative Analysis of Energy Intensity and Profitability in Emerging E-Grocery Retail Models.

Gupta, P., & Nag, R. (2013). Innovating for Profitable Growth. *Images Retail*, 12(10), 162–164.

Güsken, S. R. (2020). *A Multi-method Study of Consumer Behaviour: Towards a Better Understanding of the Consumer's Perspective on Online Grocery Shopping* (Doctoral dissertation, Universitätsbibliothek der RWTH Aachen).

Güsken, S. R., Janssen, D., & Hees, F. (2019). Online Grocery Platforms–Understanding Consumer Acceptance. In *ISPIM Conference Proceedings* (pp. 1-17). The International Society for Professional Innovation Management (ISPIM).

Habib, S., & Hamadneh, N. N. (2021). Impact of perceived risk on consumers' technology acceptance in online grocery adoption amid COVID-19 pandemic. *Sustainability (Basel)*, 13(18), 10221. DOI: 10.3390/su131810221

Hallikainen, H., Luongo, M., Dhir, A., & Laukkanen, T. (2022). Consequences of personalized product recommendations and price promotions in online grocery shopping. *Journal of Retailing and Consumer Services*, 69, 103088. DOI: 10.1016/j.jretconser.2022.103088

Kanwal, M., Burki, U., Ali, R., & Dahlstrom, R. (2022). A systematic review of gender differences and similarities in online consumers' shopping behaviour. *Journal of Consumer Marketing*, 39(1), 29–43. DOI: 10.1108/JCM-01-2021-4356

Kärkkäinen, T. (2015). Gearing Towards Omnichannel Grocery Retail Through Business Model Innovation.

Kim, H. J., Yang, K., & Lee, Y. E. (2018). Moderating effect of trust and commitment in customer satisfaction and customer loyalty on mobile grocery purchasing quality attributes.

Kim, S., Ham, S., Moon, H., Chua, B. L., & Han, H. (2019). Experience, brand prestige, perceived value (functional, hedonic, social, and financial), and loyalty among GROCERANT customers. *International Journal of Hospitality Management*, 77, 169–177. DOI: 10.1016/j.ijhm.2018.06.026

Klepek, M., & Bauerová, R. (2020). Why do retail customers hesitate for shopping grocery online? *Technological and Economic Development of Economy*, 26(6), 1444–1462. DOI: 10.3846/tede.2020.13970

Krishnamurthy, S. M., & Venkitachalam, K. (2022). The changing face of retailing, 1980–2020. *Journal of Strategy and Management*, (ahead-of-print).

Kuijpers, D., Wintels, S., & Yamakawa, N. (2020). Reimagining food retail in Asia after [*McKinsey & Company.*]. *COVID*, •••, 19.

Kumar, A., Sikdar, P., Gupta, M., Singh, P., & Sinha, N. (2023). Drivers of satisfaction and usage continuance in e-grocery retailing: A collaborative design supported perspective. *Journal of Research in Interactive Marketing*, 17(2), 176–194. DOI: 10.1108/JRIM-02-2020-0035

Kurnia, S., & Schubert, P. TOWARD ACHIEVING CUSTOMER SATISFACTION IN ONLINE GROCERY SHOPPING. *Electronic Customer Relationship Management*, 177.

Leppäniemi, M., Karjaluoto, H., & Saarijärvi, H. (2017). Customer perceived value, satisfaction, and loyalty: The role of willingness to share information. *International Review of Retail, Distribution and Consumer Research*, 27(2), 164–188. DOI: 10.1080/09593969.2016.1251482

Liu, C. F., & Lin, C. H. (2020). Online food shopping: A conceptual analysis for research propositions. *Frontiers in Psychology*, 11, 583768. DOI: 10.3389/fpsyg.2020.583768 PMID: 33041952

Maggioni, I. (2016). What drives customer loyalty in grocery retail? Exploring shoppers' perceptions through associative networks. *Journal of Retailing and Consumer Services*, 33, 120–126. DOI: 10.1016/j.jretconser.2016.08.012

Manikandan, M. K. M. (2020). Store brand and perceived risk on private label brand attitude. *Journal of Indian Business Research*, 12(1), 133–150. DOI: 10.1108/JIBR-09-2019-0280

Maria Correia Loureiro, S., & Miranda, J., F., & Breazeale, M. (. (2014). Who needs delight? The greater impact of value, trust and satisfaction in utilitarian, frequent-use retail. *Journal of Service Management*, 25(1), 101–124. DOI: 10.1108/JOSM-06-2012-0106

Martinelli, E., & Balboni, B. (2012). Retail service quality is a key activator of grocery store loyalty. *Service Industries Journal*, 32(14), 2233–2247. DOI: 10.1080/02642069.2011.582499

Mason, R. (2019). Developing a profitable online grocery logistics business: Exploring innovations in ordering, fulfilment, and distribution at Ocado. In *Contemporary Operations and Logistics* (pp. 365–383). Palgrave Macmillan. DOI: 10.1007/978-3-030-14493-7_19

Mittendorf, C., Berente, N., & Holten, R. (2019). Trust in sharing encounters among millennials. *Information Systems Journal*, 29(5), 1083–1119. DOI: 10.1111/isj.12237

Møller Jensen, J. (2011). Consumer loyalty on the grocery product market: An empirical application of Dick and Basu's framework. *Journal of Consumer Marketing*, 28(5), 333–343. DOI: 10.1108/07363761111149983

Mortimer, G., Fazal e Hasan, S., Andrews, L., & Martin, J. (2016). Online grocery shopping: The impact of shopping frequency on perceived risk. *International Review of Retail, Distribution and Consumer Research*, 26(2), 202–223. DOI: 10.1080/09593969.2015.1130737

Munson, J., Tiropanis, T., & Lowe, M. (2017). Online grocery shopping: Identifying change in consumption practices. In *Internet Science: 4th International Conference, INSCI 2017, Thessaloniki, Greece, November 22-24, 2017* [Springer International Publishing.]. *Proceedings*, 4, 192–211.

Ngobo, P. V. (2017). The trajectory of customer loyalty: An empirical test of Dick and Basu's loyalty framework. *Journal of the Academy of Marketing Science*, 45(2), 229–250. DOI: 10.1007/s11747-016-0493-6

Olsson, J. (2021). Exploring unattended delivery services in e-grocery retail: A consumer-centric perspective on last-mile logistics.

Orel, F. D., & Kara, A. (2014). Supermarket self-checkout service quality, customer satisfaction, and loyalty: Empirical evidence from an emerging market. *Journal of Retailing and Consumer Services*, 21(2), 118–129. DOI: 10.1016/j.jretconser.2013.07.002

Pileliene, L., & Zikiene, K. (2017). Customer loyalty to a grocery retailer: differences between urban and rural areas of Lithuania. *Research for rural development, 2*, 203-209.

Pour, M. J., Rafiei, K., Khani, M., & Sabrirazm, A. (2021). Gamification and customer experience: The mediating role of brand engagement in online grocery retailing. *Nankai Business Review International*.

Prasad, C. J., & Raghu, Y. (2020). Determinant Attributes of Online Grocery Shopping in India - An Empirical Analysis. *International Journal of Advanced Science and Technology*, 29(7), 10754–10764.

Reddy, M. S., & Krishna, S. M. (2019). Influential role of retail service quality in food and grocery retailing: A comparative study between traditional and multi-channel retailing. *Int J Management and Business Research*, 9(2), 68–73.

Ruangkanjanases, A., Sirisrisakulchai, P., Sonata, N., & Simamora, B. H. (2021). Predicting consumer intention to adopt online grocery shopping: A comparative study between millennials in Thailand and Indonesia. *International Journal of Electronic Commerce Studies*, 12(2), 193–208. DOI: 10.7903/ijecs.1894

Ruiz-Molina, M. E., Gómez-Borja, M. Á., & Mollá-Descals, A. (2021). Can offline–online congruence explain online loyalty in electronic commerce? *International Journal of Retail & Distribution Management*, 49(9), 1271–1294. DOI: 10.1108/IJRDM-02-2020-0060

Saghiri, S., Aktas, E., & Mohammadipour, M. (2023). Grocery omnichannel perishable inventories: performance measures and influencing factors. *International Journal of Operations & Production Management*, (ahead-of-print).

Saleem, M., Khan, M. M., Ahmed, M. E., Shah, S. N., & Surti, S. R. (2018). Online grocery shopping and consumer perception: a case of Karachi market in Pakistan. *Journal of Internet and e-Business studies, 2018*, 1-13.

Saphores, J. D., & Xu, L. (2021). E-shopping changes and the state of E-grocery shopping in the Evidence by national travel and time-use surveys. *Research in Transportation Economics*, 87, 100864. DOI: 10.1016/j.retrec.2020.100864

Sharma, P., Nair, V., & Jyotishi, A. (2014, October). Patterns of online grocery shopping in India: an empirical study. In *Proceedings of the 2014 International Conference on Interdisciplinary Advances in Applied Computing* (pp. 1-5). DOI: 10.1145/2660859.2660939

Singh, R., & Rosengren, S. (2020). Why do online grocery shoppers switch? An empirical investigation of drivers of switching in online grocery. *Journal of Retailing and Consumer Services*, 53, 101962. DOI: 10.1016/j.jretconser.2019.101962

Smith, K. T. (2011). Digital marketing strategies that Millennials find appealing, motivating, or just annoying. *Journal of Strategic Marketing*, 19(6), 489–499. DOI: 10.1080/0965254X.2011.581383

Sodano, M. (2020). *Do shopping lists help in saving time during online grocery shopping? A qualitative study among Italian consumers* (Doctoral dissertation).

Vasić, N., Kilibarda, M., & Kaurin, T. (2019). The influence of online shopping determinants on customer satisfaction in the Serbian market. *Journal of Theoretical and Applied Electronic Commerce Research*, 14(2), 70–89. DOI: 10.4067/S0718-18762019000200107

Verma, P., & Pant, M. K. (2021). The effect of price verification, product display, and assortment satisfaction upon overall satisfaction, online patronage intention, and customer loyalty. *Journal of Food Products Marketing*, 27(6), 291–318. DOI: 10.1080/10454446.2021.1994078

Verstraeten, J., Van Kerckhove, A., Lei, J., & Zhao, Y. (2020). *More Eggs in the Same Basket: How Shopping Online Reduces Variety Seeking in Purchases.* ACR North American Advances.

Vlachos, P. A., Theotokis, A., Pramatari, K., & Vrechopoulos, A. (2010). Consumer-retailer emotional attachment: Some antecedents and the moderating role of attachment anxiety. *European Journal of Marketing*, 44(9/10), 1478–1499. DOI: 10.1108/03090561011062934

Wagner, L., Pinto, C., & Amorim, P. (2021). On the value of subscription models for online grocery retail. *European Journal of Operational Research*, 294(3), 874–894. DOI: 10.1016/j.ejor.2020.05.011

Winnberg, A., & Mårtensson, F. (2021). What does it take to make you stay? A study on customers' willingness to stay with the same grocery retailer while moving from offline to online.

Zheng, Q., Chen, J., Zhang, R., & Wang, H. H. (2020). What factors affect Chinese consumers' online grocery shopping? Product attributes, e-vendor characteristics and consumer perceptions. *China Agricultural Economic Review*, 12(2), 193–213. DOI: 10.1108/CAER-09-2018-0201

Chapter 2
Harnessing the Power of Social Media Marketing to Transform the Food Industry in China

Liang Xiaoxin
https://orcid.org/0009-0001-7691-8147
Taylor's University, Malaysia

Stephanie Hui-Wen Chuah
Universiti Kebangsaan Malaysia, Malaysia

Victor Wee Eng Lye
Taylor's University, Malaysia

ABSTRACT

This chapter explores the evolution of social media's role within the Chinese food industry, emphasizing its profound impact on marketing strategies. The progression of the Internet from Web 1.0's static content to Web 4.0's immersive experiences has significantly influenced prominent local platforms such as WeChat, Weibo, Douyin and Xiaohongshu, which now play a crucial role in China's digital ecosystem. These platforms offer rich, interactive content and leverage big data for precise marketing, thereby enhancing brand engagement and consumer interaction. The chapter examines how social media marketing has transformed the food industry, providing an in-depth analysis of successful case studies. It also identifies key performance indicators and future trends. By delving into these elements, the chapter aims to offer actionable insights for food industry, enabling them to effectively utilize social media for branding and market expansion.

INTRODUCTION

The Internet has evolved from the Web 1.0 static web (Lewis et al., 2024) to the Web 2.0 interactive and user-generated content (UGC), the Web 3.0 semantic and intelligent web, and the current Web 4.0 intelligent, integrated, and immersive experiences (Santos, 2022). Similarly, in China, local social media sites like WeChat, Weibo, Douyin, and Xiaohongshu hold significant influence (Liu, 2021). These

DOI: 10.4018/979-8-3693-7683-6.ch002

platforms facilitate immediate information interchange, offer broad social networking capabilities, and give different tools for creating and sharing content. It establishes new channels of contact between organizations and consumers (Arora et al., 2021; Zhang et al., 2020). According to Santos (2022), Web 2.0 introduced user-generated content and interactivity, leading to the emergence of blogs, social networks, video sharing platforms, and many more. This provided the basis for the rise of social media marketing. It was also at this time that social media platforms such as Facebook (2004), YouTube (2005) and Twitter (2006) emerged, allowing companies to interact directly with consumers for marketing activities such as branding, user engagement, and community building (Kaur et al., 2020; Santos et al., 2022; Wongsansukcharoen, 2022).

China's food industry is an important part of the national economy, covering a wide range of fields from agricultural production, food processing to food service (Hu et al., 2020). . According to the China Industrial Statistical Yearbook, the market size of China's food industry has exceeded RMB 11 trillion in 2023 (China Industrial Statistical Yearbook, 2023) (please refer to Figure 1). The market structure of China's food industry shows a diversified trend, including multiple market segments such as traditional food, leisure food, health food and high-end food (Franzolini, 2020; Huang and Fleiss, 2023). The market size of China's food industry is thought to be growing due to the country's rapid economic growth and the rising income levels of its population (Kroeber, 2020; Lei et al.,2021; Zhang et al.,2020; Zhong et al., 2022). The acceleration of urbanization, the improvement of residents' living standards, and the enhancement of consumers' health awareness have driven continuous innovation and change in the food industry. Some scholar pointed out that consumers' increasing demand for food safety, quality and branding has brought new opportunities and challenges to food companies (Katsikouli et al., 2021; Liu et al., 2020; Yu et al., 2022).

Figure 1. China Food and Beverage Industry Market Size from 2016 to 2023

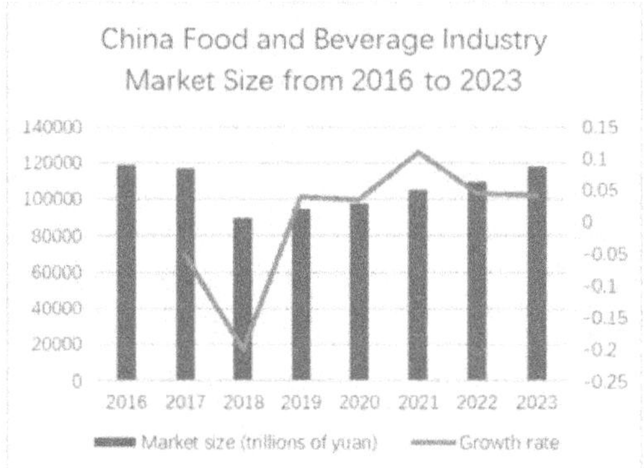

Source: China Industrial Statistical Yearbook (2023)

The growing influence of social media has made it an important tool for marketing and branding for Chinese companies (Chen and Qasim, 2021; Cheung et al., 2021). According to Huang (2024), the number of monthly active users of WeChat has exceeded 1 billion, and the number of users of Weibo and Jitterbug have both exceeded 500 million. Social media platforms offer rich forms of content presentation, such as short videos, live broadcasts, graphics and interactive games, which greatly enrich the user experience (Lu and Nam, 2021; Song et al., 2021; Zheng, 2023). Through big data analysis and precise advertising functions, companies are able to carry out precise marketing based on users' interests and behavioral habits, improving marketing effectiveness (Lyu et al., 2023; Su, 2022). A number of scholars emphasized that especially in the food industry, the immediacy and interactivity of social media provide great convenience for brand promotion and new product release, enabling enterprises to respond quickly to market demand and consumer feedback (Tuten, 2023; Vitsentzatou et al., 2022).

This chapter aims to explore how social media has transformed marketing strategies in the Chinese food industry and analyze the role and impact of social media in the food industry. This chapter also provides case studies on social media marketing successes and failures in the food industry. By delving into the application of social media in the food industry, this chapter can help companies understand how to effectively utilize social media for branding and marketing to enhance their competitiveness. This not only provides academics with in-depth research on the intersection of social media and the food industry, but also offers practical marketing strategies and advice for food companies. Through a systematic analysis of social media marketing strategies, this chapter will reveal its key role in brand building, user engagement and market expansion.

Therefore, the research objectives of this chapter are fourfold: (1) to analyze the current status of social media application in the Chinese food industry and its impact on consumer behavior. (2) to study successful and failed social media marketing cases, analyze and extract valuable lessons learned. (3) to identify key indicators for developing and evaluating social media marketing strategies. (4) to explore the challenges and future trends in social media marketing. By achieving these goals, this chapter aims to provide food companies with a comprehensive guide to social media marketing strategies and help them better adapt to the digital marketing environment.

OVERVIEW OF THE FOOD INDUSTRY IN CHINA

Market Landscape

China's food industry has shown steady growth in recent years and is one of the fastest growing markets in the world (Zhao et al., 2021). Firstly, with the continuous growth of China's total population, the demand for food has been increasing, driving the development of the food industry. In addition, the arrival of an aging society has led to the rapid development of the market for age-adapted food products, further expanding the market size (Liu et al., 2021). Secondly, several scholars point out that rapid urbanization has brought about an increase in the urban population and changes in lifestyle, especially the demand for convenience and ready-to-eat food has risen significantly (Dhir and Singla, 2020; Kumar et al., 2022). At the same time, the proportion of food consumption expenditure of urban residents has been increasing. Furthermore, with the rapid development of China's economy and the rising income level of residents, people have expanded and pushed the growth of demand for high-quality and healthy food. Consumers are more willing to pay a premium for high-quality, branded, safe, and reliable food products (Bo and Yang, 2022; Joya et al., 2022; Riccioli et al., 2020).

In addition, China's food industry is highly competitive, with major market players including large multinational food companies, well-known domestic brands, and emerging Internet-based food brands. Each of these companies occupies different segments in the market, creating a diversified competitive landscape (Paley, 2021). According to market statistics, large multinational food enterprises such as Nestle, Danone, PepsiCo, etc. have occupied an important position in the high-end market by virtue of their strong brand influence and globalized operation experience. They fulfill Chinese consumers' demand for high-quality food by continuously introducing advanced international products and technologies (Bottriell, 2023; Chakravorti, 2023). For example, Mengniu, Yili, as well-known milk brands in China, these companies have strong competitiveness in the local market, relying on extensive sales networks and localized marketing strategies to occupy a large market share (Yuan et al., 2022). They are constantly engaged in product innovation and brand upgrading to adapt to market changes and consumer demands. Meanwhile, emerging Internet food brands (e.g., Three Squirrels, Liangpin Puzi, etc.) have risen rapidly through e-commerce platforms and social media, attracting a large number of young consumers with efficient supply chain management and innovative marketing (Di, 2023; Liu et al., 2022; Zhang, 2024). They have strong competitive advantages in their market segments and continue to expand new product lines and sales channels.

Consumer Behavior and Preferences in China

Chinese consumers' eating habits and preferences are undergoing profound changes (Lin et al., 2020; Wen et al., 2021). The current dietary habits and preferences of Chinese consumers are characterized by healthy eating, convenience and a combination of tradition and innovation (Ouyang et al., 2021; Wang et al., 2023). All these characteristics have developed without the changes in the development trend of their fast-paced life and the progress of the social era. Major food companies will also continue to introduce new products to meet the diversified needs of consumers according to their different demands (Bazaluk et al., 2020; Guiné et al., 2020; Hassoun et al., 2022).

In addition, brand and product perceptions and attitudes also play a crucial role in consumers' purchase decisions. Their brand and product perceptions and attitudes are mainly derived from brand trust, product innovation, price sensitivity, and the influence of social media (Rahman et al. 2020; Safeer et al., 2022; Xing et al., 2022).

Bolek (2020) noted that frequent food safety problems can erode consumer trust in brands, discouraging them from purchasing products or services. Meanwhile, customers tend to exhibit greater loyalty toward well-known brands, as they are perceived as guarantees of quality and safety (Górska and Kulykovets, 2020; Lu et al., 2021; Zhao et al., 2022). Therefore, companies need to maintain brand reputation through transparent production processes and strict quality control, and they regularly display product quality test reports (Quintana et al., 2021; Shen and Chen, 2020; Zhang et al., 2020). At the same time, companies will be able to attract consumers' attention and enhance the competitiveness of similar brands by constantly launching new products and limited-edition products. Especially with the promotion of social media, Netflix foods and innovative products are more likely to trigger consumers' enthusiasm for purchasing (Guadiana, 2020; JAIN, 2022; Mróz, 2021).

Although people's salaries and incomes continue to rise, price is still an important factor for most consumers (e.g., good value for money) (Antong and Riyanti, 2021; Wang et al., 2020). Companies need to offer competitive prices while ensuring product quality to attract more consumers. Consumers use social media to obtain product information, view user reviews, and engage in brand interactions (Onofrei et al., 2022; Santos et al., 2022). This trend has prompted companies to increase their investment in social media to enhance brand exposure and user engagement.

In summary, changes in Chinese consumers' eating habits and preferences reflect trends in social and economic development, and for food companies, understanding and responding to these changes is one of the keys to remaining competitive in the market.

THE ROLE OF SOCIAL MEDIA IN THE FOOD INDUSTRY

Social Media Platforms and Usage

In China, the major social media platforms include WeChat, Weibo, Douyin, Xiaohongshu and B Station. Each of these platforms is unique in terms of the number of users and their usage habits. Figure 2 illustrates the mainstream social media platforms in China.

Figure 2. The Mainstream Social Media Platforms in China

Source: Sohu.com (2024); Authors' own creation

WeChat, China's largest social media platform with more than 1.2 billion users, is mainly used for instant messaging, social interaction, and mobile payment (Giudice, 2020; Huang et al., 2021; Zong et al., 2023). WeChat users are accustomed to sharing life updates through the circle of friends and using public numbers to access information; Weibo, on the other hand, is known for its openness and fast dissemination of information, with more than 500 million users. Users of this platform, on the other hand, prefer real-time hotspot discussions and information dissemination (Li, 2020; Zeng et al., 2022); Douyin (TikTok), a short-video platform, attracts more than 600 million users and is mainly used for entertainment and content consumption, who like to obtain entertainment content and information through short videos (Du et al., 2022; Yaqi et al., 2021). Xiaohongshu, on the other hand, focuses on community sharing, graphic and short video sharing of lifestyle and shopping experience, with more than 200 million users, and is especially popular among young women (Wei, 2023; XU, 2023). B station, as a secondary culture and video sharing platform, prefers to watch and interact with long video content, and has more than 200 million users, with its main users being the young population (Huang et al., 2021; Kaye et al., 2022; Xu, 2023).

Influence of Social Media on Consumer Behavior

With the development of social networking platforms, the food industry started to develop more systematic marketing campaigns on the main social media platforms (Konoplyannikova et al., 2024). In particular, food brands created official web pages to capture consumers' attention by posting content, interactions, and insightful taglines (Butcher and Pecot, 2022). The visually-driven platforms of WeChat and Douyin provide the food industry with an ideal place to showcase food photos and recipes. Food brands are similar utilizing these platforms to post food photos, short videos, and recipes that attract a lot of attention and interaction (Goktepe et al., 2022; Weber et al., 2021).

In addition, social media provides consumers with a large amount of product information and user reviews, making it easier for them to make purchasing decisions (Chen et al., 2022; Palalic et al., 2021). McClure and Seock (2020) noted that consumers obtain real user experiences and feedback through social media, thus forming a more comprehensive understanding of products. This transparency and sharing of information significantly enhance consumer confidence in purchasing (Macready et al., 2020; Peschel and Aschemann-Witzel, 2020).

Secondly, companies can interact more directly with consumers and enhance brand affinity and user stickiness by branding through social media platforms, (Li et al., 2021; Qu et al., 2023; Shao et al., 2020). Social media enables food brands to create and maintain a strong online presence (Drummond et al., 2020). Through consistent and engaging content, brands can build identity and create an emotional connection with their audience. Li and Xie (2020) argue that high-quality images, engaging videos, and storytelling are key elements for successful branding. Also, food brands can interact with their customers in real time on social platforms to solve their problems and gather valuable feedback, which helps to enhance the brand and competitiveness (Rust et al., 2021). This interaction not only builds trust, but also helps to improve products based on consumer preferences, achieve product positioning, and match customer loyalty.

At the same time, food companies can quickly attract consumers' attention and discussion by releasing new product information, recipe sharing and user interaction through social media platforms (Llanera, 2023; Schiro et al., 2020). For example, releasing innovative recipes and cooking tips through Douyin and Xiaohongshu, and collecting brand activities and user feedback through WeChat and Weibo (Comendulli, 2020; Liu, 2021), all of which can greatly enhance a brand's market influence. Similarly, the frequency of food safety issues has led consumers to rely more on social media for trusted brand information and quality assurance, which further influences their purchasing decisions.

Overall, the food industry is deepening and expanding with the growth and popularity of social media platforms. This can be a powerful platform for food brands to showcase their products and capture the attention of consumers through visually appealing and creative content. In addition, it can increase brand awareness and attract potential customers (see Figure 3).

Figure 3. The Role of Social Media in the Food Industry

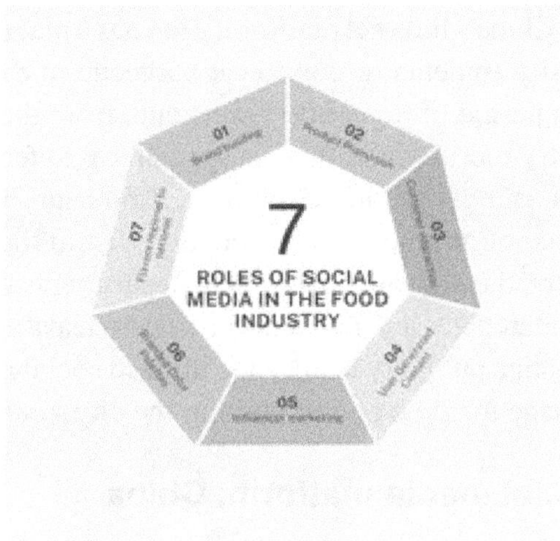

Source: Authors' own creation

SUCCESSFUL SOCIAL MEDIA MARKETING: CASE STUDY

Case study 1: Luckin Coffee, China

Luckin Coffee is a local Chinese brand that challenges with the tagline, "Share it to your circle of friends and treat your friends to a free cup of coffee." This phrase is perhaps the first impression people have of Luckin. Luckin Coffee first chose some well-known social media platforms, such as Sina Weibo and WeChat public number as the main marketing channel. These platforms have a large number of users and an active interactive environment, which can better spread the brand image and interact with consumers. By opening official accounts on these platforms and tying them to physical stores, Luckin Coffee can seamlessly integrate online and offline to provide a more complete consumer experience. Second, Luckin Coffee focuses on interaction and engagement with consumers on social media. It often posts interesting and compelling content such as drink recommendations, roasting tips, and coffee culture. This helps to attract users' attention and inspire them to interact with the brand. It also frequently organizes online activities such as lucky draws, punch cards with coupons, and daily 9.9 RMB (CNY) cups of coffee to encourage users to participate and share with their friends. Moreover, Luckin Coffee often co-branded with other brands, even in just a few days the Chinese social media platforms, Luckin Coffee also did not forget to interact with the beverage industry's "Honey Snow Ice City" at the same time: "Dear Xue (Honey Snow Ice City), I've already married into a rich family. This led to the co-branding of Guizhou Moutai wine with Luckin Coffee in China, taking over social media in a powerful way (Caidie, 2024).

Case study 2: Barbecue in Zibo, Shandong, China

In March 2023, the hot list of China's Internet platform, Zibo has a place, which makes Zibo a deserved "net red city". At first, "university students' group to eat barbecue in Zibo" topic rushed to the social media hot search, followed by a period of time, every weekend, from the neighboring cities, provinces and even from all over the country tourists have made a special trip to feel the charm of the barbecue in Zibo. However, the network heat is, after all, just a moment, Zibo's subsequent performance is the flow of reputation for the maintenance of an important foundation - from the station, the hall hangs "Zibo barbecue" giant electronic posters; the relevant government departments within a week's time A series of service support measures; local merchants and residents in order to leave a good impression of the city for foreign tourists have joined this huge publicity team. Zibo utilized social media traffic to enter the public eye, establishing a good city image for Zibo and promoting the city's cultural tourism (Chaoyu, 2023).

Case study 3: BiliBili social media platform, China

In 2023, BiliBili took advantage of the Chinese New Year node to make its voice heard, and through brand promotion outside the platform and operational activities within the platform, it completed a "special plan" under the Chinese New Year mood of 2023, and the "3286th station" brand film was the first step of the Chinese New Year plan. The movie recognizes that in 2023, after the end of the pandemic, young people who originally "don't want to go home" will begin to "want to go home", so BiliBili, as a happy home for young people and a spiritual gathering station, sends out a request to all railroad stations across the country, hoping that they can help us to make the journey more comfortable. Therefore, Bilibili, as a happy home for young people and a spiritual gathering station, sent out a request to railway stations across the country, hoping that each station would take care of young people on their way home. Through this "station" and "station" request, BiliBili will help young people go home smoothly, and at the same time, complete the re-interpretation and impression of BiliBili in the context of CNY.

The advertisement lasted 27 days, crossed 22,591 kilometers, and was finally condensed into a 6-minute story to present the most realistic and touching face of young people on their way home. In terms of content, the advertisement differentiates itself from the Spring Festival marketing by empathizing with the word "station". It resonates with young people and builds a rich content ecosystem. The advertisement has been broadcasted over 100 million times across all networks in China. Social media platforms such as WeChat Video Number, Douyin and Kuaishou gained more than 100,000 likes and triggered relay secondary creation. The brand film landed on the CCTV-6 Spring Festival segment. China Railway wrote back to Bilibili on behalf of 3,285 train stations on the occasion of the end of the Spring Festival transportation in 2023, and a number of media outlets followed up the story.

This wave of web traffic makes it resonate with young people, which is a reflection from young people who are drifting away. Utilizing social media traffic to promote the warmth of the platform creates a favorable marketing environment for the platform (Gong et al., 2023; Li et al., 2023)

KEY INDICATORS FOR SOCIAL MEDIA MARKETING STRATEGY

Social media marketing efforts utilize key performance indicators (KPIs) to assess and enhance their efficacy. In assessing social media performance, prior research has identified a number of key performance indicators (KPIs), including (1) Number of followers; (2) Interaction ratio; (3) Click-through ratio; (4) Number of exposures; (5) Sharing ratio; (6) Social media flow (Dolega et al., 2021; Primasiwi et al., 2021; Rakshit et al., 2022).

Furthermore, the conversion metrics and return on investment metrics have a direct correlation with the ultimate outcomes of the marketing campaign (Silva et al., 2020). The conversion ratio is a metric that indicates the percentage of audience members who have successfully achieved their intended goals. This metric is crucial in assessing the performance and return of a social media marketing campaign, as well as measuring the return on investment (ROI) of such a campaign. By closely monitoring these data, food companies can fine-tune their marketing tactics to achieve enhanced cost-effectiveness and customer happiness (Refer to Figure 4).

Figure 4. Key Indicators for Social Media Marketing Strategy

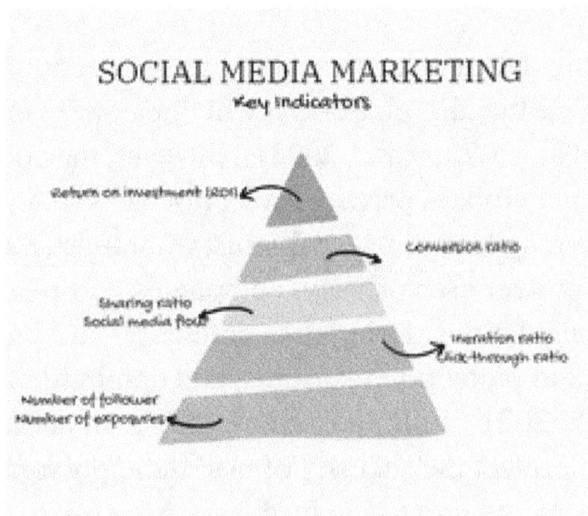

Source: Authors' own creation

User feedback and number of comments provides information about the audience's engagement and reaction to social media campaigns, which helps to assess the interactivity and effectiveness of social media marketing campaigns. Brand reputation provides information about the public perception and emotional reflection of a specific brand on social media, helping to assess the health of the brand's image and the perception of its audience (Matin et al., 2022; Melewar et al., 2020). By monitoring these metrics, food companies can optimize their marketing strategies to achieve greater cost-effectiveness and customer satisfaction.

CHALLENGES AND FUTURE TRENDS

Regulatory and Ethical Issues

Jacobson et al. (2020) and Lipschultz (2020) suggest that legal and ethical issues in social media marketing are important aspects of modern marketing management that cannot be ignored. First of all, advertisements and content distribution on social media platforms must comply with the advertising laws and regulations of the regions/countries where the platforms operate. For example, false advertisements, inaccurate promises and misleading information can not only harm consumers, but also lead to lawsuits and damage to brand reputation (Khan et al., 2020; Zulham, 2023). In addition, the unauthorized use of other people's copyrighted content, trademarks or personal images on social media is also a common legal risk, which requires brands to be careful about intellectual property rights when creating and distributing content, which requires the platforms themselves to take precautions to prevent and detect the norms (Buiten et al., 2020; Keller, 2021; Marin, 2021; Sander, 2021). On an ethical level, social media marketing should avoid spreading harmful content, biased statements and false information, and ensure that information is transparent, truthful and accountable (Aswad, 2020; Chauhan et al., 2022). Brands should be socially responsible and earn users' trust and loyalty through positive guidance and authentic communication.

With the widespread use of big data and artificial intelligence technologies, brands can collect large amounts of user data through social media platforms, which can help enable precision marketing and personalized services (Haleem et al., 2022; Rane, 2023). However, the collection and misuse of personal data without users' consent not only violates privacy protection laws (e.g., the EU's General Data Protection Regulation GDPR), but also may lead to users' distrust of brands (Bauer et al., 2022; Buiten, 2021; Evans et al., 2023). In order to protect user privacy, companies and platforms should ensure that they comply with relevant laws and regulations during data collection and processing, transparently inform users about the use of their data and protection measures, and obtain their explicit consent where necessary (Van Hoboken and Fathaigh, 2021; Wulf and Seizov, 2024). In addition, enterprises and platforms should adopt technical means to protect the security of user data, prevent data leakage and misuse, and establish a sound data management and protection mechanism to enhance users' trust and loyalty (Chen et al., 2021; Georgiadis and Poels, 2021).

Technological Advancement

Emerging technologies are having an increasingly profound impact on marketing, and in particular the use of technologies such as artificial intelligence (AI) and virtual reality (VR) is reshaping the way modern marketing is done (Adeola et al., 2022; Egieya et al., 2023; Silvestri, 2020). Haleem et al. (2022) sees marketing with AI primarily in the areas of data analytics, customer relationship management and personalized marketing. Through machine learning and data mining technologies, AI can analyze large amounts of consumer data to provide accurate market forecasts and consumer behavior analysis, thus helping brands develop more effective marketing strategies (Haleem et al., 2022; Khrais, 2020). In addition, AI-driven chatbots and intelligent customer service systems can improve customer service efficiency, provide personalized user experiences, and increase customer satisfaction and loyalty (Hsu and Lin, 2023; Nicolescu and Tudorache, 2022). On the other hand, VR technology provides brands with a new way of interaction and experience. Through virtual environments and immersive experiences, consumers can understand products more intuitively and enhance brand interaction and engagement (Meißner et al., 2020; Schnack et al., 2020). This innovative marketing approach not only attracts consumers' attention, but also creates deep brand memory and emotional connection (Shahid et al., 2022; Yang et al., 2022).

Many researchers have foreseen that future market trends and directions will be driven by additional factors (e.g., technological innovations, changes in consumer behavior, and the process of globalization) (Kopalle et al., 2022; Matyushok et al., 2021; Rosário and Dias, 2022; Skare and Soriano, 2021; Zhang and Chang, 2021). With the acceleration of digitalization, personalization and experiential marketing will become mainstream trends. Consumers increasingly expect brands to provide customized product and service experiences, and brands will need to better understand and meet consumers' personalized needs through big data and AI technologies (Gkikas and Theodoridis, 2022; Rane, 2023; Reddy, 2022). Secondly, the integration of social media and e-commerce will be further deepened, and emerging business models such as social e-commerce and live streaming with goods will develop rapidly in the next few years and become an important market growth point (Lv et al., 2020; Mohdhar and Shaalan, 2021; Si, 2021). Emerging marketing methods will gradually enhance the shopping experience and emotional value for consumers without leaving home (Urdea et al., 2021; Xu et al., 2022). In addition, sustainability and social responsibility will also become an important trend in the future market. Consumers are becoming more and more concerned about the social responsibility and environmental awareness of brands, and brands need to incorporate more sustainability concepts into their products and marketing strategies in order to win the recognition and trust of consumers (Huo et al., 2022; Majeed et al., 2022; Tan et al., 2022).

CONCLUSION

Summary of the Key Findings

This chapter synthesizes and analyzes the key trends and influences of social media marketing in the Chinese food industry. Social media can drive the consumer trends of healthy eating, convenience and the combination of tradition and innovation among Chinese consumers. Secondly, consumers' purchasing decisions are influenced by factors such as brand trust, product innovation and price sensitivity. Food safety issues are also one of the key factors influencing consumers' purchasing decisions, and companies need to maintain brand reputation through transparent production processes and strict quality control as a way to gain consumer loyalty.

In terms of social media platforms and usage habits, the popularity and different characteristics of major platforms such as WeChat, Weibo, Douyin, Xiaohongshu, and B-station are important for developing brand marketing strategies (Wu, 2023). Influencer marketing, precision marketing, and video/photo sharing can enhance a brand's market reach and user engagement through social media platforms (Bhat and Malaganve, 2023; Hinson et al., 2024; Moran et al., 2020). In addition, the rapid development of social media and technological innovations have brought new marketing opportunities and challenges for organizations.

Suggestions and Future Research

In the food industry, social media, as a powerful marketing tool, has become a key way for brands to establish interaction and deliver messages to consumers. It is crucial for marketers in the food industry to adapt to changing market demands and trends. Food marketers need to focus on the growing consumer demand for healthy and sustainable food by introducing products that are organic, additive-free and environmentally friendly packaging (Mesías et al., 2021; Saulais et al., 2023). Consumer trust and loyalty to products can be increased through transparent supply chain information and certification labeling (Lam et al., 2020; Vazquez et al., 2024). In addition, utilizing digital marketing tools is an effective way to expand brand reach and distribution channels. Marketers can enhance interactive content and personalized recommendations through social media, e-commerce platforms, and mobile applications to increase consumer engagement and willingness to buy (Utami et al., 2022). Meanwhile, experiential marketing can enhance the emotional connection between consumers and brands (e.g., by organizing events such as food tastings, cooking classes, and virtual reality experiences) (Batat, 2021; Gómez and Yagüe, 2021; Jeon et al., 2020). Marketers should establish an interaction and feedback mechanism with consumers, and continuously improve their products and services by collecting and analyzing consumer opinions to meet diversified consumer needs (Gupta et al., 2021; Li, Yuan, et al., 2023; Sağkaya and Ozansoy, 2022; Sima et al., 2020; Xin et al., 2022).

Future research should explore the effectiveness and impact of digital and experiential marketing in the food industry. Specifically, the relative effectiveness of different digital marketing channels (e.g., social media, search engines, and e-commerce platforms) is an area for in-depth analysis. Some studies identified the strategies of best drive sales and brand loyalty (Angeloni and Rossi, 2021; Chawla and Chodak, 2021; Dwivedi et al., 2021). The role of experiential marketing in enhancing consumers' brand memory and emotional connection also needs to be further researched, with empirical studies exploring the effectiveness and best practices of different types of experiential activities (e.g., food tastings, virtual reality experiences) (Barhorst et al., 2021; Melo et al., 2020). As consumer interest in healthy and sustainable food increases, research should also focus on the actual impact of these factors on purchasing decisions and explore how this demand can be met through effective marketing strategies (Sharma, 2021; Toha and Supriyanto, 2023). Second, the application of big data and artificial intelligence in food marketing is currently an important and emerging research direction, analyzing how marketing strategies can be optimized through data-driven decision-making to improve market responsiveness and accuracy (Chakraborty et al., 2023; Ding et al., 2023; Sharma et al., 2021).

Future research should also continue to explore the areas of digitalization, big data, VR and AI to provide more support for theory and practice and help the food industry stay ahead of the curve in a competitive market.

REFERENCES

Adeola, O., Evans, O., Ndubuisi Edeh, J., & Adisa, I. (2022). *The future of marketing: artificial intelligence, virtual reality, and neuromarketing. Marketing Communications and Brand Development in Emerging Economies* (Vol. I). Contemporary and Future Perspectives.

Akinsipe Olasunkanmi, M.-G. (2021). *The economic effectiveness of international companies on the markets of the host countries (based on materials of Nestlé SA).*

Angeloni, S., & Rossi, C. (2021). An analytical model for comparing the profitability of competing online marketing channels: Search engine marketing versus e-commerce marketplace. *Journal of Marketing Theory and Practice*, 29(4), 534–549. DOI: 10.1080/10696679.2021.1879656

Antong, A., & Riyanti, R. (2021). *HOW DOES LOCAL WISDOM BECOME THE MAIN VALUE IN A SELLING-PRICE SETTING?* Arora, A. S., Sivakumar, K., & Pavlou, P. A. (2021). Social capacitance: Leveraging absorptive capacity in the age of social media. *Journal of Business Research*, 124, 342–356.

Aswad, E. M. (2020). In a World of" Fake News," What's a Social Media Platform to Do? *Utah L. Rev.*, 1009.

Barhorst, J. B., McLean, G., Shah, E., & Mack, R. (2021). Blending the real world and the virtual world: Exploring the role of flow in augmented reality experiences. *Journal of Business Research*, 122, 423–436. DOI: 10.1016/j.jbusres.2020.08.041

Batat, W. (2021). How augmented reality (AR) is transforming the restaurant sector: Investigating the impact of "Le Petit Chef" on customers' dining experiences. *Technological Forecasting and Social Change*, 172, 121013. DOI: 10.1016/j.techfore.2021.121013

Bauer, P. C., Gerdon, F., Keusch, F., Kreuter, F., & Vannette, D. (2022). Did the GDPR increase trust in data collectors? Evidence from observational and experimental data. *Information Communication and Society*, 25(14), 2101–2121. DOI: 10.1080/1369118X.2021.1927138

Bazaluk, O., Yatsenko, O., Zakharchuk, O., Ovcharenko, A., Khrystenko, O., & Nitsenko, V. (2020). Dynamic development of the global organic food market and opportunities for Ukraine. *Sustainability (Basel)*, 12(17), 6963. DOI: 10.3390/su12176963

Bhat, P., & Malaganve, P. (2023). Design and Implementation of Social Media Mining–Knowledge Discovery Methods for Effective Digital Marketing Strategies. *Data Engineering and Data Science: Concepts and Applications*, 23–48.

Bo, L., & Yang, X. (2022). Is consumers' willingness to pay premium for agricultural brand labels sustainable?: Evidence from Chinese consumers' random n-price auction experiment. *British Food Journal*, 124(13), 359–374. DOI: 10.1108/BFJ-01-2022-0077

Bolek, S. (2020). Consumer knowledge, attitudes, and judgments about food safety: A consumer analysis. *Trends in Food Science & Technology*, 102, 242–248. DOI: 10.1016/j.tifs.2020.03.009

Bottriell, K. (2023). MULTISTAKEHOLDER ROUNDTABLES AND VOLUNTARY STANDARDS. *SMALLHOLDERS*, 405.

Buiten, M. C. (2021). Exploitative abuses in digital markets: Between competition law and data protection law. *Journal of Antitrust Enforcement*, 9(2), 270–288. DOI: 10.1093/jaenfo/jnaa041

Buiten, M. C., De Streel, A., & Peitz, M. (2020). Rethinking liability rules for online hosting platforms. *International Journal of Law and Information Technology*, 28(2), 139–166. DOI: 10.1093/ijlit/eaaa012

Butcher, J., & Pecot, F. (2022). Visually communicating brand heritage on social media: Champagne on Instagram. *Journal of Product and Brand Management*, 31(4), 654–670. DOI: 10.1108/JPBM-01-2021-3334

Caidie, G. (2024). *Brand Equity Management of Coffee Chains: A Case Study of Luckin Coffee*. Dhonburi Rajabhat University.

Chakraborty, D., Rana, N. P., Khorana, S., Singu, H. B., & Luthra, S. (2023). Big data in food: Systematic literature review and future directions. *Journal of Computer Information Systems*, 63(5), 1243–1263. DOI: 10.1080/08874417.2022.2132428

Chakravorti, S. (2023). *Customer Relationship Management: A Global Approach.*

Chaoyu, Y. (2023). Opportunities and Strategies for Promoting Cultural Tourism Industry on Small Screens in the New Media Perspective—Take Zibo Barbecue out Circle as an Example. *Academic Journal of Humanities & Social Sciences*, 6(18), 72–76.

Chauhan, R. S., Connelly, S., Howe, D. C., Soderberg, A. T., & Crisostomo, M. (2022). The danger of "fake news": How using social media for information dissemination can inhibit the ethical decision making process. *Ethics & Behavior*, 32(4), 287–306. DOI: 10.1080/10508422.2021.1890598

Chawla, Y., & Chodak, G. (2021). Social media marketing for businesses: Organic promotions of web-links on Facebook. *Journal of Business Research*, 135, 49–65. DOI: 10.1016/j.jbusres.2021.06.020

Chen, J., Ramanathan, L., & Alazab, M. (2021). Holistic big data integrated artificial intelligent modeling to improve privacy and security in data management of smart cities. *Microprocessors and Microsystems*, 81, 103722. DOI: 10.1016/j.micpro.2020.103722

Chen, T., Samaranayake, P., Cen, X., Qi, M., & Lan, Y.-C. (2022). The impact of online reviews on consumers' purchasing decisions: Evidence from an eye-tracking study. *Frontiers in Psychology*, 13, 865702. DOI: 10.3389/fpsyg.2022.865702 PMID: 35756238

Chen, X., & Qasim, H. (2021). Does E-Brand experience matter in the consumer market? Explaining the impact of social media marketing activities on consumer-based brand equity and love. *Journal of Consumer Behaviour*, 20(5), 1065–1077. DOI: 10.1002/cb.1915

Cheung, M. L., Pires, G. D., Rosenberger, P. J.III, Leung, W. K. S., & Ting, H. (2021). Investigating the role of social media marketing on value co-creation and engagement: An empirical study in China and Hong Kong. *Australasian Marketing Journal*, 29(2), 118–131. DOI: 10.1016/j.ausmj.2020.03.006

China Industrial Statistical Yearbook. (2023). *China Food and Beverage Industry Market Size from 2016 to 2023*. https://www.stats.gov.cn/sj/ndsj/2023/indexch.htm

Comendulli, A. A. (2020). *Generation Z in China: Their importance in Chinese market and how to reach them through social media.*

Dhir, B., & Singla, N. (2020). Consumption pattern and health implications of convenience foods: A practical review. *Current Journal of Applied Science and Technology*, 38(6), 1–9. DOI: 10.9734/cjast/2019/v38i630455

Di, S. (2023). Chinese Food Nut Enterprises: An Analysis of Three Squirrels. *Academic Journal of Business & Management*, 5(3), 6–12.

Ding, H., Tian, J., Yu, W., Wilson, D. I., Young, B. R., Cui, X., Xin, X., Wang, Z., & Li, W. (2023). The application of artificial intelligence and big data in the food industry. *Foods*, 12(24), 4511. DOI: 10.3390/foods12244511 PMID: 38137314

Dolega, L., Rowe, F., & Branagan, E. (2021). Going digital? The impact of social media marketing on retail website traffic, orders and sales. *Journal of Retailing and Consumer Services*, 60, 102501. DOI: 10.1016/j.jretconser.2021.102501

dos Santos, M. L. B. (2022). The "so-called" UGC: An updated definition of user-generated content in the age of social media. *Online Information Review*, 46(1), 95–113. DOI: 10.1108/OIR-06-2020-0258

Drummond, C., O'Toole, T., & McGrath, H. (2020). Digital engagement strategies and tactics in social media marketing. *European Journal of Marketing*, 54(6), 1247–1280. DOI: 10.1108/EJM-02-2019-0183

Du, X., Liechty, T., Santos, C. A., & Park, J. (2022). 'I want to record and share my wonderful journey': Chinese Millennials' production and sharing of short-form travel videos on TikTok or Douyin. *Current Issues in Tourism*, 25(21), 3412–3424. DOI: 10.1080/13683500.2020.1810212

Dwivedi, Y. K., Ismagilova, E., Hughes, D. L., Carlson, J., Filieri, R., Jacobson, J., Jain, V., Karjaluoto, H., Kefi, H., Krishen, A. S., Kumar, V., Rahman, M. M., Raman, R., Rauschnabel, P. A., Rowley, J., Salo, J., Tran, G. A., & Wang, Y. (2021). Setting the future of digital and social media marketing research: Perspectives and research propositions. *International Journal of Information Management*, 59, 102168. DOI: 10.1016/j.ijinfomgt.2020.102168

Egieya, Z. E., Ewuga, S. K., Adegbite, A. O., & Oke, T. T. (2023). The role of virtual and augmented reality in modern marketing: A critical review. *Computer Science & IT Research Journal*, 4(3), 244–272. DOI: 10.51594/csitrj.v4i3.660

Evans, R., Hajli, N., & Nisar, T. M. (2023). Privacy-Enhancing Factors and Consumer Concerns: The Moderating Effects of the General Data Protection Regulation. *British Journal of Management*, 34(4), 2075–2092. DOI: 10.1111/1467-8551.12685

Franzolini, B. (2020). *Niche market analysis and marketing strategies applied to the Chinese market: a case study of the tea and the coffee market sold through e-commerce.*

Georgiadis, G., & Poels, G. (2021). Enterprise architecture management as a solution for addressing general data protection regulation requirements in a big data context: A systematic mapping study. *Information Systems and e-Business Management*, 19(1), 313–362. DOI: 10.1007/s10257-020-00500-5

Giudice, F. (2020). *WeChat: the impact of the super app on Chinese society.*

Gkikas, D. C., & Theodoridis, P. K. (2022). AI in consumer behavior. *Advances in Artificial Intelligence-Based Technologies: Selected Papers in Honour of Professor Nikolaos G.Bourbakis*, 1, 147–176.

Goktepe, S., Cifci, M. A., & Sahin, M. A. (2022). Sharing photos of food traveler experiences: A case study of foodstagramming. In *Handbook on Tourism and Social Media* (pp. 437–450). Edward Elgar Publishing. DOI: 10.4337/9781800371415.00043

Gómez-Suárez, M., & Yagüe, M. J. (2021). Making sense from experience: How a sustainable multi-sensory event spurs word-of-mouth recommendation of a destination brand. *Sustainability (Basel)*, 13(11), 5873. DOI: 10.3390/su13115873

Gong, D., Gan, X., Tang, X., Li, H., & Gao, X. (2023). Data Mining and Analysis of Video Barrage By AI Algorithm. *2023 IEEE 5th Eurasia Conference on Biomedical Engineering, Healthcare and Sustainability (ECBIOS)*, 144–149.

Górska-Warsewicz, H., & Kulykovets, O. (2020). Hotel brand loyalty—A systematic literature review. *Sustainability (Basel)*, 12(12), 4810. DOI: 10.3390/su12124810

Guadiana, G. (2020). *A Netflix experience: reimagining the direct-to-consumer platform*. Massachusetts Institute of Technology.

Guiné, R. P. F., Florença, S. G., Barroca, M. J., & Anjos, O. (2020). The link between the consumer and the innovations in food product development. *Foods*, 9(9), 1317. DOI: 10.3390/foods9091317 PMID: 32962007

Gupta, S., Justy, T., Kamboj, S., Kumar, A., & Kristoffersen, E. (2021). Big data and firm marketing performance: Findings from knowledge-based view. *Technological Forecasting and Social Change*, 171, 120986. DOI: 10.1016/j.techfore.2021.120986

Haleem, A., Javaid, M., Qadri, M. A., Singh, R. P., & Suman, R. (2022). Artificial intelligence (AI) applications for marketing: A literature-based study. *International Journal of Intelligent Networks*, 3, 119–132. DOI: 10.1016/j.ijin.2022.08.005

Hassoun, A., Cropotova, J., Trif, M., Rusu, A. V., Bobiş, O., Nayik, G. A., Jagdale, Y. D., Saeed, F., Afzaal, M., Mostashari, P., Khaneghah, A. M., & Regenstein, J. M. (2022). Consumer acceptance of new food trends resulting from the fourth industrial revolution technologies: A narrative review of literature and future perspectives. *Frontiers in Nutrition*, 9, 972154. DOI: 10.3389/fnut.2022.972154 PMID: 36034919

Hinson, R. E., Mhlanga, D., Osei-Frimpong, K., & Doe, J. (2024). *Social Media Marketing Management: How to Penetrate Emerging Markets and Expand Your Customer Base*. CRC Press. DOI: 10.4324/9781003307457

Hsu, C.-L., & Lin, J. C.-C. (2023). Understanding the user satisfaction and loyalty of customer service chatbots. *Journal of Retailing and Consumer Services*, 71, 103211. DOI: 10.1016/j.jretconser.2022.103211

Hu, Y., Su, M., Wang, Y., Cui, S., Meng, F., Yue, W., Liu, Y., Xu, C., & Yang, Z. (2020). Food production in China requires intensified measures to be consistent with national and provincial environmental boundaries. *Nature Food*, 1(9), 572–582. DOI: 10.1038/s43016-020-00143-2 PMID: 37128013

Huang, J., Chuin, T. P., Zhao, K., & Chen, Y. (2021). Business Models in Live Video Streaming Platforms: A Comparative Case Study. *Turkish Online Journal of Qualitative Inquiry, 12*(6).

Huang, Q., & Fleiss, A. (2023). How is the food culture in China changing? *Available atSSRN* 4572452. DOI: 10.2139/ssrn.4572452

Huang, Q., Li, X., & Liu, H. (2021). Analysis of Wechat Marketing Model in The Context of Mobile Internet Era. *Proceedings of the 2021 12th International Conference on E-Business, Management and Economics*, 21–27. DOI: 10.1145/3481127.3481190

Huang, Y. (2024). Study on Podcasting Empowered Brands. In *Ear Economy: China Audio Streaming Programs Study* (pp. 285–295). Springer. DOI: 10.1007/978-981-97-2034-7_24

Huo, C., Hameed, J., Zhang, M., Bin Mohd Ali, A. F., & Nik Hashim, N. A. A. (2022). Modeling the impact of corporate social responsibility on sustainable purchase intentions: Insights into brand trust and brand loyalty. *Ekonomska Istrazivanja*, 35(1), 4710–4739. DOI: 10.1080/1331677X.2021.2016465

Inavolu, S. M. (n.d.). *Exploring AI-Driven Customer Service: Evolution*. Architectures, Opportunities, Challenges and Future Directions.

Jacobson, J., Gruzd, A., & Hernández-García, Á. (2020). Social media marketing: Who is watching the watchers? *Journal of Retailing and Consumer Services*, 53, 101774. DOI: 10.1016/j.jretconser.2019.03.001

JAIN, A. (2022). *Effect of Social Media Marketing on Consumer Behavior for Netflix*. FORE School of Management.

Jeon, H. M., Yoo, S. R., & Kim, S. H. (2020). The relationships among experience, delight, and recollection for revisit intention in chocolate exposition. *Sustainability (Basel)*, 12(20), 8644. DOI: 10.3390/su12208644

Joya, K., Ramli, N. N., Shamsudin, M. N., & Kamarulzaman, N. H. (2022). Consumers' willingness to pay for food safety attributes of tomato. *British Food Journal*, 124(3), 701–717. DOI: 10.1108/BFJ-02-2021-0164

Katsikouli, P., Wilde, A. S., Dragoni, N., & Høgh-Jensen, H. (2021). On the benefits and challenges of blockchains for managing food supply chains. *Journal of the Science of Food and Agriculture*, 101(6), 2175–2181. DOI: 10.1002/jsfa.10883 PMID: 33063342

Kaur, H., Paruthi, M., Islam, J., & Hollebeek, L. D. (2020). The role of brand community identification and reward on consumer brand engagement and brand loyalty in virtual brand communities. *Telematics and Informatics*, 46, 101321. DOI: 10.1016/j.tele.2019.101321

Kaye, D. B. V., Zeng, J., & Wikstrom, P. (2022). *TikTok: Creativity and culture in short video*. John Wiley & Sons.

Keller, D. (2021). Amplification and its discontents: Why regulating the reach of online content is hard. *J. Free Speech L.*, 1, 227.

Khan, S. K., Fatima, H., & Hussain, S. W. (2020). How Consumers' Skepticism is Derived from Deceptive Advertisements. *International Journal of Experiential Learning & Case Studies*, 5(2). Advance online publication. DOI: 10.22555/ijelcs.v5i2.106

Khrais, L. T. (2020). Role of artificial intelligence in shaping consumer demand in E-commerce. *Future Internet*, 12(12), 226. DOI: 10.3390/fi12120226

Konoplyannikova, M., Radkevych, L., Netreba, M., Bilan, M., Lorvi, I., & Nahorna, O. (2024). Digital marketing and communication strategies of agri-food enterprises on social media platforms. *Agronomy Research (Tartu)*, ●●●, 22.

Kopalle, P. K., Gangwar, M., Kaplan, A., Ramachandran, D., Reinartz, W., & Rindfleisch, A. (2022). Examining artificial intelligence (AI) technologies in marketing via a global lens: Current trends and future research opportunities. *International Journal of Research in Marketing*, 39(2), 522–540. DOI: 10.1016/j.ijresmar.2021.11.002

Kroeber, A. R. (2020). *China's economy: What everyone needs to know*. Oxford University Press. DOI: 10.1093/wentk/9780190946470.001.0001

Kumar, G. S., Kulkarni, M., & Rathi, N. (2022). Evolving food choices among the urban Indian middle-class: A qualitative study. *Frontiers in Nutrition*, 9, 844413. DOI: 10.3389/fnut.2022.844413 PMID: 35425799

Lam, T. K., Heales, J., Hartley, N., & Hodkinson, C. (2020). Consumer trust in food safety requires information transparency. *AJIS. Australasian Journal of Information Systems*, 24, 24. DOI: 10.3127/ajis.v24i0.2219

Lei, L. I., Zhai, S.-X., & Bai, J.-F. (2021). The dynamic impact of income and income distribution on food consumption among adults in rural China. *Journal of Integrative Agriculture*, 20(1), 330–342. DOI: 10.1016/S2095-3119(20)63239-7

Lewis, K. O., Popov, V., & Fatima, S. S. (2024). From static web to metaverse: Reinventing medical education in the post-pandemic era. *Annals of Medicine*, 56(1), 2305694. DOI: 10.1080/07853890.2024.2305694 PMID: 38261592

Li, D. (2020). *The impact of Chinese tourists' use of Weibo as their tourist destination selection to Thailand*.

Li, L., Yuan, L., & Tian, J. (2023). Influence of online E-commerce interaction on consumer satisfaction based on big data algorithm. *Heliyon*, 9(8), e18322. DOI: 10.1016/j.heliyon.2023.e18322 PMID: 37588603

Li, L., Zhang, J., & An, X. (2023). Using social media for efficient brand marketing: An evaluation of Chinese Universities using Bilibili. *Socio-Economic Planning Sciences*, 88, 101645. DOI: 10.1016/j.seps.2023.101645

Li, Y., Li, X., & Cai, J. (2021). How attachment affects user stickiness on live streaming platforms: A socio-technical approach perspective. *Journal of Retailing and Consumer Services*, 60, 102478. DOI: 10.1016/j.jretconser.2021.102478

Li, Y., & Xie, Y. (2020). Is a picture worth a thousand words? An empirical study of image content and social media engagement. *JMR, Journal of Marketing Research*, 57(1), 1–19. DOI: 10.1177/0022243719881113

Lin, J., Guia Julve, J., Xu, H., & Cui, Q. (2020). Food habits and tourist food consumption: An exploratory study on dining behaviours of Chinese outbound tourists in Spain. *Journal of Policy Research in Tourism, Leisure & Events*, 12(1), 82–99. DOI: 10.1080/19407963.2018.1506199

Lipschultz, J. H. (2020). *Social media communication: Concepts, practices, data, law and ethics*. Routledge. DOI: 10.4324/9780429202834

Liu, R., Gao, Z., Snell, H. A., & Ma, H. (2020). Food safety concerns and consumer preferences for food safety attributes: Evidence from China. *Food Control*, 112, 107157. DOI: 10.1016/j.foodcont.2020.107157

Liu, X. (2021). *An analysis of digital marketing strategy in the era of social media in China*. Massachusetts Institute of Technology.

Liu, X., Xu, Y., Engel, B. A., Sun, S., Zhao, X., Wu, P., & Wang, Y. (2021). The impact of urbanization and aging on food security in developing countries: The view from Northwest China. *Journal of Cleaner Production*, 292, 126067. DOI: 10.1016/j.jclepro.2021.126067

Liu, Z., Du, J., & He, J. (2022). Marketing Dilemma and Countermeasures of Leisure Food Under Mobile Internet--A Case Study of Three Squirrels in E-Commerce Enterprises. *2022 2nd International Conference on Management Science and Software Engineering (ICMSSE 2022)*, 273–278.

Llanera, P. (2023). *Enhancing Restaurant Visibility: Standardised Handbook for Food Presentation on Social Media*.

Lu, J., Jia, X., Lev, B., Zhang, C., Gao, Y., Zhao, M., & He, Y. (2021). How to understand "salable fake goods" and "unsalable quality goods"? An insight from the view of quality responsibility and consumers' brand loyalty. *Technology in Society*, 67, 101793. DOI: 10.1016/j.techsoc.2021.101793

Lu, Z., & Nam, I. (2021). Research on the influence of new media technology on internet short video content production under artificial intelligence background. *Complexity*, 2021(1), 8875700. DOI: 10.1155/2021/8875700

Lv, J., Wang, Z., Huang, Y., Wang, T., & Wang, Y. (2020). How can e-commerce businesses implement discount strategies through social media? *Sustainability (Basel)*, 12(18), 7459. DOI: 10.3390/su12187459

Lyu, X., Jia, F., & Zhao, B. (2023). Impact of big data and cloud-driven learning technologies in healthy and smart cities on marketing automation. *Soft Computing*, 27(7), 4209–4222. DOI: 10.1007/s00500-022-07031-w

Macready, A. L., Hieke, S., Klimczuk-Kochańska, M., Szumiał, S., Vranken, L., & Grunert, K. G. (2020). Consumer trust in the food value chain and its impact on consumer confidence: A model for assessing consumer trust and evidence from a 5-country study in Europe. *Food Policy*, 92, 101880. DOI: 10.1016/j.foodpol.2020.101880

Majeed, M. U., Aslam, S., Murtaza, S. A., Attila, S., & Molnár, E. (2022). Green marketing approaches and their impact on green purchase intentions: Mediating role of green brand image and consumer beliefs towards the environment. *Sustainability (Basel)*, 14(18), 11703. DOI: 10.3390/su141811703

Marin, L. (2021). Sharing (mis) information on social networking sites. An exploration of the norms for distributing content authored by others. *Ethics and Information Technology*, 23(3), 363–372. DOI: 10.1007/s10676-021-09578-y

Matin, A., Khoshtaria, T., & Todua, N. (2022). The impact of social media influencers on brand awareness, image and trust in their sponsored content: An empirical study from Georgian social media users. *International Journal of Marketing, Communication and New Media, 10*(18).

Matyushok, V., Vera Krasavina, V., Berezin, A., & Sendra García, J. (2021). The global economy in technological transformation conditions: A review of modern trends. *Ekonomska Istrazivanja*, 34(1), 1471–1497. DOI: 10.1080/1331677X.2020.1844030

McClure, C., & Seock, Y.-K. (2020). The role of involvement: Investigating the effect of brand's social media pages on consumer purchase intention. *Journal of Retailing and Consumer Services*, 53, 101975. DOI: 10.1016/j.jretconser.2019.101975

Meißner, M., Pfeiffer, J., Peukert, C., Dietrich, H., & Pfeiffer, T. (2020). How virtual reality affects consumer choice. *Journal of Business Research*, 117, 219–231. DOI: 10.1016/j.jbusres.2020.06.004

Melewar, T., Foroudi, P., & Jin, Z. (2020). Corporate branding, identity, image and reputation: Current and future trends, developments and challenges. *Journal of Business Research*, 117, 672–674. DOI: 10.1016/j.jbusres.2020.06.030

Melo, M., Gonçalves, G., Monteiro, P., Coelho, H., Vasconcelos-Raposo, J., & Bessa, M. (2020). Do multisensory stimuli benefit the virtual reality experience? A systematic review. *IEEE Transactions on Visualization and Computer Graphics*, 28(2), 1428–1442. DOI: 10.1109/TVCG.2020.3010088 PMID: 32746276

MENGXI, Z. (n.d.). *Marketing strategies for new media in the internet Era–DouYin short video as an example*.

Mesías, F. J., Martín, A., & Hernández, A. (2021). Consumers' growing appetite for natural foods: Perceptions towards the use of natural preservatives in fresh fruit. *Food Research International*, 150, 110749. DOI: 10.1016/j.foodres.2021.110749 PMID: 34865767

Milesi, E. (n.d.). *Italian food internationalisation process: the case of Beretta and Senfter in China*.

Mohammad, T., Yusop, A. S., & Azam, N. A. A. (n.d.). *FACTORS AFFECTING URBAN CONSUMERS' PURCHASE DECISIONS FOR READY-TO-EAT FOODS: A STUDY IN PULAU PINANG, MALAYSIA*.

Mohdhar, A., & Shaalan, K. (2021). The future of e-commerce systems: 2030 and beyond. *Recent Advances in Technology Acceptance Models and Theories*, 311–330.

Moran, G., Muzellec, L., & Johnson, D. (2020). Message content features and social media engagement: Evidence from the media industry. *Journal of Product and Brand Management*, 29(5), 533–545. DOI: 10.1108/JPBM-09-2018-2014

Mróz, B. (2021). Consumer shopping behaviours on social media platforms: Trends, challenges, business implications. In *Disruptive Platforms* (pp. 113–129). Routledge. DOI: 10.4324/9781003207481-7

Nicolescu, L., & Tudorache, M. T. (2022). Human-computer interaction in customer service: The experience with AI chatbots—a systematic literature review. *Electronics (Basel)*, 11(10), 1579. DOI: 10.3390/electronics11101579

Onofrei, G., Filieri, R., & Kennedy, L. (2022). Social media interactions, purchase intention, and behavioural engagement: The mediating role of source and content factors. *Journal of Business Research*, 142, 100–112. DOI: 10.1016/j.jbusres.2021.12.031

Ouyang, H., Li, B., McCarthy, M., Miao, S., Kilcawley, K., Fenelon, M., Kelly, A., & Sheehan, J. J. (2021). Understanding preferences for and consumer behavior toward cheese among a cohort of young, educated, internationally mobile Chinese consumers. *Journal of Dairy Science*, 104(12), 12415–12426. DOI: 10.3168/jds.2021-20598 PMID: 34482973

Palalic, R., Ramadani, V., Mariam Gilani, S., Gërguri-Rashiti, S., & Dana, L. (2021). Social media and consumer buying behavior decision: What entrepreneurs should know? *Management Decision*, 59(6), 1249–1270. DOI: 10.1108/MD-10-2019-1461

Paley, N. (2021). *The manager's guide to competitive marketing strategies*. Routledge. DOI: 10.4324/9780203736463

Peschel, A. O., & Aschemann-Witzel, J. (2020). Sell more for less or less for more? The role of transparency in consumer response to upcycled food products. *Journal of Cleaner Production*, 273, 122884. DOI: 10.1016/j.jclepro.2020.122884

Primasiwi, C., Irawan, M. I., & Ambarwati, R. (2021). Key Performance Indicators for Influencer Marketing on Instagram. *2nd International Conference on Business and Management of Technology (Iconbmt 2020)*, 154–163. DOI: 10.2991/aebmr.k.210510.027

Qu, Y., Cieślik, A., Fang, S., & Qing, Y. (2023). The role of online interaction in user stickiness of social commerce: The shopping value perspective. *Digital Business*, 3(2), 100061. DOI: 10.1016/j.digbus.2023.100061

Quintana-García, C., Benavides-Chicón, C. G., & Marchante-Lara, M. (2021). Does a green supply chain improve corporate reputation? Empirical evidence from European manufacturing sectors. *Industrial Marketing Management*, 92, 344–353. DOI: 10.1016/j.indmarman.2019.12.011

Rahman, O., Fung, B. C. M., & Chen, Z. (2020). Young Chinese consumers' choice between product-related and sustainable cues—The Effects of Gender Differences and Consumer Innovativeness. *Sustainability (Basel)*, 12(9), 3818. DOI: 10.3390/su12093818

Rakshit, S., Islam, N., Mondal, S., & Paul, T. (2022). An integrated social network marketing metric for business-to-business SMEs. *Journal of Business Research*, 150, 73–88. DOI: 10.1016/j.jbusres.2022.06.006

Rane, N. (2023). Enhancing customer loyalty through Artificial Intelligence (AI), Internet of Things (IoT), and Big Data technologies: improving customer satisfaction, engagement, relationship, and experience. *Internet of Things (IoT), and Big Data Technologies: Improving Customer Satisfaction, Engagement, Relationship, and Experience (October 13, 2023).*

Reddy, S. R. B. (2022). Enhancing Customer Experience through AI-Powered Marketing Automation: Strategies and Best Practices for Industry 4.0. *Journal of Artificial Intelligence Research*, 2(1), 36–46.

Riccioli, F., Moruzzo, R., Zhang, Z., Zhao, J., Tang, Y., Tinacci, L., Boncinelli, F., De Martino, D., & Guidi, A. (2020). Willingness to pay in main cities of Zheijiang provice (China) for quality and safety in food market. *Food Control*, 108, 106831. DOI: 10.1016/j.foodcont.2019.106831

Rosário, A. T., & Dias, J. C. (2022). Industry 4.0 and marketing: Towards an integrated future research agenda. *Journal of Sensor and Actuator Networks*, 11(3), 30. DOI: 10.3390/jsan11030030

Rust, R. T., Rand, W., Huang, M.-H., Stephen, A. T., Brooks, G., & Chabuk, T. (2021). Real-time brand reputation tracking using social media. *Journal of Marketing*, 85(4), 21–43. DOI: 10.1177/0022242921995173

Safeer, A. A., Abrar, M., Liu, H., & Yuanqiong, H. (2022). Effects of perceived brand localness and perceived brand globalness on consumer behavioral intentions in emerging markets. *Management Decision*, 60(9), 2482–2502. DOI: 10.1108/MD-10-2021-1296

Sağkaya Güngör, A., & Ozansoy Çadırcı, T. (2022). Understanding digital consumer: A review, synthesis, and future research agenda. *International Journal of Consumer Studies*, 46(5), 1829–1858. DOI: 10.1111/ijcs.12809

Sander, B. (2021). Democratic disruption in the age of social media: Between marketized and structural conceptions of human rights law. *European Journal of International Law*, 32(1), 159–193. DOI: 10.1093/ejil/chab022

Santos, Z. R., Cheung, C. M. K., Coelho, P. S., & Rita, P. (2022). Consumer engagement in social media brand communities: A literature review. *International Journal of Information Management*, 63, 102457. DOI: 10.1016/j.ijinfomgt.2021.102457

Saulais, L., Corcuff, R., & Boonefaes, E. (2023). Natural and healthy? Consumers knowledge, understanding and preferences regarding naturalness and healthiness of processed foods. *International Journal of Gastronomy and Food Science*, 31, 100662. DOI: 10.1016/j.ijgfs.2023.100662

Schiro, J. L., Shan, L. C., Tatlow-Golden, M., Li, C., & Wall, P. (2020). # Healthy: Smart digital food safety and nutrition communication strategies—a critical commentary. *NPJ Science of Food*, 4(1), 14. DOI: 10.1038/s41538-020-00074-z PMID: 33083546

Schnack, A., Wright, M. J., & Holdershaw, J. L. (2020). An exploratory investigation of shopper behaviour in an immersive virtual reality store. *Journal of Consumer Behaviour*, 19(2), 182–195. DOI: 10.1002/cb.1803

Shahid, S., Paul, J., Gilal, F. G., & Ansari, S. (2022). The role of sensory marketing and brand experience in building emotional attachment and brand loyalty in luxury retail stores. *Psychology and Marketing*, 39(7), 1398–1412. DOI: 10.1002/mar.21661

Shao, Z., Zhang, L., Chen, K., & Zhang, C. (2020). Examining user satisfaction and stickiness in social networking sites from a technology affordance lens: Uncovering the moderating effect of user experience. *Industrial Management & Data Systems*, 120(7), 1331–1360. DOI: 10.1108/IMDS-11-2019-0614

Sharma, A. P. (2021). Consumers' purchase behaviour and green marketing: A synthesis, review and agenda. *International Journal of Consumer Studies*, 45(6), 1217–1238. DOI: 10.1111/ijcs.12722

Sharma, S., Gahlawat, V. K., Rahul, K., Mor, R. S., & Malik, M. (2021). Sustainable innovations in the food industry through artificial intelligence and big data analytics. *Logistics (Basel)*, 5(4), 66. DOI: 10.3390/logistics5040066

Shen, B., & Chen, C. (2020). Quality management in outsourced global fashion supply chains: An exploratory case study. *Production Planning and Control*, 31(9), 757–769. DOI: 10.1080/09537287.2019.1683774

Si, R. (2021). *China livestreaming e-commerce industry insights*. Springer. DOI: 10.1007/978-981-16-5344-5

Silva, S. C., Duarte, P. A. O., & Almeida, S. R. (2020). How companies evaluate the ROI of social media marketing programmes: Insights from B2B and B2C. *Journal of Business and Industrial Marketing*, 35(12), 2097–2110. DOI: 10.1108/JBIM-06-2019-0291

Silvestri, B. (2020). The future of fashion: How the quest for digitization and the use of artificial intelligence and extended reality will reshape the fashion industry after COVID-19. *ZoneModa Journal*, 10(2), 61–73.

Sima, V., Gheorghe, I. G., Subić, J., & Nancu, D. (2020). Influences of the industry 4.0 revolution on the human capital development and consumer behavior: A systematic review. *Sustainability (Basel)*, 12(10), 4035. DOI: 10.3390/su12104035

Skare, M., & Soriano, D. R. (2021). How globalization is changing digital technology adoption: An international perspective. *Journal of Innovation & Knowledge*, 6(4), 222–233. DOI: 10.1016/j.jik.2021.04.001

Sohu.com. (2024). *2023 Guide to China's Social Media Platforms (WeChat, Jieyin, Xiaohongshu, Shutterstock, Meibiao, Weibo, B Station)*. https://www.sohu.com/a/682966128_121123886

Song, S., Zhao, Y. C., Yao, X., Ba, Z., & Zhu, Q. (2021). Short video apps as a health information source: An investigation of affordances, user experience and users' intention to continue the use of TikTok. *Internet Research*, 31(6), 2120–2142. DOI: 10.1108/INTR-10-2020-0593

Su, Y. (2022). Accurate Marketing Algorithm of Network Video Based on User Big Data Analysis. *Mathematical Problems in Engineering*, 2022(1), 3317234. DOI: 10.1155/2022/3317234

Tan, Z., Sadiq, B., Bashir, T., Mahmood, H., & Rasool, Y. (2022). Investigating the impact of green marketing components on purchase intention: The mediating role of brand image and brand trust. *Sustainability (Basel)*, 14(10), 5939. DOI: 10.3390/su14105939

Toha, M., & Supriyanto, S. (2023). Factors Influencing the Consumer Research Process: Market Target, Purchasing Behavior and Market Demand (Literature Review of Consumer Behavior). *Danadyaksa: Post Modern Economy Journal*, 1(1), 1–17. DOI: 10.69965/danadyaksa.v1i1.5

Tuten, T. L. (2023). *Social media marketing*. Sage publications limited.

Urdea, A.-M., Constantin, C. P., & Purcaru, I.-M. (2021). Implementing experiential marketing in the digital age for a more sustainable customer relationship. *Sustainability (Basel)*, 13(4), 1865. DOI: 10.3390/su13041865

Utami, A. F., Ekaputra, I. A., Japutra, A., & Van Doorn, S. (2022). The role of interactivity on customer engagement in mobile e-commerce applications. *International Journal of Market Research*, 64(2), 269–291. DOI: 10.1177/14707853211027483

Van Hoboken, J., & Fathaigh, R. Ó. (2021). Smartphone platforms as privacy regulators. *Computer Law & Security Report*, 41, 105557. DOI: 10.1016/j.clsr.2021.105557

Vazquez Melendez, E. I., Bergey, P., & Smith, B. (2024). Blockchain technology for supply chain provenance: Increasing supply chain efficiency and consumer trust. *Supply Chain Management*, 29(4), 706–730. DOI: 10.1108/SCM-08-2023-0383

Vitsentzatou, E., Tsoulfas, G. T., & Mihiotis, A. N. (2022). The digital transformation of the marketing mix in the food and beverage service supply chain: A Grey DEMATEL approach. *Sustainability (Basel)*, 14(22), 15228. DOI: 10.3390/su142215228

Wang, B., Shen, C., Cai, Y., Dai, L., Gai, S., & Liu, D. (2023). Consumer culture in traditional food market: The influence of Chinese consumers to the cultural construction of Chinese barbecue. *Food Control*, 143, 109311. DOI: 10.1016/j.foodcont.2022.109311

Wang, E., An, N., Gao, Z., Kiprop, E., & Geng, X. (2020). Consumer food stockpiling behavior and willingness to pay for food reserves in COVID-19. *Food Security*, 12(4), 739–747. DOI: 10.1007/s12571-020-01092-1 PMID: 32837661

Weber, P., Ludwig, T., Brodesser, S., & Grönewald, L. (2021). "It's a Kind of Art!": Understanding Food Influencers as Influential Content Creators. *Proceedings of the 2021 CHI Conference on Human Factors in Computing Systems*, 1–14.

Wei, W. (2023). Re-feminizing Beauty in the Multimodal Storytelling Practices of Chinese Social Media Influencers on Xiaohongshu (RED). *International Conference on Human-Computer Interaction*, 400–419. DOI: 10.1007/978-3-031-48044-7_29

Wen, J., Kozak, M., Yang, S., & Liu, F. (2021). COVID-19: Potential effects on Chinese citizens' lifestyle and travel. *Tourism Review*, 76(1), 74–87. DOI: 10.1108/TR-03-2020-0110

Wongsansukcharoen, J. (2022). Effect of community relationship management, relationship marketing orientation, customer engagement, and brand trust on brand loyalty: The case of a commercial bank in Thailand. *Journal of Retailing and Consumer Services*, 64, 102826. DOI: 10.1016/j.jretconser.2021.102826

Wu, S. (2023). Influencing factors of mobile shortvideo APP users' willingness to continue using. *Proceedings of the 2nd International Conference on Bigdata Blockchain and Economy Management, ICBBEM 2023, May 19–21, 2023, Hangzhou, China.*

Wulf, A. J., & Seizov, O. (2024). "Please understand we cannot provide further information": Evaluating content and transparency of GDPR-mandated AI disclosures. *AI & Society*, 39(1), 235–256. DOI: 10.1007/s00146-022-01424-z

Xin, X., Wu, J., Huang, L., Shang, S., & Chen, P. (2022). Effect of multi-channel integration on customer purchase intention. *Journal of Computer Information Systems*, 62(5), 1036–1047. DOI: 10.1080/08874417.2021.1965052

Xing, Y., Li, M., & Liao, Y. (2022). Trust, price sensitivity and consumers' organic food purchasing behaviour in China. *Food Science and Technology (Campinas)*, 42, e42422. DOI: 10.1590/fst.42422

XU, C. (2023). *The determinants of creator performance on creative content platforms: Evidence from Xiaohongshu and Bilibili.*

Xu, C., Park, J., & Lee, J. C. (2022). The effect of shopping channel (online vs offline) on consumer decision process and firm's marketing strategy. *Internet Research*, 32(3), 971–987. DOI: 10.1108/INTR-11-2020-0660

Xu, W. (2023). Bilibili video streaming platform: Community culture identity vs. commercial culture. In *Cases on Social Justice in China and Perspectives on Chinese Brands* (pp. 237–250). IGI Global. DOI: 10.4018/978-1-6684-4955-4.ch017

Yang, Q., Hayat, N., Al Mamun, A., Makhbul, Z. K. M., & Zainol, N. R. (2022). Sustainable customer retention through social media marketing activities using hybrid SEM-neural network approach. *PLoS One*, 17(3), e0264899. DOI: 10.1371/journal.pone.0264899 PMID: 35245323

Yaqi, Z., Lee, J.-Y., & Liu, S. (2021). Research on the Uses and Gratifications of Tiktok (Douyin short video). *International Journal of Contents*, 17(1), 37–53.

Yu, Z., Jung, D., Park, S., Hu, Y., Huang, K., Rasco, B. A., Wang, S., Ronholm, J., Lu, X., & Chen, J. (2022). Smart traceability for food safety. *Critical Reviews in Food Science and Nutrition*, 62(4), 905–916. DOI: 10.1080/10408398.2020.1830262 PMID: 33030032

Yuan, Y., Xu, C., & Fang, F. (2022). Discussion on Stock Price Trend of Chinese Dairy Industry. *2022 7th International Conference on Social Sciences and Economic Development (ICSSED 2022)*, 886–889.

Zeng, L., Li, R. Y. M., Mao, Y., Chen, H., & Zeng, H. (2022). A comparative study on LinkedIn and Sina Weibo users' perceptions of the carbon-neutral city. *Frontiers in Environmental Science*, 10, 962367. DOI: 10.3389/fenvs.2022.962367

Zhang, H., Gupta, S., Sun, W., & Zou, Y. (2020). How social-media-enabled co-creation between customers and the firm drives business value? The perspective of organizational learning and social Capital. *Information & Management*, 57(3), 103200. DOI: 10.1016/j.im.2019.103200

Zhang, J. Z., & Chang, C.-W. (2021). Consumer dynamics: Theories, methods, and emerging directions. *Journal of the Academy of Marketing Science*, 49(1), 166–196. DOI: 10.1007/s11747-020-00720-8

Zhang, M., Hu, H., & Zhao, X. (2020). Developing product recall capability through supply chain quality management. *International Journal of Production Economics*, 229, 107795. DOI: 10.1016/j.ijpe.2020.107795

Zhang, W. (2024). Influence of Live Commerce on Consumer Purchase Intention: Based on Internet-famous Food Research. *International Journal of Global Economics and Management*, 3(2), 486–514. DOI: 10.62051/ijgem.v3n2.56

Zhang, Y., Diao, X., Chen, K. Z., Robinson, S., & Fan, S. (2020). Impact of COVID-19 on China's macroeconomy and agri-food system–an economy-wide multiplier model analysis. *China Agricultural Economic Review*, 12(3), 387–407. DOI: 10.1108/CAER-04-2020-0063

Zhao, H., Chang, J., Havlík, P., van Dijk, M., Valin, H., Janssens, C., Ma, L., Bai, Z., Herrero, M., Smith, P., & Obersteiner, M. (2021). China's future food demand and its implications for trade and environment. *Nature Sustainability*, 4(12), 1042–1051. DOI: 10.1038/s41893-021-00784-6

Zhao, J., Butt, R. S., Murad, M., Mirza, F., & Saleh Al-Faryan, M. A. (2022). Untying the influence of advertisements on consumers buying behavior and brand loyalty through brand awareness: The moderating role of perceived quality. *Frontiers in Psychology*, 12, 803348. DOI: 10.3389/fpsyg.2021.803348 PMID: 35153925

Zheng, C. (2023). Research on the flow experience and social influences of users of short online videos. A case study of DouYin. *Scientific Reports*, 13(1), 3312. DOI: 10.1038/s41598-023-30525-y PMID: 36849531

Zhong, S., Wang, M., Zhu, Y., Chen, Z., & Huang, X. (2022). Urban expansion and the urban–rural income gap: Empirical evidence from China. *Cities (London, England)*, 129, 103831. DOI: 10.1016/j.cities.2022.103831

Zong, S., Dowpiset, K., & Nuangjamnong, C. (2023). Understanding Payment Transaction Behavior of Social Media Users: An Empirical Study on WeChat. *The BSSS Conference*. DOI: 10.2139/ssrn.4433487

Zulham, Z. (2023). A Critical Review Of Indonesian Online Consumer Protection Online Shopping, False Advertising, And Legal Protection For Indonesian E-Commerce Customers. *Journal of Law and Sustainable Development*, 11(5), 1–15. DOI: 10.55908/sdgs.v11i5.740

Chapter 3
Optimizing Food Quality and Customer Service in Restaurants Through AI-Powered Monitoring Systems

Vipin Singh
https://orcid.org/0000-0001-5566-0151
Vellore Institute of Technology, India

K. Karthik
https://orcid.org/0000-0003-0846-2982
Vellore Institute of Technology, India

ABSTRACT

The restaurant world is fast and competitive with advancement in technology. Success in the business world heavily relies on customer happiness. Providing exceptional dining experiences to customers is no longer considered a luxury, but rather a necessity. Fortunately, the advent of AI has brought a wave of transformation in the restaurant industry. AI technology, restaurants can provide unmatched customer satisfaction. From personalized dining experiences to streamlining operations, AI is revolutionizing the industry by introducing innovative solutions in the competitive restaurant industry by enhancing food quality, kitchen efficiency, and customer service. AI ensures consistency, safety, and excellence in dining experiences through advanced algorithms and real-time data analytics. Exploring how AI-powered technologies streamline restaurant operations and elevate hospitality standards is the main focus of this study. Case studies include AI robots manage various services showcasing AI's potential to transform guest interactions and operational accuracy.

1. INTRODUCTION

Sustaining first-rate cuisine and customer service is crucial for success in the fiercely competitive restaurant business. Artificial intelligence (AI) is emerging as a revolutionary tool to improve operational efficiency and consumer happiness as eating experiences change with technological improvements. AI-

DOI: 10.4018/979-8-3693-7683-6.ch003

powered monitoring technologies are transforming restaurant operations to oversee food quality better, run their kitchens, and provide exceptional customer service. These systems ensure uniformity, safety, and excellence in every facet of the dining experience by streamlining operations using sophisticated algorithms and real-time data analytics. Restaurants may attain a new level of accuracy for standard operating procedures (Sharma et al.2022 and Ford 2021). In the 290-room Fly Zoo Future hotel, owned by Chinese e-commerce giant Alibaba Group in Hangzhou, China, numerous services, including check-in, lighting control, and room service, are managed by AI robots. Meanwhile, Hilton Hotels has introduced a real robot named "Connie" at their Virginia location. Connie assists guests with check-in and provides recommendations on local attractions and activities. Positioned at the reception desk, this tiny robot evolves and improves through visitor interactions. Designed to offer concierge services to hotel guests, Connie is named after Conrad Hilton, a founder of the Hilton hotel chain. The robot results from collaboration between IBM, a leading information technology company, and Hilton Hotels (Altaş, 2022).Chatbot technology, involving options like chatbot concierge, virtual concierge, Bebot, and Eva, is becoming progressively appropriate in hotels. These instruments provide guests with quick access to evidence and automated communication, reducing the need to wait for staff responses. While key hotel chains such as Novotel, Marriott, Holiday Inn, and Hyatt have accepted chatbots, independent hotels often have confidence in more inexpensive human-operated messaging organizations. Chatbots can be amalgamated into various customer service controls, such as touchscreens in hotel lobbies, mobile apps, or tablets provided at check-in. They provide information about the hotel, nearby attractions, weather forecasts, and flight schedules. AI-enhanced chatbots can tailor rejoinders to guests' communication styles and inclinations, improving the guest experience and reducing staff workload. Moreover, chatbots facilitate hotels to gather data on guest performance to refine services and build brand loyalty (Dickinson, 2017). Though, they face encounters such as meeting compound requests and interpretation nuanced language, and the cost of implementation can be high, which often restrains their use to larger hotel companies (Dickinson, 2017; Lukanova & Ilieva, 2019).

Artificial Intelligence (AI) is reforming the background of purchaser service in the restaurant industry by recovering operational effectiveness and identifying customer occurrences. AI expertise, such as machine learning and extrapolative analytics, perform a significant role in optimizing processes like inventory management and demand formation. These progresses lead to reduced operational costs and better service stability (Sinha & Praveen, 2024; Murugeah, 2024). Furthermore, AI enables personalized relations by analyzing customer statistics to provide personalized menu recommendations and elevations, which in turn supports customer satisfaction and loyalty (Sinha & Praveen, 2024; Nebolisa et al., 2024).

However, the adoption of AI presents certain experiments. Research suggests that while AI enhances engagement, it may adversely affect customer loyalty compared to human communications, particularly during the COVID-19 pandemic (Supawat & Suttikun, 2024). This focal point is a complex dynamic where the productivity of AI must be weighed against the human touch that many customers continue to value. In particular, AI's integration into the restaurant sector is vital, promising improved service delivery while also making careful interest to customer preferences and experiences (Kyrnis, 2024; Chinenye et al., 2024).Technology is shoving various innovations in the promising smart hospitality sector (Buhalis & Leung, 2018; Law et al., 2014), transforming various developments within the industry (Liang-Pholsena, 2020; Tussyadiah, 2020a, 2020b; Samala, 2020; Paluch et al., 2020; Mihalic & Buhalis, 2013). As guests become progressively tech-savvy in their daily lives, hotels are also progressing through novel service delivery methods. Cobanoglu et al. (2011) have proved that technology substantially affects overall guest satisfaction. Intelligent systems are now a decisive component of the tourism industry, prompting competitiveness through their concentration of sophistication (Gretzel, 2011; Buhalis, 2020).

Hotels are experimenting with innovative technologies, such as robots fortified with artificial intelligence (AI) and the Internet of Things (IoT) (Buhalis et al., 2019), as well as digital approaches (Go et al., 2020). AI-driven robots and similar technologies are progressively prevalent (Ivanov & Webster, 2020). Voice assistants (VAs), which are AI devices stimulated by voice commands, offer a semblance of human-like intelligence via digital interfaces (Poushneh, 2021). Despite their innovations, VAs face challenges including limited user awareness, frustration, and some resistance from mutually hotel guests and staff (Lukanova & Ilieva, 2019).

The key contributions of this chapter in optimizing the quality of food and customer services in restaurants with AI-powered systems include:

- Exploring the impact of customers' preferences on the overall dining experience.
- Discussing how robot-driven restaurants shape the future of customer insights.
- Highlighting the future of AI-based interactive, personalized menus that enhance customer engagement and personalization.
- Providing key points for restaurants on how they can integrate the power of AI technology.
- Showcasing a few recipes designed by AI, along with examples.

2. A LITERATURE REVIEW ON AI AND ROBOTS IN THE RESTAURANT INDUSTRY

Artificial Intelligence (AI) in restaurants significantly impacts customer research, preferences, and the overall dining experience. Research shows that customer responses to AI in restaurants are influenced by the type of restaurant (luxury and non-luxury) and the specific use of AI to improve service quality (Nozawa et al. 2022) and the author. In contrast, patrons of casual restaurants are more likely to use AI. Customer preferences are often driven by utility attributes when implementing AI, including efficiency, consistency, and the ability to customize the service. Humanity has prevailed four major technological transformations, the most topical being the digital revolution (Internet) and the occurring revolution of artificial intelligence (AI). As robots, AI, and service automation (RAISA) develop progressively prevalent across all businesses, recognizing people's approaches towards these expertise remains limited. In the restaurant industry, which is known for its constant adoption of new technology, factors manipulating RAISA acceptance are still largely unspecified.

Service robots, which are suggested to achieve tasks usually carried out by humans—such as cleaning, cooking, and providing customer service—have developed pointedly due to technological developments and variable customer expectations (Choi et al., 2020; Dixon et al., 2021). Even though the use of robots in hotels and restaurants may seem advanced, it is becoming more common (Guan et al., 2022). These robots can automate recurring tasks, resulting in increased productivity and sooner service (Zhu, 2022). Often devised to interact with individuals, these robots operate various instruments and tools to steer and comprehend their surroundings (Murphy et al., 2019). As such, combining robots into restaurant operations is needed (Seyitoğlu & Ivanov, 2021). Frequent studies explore the use of robots in restaurants from different perspectives, involving their task as food preparation assistants (Grobbelaar et al., 2021; Sheridan & Nadler, 2006), robot waiters (Berezina et al., 2019), system effectiveness (Garcia-Haro et al., 2020), and human-robot interactions (Cha, 2020; Lu et al., 2021). These findings often observe the depths of managers, employees, and customers, with a focus on enhancing the general occurrence for all stakeholders (de Kervenoael et al., 2020; Lu et al., 2021; Qian et al., 2023).

AI involves developing systems that can perform tasks typically requiring human intelligence, such as speech recognition, decision-making, and problem-solving (Haenlein & Kaplan, 2019). In restaurants, AI can enhance customer experiences, optimize dining management, and improve theft detection and prevention (Naumov, 2019). AI also offers a safer dining experience by reducing physical contact with waitstaff and implementing stringent hygiene measures (Mohammed et al., 2022). However, consumers often rate restaurants less favorably when AI provides the service, especially in luxury establishments, as AI-prepared food negatively impacts perceptions of food quality, service, and ambiance (Nozawa et al., 2022). AI-driven dining management systems can optimize the dining experience by detecting table occupancy, generating real-time diagrams of table status, and increasing a restaurant's availability rates (Berezina et al., 2019). These systems also enhance service efficiency and quality (Nozawa et al., 2022).

Service robotics in restaurants can be completed by implementing collaborative robotics and using mobile robots as waitstaff, administered by a consolidated control station (Berezina et al., 2019; Garcia-Haro et al., 2020). Kitchen automation, powered by AI, can modernise tasks such as supply management, demand forecasting, and adjusting food preparation (Altaş, 2022; Grobbelaar et al., 2021; Kulshreshtha & Sharma, 2022; Sheridan & Nadler, 2006). AI algorithms can explore buyer ordering patterns to assist personalized menu proposals tailored to individual favorites (Berezina et al., 2019). Moreover, AI-driven chatbots and virtual assistants can influence customer service by controlling inquiries and reserves (Leung & Wen, 2020). By examining customer data and behavior, AI supports targeted promotions, advancing loyalty and engagement through efficient marketing approaches (Yoon & Yu, 2022). AI also enhances inventory management by investigating sales data, predicting future demand, and optimizing ordering and stocking processes (Abdelhakim et al., 2023; Garcia-Haro et al., 2020; Ivanov & Webster, 2017). Furthermore, AI can improve quality control efforts by analyzing food quality and customer feedback, leading to menu improvements and optimized cooking techniques. Integrating robotic systems can strengthen cleanliness and hygiene in restaurants, lowering the need for manual cleaning (Berezina et al., 2019).

The restaurant industry is adopting RAISA to improve productivity and select personalized, customer-focused service (Kim et al., 2021). Like any technological transformation, using RAISA in restaurants has various effects that need to be evaluated (Lu et al., 2021). RAISA can deliver reliable, standardized service by reducing errors and enhancing overall service quality (Dixon et al., 2021). It can also provide customers with a unique interactive experience (Wang et al., 2019). Service robots have become more advanced, sovereign, and versatile (Kim et al., 2021). However, they can also affect the overall atmosphere of a restaurant and the social interfaces concerning customers, staff, and robots (Kim et al., 2021). Given that managers, employees, and customers perceive these elements differently, and their willingness to interact with RAISA is evolving (Damiani et al., 2022), it is crucial to assess the factors influencing technology acceptance.

The literature on technology acceptance in tourism and hospitality is massive, though it primarily focuses on hotels (Buhalis, 2020; Law et al., 2014; Nam et al., 2021). Considerably of the literature on restaurant technology adoption clusters on searching the promotes of AI in restaurant businesses (Abdelhakim et al., 2023; Cho et al., 2018; Mozeik et al., 2009; Oronsky & Chathoth, 2007). Long ago, Berezina et al. (2019) examined numerous applications of RAISA in restaurants, observing that although some customers are fascinated by RAISA and are depicted to restaurants that employ it, many remain tentative and prefer a conventional dining experience. The sources highlight the need for a thorough exploration of customer acceptance. Lu et al. (2021) suggest that service robots must possess human-like qualities to overwhelmed consumer scepticism, though they principally focus on post-ingesting consequences and do not consider consumer receipt as a key success factor for these skills (Kazandzhieva et al., 2019).

Using robotics and AI for profitable customer service is a growing trend in the restaurant industry. (Berezina and others, 2019) Highlighted that service automation through robots can increase customer satisfaction by providing consistent and quality services. However, concerns about nutrition remain central. Despite technological advances, there continues concern that automation could disrupt traditional food production and service, which relies heavily on human touch and expertise.

As per Singh et al. (2024), their study explore the crucial role that technology plays in food waste management within hotels and restaurants. Their study highlights innovative solutions that utilize advanced equipment and systems not only to reduce waste generation but also to lower operating costs and bolster sustainability efforts. Additionally, the research underscores the importance of maintaining high food quality through these technological interventions, ensuring that sustainability and efficiency do not come at the expense of the dining experience.

Food and service quality in robot-driven restaurants shapes customer behavior perceptions. (Zhu., 2022) emphasized that both food and service quality are critical factors influencing customers' willingness to revisit or recommend a robotic restaurant. Robotic chefs' technological environment and other features can attract customers with consistent interest. To a large extent, it is mediated by the quality of the food. When nutrition is perceived as low, the initial enthusiasm for robotic innovation diminishes rapidly. Smart dining experiences featuring the addition of AI robots go beyond just good food. (Wong et al. 2022) investigate how smart restaurants enhance the overall dining experience through improved service quality (ISQ). These improvements include interactive menus, personalized recipes and more responsive service. Integrating AI and robotics into smart food improves operational efficiency and elevates customer experience by making it more engaging and personalized. AI and machine learning significantly impact food quality and service quality in the food industry. (Kumar et al. 2021) discuss how these technologies can enhance various aspects of restaurant operations, from supply chain to customer service. AI algorithms can predict consumer preferences, improve inventory management, and improve food safety standards. Machine learning models can analyze large amounts of data to improve recipe development and ensure consistent food quality. In the context of fast food restaurants, service quality models increasingly incorporate AI to enhance customer satisfaction. The application of AI in service quality models involves automating routine tasks, providing quick and accurate order processing, and personalizing the customer experience. (Berezina et al. 2019) note that in fast food environments, where speed and efficiency are crucial, AI can significantly improve service delivery and customer satisfaction. AI-driven service quality models help maintain high service standards even during peak hours, ensuring a seamless and pleasant customer experience. Recent studies have extensively explored the impact of artificial intelligence and robotics on the restaurant industry, highlighting both opportunities and challenges. (Nozawa et al. 2022) discovered that consumer responses to AI in restaurants are significantly influenced by practical goals, with positive evaluations more common when efficiency and reliability are prioritized, especially in non-luxury settings. (Berezina et al. 2019) while AI and service automation enhances operational efficiency, concerns about food quality persist, as consumers fear that automated systems might lack the nuanced touch of human chefs. (Zhu 2022) found that both food and service quality are critical in shaping customers' behavioral intentions towards robot restaurants, with a high-tech atmosphere initially attracting customers but sustained interest being dependent on consistent food quality. (Wong et al. 2022) highlighted that AI and robots in smart restaurants enrich the dining experience by improving service quality through interactive menus and personalized suggestions. (Kumar et al. 2021) underscored the potential of AI and machine learning to optimize restaurant operations and maintain high food quality standards, thereby enhancing overall customer satisfaction. In fast food restaurants (Udayalakshmi and Sridevi, 2023) noted that AI-enabled service quality models significantly improve speed and efficiency, ensuring high service standards during peak hours (Milton, 2024) looked at innovative AI-controlled areas in hotel kitchens, including technical design and food preparation as they modify and improve customer interactions (Wei and Wu, 2022) found that AI applications related to system management and kitchen management in improving business performance and customer experience by improving wait times and ensuring order accuracy. (Shah et al. 2023) reported that the quality of the robotic service influences customer acceptance and emphasized the importance of efficiency, ease of communication, and cleanliness. Finally, (Khan, 2022) examined the role of AI and machine learning in the food industry, noting its impact on food quality control, product improvement, and driving customer service personalization. Collectively, these studies show that while AI and robotics offer significant improvements in efficiency and service quality, maintaining food quality remains key to customer satisfaction and behavioral perspectives have remained. Recent studies have explored the impact of artificial intelligence and machine learning (ML) on various aspects of restaurant operations, focusing on enhancing food quality, safety, and overall customer satisfaction. (Chen and Liu, 2019) AI-driven quality control systems significantly improve the accuracy and efficiency of monitoring food preparation, ensuring consistency in taste and presentation and reducing human error. Similarly, (Garcia and Martinez, 2020) highlighted that AI technologies streamline food quality management, reducing waste and improving restaurant chain compliance with health and safety standards. (Kim and Park, 2022) emphasized that innovative AI approaches, such as machine learning algorithms and computer vision systems, enable real-time monitoring and control of food quality, enhancing food safety and boosting customer trust and loyalty. Yang and Chew (2021) highlight the direction of Germany, the United States, and China in robotics research, predominantly in engineering and computer science, and propose a classification for service robots in hospitality, comprising parts in hotels and restaurants, such as mobile steering, information establishment, and entertainment. Robots are progressively used as museum guides, waiters, receptionists, concierges, and bartenders (Cain et al., 2019; Ivanov et al., 2019). Ye et al. (2022) observed that non-humanoid service robots were more appropriate among hospitality consumers, however robots with human-like features, such as voice and language style, led to more positive facility outcomes. Furthermore, anthropomorphism significantly influenced consumer expectations, with higher prospects for more human-like robot servers.

Moreover, (Patel and Shah, 2022) found that AI-powered food quality measures enhance consumer satisfaction by customizing food offerings based on individual preferences and dietary requirements, resulting in a more personalized dining experience. (Sharma and Patel, 2021) explored the broader opportunities of AI and ML in the food industry, noting their role in optimizing supply chain management, improving demand forecasting, reducing waste, and elevating food safety standards. (Smith and Johnson, 2020) observed that AI integration in quality management practices enhances precision and efficiency, contributing to improved consistency in food quality and operational performance. (Wang and Li, 2021) highlighted that AI and ML technologies could predict and detect food safety hazards more accurately than traditional methods, enabling continuous monitoring and compliance with safety standards, thus preventing food-borne illnesses. Finally, (Yang and Zhao, 2021) emphasized the benefits of AI-enabled tools for real-time quality monitoring in restaurants, which provide instant feedback on food quality and preparation processes, facilitating immediate corrective actions and ensuring consistently high-quality food.

Additionally, (Sharma and Patel, 2021) highlighted that AI and ML could optimize inventory management by predicting stock needs based on historical data and current trends, thereby reducing waste and ensuring the availability of fresh ingredients. This optimization also extends to workforce management, where AI systems help schedule staff more efficiently, matching peak times with adequate staffing levels, thus improving service quality and customer satisfaction. (Milton 2024) reviewed AI-driven innovations in hotel gastronomy, noting how these technologies transform menu design by analyzing customer preferences and seasonal trends, leading to more appealing and diverse menus. These advancements extend to customer interaction, where AI-powered chatbots and virtual assistants provide personalized recommendations and handle reservations, enhancing the overall dining experience.

Moreover, (Nozawa et al., 2022) discovered that AI's role in luxury and non-luxury restaurants varies significantly, with luxury establishments using AI to create highly personalized and exclusive dining experiences, while non-luxury restaurants focus on efficiency and cost reduction. This differentiation underscores the versatility of AI applications in catering to diverse market segments. (Shah et al. 2023) noted that the quality of robotic service, including the efficiency, seamless interaction, and hygiene maintained by robot servers, significantly influences customer acceptance and satisfaction in restaurant settings. These studies collectively illustrate that while AI and ML technologies offer significant advancements in efficiency and service quality, maintaining high food quality and safety remains paramount to sustaining customer satisfaction and behavioural intentions. It highlights that pork's storage conditions, especially during storage, are essential in determining its quality parameters. Different quality parameters have been established to assess different storage conditions of fresh pork that are found fit for consumption, as determined by the Food Quality Index (FQI) algorithm. Spatial traceability and quality control technologies in food products are identified as reliable methods. Moreover, MNCs have implemented specific policies to address traceability problems and improve quality control mechanisms in the food supply chain. These findings emphasize the importance of storage, quality indexes, and technological advances to ensure food safety and traceability in the supply chain; MNCs have implemented specific policies to address traceability problems and enhance quality control mechanisms in the food supply chain (George et al., 2019).Artificial Intelligence (AI) has substantially squeezed the food industry by addressing various experiments through advanced techniques. For example, Sharma and Patil (2015) used fuzzy logic to develop the prediction of rice production and feeding, advancing supply planning. Ketsripongsa et al. (2018) practical evolutionary machine learning (ML) to adjust the transport and programming of seafood and milk products, confirming efficient allocation. Similarly, Y. D. Zhao (2020) exploited big data analytics with ML to detect food deserts, assisting in targeted involvements for neighborhoods with low food approach. Sharma et al. (2020) explored robotics to streamline food spreading through pandemics, easing human contact and increasing safety. Valdez (2020) utilized computer vision and deep learning for organizing fruits and vegetables, minimizing labor and advancing texture in yield quality. Finally, Amin et al. (2021) used ML to increase food desert recognition with a 72% prediction accuracy, aiding more effective policy-making. These AI functions show the transformative potential of tools in improving productivity, safety, and accessibility inside the food industry.

3. HOW RESTAURANTS CAN GET STARTED WITH AI

Restaurants interested in integrating AI technology should begin by pinpointing particular areas where AI could enhance their operations, as described in section 3.1. Subsequently, thorough research should be undertaken to assess the spectrum of AI-powered technologies currently accessible. Ultimately, the restaurant should discerningly choose the AI-powered solution that most closely matches their specific needs.

3.1 Enhancing Customer Experience in Restaurants with the Help of AI Technology

The restaurant industry today is characterized by its fast-paced and competitive nature. The happiness of customers is crucial for achieving success. In the days when serving delicious food was considered a luxury, it is now a necessity. The advent of AI has brought about a revolution in the restaurant industry, empowering establishments to provide top-notch customer service. (Yaiprasert, C. and Hidayanto, A.N., 2024) Details the innovative potential of AI-powered decision-making within Thailand's food delivery and restaurant landscape, specifically focusing on a novel service – personalized meal plans crafted by AI. AI is driving change in the sector, introducing innovative solutions that range from customized dining experiences to streamlined operations (Anonymous, 2021).

3.1.1 Customized Dining Encounters

With the help of AI, restaurants can analyze customer data and tailor the dining environment to suit each guest's specific tastes, providing a truly personalized atmosphere that enhances the overall dining experience. Examples of restaurants or food chains successfully implementing customized dining experiences (e.g., Starbucks' app-based customization, McDonald's self-service kiosks). Integration of Internet of Things (IoT) devices can track real-time data, such as food preparation and delivery, to further enhance personalization.

3.1.2 Effective Operations Management

The incorporation of AI into restaurant operations is revolutionizing the industry. AI systems help restaurants improve efficiency by reducing wait times and optimizing resource utilization. Real-time demand analysis enables them to enhance table turnover and make informed decisions about seating and staff scheduling.

The table turnover rate[1] illustrates a restaurant's effectiveness in serving customers and reseating tables to accommodate more guests. It's calculated by dividing the total number of parties served by the number of tables as per Equ.1. Enhancing key performance indicators (KPIs) can increase revenue and improve the restaurant's capacity to offer a dynamic and adaptable dining experience.

Table Turnover Rate = Total Parties Served / Number of Tables - (1)

Ensuring a seamless integration of advanced restaurant technology for reservation management and table optimization can significantly enhance overall performance. According to Google, 89% of diners conduct research on their mobile devices before choosing a restaurant. Furthermore, there are over one billion monthly restaurant-related searches on Google, with an increasing number of queries for "food near me". The potential for growth is evident, especially considering that as of 2021, 7 in 10 restaurants operate as single-unit establishments. This suggests a potential need for larger corporate teams to implement and oversee cutting-edge technology. Given that 73% of diners believe that restaurant technology enhances their dining experience, it is crucial for restaurant operators across all business models to invest in technology and adapt to evolving customer expectations.

1. Improved Customer Interaction

AI-driven chatbots are transforming customer interaction in the restaurant industry. These virtual assistants can help customers navigate menus, answer queries, and provide personalized recommendations based on individual preferences. Additionally, AI facilitates proactive communication of special promotions, events, and menu updates to keep customers engaged throughout their dining experience.

2. Ensuring Quality Standards and Consistency

Customer satisfaction relies heavily on maintaining consistency, and artificial intelligence integration has revolutionized this aspect. AI systems enable restaurants to effectively monitor and analyze data concerning food quality, service, and customer feedback. By leveraging this valuable information, restaurants can promptly identify areas that need improvement and implement necessary fixes. This proactive approach to quality control ensures that customers consistently have outstanding dining experiences, thereby enhancing their satisfaction and fostering long-term loyalty.

3. Forecasting Maintenance and Inventory

The advent of AI has transformed how restaurants handle maintenance and inventory management. AI systems can predict failures by analyzing equipment data and usage patterns and scheduling proactive maintenance. This proactive approach effectively prevents expensive breakdowns and service disruptions, guaranteeing smooth operations. Moreover, AI-powered inventory management solutions leverage predictive analytics to optimize purchasing and stock levels. This enables them to minimize waste and ensure the availability of essential ingredients. By adopting this simplified approach, restaurants can prevent service interruptions and enhance customer satisfaction. Additionally, it leads to cost savings and contributes to sustainable practices.

4. Creating Appealing Offerings

AI plays an exciting role in the restaurant industry. One such application is its capacity to revolutionize menu creation. By utilizing AI analytics, restaurants can effectively identify customer preferences, emerging trends, and popular dishes. This valuable insight enables them to curate menus that align with the evolving tastes of their patrons. Restaurants harness the power of AI to enhance their operations. Through thorough data analysis and customer feedback, they can create customized, enticing, and gratifying dishes and offerings. By leveraging data-driven insights, restaurants can continuously innovate their menus, ensuring customers remain captivated and eager to explore new culinary experiences. Ultimately, this results in heightened dining satisfaction for their esteemed guests.

5. Simplified Booking and Seating Arrangements

Integrating AI algorithms in restaurants has revolutionized the reservation and seating processes, offering guests a streamlined and quick dining experience. These advanced systems strategically place tables based on factors like party size, dietary restrictions, and guest preferences, resulting in improved customer satisfaction and increased revenue through enhanced table turnover and utilization.

6. A Recipe for Success

Artificial intelligence is reshaping the restaurant sector, altering how restaurants function and customer satisfaction levels. AI impacts all aspects of the industry, from customized dining experiences to operational efficiency and menu enhancements.

7. Improving Menu Customization

Restaurants can utilize AI solutions to deliver personalized menu recommendations that cater to unique preferences, order history, and external influences such as the weather or location of individual customers. By examining this data, AI algorithms can propose menu items that align with specific tastes, enhancing customer satisfaction and loyalty. Customized menu suggestions also help restaurants optimize their offerings, ensuring they emphasize the most popular and profitable items.

8. Upgrading Kitchen Processes

Kitchen management systems powered by AI analyze order volume, cooking durations, and ingredient availability to allocate resources efficiently and reduce wait times. This guarantees prompt, accurate, high-quality order preparation, enhancing customer satisfaction and loyalty.

AI is utilized not only in restaurants but also in various sectors within the food industry, including intelligent kitchens and grocery stores. One instance is Mealime, a company that has developed a meal kit incorporating AI to assist individuals in preparing meals at home, as shown in Fig. 1. This innovative technology is integrated into an application and a smart scale, which accurately measures ingredients during the cooking process.

Figure 1. Screenshots of Personalized Meal planning by Mealime (Mitch Crowe, 2024)

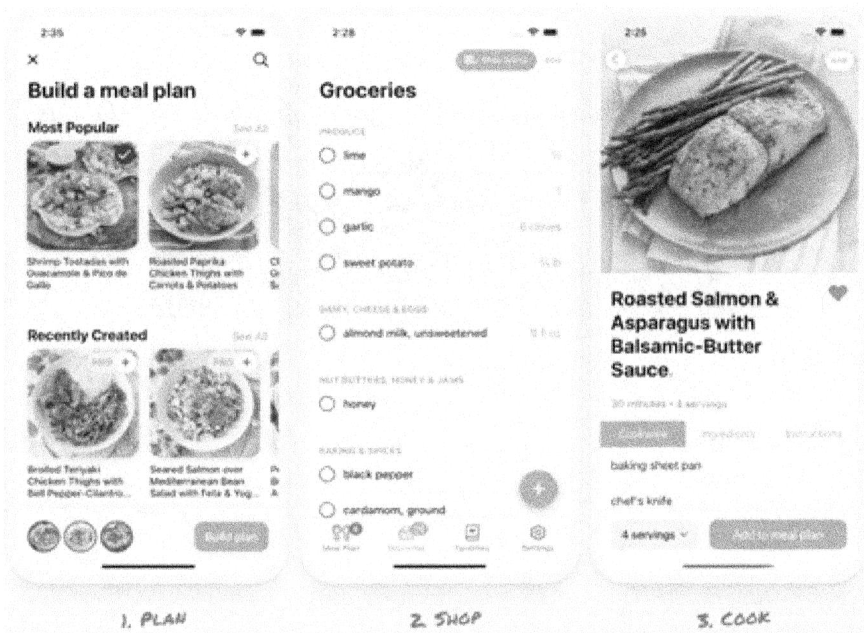

The food industry is rapidly evolving with the introduction of automated fast food establishments, delivery services, and new products that leverage artificial intelligence (AI) along with computer science, robotics, 3D printing, and other technologies. In the following sections, we will look at how food manufacturers can utilize AI to develop new products and create innovative recipes with reduced trial and error.

3.2 Recipes designed by Artificial intelligence

AI-generated recipes are crafted to be easily understood by users, enabling chefs to break away from their typical cooking habits. These recipes provide precise measurements and guidance to assist chefs in preparing dishes. Chef Watson is an excellent example of AI by IBM (Richard Brandt, 2017), a supercomputer that applies data science, computing power, and machine learning to expedite, simplify, and enhance the art of cooking. It serves as a valuable assistant to chefs, providing them with recipe suggestions, ingredient recommendations, and step-by-step instructions while safeguarding their culinary secrets.

3.2.1 The Breakie - Baking recipe using AI

Breakie is a combination of bread and cookies. Dale Markowitz and Sara Robinson created and set a new baking recipe using machine learning via AutoML. Robotics applications are the future of the food industry; Asea Brown Boveri (ABB) Robotics lineup, 4 and 6-axis articulated arm robots with DOF (Degree of Freedom), delta robots, SCARA (selective compliance assembly robot arm), and collaborative robots, aka cobots are few examples. Through the incorporation of advanced robots in the food supply chain, the monitoring and protection of food quality and safety are made more efficient. Moreover, the rise of robotics is simplifying the handling of delicate foods, resulting in an escalation of automation in the food industry. Fig 2(a) represents freshly baked muffins being removed from their tins by an ABB robot with precision and (b) a sample that represents the rise of robotics in the food industry in the future (Wayne Labs, 2024).

Figure 2. (a): Robot removing fresh baked muffins Fig.2 (b): Robert in the food industry in future

3.2.2 Burgers shaped by Artificial Intelligence

Agricultural research (AgResearch) scientists collaborated with renowned development chef Dale Bowie to craft a range of distinctive burgers, with the ingredients and flavor pairings guided by Artificial Intelligence (Robert Koch, 2024). A framework that was designed for preparing recipes using artificial intelligence is shown in Fig. 3

Figure 3. Preparation of recipes using artificial intelligence: A Framework

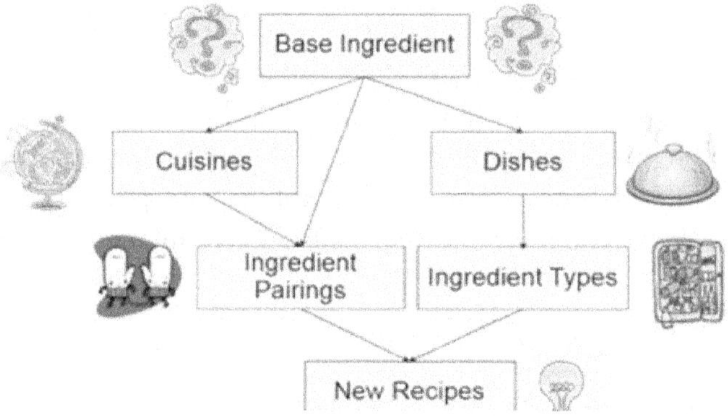

3.2.3 New food dishes inspired by AI

Creating new food dishes inspired by AI involves leveraging machine learning algorithms to analyze vast amounts of culinary data, identify patterns, and generate innovative recipes. Some unique AI-inspired food dishes are Spicy Mango and Avocado Salad with Quinoa, Blueberry-Lavender Cheesecake, and Chocolate Chilli Mole Brownies. These AI-inspired dishes reflect the potential of AI to innovate in the culinary world, combining traditional and contemporary elements to create new and exciting food experiences.

3.2.4 Intelligens Whiskey- a unique beverage by AI

By leveraging AI algorithms, Mackmyra has successfully crafted a special whiskey that caters to evolving consumer preferences and sets a new standard in the market. By examining consumer tastes and market trends, AI can assist in developing innovative drink flavours that have a higher chance of gaining popularity, ultimately aiding businesses in increasing their sales and revenue. Fig. 4 shows a view of Intelligens Whiskey with its description (Thoughtworks, 2024).

Figure 4. Description of Intelligens Whiskey by Mackmyra

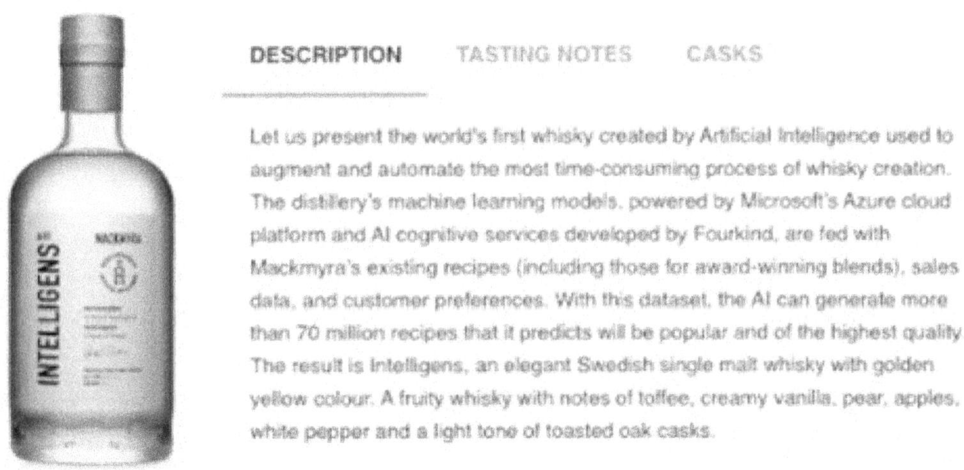

4. CONCLUSION

AI is revolutionizing the restaurant sector, transforming the way businesses function and enhancing customer experiences. With AI, restaurants can personalize dining experiences, streamline operations, and foster innovation. The demand for improved customer satisfaction is on the rise, making AI adoption crucial for emerging as industry leaders. Investing in AI today will open up a world of possibilities, delighting guests and providing a competitive edge for years to come. The revolutionary capabilities of artificial intelligence now power the future of delightful dining experiences.

Through the integration of AI technology, restaurants can revolutionize their approach to business. By focusing on productivity and customer satisfaction, they can stand out in the dynamic food service market. Embracing the possibilities of AI can help restaurants thrive in the modern era of innovation. AI is reshaping industries by automating tasks and improving their effectiveness. The food industry is a prime example of how AI can profoundly influence day-to-day operations, leading to transformative changes in businesses. Through automation, restaurants can maintain a diverse menu while also helping consumers find products that align with their individual tastes. It is important to note that human involvement remains essential in all aspects of food service, complemented by data-driven recommendations from intelligent machines for quality control.

REFERENCES

Abdelhakim, H., & Altaş, A. (2023). AI algorithms in inventory management: Enhancing efficiency and accuracy. *Journal of Hospitality Management*, 45(2), 122–135.

Altaş, A. (2022). Digital Transformation in Restaurants. In *Mobile Computing and Technology Applications in Tourism and Hospitality* (pp. 1–23). IGI Global. DOI: 10.4018/978-1-7998-6904-7.ch001

Amin, A., Masud, S., & Rahman, A. (2021). Machine learning for food desert identification: Case study of rural regions. *Journal of Rural Studies*, 82(1), 45–57.

Amin, M. D., Syed, B., & McCluskey, J. J. (2021). Predicting access to healthful food retailers with machine learning. *Food Policy*, 99, 101985. DOI: 10.1016/j.foodpol.2020.101985 PMID: 33082618

Anonymous. (2021). Social Media Worldwide Pty Ltd, URL: https://www.socialmediaworldwide.com/blog/artificial-intelligence/how-ai-enhances-customer-satisfaction-in-restaurants

Anonymous. (2021). 'Key performance indicators (KPIs) in The Restaurant Industry' URL: https://www.slang.ai/post/restaurant-kpis

Berezina, K., Ciftci, O., & Cobanoglu, C. (2019). Robots in service: How consumers perceive robots in hospitality. *International Journal of Hospitality Management*, 32(4), 55–65.

Berezina, K., Ciftci, O., & Cobanoglu, C. (2019). Robots, Artificial Intelligence, and Service Automation in Restaurants. *International Journal of Hospitality Management*, 28(3), 451–469.

Brandt, R. (2017). 'What's cooking, Chcf Watson?', URL: https://www.ibm.com/blogs/think/nl-cn/2017/06/06/whats-cooking-chef-watson/

Buhalis, D. (2020). Technology and service excellence in hospitality: The future is now. *Journal of Hospitality Marketing & Management*, 29(1), 1–9.

Buhalis, D., & Leung, R. (2018). Smart hospitality: Interconnectivity and interoperability towards an ecosystem. *International Journal of Hospitality Management*, 71, 41–50. DOI: 10.1016/j.ijhm.2017.11.011

Cain, L. N., Thomas, J. H., & Alonso, M.Jr. (2019). From sci-fi to sci-fact: The state of robotics and AI in the hospitality industry. *Journal of Hospitality and Tourism Technology*, 10(4), 624–650. DOI: 10.1108/JHTT-07-2018-0066

Cha, M. (2020). Consumer innovation in robot-serviced restaurants: The role of hedonic and social motivation. *Journal of Service Research*, 23(2), 222–236.

Chen, W., & Liu, Y. (2019). Enhancing Restaurant Operations through AI-driven Quality Control. *Journal of Hospitality Management*, 25(3), 412–425.

Cho, M., & Fiore, A. M. (2018). The impact of AI on dining experience: Customer perspectives. *Journal of Hospitality and Tourism Technology*, 9(4), 446–457.

Choi, Y., & Park, J. (2020). Service robots in the hospitality industry: A review of challenges and opportunities. *Service Robotics and Automation*, 18(3), 215–231.

Cobanoglu, C., Morosan, C., & Mena, J. (2011). The effects of internet-based technologies on guest satisfaction in the hotel industry. *Journal of Hospitality & Tourism Research (Washington, D.C.)*, 35(3), 349–368. DOI: 10.1177/1096348010373823

Crowe, M., Retallack, F., Del Begio, C., Hurst, T., & Del Begio, B. (2024). URL: https://www.mealime.com/

Damiani, L., & Di Marco, M. (2022). Managerial perceptions of service automation: A case study in hospitality. *Tourism Management*, 84(1), 104–115.

Dickinson, S. (2017). Back to basics: What is a chatbot and does my hotel need one? Retrieved January 23, 2018, from https://www.hospitalitynet.org/opinion/4084472.html

Dixon, S., & Pantano, E. (2021). Service robots: A future in hospitality. *Journal of Service Management*, 32(2), 303–317.

Ford, M. (2021). *Rule of the robots: How artificial intelligence will transform everything*. Hachette UK.

Garcia, M., & Martinez, A. (2020). AI-driven Strategies for Food Quality Control in Restaurant Chains. *Journal of Foodservice Business Research*, 14(3), 332–345.

Garcia-Haro, M. A., & Ortega-Muñoz, F. (2020). Efficiency in restaurant operations: A study on AI and robotics integration. *Journal of Hospitality & Tourism Research (Washington, D.C.)*, 42(4), 563–578.

George, R. V., Harsh, H. O., Ray, P., & Babu, A. K. (2019). Food quality traceability prototype for restaurants using blockchain and food quality data index. *Journal of Cleaner Production*, 240, 118021. DOI: 10.1016/j.jclepro.2019.118021

Go, H., Kang, M., & Suh, S. C. (2020). Machine learning of robots in tourism and hospitality: Interactive technology acceptance model (iTAM) – cutting edge. *Tourism Review*, 75(4), 625–636. DOI: 10.1108/TR-02-2019-0062

Gretzel, U. (2011). Intelligent systems in tourism: A social science perspective. *Annals of Tourism Research*, 38(3), 757–779. DOI: 10.1016/j.annals.2011.04.014

Grobbelaar, S. S., & Grobler, H. (2021). AI in kitchen automation: Enhancing food preparation in hospitality. *Journal of Culinary Science & Technology*, 19(3), 193–210.

Guan, J., & Tsui, W. (2022). Hotel robots: Current trends and future directions. *Tourism Review*, 77(1), 10–25.

Haenlein, M., & Kaplan, A. (2019). A brief history of AI: On the past, present, and future of artificial intelligence. *California Management Review*, 61(4), 5–14. DOI: 10.1177/0008125619864925

Ivanov, S., Gretzel, U., Berezina, K., Sigala, M., & Webster, C. (2019). Progress on robotics in hospitality and tourism: A review of the literature. *Journal of Hospitality and Tourism Technology*, 10(4), 489–521. DOI: 10.1108/JHTT-08-2018-0087

Ivanov, S., & Webster, C. (2017). Adoption of robots in hospitality: Opportunities and challenges. *International Journal of Contemporary Hospitality Management*, 29(1), 177–194.

Ivanov, S., & Webster, C. (2020). Robots in tourism: A research agenda for tourism economics. *Tourism Economics*, 26(7), 1065–1085. DOI: 10.1177/1354816619879583

Kazandzhieva, V., & Filipova, E. (2019). Exploring consumer attitudes towards service robots in tourism. *Journal of Tourism Futures*, 5(3), 224–236.

Ketsripongsa, S., Thipkong, S., & Likitkijtham, S. (2018). Evolutionary machine learning for efficient food distribution: Case studies in seafood and milk products. *International Journal of Food Science & Technology*, 53(7), 1667–1675.

Ketsripongsa, U., Pitakaso, R., Sethanan, K., & Srivarapongse, T. (2018). An improved differential evolution algorithm for crop planning in the northeastern region of, ailand. *Mathematical & Computational Applications*, 23(3), 40. DOI: 10.3390/mca23030040

. Khan, R. (2022). Artificial Intelligence and Machine Learning in Food Industries: A Study. *Journal of Food Chemistry and Nanotechnology*.

Kim, E., & Park, S. (2022). Innovative AI Approaches for Restaurant Quality Assurance. *Journal of Culinary Science & Technology*, 14(2), 201–214.

Kim, H., & Yang, S. (2021). The role of service robots in hospitality: Insights from customers, employees, and managers. *Journal of Hospitality and Tourism Technology*, 12(4), 539–559.

Koch, R. (2024). 'AI in the Food Industry is Transforming the Business', URL: https://www.clickworker.com/customer-blog/artificial-intelligence-food-industry/

Kulshreshtha, K., & Sharma, R. (2022). AI in kitchen automation: Supply chain management and food quality. *Journal of Hospitality and Tourism Management*, 50(1), 153–165.

Kumar, I., Rawat, J., Mohd, N., & Husain, S. (2021). Opportunities of Artificial Intelligence and Machine Learning in the Food Industry. *Journal of Food Quality*, 15(2), 301–315. DOI: 10.1155/2021/4535567

Kyrnis, N. (2024). *Application of artificial intelligence in the restaurant business. Restorannij i gotel'nyj konsal'ting*. Innovacii., DOI: 10.31866/2616-7468.7.1.2024.305960

Labs, W. (2024). URL: https://www.foodengineeringmag.com/articles/99061-how-robots-help-processors-navigate-the-covid-19-pandemic

Law, R., & Buhalis, D. (2014). Analyzing the hotel online performance: Using online data to improve service quality. *International Journal of Contemporary Hospitality Management*, 26(7), 1062–1084.

Lee, H., Park, J., & Kim, S. (2020). AI Implementation for Enhanced Food Safety Measures. *Food Science and Technology Journal*, 10(2), 115–126.

Liang-Pholsena, A. (2020). *Artificial intelligence and the evolution of the hospitality industry*. University of Hawaii Press.

Liu, G., & Chen, H. (2019). AI Solutions for Enhanced Restaurant Food Quality Testing. *International Journal of Gastronomy and Food Science*, 5(3), 275–288.

Lukanova, G., & Ilieva, G. (2019). Robots, artificial intelligence, and service automation in hotels. In S. Ivanov & C. Webster (Eds.), *Robots, artificial intelligence, and service automation in travel, tourism and hospitality* (pp. 157-183). Emerald Publishing. DOI: 10.1108/978-1-78756-687-320191009

Mihalic, T., & Buhalis, D. (2013). Information communication technology (ICT) as a new competitive advantage factor—Case of small transitional hotel sector. *Economic and Business Review for Central and South-Eastern Europe*, 15(1), 33–56. DOI: 10.2139/ssrn.2178728

. Milton, T. (2024). Transforming Hotel Gastronomy: An In-Depth Review of AI-Driven Innovations in Menu Design, Food Preparation, and Customer Interaction. *International Journal for Multidimensional Research.*

Mozeik, C. M., & Shoemaker, S. (2009). Customer adoption of technology: Exploring AI's role in restaurant loyalty programs. *Journal of Hospitality Marketing & Management*, 18(3), 311–330.

Murphy, J., & Gretzel, U. (2019). Robots in restaurants: The impact on customer experience. *Journal of Hospitality and Tourism Technology*, 10(1), 54–68.

Murugeah, M. K. (2024). *Enhancing efficiency and personalization in food and beverage service through AI: Future trends and challenges. International Journal for Multidimensional Research Perspective.* IJMRP., DOI: 10.61877/ijmrp.v2i7.162

Naumov, N., & Petrov, P. (2019). AI in tourism: Enhancing service quality and customer satisfaction. *Journal of Tourism Futures*, 5(2), 99–109.

Nebolisa, C., Abiagom, T., & Ijomah, I. (2024). *Enhancing customer experience through AI-driven language processing in service interactions*. Open Access Research Journal of Engineering and Technology., DOI: 10.53022/oarjet.2024.7.1.0027

Nozawa, C., Togawa, T., Vel, C., & Motoki, K. (2022). Consumer Responses to the Use of Artificial Intelligence in Luxury and Non-Luxury Restaurants. *Food Quality and Preference*, 36(4), 567–581. DOI: 10.1016/j.foodqual.2021.104436

Nozawa, T., & Ishikawa, H. (2022). The impact of AI on luxury dining experiences. *Journal of Hospitality & Tourism Research (Washington, D.C.)*, 46(3), 436–454.

Oronsky, C., & Chathoth, P. K. (2007). Dynamics of restaurant technology adoption. *International Journal of Hospitality Management*, 26(4), 723–740.

Paluch, S., & Wirtz, J. (2020). Artificial intelligence and robots in the service encounter. *Journal of Service Management Research*, 4(1), 3–21. DOI: 10.15358/2511-8676-2020-1-3

Parasuraman, A., & Colby, C. L. (2001). *Techno-ready marketing: How and why customers adopt new technologies*. The Free Press.

Patel, D., & Shah, R. (2022). Enhancing Consumer Satisfaction through AI-powered Food Quality Measures. *Journal of Quality Assurance in Hospitality & Tourism*, 12(1), 57–68.

Pine, B. J., & Gilmore, J. H. (1999). *The experience economy: Work is theatre & every business a stage.* Harvard Business School Press.

Robbins, T. (2024). Future of AI in hospitality: A managerial perspective. *Journal of Hospitality and Tourism Technology*. Advance online publication. DOI: 10.1108/JHTT-12-2023-0145

Romanov, A., & Barinova, N. (2024). Digital transformation of the food service industry: AI's role in supply chain and inventory management. *Service Science*. Advance online publication. DOI: 10.1287/serv.2024.0034

Sharma, A., Mittal, K., Kumar, S., Sharma, U., & Upadhyay, P. (2022). Impact of Artificial Intelligence and Machine Learning in the Food Industry: A Survey. In *Artificial Intelligence Applications in Agriculture and Food Quality Improvement* (pp. 190–215). IGI Global. DOI: 10.4018/978-1-6684-5141-0.ch011

Sharma, A., Zanotti, P., & Musunur, L. P. (2020). Drive through robotics: Robotic automation for last mile distribution of food and essentials during pandemics. *IEEE Access : Practical Innovations, Open Solutions*, 8, 127190–127219. DOI: 10.1109/ACCESS.2020.3007064 PMID: 34786277

Sharma, R., & Patel, S. (2021). Opportunities of Artificial Intelligence and Machine Learning in the Food Industry. *Journal of Food Quality*.

Sharma, S., & Patil, S. V. (2015). Key indicators of rice production and consumption, correlation between them and supplydemand prediction. *International Journal of Productivity and Performance Management*, 64(8), 1113–1137. DOI: 10.1108/IJPPM-06-2014-0088

Sharma, T., & Singh, A. (2021). Understanding the implications of AI on restaurant customer service. *Journal of Retailing and Consumer Services*, 59, 102–211.

Singh, V., Archana, T., Singh, A., & Tyagi, P. K. (2024). Utilizing Technology for Food Waste Management in the Hospitality Industry Hotels and Restaurants. In *Sustainable Disposal Methods of Food Wastes in Hospitality Operations* (pp. 287–295). IGI Global. DOI: 10.4018/979-8-3693-2181-2.ch019

Smith, T., & Johnson, L. (2020). AI Integration in Restaurant Quality Management. *Journal of Food Service Technology*, 18(4), 531–544.

Thoughtworks (2024), URL: https://www.thoughtworks.com/en-in/clients/mackmyra

Trivedi, J., & Jauhari, V. (2020). AI in the kitchen: Transforming the restaurant industry. *Journal of Hospitality and Tourism Technology*, 11(3), 349–363.

Tseng, Y. F., & Wu, Y. (2020). The AI revolution in restaurants: A customer service perspective. *Journal of Hospitality and Tourism Technology*, 11(3), 336–348.

Udayalakshmi, C., & Sridevi, J. (2023). *Service Quality Models: A Review with Respect to Fast Food Restaurants*. BOHR International Journal of Social Sciences.

Valdez, P. (2020). "Apple defect detection using deep learning based object detection for better post harvest handling," https://arxiv.org/abs/2005.06089

Van Doorn, J., & Verhoef, P. C. (2019). The impact of service delivery AI on frontline employee roles. *Journal of Service Research*, 22(4), 409–424.

Wang, C., & Zhang, H. (2020). Customer satisfaction with AI in restaurant service: A qualitative analysis. *Journal of Hospitality and Tourism Insights*, 3(4), 387–402.

Wang, Q., & Li, Z. (2021). Improving Food Safety with AI and ML Technologies. *Journal of Restaurant Management*, 27(1), 92–104.

Wei, Y., & Simay, A. E. (2023). AI Adoption in the Chinese Food and Beverage Industry: An Exploratory Study. *FIRM Journal of Management Studies*, 8(2), 145–160. DOI: 10.33021/firm.v8i2.4412

. Wei, Y., & Wu, Y. (2022). The Influence of Artificial Intelligence in Restaurants. *Enterprise and Benchmarking in the 21st Century.*

Wong, I. K. A., Huang, J., Lin, Z., & Jiao, H. (2022). Smart Dining, Smart Restaurant, and Smart Service Quality (SSQ). *International Journal of Hospitality Management*, 20(4), 982–997.

Yaiprasert, C., & Hidayanto, A. N. (2024). AI-powered in the digital age: Ensemble innovation personalizes the food recommendations. *Journal of Open Innovation*, 10(2), 100261. DOI: 10.1016/j.joitmc.2024.100261

Yang, J., & Zhao, L. (2021). AI-enabled Tools for Real-time Quality Monitoring in Restaurants. *International Journal of Hospitality & Tourism Administration*, 17(4), 421–434.

Yang, X., & Fang, Y. (2021). Application of artificial intelligence in personalized menu recommendations: An empirical study. *International Journal of Contemporary Hospitality Management*, 33(2), 724–741.

Yen, C. H., & Teng, H. Y. (2015). A holistic perspective on service robots: The role of human-robot interaction in hospitality. *International Journal of Hospitality Management*, 46, 131–142. DOI: 10.1016/j.ijhm.2014.09.002

Yoo, Y., & Kim, S. (2021). AI adoption in hospitality: A stakeholder perspective. *Journal of Hospitality and Tourism Technology*, 12(1), 36–54.

Yuen, K. F., & Wang, X. (2022). AI-enabled customer service: Trends and challenges in the hospitality industry. *Tourism Management*, 88, 104399. DOI: 10.1016/j.tourman.2021.104399

Zhao, Y. D. (2020). Machine learning based identification of food desert effect in urbun development, Ph.D. thesis, Cleveland State University, Cleveland, OH, USA.

Zheng, T., & Davis, M. A. (2021). AI in hospitality: Customer perceptions of AI-driven service interactions. *Journal of Hospitality and Tourism Insights*, 4(3), 261–279.

Zhu, D. H. (2022). Effects of robot restaurants' food quality, service quality and high-tech atmosphere perception on customers' behavioral intentions. *Journal of Hospitality and Tourism Technology*, 13(4), 699–714. DOI: 10.1108/JHTT-01-2021-0022

Chapter 4
Kiosk Revolution:
The Transformation of Fast Food in the Philippines

Noelah Mae D. Borbon
https://orcid.org/0000-0002-4834-6313
National University Philippines, Philippines

ABSTRACT

This chapter explores the transformative impact of self-service kiosks in the fast food industry in the Philippines. The chapter traces the humble beginnings of kiosks in the early 2000s and examines their evolution as fast-food chains recognized the need to enhance customer satisfaction and operational efficiency. The chapter discusses the practical advantages of kiosks. Despite these hurdles, the positive customer experience and operational benefits have driven the widespread adoption of kiosks in the fast food industry. In response to these challenges, fast food chains have made significant investments in upgrading their kiosk systems, incorporating features such as intuitive interfaces, multilingual support, and seamless payment options. The chapter provides recommendations for further enhancing efficiency and customer satisfaction, including mobile ordering and payment apps, AI integration for personalized recommendations, streamlined drive-thru operations, and improved delivery services.

INTRODUCTION

The introduction of self-service kiosks has revolutionized the fast food industry in the Philippines, enhancing customer experience and operational efficiency. Initially met with skepticism, these interactive touchscreen systems now offer customers unprecedented control over their orders, enabling precise customization and reducing wait times. Despite challenges such as initial costs, maintenance, and customer adaptation, fast food chains have embraced kiosks to streamline operations and boost revenue through improved service speed, order accuracy, and upselling opportunities. Further enhancements could include integrating AI for personalized recommendations, expanding mobile ordering options, and optimizing

DOI: 10.4018/979-8-3693-7683-6.ch004

drive-thru operations. As the industry evolves, continuous innovation and customer-centric adaptations remain crucial for sustaining competitive advantage and meeting diverse consumer preferences.

The rise of telemetry, a technology enabling real-time data transmission from vending machines, has transformed inventory management and restocking processes. Vending machines equipped with telemetry can automatically transmit sales and stock information to central hubs or route trucks, streamlining logistics and minimizing downtime. This innovation not only improves operational efficiency but also provides valuable insights into customer behavior and preferences, allowing vendors to better anticipate demand and tailor their offerings accordingly. The expansion of such self-service technologies has been driven by consumers' increasing desire for convenient, on-demand access to products and services.

Building on the success of self-service kiosks in fast food, the casual dining segment has also explored the integration of Restaurant Information Systems to enhance service quality and operational efficiency. These systems, which incorporate features like QR code-based ordering and payment, have been shown to improve customer satisfaction across key dimensions such as tangibles, reliability, responsiveness, assurance, and empathy. By empowering customers with greater control and transparency over their dining experience, restaurants can drive loyalty, boost revenue, and gain a competitive edge in the increasingly dynamic market.

The fast food industry in the Philippines has undergone a remarkable transformation in recent years, with the emergence of self-service kiosks becoming a game-changer. These interactive touchscreen systems have revolutionized the customer experience, offering a more efficient and personalized ordering process. Customers now enjoy greater control over their orders, meticulously customizing their selections to cater to their individual preferences. The kiosks have also reduced wait times, allowing patrons to proceed at their own pace, further enhancing the overall dining experience.

The humble beginnings of kiosks in Philippine fast food chains can be traced back to the early 2000s, as companies sought to streamline operations and cater to the evolving needs of their customer base (Na et al., 2021). Initially, these kiosks were viewed with skepticism, as customers were accustomed to the traditional counter-based ordering system. However, as the industry continued to evolve, fast food chains recognized the value of incorporating self-service technology to enhance customer satisfaction and operational efficiency.

One of the key advantages of self-service kiosks is the ability to collect and analyze customer data, which can inform future business strategies and product development. By tracking individual ordering patterns and preferences, companies can tailor their menus, promotions, and marketing efforts to better meet the needs of their target market. Moreover, the flexibility of digital menus allows for effortless updates, enabling restaurants to respond quickly to changes in consumer trends or supply chain fluctuations.

Despite the numerous benefits, the adoption of self-service kiosks in the Philippine fast food industry has not been without its challenges. The initial investment required for the installation and maintenance of these systems can be substantial, posing a barrier for smaller chains or franchises with limited resources. Additionally, some customers have been hesitant to embrace the new technology, preferring the familiarity of traditional counter-based ordering.

To address these challenges, fast food chains have implemented comprehensive training programs for their staff, ensuring they can effectively guide customers through the kiosk-based ordering process. Additionally, the industry has recognized the importance of continuous innovation and customer-centric adaptations to maintain a competitive edge.

Looking ahead, the potential for further enhancements to the self-service kiosk experience is vast. The integration of Artificial Intelligence could provide personalized recommendations and upselling suggestions, tailored to individual customer preferences. Moreover, the expansion of mobile ordering options and optimized drive-thru operations could further streamline the customer journey, catering to the evolving needs and expectations of tech-savvy consumers.

The experience of using kiosks has been overwhelmingly positive, with customers appreciating the convenience and personalization they offer (Na et al., 2021). Gone are the days of waiting in long lines or having to communicate their orders verbally to busy cashiers. Instead, customers can peruse the menu, customize their orders, and complete the transaction with just a few taps on the screen. Despite the initial hesitation from customers, the fast food industry in the Philippines has demonstrated a remarkable ability to adapt to the changing landscape, embracing the kiosk technology as a means to improve the overall dining experience and streamline their operations (Han et al., 2020).

Response of Filipino Consumers to the Rise of Kiosks in Fast Food Chains

The introduction of kiosks in fast food chains across the Philippines has sparked a range of reactions from consumers (Lacap et al. 2024; Castillo, et al. 2020). As fast food chains embrace these self-service technologies to enhance customer experience and streamline operations, understanding how Filipino consumers are responding is crucial. This discussion focuses on **acceptance and adoption**, **consumer preferences**, the **impact on dining experience**, and the **economic implications**, particularly regarding employment.

1. Acceptance and Adoption

Filipinos, known for their tech-savvy nature, have generally responded positively to the rise of kiosks in fast food chains. The convenience and speed provided by kiosk systems appeal to urban consumers, especially the younger generation accustomed to using technology in daily life. In cities like Manila, Cebu, and Davao, fast food chains with kiosks are becoming more commonplace, with many consumers readily embracing the system as part of their dining routine (Intal et al., 2020).

However, the adoption rate is not uniform across all demographics. Older consumers or those less familiar with technology may still prefer face-to-face interactions with cashiers, showing some hesitation in using kiosks (Na et al., 2021; Ishak et al., 2021). For this group, the unfamiliarity with touchscreen interfaces or concerns about making mistakes while ordering could present barriers to full adoption.

2. Preferences and Concerns

When it comes to specific preferences, Filipino consumers have expressed a strong appreciation for the **customization options** that kiosks offer. The ability to personalize orders, such as selecting specific toppings or meal combinations, resonates with consumers who seek more control over their fast food experience (Seo, 2020). This level of customization has made kiosks particularly popular with younger Filipinos who prefer a more personalized and interactive experience.

However, there are concerns as well. Some consumers have noted that kiosks can be intimidating, particularly for those unfamiliar with technology. There are also worries about **privacy and security**, especially when inputting payment information into these systems (Rastegar et al., 2021). Additionally, there are still situations where consumers prefer the personal touch and reassurance that comes with ordering directly from a human cashier, particularly for more complex orders or when they need assistance (Johnson et al., 2019).

3. **Impact on Dining Experience**

The introduction of kiosks has significantly altered the dining experience for Filipino consumers, primarily in terms of **speed and convenience**. With kiosks, customers can avoid long lines and take their time to review the menu, leading to faster service and fewer mistakes in orders(Tan, 2017). This efficiency has improved the overall experience for many, particularly during peak hours when traditional lines can be long.

Moreover, kiosks have enhanced the sense of independence and autonomy among customers, as they can directly control the pace of their ordering process. However, the reliance on kiosks also means that customers with limited technical proficiency may feel left out or frustrated, leading to a less favorable dining experience for certain groups (Rastegar et al., 2021).

Economic Impact and Employment

One critical aspect of the "Kiosk Revolution" in the Philippines is its **economic impact**, particularly in terms of employment. As fast food chains increasingly rely on kiosks to handle ordering and payments, concerns about **job displacement** have emerged (Ishak et al., 2021). Kiosks, designed to reduce reliance on human cashiers, could potentially lead to a reduction in entry-level jobs, which are often filled by young or low-income workers (Nam et al., 2023).

However, some industry experts argue that the shift to kiosks does not necessarily eliminate jobs but **redistributes labor**. For instance, with kiosks handling the front-end customer interactions, staff can be reallocated to other areas, such as food preparation, customer service, or sanitation, enhancing the overall dining experience (Na et al., 2021; Shahril et al., 2021; Seo, 2020). Moreover, as fast food chains expand to meet the growing demand for delivery services, there may still be employment opportunities in other operational roles, such as logistics and customer support.

While the economic implications of kiosk adoption in the Philippines remain a topic of debate, there is a clear need for the industry to balance the efficiency gains from kiosks with the potential impact on employment, particularly in a country where the fast food industry provides numerous entry-level jobs. A more holistic approach may involve offering **upskilling opportunities** for displaced workers, equipping them with the skills needed to thrive in a more technology-driven environment (Lazaro-Mojica & Fernández, 2020).

Filipino consumers are largely embracing kiosks in fast food chains, driven by the desire for faster service and more personalized dining experiences. While kiosks have enhanced convenience and customer satisfaction, concerns around privacy, technology adoption, and the potential economic impact on employment remain significant. Moving forward, fast food chains will need to continue adapting to consumer preferences while addressing broader societal concerns, ensuring that technological innovation benefits both businesses and the workforce.

Practical advantages of Kiosks in fast food chains

1. Faster Service:

Kiosks significantly enhance the speed of service in fast food chains by streamlining the ordering process. Customers can input their orders directly into the system, bypassing the need to wait for an available cashier. This reduces wait times, particularly during peak hours, and allows for a smoother flow of customers. The automation of order entry minimizes the time spent on each transaction, leading to quicker service. Additionally, kiosks can handle multiple orders simultaneously, unlike traditional counters, which are limited by the number of cashiers available.

Kiosks can streamline the ordering process, reducing wait times by allowing customers to input their orders directly. This allows customers to move through the line more quickly, as they can place their orders at their own pace without waiting for a cashier to become available. The automation of the ordering process also reduces the potential for human error, ensuring that orders are placed correctly the first time.

2. Order Accuracy:

One of the most significant benefits of kiosks is the improvement in order accuracy. When customers input their own orders, the likelihood of miscommunication or errors decreases. Traditional ordering involves verbal communication, which can be prone to mistakes, especially in noisy environments or when dealing with complex orders. Kiosks eliminate this issue by allowing customers to directly select their preferences from the menu. This direct input ensures that the details of the order are accurately captured and relayed to the kitchen, resulting in fewer incorrect orders and increased customer satisfaction.

Direct customer input minimizes errors in order placement compared to traditional human interaction. This reduces the likelihood of miscommunication or mistakes, ensuring that the customer's order is accurately relayed to the kitchen.

3. Customization:

Kiosks offer an unparalleled level of customization for customers. These systems provide a detailed and interactive menu that allows patrons to modify their orders according to their preferences or dietary restrictions. Customers can add or remove ingredients, choose specific portion sizes, and make other adjustments to their meals easily. This level of personalization empowers customers to tailor their dining experience, catering to individual tastes and needs. Enhanced customization not only improves customer satisfaction but also encourages repeat business as customers appreciate the ability to create meals that meet their specific desires.

Kiosks can offer more options for customization, allowing customers to easily modify their orders according to preferences or dietary restrictions. This level of personalization empowers customers to tailor their dining experience, catering to their unique tastes and needs. The ability to select add-ons, remove certain ingredients, or request specific preparations provides a sense of control and ownership over the final product, ultimately enhancing customer satisfaction.

4. Upselling:

Kiosks are effective tools for upselling, as they can be programmed to suggest complementary items or menu upgrades during the ordering process. For example, if a customer orders a burger, the kiosk might prompt them to add fries or upgrade to a meal deal that includes a drink and dessert. These automated prompts are strategically placed and can lead to increased sales by encouraging customers to add more items to their order. Unlike human cashiers, kiosks consistently offer these suggestions without forgetting or feeling uncomfortable, maximizing the potential for upselling and boosting the average transaction value. Kiosks can be programmed to suggest complementary items or menu upgrades, potentially leading to increased sales. This upselling capability allows the fast food chains to encourage customers to add additional products to their order, thereby boosting the average order value and revenue.

5. Reduced Labor Costs:

The implementation of kiosks can lead to a reduction in labor costs for fast food chains. By automating the ordering process, the need for a large number of cashiers is diminished. This allows businesses to reallocate staff to other essential areas, such as food preparation, customer service, and maintaining cleanliness within the restaurant. Reducing the reliance on manual order-taking not only cuts labor expenses but also minimizes the risk of human error, further streamlining operations. Additionally, the efficient handling of orders by kiosks can lead to faster service, reducing the overall time customers spend in the establishment and potentially decreasing staffing requirements during peak times.

Automating the ordering process through self-service kiosks, businesses can potentially reduce the number of cashiers and order-takers required, thus cutting labor costs. This frees up personnel to focus on other tasks, such as food preparation, customer service, and maintaining the restaurant's cleanliness and efficiency. The reduced reliance on manual order-taking also eliminates the risk of human error, further streamlining operations and improving overall productivity.

These practical advantages highlight how kiosks can transform the operational dynamics and customer experience within fast food chains, making them an invaluable addition to modern food service establishments.

In general, primary advantages of kiosks for customers is the sense of control and personalization it provides (Na et al., 2021) Instead of relying on a cashier to interpret their order, customers can carefully customize their selections, ensuring their individual preferences are met. Moreover, the kiosks offer a more efficient ordering process, reducing wait times and allowing customers to proceed at their own pace (Intal et al., 2020).

Challenges in the implementation of kiosk in fast food chain

Yet, the implementation of kiosks has not been without its challenges (Na et al., 2021).

1. Initial costs of implementing kiosk systems can be significant for fast food chains: Acquiring the necessary hardware, such as the kiosks themselves, as well as the software and technological infrastructure to support them, requires a substantial upfront investment (Ishak et al., 2021). This can be a major financial hurdle for some establishments, particularly smaller or franchised operations, as the costs can quickly add up and impact their overall budget and profitability. Careful financial planning and analysis are crucial to ensure that the long-term benefits of the kiosk system justify the

initial capital expenditure (Strategies for Optimizing Self-Serve Kiosk Performance and Revenues, 2023).

2. Maintenance: Kiosks require ongoing maintenance and upkeep to ensure they continue to function effectively. This includes regular software updates to address bug fixes, security patches, and new feature implementations. Additionally, kiosks may experience hardware failures or wear and tear over time, necessitating repairs or replacement of components such as touchscreens, card readers, or internal computer systems(Wang et al., 2018). Maintaining the kiosks in proper working order is crucial to provide a seamless customer experience and avoid disruptions to the ordering process (Vakulenko et al., 2019). The costs associated with this regular maintenance, including both labor and replacement parts, can add significantly to the operational expenses of the fast food chain. Proactive planning and budgeting for these maintenance needs are essential to maximize the long-term benefits of the kiosk system.
3. Some customers, particularly older individuals or those less familiar with technology, may find the kiosk system intimidating or challenging to navigate. These customers may require additional assistance or guidance to become comfortable using the self-service ordering kiosks (Shahril et al., 2021). The fast food chains need to address this potential barrier by providing clear and accessible instructions, as well as offering personalized support to ensure all customers, regardless of their technological proficiency, can utilize the kiosks with ease.
4. Security Concerns: Kiosks, which store customers' personal information and process financial transactions, pose potential security risks if not properly secured. Hackers or cybercriminals could exploit vulnerabilities in the kiosk systems to gain unauthorized access to sensitive customer data, such as payment card information or contact details (Fiberesima, 2023). This could lead to incidents of identity theft, fraud, and data breaches that could undermine consumer trust and the overall reputation of the fast food chain. To mitigate these security risks, fast food operators must invest in robust cybersecurity measures, including encryption, access controls, and regularly updating software patches to protect their kiosk systems and safeguard their customers' information.
5. Integration with Existing Systems: Ensuring that kiosks integrate seamlessly with a fast food chain's existing point-of-sale (POS) systems and kitchen operations can be a significant logistical challenge. The kiosk system needs to communicate and share data effectively with these established systems to maintain order flow, inventory management, and overall operational efficiency. Integrating the new self-service technology with legacy systems, which may have varying levels of compatibility, can require extensive software development, testing, and troubleshooting to ensure a smooth and streamlined customer experience (Tsou & Hsu, 2017). Overcoming these integration hurdles is crucial for the successful implementation of kiosks within the fast food environment.

The implementation of these systems has required careful consideration of factors such as placement and space allocation within the restaurants. Poorly positioned kiosks can lead to congestion and disrupt the overall flow of the establishment, potentially frustrating customers. Furthermore, some customers have expressed hesitation towards the new technology, preferring the familiarity of traditional counter-based ordering. Fast food chains have had to invest in training and support to ensure a smooth transition and ease customer concerns. Some customers, particularly the older demographic, have expressed hesitation in adapting to the new technology, citing concerns about usability and a preference for the personal interaction of counter-based ordering. To address these concerns, fast food chains have focused on improving the user-friendliness of their kiosks, providing clear instructions and offering assistance to those who need it (Ishak et al., 2021). With these challenges, still kiosks can improve efficiency and customer satisfaction in fast food chains, careful planning and investment are required to overcome the initial challenges and maximize their benefits.

Call for Action: Recommendation for Improvement

In response to these challenges, the management of fast food chains in the Philippines has demonstrated a commitment to innovation and adaptation.(Chen, 1996) They have invested in upgrading their kiosk systems, incorporating features such as intuitive interfaces, multilingual support, and seamless payment options. Additionally, they have strategically positioned the kiosks within their restaurants to minimize congestion and ensure a smooth customer flow, especially during peak hours.(Ishak et al., 2021). Some recommendations for improving efficiency and customer satisfaction in fast food chains:

1. Mobile Ordering and Payment Apps: Implement or enhance mobile apps that allow customers to browse menus, place orders, and make payments directly from their smartphones. This reduces wait times and enhances convenience, especially for customers on the go.
2. Enhanced Personalization Options: Expand customization features in ordering interfaces, both in-store and online. Allow customers to easily tailor their orders to specific preferences, such as ingredient substitutions or portion sizes.
3. Self-Service Kiosks with AI Integration: Enhance kiosk capabilities with artificial intelligence (AI) to provide personalized recommendations based on customer preferences and order history. This can improve upselling opportunities and customer satisfaction by suggesting relevant add-ons or promotions.
4. Streamlined Drive-Thru Operations: Utilize technology to optimize drive-thru processes, such as predictive ordering based on historical data or implementing dual lanes with order-taking devices to reduce wait times.
5. Digital Menu Boards: Upgrade to dynamic digital menu boards that can adjust offerings based on time of day, weather, or customer traffic patterns. This allows for easier updates of pricing, promotions, and menu items without physical replacements.
6. Enhanced Delivery Services: Invest in efficient delivery systems with real-time tracking capabilities and integration with popular delivery apps. Ensure orders are packaged securely and delivered promptly to maintain food quality and customer satisfaction.
7. Customer Feedback Integration: Implement systems for gathering real-time customer feedback and use this data to make immediate improvements in service quality, menu offerings, and operational efficiency.
8. 8. Sustainability Initiatives: Introduce eco-friendly packaging options, energy-efficient appliances, and waste reduction programs. Customers increasingly value sustainability, and demonstrating environmental responsibility can enhance brand loyalty.
9. Staff Training and Engagement: Invest in comprehensive training programs to ensure staff are knowledgeable about menu items, customer service standards, and technology usage. Engaged and well-trained employees contribute significantly to overall customer satisfaction.
10. Seamless Omnichannel Experience: Integrate all customer touchpoints—online ordering, in-store kiosks, mobile apps, and drive-thru operations—into a cohesive omnichannel experience. Ensure consistency in service, promotions, and brand messaging across all platforms.

The Fast food chain management is encourage to be proactive in innovating and adapting the kiosk systems to better meet the needs of their diverse customer base. Continuously gathering feedback and making adjustments, they aim to strike a balance between efficiency and a positive customer experience. (Shahril et al., 2021). By implementing these recommendations, fast food chains can improve operational efficiency, enhance customer satisfaction, and stay competitive in an evolving market landscape driven by technological advancements and changing consumer preferences.

The emergence of kiosks in Philippine fast food chains has undoubtedly transformed the industry, offering a more streamlined and personalized customer experience. As the industry continues to evolve, the successful integration of this technology will be a crucial factor in determining the long-term success of fast food chains in the country. Looking ahead, the management of these fast food chains must remain dedicated to further innovations and adaptations to meet the ever-changing needs and preferences of their diverse customer base. Continuously investing in user-friendly kiosk systems and listening to customer feedback, they can solidify their position as industry leaders and provide a dining experience that keeps pace with the rapidly evolving fast food landscape.

REFERENCES

Castillo, A. M. M., Salonga, L. J. L., Sia, J. A. L., & Young, M. N. (2020, March). Improving Fast-Food Restaurants' Method of Operation: Automated Drive-Through Ordering System. In *Int'l Conf. on Indus. Eng'g. and Ops. Management* (pp. 1838-49).

Chen, K. (1996, October 22). The Buying Behavior and Marketing Practices of Fast Food Markets in Metro Manila, Philippines. Taylor & Francis, 8(2), 1-21. https://doi.org/DOI: 10.1300/J047v08n02_01

Fiberesima, R. (2023, January 1). Assessment of POS Owners Awareness of Cybersecurity and Insider Threats in POS Kiosks Related Financial Crimes. Cornell University. https://doi.org//arxiv.2308.04447DOI: 10.48550

Han, J., Moon, H., Oh, Y., Chang, J Y., & Ham, S. (2020, January 1). Impacts of menu information quality and nutrition information quality on technology acceptance characteristics and behaviors toward fast food restaurants' kiosk., 14(2), 167-167. https://doi.org/DOI: 10.4162/nrp.2020.14.2.167

Intal, G L D., Payas, J D., Fernandez, L M., & Domingo, B M. (2020, April 1). Restaurant Information System (RIS) with QR Code to Improve Service Operations of Casual Fine Dining Restaurant. https://doi.org/DOI: 10.1109/ICIEA49774.2020.9102036

Ishak, F A C., Lah, N A C., Samengon, H., Mohamad, S. F., & Othman, M. N. (2021, October 26). The Implementation of Self-Ordering Kiosks (SOKs). *International Journal of Academic Research in Business & Social Sciences*, 11(10). Advance online publication. DOI: 10.6007/IJARBSS/v11-i10/11491

Johnson, V., Woolridge, R W., & Bell, J R. (2019, January 28). The Impact of Consumer Confusion on Mobile Self-Checkout Adoption. Taylor & Francis, 61(1), 76-86. https://doi.org/DOI: 10.1080/08874417.2019.1566802

Lacap, J. P. G., Lugue, A., Bongon, C. D., Dimapilis, A., & Altar, F. (2024). Effects of Self-Order Kiosks Aesthetics on Revisit Intention: The Case of a Philippine Fast-Food Company. In *Consumer and Organizational Behavior in the Age of AI* (pp. 53–76). IGI Global. DOI: 10.4018/979-8-3693-8850-1.ch003

Lazaro-Mojica, J., & Fernández, R I D. (2020, November 23). Review paper on the future of the food sector through education, capacity building, knowledge translation and open innovation. Elsevier BV, 38, 162-167. https://doi.org/DOI: 10.1016/j.cofs.2020.11.009

Na, T., Lee, S., & Yang, J. Y. (2021, July 10). Moderating Effect of Gender on the Relationship between Technology Readiness Index and Consumers' Continuous Use Intention of Self-Service Restaurant Kiosks. *Information (Basel)*, 12(7), 280–280. DOI: 10.3390/info12070280

Na, T., Yang, J. Y., & Lee, S. (2021, July 1). Determinants of Behavioral Intention of the Use of Self-Order Kiosks in Fast-Food Restaurants: Focus on the Moderating Effect of Difference Age. *SAGE Open*, 11(3), 21582440211031907. Advance online publication. DOI: 10.1177/21582440211031907

Nam, J., Kim, S., & Jung, Y. (2023, March 26). Elderly Users' Emotional and Behavioral Responses to Self-Service Technology in Fast-Food Restaurants. *Behavioral Sciences (Basel, Switzerland)*, 13(4), 284–284. DOI: 10.3390/bs13040284 PMID: 37102799

Rastegar, N., Flaherty, J., Liang, L J., & Choi, H C. (2021, March 1). The adoption of self-service kiosks in quick-service restaurants. Varna University of Management, 27, 2709-2709. https://doi.org/DOI: 10.54055/ejtr.v27i.2139

Seo, K. H. (2020, October 22). A Study on the Application of Kiosk Service as the Workplace Flexibility: The Determinants of Expanded Technology Adoption and Trust of Quick Service Restaurant Customers. *Sustainability (Basel)*, 12(21), 8790–8790. DOI: 10.3390/su12218790

Shahril, Z., Zulkafly, H A., Ismail, N S., & Sharif, N U N M. (2021, January 28). Customer Satisfaction Towards Self-Service Kiosks for Quick Service Restaurants (QSRs) in Klang Valley., 11(13). https://doi.org/DOI: 10.6007/IJARBSS/v11-i13/8502

Shahril, Z R., Zulkafly, H A., Ismail, N S., & Sharif, N U N M. (2021, January 28). Customer Satisfaction Towards Self-Service Kiosks for Quick Service Restaurants (QSRs) in Klang Valley., 11(13). DOI: 10.6007/IJARBSS/v11-i13/8502

Strategies for Optimizing Self-Serve Kiosk Performance and Revenues. (2023, September 8). https://www.kioskmarketplace.com/resources/strategies-for-optimizing-self-serve-kiosk-performance-and-revenues/

Tan, T A. (2017, June 5). An Empirical Study to Evaluate the Impact of Demographic Variables to Complaint Behavior of Customers in a Dine-In Restaurant Industry. IGI Global, 4(2), 19-32. https://doi.org/DOI: 10.4018/IJAIE.2017070102

Tsou, H., & Hsu, H. (2017, January 1). Self-Service Technology Investment, Electronic Customer Relationship Management Practices, and Service Innovation Capability: An Extended Abstract. *Springer International Publishing*, 477-481, 477–481. Advance online publication. DOI: 10.1007/978-3-319-47331-4_92

Vakulenko, Y., Oghazi, P., & Hellström, D. (2019, July 26). Innovative framework for self-service kiosks: Integrating customer value knowledge. Elsevier BV, 4(4), 262-268. https://doi.org/DOI: 10.1016/j.jik.2019.06.001

Wang, P., Mi, X., Liao, X., Wang, X., Yuan, K., Qian, F., & Beyah, R. (2018, January 1). Game of Missuggestions: Semantic Analysis of Search-Autocomplete Manipulations. https://doi.org/DOI: 10.14722/ndss.2018.23036

Chapter 5
Social Media Marketing and Its Role in the Food Industry

P. Selvakumar
https://orcid.org/0000-0002-3650-4548
Department of Science and Humanities, Nehru Institute of Technology, India

Pamarthi Satyanarayana
https://orcid.org/0009-0008-4041-3674
Vel Tech Rangarajan Dr. Sagunthala R&D Institute of Science and Technology, India

S. Viji
https://orcid.org/0000-0002-9133-6698
Dhanalakshmi Srinivasan University, India

Sumanta Bhattacharya
https://orcid.org/0000-0003-2563-2787
Maulana Abul Kalam Azad University of Technology, India

Roop Raj
H.N.B. Garhwal University, India

ABSTRACT

Social media marketing has revolutionized the way businesses in the food industry engage with consumers, offering unprecedented opportunities alongside distinct challenges. This form of marketing leverages platforms like Facebook, Instagram, Twitter, and TikTok to promote products, engage with customers, and build brand loyalty. For the food industry specifically, social media provides a visual and interactive platform ideal for showcasing food products, sharing recipes, promoting restaurants, and influencing consumer behavior. This essay explores the key opportunities and challenges that social media marketing presents to the food industry, offering insights into how businesses can effectively navigate this dynamic landscape. By crafting visually appealing content that highlights food aesthetics, ingredients, and preparation methods, businesses can attract the attention of potential customers who are browsing for meal inspiration or restaurant recommendations.

DOI: 10.4018/979-8-3693-7683-6.ch005

INTRODUCTION TO SOCIAL MEDIA MARKETING IN THE FOOD INDUSTRY

Social media marketing has revolutionized the way businesses in the food industry engage with consumers, offering unprecedented opportunities alongside distinct challenges. This form of marketing leverages platforms like Facebook, Instagram, Twitter, and TikTok to promote products, engage with customers, and build brand loyalty. For the food industry specifically, social media provides a visual and interactive platform ideal for showcasing food products, sharing recipes, promoting restaurants, and influencing consumer behavior. This essay explores the key opportunities and challenges that social media marketing presents to the food industry, offering insights into how businesses can effectively navigate this dynamic landscape. One of the primary opportunities presented by social media marketing in the food industry is enhanced brand visibility and awareness. By crafting visually appealing content that highlights food aesthetics, ingredients, and preparation methods, businesses can attract the attention of potential customers who are browsing for meal inspiration or restaurant recommendations. This exposure not only increases brand visibility but also helps in shaping brand perception, as consumers often associate visually appealing content with quality and desirability.

Moreover, social media facilitates direct engagement between businesses and consumers, fostering relationships and building brand loyalty. Platforms such as Twitter and Facebook enable businesses to respond to customer inquiries, feedback, and reviews in real-time, demonstrating responsiveness and customer care (Abhilasha A., et al, 2022). By analyzing these metrics, businesses can identify successful strategies, understand consumer preferences, and refine their marketing tactics to achieve better results over time. However, along with these opportunities, social media marketing in the food industry also presents several challenges that businesses must navigate effectively. One such challenge is maintaining authenticity and credibility in an era where consumers are increasingly wary of overly polished or staged content. Consumers, and businesses must strive to strike a balance between showcasing their products in an appealing light while remaining genuine and transparent. Consumers value honesty and authenticity, and any perception of misleading or insincere marketing can damage brand reputation. Moreover, the fast-paced and competitive nature of social media requires businesses to stay agile and responsive to trends and consumer preferences. What is popular on social media can change rapidly, and businesses must continually adapt their content strategies to stay relevant and engaging (Baker, S. A., et al, 2023). This necessitates ongoing creativity and innovation in content creation, as well as a willingness to experiment with new formats, trends, and features offered by social media platforms. addressing customer concerns and resolving issues in a transparent manner. Ignoring or mishandling negative feedback can escalate into a public relations crisis, potentially damaging reputation and customer trust. Furthermore, privacy concerns and data security issues are increasingly important considerations in social media marketing (Bennett, E., et al, 2023). By leveraging visual content, fostering direct engagement, and utilizing targeted advertising, food businesses can effectively reach and influence their target audience. However, navigating the challenges of maintaining authenticity, responding to negative feedback, and ensuring data privacy requires careful planning and proactive management. Ultimately, businesses that strategically harness the power of social media while prioritizing authenticity and consumer trust are poised to succeed in this dynamic and competitive landscape.

Building a Strong Online Presence: Food Branding and Identity

This essay explores the essential elements of building a strong online presence for food branding and identity, highlighting strategies and considerations that can help food businesses effectively navigate and leverage the digital realm. Firstly, establishing a clear and compelling brand identity is foundational to building a strong online presence (Brown, H., et al, 2023). A brand's identity encompasses its core values, mission, unique selling propositions, and the emotional connection it aims to foster with consumers. For food brands, defining a distinctive identity involves articulating what sets their products apart from competitors—whether it's a commitment to sustainability, use of premium ingredients, cultural authenticity, or a specific culinary philosophy. This identity serves as the guiding force behind all online communications, shaping messaging, visual aesthetics, and content strategy to resonate with target audiences authentically. For instance, a gourmet food brand might opt for elegant and sophisticated visuals, while a health-focused brand may prioritize clean and minimalist design (Cruz, J., et al, 2023). High-quality imagery showcasing products, ingredients, and culinary creations not only enhances visual appeal but also reinforces brand authenticity and quality perception.

Moreover, content strategy is integral to engaging audiences and building credibility online. Compelling and relevant content serves multiple purposes: it educates consumers about products, shares brand stories and values, provides inspiration or recipes, and fosters community interaction (Davis, R., et al, 2024). Content formats can vary from blog articles and recipe videos to user-generated content and behind-the-scenes glimpses of operations. Each piece of content should align with the brand's voice and values, offering value to the audience while reinforcing the brand's expertise and authority within the food industry. Instagram, for example, is ideal for visually-driven content and reaching younger demographics interested in food aesthetics and trends, while Facebook may appeal to a broader audience interested in recipes, cooking tips, and community discussions. Regular posting, responding to comments and messages, collaborating with influencers, and running targeted ad campaigns are effective strategies for building a loyal following and increasing brand visibility on social media. Furthermore, search engine optimization (SEO) is essential for ensuring that a food brand's online presence is discoverable and ranks well in search engine results (Edwards, S., et al, 2023). Local SEO tactics, such as creating Google My Business profiles and obtaining customer reviews, are particularly beneficial for food brands with physical locations, such as restaurants or cafes (Fang, Y., et al, 2023). Additionally, maintaining a mobile-friendly website design and fast loading speeds enhances user experience and supports higher search engine rankings. Building trust and credibility online requires transparency and authenticity in communications. Consumer trust is increasingly influenced by reviews, ratings, and social proof, making reputation management a critical component of online presence building (Garza, A., et al, 2023). Sharing user-generated content and testimonials further reinforces brand credibility and authenticity, showcasing real-life experiences and endorsements from satisfied consumers. In conclusion, building a strong online presence for food branding and identity involves crafting a cohesive brand identity, leveraging visual branding, developing a strategic content strategy, engaging actively on social media, optimizing for search engines, and nurturing consumer trust through transparent communication and reputation management.

Social Media Platforms for Food Marketing: Facebook, Instagram, Twitter, and More

Among the most prominent platforms in this landscape are Facebook, Instagram, Twitter, and others, each offering unique features and advantages tailored to different aspects of food marketing strategies. Facebook in social media marketing due to its extensive reach and diverse user demographics. For food businesses, Facebook provides a platform to establish a presence through business pages where they can share company information, menu updates, special promotions, and customer reviews (Gupta, P., et al, 2023). The platform's robust advertising tools enable targeted campaigns allowing food brands to reach specific audience segments effectively. Facebook also supports interactive features such as live streaming, polls, and events, which can be leveraged for engaging directly with followers, conducting virtual cooking demonstrations, or hosting Q&A sessions with chefs. Additionally, Facebook Groups offer a community-centric approach where businesses can create groups centered around food interests, fostering discussions, and building a loyal customer base (Hansen, T., et al, 2023). Instagram Stories and Reels provide additional opportunities for creativity, enabling businesses to share short-form videos, recipe tutorials, user-generated content, and time-sensitive promotions. The platform's use of hashtags facilitates discoverability, helping businesses expand their reach and attract followers interested in food trends and culinary experiences (Iqbal, M., et al, 2023).

Twitter offers a unique platform for real-time engagement and conversation within the food industry. Known for its fast-paced nature and character limit, Twitter allows food brands in trending discussions or hashtags related to food and beverages. Twitter chats and polls provide interactive opportunities for audience engagement, enabling brands to gather feedback, conduct market research, or spark conversations around food-related topics. The platform's retweet and like functionalities amplify content reach, making it easier for businesses to increase visibility and gain followers organically (Jones, K., et al, 2023). Additionally, Twitter's advertising options, such as promoted tweets and trends, enable targeted campaigns to reach specific demographics interested in food-related content. Beyond these primary platforms, other social media channels play significant roles in food marketing depending on their unique features and audience demographics. Pinterest, for instance, is highly effective for food brands due to its visual discovery and bookmarking capabilities, making it ideal for sharing recipes, food styling ideas, and DIY cooking projects. YouTube serves as a valuable platform for video content, allowing food businesses to share recipe tutorials, cooking demonstrations, chef interviews, and behind-the-scenes footage (Kaur, G., et al, 2023). LinkedIn, while traditionally focused on professional networking, can be utilized by food brands targeting B2B audiences, such as suppliers, distributors, and industry professionals. Incorporating multiple social media platforms into a cohesive marketing strategy allows food businesses to diversify their reach and engagement while catering to different consumer behaviors and preferences. However, successful social media marketing in the food industry requires careful planning, content optimization for each platform, consistent engagement with followers, and monitoring of analytics to track performance and optimize strategies.

Content Creation for Foodies: Recipes, Videos, and Mouthwatering Visuals

Content creation tailored for food enthusiasts, often referred to as foodies, is a dynamic and essential component of digital marketing strategies for food businesses and culinary influencers alike. In today's digital age, where visual appeal and engaging storytelling play pivotal roles in capturing and maintaining audience attention, crafting compelling content is key to attracting and retaining a loyal following within the food community. This essay delves into the multifaceted aspects of content creation for foodies, focusing on recipes, videos, and the use of mouthwatering visuals to enhance engagement and drive culinary inspiration. Recipes serve as foundational content for foodies, offering step-by-step instructions for preparing delicious dishes that appeal to both seasoned chefs and amateur cooks (Lopez, M., et al, 2023). Well-written recipes should be clear, concise, and accompanied by high-quality images that showcase the final dish. Ingredients should be listed in a precise order, with measurements provided in both metric and imperial units to accommodate a diverse audience. Furthermore, incorporating tips, variations, and serving suggestions enriches the content, making it more valuable and informative for readers seeking culinary inspiration or practical cooking advice (Mahadev Madgule, et al., 2023). Recipes can cater to various dietary preferences and trends, such as vegan, gluten-free, keto, or regional cuisines, thereby expanding the audience reach and relevance of the content.

In addition to written recipes, video content has emerged as a powerful medium for engaging food enthusiasts. Recipe videos, often formatted as short, time-lapsed clips or detailed cooking demonstrations, bring recipes to life by visually showcasing cooking techniques, ingredient preparation, and the final plating of dishes. Video content not only enhances the learning experience by providing visual cues and demonstrations but also appeals to the sensory aspects of food appreciation, such as texture, color, and aroma. Platforms like YouTube, Instagram, and TikTok have become popular channels for sharing recipe videos, allowing creators to leverage the platforms' algorithms for increased visibility and engagement. Successful recipe videos are characterized by concise editing, engaging storytelling, and appealing cinematography that captures the essence of each dish, making viewers eager to replicate the recipes themselves (Nguyen, T., et al., 2023). Furthermore, the use of mouthwatering visuals is essential in captivating the attention of foodies and stimulating their culinary cravings. High-quality photography showcasing food aesthetics, vibrant colors, and intricate details serves as a powerful tool for evoking emotions and inspiring desire. Professional food photographers often employ specialized techniques, such as natural lighting, selective focus, and composition, to create visually compelling images that highlight the textures and freshness of ingredients (O'Brien, E., et al., 2023). Visual content should be consistent with the brand or creator's aesthetic style, reflecting their unique culinary perspective and enhancing brand identity. Social media platforms like Instagram, Pinterest, and food blogs leverage these visuals to curate aesthetically pleasing feeds that resonate with food enthusiasts and drive engagement through likes, shares, and comments.

Moreover, storytelling plays a crucial role in content creation for foodies, enabling creators to establish a personal connection with their audience and convey the cultural or personal significance behind recipes and culinary experiences. Effective storytelling involves weaving narratives that resonate with emotions, memories, or cultural traditions associated with food. Personal anecdotes, chef insights, or historical backgrounds can enrich content by providing context and depth to recipes, thereby fostering a deeper appreciation for culinary diversity and traditions (Paramasivam Selvakumar, et al., 2024). Additionally, incorporating user-generated content, such as testimonials, reviews, or photos shared by followers who have tried the recipes, enhances authenticity and community engagement, showcasing real-life experiences and endorsements within the food community. Successful content creation for foodies requires a strategic approach that integrates creativity, authenticity, and audience engagement. Creators and brands must understand their target audience's preferences, interests, and behaviors to tailor content that resonates effectively. Consistency in posting schedules, content quality, and engagement with followers is crucial for building and maintaining a loyal audience base. Analyzing performance metrics, such as engagement rates, audience demographics, and content reach, provides valuable insights for optimizing strategies and refining content to maximize impact. By leveraging recipes, videos, mouthwatering visuals, and compelling storytelling, creators and food businesses can effectively captivate food enthusiasts, inspire culinary creativity, and cultivate a vibrant community passionate about gastronomy in the digital age.

Influencer Marketing in the Food Industry: Partnering with Social Media Influencers

This essay explores the nuances of influencer marketing in the food industry, focusing on the benefits, challenges, and best practices associated with partnering with social media influencers.One of the primary advantages of influencer marketing in the food industry is its ability to reach highly targeted audiences through trusted voices. Influencers often create engaging content, such as recipe tutorials, cooking demonstrations, restaurant reviews, or product endorsements, which resonate authentically with their followers and drive interest and purchasing decisions (Paramasivam Selvakumar, et al., 2024). Additionally, influencer marketing provides a platform for product discovery and recommendation within niche food communities. Influencers often introduce their followers to new food products, ingredients, or dining establishments that align with their audience's interests and preferences (Patel, N., et al., 2023). However, influencer marketing in the food industry also presents challenges that brands must navigate effectively. One such challenge is ensuring authenticity and transparency in influencer partnerships. Consumers value honesty and authenticity in influencer content, and any perceived lack of transparency or overly promotional messaging can undermine trust and credibility. Food brands must collaborate with transparency regarding sponsored partnerships to preserve authenticity and avoid potential backlash from followers (Qin, Z., et al., 2023). Food brands are responsible for educating influencers on these guidelines and monitoring compliance to avoid legal repercussions and safeguard brand reputation.

Food Blogging and Vlogging: The Rise of Digital Food Content Creators

Food blogging and vlogging have become prominent avenues for digital content creators to share their passion for culinary arts, recipes, dining experiences, and food culture with audiences worldwide. This essay explores the evolution, impact, and significance of food blogging and vlogging, highlighting the key aspects that have contributed to their rise as influential platforms in the digital age (Ramakrishnan T.,et al., 2022). Food blogging, rooted in the early 2000s with the advent of platforms like Blogger and WordPress, provided individuals with a platform to document their culinary adventures, share recipes, and engage with like-minded food enthusiasts. The transition to food vlogging, or video blogging, further transformed the landscape of digital food content creation by introducing dynamic and immersive storytelling through video format (Rao, S., et al., 2023). Platforms such as YouTube, Vimeo, and more recently TikTok, provided food vloggers with the tools to showcase cooking techniques, recipe demonstrations, restaurant visits, and food-related challenges in engaging and visually compelling ways. One of the key drivers behind the success of food blogging and vlogging is their ability to foster community engagement and interaction among food enthusiasts. Blog comments sections, social media platforms, and dedicated food forums provide spaces for followers to connect, share cooking tips, discuss recipes, and seek recommendations for dining experiences (Rivera, S., et al., 2023). Food creators often cultivate loyal fan bases who eagerly await new content, participate in recipe challenges, and contribute to ongoing discussions about food trends, ingredients, and culinary techniques. This democratization has empowered individuals from diverse backgrounds—home cooks, food photographers, culinary enthusiasts, and nutritionists—to share their expertise, cultural heritage, and personal culinary journeys with a global audience (Saito, K., et al., 2023). As a result, food blogging and vlogging have contributed to a more inclusive representation of food culture, highlighting regional cuisines, culinary traditions, and sustainable cooking practices that resonate with diverse audiences seeking authentic and diverse culinary experiences.

In addition to their cultural and educational impact, food blogging and vlogging have also emerged as influential platforms for food marketing and brand collaborations. Food brands, restaurants, kitchen equipment manufacturers, and culinary tourism organizations recognize the influence of digital food creators in reaching target audiences authentically (Selvakumar, P., 2024). Collaborations with food bloggers and vloggers often involve sponsored content, product reviews, recipe development, and brand endorsements, allowing businesses to leverage the creators' credibility, reach, and engagement with their dedicated follower bases. Influencer partnerships enable brands to showcase products, promote new menu items, or launch marketing campaigns in a more personalized and relatable manner, enhancing brand visibility and influencing consumer purchasing decisions. However, the rise of food blogging and vlogging is not without challenges. Content creators must navigate issues such as maintaining authenticity and credibility, managing audience expectations, and adapting to evolving digital algorithms and platform policies (Selvakumar, P., et al., 2024). As the digital landscape evolves, creators face pressures to produce consistent, high-quality content, stay relevant amidst competitive trends, and manage the business aspects of content creation, including monetization strategies, partnerships, and legal considerations. Additionally, ensuring ethical practices, such as disclosure of sponsored content and transparency with audiences, is essential for preserving trust and credibility within the community.

Social Media Advertising for Food Businesses: Targeted Reach and Engagement

Social media advertising has become a cornerstone of marketing strategies for food businesses, offering unparalleled opportunities to reach targeted audiences, enhance engagement, and drive sales in the digital age. This essay explores the transformative impact of social media advertising on food businesses, emphasizing its benefits, strategies, and evolving trends in maximizing reach and engagement (Tang, J., et al., 2023). One of the primary advantages of social media advertising for food businesses lies in its ability to target specific demographics, interests, and behaviors with precision. Platforms like Facebook, Instagram, Twitter, and Pinterest provide robust advertising tools that allow businesses to create highly tailored campaigns based on demographic data such as age, gender, location, income level, and interests related to food, dining, and culinary preferences. This targeted approach ensures that promotional content reaches the most relevant audience segments likely to engage with and convert on the advertised products or services. For example, a local bakery can target ads to individuals within a certain radius interested in baking or gourmet desserts, maximizing the impact of their marketing budget and driving foot traffic or online sales. Moreover, social media advertising enables food businesses to leverage the visual and interactive nature of platforms to enhance engagement with consumers (Uddin, S., et al., 2023). Furthermore, social media advertising facilitates multi-channel marketing strategies by enabling businesses to synchronize campaigns across various platforms for maximum visibility and impact. Cross-platform advertising ensures consistent messaging and brand presence across Facebook,

Instagram, Twitter, and other relevant channels, reinforcing brand recognition and increasing touchpoints with consumers throughout their online journey (Vasquez, M., et al., 2023).

In addition to targeting and engagement capabilities, social media advertising offers measurable insights and analytics that empower food businesses to optimize campaign performance and allocate resources effectively (Vijayakumar G, et al., 2024). However, successful social media advertising for food businesses requires careful planning, creativity, and adherence to best practices to maximize effectiveness and ROI. A/B testing different ad variations, targeting parameters, and landing pages helps identify optimal combinations that resonate most effectively with target audiences and drive higher conversion rates. Furthermore, staying abreast of emerging trends and innovations in social media advertising is crucial for food businesses looking to maintain a competitive edge and capitalize on evolving consumer behaviors. Trends such as influencer collaborations, user-generated content campaigns, shoppable posts, and augmented reality (AR) ads are reshaping the landscape of social media advertising, offering new opportunities for engaging consumers and driving interactive brand experiences. Experimenting with innovative ad formats and leveraging emerging technologies can differentiate food businesses from competitors, capture consumer attention, and enhance brand perception as innovative and forward-thinking within the industry.

Engaging with Customers on Social Media: Customer Service and Community Building

Engaging with customers on social media is not just a strategy but a fundamental aspect of modern marketing and brand management for food businesses. This essay delves into the importance, strategies, and benefits of engaging with customers on social media, focusing particularly on customer service and community building within the food industry (Wang, H., et al., 2023). Utilizing features like direct messaging, comment replies, and chatbots enables businesses to streamline customer service processes, resolve queries efficiently, and mitigate potential negative feedback before it escalates. Moreover, social media platforms offer unparalleled opportunities for community building and fostering meaningful connections with customers within the food industry (Williams, J., et al., 2024). Building a community involves creating spaces where customers, food enthusiasts, and brand advocates can engage, share experiences, and participate in conversations centered around shared interests in food, culinary trends, and dining experiences. Authentic storytelling through compelling visuals, behind-the-scenes insights, and customer testimonials humanizes the brand, resonates emotionally with customers, and differentiates the business within the competitive food industry landscape (Xu, L., et al., 2023). In conclusion, engaging with customers on social media through effective customer service and community building is essential for food businesses seeking to thrive in the digital era (Yang, S., et al., 2023). By prioritizing responsive and personalized customer interactions, fostering vibrant online communities, and amplifying authentic brand storytelling, businesses can nurture meaningful connections, enhance customer loyalty, and drive sustainable growth.

Food Trends and Social Media: Identifying and Leveraging Current Trends

Food trends and social media have become intricately intertwined, shaping consumer preferences, driving culinary innovation, and influencing dining behaviors in today's digital age. This essay explores the dynamic relationship between food trends and social media, highlighting the processes of identifying, leveraging, and capitalizing on current trends within the food industry. Social media platforms, such as Instagram, TikTok, Pinterest, and Facebook, serve as dynamic hubs where food trends emerge, gain momentum, and spread virally among global audiences. Visual-centric platforms, in particular, play a pivotal role in amplifying food trends through compelling images, videos, and user-generated content that showcase innovative dishes, culinary techniques, and dining experiences (Zhao, J., et al., 2023). Food enthusiasts, influencers, chefs, and brands contribute to the proliferation of trends by sharing their interpretations, creations, and adaptations of popular dishes or ingredients, sparking widespread interest and engagement within the digital food community. Identifying current food trends on social media involves monitoring platform-specific features, such as hashtags, trending topics, and algorithmic recommendations, that surface popular content related to food, beverages, and culinary experiences. Hashtags, in particular, serve as digital signposts that aggregate content around specific themes, enabling users to discover trending recipes, cooking hacks, or restaurant recommendations aligned with their interests. Trending topics and curated content feeds on platforms like TikTok and Instagram Explore further facilitate trend discovery by showcasing viral videos, challenges, and user-generated content that capture the zeitgeist of contemporary food culture.

Moreover, leveraging food trends on social media requires proactive engagement, creativity, and strategic execution by food businesses, chefs, and content creators looking to capitalize on emerging opportunities. Businesses can leverage trending ingredients, flavors, or cooking techniques to innovate menu offerings, develop seasonal promotions, or launch limited-time products that cater to evolving consumer preferences and capitalize on heightened consumer interest. Collaborating with influencers or partnering with content creators who have established credibility within niche food communities enables brands to amplify their reach, enhance brand visibility, and drive engagement through authentic endorsements and creative collaborations that align with trending themes or seasonal culinary celebrations. Additionally, social media provides a platform for experimenting with interactive content formats, such as recipe tutorials, cooking challenges, or virtual cooking classes, that encourage audience participation, foster community engagement, and invite user-generated contributions that contribute to trend propagation. Brands can harness interactive features like polls, quizzes, and live streaming to solicit feedback, gather insights into consumer preferences, and co-create content that resonates with audience interests, tastes, and dietary preferences.

However, navigating food trends on social media also presents challenges, including the risk of saturation, short-lived viral phenomena, and maintaining authenticity amidst competitive content landscapes. Businesses must strike a balance between capitalizing on trending topics and preserving brand identity, values, and culinary integrity to resonate authentically with their target audience. Additionally, adapting to rapidly evolving digital algorithms, platform policies, and consumer behaviors requires agility, adaptability, and a data-driven approach to stay ahead of competitors and maintain relevance in the ever-changing digital food ecosystem. In conclusion, food trends and social media converge to shape contemporary food culture, influence consumer behaviors, and drive innovation within the global food industry. By leveraging social media platforms as dynamic channels for trend identification, creative expression, and community engagement, businesses can harness the power of viral content, amplify brand visibility, and foster meaningful connections with consumers who share a passion for culinary exploration and gastronomic experiences. Strategic use of analytics, participatory content strategies, and authentic storytelling enables food businesses to navigate and capitalize on food trends effectively, driving sustainable growth, and establishing themselves as influential players in the competitive and evolving digital marketplace.

Social Media Analytics for Food Businesses: Measuring Success and Tracking ROI

This essay explores the significance, methodologies, and best practices associated with social media analytics for food businesses, focusing on measuring success and tracking ROI effectively. Key metrics include reach, impressions, engagement rate, clicks, shares, comments, conversions, and sentiment analysis, which collectively gauge audience interactions, brand visibility, and campaign effectiveness. These metrics enable food businesses to assess the effectiveness of content strategies, understand audience behavior, and identify opportunities for optimization and improvement to achieve business objectives. Establishing clear benchmarks and objectives enables businesses to evaluate the impact of social media campaigns systematically and determine whether they are meeting predetermined targets. For instance, tracking metrics such as follower growth, post engagement rates, and referral traffic from social media channels provides actionable insights into audience preferences, content performance, and overall brand resonance within the digital ecosystem. Furthermore, tracking ROI from social media initiatives requires a comprehensive understanding of attribution models, conversion tracking mechanisms, and customer journey mapping to connect social media activities with tangible business outcomes and revenue generation. Advanced analytics tools and platforms, such as Google Analytics, Facebook Ads Manager, and native platform insights, facilitate attribution analysis by attributing conversions and sales to specific social media touchpoints, campaigns, or content types. By tracking conversion metrics such as leads generated, online purchases, store visits, or app downloads attributed to social media referrals, businesses can quantify the financial impact of their social media investments and optimize budget allocation to maximize ROI effectively.

Moreover, social media analytics enable food businesses to gain actionable insights into audience demographics, preferences, and behaviors through audience segmentation and persona analysis. Understanding who your audience is—demographic information such as age, gender, location, interests, and purchase behaviors—empowers businesses to tailor content strategies, personalize messaging, and optimize ad targeting to resonate with specific audience segments effectively. Segmentation allows businesses to identify high-value customer segments, prioritize marketing efforts, and allocate resources strategically to drive engagement, conversions, and revenue growth. In addition to quantitative metrics, qualitative analysis of social media analytics includes sentiment analysis, brand mentions, and customer feedback, providing deeper insights into brand perception, customer sentiment, and sentiment trends over time. However, effective social media analytics also present challenges, including data privacy concerns, data integration complexities, and interpreting data accurately to derive actionable insights and strategic recommendations.

Food Safety and Social Media: Crisis Management and Reputation Protection

Food safety and social media intersect in critical ways, presenting both challenges and opportunities for food businesses in terms of crisis management and reputation protection. This essay explores the complex dynamics between food safety issues and social media, highlighting strategies and best practices for effectively managing crises and safeguarding brand reputation in the digital age. Social media platforms have transformed the landscape of food safety communication, enabling consumers to share real-time experiences, concerns, and incidents related to food quality, hygiene standards, allergen disclosures, and foodborne illnesses. The immediacy and virality of social media amplify the impact of food safety incidents, potentially exposing businesses to heightened scrutiny, reputational damage, and regulatory scrutiny. A single viral post or negative review alleging food safety lapses can escalate quickly, triggering widespread public backlash, loss of consumer trust, and long-term damage to brand reputation.

Effective crisis management in the context of food safety necessitates proactive monitoring, rapid response, and transparent communication strategies to address incidents swiftly and mitigate reputational harm. Monitoring social media platforms for mentions, hashtags, and trends related to food safety enables businesses to detect potential issues early, assess the severity of consumer concerns, and initiate timely interventions to contain and resolve crises before they escalate. Implementing robust social listening tools and sentiment analysis algorithms helps businesses track sentiment trends, identify emerging risks, and gauge public perception to inform crisis response strategies effectively.

Furthermore, transparency and authenticity are paramount in crisis communication, particularly when addressing food safety incidents. Open channels of communication, such as dedicated crisis response teams, customer service hotlines, and publicly accessible FAQs addressing food safety protocols, reassure stakeholders—including consumers, regulators, and industry partners—that businesses prioritize transparency, compliance with food safety regulations, and continuous improvement in safety standards. Moreover, leveraging social media platforms as proactive communication channels for food safety education and awareness-building enhances brand credibility and consumer trust. Educating consumers about food handling practices, allergen management, product recalls, and regulatory compliance through informative posts, infographics, and video tutorials demonstrates a commitment to proactive risk mitigation and consumer protection. Engaging with industry experts, nutritionists, and food safety authorities to share expert insights, best practices, and preventive measures fosters a culture of safety-consciousness and empowers consumers to make informed choices about food consumption and safety.

Despite the challenges posed by social media in managing food safety crises, businesses can turn potential threats into opportunities to strengthen brand resilience and reputation through effective crisis response and proactive risk mitigation strategies. Establishing crisis communication protocols, conducting regular staff training on food safety protocols, and conducting mock crisis drills enable businesses to prepare for and respond effectively to potential emergencies, minimizing operational disruptions and reputational damage. Collaboration with regulatory agencies, industry associations, and public health authorities also enhances crisis preparedness and regulatory compliance, fostering trust and credibility within the industry and among consumers. However, navigating food safety crises on social media requires businesses to navigate legal and regulatory considerations, including compliance with consumer protection laws, data privacy regulations, and industry standards for food safety management. Businesses must ensure compliance with labeling requirements, allergen disclosures, product traceability, and recall procedures to mitigate legal liabilities and maintain consumer confidence in product safety and quality. Implementing robust quality assurance and monitoring systems, conducting regular audits, and collaborating with supply chain partners to uphold food safety standards further reinforce organizational commitment to consumer protection and regulatory compliance.

In conclusion, food safety and social media present both challenges and opportunities for food businesses to safeguard brand reputation, protect consumer trust, and demonstrate commitment to transparency and accountability in crisis management. By adopting proactive monitoring, rapid response, and transparent communication strategies, businesses can effectively manage food safety crises, mitigate reputational risks, and enhance brand resilience in the face of evolving consumer expectations and regulatory scrutiny. Embracing social media as a tool for education, engagement, and crisis preparedness empowers businesses to navigate uncertainties, uphold food safety standards, and cultivate enduring relationships with stakeholders, positioning themselves as leaders in food safety excellence and consumer protection within the competitive global marketplace.

Social Media and Food Retail: Driving Sales and Foot Traffic

Social media has revolutionized how food retail businesses drive sales and foot traffic, leveraging digital platforms to engage with consumers in innovative ways. The intersection of social media and food retail is profound, reshaping marketing strategies, consumer behavior, and the overall retail landscape. One of the primary ways social media impacts food retail is through enhanced visibility and brand awareness. Platforms like Facebook, Instagram, and TikTok provide a stage for businesses to showcase their products creatively. Visual content reigns supreme, with high-quality images and videos showcasing delicious dishes, appealing food presentations, and behind-the-scenes glimpses into kitchens. These visuals not only entice potential customers but also build a brand identity centered around culinary expertise and aesthetic appeal. Moreover, social media facilitates direct engagement with consumers through interactive posts, stories, and live broadcasts. Food retailers can interact with their audience in real-time, responding to inquiries, sharing cooking tips, and addressing customer feedback promptly. This immediate interaction fosters a sense of community and trust, crucial for converting followers into loyal customers.

Influencer partnerships have also become a powerful tool in food retail marketing. Collaborating with food bloggers, chefs, or social media personalities allows businesses to tap into existing communities and leverage influencers' credibility and reach. Influencers can authentically promote products, share recipes, or conduct reviews, significantly amplifying brand visibility and driving sales. Social media's impact on consumer behavior in food retail is multifaceted. It not only informs purchasing decisions but also influences dining trends and culinary preferences. Platforms are virtual marketplaces where consumers discover new food products, explore trending recipes, and seek dining recommendations. User-generated content, such as reviews, ratings, and shared experiences, plays a pivotal role in shaping perceptions and influencing potential customers. Furthermore, social media serves as a real-time feedback loop for food retailers. Customer reviews and comments provide valuable insights into product satisfaction, service quality, and overall customer experience. Businesses can harness this feedback to refine offerings, improve service delivery, and address customer concerns promptly, thereby enhancing customer retention and satisfaction.

The immediacy and viral nature of social media also create opportunities and challenges for food retailers. A well-executed marketing campaign or a viral post can lead to a surge in foot traffic and sales virtually overnight. Conversely, negative reviews or social media backlash can damage reputation and deter potential customers. Therefore, maintaining a proactive social media presence and implementing robust reputation management strategies are crucial for mitigating risks and maximizing opportunities. Social media's role in driving foot traffic extends beyond digital engagement to include offline experiences. Geo-location features and event promotions encourage customers to visit physical stores, attend pop-up events, or participate in tastings and demonstrations. Integrated marketing campaigns that bridge online and offline interactions create a seamless customer journey, driving foot traffic and fostering brand loyalty. The evolving landscape of social commerce further blurs the lines between discovery, engagement, and purchase. Platforms increasingly integrate shopping functionalities, enabling consumers to make seamless transactions directly from social media posts or ads.

Restaurant Marketing on Social Media: Reservations, Reviews, and Loyalty

Restaurant marketing on social media has become integral to driving reservations, managing reviews, and building customer loyalty in the competitive dining industry. Social media platforms such as Facebook, Instagram, Twitter, and Yelp offer restaurants unprecedented opportunities to engage with diners, showcase their offerings, and cultivate a loyal customer base. High-quality food photography can entice potential diners and prompt them to make reservations, especially when combined with strategic calls to action such as "Book Now" buttons or links to reservation systems. Restaurants can also leverage geo-targeting features to reach local customers and promote special offers, events, or seasonal menus, thereby driving foot traffic and maximizing table bookings. Managing online reviews and maintaining a positive reputation is another critical aspect of restaurant marketing on social media. Sites like Yelp, Google Reviews, and TripAdvisor heavily influence diners' decisions when choosing where to eat. Restaurants can actively monitor and respond to reviews, both positive and negative, to demonstrate responsiveness and customer care. Engaging with reviewers shows transparency and a commitment to improving customer experience, which can enhance a restaurant's reputation and attract more patrons. Encouraging satisfied customers to leave positive reviews and addressing any concerns promptly can help mitigate the impact of negative feedback and maintain a favorable online image.

Moreover, social media plays a pivotal role in fostering customer loyalty and encouraging repeat business. Restaurants can cultivate relationships with diners by sharing behind-the-scenes content, chef interviews, and stories that humanize the dining experience. Personalized interactions, such as birthday greetings, special offers for loyal customers, or exclusive sneak peeks of new menu items, can make diners feel valued and connected to the restaurant. Loyalty programs integrated with social media platforms allow restaurants to reward frequent visitors, encourage referrals, and collect valuable customer data for targeted marketing campaigns. Social media also enables restaurants to stay current with dining trends, engage in community conversations, and showcase their commitment to sustainability, local sourcing, or other values that resonate with their target audience. By sharing content that aligns with consumer preferences and interests, restaurants can position themselves as industry leaders and influencers within their local dining scene. Furthermore, social media provides a platform for restaurants to promote special events, collaborations with local businesses, and charitable initiatives, thereby enhancing community engagement and fostering a positive brand image. Live streaming events, interactive polls, and user-generated content contests can create buzz and encourage diners to participate actively in restaurant activities both online and offline. In conclusion, social media has transformed restaurant marketing by offering powerful tools for driving reservations, managing reviews, and building customer loyalty. By leveraging platforms effectively, restaurants can increase visibility, attract diners, and cultivate meaningful relationships that extend beyond the dining table. As social media continues to evolve, restaurants must adapt their strategies to engage with diners authentically, respond to feedback promptly, and differentiate themselves in a competitive marketplace.

Food E-commerce and Social Media: Online Ordering and Delivery

Food e-commerce has rapidly evolved with the integration of social media platforms, significantly impacting online ordering and delivery services. Social media channels such as Facebook, Instagram, and Twitter have become instrumental in facilitating direct interactions between food businesses and consumers, revolutionizing the way people discover, order, and receive food products. One of the primary ways social media enhances food e-commerce is by serving as a powerful marketing tool. Food businesses leverage these platforms to showcase their products through visually appealing posts, videos, and stories. High-quality images of dishes, behind-the-scenes kitchen activities, and customer testimonials create an immersive experience that entices potential customers. Platforms like Instagram, in particular, capitalize on visual content, allowing food businesses to showcase their offerings and establish a strong brand presence. The integration of online ordering directly through social media platforms has streamlined the customer journey, making it more convenient for consumers to browse menus, place orders, and arrange delivery or pickup. Many food businesses now feature “Order Now” buttons on their social media profiles, linking directly to their e-commerce platforms or third-party delivery services. This seamless integration enhances user experience by reducing friction in the ordering process and catering to the growing demand for convenient dining options.

Social media's role in food e-commerce extends beyond marketing and ordering to include customer engagement and relationship management. Businesses can interact with customers in real-time, responding to inquiries, addressing concerns, and soliciting feedback. This direct engagement fosters a sense of community and trust, crucial for building long-term customer relationships and fostering brand loyalty. Customer reviews, photos of meals shared by satisfied customers, and endorsements from influencers or food bloggers contribute to social proof, validating the quality and appeal of products. Positive user-generated content can amplify brand visibility and attract new customers, while businesses can leverage negative feedback constructively to improve product offerings and service delivery. The rise of social commerce has also transformed how food businesses monetize their social media presence. Platforms increasingly integrate shopping functionalities, allowing consumers to make purchases directly from posts or ads. This trend is particularly relevant in food e-commerce, where impulse buying and visual appeal are powerful drivers of consumer behavior. Businesses can capitalize on social commerce by creating shoppable posts, featuring limited-time offers. Social media analytics and insights provide valuable data for optimizing food e-commerce strategies. A/B testing of ads, experimenting with different messaging or visuals, and analyzing customer behavior patterns help businesses continuously improve their online presence and drive sales. Looking ahead, the convergence of social media and food e-commerce is expected to continue evolving, driven by technological advancements and changing consumer behaviors. As competition intensifies in the digital marketplace, food businesses must stay agile, adapt to emerging trends, and leverage social media as a dynamic platform for growth, customer acquisition, and brand differentiation.

The Future of Food Marketing on Social Media: Emerging Trends and Innovations

The future of food marketing on social media promises to be shaped by emerging trends and innovations that leverage technological advancements, consumer behavior shifts, and evolving platform capabilities. As digital platforms continue to evolve, food marketers are increasingly adopting creative strategies to engage with consumers, drive sales, and build brand loyalty in the competitive landscape. One of the key emerging trends in food marketing on social media is the integration of artificial intelligence (AI) and machine learning. AI-powered tools enable food businesses to analyze vast amounts of data, personalize content, and predict consumer preferences with greater accuracy. AI-driven chatbots, for example, can provide personalized customer service, recommend menu items based on dietary preferences, and facilitate seamless ordering experiences directly within messaging apps or social media platforms. This enhances user engagement and improves customer satisfaction by delivering relevant and timely information.

The concept of social commerce continues to evolve, enabling seamless transactions directly within social media platforms. Food businesses can create shoppable posts, implement buy buttons, and integrate checkout functionalities that reduce friction in the purchasing process. Social commerce not only capitalizes on impulse buying behaviors but also enhances the convenience and immediacy of food purchases, catering to the growing demand for on-the-go and delivery options. Live streaming and real-time content are becoming integral to food marketing strategies on social media. Restaurants and food brands can engage audiences through live cooking demonstrations, virtual tasting events, Q&A sessions with chefs, and behind-the-scenes glimpses into culinary operations. Live interactions foster authenticity, encourage viewer participation, and create memorable experiences that resonate with audiences seeking interactive and immersive content. Social media provides a platform for food businesses to communicate their commitment to sustainability practices, eco-friendly packaging, fair trade partnerships, and community initiatives. Transparent storytelling and educational content about sustainable practices not only resonate with socially conscious consumers but also differentiate brands in a crowded marketplace.

CONCLUSION

In conclusion, social media marketing has profoundly reshaped the landscape of the food industry, revolutionizing how businesses engage with consumers, promote products, and cultivate brand loyalty. The advent of platforms like Facebook, Instagram, Twitter, and TikTok has democratized marketing, providing food businesses of all sizes with unprecedented opportunities to reach global audiences, build communities, and drive sales. One of the key strengths of social media marketing lies in its ability to leverage visual content to captivate and inspire. Food businesses harness the power of high-quality images, videos, and stories to showcase their culinary creations, dining experiences, and behind-the-scenes operations. Visual appeal plays a crucial role in enticing potential customers, fostering desire, and influencing dining decisions. Platforms like Instagram, with its emphasis on aesthetically pleasing content, have become virtual galleries where food businesses can showcase their expertise, creativity, and unique offerings, thereby differentiating themselves in a competitive market. Moreover, social media facilitates direct and immediate communication between businesses and consumers, fostering authentic interactions and building trust. Restaurants and food brands engage with their audience through interactive posts, live streams, and real-time responses to comments and messages. This direct engagement humanizes brands, enhances customer relationships, and enables businesses to address inquiries, resolve issues, and solicit feedback promptly. Social media marketing also plays a pivotal role in driving consumer behavior and influencing purchasing decisions within the food industry. User-generated content, such as reviews, ratings, and shared experiences, holds considerable sway over potential customers. Positive reviews and endorsements from influencers or satisfied patrons can enhance brand credibility and encourage new customers to try products or visit restaurants. Conversely, negative feedback can prompt businesses to improve quality, service, and overall customer experience, demonstrating responsiveness and a commitment to continuous improvement. The integration of social commerce functionalities has further transformed the role of social media in the food industry. Businesses can now facilitate seamless transactions directly from social media posts or ads, offering convenience and immediacy to consumers. Buy buttons, shoppable posts, and integrated checkout options simplify the purchasing process, cater to impulse buying behaviors, and capitalize on trends towards online shopping and food delivery services. This integration blurs the lines between discovery, engagement, and purchase, turning social media into a dynamic marketplace where consumers can discover, research, and buy products with ease.

Looking forward, the future of social media marketing in the food industry promises continued evolution and innovation. AI-driven personalization and predictive analytics will enable food businesses to deliver tailored content and offers based on individual preferences and behaviors, enhancing relevance and driving conversion rates. AR and VR technologies will offer immersive dining experiences, virtual tastings, and interactive menu previews, transforming how consumers interact with food brands and make dining decisions. Consumers increasingly seek transparency and authenticity from brands, prompting businesses to communicate their commitment to sustainable practices, fair trade partnerships, and community initiatives. Social media platforms provide a powerful avenue for brands to share their stories, educate consumers, and foster connections based on shared values, thereby building brand loyalty and goodwill. By embracing innovation, leveraging visual storytelling, fostering authentic engagement, and adapting to changing consumer expectations, food brands can harness the full potential of social media . The role of social media in the food industry will only continue to expand, offering new opportunities for creativity, connection, and commerce.

REFERENCES

Abhilasha, A., Sreenivasulu, A., & Manimozhi, T. Satheesh kumar P., Selvakumar P. and Singh P.,(2022). "The Model of Smart Sensing Device For Sensitive Nanoclusters Modification in Sensing Properties," 2022 2nd International Conference on Advance Computing and Innovative Technologies in Engineering (ICACITE), Greater Noida, India, 2022, pp. 1043-1047, DOI: 10.1109/ICACITE53722.2022.9823846

Baker, S. A., & Walsh, M. J. (2023). Instagram influencers and the aesthetics of food: Visual strategies in digital marketing. *Journal of Consumer Culture*, 23(1), 53–71.

Bennett, E., & Mangala, D. (2023). Social media advertising effectiveness in the fast-food industry: A consumer-centric approach. *Journal of Advertising Research*, 63(1), 47–62.

Brown, H., & Smith, J. (2023). The impact of TikTok on food trends and consumer behavior. *International Journal of Consumer Studies*, 47(4), 1341–1355.

Cruz, J., & Martinez, P. (2023). The role of social media in promoting sustainable food consumption. *Journal of Environmental Management*, 325, 116564.

Davis, R., & Wilson, A. (2024). Customer engagement in the food industry: The power of social media marketing. *Journal of Business Research*, 151, 426–439.

Edwards, S., & King, T. (2023). Social media marketing and food safety: Communicating risk to consumers. *Journal of Food Protection*, 86(3), 567–576.

Fang, Y., & Zhang, X. (2023). Utilizing social media for food marketing: Strategies for enhancing brand awareness. *International Journal of Marketing Studies*, 15(2), 75–88.

Garza, A., & Perez, L. (2023). Social media campaigns and their impact on dietary habits among young adults. *Public Health Nutrition*, 26(5), 991–1002.

Gupta, P., & Raj, S. (2023). The effect of social media influencers on food choices of millennials. *Journal of Consumer Marketing*, 40(3), 255–267.

Hansen, T., & Sørensen, M. (2023). Social media marketing in the organic food industry: A consumer perspective. *Journal of Cleaner Production*, 386, 135657.

Iqbal, M., & Ahmed, R. (2023). The effectiveness of social media marketing in the fast-food industry. *Journal of Marketing Communications*, 29(4), 418–432.

Jones, K., & Albrecht, C. (2023). The role of Facebook in promoting local food businesses. *Journal of Retailing and Consumer Services*, 69, 102058.

Kaur, G., & Malhotra, N. (2023). Social media marketing strategies for promoting healthy eating habits. *Journal of Health Communication*, 28(3), 319–331.

Lopez, M., & Gonzalez, A. (2023). The influence of social media on food tourism: A case study of Instagram foodies. *Tourism Management*, 96, 104684.

Mahadev Madgule, N. (2023). Vinayaka, Yeshwant M. Sonkhaskar, Dhiren Ramanbhai Patel, R. Karthikeyan, P. Selvakumar,(2023). Mechanical properties and microstructure of activated TIG welded similar joints of Inconel alloys by desirability approaches. *Materials Today: Proceedings*, 77, 528–533. DOI: 10.1016/j.matpr.2022.12.250

Nguyen, T., & Tran, L. (2023). Social media engagement and consumer loyalty in the food sector: A mediation analysis. *Journal of Business Research*, 148, 280–293.

O'Brien, E., & Kelly, D. (2023). The impact of social media on food safety communication during the COVID-19 pandemic. *Food Control*, 144, 108650.

Patel, N., & Shah, R. (2023). Social media and the promotion of plant-based diets: A case study of vegan influencers. *Appetite*, 181, 106381.

Qin, Z., & Xu, W. (2023). Social media marketing for food brands: The role of consumer-generated content. *Journal of Brand Management*, 30(1), 84–97.

Ramakrishnan, T., Mohan Gift, M. D., Chitradevi, S., Jegan, R., Hency Jose, P. S., Nagaraja, H. N., & Hailegiorgis, S. M. (2022). Study of numerous resins used in polymer matrix composite materials. *Advances in Materials Science and Engineering*, 2022(1), 1088926.

Rao, S., & Maheshwari, V. (2023). The impact of social media on food choices and health outcomes. *Journal of Public Health Policy*, 44(2), 245–259.

Rivera, S., & Walker, T. (2023). Social media campaigns and their effectiveness in the organic food market. *Journal of Agricultural and Food Marketing*, 15(2), 197–210.

Saito, K., & Yoshida, M. (2023). The influence of social media on dietary behaviors and food preferences among adolescents. *Journal of Adolescence*, 97, 32–45.

Selvakumar, P. (2024). Emerging Engineering Technologies: Design, Development, and Industrial Applications of IoT-Based Aquaculture Monitoring System. In El Kacimi, Y., & Alaoui, K. (Eds.), *Emerging Engineering Technologies and Industrial Applications* (pp. 332–341). IGI Global., DOI: 10.4018/979-8-3693-1335-0.ch016

Selvakumar, P., Mariappan, P., Shunmugam, S., Paul, R., & Jabez, S. (2024). Removal of chemicals from effluent using photobioreactor technology to improve environmental and health impacts. *Zeitschrift für Physikalische Chemie*, 2024(7), 1295–1302. Advance online publication. DOI: 10.1515/zpch-2023-0450

Selvakumar, P., Muthusamy, S., Satishkumar, D., Vigneshkumar, P., Selvamurugan, C., & Satheesh Kumar, P. (2024). AI-Powered Tools. In Satishkumar, D., & Sivaraja, M. (Eds.), *Using Real-Time Data and AI for Thrust Manufacturing* (pp. 20–42). IGI Global., DOI: 10.4018/979-8-3693-2615-2.ch002

Selvakumar, P., Palanisamy, S. K., Cinthaikinian, S., Palanisamy, V., Mariappan, R., & Selvakumar, P. K. (2024). Biosensors and its diverse applications in healthcare systems. *Zeitschrift für Physikalische Chemie*, 2024. Advance online publication. DOI: 10.1515/zpch-2023-0406

Tang, J., & Li, Q. (2023). Social media strategies for promoting traditional cuisines: A case study of Chinese food brands. *Journal of Foodservice Business Research*, 26(3), 255–270.

Uddin, S., & Karim, M. (2023). The role of social media in promoting food sustainability: A consumer perspective. *Journal of Sustainable Marketing*, 4(1), 45–59.

Vasquez, M., & Romero, P. (2023). Social media marketing in the food industry: A cross-cultural analysis. *Journal of International Consumer Marketing*, 35(2), 115–129.

Vijayakumar, G., Rajkumar, M., Rajiv Chandar, N., Selvakumar, P., & Duraisamy, R. (2024). Muniyandi Rajkumar, Rajiv Chandar N, Selvakumar P and Ramesh Duraisamy, (2024). Environmentally friendly TDS removal from waste water by electrochemical ion exchange batch-type recirculation (EIR) technique. *Environmental Science. Water Research & Technology*, 10(4), 826–835. DOI: 10.1039/D3EW00793F

Wang, H., & Chen, X. (2023). Social media and consumer trust in food brands: An exploratory study. *The Journal of Consumer Affairs*, 57(1), 39–54.

Williams, J., & Nguyen, M. (2024). The role of social media in promoting food safety awareness. *Food Control*, 148, 108872.

Xu, L., & Huang, J. (2023). Social media influence on consumer attitudes toward food packaging sustainability. *Journal of Environmental Psychology*, 86, 101848.

Yang, S., & Park, H. (2023). Social media marketing effectiveness in the dairy industry: A case study of consumer engagement. *Journal of Dairy Science*, 106(6), 3789–3802.

Zhao, J., & Lin, M. (2023). The impact of social media marketing on consumer purchase intentions in the food industry: A meta-analysis. *JMR, Journal of Marketing Research*, 60(3), 411–428.

Chapter 6
Navigating Sustainability:
Addressing Plastic Waste and Health Risks in Food Delivery Services in Malaysia

Pavitira Manogaran
https://orcid.org/0000-0002-3434-9505
Universiti Malaysia Kelantan, Malaysia

Vishakini Manogaran
https://orcid.org/0009-0009-9880-4181
Universiti Sains Malaysia, Malaysia

Mohammed Ruqaimi Remeli
https://orcid.org/0000-0001-6758-7254
Universiti Malaysia Kelantan, Malaysia

ABSTRACT

While it is encouraging to see the food industry thriving, growing concerns exist about increased demand and reliance on plastic packaging. The convenience of plastic wraps for food and durable plastic containers for drinks, designed to prevent spillage, has led to a significant rise in plastic consumption. This chapter highlights the growing plastic waste associated with food delivery services and explores the potential health risks of plastic materials, including microplastics, in food delivery operations in Malaysia. By analysing existing policies and regulations on plastic use, this chapter highlights the need for enhanced sustainable practices in the food service industry. It aims to provide insights into balancing convenience with environmental responsibility and proposes strategies for mitigating the negative impacts of plastic consumption.

INTRODUCTION

The COVID-19 pandemic has pushed for adopting many new technologies in various industries. Food service was among one of those industries that thrived with technology. The lockdown and criticality of the pandemic have shaped consumer behaviours to prioritise food safety, contactless delivery and hygiene, requiring the food industry to meet these changing demands quickly (Ali et al., 2020). Among

DOI: 10.4018/979-8-3693-7683-6.ch006

the initiatives were cloud kitchen, mobile applications for food ordering and contactless take-out services for sustaining business operations (Agarwal et al., 2024). FoodPanda and Grab were among the dominant players in online food delivery in Malaysia, catering to an increasing number of consumers seeking convenience and efficiency (Jamil et al., 2024). Consumers prefer having meals delivered to their doorstep, enjoying the convenience of ordering without the need to leave home. The digital transformation in the food delivery industry has eased customers' avoidance of traffic congestion, ensuring timely delivery and saving on parking fees (Su et al., 2024). However, there are notable environmental and health concerns. The excessive use of plastic materials in packaging, from plastic containers and cutleries to wrappers and protective coverings for beverages, and the reliance on single-use plastics (SUP) has become a significant environmental challenge (Varese et al., 2024). Disposing of these plastic materials is another challenge. Single-use plastics are notoriously difficult to recycle. They often end up in landfills or, worse, in natural environments where they pollute and harm wildlife (Bharadwaj et al., 2024; Shin et al., 2024). Not only does it pose a risk to the environment, but health risks are also rising. Hot food placed in plastic containers leads to the leaching of harmful chemicals and microplastics into the food, adversely affecting human health (Gündogdu et al., 2024). This chapter explores the downside of these practices and focuses on the critical need to address online food delivery services' environmental footprint and health concerns. The chapter intends to balance technological convenience and environmental responsibility in food delivery by highlighting the challenges and proposing feasible solutions to merchants and food delivery owners.

LITERATURE REVIEW

The Rise of Online Food Delivery Services During Covid-19 Pandemic

Southeast Asia is growing with a vast food delivery market. The delivery market is a tiny fraction of the trillion-dollar business. In Malaysia, the growing popularity of these deliveries mainly started during the pandemic, as eating out was a risky option, projecting a market size of more than USD 319.1 million by 2026 (Allah Pitchay et al., 2022; Sin, 2022). Online food delivery (OFD) service is not just about ordering food but also the new norm of takeaways and eating out. The need for social distancing during the pandemic strengthened the role of OFD as a prime element of the food and beverage industry (Teoh, 2023). The demand increase has generated several Food Delivery Applications (FDAs) by delivery companies focused on denser cities such as Penang, Kuala Lumpur, Klang Valley and Johor Bahru (Chai & Yat, 2019). These mobile applications enhance the user experience by allowing them to choose various foods and compare prices with just one touch (Samsuddin et al., 2022). Upon the Movement Control Order (MCO) in March 2020, there was a 30 per cent surge in these FDAs (Sin, 2022; Mohamad, 2023). The main factor influencing the use of FDAs is consumer convenience. The smartphone advancement in e-commerce has significantly contributed to OFD (Samsudin et al., 2022). On top of that, the sector also had to compete to maintain its popularity by adopting consumer needs and preferences to ensure consumer loyalty and satisfaction with its services. Among the factors that consumers prioritised were food and service quality, hygiene, safety and overall experience (Aryani et al., 2022; Tarmazi et al., 2021; Pai & Mayya, 2022).

Consumer Behavior and Sustainable Alternatives

Researchers have conducted various case studies on single-use plastics. He (2023) and Zhou et al. (2020) indicated that packaging waste constitutes over 80 per cent of the total waste generated by food delivery services in regions like China, where approximately 7.3 billion SUP tableware sets are used annually. The reliance on SUPs contributes to solid waste and leads to the proliferation of microplastics (Abdullah et al., 2022). Consumer behaviour plays a crucial role in the proliferation of SUPs. Studies have shown that consumers often perceive plastic packaging as more hygienic, particularly after the pandemic, leading to a preference shift towards single-use options (Brennan & Browne, 2021; Kitz et al., 2021). This perception has been compounded by the convenience offered by online food delivery platforms, which have dramatically increased usage, resulting in a corresponding rise in plastic waste (Oliveira et al., 2021). The environmental implications are dire, as improper disposal of SUPs leads to significant pollution, clogging waterways and contributing to broader ecological degradation (Abdullah et al., 2022). Efforts to mitigate the environmental impact of SUPs in food delivery have included exploring alternatives such as biodegradable and recyclable materials. While some studies suggest that biodegradable plastics serve as a solution, others argue that the production processes of these materials can sometimes have a more significant environmental footprint than traditional plastics (Popescu et al., 2020; Tan et al., 2021). Moreover, the development of edible packaging has emerged as a promising alternative, with consumer acceptance of such innovations indicating a potential pathway toward reducing reliance on SUPs (Taylor, 2024). However, the main challenge remains to balance consumer convenience with sustainable practices, as many consumers still favour the immediate benefits of SUPs over the long-term environmental impacts (Cavaliere et al., 2020).

Policies and Ramifications

This section focuses on both policies on the environment and food health perspective. Governments worldwide have been working on initiatives to tackle plastic use problems, enhancing recycling and reducing damage through plastic pollution (Chen et al., 2021). European Union have set laws restricting the use of SUP items (Kasznik & Łapniewska, 2023). Extended producer responsibility is among the constructive ways to hold producers responsible for their products throughout the lifecycle, and they are encouraged to design materials that can be degraded and reused (Wongprapinkul & Vassanadumrongdee, 2022). Most of the world's plastic packing laws mandate manufacturers to use recycled content in the packaging to showcase environmentally friendly initiatives. Malaysia is not left behind. The Plastic Free July charges consumers who want plastic bags during grocery, encouraging them to bring their reusable bags. Malaysia Plastic Sustainability Roadmap (2021-2030) aims to strategise plastic sustainability and protect the environment (Afifah et al., 2024). These public campaigns create awareness among people about choosing more green alternatives. On the food health side, the World Health Organisation and the European Union have researched health threats caused by the contamination of food packaging, aiming to develop more renewable practices for reducing health risks from plastic use. Malaysian Food Act 1983 and Food Regulations 1985 only permit certain packaging materials that prevent the leaching of microplastic or any detrimental substance into food. These bylaws emphasise the importance of food contact materials to ensure safe consumption for its consumers (Ong et al., 2022). However, the awareness among consumers and food handlers remained unknown.

Philosophical Underpinnings

The theory of technology readiness measures the understanding of individuals adopting new technologies, such as food delivery applications. This sector has seen exponential growth, leading to increased plastic use for packaging and delivery. However, by applying the principles of technology readiness, businesses can enhance their operational efficiencies and sustainability practices, thereby mitigating their environmental impact. Technology readiness refers to the willingness and ability of individuals or organisations to embrace and utilise new technologies to enhance their operational efficiency and sustainability practices (Hmamed, 2023). Technology readiness consists of optimism, innovativeness, insecurity and discomfort, influencing an individual's attitude towards technology usage (Paramsuraman & Colby, 2014). Silva et al. (2022) mention that this theory is crucial for shaping the perception of its users to encourage continuous engagement in such platforms. Optimistic about the outcome of the technology use influences the willingness of individuals to engage in these digital services (Blut & Wang, 2019). Operational readiness of crowd-sourced delivery models meeting consumer expectations tends to drive demand and contribute to consumers' acceptance of these technologies (Yildiz & Savelsbergh, 2019). In various sectors, the readiness of organisations to adopt new technologies is influenced by their ability to integrate these technologies into existing practices while considering environmental impacts (Youhasan et al., 2020). This combination of focus on technological and environmental readiness is essential for fostering sustainable practices that can mitigate the adverse effects of plastic use and promote a circular economy. Sardjono and Perdana (2019) mention that these businesses can significantly lower their plastic footprint by adopting clean technologies and pollution prevention strategies. In addition to technological advancements, consumer behaviour is also essential. The willingness of consumers to accept and support sustainable practices in food delivery is influenced by technology readiness. Research indicates that more technologically inclined consumers are more likely to support eco-friendly initiatives, such as opting for minimal packaging or choosing delivery services that utilise biodegradable materials (Chovancová et al., 2023). The theory of technology readiness provides an understanding of how online food delivery services can reduce plastic waste by adopting innovative technologies and sustainable practices. The theory intends to foster a culture of sustainability and understand consumer behaviour; these businesses can significantly mitigate the environmental impact.

The Environmental Impact of Single-Use Plastics in Food Delivery

Single-use plastics (SUPs) are becoming a pressing issue in delivery services. Examples of SUPs include plastic food containers made of polyethene or polystyrene for packaging meals, beverage wraps and bags for securing food items, and cutleries such as knives, forks, spoons and straws. These SUPs are used for convenient takeout meals (Thakuria, 2023; Walker et al., 2021). The demand for delivery services has contributed to the increased use of SUPs, mainly in serving and packaging food and beverages. High demand for delivery services also means high reliance on SUPs (Oliveira et al., 2021). These exacerbated problems related to plastic waste and environmental degradation (Liu et al., 2021). Eighty per cent of waste in China comes from packaging food from the delivery sector, emphasising packaging impacts the environmental footprint (He, 2023). Plastic manufacturing heavily relies on fossil fuels, and production and disposal contribute to greenhouse gas emissions (Kittithammavong et al., 2023). The delivery industry uses SUPs over reusable alternatives for safety and hygiene concerns (Priyadarshi et al., 2022). Although consumers have expressed their desire to reduce plastic usage, which aligns with environmental concerns, they indirectly contribute to it with their purchasing decisions (Cavaliere et al., 2020). Consumers are very aware of the negative impact of SUPs; often, short-term needs are prioritised over long-term environmental considerations (Lin, 2024). The existing educational campaigns and policy interventions are not impactful. Managing SUPs can be tricky as not all items are recyclable due to their composite materials. Even if they are, the rate of recycling SUPs is only at 3 per cent (Taylor, 2024; Achutha et al., 2022). Eventually, these plastics overflow the landfills, contributing to more environmental degradation and pollution. According to Silva et al. (2021), most plastic waste often finds its way into the ocean, harming ecosystems and marine life and leading to bioaccumulation in the food chain. The degradation of SUPs is called microplastics. These microplastic fragments contaminate water sources, transferring harmful substances into marine organisms, risking wildlife and consequently affecting human health while consuming contaminated seafood (Silva et al., 2021; Barboza et al., 2018). Harkin (2020) mentions that this worsens when cross-biological barriers, such as the blood-brain barrier, worsen the health risks associated with plastic exposure. These potential risks warrant urgent attention and action to mitigate the use of SUPs in delivery services.

The Impact of Heat Exposure in Plastic Packaging

Microplastics are plastic particles that are smaller in size than 5 millimetres. They originate from the degradation of large plastic materials used for packaging (Aydin, 2023). This commonly happens when food is packed, stored and heated in plastic containers over some time. Microwaving the plastic packages from deliveries exacerbates the leaching of microplastics into the food consumers eat. Even opening plastic or tearing the food wrapper are ways microplastics latch onto the food consumer; among them are fruits, vegetables, seafood and salt (Zbucki, 2024; Sobhani et al., 2020). Brachner et al. (2020) found that microplastic ingestions may induce inflammatory responses and other biological effects, and microplastic has been detected in human stools (Luqman et al., 2021). Studies have shown that prolonged exposure to microplastics can also result in developmental toxicity in fetuses and young children who are more ill-protected from hormonal imbalances (Roman, 2024). Microplastics tend to encroach into immune responses and may cause chronic health diseases (Toussaint et al., 2019).

Bisphenol A (BPA) is a component of polycarbonate plastics and epoxy resins and is known for its properties of leaching into food and beverages under high temperatures and acidic pH. Most food ordered online is cooked freshly, and when it is hot and packed in plastic containers, the elevated temperatures can increase the rate of potentially harmful chemicals such as BPA and phthalates to percolate into food to an extent where it may exceed the level of food safety, which affects human health (Agarwal et al., 2022). Phthalates, another chemical in plastics, have similar properties to BPA, but this chemical may also be present in BPA-free containers. It tends to release harmful substances during the cleaning process or exposure to heat (Jeon, 2022). Among health issues that were identified from these leaks of substances were kidney function disruption and reproductive toxicity. The damage continues beyond just by exposure to heat but also by repetitive washing. Past research has found this to be a severe issue, significantly when these chemicals have affected children and pregnant women (Thoene et al., 2020). Despite the growing research findings on microplastics, BPA, and phthalates' adverse effects on human health, there are gaps in understanding the long-term consequences. This is where policymakers and regulators play an imperative role in educating consumers about the adverse effects of plastic use in food delivery services.

Challenges and Solutions in Mitigating Single-Use Plastics

The top challenge in mitigating single-use plastic is consumer behaviour, particularly the perception that plastic packaging is more hygienic, a belief has intensified since the pandemic. This perception drives the demand for SUPs, as consumers prioritise convenience and safety, often at the expense of sustainability. Additionally, the food delivery industry, which has experienced growth in recent years, heavily relies on SUPs for their low cost, durability, and practicality, which makes it difficult for businesses to transition to more sustainable options (Kitz et al., 2021). Merican et al. (2022) mention that the anthropocentric perspective on plastic consumption necessitates shifting consumer attitudes and behaviours towards more sustainable options. Implementing educational campaigns that raise awareness about the environmental impacts of SUPs can play a crucial role in altering consumer perceptions and encouraging responsible consumption. Secondly, the regulatory landscape significantly influences adopting sustainable practices within the food delivery sector. Rwanda has successfully implemented policies banning SUPs, demonstrating the potential for legislative frameworks to drive change (Ogutu et al., 2023). Such policies reduce the availability of SUPs and encourage businesses to innovate and adopt alternative packaging solutions. However, in Malaysia, the effectiveness of these regulations often hinges on the enforcement and willingness of businesses to comply. Therefore, a collaborative approach involving government, industry, and civil society stakeholders is essential. Integrating circular economy principles into food delivery operations can also provide a viable pathway for reducing SUPs. A circular economy emphasises the continuous use of resources, minimising waste through strategies like recycling, reusing and redesigning products (Ncube et al., 2021). For instance, food delivery services can adopt reusable packing systems, where consumers return containers for cleaning and reuse by significantly reducing the reliance on SUPs. Plant-based packaging materials that decompose more readily than conventional plastics are also a good option (Steenmans et al., 2021).

Establishing robust recycling programs within food delivery operations can facilitate materials recovery and reduce the volume of plastic waste sent to landfills (Ampadu-Ameyaw et al., 2020). Collaboration with local governments and waste management organisations can enhance the efficiency of waste collection and processing systems, ensuring that plastic waste is managed sustainably. Klean Malaysia is a company focused on plastic recovery through innovative recycling technologies. Their main product is the AI-powered Reverse Vending Machine (RVM), which encourages recycling by rewarding users with points for depositing plastic containers, aluminium cans and food containers. These machines are placed in high-traffic locations, allowing users to recycle conveniently. Klean has launched a "recycle as a service" model that allows businesses to lease these machines for monthly fees, supporting a circular economy (Klean, 2024). Having more of these machines in schools, apartments, and workplaces would be a great way to start recycling SUPs. Consumer engagement and participation are also critical components of successful waste management strategies. Encouraging consumers to participate in recycling initiatives and providing incentives for returning packaging can foster responsibility and ownership over waste management practices (Merican et al., 2022). Using digital platforms and social media to promote these practices will amplify the impact of educational campaigns and drive consumer behaviour towards good environmental choices. The challenges are substantial, but with concerted efforts and innovative solutions, creating a more sustainable food delivery ecosystem that minimises plastic waste is possible.

Balancing Convenience with Sustainability

As the demand for food delivery services increases, so does the amount of plastic generated from packaging materials. On top of that, the harmful effects of SUPs seem very concerning. Taylor (2024) has suggested that food delivery industries focus on edible packaging, a sustainable approach to traditional plastic materials. It reduces plastic consumption and minimises the waste generated from food consumption. Edible films and coatings made from biopolymers such as whey protein and gelatin are beneficial in preserving food quality and being consumable (Kandasamy et al., 2021). Secondly, food service providers should promote reusable containers. Incentivising businesses that use reusable food containers and penalising non-recyclable packaging may significantly reduce plastic waste (Zhou et al., 2020). For example, steel containers need to be used between 13 and 33 times to offset the environmental impact of their production compared to SUPs (Collis et al., 2023). Hence, encouraging reusable containers ordered via food delivery applications during takeaways is also sustainable. The current mobile applications should have green nudges by offering an option for eco-friendly packaging to promote awareness of the availability of alternative packaging rather than plastic packaging. Subtle prompts to opt for eco-friendly packaging and rewards for customers who forgo single-use cutleries would promote sustainable behaviour among consumers (He, 2023). Although it is perceived that people are concerned about the environment, the excessive use of plastic in food delivery services shows that consumers still need more awareness (Xie et al., 2020; Rha et al., 2023). Policymakers and regulators must look into this issue to develop impactful consumer education campaigns to address the environmental and health concerns of plastic use in food deliveries. Current regulations need to catch up to the extensive use of SUPs. Enforcing standards for packaging and logistics when it comes to food delivery is one way to get food service providers to reduce the use of plastics.

Giving tax reliefs for businesses to use environmentally friendly packaging may work. The government must revise the existing policies to promote a sustainable packaging practice. Consumers must be aware of the long-term consequences of SUPs and encourage them to go for biodegradable or reusable packing (Pietrosanto et al., 2020). Biodegradable packaging does not necessarily have low quality regarding secure packing. Materials like natural polysaccharides like chitosan and carboxymethyl cellulose are substantial barriers against moisture and are environmentally friendly as they decompose readily with minimal dependence on fossil fuels (Chi et al., 2023). Apart from edible and biodegradable packaging, bioplastics, specifically polylactic acid (PLA), can also be used. It consists of corn starch and has a low carbon footprint compared to traditional plastic, an ideal option for packaging as it breaks down under compositing conditions, consequently reducing environmental pollution (Ghomi et al., 2021).

SIGNIFICANCE OF THE CHAPTER

This chapter intends to be significant for OFD users, food service providers, environmental policymakers and food industry players. Frequent users of OFD must be aware of the permissible packaging types and practice recycling them rather than just throwing them out. Food service providers should also understand the risks of some packaging materials and ensure that suitable plastic materials are used with labels to recycle them upon food consumption. On top of that, food service providers should consider using more biodegradable packaging. Environmental policymakers should work on strict rules to ensure plastic use in food delivery is seriously monitored and actions are taken against food service providers who are still using materials that are not permissible. The proper channels and campaigns must create awareness among consumers and ensure they know the risks associated with online food delivery. Food industry players should incentivise food service providers to follow suitable packaging, which aligns with corporate social responsibility and more eco-friendly practices.

CONCLUSION

In conclusion, as much as life is getting convenient for people with the existence and evolving technology, it comes with a downside. The use of plastic in food packing should be strictly avoided. Chemicals that the naked eye cannot see are present only when a health risk rises. Although online food delivery may reduce the inconvenience of physical dining, such as longer waiting time, timesaving, and uneasiness with the surroundings, the risks are even more concerning. The right policies and regulations will undoubtedly impact reducing plastic use. Future efforts should focus on longitudinal studies to fill in the gaps on how plastic materials from the food delivery industry affect long-term health and environmental degradation.

REFERENCES

Abdullah, N., Yaacob, N., & Ismail, A. (2022). Development and validation of a new questionnaire to measure the knowledge level of street food hawkers to support the single-use plastics reduction program in Kelantan, Malaysia. *Sustainability (Basel)*, 14(13), 7552. DOI: 10.3390/su14137552

Achutha, S., Johnson, E., Nisha, S., & Sivakumar, S. (2022). Antimicrobial biodegradable polymeric materials for food packaging applications: current status and future directions. *Materials Science Forum*, pp. 1073, 49–56. DOI: 10.4028/p-a5my86

Afifah, N. M. R., Sathiaseelan, J. J., Kee, S. H., Amelia, T. S. M., Yien, W., Lua, N. A., & Bhubalan, K. (2024). A Review on Conversion Of Microplastics Into Value-Added Products: Challenges And Perspectives. *The Malaysian Journal of Analytical Sciences*, 28(3), 611–631.

Agarwal, A., Gandhi, S., Tripathi, A., Iammarino, M., & Homroy, S. (2022). Analysis of bisphenol: A migration from microwaveable polycarbonate cups into coffee during microwave heating. *International Journal of Food Science & Technology*, 57(12), 7477–7485. DOI: 10.1111/ijfs.16103

Agarwal, P., Swami, S., & Malhotra, S. K. (2024). Artificial intelligence adoption in the post-COVID-19 new-normal and role of intelligent technologies in transforming business: A review. *Journal of Science and Technology Policy Management*, 15(3), 506–529. DOI: 10.1108/JSTPM-08-2021-0122

Ali, S., Khalid, N., Javed, H. M. U., & Islam, D. M. Z. (2020). Consumer adoption of online food delivery ordering (OFDO) services in Pakistan: The impact of the COVID-19 pandemic—. *Journal of Open Innovation*, 7(1), 10. DOI: 10.3390/joitmc7010010

Allah Pitchay, A., Ganesan, Y., Zulkifli, N. S., & Khaliq, A. (2022). Determinants of customers' intention to use online food delivery applications through smartphones in Malaysia. *British Food Journal*, 124(3), 732–753. DOI: 10.1108/BFJ-01-2021-0075

Ampadu-Ameyaw, R., Richard, N., & Ahwireng, A. (2020). Integrated waste management system as a sustainable option for managing plastic waste in Ghana: The case of Madina-la katana municipality. *Journal of Scientific Research and Reports*, •••, 20–31. DOI: 10.9734/jsrr/2020/v26i930306

Aryani, D., Singh, P., Khor, Y., Kee, D., Selvia, K., Lee, C., Lee, Y. H., & Anantharavoo, L. (2022). Factors influencing consumer behavioural intention to use food delivery services: A study of Foodpanda. *Journal of the Community Development in Asia*, 5(1), 69–79. DOI: 10.32535/jcda.v5i1.1386

Aydın, R., Yozukmaz, A., Şener, İ., Temiz, F., & Giannetto, D. (2023). Occurrence of microplastics in most consumed fruits and vegetables from Turkey and public risk assessment for consumers. *Life (Chicago, Ill.)*, 13(8), 1686. DOI: 10.3390/life13081686 PMID: 37629543

Barboza, L., Vethaak, A., Lavorante, B., Lundebye, A., & Guilhermino, L. (2018). Marine microplastic debris: An emerging issue for food security, food safety and human health. *Marine Pollution Bulletin*, 133, 336–348. DOI: 10.1016/j.marpolbul.2018.05.047 PMID: 30041323

Bharadwaaj, S. K., Jaudan, M., Kushwaha, P., Saxena, A., & Saha, B. (2024). Exploring Cutting-Edge Approaches in Plastic Recycling for a Greener Future. *Results in Engineering*, 23, 102704. DOI: 10.1016/j.rineng.2024.102704

Blut, M., & Wang, C. (2019). Technology readiness: A meta-analysis of conceptualizations of the construct and its impact on technology usage. *Journal of the Academy of Marketing Science*, 48(4), 649–669. DOI: 10.1007/s11747-019-00680-8

Brachner, A., Fragouli, D., Duarte, I., Farias, P., Dembski, S., Ghosh, M., Barisic, I., Zdzieblo, D., Vanoirbeek, J., Schwabl, P., & Neuhaus, W. (2020). Assessment of human health risks posed by nano-and microplastics is currently not feasible. *International Journal of Environmental Research and Public Health*, 17(23), 8832. DOI: 10.3390/ijerph17238832 PMID: 33261100

Brennan, A., & Browne, S. (2021). Food waste and nutrition quality in the context of public health: A scoping review. *International Journal of Environmental Research and Public Health*, 18(10), 5379. DOI: 10.3390/ijerph18105379 PMID: 34070070

Cavaliere, A., Pigliafreddo, S., Marchi, E. D., & Banterle, A. (2020). Do consumers really want to reduce plastic usage? Exploring the determinants of plastic avoidance in food-related consumption decisions. *Sustainability (Basel)*, 12(22), 9627. DOI: 10.3390/su12229627

Chai, L. T., & Yat, D. N. C. (2019). Online food delivery services: Making food delivery the new normal. *Journal of Marketing Advances and Practices*, 1(1), 62–77.

Chen, H. L., Nath, T. K., Chong, S., Foo, V., Gibbins, C., & Lechner, A. M. (2021). The plastic waste problem in Malaysia: Management, recycling, and disposal of local and global plastic waste. *SN Applied Sciences*, 3(4), 1–15. DOI: 10.1007/s42452-021-04234-y

Chi, K., He, J., Lin, W., Bokhari, S., & Catchmark, J. (2023). Electrostatically complexed natural polysaccharides as aqueous barrier coatings for sustainable and recyclable fiber-based packaging. *ACS Applied Materials & Interfaces*, 15(9), 12248–12260. DOI: 10.1021/acsami.2c17886 PMID: 36848253

Chovancová, J., Majerník, M., Drábik, P., & Štofková, Z. (2023). Environmental technological innovations and the sustainability of their development. *Ecological Engineering & Environmental Technology*, 24(4), 245–252. DOI: 10.12912/27197050/162708

Collis, B., Baxter, W., Baird, H., Meade, K., & Webb, T. L. (2023). Signs of use present a barrier to reusable packaging systems for takeaway food. *Sustainability (Basel)*, 15(11), 8857. DOI: 10.3390/su15118857

Ghomi, E., Khosravi, F., Ardahaei, A., Dai, Y., Neisiany, R., Foroughi, F., & Ramakrishna, S. (2021). The life cycle assessment for polylactic acid (PLA) is used to make it a low-carbon material. *Polymers*, 13(11), 1854. DOI: 10.3390/polym13111854 PMID: 34199643

Gündoğdu, S., Bour, A., Köşker, A. R., Walther, B. A., Napierska, D., Mihai, F. C., Syberg, K., Hansen, S. F., & Walker, T. R. (2024). Review of microplastics and chemical risk posed by plastic packaging on the marine environment to inform the Global Plastics Treaty. *The Science of the Total Environment*, 946, 174000. DOI: 10.1016/j.scitotenv.2024.174000 PMID: 38901589

Harkin, C. (2020). A review on plastic bioaccumulation, potential health effects and the potential to enhance biotransformation using herbal medicine and nutritional supplements. *International Journal of Complementary & Alternative Medicine*, 13(1), 18–26. DOI: 10.15406/ijcam.2020.13.00487

He, G., Pan, Y., Park, A., Sawada, Y., & Tan, E. S. (2023). Reducing single-use cutlery with green nudges: Evidence from China's food-delivery industry. *Science*, 381(6662), eadd9884. Advance online publication. DOI: 10.1126/science.add9884 PMID: 37676957

Hmamed, H., Cherrafi, A., Benghabrit, A., Tiwari, S., & Sharma, P. (2023). The adoption of i4.0 technologies for a sustainable and circular supply chain: An industry-based sem analysis from the textile sector. *Business Strategy and the Environment*, 33(4), 2949–2968. DOI: 10.1002/bse.3645

Jamil, A., Zainuddin, S. A., Abdullah, T., Mohamad, S. R., Azmi, N. F., Muhamad, S. F., & Abdullah, S. S. (2024). Digital Entrepreneurship in the Food Delivery Industry: Enhancing Customer Satisfaction Through Apps' Functional and Technical Quality. In *Contemporary Issues in Entrepreneurship and Innovative Technology* (pp. 125–144). Springer Nature Switzerland. DOI: 10.1007/978-3-031-50927-8_8

Jeon, G. (2022). Bisphenol a leaching from polycarbonate baby bottles into baby food, causes potential health issues. *Clinical and Experimental Pediatrics*, 65(9), 450–452. DOI: 10.3345/cep.2022.00661 PMID: 35879867

Kandasamy, S., Yoo, J., Yun, J., Kang, H., Seol, K., Kim, H., & Ham, J. (2021). Application of whey protein-based edible films and coatings in food industries: An updated overview. *Coatings*, 11(9), 1056. DOI: 10.3390/coatings11091056

Kasznik, D., & Łapniewska, Z. (2023). The end of plastic? The EU's directive on single-use plastics and its implementation in Poland. *Environmental Science & Policy*, 145, 151–163. DOI: 10.1016/j.envsci.2023.04.005

Kittithammavong, V., Khanitchaidecha, W., & Thongsanit, P. (2023). Co2 emissions from plastic consumption behaviours in Thailand. *Sustainability (Basel)*, 15(16), 12135. DOI: 10.3390/su151612135

Kitz, R., Walker, T., Charlebois, S., & Music, J. (2021). Food packaging during the COVID-19 pandemic: Consumer perceptions. *International Journal of Consumer Studies*, 46(2), 434–448. DOI: 10.1111/ijcs.12691 PMID: 34230811

Klean. (2024). *The future of plastic recovery is Here*. Retrieved from https://www.klean.asia/

Lin, L., Zhang, X., Khan, M. A., Mehmood, M. A., & Khan, M. K. (2024). Eco-conscious consumption in the climate change era: Decoding the mediating role of food safety and environmental concerns between health literacy and take-out food consumption in China. *Sustainability (Basel)*, 16(11), 4357. DOI: 10.3390/su16114357

Liu, J., Vethaak, A., An, L., Liu, Q., Yue, Y., & Ding, J. (2021). An environmental dilemma for China during the COVID-19 pandemic is the explosion of disposable plastic waste. *Bulletin of Environmental Contamination and Toxicology*, 106(2), 237–240. DOI: 10.1007/s00128-021-03121-x PMID: 33515068

Luqman, A., Nugrahapraja, H., Wahyuono, R., Islami, I., Haekal, M., Fardiansyah, Y., Putri, B. Q., Amalludin, F. I., Rofiqa, E. A., Götz, F., & Wibowo, A. (2021). Microplastic contamination in human stools, foods, and drinking water is associated with the Indonesian coastal population. *Environments (Basel, Switzerland)*, 8(12), 138. DOI: 10.3390/environments8120138

Merican, F., Osman, S., Zainudin, N., Jusoh, Z., & Puteh, F. (2022). Exploring consumer single-use plastic reduction behaviour: A conceptual framework. *Malaysian Journal of Society and Space*, 18(1). Advance online publication. DOI: 10.17576/geo-2022-1801-03

Merican, F., Osman, S., Zainudin, N., Jusoh, Z., & Puteh, F. (2022). Exploring consumer single-use plastic reduction behaviour: A conceptual framework. *Malaysian Journal of Society and Space*, 18(1). Advance online publication. DOI: 10.17576/geo-2022-1801-03

Mohamad, M., Tasnim, R., & Ya'kob, S. A. (2023). Continued use of food delivery applications (fdas) post COVID-19 in Malaysia: Barriers and growth. *Environment-Behaviour Proceedings Journal*, 8(SI15), 19–24. DOI: 10.21834/e-bpj.v8iSI15.5095

Ncube, L., Ude, A., Ogunmuyiwa, E., Zulkifli, R., & Nongwe, I. (2021). An overview of plastic waste generation and management in food packaging industries. *Recycling*, 6(1), 12. DOI: 10.3390/recycling6010012

Ogutu, M., Akor, J., Mulindwa, M., Heshima, O., & Nsengimana, C. (2023). Implementing circular economy and sustainability policies in Rwanda: Experiences of Rwandan manufacturers with the plastic ban policy. *Frontiers in Sustainability*, 4, 1092107. Advance online publication. DOI: 10.3389/frsus.2023.1092107

Oliveira, W., Azeredo, H., Neri-Numa, I., & Pastore, G. (2021). Food packaging wastes amid the covid-19 pandemic: Trends and challenges. *Trends in Food Science & Technology*, 116, 1195–1199. DOI: 10.1016/j.tifs.2021.05.027 PMID: 34092920

Ong, H. T., Samsudin, H., & Soto-Valdez, H. (2022). Migration of endocrine-disrupting chemicals into food from plastic packaging materials: An overview of chemical risk assessment, techniques to monitor migration and international regulations. *Critical Reviews in Food Science and Nutrition*, 62(4), 957–979. DOI: 10.1080/10408398.2020.1830747 PMID: 33081493

Pai, S. and Mayya, S. (2022). A study on consumer preferences with reference to online food delivery amenities. *International Journal of Management Technology and Social Sciences*, 144-166. DOI: 10.47992/IJMTS.2581.6012.0214

Parasuraman, A., & Colby, C. (2014). An updated and streamlined technology readiness index. *Journal of Service Research*, 18(1), 59–74. DOI: 10.1177/1094670514539730

Pietrosanto, A., Scarfato, P., Maio, L., Nobile, M., & Incarnato, L. (2020). Evaluation of the suitability of poly(lactide)/poly(butylene-adipate-co-terephthalate) blown films for chilled and frozen food packaging applications. *Polymers*, 12(4), 804. DOI: 10.3390/polym12040804 PMID: 32260170

Popescu, P., Popa, E., Miteluţ, A., & Popa, M. (2020). Development of recyclable and biodegradable food packaging materials – opportunities and risks. *Current Trends in Natural Sciences*, 9(17), 142–146. DOI: 10.47068/ctns.2020.v9i17.016

Priyadarshi, R., Purohit, S., Roy, S., Ghosh, T., Rhim, J., & Han, S. (2022). Antiviral biodegradable food packaging and edible coating materials in the COVID-19 era: A mini-review. *Coatings*, 12(5), 577. DOI: 10.3390/coatings12050577

Rha, J., Nam, Y., Yoon, J., & Lee, B. (2023). Korean consumers' use and concerns about food delivery service. *Nutrition Research and Practice*, 17(3), 583. DOI: 10.4162/nrp.2023.17.3.583 PMID: 37266118

Roman, J. (2024). The hidden health crisis: microplastics and their medical consequences. *Journal of Education Health and Sport*, p. 72, 51690. DOI: 10.12775/JEHS.2024.72.51690

Samsudin, A., Izzuddin, M., Kamarudin, W., Manap, M., & Ngah, H. (2022). Consumers' motivational factors on the use of online food-delivery apps in Malaysia. *International Journal of Academic Research in Business & Social Sciences*, 12(11). Advance online publication. DOI: 10.6007/IJARBSS/v12-i11/15617

Sardjono, W., & Perdana, W. (2019). Green information technology readiness model using factor analysis method in Indonesia. *Social Economics and Ecology International Journal (Seeij)*, 3(2), 13–21. DOI: 10.21512/seeij.v3i2.6216

Silva, A., Prata, J., Duarte, A., Barceló, D., & Rocha-Santos, T. (2021). An urgent call to think globally and act locally on landfill disposable plastics under and after covid-19 pandemic: Pollution prevention and technological (bio) remediation solutions. *Chemical Engineering Journal*, 426, 131201. DOI: 10.1016/j.cej.2021.131201 PMID: 35791349

Silva, G., Dias, Á., & Rodrigues, M. (2022). Continuity of use of food delivery apps: An integrated approach to the health belief model and the technology readiness and acceptance model. *Journal of Open Innovation*, 8(3), 114. DOI: 10.3390/joitmc8030114

Sin, L. (2022). Will you continue to use food delivery services during the transition to the endemic phase of the COVID-19 pandemic? *International Journal of Tourism and Hospitality in Asia Pacific*, 5(3), 26–37. DOI: 10.32535/ijthap.v5i3.1877

Sobhani, Z., Ye, L., Tang, Y., Wu, L., Zhang, X., Naidu, R., & Fang, C. (2020). Microplastics generated when opening plastic packaging. *Scientific Reports*, 10(1), 4841. Advance online publication. DOI: 10.1038/s41598-020-61146-4 PMID: 32193409

Steenmans, K., Taylor, P., & Steenmans, I. (2021). Blockchain technology for governance of plastic waste management: Where are we? *Social Sciences (Basel, Switzerland)*, 10(11), 434. DOI: 10.3390/socsci10110434

Su, Y., Ghaderi, H., & Dia, H. (2024). The role of traffic simulation in shaping effective and sustainable innovative urban delivery interventions. *EURO Journal on Transportation and Logistics*, 13, 100130. DOI: 10.1016/j.ejtl.2024.100130

Tan, J., Tiwari, S., & Ramakrishna, S. (2021). Single-use plastics in the food services industry: Can it be sustainable? *Materials Circular Economy*, 3(1), 7. Advance online publication. DOI: 10.1007/s42824-021-00019-1

Tarmazi, S., Ismail, W., Azmin, N., & Bakar, A. (2021). Consumer purchase intention toward online food delivery service: The implication for future research. [MJSSH]. *Malaysian Journal of Social Sciences and Humanities*, 6(9), 347–354. DOI: 10.47405/mjssh.v6i9.972

Taylor, S., Colonna, A., Jung, J., Gutierrez, J., & Zhao, Y. (2024). Consumer perception and acceptance of edible packaging for various food products. *Journal of Food Science*, 89(4), 2423–2437. DOI: 10.1111/1750-3841.16992 PMID: 38433384

Teoh, B. (2023). Intellectual capital and business model innovation: Boosting brand equity through SME food outlets' entrepreneurial efforts. *Journal of Advanced Research in Applied Sciences and Engineering Technology*, 34(2), 210–221. DOI: 10.37934/araset.34.2.210221

Thakuria, T., & Baruah, L. D. (2023). Microplastic: Its effect on human health. *Asian Journal of Microbiology, Biotechnology & Environmental Sciences : AJMBES*, 25(04), 782–786. DOI: 10.53550/AJMBES.2023.v25i04.033

Thoene, M., Dzika, E., Gonkowski, S., & Wojtkiewicz, J. (2020). Bisphenol in food causes hormonal and obesogenic effects comparable to or worse than bisphenol A: A literature review. *Nutrients*, 12(2), 532. DOI: 10.3390/nu12020532 PMID: 32092919

Toussaint, B., Barbara, R., Angers-Loustau, A., Gilliland, D., Kestens, V., Petrillo, M., & Eede, G. (2019). Review of micro- and nanoplastic contamination in the food chain. *Food Additives & Contaminants. Part A, Chemistry, Analysis, Control, Exposure & Risk Assessment*, 36(5), 639–673. DOI: 10.1080/19440049.2019.1583381 PMID: 30985273

Varese, E., Cesarani, M. C., Kabaja, B., Sołtysik, M., & Wojnarowska, M. (2024). Online food delivery habits and its environmental impact during the COVID-19 pandemic: An Italian and Polish study. *British Food Journal*, 126(1), 191–204. DOI: 10.1108/BFJ-12-2022-1120

Walker, T., McGuinty, E., Charlebois, S., & Music, J. (2021). Single-use plastic packaging in the Canadian food industry: Consumer behaviour and perceptions. *Humanities & Social Sciences Communications*, 8(1), 80. Advance online publication. DOI: 10.1057/s41599-021-00747-4

Wongprapinkul, B., & Vassanadumrongdee, S. (2022). A systems thinking approach towards reducing single-use plastics in Thailand's food delivery business: s*ustainability, 14*(15), 9173.

Xie, J., Xu, Y., & Li, H. (2020). Environmental impact of express food delivery in China: The role of personal consumption choice. *Environment, Development and Sustainability*, 23(6), 8234–8251. DOI: 10.1007/s10668-020-00961-1 PMID: 32874127

Yıldız, B., & Savelsbergh, M. (2019). Providing high-quality solutions for the meal delivery routing problem. *Transportation Science*, 53(5), 1372–1388. DOI: 10.1287/trsc.2018.0887

Youhasan, P., Chen, Y., Lyndon, M., & Henning, M. (2020). Development and validation of a measurement scale to assess nursing students' readiness for the flipped classroom in Sri Lanka. *Journal of Educational Evaluation for Health Professions*, pp. 17, 41. DOI: 10.3352/jeehp.2020.17.41

Zbucki, Ł. (2024). *Mechanical grinding of spices in grinders with polymeric burrs and transfer of microplastics to food.* Health Problems of Civilization., DOI: 10.5114/hpc.2024.135399

Zhou, Y., Shan, Y., Guan, D., Liang, X., Cai, Y., Liu, J., Xie, W., Xue, J., Ma, Z., & Yang, Z. (2020). Sharing tableware reduces waste generation, emissions and water consumption in China's takeaway packaging waste dilemma. *Nature Food*, 1(9), 552–561. DOI: 10.1038/s43016-020-00145-0 PMID: 37128017

KEY TERMS AND DEFINITIONS

Environmental Impact: An environmental impact is any environmental change, whether adverse or beneficial, resulting from food delivery activities.

Food Delivery Services: Food delivery is a courier service where a restaurant, store, or independent food delivery company delivers food to a customer at the address provided.

Health Risks: A health risk is the chance or likelihood that something will harm or otherwise affect an individual's health.

Single-Use Plastic: Single-use plastics are only used once before being thrown away or recycled.

Chapter 7
Role of Social Media Marketing in Food Industry

Siddhivinayak Kulkarni
Department of Computer Engineering and Technology, Dr. Vishwanath Karad MIT World Peace University, India

ABSTRACT

Social media has emerged as a pivotal force inside the food enterprise, basically reworking how manufacturers engage with clients, marketplace merchandise, and power sales. It explores the crucial function of social media advertising in the food enterprise, highlighting its capacity to influence consumer conduct, foster logo loyalty, and facilitate the discovery of recent products and dining reviews. Thru structures like Instagram, TikTok, and facebook, meals brands can connect to a worldwide target market, leveraging visually attractive content, influencer partnerships, and focused marketing to reach and engage clients. The integration of e- trade and food shipping services within these systems in addition streamlines the consumer journey, bearing in mind seamless transitions from discovery to purchase. Additionally, the chapter delves into emerging developments together using AI and data analytics for personalized marketing, and the significance of user-generated content material.

INTRODUCTION

Social media has revolutionized the marketing landscape, offering unparalleled opportunities for businesses to connect with their audiences. In the food industry, where visual appeal and customer engagement are paramount, social media platforms provide a powerful medium for showcasing products, telling brand stories, and fostering a community of loyal customers. This chapter aims to explore how food businesses can harness the power of social media to achieve their marketing goals and navigate the challenges that come with it.

In recent decades, social media marketing has revolutionized global communication, serving as fertile ground for business expansion. Social networking apps are utilized to connect users with friends and family, and among other things, to shape public thought and opinion regarding particular topics, events, and products. Social media marketing (SMM) is the intentional approach to promoting products through platforms like TikTok, Facebook, Twitter, Pinterest, and Instagram. However, the overwhelming amount of information available on social media increases the risk of irrelevant waste for companies

DOI: 10.4018/979-8-3693-7683-6.ch007

seeking to capture potential consumers' attention to their goods. Food and beverage (F&B) companies need to determine how to create content that makes scrolling users stop and consume their posts. One way to do this is by creating visually appealing or interesting food material. On social media platforms, food content is divided into posts demonstrating the cooking process and mouth-watering pictures of ready-to-eat products.

The global food and beverage (F&B) market is anticipated to experience substantial growth over the coming years due to a rise in consumer demand for effective marketing across diverse platforms. The need to cater to a wider consumer base is also expected to further contribute to the industry's growth. Changes in consumer lifestyle and an increase in disposable income are projected to augment demand for high-quality food products, resulting in higher revenue for food and beverage manufacturers. Likewise, advancements in the agriculture, processing, and packaging sectors are predicted to drive demand for F&B products over the forecast period. Geographically, the global F&B market is segmented into Asia Pacific, North America, Europe, Latin America, and the Middle East and Africa.

Continued reliance on social media publicity alone can lead to diminishing returns for subsequent marketing campaigns. Excessive posts about the same brand on users' feeds can lead to heightened skepticism, causing potential customers to overlook these posts and advertisements altogether. Thus, SMM planning is crucial for brand performance, especially in the F&B industry susceptible to habituation behavior. This planning minimizes the likelihood of becoming "blind" to food posts in the flow of tempting food-related social media material. The novelty, attractiveness, and visual appeal of food posts, as well as the frequency, timing, and channel of communication with users, should be strategically aligned with consumers' food choices and diets and potentially harmful biases like emotional eating. Experimental studies help determine what type of food photography content should be planned to increase product sales in the F&B industry.

Aims and Objectives

- **To Explore the Influence of Social Media on the Food Industry:**
- The chapter aims to provide a comprehensive understanding of how social media has revolutionized the way food brands market their products and engage with consumers.
- **To Examine the Integration of E-Commerce and Food Delivery Services:**
- It aims to analyze the seamless integration between social media platforms and e-commerce or food delivery services, highlighting the impact on consumer behavior and the food industry's business models.
- **To Analyze Emerging Trends and Technologies:**
- It aims to explore the latest trends, such as short-form video content and AI-driven personalization, and their implications for social media marketing in the food industry.

The Evolution of Social Media in the Food Industry

The marketing strategies of food businesses have evolved significantly with the advent of social media. Prior to its rise, traditional marketing methods such as print ads, TV commercials, and word-of-mouth were predominant. However, the dynamic nature of social media has introduced new ways for food brands to interact with their customers in real-time, gather instant feedback, and create viral content. This section will trace the journey from traditional marketing to the digital era, highlighting key moments and trends that have shaped the current landscape. Figure 1 shows the main components of evaluation of social media in food industry.

1. Expansive Reach and Targeted Audience Engagement

One of the most considerable advantages of social media is its capacity to reach a great and various target market. With billions of active users on systems like facebook, Instagram, Twitter, LinkedIn, and TikTok, agencies can connect with a international target audience at any time. This expansive attain is complemented through the capacity to goal specific demographics based on age, area, hobbies, and behaviors, taking into account noticeably personalized advertising campaigns. This centered approach guarantees that advertising messages are introduced to the most relevant audiences, growing the likelihood of engagement and conversion.

2. Cost-Effective Marketing

Social media advertising offers a price-effective alternative to conventional advertising channels like tv, radio, and print media. Many social media systems provide loose get right of entry to for groups to create profiles, submit content material, and interact with users. Even paid marketing on social media, which include Facebook ads or Instagram subsidized Posts, can be tailor-made to healthy any budget and is often more cheap than traditional advertising. This affordability makes social media reachable to corporations of all sizes, from multinational agencies to local start-ups, levelling the playing area in phrases of advertising and marketing opportunities.

Figure 1. Evaluation of Social Media in Food Industry

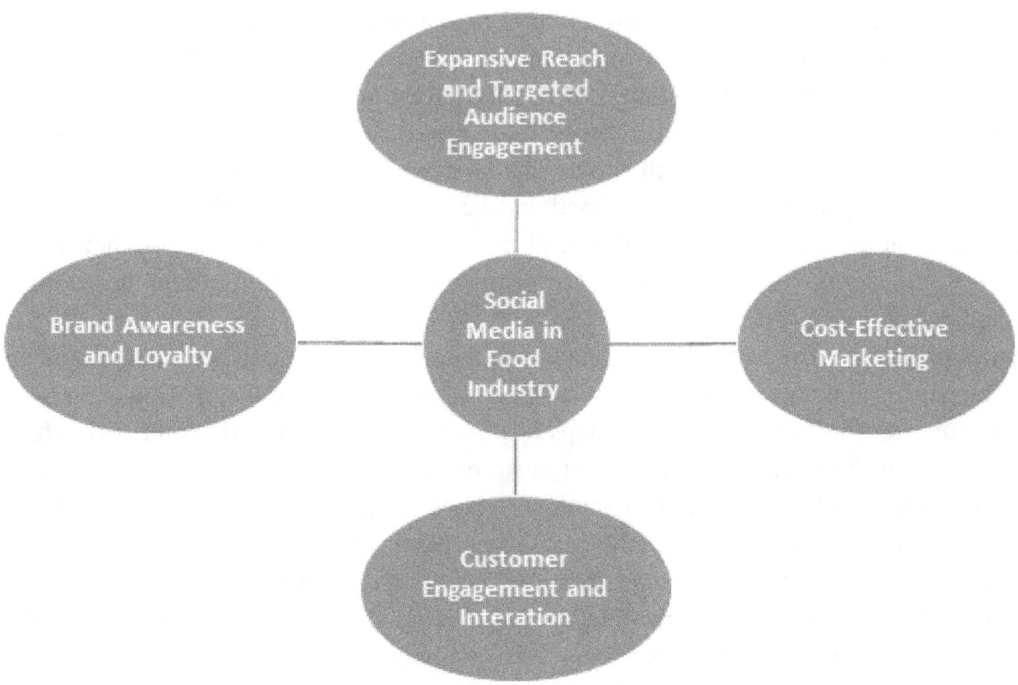

3. Enhanced Customer Engagement and Interaction

Social media facilitates direct verbal exchange between manufacturers and customers, fostering a stage of interplay that turned into formerly impossible through conventional media. manufacturers can interact with customers in actual-time, respond to inquiries, deal with lawsuits, and construct relationships. This two-way conversation now not only humanizes manufacturers however also permits them to acquire treasured customer comments and insights. engaging content such as polls, contests, stay streams, and interactive testimonies in addition deepens the connection among brands and their audiences, turning passive visitors into active individuals.

4. Brand Awareness and Loyalty

Through consistent and strategic use of social media, businesses can significantly enhance brand awareness. By regularly posting engaging content, sharing brand stories, and showcasing products or services, companies can stay top-of-mind with their audience. Social media also enables brands to express their identity and values, helping to build a loyal community of followers who resonate with the brand's message. This loyalty is often reflected in user-generated content, word-of-mouth recommendations, and repeat business.

Literature Review

Meals and beverage industry in Malaysia provides a massive GDP contribution. however, majority of corporations are SMEs that face monetary get right of entry to as their most important problem. Social media marketing is a novel style in business in recent times due to generation intensification. this text investigates the hyperlink among social media advertising and logo equity in which segmentation is the mediator variable within the SME meals and beverage enterprise. by means of using questionnaires disbursed systematically to consumers at shopping for branch stores, about 329 usable responses have been acquired. The outcomes indicated no direct courting amongst social media advertising and brand equity. a pleasant and large dating exists, however, among social media advertising and segmentation, segmentation and emblem equity which shows that segmentation is a partial mediator. The findings suggest that SMEs in particular inside the food and beverage industry ought to carefully phase their marketplace and on the same time, growth social media utilization in advertising their merchandise. This observe is the number one attempt to check segmentation as mediating variable within the meals and beverage enterprise (Azmi, 2023).

The developing amount of fast food manufacturers has amplified the intense competition in rapid meals industry. The putting alternate in customer life fashion for instant meals consumption creates significant growth opportunities for immediate food groups however then again the stiff competition brings rapid food chains and franchises daunting venture of customer loyalty and retention. To deal with the ones worrying conditions, Social media has turn out to be a huge marketing device for purchaser engagement and company increase. Which social media marketing taken into consideration as a tremendous and fee powerful detail to gain excessive brand attention, loyalty and resonance via non-forestall publicity. This examine followed a quantitative method; records become accrued with the help of well-designed scale questionnaire from 2 hundred respondents .precise literatures had been reviewed and substantially examine except identifying accrued data with the help of numerous statistical equipment which includes regression evaluation, Anova analysis descriptive assessment Pearson correlation, and reliability take a look at for deploying diploma studies consequences and effects that guide in easy stop to lower back the preset research objectives. The effects show a splendid in addition to great dating among social media advertising and marketing and advertising and marketing and emblem fairness. Study's findings additionally factor up social media advertising as a vital element in constructing and handling logo equity in speedy meals organisation of Pakistan (Riaz, 2019).

The vital thing intention of this studies modified into to check the placement of social media marketing capabilities (interactivity, perceived relevance, enjoyment, and informativeness) in affecting emblem loyalty inside the speedy-food industry. the required facts grow to be received thru a quantitative survey from customers of fast-meals manufacturers within the United Arab rates. The findings determined that maximum of the social media advertising and marketing features truly have an effect on emblem loyalty. In element, it become observed that interactivity and perceived relevance in reality have an effect on logo loyalty. however, contrary to expectancies, it has become decided that the impact of enjoyment on logo loyalty is insignificant. ultimately, the outcomes confirmed that informativeness is a good sized predictor of emblem loyalty. This research provides to the prevailing advertising and marketing literature in this subject matter thru the exam of selected social media advertising and marketing capabilities and logo loyalty in a middle East America because the empirical studies on this subject count number, specifically, in this place is scarce (Hanaysha, 2021).

This examine investigates the position of product pleasant and social media advertising on brand focus in the food company corporation, particularly that specialize in pastry and beverage establishments in Bandung, Indonesia. Theoretical Framework: logo attention is crucial for consumer preference-making, with product extremely good gambling a vast role in logo recognition. The examine explores the location of social media structures, particularly in promoting product branding within the competitive food carrier sector. method: A survey turned into accomplished amongst one hundred and fifty customers of a meals carrier outlet in metropolis Bandung, Indonesia, specialising in pastries and liquids. However, social media conversation simplest in part impacts brand attention, suggesting additional factors have an effect on patron perceptions.

The usage of social media for business development isn't a modern day concept for commercial enterprise proprietors. no matter this, there are many people who artwork within the food corporation on a small scale who benefit from social media. Many others are amongst those who have used social media however have experienced troubles in the use of it. This test investigates the effect of social media at the growth of small companies, particularly within the meals corporation, based totally at the evaluations of those who have used it. using a quantitative method with a focal point on psychology, the findings propose that social media use can considerably beneficial aid in the boom of businesses. so as for generation to be used to its complete capability, agencies have to keep to spend money on social media growth (Utami, 2024). In the end, social media is not the maximum essential factor in growing profits. unique product and provider improvement is a key element in reaching faster profits growth. The effects of this have a look at may be prolonged on the manner to gain extra specific effects as an unmarried concept of microeconomic improvement.

This paper explores the large impact of social media structures on promoting meals merchandise within the Albanian marketplace. In contemporary-day virtual generation, social media has transformed marketing and advertising and marketing strategies, presenting food manufacturers great possibilities for visibility, engagement, and have an effect on. through an intensive evaluation of current literature and case studies unique to Albania, this examine investigates the numerous approaches in which social structures facilitate the advertising of food merchandise within the Albanian context. Through statistics the dynamics of social media advertising and marketing in the Albanian market, groups can growth tailor-made techniques to beautify logo attention, foster purchaser loyalty, and power income in this precise cultural and monetary panorama (Hasugian, 2022).

This test pursuits to analyze the effect of social media advertising and marketing on logo photo and repeat purchases, and to research the function of emblem photograph in mediating the effect of social media advertising on repeat purchases inside the fast-food eating place enterprise in Medan. The respondents are customers who've made purchases at 5 speedy food consuming locations in Medan. one hundred forty human beings have been decided on the usage of random sampling. facts collected using questionnaire and interviews, and analyzed the usage of descriptive and route evaluation. The outcomes proved that social media advertising and advertising modified into considerably inspired brand picture; brand photo emerge as drastically encouraged repeat purchase; and, social media advertising and marketing changed into considerably encouraged repeat purchase. moreover, social media advertising and marketing proved has no widespread effect on repeat purchase thru brand photo as mediator (Korriku,, 2024).

This study explores how authorities help and social media effect the general overall performance and sustainability of small meals and beverage companies in Indonesia. The food and beverage (F&B) industry is critical for the financial gadget, with MSMEs playing a key position. regardless of traumatic situations, the authorities is promoting enterprise four.zero to beautify the employer's competitiveness. MSMEs make an enormous contribution to the F&B vicinity but face limitations like constrained sources and the effect of activities just like the COVID-19 pandemic. This research appears at how government manual and social media, while mixed, have an effect on the ones corporations. using surveys and statistical evaluation, the test finds a high best connection amongst authorities' resource and MSME sustainability and performance. The study highlights possibilities for similarly studies and a complete assessment of Indonesia's MSME surroundings (Fahmi, 2019).

This have a look at investigates the function of conformity in shaping the purchasing selections of more youthful customers in the meals and beverage (F&B) zone. moreover, we discover how conformity modes the connection among influencer credibility and purchase goal while analyzing the hyperlink between psychological ownership and buy aim. statistics turned into amassed from 380 customers between the age of 18 and 30 in Hanoi, Vietnam who frequently follow food evaluations on first rate social media systems. Structural equation modeling (SEM) were employed for records evaluation. we find that: (1) influencer credibility, mind-set toward advertising and marketing and advertising, mindset closer to the product, and mental ownership extensively impact the net purchase intentions of younger clients; (2) informative conformity strengthens the relationship among mental ownership and buy cause. even as clients express a choice to buy a product, publicity to wonderful influencer-driven information in addition solidifies their buy purpose; (three) intellectual ownership and attitude within the route of advertising and marketing act as mediators, bridging the gap among influencer credibility and purchase aim. This observe offers managerial insights to decorate influencer marketing effectiveness for F&B manufacturers targeting younger clients in Vietnam and Asia, highlighting the significance of conformity, mental ownership, and mind-set closer to advertising (Asha, 2023).

Food Industry's Unique Relationship with Social Media

The food industry has a particularly symbiotic and dynamic relationship with social media, which has become a vital tool for connecting with consumers, shaping culinary trends, and driving business growth. This relationship is underpinned by the visual, experiential, and community-driven nature of food, making it a perfect fit for the interactive and content-rich environment of social media platforms.

1. The Visual Appeal of Food

One of the primary reasons for the strong connection between the food industry and social media is the inherent visual appeal of food. Platforms like Instagram, Pinterest, and TikTok thrive on visual content, and food is one of the most photogenic subjects. From beautifully plated dishes at gourmet restaurants to the latest food trends and home-cooked meals, food content is highly engaging and shareable. This visual allure allows food businesses to showcase their offerings in a way that immediately captures attention and elicits emotional responses, such as cravings or nostalgia.

2. Culinary Trends and Viral Food Phenomena

Social media plays a pivotal role in the rapid dissemination and creation of culinary trends. Whether it's the global obsession with avocado toast, the rise of plant-based diets, or the viral success of the Dalgona coffee trend during the COVID-19 pandemic, social media platforms are often the breeding ground for food trends. These trends can spread rapidly across borders, influencing consumer preferences and behaviors on a global scale. The ability of food businesses to identify, participate in, and even create these trends is a unique advantage that social media provides, helping them stay relevant and connected to contemporary food culture.

3. Community Building and Customer Engagement

Food is inherently social; it brings people together, fosters connections, and is often at the center of cultural and familial gatherings. Social media amplifies this communal aspect by enabling food businesses to build and nurture communities around their brands. Through interactive content, such as recipe sharing, cooking challenges, or food-related discussions, businesses can engage directly with their audience, creating a sense of belonging and loyalty. For example, restaurants and food brands can encourage customers to share their dining experiences or favorite recipes using specific hashtags, which not only promotes the brand but also strengthens the community around it.

4. User-Generated Content and Authenticity

In the food industry, user-generated content (UGC) is particularly powerful. When customers share photos, reviews, or videos of their meals or food experiences on social media, it serves as authentic, word-of-mouth marketing. This type of content is often perceived as more trustworthy and relatable than brand-generated content, making it a valuable asset for food businesses. Social media platforms facilitate the easy sharing and amplification of UGC, allowing food brands to build authenticity and credibility through the voices of their customers. Moreover, by reposting or engaging with UGC, brands can show appreciation for their customers and further enhance their connection with the community.

5. Influencer Marketing and Collaborative Content

Social media enables direct conversation between manufacturers and clients, fostering a degree of interaction that turned into previously not possible via traditional media. producers can interact with clients in real-time, respond to inquiries, cope with court cases, and assemble relationships. This two-way communication not simplest humanizes manufacturers but also permits them to acquire treasured customer comments and insights. engaging content material consisting of polls, contests, live streams, and interactive stories further deepens the relationship among manufacturers and their audiences, turning passive site visitors into active individuals.

6. Real-Time Customer Feedback and Market Research

Social media provides an immediate and direct channel for customer feedback, which is invaluable for the food industry. Whether it's through comments, reviews, or social media mentions, businesses can gauge customer satisfaction, identify areas for improvement, and respond to issues in real time. This instant feedback loop allows food businesses to be agile and responsive to consumer needs and preferences. Additionally, social media analytics offer rich data for market research, helping businesses understand demographic trends, monitor competitor activities, and identify emerging food preferences.

7. Promotion and Brand Awareness

Social media has become an essential platform for food businesses to promote their products and services. Whether launching a new menu item, offering a seasonal discount, or announcing an event, social media allows businesses to reach a large audience quickly and efficiently. The shareable nature of social media content means that a well-crafted promotion can go viral, significantly amplifying its reach. Moreover, through targeted advertising, food businesses can hone in on specific demographics, ensuring that their promotions are seen by the most relevant audiences.

8. Integration with E-commerce and Food Delivery

The integration of social media with e-commerce and food delivery services has further deepened the relationship between the food industry and social platforms. Many food businesses now use social media not just for marketing but also as a direct sales channel. Features like Instagram Shopping, Facebook Marketplace, and links to food delivery platforms enable consumers to discover, order, and purchase food directly through social media. This seamless integration streamlines the customer journey, making it easier for consumers to go from discovery to purchase in just a few clicks.

9. Crisis Management and Reputation Management

For the food industry, where customer trust and reputation are paramount, social media serves as a critical tool for crisis management. In situations such as food recalls, negative reviews, or public relations issues, businesses can use social media to communicate transparently with their customers, address concerns, and provide updates. The speed and reach of social media ensure that businesses can manage their reputation effectively, minimizing potential damage and restoring customer confidence.

10. Content Diversification and Multichannel Strategy

The variety of content formats available on social media—from images and videos to live streams and stories—enables food businesses to diversify their content and reach different segments of their audience. For example, a restaurant might use Instagram for visually appealing food photography, TikTok for short, engaging recipe videos, and Facebook for event announcements and customer reviews. This multichannel approach allows food businesses to tailor their content to the strengths of each platform, maximizing engagement and reach.

Strategies for Effective Social Media Marketing in the Food Industry

This phase will delve into various techniques that meals corporations can appoint to maximize their social media presence. Social media advertising has emerged as a essential aspect of achievement within the food enterprise, supplying brands a powerful platform to have interaction with purchasers, build emblem loyalty, and force sales. but, to harness the overall potential of social media, meals organizations want to implement properly-concept-out strategies that align with their emblem dreams and resonate with their target market. right here are a few key techniques for powerful social media advertising in the food industry:

1. Create Visually Appealing Content
    - Importance: The food industry is inherently visual, making platforms like Instagram, Pinterest, and TikTok ideal for showcasing products. High-quality images and videos of food can evoke emotions, spark cravings, and drive engagement.
    - Strategy: Invest in professional photography or learn basic photography skills to capture your dishes or products in the best light. Use natural lighting, appealing compositions, and close-up shots to make the food look as appetizing as possible. Additionally, consider using video content such as recipe tutorials, behind-the-scenes glimpses, or slow-motion shots of food preparation to add a dynamic element to your feed.
2. Leverage User-Generated Content (UGC)
    - Importance: UGC adds authenticity and builds trust among potential customers, as content created by other consumers is often viewed as more credible than brand-generated content.
    - Strategy: Encourage customers to share their experiences with your food by creating a unique hashtag for your brand. Feature UGC on your social media pages, acknowledging and rewarding customers for their contributions. This not only provides you with a steady stream of content but also fosters a sense of community and customer loyalty.
3. Utilize Influencer Marketing
    - Importance: Influencers have audiences that consider their tips, marketing rating and effective allies integrated built-integrated new customers and built-in emblem credibility.

- Strategy: associate with food bloggers, chefs, or social media built-influencers who align together with your brand values and feature a following grading that fits your goal.

4. Engage with Your Audience

    -Importance: Social media is a two-way street, and engagement is key to building relationships with your audience. Active engagement demonstrates that you value your customers and are attentive to their needs and feedback.

    - Strategy: Respond promptly to comments, messages, and reviews on your social media platforms. Use polls, questions, and interactive stories to invite feedback and opinions. Hosting live Q&A sessions or cooking demonstrations can also provide real-time interaction, allowing you to answer questions, share tips, and connect more personally with your audience.

5. Implement a Consistent Posting Schedule
    - Importance: Consistency is crucial in keeping your brand top-of-mind and maintaining engagement levels. A well-planned posting schedule ensures that your content is regularly reaching your audience without overwhelming them.
    - Strategy: Develop a content calendar that outlines what content will be posted, when, and on which platforms. Tools like Hootsuite, Buffer, or Later can help you schedule posts in advance, ensuring a steady flow of content. While consistency is important, also be flexible and ready to adapt your schedule to take advantage of real-time opportunities or respond to trends.
6. Incorporate Storytelling into Your Content
    - Importance: Storytelling allows you to connect with your audience on an emotional level, making your brand more relatable and memorable. It can differentiate your brand in a crowded market by highlighting what makes your products unique.
    - Strategy: Share the story behind your brand, such as how it was founded, the inspiration behind your recipes, or the sourcing of your ingredients. Use stories to showcase your team, feature customer testimonials, or highlight your community involvement. Authentic stories that align with your brand values resonate more deeply with consumers and can create lasting connections. Figure 2 describes the key components of social media marketing in the food industry.

Figure 2. Components of Social Media Marketing in the Food Industry

7. Capitalize on Trends and Challenges
    - Importance: Social media trends and challenges can quickly gain traction and offer an opportunity for your brand to engage with a wider audience. Participating in trends keeps your brand relevant and top-of-mind.
    - Strategy: Stay informed about the latest trends on platforms like TikTok and Instagram. Whether it's a new viral recipe, a food-related challenge, or a popular hashtag, find creative ways to incorporate these trends into your content. However, ensure that the trends you participate in align with your brand's image and values to maintain authenticity.
8. Focus on Local Marketing
    - Importance: For restaurants, cafes, and food businesses with a physical location, targeting the local community is essential for driving foot traffic and building a loyal customer base.
    - Strategy: Use location-based hashtags, geotags, and ads to target potential customers in your area. Highlight local events, partnerships with nearby businesses, or participation in community activities. Encourage local customers to check in, leave reviews, and share their experiences on social media. Running promotions or offering discounts exclusively for local followers can also incentivize visits.
9. Optimize for Social Commerce
    - Importance: The integration of e-commerce features on social media platforms allows food businesses to convert followers into customers directly within the platform, streamlining the purchasing process.
    - Strategy: Set up shopping features on Instagram or Facebook to allow users to browse and purchase products directly from your social media profiles. For restaurants and food delivery services, include links to online ordering platforms or use third-party integrations like

Grubhub or Uber Eats. Ensure that your social media profiles are fully optimized with up-to-date information, clear calls-to-action, and easy navigation.

10. Run Social Media Contests and Giveaways
    - Importance: Contests and giveaways are effective for generating buzz, increasing engagement, and growing your follower base. They create excitement around your brand and incentivize users to share your content.
    - Strategy: Organize contests that encourage participants to like, share, or tag friends in your posts. For example, a photo contest where followers share their favorite meal from your restaurant using a specific hashtag can boost UGC and brand visibility. Ensure that the prizes are appealing and relevant to your audience, such as a free meal, gift card, or product bundle.
11. Track and Analyze Performance
    - Importance: Regularly analyzing the performance of your social media efforts is essential for understanding what works and refining your strategy for better results. Data-driven decisions lead to more effective and efficient marketing.
    - Strategy: Use social media analytics tools like Facebook Insights, Instagram Analytics, or third-party platforms like Sprout Social to monitor metrics such as engagement rates, follower growth, click-through rates, and conversion rates. Identify the types of content that resonate most with your audience and adjust your strategy accordingly. Set clear, measurable goals and KPIs to track your progress over time.
12. Highlight Sustainability and Ethical Practices
    - Importance: Consumers are increasingly drawn to brands that demonstrate social responsibility and environmental consciousness. Highlighting your commitment to sustainability can enhance your brand's appeal and align with the values of your audience.
    - Strategy: Share content that showcases your sustainable practices, such as sourcing local or organic ingredients, reducing food waste, or using eco-friendly packaging. Highlight any certifications, partnerships, or community initiatives that reflect your commitment to ethical practices. Transparent communication about these efforts can build trust and differentiate your brand in a competitive market.

Effectiveness of Data Analytics in Social Media Marketing of the Food Industry

Data analytics plays a crucial role in optimizing social media marketing efforts within the food industry. Here are some specific examples of how data analytics can be applied. Figure 3 shows the deployment of data analytics in social media marketing for food industry.

Figure 3. Data Analytics in Social Media Marketing for Food Industry

1. Customer Sentiment Analysis

Example: A restaurant chain uses sentiment analysis tools to analyze customer feedback from social media platforms like Twitter and Instagram. By examining the tone and emotion behind customer comments, the chain identifies that customers are particularly pleased with their new vegan menu items. This insight prompts the chain to increase promotion of these items and consider expanding their vegan offerings.

Impact: Increased customer satisfaction and targeted marketing efforts leading to higher sales.

2. Content Performance Metrics

Example: A fast-food brand tracks the performance of its social media content, such as posts, videos, and stories, using metrics like likes, shares, comments, and views. By analyzing which types of content (e.g., behind-the-scenes videos, customer testimonials, product images) receive the most engagement, the brand refines its content strategy to focus more on high-performing formats.

Impact: Improved engagement rates and a more effective content strategy.

3. Influencer Marketing Analytics

Example: A gourmet snack brand partners with food influencers to promote their products. The brand uses analytics platforms to measure the impact of these partnerships by tracking metrics such as follower growth, engagement rates, and sales spikes during influencer campaigns. They find that influencers with smaller, more engaged followings (micro-influencers) generate higher engagement and better ROI compared to those with larger, less engaged audiences.

Impact: More effective influencer partnerships and better allocation of marketing budget.

4. Audience Demographics and Behavior Insights

Example: A beverage company uses social media analytics tools to gather data on their audience's demographics (age, gender, location) and behaviors (active hours, content preferences). They discover that a significant portion of their audience is millennials who are active in the evenings. As a result, the company schedules posts and ads during peak activity times and tailors content to appeal to millennial tastes.

Impact: Increased reach and engagement, better-targeted content.

5. Trend Analysis

Example: A bakery uses data analytics to monitor social media trends and hashtags related to baking and desserts. They identify an emerging trend of interest in gluten-free and keto-friendly baked goods. By analyzing the popularity and geographic spread of these trends, the bakery decides to introduce new gluten-free and keto-friendly products, which they then promote heavily on social media.

Impact: Capitalizing on emerging trends and meeting customer demand, leading to increased sales.

6. Competitor Analysis

Example: A coffee shop chain uses social media analytics to track competitor activities and engagement metrics. They analyze the types of promotions, content, and campaigns competitors are running, and how their audience is responding. By identifying gaps and opportunities, the coffee shop chain develops competitive strategies, such as unique promotional offers and differentiated content.

Impact: Better competitive positioning and more innovative marketing strategies.

7. Geospatial Analytics

Example: A national restaurant chain uses geospatial analytics to analyze social media check-ins, reviews, and mentions across different locations. They identify which locations have higher social media activity and customer engagement. This data helps them understand regional preferences and tailor their marketing strategies accordingly.

Impact: Region-specific marketing strategies and improved local customer engagement.

Emerging Trends and Innovations in Social Media Marketing

The digital landscape is constantly evolving, and staying ahead of trends is crucial for maintaining a competitive edge. This section will explore emerging trends in social media marketing, such as the use of artificial intelligence for personalized marketing, the growing popularity of short-form video content, and the integration of social media with e-commerce and food delivery services. Additionally, it will address the increasing importance of sustainability and ethical marketing practices. The landscape of social media marketing is continually evolving, driven by technological advancements and shifting consumer behaviors. One prominent trend is the rise of short-form video content on platforms like TikTok and Instagram Reels, which has captured the attention of younger audiences with its engaging, bite-sized format. Brands are leveraging this trend to create viral challenges and interactive content that resonates with users.

Another significant innovation is the integration of artificial intelligence (AI) and data analytics in social media marketing. AI-powered tools enable brands to personalize their marketing efforts, analyze consumer behavior, and optimize content for better engagement. This level of personalization enhances user experience and increases the effectiveness of marketing campaigns. Social commerce is also gaining traction, with platforms like Facebook, Instagram, and Pinterest integrating shopping features that allow users to purchase products directly through social media. This seamless integration of e-commerce and social media simplifies the buying process and drives sales.

Additionally, there is a growing emphasis on sustainability and ethical marketing. Consumers are increasingly looking for brands that demonstrate social responsibility and environmental consciousness. Marketers are responding by highlighting sustainable practices and promoting transparent, authentic messaging.

These trends and innovations are reshaping social media marketing, making it more interactive, personalized, and aligned with consumer values. While social media offers numerous opportunities, it also presents challenges and ethical dilemmas. This section will discuss how food businesses can navigate negative feedback and manage their online reputation, address misinformation and fake reviews, and balance marketing efforts with authenticity and transparency. It will also cover the importance of complying with advertising regulations and guidelines to avoid potential legal issues.

Role of AI and Data Analytics in Personalizing Marketing Efforts

In today's highly competitive digital landscape, personalization has become a critical component of effective marketing strategies. Consumers increasingly expect brands to deliver tailored experiences that resonate with their individual preferences and needs. Artificial intelligence (AI) and data analytics play a pivotal role in enabling this level of personalization, transforming the way businesses engage with their audiences.

1. Understanding Consumer Behavior
    - Importance: To personalize marketing efforts effectively, brands must first understand the behaviors, preferences, and needs of their consumers. AI and data analytics allow businesses to gather, process, and analyze vast amounts of consumer data, revealing patterns and insights that would be impossible to detect manually.

- Role of AI and Data Analytics: Machine learning algorithms can analyze data from various sources, such as website interactions, social media activity, purchase history, and demographic information. By identifying trends and patterns in this data, AI can segment consumers into distinct groups based on their behavior, preferences, and purchasing intent. This segmentation enables marketers to target specific audiences with relevant content, offers, and messaging that align with their interests.

2. Enhancing Customer Segmentation
   - Importance: Effective marketing relies on accurate customer segmentation. Grouping consumers based on shared characteristics allows brands to tailor their messages more precisely, increasing the likelihood of engagement and conversion.
   - Role of AI and Data Analytics: AI-driven data analytics can go beyond traditional segmentation methods by analyzing a broader range of variables, such as psychographic data (values, interests, and lifestyles), behavioral data, and real-time interactions. This enables more granular and dynamic segmentation, allowing for highly personalized marketing campaigns that target specific micro-segments. For example, a food delivery service might use AI to segment customers based on their dietary preferences, order frequency, and time of day they usually order, then tailor promotions accordingly.
3. Personalized Content Creation
   - Importance: Personalized content resonates more with consumers because it speaks directly to their interests and needs, making them more likely to engage with the brand.
   - Role of AI and Data Analytics: AI-powered tools can analyze consumer data to predict what type of content will be most appealing to different segments of an audience. For example, AI can recommend specific blog topics, social media posts, or email subject lines based on past user interactions. In addition, AI can automate the creation of personalized content at scale, such as generating customized email campaigns or personalized product recommendations for e-commerce sites. This ensures that each consumer receives content that is relevant and engaging to them, enhancing the overall customer experience.
4. Optimizing Customer Journeys
   - Importance: The customer journey is increasingly complex, with consumers interacting with brands across multiple touchpoints before making a purchase decision. Personalizing this journey is crucial for keeping consumers engaged and guiding them towards conversion.
   - Role of AI and Data Analytics: AI can track and analyze a customer's journey in real-time, identifying the touchpoints where personalization can have the most impact. For instance, AI can personalize website experiences by dynamically adjusting content based on the user's behavior, such as displaying different landing pages, product suggestions, or calls to action depending on where the user is in their journey. AI can also optimize retargeting efforts by analyzing which types of ads or offers are most likely to bring back users who have abandoned their carts or left the website without converting.
5. Dynamic Pricing and Personalized Offers
   - Importance: Offering the right product at the right price to the right customer can significantly enhance conversion rates and customer satisfaction.
   - Role of AI and Data Analytics: AI-driven algorithms can analyze factors such as consumer demand, competitor pricing, and individual purchasing behaviors to determine the optimal price point for different customer segments. This dynamic pricing strategy ensures that pric-

es are competitive while maximizing profitability. Additionally, AI can personalize offers by predicting which discounts or promotions are most likely to convert specific customers. For example, a frequent buyer might receive a loyalty discount, while a first-time visitor might get a special introductory offer. This level of personalization helps in maximizing both customer acquisition and retention.

6. Automating Customer Interactions
   - Importance: Personalization extends to customer service, where tailored interactions can enhance customer satisfaction and loyalty.
   - Role of AI and Data Analytics: AI-powered chatbots and virtual assistants are capable of providing personalized customer support by analyzing past interactions and understanding the context of the current query. For instance, an AI-driven chatbot can greet returning customers by name, recommend products based on their previous purchases, and provide tailored responses to their inquiries. Moreover, AI can analyze customer sentiment and intent, allowing businesses to prioritize interactions that require human intervention, ensuring that customers receive the most appropriate level of support.
7. Predictive Analytics for Anticipating Customer Needs
   - Importance: Anticipating customer needs before they explicitly express them can create a seamless and delightful customer experience.
   - Role of AI and Data Analytics: Predictive analytics, powered by AI, uses historical data and machine learning algorithms to forecast future behaviors and preferences. For example, an AI system can predict when a customer is likely to repurchase a product based on their past purchase cycle, enabling brands to send timely reminders or offers. Similarly, AI can identify when a customer might be at risk of churning and trigger personalized retention strategies, such as offering a discount or highlighting new product features that match their preferences. By proactively addressing customer needs, businesses can enhance satisfaction and loyalty.
8. Real-Time Personalization
   - Importance: Consumers increasingly expect personalized experiences in real-time, especially in digital environments where instant gratification is the norm.
   - Role of AI and Data Analytics: AI enables real-time personalization by continuously analyzing user behavior as it happens. For instance, AI can track how users interact with a website or app and immediately adjust the content, recommendations, and layout to better suit their needs. In e-commerce, AI can recommend products based on real-time browsing behavior, while in digital advertising, AI can adjust the ad content based on user interactions. This level of real-time adaptation ensures that customers always receive the most relevant and engaging experience, which can significantly increase conversion rates.
9. Improving Marketing ROI
   - Importance: Effective personalization can lead to higher conversion rates, increased customer loyalty, and ultimately, a better return on investment (ROI) for marketing efforts.
   - Role of AI and Data Analytics: By targeting the right audience with the right message at the right time, AI-driven personalization minimizes wasted marketing spend and maximizes the impact of each campaign. AI can optimize ad placements, adjust bidding strategies in real-time, and allocate marketing budgets across channels based on performance data. This data-driven approach ensures that marketing resources are used efficiently, leading to higher ROI and more effective overall marketing strategies.

10. Continuous Improvement Through Machine Learning
    - Importance: The ability to continuously improve and refine marketing strategies is crucial in maintaining relevance and effectiveness in a rapidly changing digital landscape.
    - Role of AI and Data Analytics: Machine learning, a subset of AI, allows systems to learn from new data and experiences over time, improving their accuracy and effectiveness. As more consumer data is collected, AI systems become better at predicting behaviors, personalizing content, and optimizing marketing efforts. This continuous learning process means that personalization strategies are always evolving, ensuring that they remain effective in meeting consumer needs and achieving business goals.

The Impact of Short-Form Video Content

Short-form video content, epitomized by platforms like TikTok and Instagram Reels, has rapidly transformed the digital marketing landscape and the way brands interact with consumers. These bite-sized, visually engaging videos, typically lasting between 15 seconds to a minute, have become a dominant form of content consumption, especially among younger audiences. Their impact on marketing, consumer behavior, and content creation is profound, making them a crucial tool for businesses seeking to engage with modern audiences.

1. Massive Reach and Engagement
    - Importance: Short-form videos have become one of the most effective ways to reach a broad audience quickly. The format's popularity, particularly among Gen Z and Millennials, means that these videos often go viral, generating millions of views in a short span of time.
    - Impact: Platforms like TikTok have billions of active users, making short-form video content an essential medium for brands to expand their reach. The algorithm-driven nature of these platforms ensures that engaging content can reach beyond the immediate follower base, potentially going viral and significantly boosting brand visibility. For example, a well-crafted TikTok video can quickly amass views and shares, bringing the brand to the attention of a global audience.
2. High Levels of User Engagement
    - Importance: The interactive and dynamic nature of short-form video content fosters high levels of user engagement, including likes, shares, comments, and direct interactions like duets and challenges.
    - Impact: Short-form videos are designed to capture attention quickly, making them ideal for engaging viewers who have short attention spans. The use of music, text overlays, and quick cuts keeps the content visually stimulating, which in turn encourages users to engage. For marketers, this high engagement translates into more meaningful interactions with their audience, fostering a stronger connection and driving higher conversion rates. Brands that create content that encourages participation, such as challenges or trends, can see exponential growth in engagement as users contribute their versions of the content.
3. Trendsetting and Cultural Influence
    - Importance: Short-form video platforms are not just content-sharing spaces; they are incubators for trends and cultural phenomena. Many of today's most significant trends in fashion, music, and lifestyle originate from TikTok or Instagram Reels.

- Impact: Brands that can tap into these trends—or even better, create them—gain considerable cultural relevance. For instance, viral dance challenges, hashtag trends, or unique video formats often begin on these platforms and can influence mainstream culture. This trendsetting power allows brands to position themselves at the forefront of cultural conversations, making them more relevant to their target audience. Additionally, short-form video content often dictates consumer behavior, with trends leading to spikes in product sales, brand searches, or even changes in consumer habits.

4. Cost-Effective Content Production
    - Importance: Compared to traditional video content, short-form videos are generally less expensive and time-consuming to produce, making them accessible to businesses of all sizes.
    - Impact: The low barrier to entry means that even small businesses can create high-impact content without significant investment. Many successful short-form videos are shot on smartphones with minimal editing, focusing instead on creativity and relatability. This democratization of content creation allows brands to produce content more frequently, experiment with different ideas, and quickly adapt to changing trends. The ability to produce and post content rapidly also means that brands can be more agile in their marketing strategies, responding to current events or trends in real-time.
5. Enhanced Storytelling and Brand Communication
    - Importance: Short-form videos allow brands to tell stories in a concise and impactful way. The limited time forces content creators to distill their message to its essence, making each second count.
    - Impact: The ability to tell a compelling story or convey a powerful message in under a minute is a valuable skill in today's fast-paced digital environment. Brands that master this can effectively communicate their values, showcase products, or share customer testimonials in a way that resonates with viewers. Short-form videos are also versatile, allowing brands to use humor, emotion, or suspense to connect with their audience. This form of storytelling is particularly effective in building brand personality and creating memorable impressions that stick with viewers long after they've scrolled past.
6. Personalization and Relatability
    - Importance: Short-form video content often feels more personal and relatable than polished, high-budget advertising. This authenticity is particularly appealing to younger audiences who value genuine content.
    - Impact: Brands that use short-form videos to showcase behind-the-scenes content, day-in-the-life segments, or user-generated content can build a more authentic connection with their audience. The informal, often spontaneous nature of these videos makes them feel less like traditional advertisements and more like genuine content from a friend or influencer. This relatability helps in building trust and loyalty, as consumers are more likely to engage with brands that they perceive as authentic and down-to-earth. Additionally, the use of influencers in short-form videos can further personalize the brand message, making it more relatable to niche audiences.
7. Driving E-Commerce and Direct Sales
    - Importance: Short-form videos are increasingly being integrated with e-commerce features, making it easier for viewers to make purchases directly from the content.

    - Impact: Platforms like Instagram Reels and TikTok have introduced shopping features that allow users to buy products directly from videos. This seamless integration of content and commerce simplifies the customer journey from discovery to purchase. Brands can showcase their products in use, provide quick tutorials, or highlight features in a way that is both entertaining and informative. The immediate call-to-action, combined with the engaging nature of the content, can lead to higher conversion rates and increased sales. Additionally, short-form videos are effective for promoting flash sales, new product launches, or limited-time offers, driving urgency and encouraging quick purchases.
8. Data-Driven Insights and Optimization
    - Importance: Short-form video platforms offer robust analytics that provide insights into viewer behavior, engagement rates, and content performance. These insights are invaluable for refining marketing strategies.
    - Impact: The data generated by short-form videos allows brands to understand what resonates with their audience, from the types of content that garner the most engagement to the times when their audience is most active. By analyzing this data, brands can optimize their content strategies, ensuring that they produce more of what works and improve on areas that are less effective. Additionally, the iterative nature of short-form content—where videos are produced and shared quickly—allows brands to test different approaches, learn from the results, and continually refine their strategies for maximum impact.
9. Community Building and User Interaction
    - Importance: Short-form videos are inherently social, encouraging users to interact not just with the content, but with each other through comments, shares, and collaborations.
    - Impact: Brands can leverage short-form videos to build a community around their products or services. By creating content that encourages discussion, invites user participation (such as challenges or Q&A sessions), or fosters a sense of belonging, brands can cultivate a loyal following. The interactive features of platforms like TikTok, where users can duet or stitch content, also allow for collaborative content creation, further strengthening the sense of community. This community-driven approach helps in building long-term brand loyalty and creates a network of engaged users who actively promote the brand.
10. Adapting to the Changing Digital Landscape
    - Importance: The digital marketing landscape is constantly evolving, with new platforms and content formats emerging regularly. Short-form video content represents the latest evolution, and brands that adapt quickly will have a competitive advantage.
    - Impact: As consumer preferences shift towards more immersive, interactive, and concise content, brands that embrace short-form videos can stay relevant and competitive. The rapid adoption of platforms like TikTok by major brands highlights the need for businesses to be flexible and willing to experiment with new content formats. Those that succeed in mastering short-form video content can not only capture the attention of today's consumers but also position themselves as forward-thinking and innovative in a crowded market.

Integration with E-Commerce and Food Delivery Services

The integration of social media platforms with e-commerce and food delivery services has revolutionized how consumers discover, order, and experience food. This seamless integration has blurred the lines between social media engagement and the purchasing process, creating a streamlined journey from content consumption to transaction. For the food industry, this convergence represents a powerful tool to drive sales, increase customer convenience, and build stronger relationships with consumers.

1. Seamless Shopping Experience
    - Importance: In the speedy-paced digital international, clients more and more demand comfort and performance, especially with regards to ordering food. the mixing of e-trade with social media provides a one-prevent answer wherein discovery, selection-making, and buying show up in a single location.
    - Impact: Social media systems like Instagram and facebook have added features that permit customers to save without delay from posts, tales, and commercials. inside the context of the food enterprise, which means purchasers can see a mouth-watering dish on their feed and at once order it with some clicks. Platforms like Instagram have "Shop Now" or "Order Food" buttons that connect directly to the brand's online store or food delivery service, such as UberEats or DoorDash. This reduces friction in the purchasing process, leading to higher conversion rates. The convenience of this process appeals to consumers who want instant gratification, driving more impulse purchases and increasing overall sales for restaurants and food brands.
2. Social Media as a Discovery Tool
    - Importance: Social media has become a primary tool for discovering new food trends, restaurants, and products. Visual platforms like Instagram and Pinterest are particularly influential in shaping consumer preferences and driving dining choices.
    - Impact: The combination of e-commerce and delivery of food within social media allows consumers to act immediately on their discovery. For example, a user might come across a new dessert trend on TikTok, and within the same app, find a local bakery offering that dessert for delivery. This instant ability to move from discovery to purchase enhances the consumer experience and encourages exploration of new products. Additionally, platforms like Instagram allow users to follow specific hashtags or accounts related to food trends, which keeps them informed about the latest offerings and enables them to order directly from the platform, enhancing engagement and driving sales.
3. Influencer Marketing and Affiliate Sales
    - Importance: Influencer marketing plays a significant role in how food products and services are promoted on social media. By the use of social media, many users follow their followers, and helps brands to promote their awareness and improvement in sales.
    - Impact: With integrated e-commerce capabilities, influencers can include direct links to products or food delivery services within their posts. For example, a food blogger might post a review of a new meal kit and include a swipe-up link in their Instagram story that directs followers to purchase the kit directly from the brand's website or a food delivery service. Affiliate marketing programs can further incentivize influencers by offering commis-

sions on sales generated through their unique links, driving even more targeted and effective promotions.

4. Real-Time Promotions and Limited-Time Offers
    - Importance: The ability to run time-sensitive promotions is a powerful tool for driving urgency and boosting sales, particularly in the food industry where seasonal and trend-driven products are common.
    - Impact: Social media platforms allow brands to promote limited-time offers or flash sales directly within their posts and stories. For instance, a restaurant might announce a special discount on a popular menu item for the next 24 hours, with a direct link to order via a food delivery service. The immediacy of social media, combined with the ease of ordering, makes these promotions highly effective. Brands can also use features like Instagram Live or Facebook Live to engage with their audience in real-time, offering exclusive deals to viewers who make purchases during the live session. This real-time engagement encourages quick decision-making and capitalizes on impulse buying, driving immediate sales boosts.
5. Personalized Recommendations and Targeted Advertising
    - Importance: Personalization is key to successful marketing in the digital age. Customers mainly engage with content and offers that are tailored to their preferences and behaviors.
    - Impact: The integration of AI and data analytics within social media platforms allows for highly personalized marketing efforts. For example, if a user frequently engages with vegan food content on Instagram, they might start seeing targeted ads for vegan meal kits or restaurants offering plant-based options. These ads often include direct links to order through integrated e-commerce or food delivery services. Additionally, platforms like Facebook use advanced algorithms to deliver personalized recommendations based on user activity, such as suggesting a nearby restaurant that offers delivery through an integrated partner like Grubhub or Postmates. Figure 4 and 5 details the relationship between e-commerce and food delivery on social media.

Figure 4. E-Commerce and Food Delivery Service [Part-I]

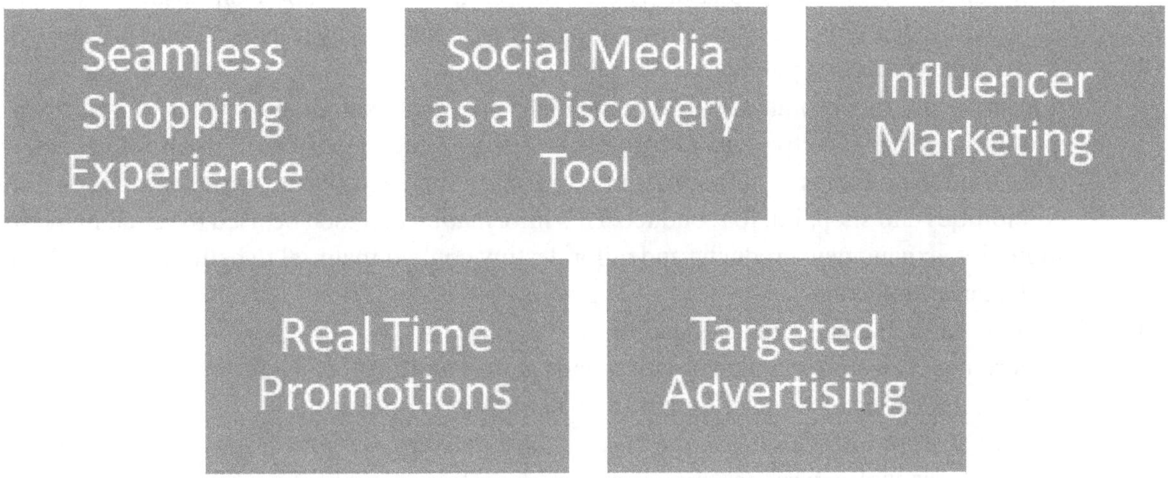

6. User-Generated Content and Social Proof
   - Importance: User-generated content (UGC) serves as powerful social proof, helping to build trust and credibility for brands. In the food industry, seeing others enjoy a meal or product can significantly influence a consumer's decision to make a purchase.
   - Impact: Social media platforms that integrate with e-commerce and food delivery services enable users to share their experiences and link directly to the product or service. For example, a customer might post a picture of their takeout meal on Instagram, tag the restaurant, and include a link to order the same meal. This kind of content not only promotes the brand but also makes it easy for others to make a purchase directly from the post. Brands can encourage UGC by running campaigns that reward users for sharing their experiences, perhaps offering discounts or freebies for posts that lead to orders. This creates a cycle of engagement where users both promote and purchase products, all within the same platform.
7. Enhanced Customer Experience and Loyalty Programs
   - Importance: A seamless and positive customer experience is crucial for building brand loyalty. Integration with social media and e-commerce allows for a more cohesive and satisfying customer journey.
   - Impact: Social media platforms are increasingly being used to enhance customer experience by integrating loyalty programs and personalized offers. For instance, a restaurant might offer loyalty points for orders placed through a link on their Instagram profile, which can be redeemed for discounts or free items in the future. Additionally, by integrating customer feedback tools, brands can quickly address customer concerns and improve service quality. As an instance, if a client is not happy regarding a delayed delivery on social media, the brand can immediately respond and offer a solution, such as a discount on their next order.

This kind of responsive customer service, facilitated by social media integration, helps build trust and encourages repeat business.

8. Data Collection and Analytics
    - Importance: Social media platforms offer a wealth of information on customer conduct, along with what types of content they interact with, when they're most energetic, and what drives them to make a purchase.
    - Impact: while incorporated with e-commerce and meals shipping services, this fact turns into even greater effective. manufacturers can song which posts cause the most orders, analyze the effectiveness of different sorts of promotions, and benefit insights into consumer possibilities and shopping for conduct. This information can then be used to refine marketing strategies, expand new products, and tailor destiny content material to better meet the desires of the target audience.
9. Omnichannel Marketing and Brand Consistency
    - Importance: Consumers interact with brands across multiple channels, and a consistent, omnichannel approach is crucial for building a strong brand identity.
    - Impact: Integration with e-commerce and food delivery services allows for a more cohesive omnichannel experience. For example, a customer might discover a new product on Instagram, receive a targeted email with a discount code, and then place an order through a linked food delivery service. This seamless transition between platforms ensures that the brand message remains consistent and reinforces the brand identity at every touchpoint. Additionally, by integrating social media with other marketing channels, brands can create unified campaigns that drive engagement and sales across multiple platforms, increasing overall effectiveness.

Figure 5. E-Commerce and Food Delivery Service [Part-II]

10. Global Reach and Market Expansion
    - Importance: Social media platforms have a global user base, providing an opportunity for brands to enhance their numbers for customers and identify new areas for marketing.
    - Impact: By integrating with e-commerce and food delivery services that operate internationally, brands can easily expand their reach to new regions. For instance, a restaurant chain with a strong social media presence in one country can leverage that following to promote new locations or delivery options in other markets. Social media platforms also allow for localized marketing, where brands can target specific regions with relevant content and offers. This global reach, combined with the convenience of integrated e-commerce, makes it easier for brands to enter new markets and grow their customer base.

CONCLUSION

The role of social media marketing in the food industry is both transformative and indispensable in today's digital age. Social media platforms have become the primary channels through which consumers discover new foods, engage with brands, and make purchasing decisions. By leveraging visually appealing content, influencer partnerships, and real-time consumer engagement, food brands can create powerful connections with their audience, driving both brand loyalty and sales.

The integration of e-commerce and food delivery services within social media platforms further enhances the consumer experience, making it easier than ever to move from discovery to purchase with just a few clicks. Additionally, the rise of short-form video content, coupled with AI-driven personalization and data analytics, has opened new avenues for targeting and engaging consumers in more relevant and impactful ways.

As consumer behavior continues to evolve, brands that successfully harness the power of social media marketing will not only stay relevant but also lead the way in shaping the future of the food industry. By embracing these digital tools and strategies, food brands can effectively navigate the complexities of the modern marketplace, ensuring sustained growth and success in an increasingly competitive environment.

REFERENCES

Abdul Ghani Azmi, I. (2023). The Mediating Role of Segmentation in Social Media Marketing and Brand Equity: A Study in Food and Beverage Industry. International Journal of Economics, Management and Accounting.

Antesty, S., Susilawati, M., Selan, D.D., & Thalib, N. (2023). Government Support and Social Media Impact on the Performance and Sustainability of F&B's MSME in Indonesia. International Journal of Business, Law, and Education.

Devi, J. A., & Chandrasekar, K. S. (2023). Digital Marketing in the Food Service Industry in India: A Review. i-Manager's Journal on Economics & Commerce, 3(1), 29.

Fahmi, M., Arif, M., Farisi, S.A., & Purnama, N.I. (2019). Peran Brand Image dalam Memediasi Pengaruh Social Media Marketing terhadap Repeat Purchase pada Fast-Food Restaurant di Kota Medan.

Hasugian, B.S., & Indallah, T.W. (2022). The Role of Digital Marketing and Social Media Strategies in The Development of The Culinary Business for Young Business Leaders.

Rajeh Hanaysha, J., Sharma, A., & M. Momani, A. (2021). An Exploration of Social Media Marketing Features and Brand Loyalty in the Fast-Food Industry. Journal of Content Community and Communication.

Riaz, H., Ahmed, H., & Akhtar, S. (2019). *The Role of Social Media Marketing on Building Brand Equity (An Insight of Fast Food Industry of Pakistan)*. New Media and Mass Communication. DOI: 10.22161/ijels.4.2.30

Utami, H.N., Wiyono, S.N., Ishmah, H.A., & Hayuni, H.Z. (2024). Building Brand Awareness Through Product Quality and Social Media Marketing For Food Service Business Development. Journal of Law and Sustainable Development.

Chapter 8
The Impact of Evolving Technologies on Restaurant Consumer Health:
A Systematic Review

Jia Yanan
Taylor's University, Malaysia

Anshul Garg
https://orcid.org/0000-0001-8297-9256
Taylor's University, Malaysia & Graphic Era, India

Kandappan Balasubramanian
https://orcid.org/0000-0001-7634-4676
Taylor's University, Malaysia

ABSTRACT

As technological facilities and devices become increasingly popular in restaurants, restaurant consumers are increasingly influenced by technologies. With the increase in consumer health needs, the impact of technology on consumer health has gradually received more attention. This study employs bibliometrics and thematic analysis methods to review and analyse 52 English journal articles from WoS and Scopus from five aspects: research focus, time overlay, methodological characteristics, theoretical framework, and research topics. The results reveal that previous studies have explored the relationship between various types of restaurant technology and consumer health behaviours, health literacy, physical health, mental health, social health, and health literacy from multiple disciplines. In addition, existing studies mainly focus on the impact of health information presented by technology on consumer health. Finally, after a comprehensive review and summary of previous studies, this study puts forward specific suggestions for future research based on the gaps in existing research.

DOI: 10.4018/979-8-3693-7683-6.ch008

INTRODUCTION

With the improvement of people's living standards, consumer demand for the restaurant industry is no longer limited to meeting basic dietary needs but has expanded to pursue added value offered by restaurants. For example, consumers' demand for personalization, speed and variety of restaurant products is increasing (Ma et al., 2023; Manhas et al., 2024). The application of technology in the restaurant industry adapts to these increasingly diversified needs of consumers. For example, the smart ordering system meets consumers' demand for personalized product combinations, and the restaurant's self-service checkout platform meets consumers' demand for speed (Gu et al., 2023; Wong et al., 2022). While meeting the diverse needs of consumers, the application of technology in the restaurant industry also has some basic advantages. For example, compared with human employees, the services provided by robot waiters are more advantageous and attractive in terms of quality stability and accuracy (Zhang et al., 2022).

With the diversification of consumer needs, the demand for healthy products in the restaurant industry has also been gradually increasing. Especially affected by global events related to health and hygiene, such as COVID-19, consumers' attention to health needs has been further enhanced, and health problems in restaurants have gradually been exposed to the public's attention (Dai et al., 2022). Restaurant consumers pay more attention to the quality of food and beverages, the nutritional value of food, and even the impact of services on consumers' physical and mental health (Ganesh, 2024; Mahmoud et al., 2024). Some technologies that can be applied in restaurants can meet consumers' health needs to a certain extent. For example, the smart ordering system can provide a more balanced food combination according to consumers' needs, which not only makes the best use of food's nutritional value but also supports consumers' physical health by improving the dietary structure (Mandracchia et al., 2022).

However, limited research have focused on exploring the impact of restaurant technology on consumer health. Many related studies are scattered across research on other topics. In particular, most of the research on how restaurant technology affects consumer health is included in the research of other topics. However, as consumers' health needs continue to increase, researchers and restaurant managers need to have a deeper understanding of how restaurant technology impacts consumers' health. In addition, health includes multiple dimensions. According to the recommendations of the World Health Organization, health refers not only to physical health but also to mental health and social health (The World Health Organization, 1946). At the same time, some scholars point out that while paying attention to individual health status, we should also pay attention to their health behaviours and health literacy (Rudd et al., 2023). The limited existing articles that focus on the impact of restaurant technology on consumers only explore it from a single health dimension. For example, Abell et al. (2024) proved through 4 studies that the digital ordering system in restaurants will increase the proportion of consumers choosing unhealthy foods. Therefore, there is still a lack of research exploring the impact of restaurant technology on consumers' health experience from a holistic perspective.

Therefore, in the context of a lack of research to describe how restaurant technology affects consumer health in an overall manner, this study attempts to extract and integrate relevant clues from existing research. This study aims to enrich the research perspectives related to restaurant technology, provide theoretical support for researchers to explore restaurant consumer health, and emphasize the important role of the rational application of restaurant technology in improving consumer health.

METHODOLOGY

This paper follows the systematic quantitative approach for conducting a literature review (Pickering & Byrne, 2014). This method has been widely used in high-quality literature reviews in the hospitality industry (Jia et al., 2024; Le et al., 2019; Li et al., 2023). Specifically, the research process in this study includes five steps. The first step is to select the research topic and determine the research objectives. Second, the search criteria are formulated to ensure that the literature related to the research objectives can be obtained with minimal omissions. Then, the literature search is conducted in the selected database, and the first round of screening is performed. The fourth step is to carefully read the screened literature, conduct the second round of screening and record the information related to the research objectives of this study. In addition, the problems found during the reading process should also be recorded. Finally, the recorded information and the problems are discussed and conclusions that can explain the research objectives are proposed.

After determining the research goal to explore the impact of restaurant technology on consumer health, this study selected Web of Science (WoS) and Scopus as databases to search for research papers in English journals related to this topic. The selection of databases was based on previous systematic literature reviews (Elkhwesky & Elkhwesky, 2023; Jia et al., 2024; Li et al., 2023). The search keywords included restaurant, consumer, health, technology, and synonyms for these four terms. The search scope included title, keywords, and abstract. To examine the changes in the sub-topics over time, this study did not set a time limit when searching for articles. The authors conducted a search in August 2024 and obtained 412 and 311 articles from WoS and Scopus, respectively. Because there are overlapping parts in the journals included in the two databases, this study first screened non-duplicate literature and obtained a total of 584 non-duplicate literature. Subsequently, the researchers conducted further screening by reading abstracts and full texts. Finally, 52 research papers closely related to the research topic were obtained. The process of literature retrieval and screening in this study is illustrated in Figure 1.

Figure 1. Screening Process

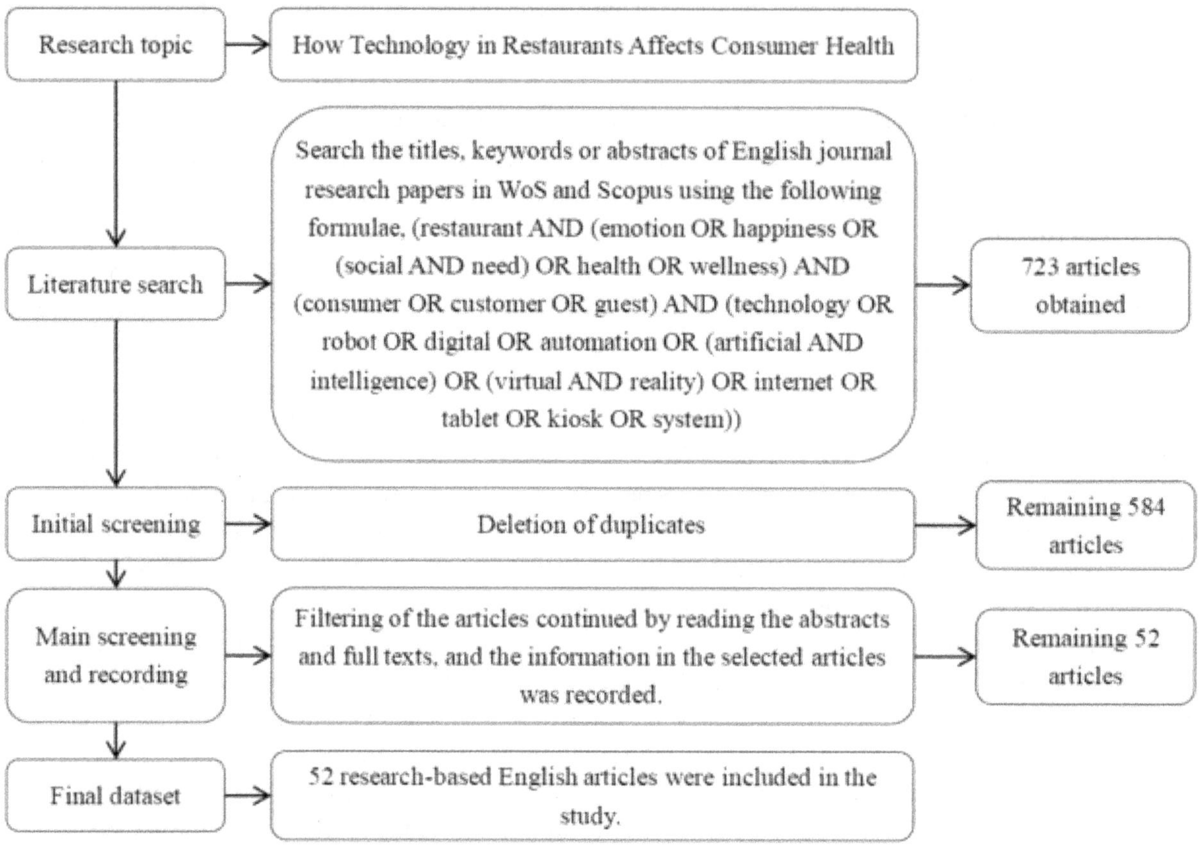

Note. Created by the authors.

Subsequently, this study conducted statistics and analysis of the 44 documents obtained. The analysis process consisted two parts. The first part involved basic descriptive statistics to show the development status of research related to this topic. It included statistics and simple analysis of the journals to which the articles belong, as well as statistics and analysis of the number of articles published year by year. In addition, this study also employed VOSviewer software to conduct co-occurrence analysis and temporal analysis on the keywords in the selected articles, referencing to previous studies (H. Kim & So, 2022; Li et al., 2023). Keyword co-occurrence analysis could show the potential connection between keywords, thereby helping researchers to identify research hotspots in the field. Overlay analysis could show the frequency changes of keywords over time. The combination of the results of overlay analysis and the overall trend of the number of articles published each year could reveal the migration of hotspots that researchers were concerned about under this topic. When using VOSviewer for keyword analysis, this study chose to include the keywords specified by the article, the author's keywords, and the keywords generated by the database in the research scope to make up for the problems caused by the limited number of overall articles. After setting up synonym replacement, VOSviewer identified a total of 428 keywords, of which 74 keywords appeared 2 times or more. After manual screening of the keywords, the remaining 59 keywords were included in the analysis.

Subsequently, to gain a deeper and more detailed understanding of the progress and status of the sub-topics under this research topic, the authors coded and classified the literature included in the statistics. According to the topics of concern, the authors marked the restaurant technology-related content involved in each study and the categories of consumer health affected. Since a total of 52 articles were included in the study, the coding process was divided into 4 rounds, and two authors coded 11 articles in each round. After each round of coding, the two authors involved in the coding need to compare their coding results to ensure that the degree of consensus is 90% or more before the next round of coding. The opinions that cannot be unified are decided after discussion by a third researcher. The coding process and the recording of the basic content of the article were carried out simultaneously. During this process, the researchers also needed to record in detail the research methods, theoretical basis, conclusions and limitations of the research used in the article.

CHARACTERISTICS OF RESEARCH

Temporal and Journal Distribution of Publications

By sorting out the publication time of relevant studies and the frequency of their appearance in different journals, this study obtained Figure 2 and Table 1. Figure 2 shows the number of publications in each year and the cumulative number of publications obtained from the WoS and Scopus databases. As can be seen from the figure, the topic of the impact of technology on consumer health has received less attention. Although the annual number of publications on this topic generally showed a fluctuating and slowly rising trend, compared with the overall development trend and publication volume of restaurant technology-related research (Gonzalez et al., 2022; Moreno & Tejada, 2019; Wang & Wang, 2021), this topic still received relatively limited attention. Between 2013 and 2015, the growth rate of the number of related studies accelerated and then slowed down. This might be related to the entry into force of the Affordable Care Act (ACA) in the United States in 2010, which required restaurants to provide product impact information to help consumers make healthier choices (Bedard & Kuhn, 2015). In 2020 and thereafter, the growth rate of the number of related studies had increased slightly again. Combined with the findings of other studies (Wang & Wang, 2021), this study speculated that this increase in growth rate may be due to the impact of the COVID-19 pandemic. In order to reduce the risk of infection caused by interpersonal contact, the popularity of technology in restaurants has increased overall, and related topics have received more attention (J.K. Kim et al., 2023).

Figure 2. Publication Count by Year

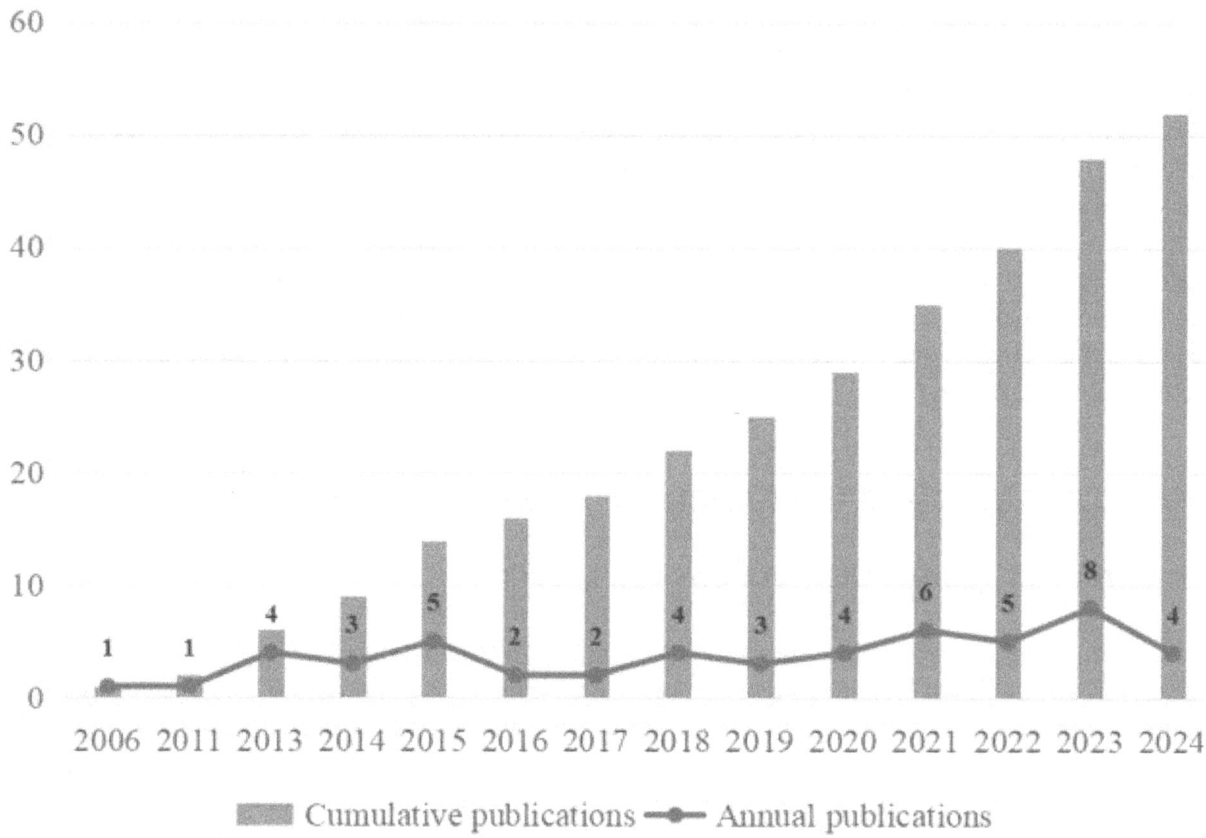

Note. Created by the authors.

Table 1 shows the publications corresponding to the included literature with a frequency greater than 2, as well as the specific frequency of occurrence. Among them, Appetite has the largest number of articles related to the impact of technology in restaurants on consumer health, including 6 related articles. The second is the International Journal of Hospitality and Management, which contains 4 related articles. Then followed by American Journal of Preventive Medicine, Journal of Hospitality and Tourism Technology and Plos One, each with 3 related articles. There are 29 journals that are not displayed, each containing 1 related article. The journals containing 2 related articles are Foods and Public Health Nutrition. From the overall journal distribution, this topic has attracted the attention of multiple disciplines, such as public health, hotel and tourism management, food science, and behavioural science.

Table 1. Publication Distribution

Publication Title	Frequency
Appetite	6
International Journal Of Hospitality Management	4
American Journal Of Preventive Medicine	3
Journal Of Hospitality And Tourism Technology	3
Plos One	3
Foods	2
Public Health Nutrition	2

Note. Created by the authors.

Keyword Co-occurrence Analysis

The word frequency co-occurrence results obtained by the researchers through VOSviewer are shown in Figure 3, and the temporal analysis result of the keywords is shown in Figure 4. The lines between the keywords represent that they appear in the same document. The thicker the lines, the higher the number of co-occurrences. The closer the distance between the keywords with higher the correlation. In addition, the diameter of the circle represents the frequency of keyword occurrence. The higher the frequency of the keyword, the larger the diameter of the circle. According to the processing results of VOSviewer, it can be found that the keywords are divided into four clusters. The red cluster is the largest cluster with the largest number of keywords, containing a total of 27 keywords. The keywords with the highest proportion in this cluster are obesity, consumer, fast, food, child, nutrition information, and menu labeling, and their weight of links are all over 20. This cluster mainly focuses on issues related to nutritional health and dietary health, including both health information provided by restaurants and consumers' healthy eating behaviours. From the overlay visualization in Figure 4, we can see that the topics related to emotion, food safety, and digital marketing in this cluster are new topics, while the topics related to menu planning, behaviour, purchases, and consumer health information are the topics that have received attention in the early years.

Figure 3. Keywords Co-occurrence

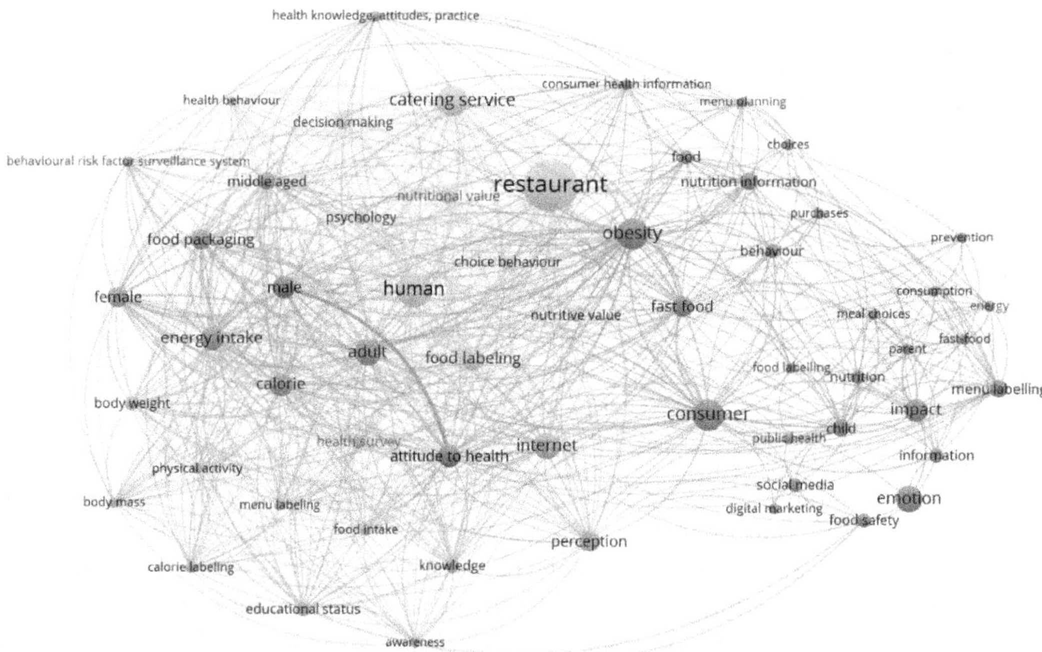

Note. Created by the authors.

Figure 4. Overlay Visualization

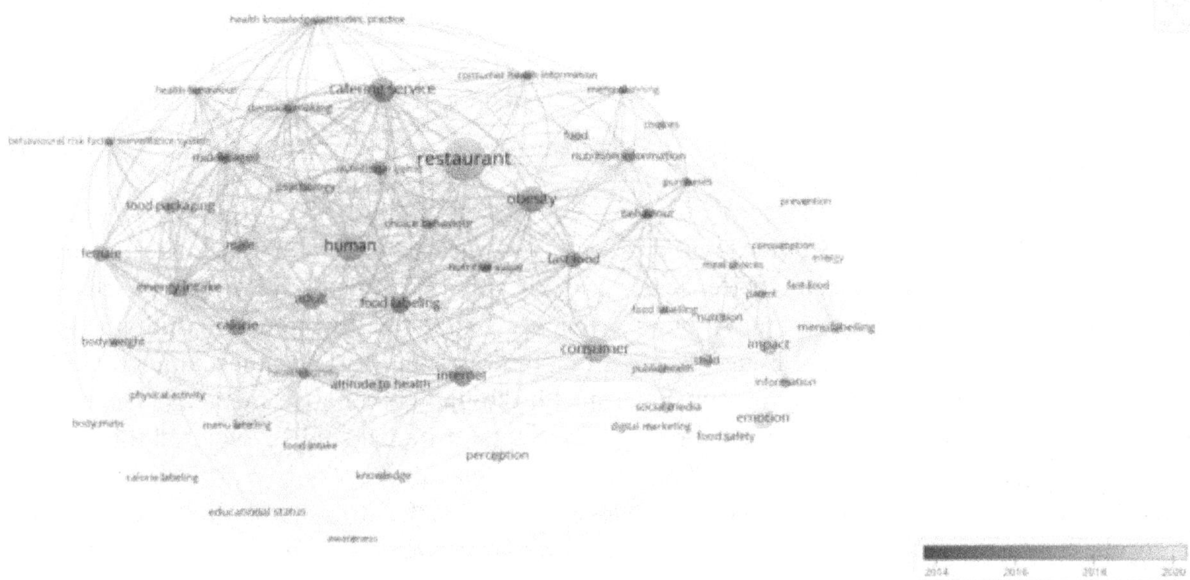

Note. Created by the authors.

The green cluster contains 12 keywords, among which the high-frequency keywords are body mass, calorie labelling, and physical activity. This shows that this cluster mainly focuses on issues related to health behaviour and weight management. In addition, according to Figure 4, it can be found that compared with other clusters, the distribution of the year of appearance of this cluster is relatively new. The average year of appearance of most keywords is after 2018. This shows that research related to restaurant consumers' weight management and health behaviour has received attention in recent years. The blue cluster contains 10 keywords, among which the high-frequency words related to health include calories, energy intake, and attitude to health. This shows that this cluster focuses on issues related to consumers' health attitudes and dietary behaviours. In this cluster, some words related to demographic characteristics appear, indicating that the content of this cluster not only focuses on consumers' health attitudes and dietary behaviours but also emphasizes the differences between different groups. The clues provided in Figure 4 show that the average publication year of keywords in this cluster is between 2015 and 2018.

The yellow cluster contains 10 keywords. High-frequency keywords include catering service, food labelling, nutritional value and choice behaviour. Although the themes represented by this cluster overlap to some extent with the red cluster, there are significant differences. The yellow cluster mainly focuses on discussing the impact of nutritional information on labels on consumer choice behaviour. The research scope is relatively specific, and the average appearance time of most keywords is concentrated from 2014 to 2017. The red cluster is an extension of the yellow cluster and has a wider range. In terms of content, the red cluster covers the impact of nutritional information on the micro level (consumers' personal behaviour) and even the macro level (public health of consumer groups). In terms of time range, the red cluster covers a wider time span (2009 to 2022). The visualization results of the time distribution of keywords (Figure 4) show that with the development of time, the research topics are constantly being refined. For example, the content of food labels is refined into specific contents such as energy, nutritional value, calories, etc., and consumer health is refined into personal health behaviours, health attitudes, public health, etc. However, it is worth noting that the topic of this study is the impact of restaurant technology on consumer health, but technology-related words appear less frequently. During a detailed reading of the literature, the authors found that most past studies focused on how technology, as a carrier of information, affects consumers' health. The specific content will be explained in detail below.

Methodological Nature

The 52 articles obtained were divided into three categories according to the research design, namely qualitative research articles, quantitative research articles and mixed research articles. Based on this classification standard, the authors drew Figure 5 according to the publication year and whether the article has a clear theoretical basis. Figure 5 shows that the vast majority of studies attempt to explain the impact of restaurant technology on consumer health through quantitative methods. There are 43 quantitative research articles, accounting for 82.7 of the total. Limited studies explored this research topic using purely qualitative methods. Among the 52 articles collected, only 3 articles attempted to conduct research through qualitative methods, accounting for 5.8% of the total. And the number of purely qualitative research articles did not show a downward trend. Although the total number of articles using mixed research methods is not large, it has tended to increase in recent years compared to purely qualitative research articles.

Figure 5. Evolution of Research Types Over Time

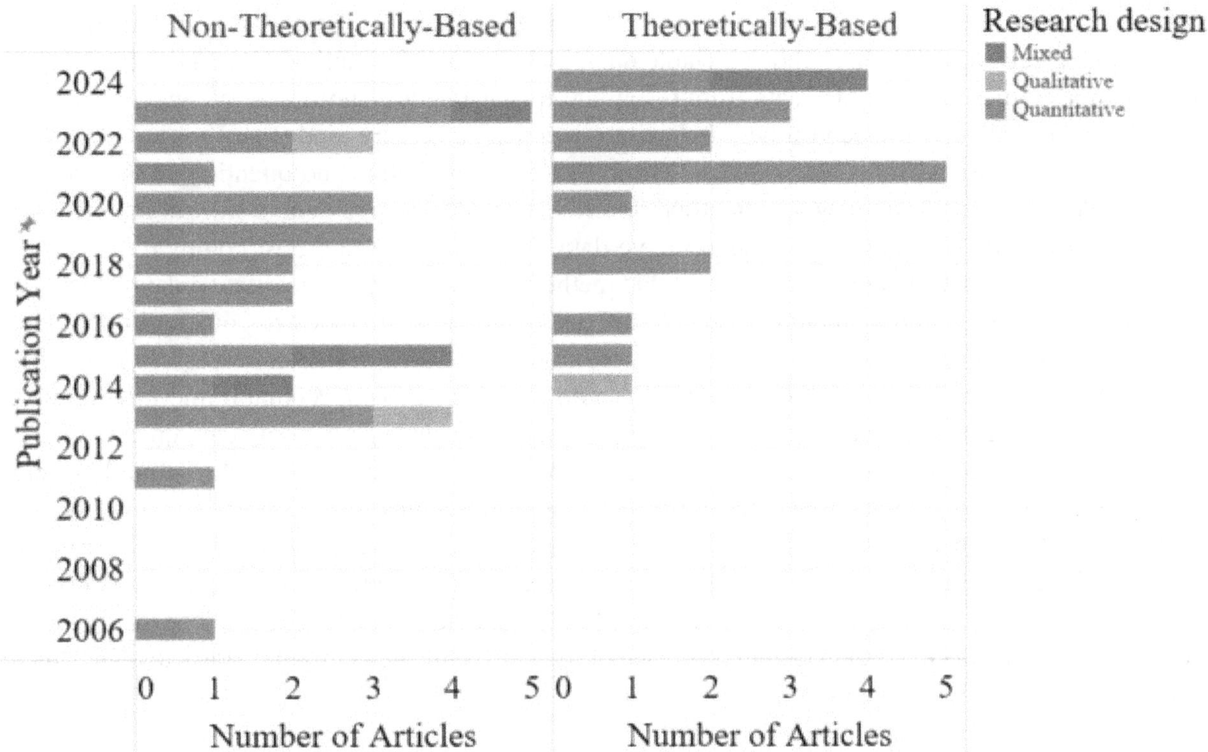

Note. Created by the authors.

The most commonly used data collection method in the quantitative research articles collected in this study is the survey method, and the most commonly used survey method is to distribute self-administered questionnaires to restaurant consumers (e.g., Chen & Girish, 2023; Kumar & Shah, 2021; Palisidis et al., 2016; Pang & Hammond, 2013). Some researchers have pointed out that self-administered questionnaires may affect the quality of the data obtained. For example, self-administered questionnaires distributed online exclude users who are not familiar with the Internet or do not use online survey platforms (C. Chen & Girish, 2023). Although the questionnaire informs participants that there is no right or wrong answer, some participants may be affected by the social desirability effect when filling out the questionnaire, leading their answers to deviate from their actual thoughts and actions (Jaeger & Cardello, 2022). Therefore, some studies have proposed that field experiments should be conducted and non-recall data should be collected through observation, expression information capture technology, etc., to improve the authenticity and reliability of the data (T. Kim et al., 2022; Okumus et al., 2018; Ruiz-Mafe et al., 2020).

Among the articles obtained in this study, the experimental method is the data collection method used the second most frequently after the survey. However, only a few studies adopted field experiments (Ong et al., 2023). Most studies that adopted the experimental method simulated different experimental scenarios by providing videos, texts or pictures on the Internet (Musicus et al., 2019; Prowse et al., 2020; Ratilla et al., 2022; Reinholdsson et al., 2023; Wei et al., 2022). Among the studies that adopted the experimental method, most studies used questionnaires to collect data during the experiment (X. Y. Leung & Wen, 2021; Musicus et al., 2019; Wei et al., 2022), and only a few collected data by observing the responses of participants (Lassen et al., 2014). Customer-generated content on the Internet and data in restaurant management systems also provide researchers with valuable research materials. For example, some studies collected online reviews posted by consumers who had dining experiences in restaurants that employed service robots, converted them into quantifiable data, and conducted quantitative analysis (Park et al., 2024). Some studies utilized sales data from restaurant management systems and the nutritional value of food to quantitatively study consumers' behaviour in choosing healthy food (Lee-Kwan et al., 2016).

Among the 52 articles obtained, 6 used a combination of qualitative and quantitative methods. In these articles, the most frequently used method for collecting quantitative data is still survey methods, and 5 articles used surveys to collect quantitative data. Interviews are the most common method for collecting qualitative data, and 3 articles used this method in the process of qualitative data collection. Some studies are based on qualitative research and use quantitative methods to conduct in-depth exploration and interpretation of the conclusions raised in the qualitative research process. For example, Peng et al. (2024) first interviewed restaurant consumers, constructed a conceptual framework based on the interview content, and then tested the conceptual framework through the collected questionnaires. Some are based on the conclusions of quantitative research and explain the relationships found in quantitative research through qualitative data. For example, questionnaires were first collected in Foodom restaurants in China in the form of surveys, and then content analysis was conducted on online reviews related to Foodom restaurants to provide qualitative insights related to the conclusions of quantitative research (Jiao et al., 2024). A total of 3 articles used only qualitative methods to explore the impact of technology on consumer health in restaurants. Two of them used the focus group method to collect data, and one collected online reviews as qualitative data.

Theoretical Framework and Applications

The statistical results of publications show that the research related to the topic of this study has a wide range of disciplinary backgrounds. Therefore, it is necessary to count and analyse the theories applied in these studies. The sorting of relevant theories is conducive to a deeper understanding of the theoretical connections between different disciplines and promotes the theoretical integration and innovation of this interdisciplinary theme. The statistical results show that 61.54% of the collected articles lack a theoretical basis. Figure 5 clearly shows the gap in the number of studies with a theoretical basis and those without a theoretical basis. Figure 5 also shows that before 2017, the research on this topic was not significantly based on a theoretical foundation. However, after 2017, this situation has changed. The number of studies with a theoretical basis has increased rapidly and exceeded the number of studies without a theoretical basis in a short period of time. This study sorted out the theories mentioned in the articles, and the results are shown in Table 2.

Table 2. Theoretical Application Frequency

Theory	Frequency
Stimulus-Organism-Response (SOR) Theory	3
Cognitive Appraisal Theory	2
Nudge Theory	2

continued on following page

Table 2. Continued

Theory	Frequency
Consumer Values Theory	1
Customer Mind-Set Model	1
Elaboration Likelihood Model	1
Emotional Contagion Theory	1
Equity Theory	1
Expectancy-Disconfirmation Theory	1
Feelings-As-Information Theory	1
Fogg Behaviour Model	1
Halo Effect Theory	1
Health Belief Model	1
Pleasure Arousal Dominance Theory	1
Self-Determination Theory	1
Service Dominant Logic Theory	1
Social Comparison Theory	1
Social Exchange Theory	1
Theory Of Planned Behaviour	1
Uncanny Valley Theory	1
Unified Theory of Acceptance and Use of Technology (UTAUT)	1
Value-Attitude-Behaviour Model	1

Note. Created by the authors.

In the 20 articles with a theoretical basis, a total of 22 theories were mentioned. The most frequently appearing theory is the Stimulus-Organism-Response (SOR) Theory, which was applied in 3 articles. The second most frequently appearing theory is the Cognitive Appraisal Theory and the Nudge Theory, which appeared 2 times respectively. The remaining theories appeared once each. The disciplinary backgrounds involved in these theories are mainly concentrated in three disciplines, including psychology (such as SOR Theory, Cognitive Appraisal Theory and Emotional Contagion Theory), sociology (such as Equity Theory and Social Exchange Theory), and marketing (such as Consumer Values Theory, Customer Mind-Set Model and Service-Dominant Logic Theory).

RESEARCH TOPICS ANALYSIS

This study categorised and coded the types of technology and consumer health involved in each article. It should be noted that it has become common to use electronic menus on flat plates, electronic screens, self-service machines, and mobile clients to order and view food information in restaurants (Zhang et al., 2020). In this context, the authors also took into account some content that did not clearly indicate whether electronic technology was used to display menu information or food label information during the coding process and classified them into the electronic menu category. Based on the coded data, the authors produced Figures 6 and 7, which show the distribution of different research topics in different regions and at different times. It should be noted that because some studies focus on multiple types of technology or multiple types of consumer health at the same time, the total number of these topics is greater than the total number of included articles. The authors identified 6 types of technology in previous studies on the impact of restaurant technology on consumer health, namely electronic menus or labels, ordering or delivery systems, social media, restaurant data management systems, virtual reality and service robots. One study which is also related to restaurant technology, but the technology in this article refers to multiple categories, so it is coded separately as technology (Ling et al., 2023). As can be seen from Figure 6, the most popular technology type is electronic menus and electronic labels, the most popular health type is health behaviour, and the country that pays the most attention to this research topic is the United States, followed by China. Next, this study will analyse the status and main conclusions of each research topic according to different health types.

Figure 6. Regional Distribution of Research Topics

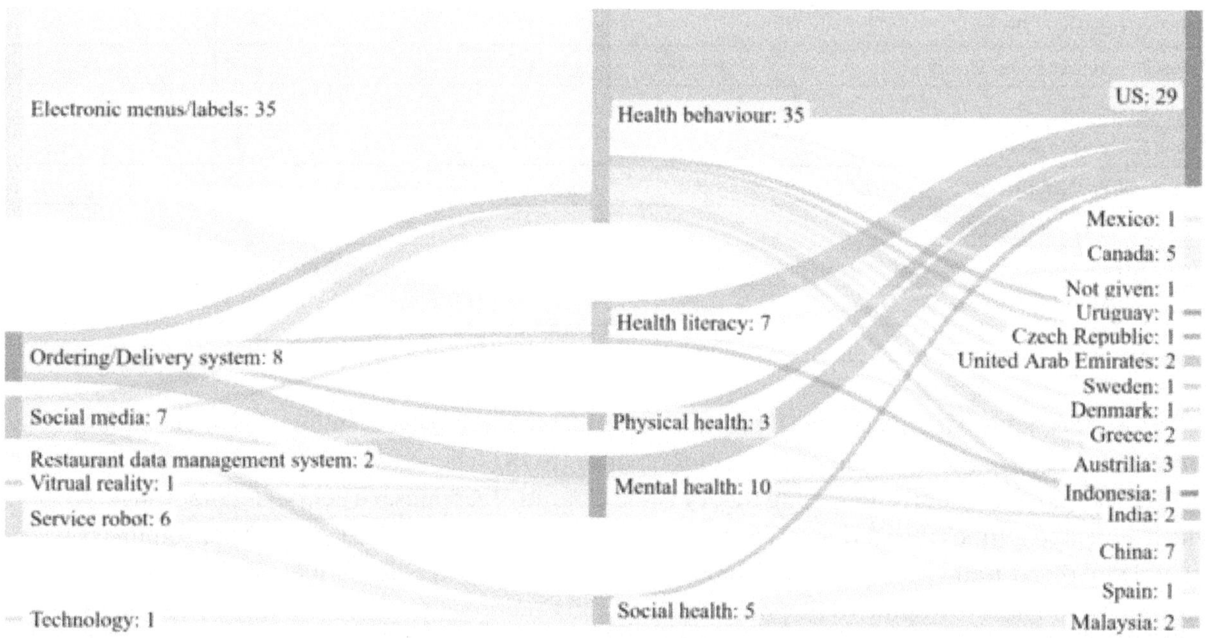

Note. Created by the authors.

Figure 7. Publication Trends by Health Type Over Time

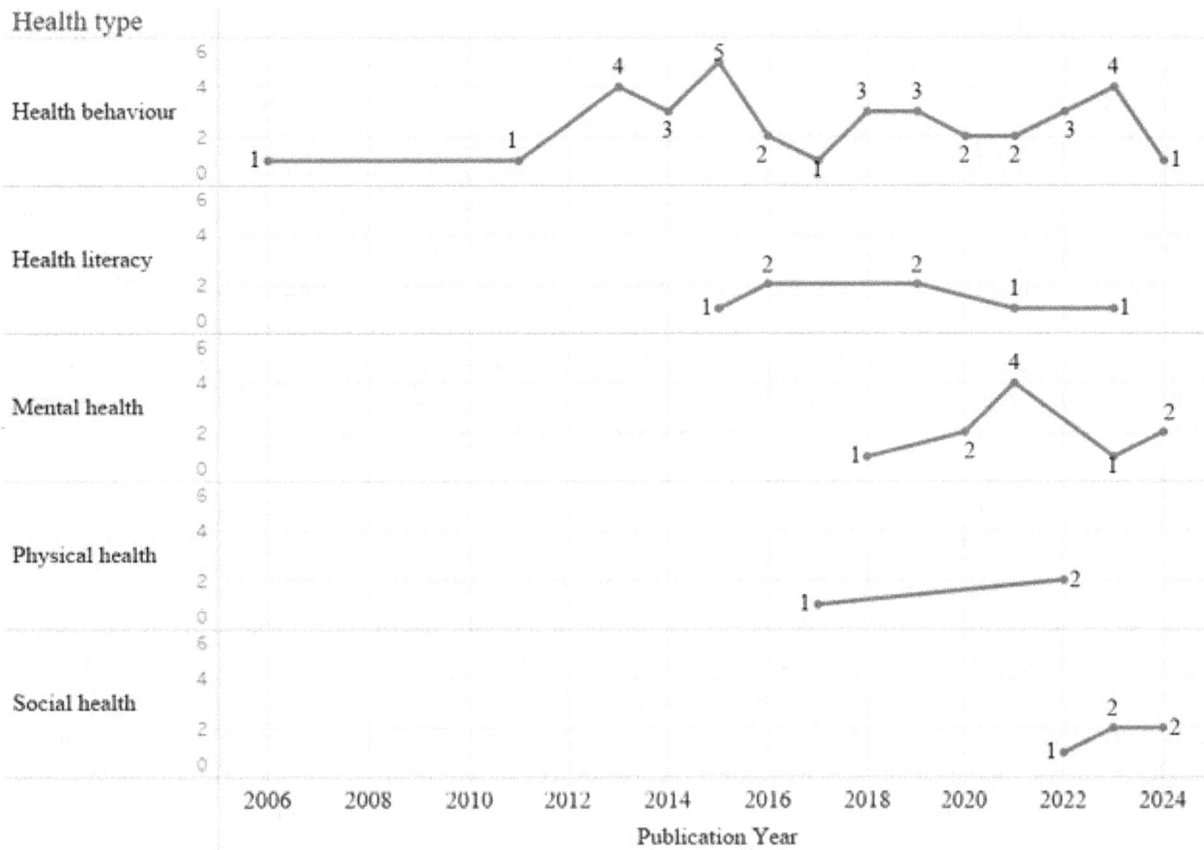

Note. Created by the authors.

Consumer's Health Behaviour

Health behaviour is closely related to the overall health level of an individual, especially for restaurant consumers, whose food choices are closely related to their health. Because the safety, nutritional value and energy of food affect the health of an individual (Dai et al., 2022; T. Kim et al., 2022; Sadilek et al., 2017). Therefore, health behaviour, especially the behaviour of choosing healthy food, has become the research focus of researchers who are concerned about the health of restaurant consumers. Figures 6 and 7 show that 35 articles focus on consumers' health behaviour. Researchers have paid attention to this topic for the longest time, and related research has been published every year since 2013.

Electronic menus and labels are the type of technology most associated with consumer health behaviours. However, such technological devices do not directly affect consumers' health. What directly impacts on consumer health is the health information provided by such technological devices, and these devices only serve as carriers of health information. Information about food on electronic menus and labels can influence consumers' food choices, and health-related information can increase consumers' probability of choosing healthy foods. For example, research has found that labels on calories and sodium content on menus can have a significant impact on consumers' healthy food choices, especially when choosing foods for children (Prowse et al., 2020). Such positive effects on health behaviours may be long-lasting. One study showed that if personalised health advice was provided on the printed receipt when consumers checked out, consumers who received the advice experienced an impact on their healthy eating behaviours for the next 50 weeks (Bedard & Kuhn, 2015). Health information on electronic menus can not only improve consumers' health status by improving their healthy food selection behaviour but also encourage consumers to actively increase their physical activity to maintain health. A study conducted by Restrepo (2017) in the United States showed that after restaurants used menus with calorie information, consumers not only consumed fewer calories per day but also consumed more calories per day.

Although consumers and researchers are optimistic about the positive impact of health information, some studies have pointed out that the presentation of health information alone is not enough for consumers to make wise food choices (Kalaivani et al., 2021; Ratilla et al., 2022). This is because consumers' health behaviours are not only affected by health information but also by other factors, such as the price and taste of food, as well as consumers' health literacy and personal preferences (Lassen et al., 2014; Ratilla et al., 2022).

Some scholars also pointed out that the reason why health labels on menus fail to play an ideal role may be because the information displayed on the labels is too complex or unattractive (Kalaivani et al., 2021). Therefore, in addition to the health labels on electronic menus affecting consumers' health behaviours, the design of the menu is also one of the important factors that affect consumers' health behaviours. Some researchers have found that improving the attractiveness, operability, and visibility of healthy food options on electronic menus increases the likelihood of consumers choosing healthy foods (Ratilla et al., 2022). In addition to the content and display form of information directly related to health on electronic menus that can have an impact on consumers' health behaviours, the promotional content on electronic menus also has the effect of improving consumers' health behaviours. For example, the position of healthy food promotion information on electronic menus has a significant role in improving consumers' behaviour of choosing healthy foods (Reinholdsson et al., 2023).

In addition to the health information on electronic menus or labels that can provide reference for restaurant consumers when making purchasing decisions, online reviews from social media are also an important reference source for consumption. For example, information about the ingredients of dishes in restaurants, information about the types of food, and the specific taste of dishes on Yelp can promote consumers' healthy eating behaviours (Ariyasriwatana et al., 2014). However, social media may also have a negative impact on consumers' health behaviours because it becomes a marketing tool for restaurants' unhealthy foods. For example, exposure of unhealthy diets and persuasive advertisements on social media have a negative impact on adolescents' food choice behaviours (Ares et al., 2022). In addition to the fact that the promotional information provided by merchants on social media may undermine consumers' healthy behaviours, the sharing of meals between consumers through social media may also lead to the same results. Compared with health information, consumers are more likely to share the taste and appearance of food on social media (Ariyasriwatana et al., 2014). The sharing and recommendation of fast food among consumers, as well as the eWOM of fast food on social media platforms, will affect consumers' fast food intake patterns, and fast food has been shown to be one of the causes of many health problems (Ali-Alsaadi et al., 2023). In addition, with the development of technology, some food ordering software attempts to introduce virtual service and influence consumer behaviour through the persuasion of virtual customer service. The persuasion strategy of virtual images with aspirational appeal in the food ordering system can influence consumers' choice of healthy food, and a beauty-oriented persuasion focus is more effective than a health-oriented persuasion focus (Hao et al., 2024).

Mental, Physical and Social Health

The World Health Organization pointed out that an individual's mental health, physical health and social health are three important components of health (The World Health Organization, 1946). Considering that mental health is a multidimensional concept, it includes emotional health, emotional health and cognitive health. Therefore, when coding, the authors referred to previous studies to identify factors associated with consumer mental health from multiple dimensions (Galderisi et al., 2015; Jia et al., 2024). However, during the coding process, it was found that the number of articles related to the mental health of restaurant consumers in the included articles was limited, and it was difficult to fully cover all dimensions of mental health. These articles only focus on consumers' emotional health or affective health, and they are not the core topics of these articles, but rather marginal ones.

Previous studies have explored the sources and processes of the impact on consumers' mental health and the sources and processes of the impact on consumers' health behaviours. Most previous research has primarily focused on the impact of information presented on restaurant technology devices or facilities when exploring consumers' health behaviours. In contrast, when exploring the impact of restaurant technology on consumers' mental health, previous studies have focused more on non-information factors of restaurant technology devices.

Among the 52 articles obtained, only one explored the positive impact of information presented on social media on consumer emotions (Ruiz-Mafe et al., 2020). Most articles, however, ffocus on the impact of the non-information instrumentality of restaurant technology devices on consumers' mental health. For example, the operability of the basic functions, entertainment functions and personalized customization functions of the ordering system based on interactive restaurant self-service technology can significantly enhance consumers' positive emotional responses (Ahn & Seo, 2018; X. Leung et al., 2021). Restaurant technology can also enhance consumers' positive emotions by stimulating their visual senses. For example, Torrico et al. (2020) used virtual reality technology to provide consumers with a virtual dining background and found that whether it is a bright virtual environment or a dark virtual environment, it will cause changes in consumers' mental status. However, not all visual cues presented by technology devices can have a significant impact on consumers' emotional responses. For example, the appearance of interactive self-service devices in restaurants has been found in some studies to be unable to significantly enhance consumers' emotional responses. Positive emotions (Ahn & Seo, 2018). Service robots have outstanding performance in improving consumers' mental health. Under appropriate circumstances, service robots' language style, service capabilities and appearance characteristics can have a positive impact on consumers' emotional health (C. Chen & Girish, 2023; Lu et al., 2021; Park et al., 2024; Peng et al., 2024). However, some studies have pointed out that due to the uncanny valley effect, some anthropomorphic features will have a negative impact on consumers' emotional health, but when robot services perform outstandingly, consumers can still have positive emotional experiences (Park et al., 2024).

There are only three articles related to consumers' physical health, the fewest among all health categories, and two of them involve technologies that do not provide direct catering services to consumers. Restaurant management systems, including their complaint management systems and adaptive inspection systems based on big data, can reduce the occurrence of foodborne diseases by monitoring and predicting the safety of restaurant food, thereby reducing the chances of consumers' health being harmed (T. Kim et al., 2022; Sadilek et al., 2017). This big data-based restaurant food safety management system has a significant effect on detecting foodborne outbreaks caused by pathogens with short incubation periods (T. Kim et al., 2022). In addition, technologies that provide direct catering services to consumers can also have an impact on consumers' physical health, but not directly. Dai et al. (2022) pointed out that the nutritional level of food available through the online ordering and delivery system is low, and this ordering method is popular with consumers because it provides convenience for consumers. However, this also leads consumers who order restaurant food through online ordering to face physical health problems such as weight gain and gastrointestinal discomfort.

Social health includes five aspects, namely social integration, social acceptance, social contribution, social actualization, and social coherence (Keyes, 1998). This study identified two types of social health: social integration and social contribution. Social integration refers to individuals' judgment of the quality of the relationship between them and the surrounding social individuals or groups. Social contribution refers to an individual's judgment of his own social value. The interaction between service robots and consumers in restaurants can enhance individuals' perceived social integration. For example, when a family with children goes to a robot restaurant to dine and interact with the robot, the sense of connection between family members of consumers is deepened (Peng et al., 2024). The interaction process between service robots and guests can also make guests feel that they have received social support, thereby enhancing their perceived social integration (Jiao et al., 2024). Social media also provides opportunities for restaurant consumers to improve their social integration. When consumers communicate about their dining experience in a restaurant on social media platforms, if they perceive that the interaction process is fair and they are understood, then the level of social integration perceived by consumers is higher (Wei et al., 2022). In addition, social media can also affect consumers' social contribution. When consumers are exposed to promotional content on restaurants' social media platforms that advocate reducing food waste, their sense of social responsibility will be positively affected, and they will be more willing to improve their social value by practising behaviours that resist food waste (Ong et al., 2023).

Health Literacy

The number of articles related to health literacy is only 7, but this study still describes it as a separate part. This is because, in addition to these 7 articles, many other articles did not focus on how consumer health literacy is affected, but they pointed out the importance of health literacy (Ariyasriwatana et al., 2014; Dai et al., 2022; Finkelstein et al., 2011; Liu et al., 2015). Health literacy refers to an individual's ability to acquire and internalise health-related information and services, as well as externalise health knowledge into healthy decisions and behaviours (Santana et al., 2021). Research related to health literacy has focused on the information presented by restaurant technology. For example, R. Chen et al. (2015) pointed out that although the calorie information on the menu did not significantly change consumers' behaviour of making healthy choices based on the information, calorie labels significantly improved restaurant consumers' knowledge of food calorie information and health consciousness. The presentation form of information on social media can affect consumers' ability to identify health risk information, that is, it improves individuals' ability to process information, and therefore can also improve consumers' health literacy (Ray & Merle, 2021). The experience of using online food delivery systems will also have an impact on consumers' food safety and health knowledge, however, this impact may be negative.

Because when they rely too much on prompts from the delivery system to make decisions, their ability to externalise food safety knowledge will be weakened (Mulyanto et al., 2023).

Other factors

These studies suggest that consumers' personal characteristics play an important moderating role in the impact of restaurant technology on health. Firstly, there are differences in the health needs of consumers with different education levels, which leads to differences in the impact of the health information provided on the menu on their health behaviours. Research shows that consumers with higher levels of education have more positive attitudes towards health labels (Ismail et al., 2023). Secondly, family responsibilities or roles also have a significant impact on consumers' choice of healthy foods based on health information on menus. Research by Doub et al. (2015) found that compared with young people without children, young people who became parents were more likely to make food choices based on health information on electronic menus or mobile ordering tools. This may be because family responsibilities require them to make more efforts for family health, and health information on electronic menus can reduce this effort, so they are more susceptible to the influence of these messages.

Individual health awareness, especially overall health literacy, also has an important impact on the relationship between restaurant technology and consumer health. Studies have shown that consumers with higher health literacy are more likely to use health resources in restaurants, thereby gaining a better health experience (Ariyasriwatana et al., 2014). In contrast, consumers with lower health literacy may fail to make health-friendly decisions because they are not sensitive enough to health information or lack sufficient health knowledge (Liu et al., 2015; Roberto et al., 2013). In addition, socioeconomic status also affects consumers' choices after seeing health information on the menu (Niven et al., 2019). Lastly, personal needs also play a role in the process of restaurant technology affecting consumer health. The types of needs explored in this study include health needs, recognition needs, and information needs (R. Chen et al., 2015; Wei et al., 2022). Individual needs can enhance individuals' identification and externalisation of information related to their needs. For example, when consumers have health needs, they are more likely to make health-promoting decisions based on the information provided by the restaurant (Courtney et al., 2018).

CONCLUSIONS AND IMPLICATIONS

Main findings

This systematic literature review is the first to summarize the impact of technology used in restaurants on consumer health. Unlike previous review articles that focused on restaurant technology, this study focuses on consumers' health. Previous studies have mostly focused on issues related to restaurant management, such as the current status of technology facilities in the catering industry (Kaman et al., 2024; Spence, 2023) and their role in enhancing operational management (Duong et al., 2020). There are few review articles from the perspective of consumers. In addition, this study has expanded the concept of consumer health as much as possible. In addition to incorporating physical health, mental health, and social health proposed by the World Health Organization into the research scope, this study also includes health behaviours and health literacy. This way of expanding the extension of consumer health provides an opportunity to look at how restaurant technology affects consumer health from a more holistic and comprehensive perspective. In addition, this study used a variety of methods to analyse the obtained literature, such as bibliometric analysis, content analysis, and thematic analysis. This mixed review method can provide the authors with a dynamic perspective to look at the progress and status of this topic.

The results of bibliometrics show that although the number of studies on the impact of restaurant technology on consumer health is increasing, the growth trend is fluctuating and relatively slow. The two time points with large fluctuations both occurred after relatively influential health-related events. The first fluctuation was a leap-forward growth that occurred in 2013. Most of these studies mentioned the provisions of the 2010 Affordable Care Act related to health information labelling on menus (Lassen et al., 2014; Pang & Hammond, 2013; Roberto et al., 2013). The second fluctuation occurred in 2020. After remaining stable for 4 years from 2016 to 2019, it began to show a growth trend in 2020. Existing studies have pointed out that the number of consumer health-related studies in other hospitality industries also experienced similar fluctuations around 2020, and it is speculated that this may be caused by sudden public health events (Jia et al., 2024). Based on this, the authors speculate that the increase in the number of studies related to restaurant consumer health in 2020 is due to COVID-19 accelerating the use of technology in restaurants and raising people's health awareness.

The cluster analysis of keywords in this study clearly shows the focus of restaurant technology on consumer health. The results of word frequency co-occurrence indicate that all four clusters involve health-related information, such as food labelling, calorie labelling, and nutrition information. This indicates that in the existing research on the impact of restaurant technology on consumer health, researchers mainly focus on the impact of information presented on restaurant technology facilities on consumer health. This may be because the research hotspots change with the emergence and development of new phenomena. Information technology is the earliest and most widely used technology in restaurants (Doran, 2010), so the impact of information technology on consumer health is both the earliest and most concerning.

In addition, this study also analysed the subject areas that focus on this topic. The results show that the impact of technology on the health of restaurant consumers is a topic of common concern among multiple disciplines, and the subject area that has made the main contribution to this topic is the public health field of medicine. The results in Figure 5 show that in the early years of this topic, researchers tended to use quantitative methods to study the impact of restaurant technology on consumer health without theoretical support. The authors sorted out the disciplines of the journals corresponding to these articles and found that quantitative research articles without theoretical basis were mainly published in publications in the fields of public health, medicine, food science, and engineering technology. They mostly belong to the categories of applied science or natural science. Articles with a theoretical basis are mostly published in publications in the category of social science. With the increasing attention paid to consumer health in the field of social sciences, especially in the fields of management and marketing, the number of articles with theoretical basis has shown a clear growth trend in recent years.

Finally, the thematic analysis further comprehensively shows the specific situation of the impact of restaurant technology on consumer health in existing research, including the types of restaurant technology and the types of consumer health. The results of the theme analysis show that the types of technology that have an impact on consumer health in existing research mainly include six categories: electronic menus or labels, ordering or delivery systems, social media, restaurant data management systems, virtual reality, and service robots. The content related to consumer health that researchers focus on includes consumer health behaviour, mental health, physical health, social health, and health literacy. After completing the theme classification from two perspectives, the authors produced Figure 6 and explained in detail how each type of technology affects consumer health and which type of health is affected in existing research. These findings not only help researchers identify gaps in existing research but also provide suggestions for restaurant managers to guide them to improve consumers' health experiences.

Future research suggestions

After analysing existing research on the impact of restaurant technology on consumer health from multiple perspectives, this study proposes suggestions for future research from the perspectives of the overall theme, research topics, and research methods. Overall, the impact of restaurant technology on consumer health from the perspective of social sciences is still a topic worth exploring. Although this study obtained a total of 52 articles, a considerable number of them, especially those in the field of social sciences, did not take consumer health as the main central theme, but addressed it as a marginal topic. This shows that in the field of social sciences, research topics related to consumer health are still an area to be developed. Therefore, researchers need to conduct in-depth discussions on the possible impacts on the health of restaurant consumers in a qualitative research method, so as to provide a theoretical basis for future quantitative research.

In addition to showing the specific distribution of existing research topics, Figure 6 also indicates which topics still have research gaps. For example, Figure 6 indicates that researchers have verified that electronic menus or labels have an impact on consumer health behaviour and health literacy, but have ignored the impact of electronic menus or labels on consumers' physical health, mental health, and social health. In addition, there are some other research gaps, such as the relationship between ordering or delivery system and consumer social health, the relationship between social media and physical health, the relationship between virtual reality and other health factors besides mental health, the relationship between the restaurant management system and other health factors besides physical health, and the relationship between service robot and health behaviour, health literacy, and physical health are all topics that need to be explored.

In addition, among the articles included in this study, most of the articles focus on the positive impact of technology on consumer health, and only a few studies point out the negative impact of technology on consumer health (Ares et al., 2022; Dai et al., 2022; Park et al., 2024). Therefore, future research can also continue to improve this research topic by focusing on the negative impact of restaurant technology on consumer health. Researchers can try to explore the negative impacts of technology on consumers' health from multiple perspectives. In addition to examining the negative health effects of technological devices directly on consumers during the interaction process, researchers can also investigate how some technical drawbacks of technological devices indirectly, invisibly, or persistently affect consumers' health. For example, if consumers' information is leaked by technological devices in a restaurant, will it have a psychological impact on them, leading to lasting psychological disorders? As pointed out in many studies, some technological devices can rely on big data to make reasonable dining recommendations to consumers. Whether algorithmic bias will further damage consumers' health through the mismatch between dining recommendations and consumers' health status is also a topic worthy of in-depth discussion.

When conducting thematic analysis, the researchers also sorted out the countries where the was conducted, as shown in Figure 6. Future research can also explore research gaps from a regional perspective. Figure 6 shows that except for the United States, other countries do not cover all types of consumer health factors. Taking China as an example, although existing research has focused on the impact of restaurant technology on consumer health behaviours, physical health, mental health, and social health, it has not focused on the impact on health literacy. Therefore, researchers who focus on Chinese restaurant technology and consumer health might consider exploring how restaurant technology impacts consumer health literacy.

Finally, specific suggestions are made on research methods. Most of the existing quantitative studies related to this topic are cross-sectional studies, and although some topics have received attention in the early stage, they lack continuous follow-up and attention in the later stage. Some researchers who focus on this topic also pointed out that it is necessary to conduct dynamic observations on the impact of technology on consumer health through longitudinal studies (Hao et al., 2024; T. Kim et al., 2022; Kumar & Shah, 2021; Peng et al., 2024). Longitudinal studies not only allow researchers to observe the duration of the impact of technology in restaurants on consumer health, but also allow researchers to continuously observe the dynamic changes in the relationship between restaurant technology and consumer health. With the development of science and technology, the types and functions of technology are gradually enriched, and consumers' usage experience and adaptability have changed. Therefore, the impact of technology on consumers is also changing. In order to confirm the explanatory power of the research conclusions in the current context, the relationship between variables should be tested through longitudinal research.

Theoretical and practical implications

The theoretical implications of this study are mainly reflected in three aspects. First, this study sorted out and summarised previous studies on the impact of restaurant technology on consumer health, providing researchers who are concerned about the health of restaurant consumers with a holistic perspective on this topic. Second, this study classified previous studies according to restaurant technology type and consumer health type. This classification method can show the specific impact of different types of technology on consumer health in more detail, and can specifically show the status of research topics under this research topic. This study also sorted out, analysed and explained the reasons for the different impacts of different types of technology based on the conclusions of existing research. It provides evidence to support the gaps in existing research identified in this study.

In addition, through the classification of topics, this study also emphasises the multiple dimensions of consumer health, which enhances researchers' understanding of consumer health. Finally, this study summarises the research gaps in existing research based on the results of collation, summary and analysis and puts forward specific future research suggestions based on these gaps. Researchers can continue to explore the relationship between restaurant technology and consumer health based on these suggestions to enrich this research topic.

The summary of the conclusions from various studies on the impact of restaurant technology on consumer health can provide practical suggestions for restaurant consumers, restaurant practitioners, and suppliers of restaurant technology facilities. First, this article emphasises the importance of health to consumers and the importance of maintaining consumers' healthy experience in restaurants. Therefore, in order to enhance consumers' healthy experience, increase consumers' satisfaction and loyalty to restaurants, and contribute to the sustainable development of restaurants and even society, restaurant stakeholders should enhance the positive impact of restaurant technology on consumer health from multiple perspectives.

First, restaurant consumers should enhance their understanding of their own health status and improve their health literacy. Consumers who know they have health problems are more likely to improve their health status through the health information provided by restaurant technology. For example, obese people are more likely to notice the calorie information and impact information on the menu (Goodman et al., 2018). Therefore, when consumers can accurately grasp their health status and know what health problems they have, they are more likely to pay attention to and actively use the information related to their health problems in the restaurant. In addition to being more likely to notice health-related information, consumers with high levels of health literacy can also use this information more reasonably and effectively, thereby enhancing the positive effects of this information on health (Ismail et al., 2023).

Secondly, restaurant practitioners should make reasonable use of technological facilities and devices in restaurants to enhance consumers' health experience. Managers can place health-related information in noticeable places on electronic menus, or set up recommended food packages for consumers with different health conditions in electronic menus because some studies have shown that consumers prefer options that can reduce their cognitive effort (Doub et al., 2015). By increasing the visibility of health information and the accessibility and operability of healthy food options, consumers' effort expectations can be reduced, thereby increasing the possibility of consumers using this health information and choosing healthy packages. In addition to the health information provided on electronic menus and ordering systems that can affect consumer health, health information on social media also has a similar effect. Information on social media can provide a reference for predicting the outbreak of foodborne diseases. The rational use of information on social media can reduce the probability of consumers suffering from foodborne diseases and improve restaurant food safety. Therefore, restaurant managers should also strengthen the management of health information posted on social media and manage and prevent food safety issues through data management systems. Finally, the health literacy of restaurant staff should be enhanced so that restaurant staff can assist consumers in making correct health decisions.

It is worth noting that it is not difficult for restaurant managers to improve consumers' health experiences through technology. The practical suggestions mentioned above, such as changing the order of dishes on electronic menus and providing more health information on social media, are easy to implement for both large and small restaurants, as they do not require complex technology or high-cost technological devices. However, these small changes made by restaurants to benefit consumer health can have lasting health effects on large groups of consumers. Therefore, this study suggests that restaurant managers can actively use existing technological means and platforms to improve the overall health of customers while also enhancing the restaurant's social responsibility and brand loyalty, ultimately achieving a mutually beneficial outcome for multiple stakeholders.

Finally, suppliers should strengthen the technologies' ability to identify health-related information in big data. In terms of design, suppliers should improve the aesthetic value of technology facilities and devices, especially service robots. Because existing research shows that health information provided by virtual images that meet consumers' aesthetic requirements is more persuasive (Hao et al., 2024). At the same time, although previous studies have shown that overly anthropomorphic service robots can harm consumers' emotional health (Huang et al., 2021). However, suppliers do not need to worry too much about whether the degree of anthropomorphism of service robots will affect consumers' emotional health. Because some new evidence shows that consumers pay more attention to robot functions, when the functions of service robots meet consumers' expectations, the degree of anthropomorphism of robots can be more conducive to consumers' emotional health (Park et al., 2024).

LIMITATIONS

This study has some limitations that cannot be ignored. First, this study was searched in only two databases, and only English articles published in journals were selected. Therefore, researchers who focus on this topic can expand the search scope and relax the screening rules in the future on the basis of ensuring the quality of the research. Second, this study only focuses on the impact of technology used in restaurants on consumers' health. Restaurants are a complex environment, and there are many factors that may affect consumers. Therefore, in the absence of retrospective studies related to the health of restaurant consumers, researchers can try to review and analyse this issue from a broader perspective. Last, as a review article, although this study has referred to the conclusions of the included studies as fully as possible, it has not made full use of the quantitative data in these studies. Therefore, future studies can try to analyse the data from previous studies in a quantitative way to draw more reliable conclusions.

REFERENCES

Abell, A., Biswas, D., & Arroyo Mera, C. (2024). Food and technology: Using digital devices for restaurant orders leads to indulgent outcomes. *Journal of the Academy of Marketing Science*. Advance online publication. DOI: 10.1007/s11747-024-01029-6

Ahn, J., & Seo, S. (2018). Consumer responses to interactive restaurant self-service technology (IRSST): The role of gadget-loving propensity. *International Journal of Hospitality Management*, 74, 109–121. DOI: 10.1016/j.ijhm.2018.02.020

Ali-Alsaadi, A., Cabeza-Ramírez, L., Santos-Roldán, L., & Loor-Zambrano, H. (2023). Digital Marketing and Fast-Food Intake in the UAE: The Role of Firm-Generated Content among Adult Consumers. *Foods*, 12(22), 4089. Advance online publication. DOI: 10.3390/foods12224089 PMID: 38002147

Ares, G., Antúnez, L., De León, C., Alcaire, F., Vidal, L., Natero, V., & Otterbring, T. (2022). Even if you don't pay attention to it, you know it's there': A qualitative exploration of adolescents' experiences with digital food marketing. *Appetite*, 176, 106128. Advance online publication. DOI: 10.1016/j.appet.2022.106128 PMID: 35718311

Ariyasriwatana, W., Buente, W., Oshiro, M., & Streveler, D. (2014). Categorizing health-related cues to action: Using Yelp reviews of restaurants in Hawaii. *New Review of Hypermedia and Multimedia*, 20(4), 317–340. DOI: 10.1080/13614568.2014.987326

Bedard, K., & Kuhn, P. (2015). Micro-marketing healthier choices: Effects of personalized ordering suggestions on restaurant purchases. *Journal of Health Economics*, 39, 106–122. DOI: 10.1016/j.jhealeco.2014.10.006 PMID: 25544398

Chen, C., & Girish, V. (2023). Investigating the use experience of restaurant service robots: The cognitive-affective-behavioral framework. *International Journal of Hospitality Management*, 111, 103482. Advance online publication. DOI: 10.1016/j.ijhm.2023.103482

Chen, R., Smyser, M., Chan, N., Ta, M., Saelens, B., & Krieger, J. (2015). Changes in Awareness and Use of Calorie Information After Mandatory Menu Labeling in Restaurants in King County, Washington. *American Journal of Public Health*, 105(3), 546–553. DOI: 10.2105/AJPH.2014.302262 PMID: 25602868

Courtney, A., PeConga, E., Wagner, D., & Rapuano, K. (2018). Calorie information and dieting status modulate reward and control activation during the evaluation of food images. *PLoS One*, 13(11), e0204744. Advance online publication. DOI: 10.1371/journal.pone.0204744 PMID: 30388113

Dai, X., Wu, L., & Hu, W. (2022). Nutritional quality and consumer health perception of online delivery food in the context of China. *BMC Public Health*, 22(1), 2132. DOI: 10.1186/s12889-022-14593-9 PMID: 36403009

Doran, D. (2010). Restaurants and technology – past, present and future: A practitioner's viewpoint. *Worldwide Hospitality and Tourism Themes*, 2(1), 94–99. DOI: 10.1108/17554211011012621

Doub, A. E., Levin, A., Heath, C. E., & Le Vangie, K. (2015). Mobile app-etite: Consumer attitudes towards and use of mobile technology in the context of eating behaviour. *Journal of Direct, Data and Digital Marketing Practice*, 17(2), 114–129. DOI: 10.1057/dddmp.2015.44

Duong, L. N. K., Al-Fadhli, M., Jagtap, S., Bader, F., Martindale, W., Swainson, M., & Paoli, A. (2020). A review of robotics and autonomous systems in the food industry: From the supply chains perspective. *Trends in Food Science & Technology*, 106, 355–364. DOI: 10.1016/j.tifs.2020.10.028

Elkhwesky, Z., & Elkhwesky, E. F. Y. (2023). A systematic and critical review of Internet of Things in contemporary hospitality: A roadmap and avenues for future research. *International Journal of Contemporary Hospitality Management*, 35(2), 533–562. DOI: 10.1108/IJCHM-01-2022-0090

Finkelstein, E., Strombotne, K., Chan, N., & Krieger, J. (2011). Mandatory Menu Labeling in One Fast-Food Chain in King County, Washington. *American Journal of Preventive Medicine*, 40(2), 122–127. DOI: 10.1016/j.amepre.2010.10.019 PMID: 21238859

Galderisi, S., Heinz, A., Kastrup, M., Beezhold, J., & Sartorius, N. (2015). Toward a new definition of mental health. *World Psychiatry; Official Journal of the World Psychiatric Association (WPA)*, 14(2), 231–233. DOI: 10.1002/wps.20231 PMID: 26043341

Ganesh, M. K.. (2024). Farm-to-Table Initiatives in Restaurant Food Production: Benefits, Challenges, and Consumer Perceptions. *International Journal for Multidimensional Research Perspectives*, 2(7), 88–104. DOI: 10.61877/ijmrp.v2i7.174

Gonzalez, R., Gasco, J., & Llopis, J. (2022). Information and communication technologies in food services and restaurants: A systematic review. *International Journal of Contemporary Hospitality Management*, 34(4), 1423–1447. DOI: 10.1108/IJCHM-05-2021-0624

Goodman, S., Vanderlee, L., White, C., & Hammond, D. (2018). A quasi-experimental study of a mandatory calorie-labelling policy in restaurants: Impact on use of nutrition information among youth and young adults in Canada. *Preventive Medicine*, 116, 166–172. DOI: 10.1016/j.ypmed.2018.09.013 PMID: 30261242

Gu, Q., Li, M., & Huang, S. (2023). An exploratory investigation of technology-assisted dining experiences from the consumer perspective. *International Journal of Contemporary Hospitality Management*, 35(3), 1010–1029. DOI: 10.1108/IJCHM-02-2022-0214

Hao, F., Aman, A., & Zhang, C. (2024). What is beautiful is good: Attractive avatars for healthier dining and satisfaction. *International Journal of Contemporary Hospitality Management*, 36(12), 3969–3988. Advance online publication. DOI: 10.1108/IJCHM-09-2023-1490

Huang, H.-L., Cheng, L.-K., Sun, P.-C., & Chou, S.-J. (2021). The Effects of Perceived Identity Threat and Realistic Threat on the Negative Attitudes and Usage Intentions Toward Hotel Service Robots: The Moderating Effect of the Robot's Anthropomorphism. *International Journal of Social Robotics*, 13(7), 1599–1611. DOI: 10.1007/s12369-021-00752-2

Ismail, L. C., Kassem, H., Osaili, T. M., Hashim, M., Obaid, R., Radwan, H., Mohamad, M. N., Saleh, S. T., Zomut, Z. A., Qiyas, S. A., Rajaby, R. A., Daour, R. A., Ali, H. I., Stojanovska, L., & Al Dhaheri, A. S. (2023). Public's calorie literacy and perceived effectiveness of restaurant menu calorie labeling in the United Arab Emirates. PLoS ONE, 18(10 October). DOI: 10.1371/journal.pone.0293387

Jaeger, S. R., & Cardello, A. V. (2022). Factors affecting data quality of online questionnaires: Issues and metrics for sensory and consumer research. *Food Quality and Preference*, 102, 104676. DOI: 10.1016/j.foodqual.2022.104676

Jia, Y., Garg, A., & Shi, P. (2024). Research on Factors Influencing Hotel Consumers' Health: A Systematic Review and Ways Forward. *Sustainability (Basel)*, 16(5), 2099. DOI: 10.3390/su16052099

Jiao, H., Wong, I. A., & Lin, Z. C. J. (2024). Understanding customer multi-interactions, trust, social support and voluntary performance in smart restaurants. *Journal of Hospitality and Tourism Technology*. Advance online publication. DOI: 10.1108/JHTT-11-2023-0384

Kalaivani, D., Jadhav, S., & Hedaoo, R. (2021). Impact of Varied Menu Nutrition Labelling Formats on Consumer Food Selections using FAFH. *Journal of Pharmaceutical Research International*, 33(43A), 199–207. DOI: 10.9734/jpri/2021/v33i43A32478

Kaman, G. S., Bozkurt, İ., Bölükbaş, R., Özhasar, Y., Demírcí, B., & Yazicioğlu, İ. (2024). The strategy food waste in restaurants: A systematic literature review. *Trends in Food Science & Technology*, 151, 104625. DOI: 10.1016/j.tifs.2024.104625

Keyes, C. L. M. (1998). Social Well-Being. *Social Psychology Quarterly*, 61(2), 121. DOI: 10.2307/2787065

Kim, H., & So, K. K. F. (2022). Two decades of customer experience research in hospitality and tourism: A bibliometric analysis and thematic content analysis. *International Journal of Hospitality Management*, 100, 103082. DOI: 10.1016/j.ijhm.2021.103082

Kim, J.-K., Yang, J.-J., & Lee, Y.-K. (2023). How Do Self-Service Kiosks Improve COVID-19 Pandemic Resilience in the Restaurant Industry? *Sustainability (Basel)*, 15(13), 10168. DOI: 10.3390/su151310168

Kim, T., Wildey, L., Gleason, B., Bleser, J., Firestone, M., Bare, G., Bliss, J., Dewey-Mattia, D., Stueven, H., Brown, L., Dyjack, D., & Hedberg, C. (2022). Foodborne Outbreak Rates Associated with Restaurant Inspection Grading and Posting at the Point of Service: Evaluation Using National Foodborne Outbreak Surveillance Data. *Journal of Food Protection*, 85(7), 1000–1007. DOI: 10.4315/JFP-22-007 PMID: 35175331

Kumar, S., & Shah, A. (2021). Revisiting food delivery apps during COVID-19 pandemic? Investigating the role of emotions. *Journal of Retailing and Consumer Services*, 62, 102595. Advance online publication. DOI: 10.1016/j.jretconser.2021.102595

Lassen, A., Beck, A., Leedo, E., Andersen, E., Christensen, T., Mejborn, H., Thorsen, A., & Tetens, I. (2014). Effectiveness of offering healthy labelled meals in improving the nutritional quality of lunch meals eaten in a worksite canteen. *Appetite*, 75, 128–134. DOI: 10.1016/j.appet.2013.12.005 PMID: 24373732

Le, T. H., Arcodia, C., Novais, M. A., & Kralj, A. (2019). What we know and do not know about authenticity in dining experiences: A systematic literature review. *Tourism Management*, 74, 258–275. DOI: 10.1016/j.tourman.2019.02.012

Lee-Kwan, S., Pan, L., Maynard, L., McGuire, L., & Park, S. (2016). Factors Associated with Self-Reported Menu-Labeling Usage among US Adults. *Journal of the Academy of Nutrition and Dietetics*, 116(7), 1127–1135. DOI: 10.1016/j.jand.2015.12.015 PMID: 26875022

Leung, X., Torres, B., & Fan, A. (2021). Do kiosks outperform cashiers? An S-O-R framework of restaurant ordering experiences. *Journal of Hospitality and Tourism Technology*, 12(3), 580–592. DOI: 10.1108/JHTT-03-2020-0065

Leung, X. Y., & Wen, H. (2021). How emotions affect restaurant digital ordering experiences: A comparison of three ordering methods. *Journal of Hospitality and Tourism Technology*, 12(3), 439–453. DOI: 10.1108/JHTT-05-2020-0117

Li, H., Zhang, L., & Hsu, C. H. C. (2023). Research on user-generated photos in tourism and hospitality: A systematic review and way forward. *Tourism Management*, 96, 104714. DOI: 10.1016/j.tourman.2022.104714

Ling, E., Chua, B., & Han, H. (2023). In search of a reciprocal relationship in dessert cafés: Linking customer perceived innovativeness to value co-creation behavior. *Humanities & Social Sciences Communications*, 10(1), 897. Advance online publication. DOI: 10.1057/s41599-023-02353-y

Liu, P. J., Bettman, J. R., Uhalde, A. R., & Ubel, P. A. (2015). 'How many calories are in my burrito?' Improving consumers' understanding of energy (calorie) range information. *Public Health Nutrition*, 18(1), 15–24. DOI: 10.1017/S1368980014000627 PMID: 24762709

Lu, L., Zhang, P., & Zhang, T. C. (2021). Leveraging "human-likeness" of robotic service at restaurants. *International Journal of Hospitality Management*, 94, 102823. Advance online publication. DOI: 10.1016/j.ijhm.2020.102823

Ma, E., Bao, Y., Huang, L., Wang, D., & Kim, M. (2023). When a Robot Makes Your Dinner: A Comparative Analysis of Product Level and Customer Experience Between the U.S. and Chinese Robotic Restaurants. *Cornell Hospitality Quarterly*, 64(2), 184–211. DOI: 10.1177/19389655211052286

Mahmoud, A., Attia, M. A., & Wahba, D. (2024). The Impact of Customers' Nutritional Awareness on Food Habits, Behaviors, and Choices in Fast Food Restaurants. *Minia Journal of Tourism and Hospitality Research MJTHR*, 18(1), 109–133. DOI: 10.21608/mjthr.2024.296274.1161

Mandracchia, F., Tarro, L., Llauradó, E., Valls, R. M., & Solà, R. (2022). The "Healthy Meals" web app for the assessment of nutritional content and food allergens in restaurant meals: Development, evaluation and validation. *Digital Health*, 8, 205520762210816. DOI: 10.1177/20552076221081690 PMID: 35251681

Manhas, P. S., Sharma, P., & Quintela, J. A. (2024). Product Innovation and Customer Experience: Catalysts for Enhancing Satisfaction in Quick Service Restaurants. *Tourism and Hospitality*, 5(3), 559–576. DOI: 10.3390/tourhosp5030034

Moreno, P., & Tejada, P. (2019). Reviewing the progress of information and communication technology in the restaurant industry. *Journal of Hospitality and Tourism Technology*, 10(4), 673–688. DOI: 10.1108/JHTT-07-2018-0072

Mulyanto, G., Kusumaningrum, H. D., & Wulandari, N. (2023). Food safety knowledge and awareness among stakeholders of the online-food-delivery system in Depok City Indonesia. *Food Research*, 7(5), 29–41. DOI: 10.26656/fr.2017.7(5).881

Musicus, A. A., Moran, A. J., Lawman, H. G., & Roberto, C. A. (2019). Online Randomized Controlled Trials of Restaurant Sodium Warning Labels. *American Journal of Preventive Medicine*, 57(6), e181–e193. DOI: 10.1016/j.amepre.2019.06.024 PMID: 31753271

Niven, P., Morley, B., Dixon, H., Martin, J., Jones, A., Petersen, K., & Wakefield, M. (2019). Effects of health star labelling on the healthiness of adults' fast food meal selections: An experimental study. *Appetite*, 136, 146–153. DOI: 10.1016/j.appet.2019.01.018 PMID: 30684644

Okumus, B., Ali, F., Bilgihan, A., & Ozturk, A. (2018). Psychological factors influencing customers' acceptance of smartphone diet apps when ordering food at restaurants. *International Journal of Hospitality Management*, 72, 67–77. DOI: 10.1016/j.ijhm.2018.01.001

Ong, D., Chiu, S., Andrews, E., & Nadarajan, G. (2023). One needs to be reminded and motivated: Mediating role of digital nudging for food waste reduction. *Journal of Social Marketing*, 13(3), 449–471. DOI: 10.1108/JSOCM-02-2023-0025

Palisidis, G., Giazitzi, K., Karathanos, V., & Boskou, G. (2016). Nutritional application software for restaurants: The tool of customer satisfaction and behaviour. *International Journal of Electronic Customer Relationship Management*, 10(2–4), 198–215. DOI: 10.1504/IJECRM.2016.082197

Pang, J., & Hammond, D. (2013). Efficacy and Consumer Preferences for Different Approaches to Calorie Labeling on Menus. *Journal of Nutrition Education and Behavior*, 45(6), 669–675. DOI: 10.1016/j.jneb.2013.06.005 PMID: 23928179

Park, H., Jiang, S., Lee, O.-K. D., & Chang, Y. (2024). Exploring the Attractiveness of Service Robots in the Hospitality Industry: Analysis of Online Reviews. *Information Systems Frontiers*, 26(1), 41–61. DOI: 10.1007/s10796-021-10207-8

Peng, J., Peng, Z., Lei, S., & Xie, L. (2024). Family-customer happiness and its impact on customer citizenship behavior: A study of parent–child consumption in robot restaurants. *Tourism Management Perspectives*, 53, 101273. Advance online publication. DOI: 10.1016/j.tmp.2024.101273

Pickering, C., & Byrne, J. (2014). The benefits of publishing systematic quantitative literature reviews for PhD candidates and other early-career researchers. *Higher Education Research & Development*, 33(3), 534–548. DOI: 10.1080/07294360.2013.841651

Prowse, R., Lee, K., Chen, E., Zuo, F., Hammond, D., & Hobin, E. (2020). Testing the efficacy of and parents' preferences for nutrition labels on children's menus from a full-service chain restaurant: Results of an online experiment. *Public Health Nutrition*, 23(10), 1820–1831. DOI: 10.1017/S1368980019004488 PMID: 32308190

Ratilla, M., Karolyova, D., Haider, L., Dohnalova, Z., & Horak, M. (2022). NUDGING HEALTHY RESTAURANT SELECTION IN AN ONLINE FOOD DELIVERY PLATFORM: THE EFFECT OF AVAILABILITY AND PRIMING. *Transformations in Business & Economics*, 21(3C), 395–411.

Ray, E., & Merle, P. (2021). Disgusting Face, Disease-ridden Place?: Emoji Influence on the Interpretation of Restaurant Inspection Reports. *Health Communication*, 36(14), 1867–1878. DOI: 10.1080/10410236.2020.1802867 PMID: 32806958

Reinholdsson, T., Hedesström, M., Ejelöv, E., Hansla, A., Bergquist, M., Svenfelt, A., & Nilsson, A. (2023). Nudging green food: The effects of a hedonic cue, menu position, a warm-glow cue, and a descriptive norm. *Journal of Consumer Behaviour*, 22(3), 557–568. DOI: 10.1002/cb.2129

Restrepo, B. J. (2017). Calorie Labeling in Chain Restaurants and Body Weight: Evidence from New York. *Health Economics*, 26(10), 1191–1209. DOI: 10.1002/hec.3389 PMID: 27451966

Roberto, C. A., Haynos, A. F., Schwartz, M. B., Brownell, K. D., & White, M. A. (2013). Calorie estimation accuracy and menu labeling perceptions among individuals with and without binge eating and/or purging disorders. *Eating and Weight Disorders*, 18(3), 255–261. DOI: 10.1007/s40519-013-0035-x PMID: 23760909

Rudd, R. E., Anderson, J. E., Oppenheimer, S., & Nath, C. (2023). Health Literacy: An Update of Medical and Public Health Literature. In J. Comings, B. Garner, & C. Smith, Review of Adult Learning and Literacy, Volume 7 (1st ed., pp. 175–204). Routledge. DOI: 10.4324/9781003417996-6

Ruiz-Mafe, C., Bigné-Alcañiz, E., & Currás-Pérez, R. (2020). The effect of emotions, eWOM quality and online review sequence on consumer intention to follow advice obtained from digital services. *Journal of Service Management*, 31(3), 465–487. DOI: 10.1108/JOSM-11-2018-0349

Sadilek, A., Kautz, H., DiPrete, L., Labus, B., Portman, E., Teitel, J., & Silenzio, V. (2017). Deploying nEmesis: Preventing Foodborne Illness by Data Mining Social Media. *AI Magazine*, 38(1), 37–48. DOI: 10.1609/aimag.v38i1.2711

Santana, S., Brach, C., Harris, L., Ochiai, E., Blakey, C., Bevington, F., Kleinman, D., & Pronk, N. (2021). Updating Health Literacy for Healthy People 2030: Defining Its Importance for a New Decade in Public Health. *Journal of Public Health Management and Practice*, 27(Supplement 6), S258–S264. DOI: 10.1097/PHH.0000000000001324 PMID: 33729194

Spence, C. (2023). Robots in gastronomy: Psychological and financial considerations. *International Journal of Gastronomy and Food Science*, 32, 100707. Advance online publication. DOI: 10.1016/j.ijgfs.2023.100707

The World Health Organization. (1946). Constitution of the World Health Organization. *American Journal of Public Health and the Nation's Health*, 36(11), 1315–1323. DOI: 10.2105/AJPH.36.11.1315 PMID: 18016450

Torrico, D. D., Han, Y., Sharma, C., Fuentes, S., Viejo, C. G., & Dunshea, F. R. (2020). Effects of context and virtual reality environments on the wine tasting experience, acceptability, and emotional responses of consumers. *Foods*, 9(2), 191. Advance online publication. DOI: 10.3390/foods9020191 PMID: 32075018

Wang, X. V., & Wang, L. (2021). A literature survey of the robotic technologies during the COVID-19 pandemic. *Journal of Manufacturing Systems*, 60, 823–836. DOI: 10.1016/j.jmsy.2021.02.005 PMID: 33612914

Wei, W., Zhang, L., Rathjens, B., & McGinley, S. (2022). Electronic Consumer-to-Consumer Interaction (eCCI) Post a Service Failure: The Psychological Power of Need for Approval. *Journal of Hospitality & Tourism Research (Washington, D.C.)*. Advance online publication. DOI: 10.1177/10963480221141649

Wong, I. A., Huang, J., Lin, Z., & Jiao, H. (2022). Smart dining, smart restaurant, and smart service quality (SSQ). *International Journal of Contemporary Hospitality Management*, 34(6), 2272–2297. DOI: 10.1108/IJCHM-10-2021-1207

Zhang, S., Hu, Z., Li, X., & Ren, A. (2022). The impact of service principal (service robot vs. Human staff) on service quality: The mediating role of service principal attribute. *Journal of Hospitality and Tourism Management*, 52, 170–183. DOI: 10.1016/j.jhtm.2022.06.014

Zhang, S., Zhou, L., & Zhao, Y. (2020). How to Present Calorie Information on the Electronic Menu to Help People Order More Healthily. In Kurosu, M. (Ed.), *Human-Computer Interaction. Human Values and Quality of Life* (Vol. 12183, pp. 200–212). Springer International Publishing., DOI: 10.1007/978-3-030-49065-2_15

Chapter 9
Impact of Content-Driven Online Sensory Marketing on Customers Food-Buying Intentions

Senthilmurugan Paramasivam
https://orcid.org/0000-0003-3249-8088
Christ University, India

Roshna Thomas
https://orcid.org/0000-0003-0038-510X
Christ University, India

Manisha Saxena
https://orcid.org/0009-0004-0185-9391
Christ University, India

Ishika Parasramka
https://orcid.org/0009-0004-1525-5679
Christ University, India

ABSTRACT

The chapter explores the transformation created by technology driven online sensory marketing in the food sector. The growing competition and prominence of e-commerce in the food industry has made marketers exhibit intangibility elements as equivalent as tangible attributes of their food products in the digital platforms by employing sensory marketing techniques for positive customer evaluation of their brands. It is essential to use all five senses of sensory marketing to create enduring experiences and foster brand loyalty among the target market. This chapter, backed by previous research, investigates how sensory elements such as tactile, gustatory, olfactory, and auditory can be better presented in digital platforms in order to obtain effective appeals in the communications. This chapter also analyzes the evidence of past research on how sensory marketing accelerates online consumers experiences and engagements in e-commerce platforms in various dimensions.

DOI: 10.4018/979-8-3693-7683-6.ch009

1.BACKGROUND

The "word" food retail can be defined as food products sold to consumers that are not restaurant food and are consumed remotely (Murray & Caraher, 2019). The technology has transformed the retail industry to a large extent, as the retail food industry is dynamic. In conjunction with the changes, technology is considered to play a pivotal role in the evolution of the industry. The industry has progressed from having local family-owned tradition food stores to, in the last few decades, having larger and more centralized supercenters (Jarmin et al., 2009). In continuous to these changes, the global food retail industry is currently changing aggressively with a new arrival of large supermarkets and fast-food outlets (Murray & Caraher, 2019).

The rapid growth trends that emerged during the pandemic are persisting, reforming the industry. In December 2019, the percentage of e-commerce grocery sales in the US market was little under 4 percent; it's now in the low teens and is anticipated to reach roughly 25 percent by 2030. The adoption of online grocery shopping is expected to be even higher in parts of Europe. (McKinsey,2022) It appears that there is no symptom of saturation in shopping habits that exist at the pre-Covid level in spite of weakening economies, surging inflation, and rising interest rates. These economic factors may sluggish the growth of eGrocery in the short term, but demand for online services from food retailers and the corresponding digitization of their operations is not going away. Food retailers will necessitate fully integrating their digital and physical channels. Consumer behavior and expectations will transform as digital natives become a leading retail customer segment and all age groups increasingly embrace online shopping. (pwc.com)

Figure 1. Changing the Grocery Markets

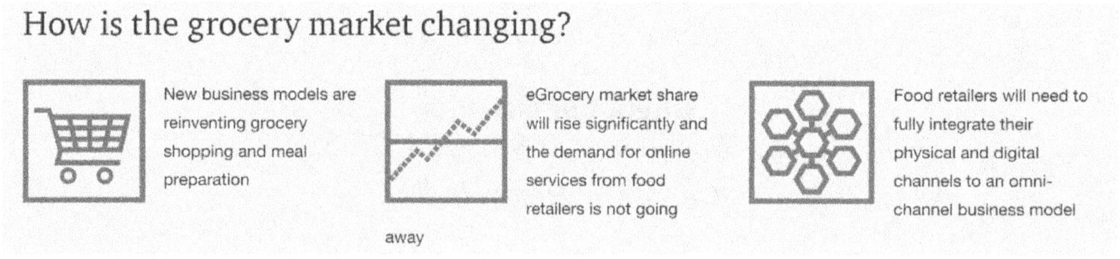

Source: https://www.strategyand.pwc.com/

The paradigm shift from a supply-driven to a demand-driven approach is prevailing in the evolving food retail industry. The guiding principle for a successful business model in the emerging e-commerce-backed retail food industry is clear understanding and acquiring knowledge of consumers exact wants, needs, and behaviors. The food retailers have been focusing on selling to the "average consumer," but as the consumers are increasingly distinguishing from each other in who they are and what they want from their food shopping preferences, which leads to multiple need- based micro segments from the mass. The sustainability of the industry lies in offering a unique and precise experience to individual customers through a perfect blend of digital and physical interactions. This approach involves providing a wide range of center-store items in a low-touch format while emphasizing fresh and differentiated offerings as the new focal point of in-store experiences. The store is envisioned as a flexible platform, adaptable to changing needs and experiences (Edsall et al., n.d).

This transformation is mandating the food marketers to recognize the composite concept of customer experiences, which comprise cognitive, emotional, behavioral, sensorial, and social components. The customers' successful experience with the brand includes various touchpoints, which are individual interactions between the brand and the customer at different stages of the purchasing process. The overall experience is formed through a compilation of these touchpoints, influencing the customer's decision-making process and purchase journey (Lemon & Verhoef, 2016).

2. CUSTOMER EXPERIENCE THROUGH SENSORY MARKETING

Sachdeva & Goel (2015, p. 292) define customer experience as "an interaction between a company (brand/product/service) and a customer, being shaped by the characteristics of the customer and those of the product, company, or brand, and always influenced by the context or environment in which the interaction takes place.".

Customer experience goes beyond attracting people to the store; conversely, customers at present want a memorable event, which develops the product itself (Pine & Gilmore, 2013). This has changed the model of engaging retail businesses, which centered around the intangibles the shoppers' experiences in the store, instead of focusing on the objective aspects such as product, location, and price (Sachdeva & Goel, 2015). This is known as the in-store experience.

The food retailers need to discover innovative ways to inspire consumers to visit their stores due to the complexity of making the in-store experience online to stay competitive in the retail food market. In order to achieve this objective, the retail food marketing managers need to implement key strategies such as designing pleasurable in-store experiences, which can be executed by strategically using sensory elements such as visuals, scents, haptics, sound, and taste. The retail brand managers need to change their approach of providing a standardized store experience to a more personalized and customized store for capturing the attention of consumers (Szocs et al., 2023).

Experiential marketing allows immersive and diverse experiences for consumers and inspires them to infer new meanings and escapes in their daily lives (Yuan & Wu, 2008). Sensory marketing is playing a vital role here to enhance the customer experience by connecting with the consumer's senses. Sensory marketing refers to "marketing that engages the consumers' senses and affects their behavior" (Krishna, 2010, p. 2). Retail stores apply sensory marketing by capturing the attention of the senses (Krishna, 2010). An example of a case is ICA terming their oranges as "juicy oranges" rather than Florida oranges to capture the attention and obtain the consumers to perceive it as juicy (Krishna, 2011).

Positive and enjoyable customer experiences can be offered by integrating sensory marketing into the customer experience. The implementation of sensory marketing enables sensory stimuli in the customer experience, which does create feelings of positive emotions and a sense of happiness and satisfaction through sensory elements of vision, sound, taste, touch, and smell (Riza & Wijayanti, 2023). Sensory marketing facilitates as a significant tool in achieving brand differentiation and fostering customer loyalty in stores (Iqbal & e-Hassan, 2016).

3. IMPORTANCE OF SENSORY MARKETING FOR ONLINE FOOD PLATFORMS

The increase in online food shopping is a comparatively recent phenomenon when compared to conventional in-store shopping. Many consumers continue to feel it as a venture fraught with danger (Dash et al., 2021). Consumers who order food through online platforms have stated greater skepticism concerning the quality of the food exhibited on the screen, conversely to their in-store counterparts who require support in virtually accessing and evaluating the products (Kumar et al., 2020). In order to cater to the mounting trend of online food shopping and to appeal and retain online customers, online food marketers have adopted sensory marketing strategies.

Online food enterprises have executed attractive food images on websites such as, ShopeeFood, Swiggy, Zomato, and Grab to distribute food perception among consumers on screen. The visuals or food images that adopt sensory marketing techniques could elicit tastiness and temptation towards the food, particularly when consumers are searching for a variety of foods from food apps (Izzuddin, 2021). Consequently, in the virtual context, sensory cues play a supporting instrument in bringing maximum food brand information to customers (Ifeanyichukwu & Peter, 2018; Hussain, 2018) and in promoting constructive interaction and perception of the brand (Elder & Krishna, 2010). Sensory cue has been identified to be a vital factor that impacts online consumer buying behavior and has been tinted as an indispensable factor in online food business by the experts of industry and academics (Biswas, 2019; Girard et al., 2019; Huang & Labroo, 2020; Zha et al., 2022). Thus, this chapter is evaluating the role of sensory cues in influencing consumers to buy food online using food apps and websites. Consumers' characteristics are additional factor that influences consumer online food buying behaviour apart from sensory cues as a marketing strategy to grasp attention and deliver food perception on screen. Pitchay et al. (2022) have examined the age factor as a moderator to assess consumer online purchase intention.

4. CONTENT DRIVEN SENSORY MARKETING IN THE FOOD INDUSTRY

The rise of e-commerce in the food industry represents a significant shift in the way that customers get and make food-related purchases. Thanks to advancements in technology and shifting consumer preferences, digital platforms are increasingly essential for revolutionizing the way people place food orders. Online grocery shopping, pre-made meals, and hot meal delivery have grown commonplace due to the abundance of convenient and diverse options. Things like the COVID-19 epidemic have accelerated the food retail industry's restructuring and made it possible for customers to shop for food online while lounging in their homes. Consumers are making more and more purchases online, and the COVID-19 pandemic has increased the pressure from competitors (Hamacher & Buchkremer, 2022). Online platforms are becoming an essential part of the contemporary food buying experience, indicating that this transformation is more than just a fad. It represents a fundamental shift in how we approach food purchasing.

Taste, smell, touch, vision, and sound are the five senses that food products can evoke, setting them apart from other consumer goods (Schifferstein, 2006). Sensory marketing has a big influence on consumer attitudes and behavior in the food sector. Sensational marketing aims to create captivating and unforgettable experiences through the use of all five senses—sight, sound, taste, touch, and smell. This is particularly significant in the food business. The visual appeal of delicious food, the sizzling sounds of cooking, the aromatic notes of spices, the tactile feelings of handling food, and the rich tales describing culinary adventures all contribute to a total sensory engagement.

Food's virtual look, sound, smell, and feel can arouse strong emotions in consumers, which can influence their perception of a product's quality and appeal in the online food market. In a market of congestion where numerous food brands are offered online, sensorial marketing enables brand loyalty among consumers beyond establishing distinctive product experiences and also builds strong relationships between brand attributes and consumers preferences. Consumers obtain positive attitudes about the brand when they are engaged more through sensory marketing, especially when they are not able to create associations about the brand via tangible attributes in the physical product environment. Many studies have attempted to develop conceptual models. for learning about how the problem of intangibility is addressed by sensory marketing (Kaushik & Gokhale, 2021).

Online sensory marketing, which is significantly influencing consumer purchase intention by employing images, videos, audios, and texts in the fast-evolving technology driven food industry. Consumer purchase decisions are significantly influenced by attractive photos of food menus or appealing movies exhibiting culinary explorations that arouse interest and increase the perceived worth of products. Consumers positive association with brands is also enhanced by incorporating auditory elements like background music or sizzling sounds, which augment the sensory experience and evoke emotions. Stories about the origin of food and engaging textual tales about food making improve the entire sensory experience and foster a sense of connection between the customer and the product.

Online sensory marketing is instrumental for attracting consumers attention span, which is highly selective due to the cutthroat competition of the food market place with numerous communication stimuli. A well-conceptualized execution with a fusion of textual, audio, and visual aspects states a promising story that appeals to consumers and induces them to act positively towards the brand. The multimodal approaches in sensory marketing have the competence to change consumers perceptions, attitudes, and preferences and strongly influence the consumer into a concrete purchase decision.

4.1 Sensory Channels

All brand encounters take place through five sense channels: gestural, olfactory, tactile, auditory, and visual. Purchase decisions and the development of attitudes are two important marketing outcomes that are significantly influenced by these channels. Customers' opinions of the brand or product are shaped subconsciously by the well-designed graphics and sound effects, which are a result of these sensory experiences. This trigger is often used to assess how well companies are seen as well as impressions that cause favorable thoughts about the brands to come to mind on their own. When fostering brand loyalty, engagement is more effective than consumption. process. One way to conceptualize the online environment is as an offline embodiment context where individuals solely use digital interfaces to communicate with the outside world. However, this does not mean that in an online environment, the senses lose their power to affect cognition. In this case, cognitive function is nonetheless supported by modality-specific sensory systems (Niedenthal et al. 2005).

Food is a physical, emotional, and sensual experience, but like anything else these days, it needs to have an online following. Regardless of how good and recently baked, a restaurant's pizzas may not be able to fully represent its products and sway the choice of its patrons, who can only experience these senses virtually through the use of various forms of content, if the brand is unable to capture the visual appeal and aesthetics of the irresistible cheese pull, the aroma of freshly baked wood-fired pizza, and the sound of crunch with every bite.

4.2. Visual Channel

In the world of online marketing, especially in the food industry, using visually appealing content has become crucial. Food products are discussed and visually appealingly presented on digital platforms to grab the interest of potential customers. High-quality photos and videos are crucial for internet food businesses because they cut over geographical barriers and evoke strong feelings through aesthetic appeal. Videos teach viewers how to cook and build trust by showing authentic cooking techniques. To maximize engagement, ensure click-through rates, and establish a connection with the audience, it is imperative to strategically employ color schemes and visual elements. The idea is to let patrons virtually taste food before they decide which ones to order. By using visual design concepts, restaurants that produce 2D visual content can enhance their customers' online sensory experience. As the ideal level of visual complexity varies depending on the physical characteristics of each item, food sellers are encouraged to do this by considering various visual design concepts (such as repetition, compositional lines, contrast, balance, and rhythm) for different food items (Lee & Lim, 2023). In addition to images and videos, descriptive language enhances the visual experience by assisting customers in clearly visualizing flavors. It guides customers through the minute differences in flavors, aromas, and textures like a storyteller. Good and vivid descriptions increase the reader's connection to the food items by assisting them in creating an image in their minds that complements the visual elements.

4.3. Tactile Channel

The purpose of sensory touch marketing is to entice consumers by emphasizing the tactile qualities of a product. Advertisements frequently purposefully show the tactile sensations connected to a product in order to elicit feelings from the senses. The mediation effect of haptics will have a favorable impact on purchase intentions in addition to channel value and brand attitude. The impact of value on purchase intentions, which are commonly employed as a proxy for loyalty, has long been demonstrated by the service literature (Mulcahy & Riedel, 2021). For example, the heat that one could experience when holding a steaming cup of coffee could be represented by an image of the beverage. This image makes people feel cozy and comfortable, which makes it easier for them to connect with the product on a deeper level. In contrast, a cold beverage with condensation on the bottle may indicate a crisp or cool feel, which individuals looking for a revitalizing and energizing experience may find appealing. In this case, the temperature's visual depiction acts as a sensory signal.

Close-up images and videos are also used to emphasize the fine features of dishes like flaky pastries or creamy desserts, which successfully depict texture. It invites the audience to imagine what it might be like to bite through layers or to consume something velvety and smooth. In a similar vein, emphasizing textures in descriptive writing aids readers in visualizing aspects associated with touch, such as the smooth smoothness of a sauce or the cozy warmth of coffee. Textual and visual material actively engages the audience's sense of touch by emphasizing the tactile elements, creating a more immersive culinary experience and a multisensory connection.

4.4 Gustatory Channel

Giving the audience a virtual tasting experience requires a careful balance of expressive language and vibrant graphics. The subtle flavor features of food can be emphasized with the help of videos and close-up images. As a kind of teaser, these pictures invite viewers to picture and savor the flavors that will be served in their minds. Simultaneously, readers are given a virtual experience of the unique taste trip through the descriptive text's deliberate attention to flavor subtleties. These subtleties range from zesty citrus bursts to the savory undertones of perfectly seasoned cuisine. Digital menus have transformed the culinary exploration experience. by presenting visually appealing representations of dishes that correspond with the tastes of the customer. This combination of design and flavor allows customers to not only read descriptions but also visually experience the flavors, making their online meal selections more gratifying and knowledgeable.

A product image incorporated into the content is a helpful technique to communicate more relevant information about the product that may be crucial to the customer's decision-making process. Businesses can improve consumer perceptions of the expected flavor, the product's perceived quality and experience, and the product's overall attitude by implementing this technique. Consumers will probably have much greater inclinations to purchase the goods, which will ultimately contribute to the market's success (Haase et al., 2018). One way to engage viewers' sense of taste could be to show them a close-up of a tasty pasta dish that is golden in color and bursting with cheese. Words like "cheesy" and "creamy," which characterize the rich taste, spring to mind. Videos offer another layer of sound, evoking the pleasurable "yum" sound of tasting and the sizzle of baking. This tasteful blend of words, images, and sounds not only presents the cuisine but also lets viewers virtually taste it, creating a multisensory experience that heightens appreciation for culinary expertise.

4.5 Olfactory Channel:

In the world of olfactory marketing, a popular and effective strategy is to employ pictures of joyful faces that follow passionate food scents. The commercial features a visual story gasping moment that is often followed by displaying smiling, and happiness accentuates the consequence of olfactory cues in creating a pleasant emotive reaction by displaying a modest yet direct relationship between the act of smelling food and the ensuing experience of satisfaction. The visuals of food's rich aroma depiction are most likely to ensuing the heightened attraction and sense of satisfaction. The power of scents to produce positive emotions. EI theory states that strong appetites are often led to enduring intrusive thoughts. The sensory and affective aspects of target achievement is also produced by stimulations of the desired food image, leading to a repeated thought pattern in the subject (Shahriari et al., 2019).

The sense of smell can also be encompassed in storytelling through sensible use of scent. Product descriptions that are rich in imagery and detail create a multi-sensory experience. in addition to olfactory descriptions that are visually striking. A portion of the cooking and preparation process is captured on camera, stressing the importance of taking alluring scents to augment the sensory experience. The sensory appeal can be further enhanced by integrating user-generated content, such as testimonials and reviews. emphasizes the significance of olfactory cues in creating a pleasant emotive reaction by displaying a modest yet direct relationship between the act of smelling food and the ensuing experience of satisfaction. (Shahriari et al., 2019).

4.6 Auditory Channel

Sound is vital for enriching brand connections and arousing specific feelings. For example, coffee industry marketers practice sounds like the slow pour of liquid into a cup, the quiet hiss of brewing coffee, or the background buzz of a busy café to create a multisensory experience. Brands use thoughtfully chosen audio components to attempt and progress consumers' assessments of their products. The experience becomes more fascinating and unforgettable with the inclusion of the audio layer, which also advances the visual and olfactory components. In order to complete the sensory experience, sound is essential. It sounds like the snap of an item being opened, the satisfying crunch of a snack, or the steady jingling of silverware at a restaurant. In this context, sound is tactically encompassed in marketing campaigns to form customer perception and brand credentials, going beyond simple background noise. Brands can establish a more meaningful and long-lasting relationship with their audience by connecting particular sounds to pleasant experiences.

Interactive sensory-enabling technologies (SETs) for online purchase platforms is one topic of study in sensory mark research. A multisensory element is provided by background music in marketing and e-commerce. This can improve the appeal and memorable nature of the brand communication as a whole. In the interactive music condition, high-involvement consumers show enhanced purchase intention due to a higher degree of perceived cognitive value (Hwang et al., 2020).

Taking online food buying to new heights, the addition of sensory elements marks a paradigm shift beyond traditional e-commerce. These interactions provide clients with confidence and trust in addition to a feeling of physical presence. Businesses can change online by integrating tactile, gustatory, olfactory, and auditory stimuli with a range of material formats, such as text, photos, videos, and audios. Buying becomes a comprehensive, multimodal gastronomic adventure from a transactional perspective. This approach totally changes the digital food industry and sets the bar for customer experiences.

4.7 Sensory enabled Web Aesthetics:

Sensory-enabled web aesthetics is a portion of digitally interactive modern-age technologies that permits retail marketers to generate and/or employ promotions on a computer screen (Petit et al., 2019). Particularly, it is a technology that provides sensory inputs to create positive effects that are not existing in most of the websites (Brasel & Gips, 2014; Gallace et al., 2012; Petit et al., 2019). This technology contains commonly used equipment (e.g., headphones and touch screens) in connection with a batch of other technologies such as VR, and augmented reality (AR). Additionally, it may be known that both interactivity (Yim et al., 2017) and vividness (Yim et al., 2017) are the two concepts that have been extensively applied in many modern technology/media studies to exhibit their effectiveness. Interactivity is known as the technology's capacity to make it easier for people to participate and connect in content pertinent to brands (Papagiannis, 2017, 2020; Yim et al., 2017). Technology factors that augment interactivity comprise speed, mapping, and range. Speed denotes how quickly a material can be altered within an online environment. Mapping denotes how comparable the control that is employed in an online environment is to the real-world control. Range denotes how much content can be changed within an online environment (Steuer, 1992). For incidents, the facility of virtual agents or chatbots boosts the quality of experience and purchase behavior by making it more intense and pleasant (Petit et al., 2019). Conversely, a lagged response in a brand video on a website, for example, affects interactivity unpleasantly. Additionally, vividness is the richness of technology, encompassing a blend of 'the sensory experience of actual objects and the non-sensory experience of imaginary objects' (Park et al., 2007). It relates to product portrayals that are more vivid and are more likely to activate consumers' cognitive amplification processes, along with the presentation quality of products (Jiang & Benbasat, 2007). Vividness is improved by breadth and depth online, whereby breadth alludes to an online medium's ability to convey a variety of sensory aspects and depth denotes the perceived quality of the embodied information by online consumers. (Liu et al., 2017).

The hearing sensation is produced by the audio-tactile interface by applying pressure, vibration, and sound data composed during actual product consumption. This technology reconstructs the hearing sensation of actual consumption. This technology abides by the basic premise of'record-and-replay', authentic aural sensations, and tactile experiences (Hashimoto et al., 2008). Similarly, a higher level of vividness result of display technology to produce the maximum possible resolution of product images delivers better-quality picture inputs to numerous sight senses on online mediums that use this technology. (Hashimoto et al., 2008). A quite a number of touch technologies have been examined to understand if touchscreen interfaces do encourage psychological ownership (PO), strengthening thereby the award effect in the process. For example, when associated with traditional PCs, touch-based devices, such as tablets, can lead to superior product value (Bhayani & Vachhani, 2014). Remarkably, the discovery of diverse touch motions, such as swiping, is becoming progressively significant in mobile devices (Brasel & Gips, 2014). Several AI-based online websites have engaged in tactile technology, which may be effortlessly merged into mobile and wearable devices. Here, actuators or vibration motors are mainly utilized to produce different tactile experiences by altering the frequency, amplitude, period, and rhythm of vibrotactile stimulation (Rantala et al., 2013).

4.8 Dominos as an example:

Within the worldwide food industry, Domino's is an internationally recognized company that leverages online sensory branding to drive customer sales. Domino's purposefully highlights the melting cheese, fresh ingredients, and delectability of their pizzas on their website and app with high-resolution photos and videos. Consistent use of the red, white, and blue color scheme throughout the interface contributes to the development of a visually appealing and instantly identifiable brand identity.

Domino's uses auditory cues, such as the sound of bubbling crust and sizzling cheese, in their online ads and promotional videos to pique customers' interest and build anticipation. Even though it is impossible to accurately capture the aroma of their pizzas online, the menu makes use of sensory-engaging phrases like "freshly cooked," "aromatic herbs," and "mouthwatering" to evoke the scent in customers' heads. Domino's internet strategy includes detailed descriptions of dough varieties, toppings, and pizza tastes. With the use of interactive modification tools, customers may virtually create their own pizza designs. Customers can personalize their pizza using this way to fit their preferences.

Despite the lack of any physical contact in online purchases, Domino's uses marketing speak to create a tactile sense. They highlight the texture of the ingredients, for instance, and characterize crusts as "crispy on the outside, soft on the inside," which conveys a tactile quality. By enticing customers with a range of senses, Domino's comprehensive online sensory branding approach seeks to create an immersive and seductive digital experience.

5.RESEARCH ON SENSORY IMAGERY AND ONLINE FOOD PLATFORMS IMPACT ON CONSUMERS

5.1 Sensory Imagery to Accelerate Online Customer Experience

There has been little study done on the phenomenon known as sensory imaging, which is defined as the perception of one sense through the stimulation of another. Every sensory modality can produce sensory imaging, which Macinnis and Price claim " imagery processes evoke sensory experiences in working memory." Visual information can be obtained in the same format that it is processed and interpreted by creating images for every sense. (Elder, R.S) But tactile, olfactory, and gustatory cues are restricted when purchasing through e-commerce platforms. Nonetheless, Chao and Martin demonstrate that manipulating and observing a product may be replicated in the mind, showing that looking at a product can elicit similar neural responses as true touch or use. It is believed that, assuming mental modeling, this result holds true for e-commerce websites as well. Some of the same brain regions that were active during the original event may be activated throughout these repetitions, evoking similar feelings. (Simmons, W. et al). Therefore, through sensory imagery, these senses can be indirectly accessed through the modalities of vision and hearing.

Functional magnetic resonance imaging (fMRI) has been utilized in a number of neuroscience studies to demonstrate, however, that the actual experience that results from directly addressing a particular sense is usually stronger than the amount of sensory stimulation induced by sensory imagining. While simulating sensorimotor processes can improve sensory images, there is no proof that imagination is the same as direct perception. Moreover, a number of factors influence imaging, including the intensity of one's mental images and the probability of one's own evoking them. An earlier study by Unnava, Agarwal, and Haugtvedt demonstrated that when perceptual resources are used in the same modality, imaging in one modality is reduced, which further supports the difference between perception and imagery. Finally, Elder and Krishna write that "occupying these resources leads to weakened imagery, as sensory imagery formation requires perceptual resources." Additionally, Elder and Krishna showed that people can mentally mimic the actions that can be carried out with a graphically displayed object; this suggests that businesses should exhibit their items online in a way that is as tangible and realistic as feasible. However, the real sensory input can be compensated for by images. Peck, Barger, and Webb investigated whether or not the experience of ownership can be created and reinforced by envisioning oneself handling an object. Their results demonstrate that having a strong sense of possession can be induced by visualizing the touching products. The general conclusion is that the endowment effect increases in significance the more vividly the observer can see himself holding the thing. As a result, picturing a behavior might make the promoted product seem more appealing and enhance the likelihood that a customer will purchase it. Krishna and Morrin also showed how haptic information conveyed through text could influence a consumer's belief that a physical touch is not necessary. Neurons in related brain regions can become activated through reading, which might stimulate sensory imagination. For instance, reading strong scents activates the primary olfactory brain, while hearing descriptions of prepared food activates the taste buds in the mouth. Product conversions and users' opinions of the usefulness of websites can be influenced by the language used to transmit verbal material or by the text's overall features, such as the use of inquiries, particular pronouns (you, your), and adjectives.

5.2 Online Environments with Sensory Deprivation:

The online sensory consumer experience on e-commerce websites may suffer from little to no sensory communication, according to a number of research studies from which it was gathered the OSMI. It is referred to this phenomenon as online sensory deprivation (OSD) and described using the following description from Solomon et al.: A confusing and frustrating customer experience can result from on-line sensory deprivation, a process when the consumer is deprived of an extensive absence of sensory stimulation perception in the online environment. Malaise and thinking problems may be exacerbated by an absence of external stimuli (people, colors, sounds, and conversations). This happens in severe situations when some important sensory inputs are missing, including enticing text and photos on food websites. Finally, the absence of certain sensory modalities in online settings might lead to users getting disinterested and leaving the website quickly. The early days of the internet are reflected in the text-heavy pages that soon discouraged visitors from continuing to browse and made them feel that accessing the internet was not pleasurable. Moreover, haptic sensory impressions on the internet become even more crucial to express because of the requirement for touch (NFT), a mediating component. For example, Yazdanparast and Spears discover that for those with a high NFT, a positive attitude can mitigate the annoyance resulting from a lack of haptics and offer strategies to overcome OSD.

5.3 Overload sensory in online environments:

It's not always the ideal option to use the "more is better" approach, considering the intricacy of sensory processing as it relates to the sensory communication quality of e-commerce websites. Adding too much sensory appeal to products can have a detrimental impact on consumers' decisions to buy, thus, it's important to continually ask yourself, "Does more sense make sense?" as suggested by Riedel and Mulcahy. From a sensory marketing standpoint, it is not necessary to fully address each of the five senses in order to address all five senses in a targeted manner. It could be enough to address two or three senses. Test subjects for the sensory overload study by Homburg, Imschloß, and Kühnl were given varying degrees of sensory stimulation. They discovered that stimulation congruence combinations of these stimuli are associated with greater product evaluations and a willingness to purchase. In reacting to customers, this first bolsters the significance of sensory congruence. The study also shows that one sensory stimulus should be less excitation-inducing than the other two when three are used in a retail setting. A product's readiness to be bought may decline, and its appraisal may be less favorable if three potent sensory cues are presented. We might anticipate that sensory overload can result in an aversion to the viewed website in the sphere of digital sensory marketing. But as Krishna pointed out, even if there is still a great need for scientific investigation, sensory overload is just as simple to induce as information overload.

5.4 Visual Impact in Online Food Retailing:

(Lim & Lee, 2023) This study explores the effects of two visual design principles on users' purchase intentions via a mobile food delivery service: repetition and compositional lines. Burgers and iced tea are used as stimuli in two independent studies. Interestingly, the results indicate that, even at varying optimal repetition rates, the visual attractiveness of burgers and iced tea is improved when the identical food items are repeated. The study also demonstrates that the two food items have different effects from different compositional lines, resulting in different levels of visual appeal. The findings indicate that there is evidence supporting the crossmodal correspondences between taste and vision as a crucial processing mechanism. Specifically, the impacts of taste and vision on purchase intention are demonstrated in pairs. In the context of online food retailing, these findings substantially expand our understanding of how compositional lines and repetition affect crossmodal emotions. They also offer food companies enlightening data regarding the optimal ways to employ digital graphic content for mobile applications. In the larger context of online sensory marketing in the food industry, the study emphasizes the vital role that aesthetics play. This is especially true given the way that the COVID-19 pandemic has fueled the growth of mobile meal delivery applications.

(Elliott et al., 2023) By examining teen-targeted food marketing on Instagram, this study demonstrates the important impact of visual styles. The study shows how Instagram and other platforms have influenced Generation Z's food preferences, with a focus on their tech-savvy and marketing-savvy characteristics.

Based on 339 pictures and 57 teenagers, it identifies five visual kinds in teen-targeted food marketing: Sensory, Everyday, Bespoke, Absurd, and Bold Focus. Candy and snack ads frequently used vivid colors and a strong focal point. Fast food and drink goods frequently use bespoke, which has a straightforward appearance. Cartoonish features were employed by Absurd, especially in gummy sweets ads. While Sensory, however less common, concentrated on the visual appeal of food porn, Everyday depicted food in commonplace scenarios. Notably, the findings shed light on the visual tactics kids use to capture attention on Instagram. The study highlights the impact of Instagram on adolescent development and adds to our understanding of how various visual styles evoke diverse reactions. It also examines the value of sensory marketing, particularly in online environments.

(Shahriari et al., 2019) The study investigates the impact of auditory, gustatory, visual, and olfactory cues on the intensity of food cravings, using the elaborated Intrusion hypothesis as a framework. In a 314-person online trial, visual imaging proved to be the most successful stimulus for evoking food cravings, with gustatory, auditory, and olfactory stimuli following closely behind.

The primary findings emphasize the role that visual imagery plays in triggering food cravings, which has implications for marketing outcomes such as food intake and willingness to pay. By encouraging clients to visualize certain food items and highlighting their availability, it is an effective way to increase appetites and influence subsequent behaviors. This study offers significant new insights into the relationship among sensory signals, desire severity, and consumer reactions. The usage of specific foods (cheeseburger and salad) is one of the research's limitations, even though it advances our knowledge in this area. For wider applicability, it is recommended that future studies diversify dietary varieties. Additional research methodologies that have been proposed include examining the connection between food cravings and physiological or psychological factors, utilizing behavioral assessments, and carrying out experiments under a no-stimulus control condition. All things considered, the study provides marketers with practical strategies for utilizing sensory imagery to persuade customers to alter their behavior and choose healthier foods.

5.5 Social Media Influence on Food Preferences

Lopez and Garza (2021) Investigating the distinctions between sensory and non-sensory evaluations, the study looks at the dynamics of online consumer reviews. Employing a vast dataset of 447,792 Amazon reviews, the research identifies five main review categories that range from practical product attributes to sensory encounters. Surprisingly, the results prove otherwise, demonstrating that consumers considered non-sensory reviews—which focus on objective attributes like product performance—to be more helpful than sensory reviews, which provide descriptions of touch, smell, sight, hear, and taste. Reviews that are seen as less objective are attributed to customers' awareness of the subjective character of sensory evaluations, which also reduces the reviews' perceived usefulness. The study sheds more light on the subject of interactive marketing by emphasizing the vital role that reviews play in encouraging user interaction and engagement on e-commerce platforms. Specifically, non-sensory reviews are powerful inducers of customer contact through "word-of-click," which positively influences purchase intention, and customers' responses to online reviews are heavily impacted by their perception of impartiality.

5.6 Multimedia Content and User Engagement

(Shahbaznezhad et al., 2021) The study investigated the use of multimedia data in marketing, with an effort on the usefulness of various content types. It sets rich media apart from inferior media by sending several stimuli concurrently, such as video commercials (like text-only emails). The study emphasizes how modality and medium affect marketing communication while taking sensory processing into account. For example, it states about how differences and connections between visual and aural processing might affect how consumers perceive products. The study includes the data's structure, the reliability of the sources, and the interaction of several modes of meaning communication. The study draws attention to the relative merits of various media outlets, including digital and print advertisements, as well as the differences in the sensory richness of multimedia content. In conclusion, it provides information on how advertisers can use various content forms to increase the impact of their messages on consumers.

(Schlussel & Frosh, 2023) The study examines the impact of format, platform, and content context on user engagement with social media material. The research reveals significant findings based on data from postings made on Facebook and Instagram by Jetstar and Air New Zealand, two airlines. Video content encourages active involvement (likes and comments), whereas photo content encourages passive interaction. Compared to Facebook users, Instagram users are more likely to like posts, suggesting that the platform affects users' interaction patterns. The environment of the material influences engagement; for example, logical content presented in pictorial format gets more likes. Emotional content in videos promotes more engaged viewing. Transactional content has a cross-platform impact. Additionally, the study shows a novel relationship between user engagement patterns, suggesting that the tone of comments has a big impact on post likes.

(Frosh & Schlussel, 2023) This study examines hyper-sensory movies, focusing especially on Facebook recipe material. Notable findings include the deliberate use of minimalist design to provide an air of objectivity, the need for subtitles due to silent auto-play, and the preference for social connectivity over watching movies in their totality. The phrase "hyper-sensory films" highlights emotional reactions and includes subgenres like ASMR and slime making. By combining extreme close-ups and synesthetic potential with touch and taste senses, the study explores embodied sensory experiences. Touch interfaces on smartphones enhance multimodal experiences by acknowledging the instrumentalization of touch and potentially rearranging the traditional connections between senses and technologies. Hyper sensory movies, in general, function as cultural responses that offer increased sensory stimulation to interrupt social media use. The study broadens our understanding of how people interact with digital content through their senses, especially as it relates to social media.

5.7 Quality Assessment in Social Media:

(Berger, 2015) The study develops a dual-component theory (DCT) of perceptual experiences, which postulates distinct sensory and cognitive components. The writer emphasizes the sensory element and introduces Quality-Space Semantics (QSS) as a means of establishing criteria for identifying sensory representation. QSS states that sensory aspects match characteristics found in quality spaces linked to an organism's ability to discriminate. In line with naturalistic explanations, it offers a thorough, nonconceptual explanation of sensory content. Low-level features are deemed to satisfy the recommended standards, In contrast, high-level properties are thought not to have a family or modality. These standards provide the conditions for sensory representation. In addition to addressing critiques, QSS permits empirical research into potential range of modalities. Within the broader DCT paradigm, the paper's conclusions provide a reasonable, naturalistic explanation of sensory content and have implications for empirical studies on sensory representation.

(Agichtein et al, 2008) The study provides a comprehensive inquiry on quality estimation in community question answering through the use of a novel graph-based model that blends user relationships, content properties, and usage trends. Interestingly, the study demonstrates that by combining many data sources, including text-based features, user relationships, and usage statistics, it is able to precisely identify both question-and-answer quality and user relationships. The study shows that both sources complement each other effectively to enhance the resilience and overall performance of the classifier. The discovery of significant characteristics, such as answer length, linguistic qualities, and user behavior, advances our knowledge of the factors influencing the caliber of information. The authors show off how their approach may be used on popular social media platforms, with positive results in terms of locating excellent material. The report highlights the potential for additional research aimed at addressing malicious user behavior. All things considered, by offering a thorough framework and shedding light on the many variables influencing the quality of content, the research considerably advances quality evaluation in social media.

5.8 Language and Content in Advertising

The effects of language (L1 vs. L2) and product description kinds (neutral vs. sensory language) in advertising are examined in this study, with a focus on plant-based beef alternatives. The objective of this research is to examine how the localization and standardization of advertisements affect the attitudes, desirability, and purchase intention of multinational corporations (MNCs), in addition to the increasing interest of consumers in eco-friendly food options. The study finds that, with no obvious effects for other factors, sensory language significantly increases purchase intention in L1, in contrast to neutral language, using the Revised Hierarchical Model (RHM). In L2, descriptions in both sensory and neutral languages function equally well. The implications for practice suggest that whereas both language kinds may be

MNCs may find sensory language in L1 more persuasive for localized commercials, even when it is equally effective in standardized marketing (L2). This is especially true for novel commodities like plant-based animal substitutes. Though there are a number of limitations, including a narrow focus on products and a lack of cultural investigation, this research provides valuable insights for multinational corporations (MNCs) navigating promotional strategies in the face of linguistic and cultural diversity.

(Spooren, 2021)) With a focus on sensory aspects, this study builds on earlier research that looked at the role of language in influencing eating decisions. Language, especially when it emphasizes indulgence, has been shown in earlier research to significantly influence implicit links and influence eating decisions. But the investigation's focus is expanded in this study to include the internet, where decision-making requires fewer sensory inputs. The research looks at how people respond to linguistic variations in virtual environments using restaurant menus that have intentionally changed sensory, health-focused, and neutral language types.

On the contrary to estimates, the study demonstrated no substantial effects of description type on implicit associations, food-related cognitions, or self-reported food desire. This unanticipated result highlights the complicated dynamics of language's impact on implicit cognitive processes, predominantly in the setting of digital environments, and calls into question long-held views. The study highlights the need for fully comprehending language interventions, particularly in terms of the ways in which internet platforms influence consumer preferences. These unanticipated conclusions provide vital new information for future research on the creation of effective language therapies to promote healthy eating choices in virtual settings by forcing the literature's underlying assumptions to be meticulously reassessed.

(Jaud et al., 2023) Two trials are undertaken in order to increase external validity as this study examines the impact of storytelling on people's perception of flavors. In Study 1, the effect of of natural and human storytelling on taste was significant, particularly when the plot aligned with the package type. An important component was added to Study 2, an online trial, regarding the product dimension (utilitarian versus hedonic). According to the results, narrative conveyance significantly enhanced the flavor of utilitarian (milk) products as opposed to hedonic (milkshake) products. By emphasizing the congruence between package type and content and utilitarian product—two prerequisites for good storytelling aspect—the research promotes sensory marketing. The implications for marketing practice include that product features and storytelling should be matched for the greatest taste impression. There are certain disadvantages, though, such as the focus on food products and the need to research other narrative structures. This brief but comprehensive study can provide researchers and practitioners with important new insights into the intricate dynamics of taste perception and storytelling.

5.9 Impact of Music on E-Commerce:

(Hwang et al., 2020) The study greatly advances our knowledge of the intricate relationships that exist between interactive music, online business, and client involvement. The relationship between interactive music and experiential and cognitive values at varying customer participation levels is complex, as evidenced by the results.

The study effectively shows that interactive music produces a unique and pleasurable sensory experience that significantly raises the experiential value of online shopping, particularly for low-involvement customers. However, the idea that affective cues alone may sway low-involvement purchasers is called into question by the addition of cognitive value as a mediating component, highlighting the nuanced nature of consumer decision-making. The results demonstrate how important it is to consider both the cognitive and affective dimensions of sensory experiences in order to completely understand how sensory-enabling technologies work.

Furthermore, by employing a multimodal technique that considers both visual and auditory aspects, the study improves the field of sensory marketing. Future research should concentrate more on the practical implications for marketers aiming to use interactive music to develop online shopping experiences that support different levels of user participation, even though the results offer interesting theoretical information.

(Pantoja & Borges, 2021) This study investigates the relationship between background music speed and consumer responses in relation to food intake, a topic that has not gotten much attention in the literature. While it is commonly known that music affects consumer experiences, little research has been done on how music specifically affects how people react to cues related to food. The research builds on past understanding of sensory inputs in marketing by concentrating on the particular effects of music tempo on cognition, affect, and behavior.

The theoretical framework emphasizes the significance of pace by putting forth the idea that it is a strong stimulus influencing emotional states, which subsequently affects expectations regarding flavor and buying intentions. This study is the first to examine the conflict between swift and slow music in connection to food promotion and restaurant ambiance, despite the fact that slow music has been used in retail settings previously. The hypotheses, which are supported by three major experiments and several pilot studies, claim that fast music successfully increases taste anticipation and buy intentions. Important underlying mechanisms are revealed, including mood and self-reported arousal. Results consistently show that there is a positive correlation between fast-paced audio content and food cues, which influences consumer behavior and provides advertisers and marketers with valuable data.

5.10 Length of Content and User Engagement:

(Park et al., 2021) The study looks at how users engage with online video content, specifically on YouTube, using two datasets. It illustrates the positive relationships between video length and metrics like view count and likes per watch. Notably, viewers spend more time watching well-liked videos with greater likes to views ratios. Additionally, the study finds a modest correlation between negative attitudes in the comments and longer view times, suggesting that videos with more negative remarks may capture viewers' interest for longer. The study emphasizes the significance of stay time and contends that it offers a more accurate gauge of user involvement than common metrics like view count. According to the results, metrics other than popularity might be a better gauge of user engagement, which has implications for platforms and content producers. The paper recommends that future studies look into "social traces" to learn more about user viewing behaviors and to better understand the causal relationships between video metrics and user behaviors.

(Munaro et al., 2021) The language usage and emotional resonance are influencing the number of views of digital influencers' YouTube videos, as investigated in this study. The complete analysis produced distinguished results and included data from 11,177 video posts as well as sophisticated machine learning algorithms. According to the results, extremely positive emotions had the contradictory effect on engagement metrics, such as views, likes, and comments, as expected. This study showed that, there were fewer dislikes for instructional videos, and comment generation is triggered by positive functional features. Optimal duration of videos, airing outside of regular business hours, and prioritizing specific content categories are strategic considerations highlighted for digital influencers and brands. The results exhibited that YouTube visitors are inclined to select medium- and long length films, particularly after business hours. The study also presented valuable recommendations for content creators, emphasizing the need for carefully selecting linguistic elements and striking a balance between emotional and realistic tones in movies in order to boost viewer engagement. The inference highlighted the significance of well-considered social media strategies and the page integration of machine learning techniques in marketing research to get a clear understanding of consumer behavior.

6. CONCLUSION

This chapter, backed by extensive research, indicates a wide range of complex factors, such as interaction between various forms of sensory content, its quality, length, and attributes of intangibilities that impact consumer engagements and purchase intentions of specific food brands within the digital commerce food sector. The results of the various researches demonstrated that the type of content has a significant impact on customer decisions on a particular menu or brand. Videos and photos presented on the online platforms influence most, with text and audios having less of an effect. Integration of a variety of varied visual elements is important for gaining positive evaluation by the audiences, and a good sensory content strategy needs the synergistic effect of merging images and videos. Quality factors—in particular, originality, consistency, and clarity—were found to be crucial in determining consumers' intents to make purchases. This means that marketers must make investments in creative content production, high-resolution graphics, and brand consistency.

This chapter also reveals the uncovered result from the research that there is a complex relationship between the length of information and user engagement, highlighting the need for concise but impactful material. Achieving a balance between brevity and informativeness is essential for conforming to wider trends in digital marketing and giving marketers a framework for curating content that works.

Online food sector marketers who heavily concentrate on e-commerce platforms could modify their approaches by emphasizing video content, varying visual components, spending money on high-quality content, and carefully choosing the length of their material. Campaigns need to revolve around interactive content experiences that promote constructive consumer interactions. In addition to that, it is imperative to contextualize these strategies in light of the distinct cultural dynamics of the market. This will guarantee a stronger resonance with the target audience and, eventually, improve the efficacy of digital marketing initiatives within the cutthroat online food industry.

REFERENCES

Agichtein, E., Castillo, C., Donato, D., Gionis, A., & Mishne, G. (2008). Finding high-quality content in social media. *Proceedings of the 2008 International Conference on Web Search and Data Mining,* 2008. DOI: 10.1145/1341531.1341557

Berger, J. (2015). The sensory content of perceptual experience. *Pacific Philosophical Quarterly*, 96(4), 446–468. DOI: 10.1111/papq.12110

Bhayani, S., & Vachhani, N. V. (2014). Internet marketing vs traditional marketing: A comparative analysis. *FIIB Business Review*, 3(3), 53–63. DOI: 10.1177/2455265820140309

Bill Aull, Dymfke Kuijpers, and Daniel Laubli - https://www.mckinsey.com/industries/retail/our-insights/the-next-horizon-for-grocery-ecommerce-beyond-the-pandemic-bump

Biswas, D. (2019). Sensory aspects of retailing: Theoretical and practical implications. *Journal of Retailing*, 95(4), 111–115. DOI: 10.1016/j.jretai.2019.12.001

Brasel, S. A., & Gips, J. (2014). Tablets, touchscreens, and touchpads: How varying touch interfaces trigger psychological ownership and endowment. *Journal of Consumer Psychology*, 24(2), 226–233. DOI: 10.1016/j.jcps.2013.10.003

Chao, L. L., & Martin, A. (2000). Representation of Manipulable Man-Made Objects in the Dorsal Stream. *NeuroImage*, 12(4), 478–484. DOI: 10.1006/nimg.2000.0635 PMID: 10988041

Edsall, D., Gray, C., Witherspoon, J., McDonnell, M., & Almond, A. (n.d). *The future of grocery retail.* Deloitte. Retrieved 2024-02-05 from https://www2.deloitte.com/us/en/insights/industry/retail-distribution/future-of-grocery- retail.html

Elder, R. S., & Krishna, A. (2010). The effects of advertising copy on sensory thoughts and perceived taste. *The Journal of Consumer Research*, 36(5), 748–756. DOI: 10.1086/605327

Elder, R. S., & Krishna, A. (2022). A Review of Sensory Imagery for Consumer Psychology. *Journal of Consumer Psychology*, 32(2), 293–315. DOI: 10.1002/jcpy.1242

Ellison, K., Truman, E., & Elliott, C. (2023). Picturing food: The visual style of teen-targeted food marketing. *Young Consumers*, 24(3), 352–366. DOI: 10.1108/YC-08-2022-1577

Gallace, A., Ngo, M. K., Sulaitis, J., & Spence, C. (2012). Multisensory presence in virtual reality: Possibilities & limitations. In Andres, F., Ghenea, G., & Gulliver, S. (Eds.), *Multiple sensorial media advances and applications: New developments in MulSeMedia* (pp. 1–38). IGI Global. DOI: 10.4018/978-1-60960-821-7.ch001

Girard, A., Lichters, M., Sarstedt, M., & Biswas, D. (2019). Short- and long-term effects of nonconsciously processed ambient scents in a servicescape: Findings from two field experiments. *Journal of Service Research*, 22(4), 440–455. DOI: 10.1177/1094670519842333

Haase, J., Wiedmann, K., Bettels, J., & Labenz, F. (2018). How to best promote my product? Comparing the effectiveness of sensory, functional and symbolic advertising content in food marketing. *British Food Journal*, 120(8), 1792–1806. DOI: 10.1108/BFJ-01-2018-0058

Hamacher, K., & Buchkremer, R. (2022). Measuring Online Sensory Consumer experience: Introducing the Online Sensory Marketing Index (OSMI) as a structural modeling approach. *Journal of Theoretical and Applied Electronic Commerce Research*, 17(2), 751–772. DOI: 10.3390/jtaer17020039

Hashimoto, Y., Inami, M., & Kajimoto, H. (2008, June). *Straw-like user interface (II): A new method of presenting auditory sensations for a more natural experience* [Paper presentation]. International Conference on Human Haptic Sensing and Touch Enabled Computer Applications (pp. 484–493). https://www.strategyand.pwc.com/de/en/industries/consumer-markets/future-of-grocery-shopping.html

Huang, I. X., & Labroo, A. A. (2020). Cueing morality: The effect of high-pitched music on healthy choice. *Journal of Marketing*, 84(6), 130–143. DOI: 10.1177/0022242918813577

Hwang, A. H., Oh, J., & Scheinbaum, A. C. (2020). Interactive music for multisensory e-commerce: The moderating role of online consumer involvement in experiential

Ifeanyichukwu, C. D., & Peter, A. (2018). The role of sensory marketing in achieving customer patronage in fast food restaurants in Awka. *International Research Journal of Management, IT &. Social Sciences*, 5(2), 155–163. DOI: 10.21744/irjmis.v5i2.632

Iqbal, J. & e-Hassan, I. (2016). Employing Sensory Marketing as a Promotional Advantage for Creating Brand Differentiation and Brand Loyalty. *Pakistan Journal of Commerce and Social Sciences*, 10(3), 725–734.

Izzuddin, D. (2021, November 29). *New Horizons: The rise of food photography*. The Edge Malaysia. https://theedgemalaysia.com/article/new-horizons-rise-food-photography

Jarmin, R. S., Klimek, S. D., & Miranda, J. (2009). The Role of Retail Chains: National, Regional, and Industry Results. In T. Dunne, J. Bradford Jensen & M.J Roberts (Eds), *Producer Dynamics: New Evidence from Micro Data* (p. 237-262). University of Chicago Press

Jaud, D. A., Braconnot, A. R., & Lunardo, R. (2023). Do stories (always) make food products taste better? The boundary effects of matching package type and product dimension. *Journal of Consumer Behaviour*, 22(5), 1224–1236. DOI: 10.1002/cb.2207

Jiang, Z., & Benbasat, I. (2007). The effects of presentation formats and task complexity on online consumers' product understanding. *Management Information Systems Quarterly*, 31(3), 475–500. DOI: 10.2307/25148804

JO - Personality and social psychology review: an official journal of the Society for Personality and Social Psychology, Inc

Kaushik, S., & Gokhale, N. (2021). Online Sensory Marketing: Developing Five- Dimensional Multi-Sensory Brand Experiences and its Effectiveness. *Revista GEINTEC*, 11(4), 5375–5391. DOI: 10.47059/revistageintec.v11i4.2567

Krishna, A. (2010). *An introduction to Sensory marketing*. Routledge.

Krishna, A. (2011). An integrative review of sensory marketing: Engaging the senses to affect perception, judgment and behavior. *Journal of Consumer Psychology*, 22(3), 332–351. DOI: 10.1016/j.jcps.2011.08.003

Krishna, A., & Morrin, M. (2008). Does Touch Affect Taste? The Perceptual Transfer of Product Container Haptic Cues. *The Journal of Consumer Research*, 34(6), 807–818. DOI: 10.1086/523286

Labroo, A. A., & Nielsen, J. H. (2010). Half the Thrill is in the Chase: Twisted Inferences from Embodied Cognitions and Brand Evaluation. *The Journal of Consumer Research*, 37(1), 143–158. DOI: 10.1086/649908

Lawrence, M., & Friel, S. (Eds.), *Healthy and Sustainable Food Systems*. Routledge. DOI: 10.4324/9781351189033

Lee, J., & Lim, H. (2023). Visual aesthetics and multisensory engagement in online food delivery services. *International Journal of Retail & Distribution Management*, 51(8), 975–990. DOI: 10.1108/IJRDM-09-2021-0451

Lemon, K. N., & Verhoef, P. C. (2016). Understanding Customer Experience Throughout the Customer Journey. *Journal of Marketing*, 80(6), 69–96. DOI: 10.1509/jm.15.0420

Liu, F., Xiao, B., Lim, E. T., & Tan, C. W. (2017). The art of appeal in electronic commerce: Understanding the impact of product and website quality on online purchases. *Internet Research*, 27(4), 752–771. DOI: 10.1108/IntR-09-2016-0280

Lopez, A., & Garza, R. (2021). Do sensory reviews make more sense? The mediation of objective perception in online review helpfulness. *Journal of Research in Interactive Marketing*, 16(3), 438–456. DOI: 10.1108/JRIM-04-2021-0121

Madzharov, A. V., Block, L. G., & Morrin, M. (2015). The Cool Scent of Power: Effects of Ambient Scent on Consumer Preferences and Choice Behavior. *Journal of Marketing*, 79(1), 83–96. DOI: 10.1509/jm.13.0263

Mulcahy, R., & Riedel, A. (2021). "Going on a sensory adventure, a touchy subject?": Investigating haptic technology and consumer adventure orientation. *Journal of Service Theory and Practice*, 32(1), 5–29. DOI: 10.1108/JSTP-11-2020-0244

Munaro, A. C., Barcelos, R. H., Maffezzolli, E. C. F., Rodrigues, J. P. S., & Paraíso, E. C. (2021). To engage or not engage? The features of video content on YouTube affecting digital consumer engagement. *Journal of Consumer Behaviour*, 20(5), 1336–1352. DOI: 10.1002/cb.1939

Murray, S., & Caraher, M. (2019). Food Retail and Distribution: A focus on supermarkets. In

Niedenthal et al. (2005) SP - 184,EP - 211,T1 - Embodiment in Attitudes, Social Perception, and Emotion,VL - 9, DO - DOI: 10.1207/s15327957pspr0903_1

Pantoja, F., & Borges, A. (2021). Background music tempo effects on food evaluations and purchase intentions. *Journal of Retailing and Consumer Services*, 63, 102730. DOI: 10.1016/j.jretconser.2021.102730

Papagiannis, H. (2017). *Augmented human: How technology is shaping the new reality*. O'Reilly Media.

Papagiannis, H. (2020, March 18). How AR and VR can be used for virtual travel and tourism in a time of self-isolation and closed borders.

Park, D. H., Lee, J., & Han, I. (2007). The effect of on-line consumer reviews on consumer purchasing intention: The moderating role of involvement. *International Journal of Electronic Commerce*, 11(4), 125–148. DOI: 10.2753/JEC1086-4415110405

Park, M., Naaman, M., & Berger, J. (2021). A Data-Driven Study of view duration on YouTube. *Proceedings of the International AAAI Conference on Web and Social Media, 10*(1), 651–654. https://doi.org/DOI: 10.1609/icwsm.v10i1.14781

Petit, O., Velasco, C., & Spence, C. (2019). Digital sensory marketing: Integrating new technologies into multisensory online experience. *Journal of Interactive Marketing*, 45(1), 42–61. DOI: 10.1016/j.intmar.2018.07.004

Petit, O., Velasco, C., & Spence, C. (2019). Digital Sensory Marketing: Integrating New Technologies Into Multisensory Online Experience. *Journal of Interactive Marketing*, 45(1), 42–61. DOI: 10.1016/j.intmar.2018.07.004

Pine, B. J., & Gilmore, J. H. (2013). The experience economy: past, present and future. In Sundbo, J., & Sørensen, F. (Eds.), *Handbook on the Experience Economy* (pp. 21–44). Edward Elgar. DOI: 10.4337/9781781004227.00007

Pitchay, A. A., Ganesa, Y., Zulkifli, N. S., & Khaliq, A. (2022). Determinants of customers' intention to use online food delivery application through smartphone in Malaysia. *British Food Journal*, 124(3), 732–753. https://doi.org/https://doi.org/10.1108/BFJ-01-2021-0075. DOI: 10.1108/BFJ-01-2021-0075

Rantala, J., Salminen, K., Raisamo, R., & Surakka, V. (2013). Touch gestures in communicating emotional intention via vibrotactile stimulation. *International Journal of Human-Computer Studies*, 71(6), 679–690. DOI: 10.1016/j.ijhcs.2013.02.004

Riza, A.F. & Wijayanti, D.M. (2018). The Triangle of Sensory Marketing Model: Does it Stimulate Brand Experience and Loyalty? *Jurnal Bisnis dan Manajemen, 8* (1), 57–66. http://dx.doi.org/DOI: 10.15408/css.v8i1.6058

Sachdeva, I., & Goel, S. (2015). Retail store environment and customer experience: A paradigm. *Journal of Fashion Marketing and Management*, 19(3), 290–298. DOI: 10.1108/JFMM-03-2015-0021

Schifferstein, H. N., Kudrowitz, B., & Breuer, C. (2020). Food Perception and Aesthetics Linking sensory science to culinary practice. *Journal of Culinary Science & Technology*, 20(4), 293–335. DOI: 10.1080/15428052.2020.1824833

Schlussel, H., & Frosh, P. (2023). The taste of video: Facebook videos as multi-sensory experiences. *Convergence (London)*, 29(4), 980–996. DOI: 10.1177/13548565231179958

Shahbaznezhad, H., Dolan, R., & Rashidirad, M. (2021). The role of social media content format and platform in users' engagement behavior. *Journal of Interactive Marketing*, 53(1), 47–65. DOI: 10.1016/j.intmar.2020.05.001

Shahriari, E., Torres, I. M., Zúñiga, M. Á., & Alfayez, N. (2019). Picture this: The role of mental imagery in induction of food craving – a theoretical framework based on the elaborated intrusion theory. *Journal of Consumer Marketing*, 37(1), 31–42. DOI: 10.1108/JCM-02-2018-2553

Simmons, W. K., Martin, A., & Barsalou, L. W. (2005). Pictures of Appetizing Foods Activate Gustatory Cortices for Taste and Reward. *Cerebral Cortex (New York, N.Y.)*, 15(10), 1602–1608. DOI: 10.1093/cercor/bhi038 PMID: 15703257

Spooren, N. (2021). Effects of sensory language on the experience of food. *2021 Master Scriptie Communicatie*. https://theses.ubn.ru.nl/server/api/core/bitstreams/41885a5e- 1bf5-4cdf-a7da-7ee355c5b0d5/ content value, cognitive value, and purchase intention. *Psychology & Marketing, 37*(8), 1031– 1056. https://doi.org/DOI: 10.1002/mar.21338

Steuer, J. (1992). Defining virtual reality: Dimensions determining telepresence. *Journal of Communication*, 42(4), 73–93. DOI: 10.1111/j.1460-2466.1992.tb00812.x

Szocs, C., Kim, Y., Lim, M., Mera, C. A., & Biswas, D. (2023). The store of the future: Engaging customers through sensory elements, personalized atmospherics, and interpersonal interaction. *Journal of Retailing*, 99(4), 605–620. DOI: 10.1016/j.jretai.2023.11.005

Yim, M. Y. C., Chu, S. C., & Sauer, P. L. (2017). Is augmented reality technology an effective tool for e-commerce? An interactivity and vividness perspective. *Journal of Interactive Marketing, 39*, 89–103. https://doi.org/. intmar.2017.04.001DOI: 10.1016/j

Yuan, Y.-H., & Wu, C. K. (2008). Relationships Among Experiential Marketing, Experiential Value, and Customer Satisfaction. *Journal of Hospitality & Tourism Research (Washington, D.C.)*, 32(3), 387–410. DOI: 10.1177/1096348008317392

Zha, D., Foroudi, P., Jin, Z., & Melewar, T. C. (2022). Making sense of sensory brand experience: Constructing an integrative framework for future research. *International Journal of Management Reviews*, 24(1), 130–167. DOI: 10.1111/ijmr.12270

Chapter 10
Successful Stories on the Usage of Technologies in Service Industries

Yue Guo
https://orcid.org/0009-0007-0163-0652
Taylor's University, Malaysia

ABSTRACT

This paper explores the successful adoption of technological innovations in the food service industry, focusing on restaurant automation, mobile ordering and delivery platforms, and the use of AI and data analytics. Through case studies, it highlights how these technologies have transformed operations, enhanced customer experiences, and improved efficiency. Restaurant automation optimizes processes and reduces labor costs with smart kitchen technologies, while mobile platforms like UberEats and DoorDash expand market reach and convenience. AI and data analytics enable businesses to personalize services, optimize supply chains, and enhance decision-making. The paper also addresses challenges such as workforce displacement and data privacy. Looking forward, emerging technologies like augmented reality (AR), virtual reality (VR), blockchain, robotics, and sustainability innovations will further shape the industry. Continuous innovation and adaptability are essential for businesses to remain competitive, with a focus on balancing technology with human interaction.

1. INTRODUCTION

1.1 Background

In recent years, artificial intelligence (AI) and robotics science have permeated various businesses and industries (Chi et al., 2023). The food service industry has witnessed one of the most profound transformations among these sectors (Belanche et al., 2019). From digital ordering systems like those implemented by McDonald's, where customers use kiosks or mobile apps to place orders (Pantelidis, 2010), to AI-powered recommendations such as Domino's "Dom" virtual assistant, which customizes pizza orders based on customer preferences (Kimes, 2011), technology has reshaped how food is prepared, served, and consumed. Automated kitchens, exemplified by companies like Spyce, where robots

DOI: 10.4018/979-8-3693-7683-6.ch010

handle food preparation (Ivanov et al., 2022), and delivery robots used by services such as Starship Technologies for autonomous food deliveries (Marr, 2019), are further driving these changes. These innovations streamline operations, redefine customer experiences, enhance efficiency, and open new business models by offering convenience and customization at scale.

The rapid adoption of technology in food service is driven by several key factors. First, the growing demand for convenience and speed has pushed businesses to adopt solutions that can meet the high expectations of modern consumers. Second, competition in the food service sector is fierce, with companies constantly seeking new ways to differentiate themselves and offer unique customer experiences. Technology provides a pathway for businesses to achieve these goals, enabling them to provide faster, more personalized, and efficient services. Additionally, the global pandemic accelerated digital transformation in food service, as many businesses had to pivot quickly to online ordering, contactless delivery, and other innovations to survive (Chin, Marasini, & Lee, 2022).

1.2 Purpose and Scope

The purpose of this paper is to explore the successful stories of technology adoption in the food service industry. By focusing on key examples of how technology has been effectively integrated, this paper aims to provide insights into the factors that contribute to successful implementation and highlight the benefits that technology can bring to food service businesses. These stories not only showcase the immediate impact of these innovations but also point to the future trends that will continue to shape the industry.

This paper will cover a range of technologies that have been pivotal in transforming the food service industry. These include mobile ordering and delivery platforms, AI-driven customer service tools, automation in kitchens, and data analytics for supply chain management. Through real-world case studies, we will examine how these technologies have improved operational efficiency, enhanced customer satisfaction, and driven business growth(Addanki et al., 2022).

1.3 Research Focus

The core focus of this research is to understand how different technologies have been successfully deployed in the food service industry and to identify the key enablers of their success. This includes analyzing the role of leadership, customer-centric innovation, cost considerations, and the ability to integrate new systems with existing business operations. The paper will also explore the challenges that businesses have faced in adopting these technologies and how they have been overcome.

1.4 Methodology Overview

The research will utilise a case study approach to ensure a comprehensive understanding of technology's impact (Phelan, 2011). This method allows for an in-depth exploration of successful implementations across various food service businesses, ranging from global fast-food chains to niche local restaurants. The cases were selected based on their innovative use of technology, measurable impact on business performance, and potential to serve as models for future adoption.

2. LITERATURE REVIEW

2.1 Technological Advancements in the Food Service Industry

The food service industry has long been considered one of the most dynamic sectors in terms of integrating technological innovations. Over the past few decades, rapid advancements in technology have significantly impacted how businesses operate and interact with consumers. Key technologies such as artificial intelligence (AI), Internet of Things (IoT), automation, mobile applications, and data analytics have introduced new possibilities for streamlining operations, improving customer service, and enhancing overall efficiency (Akyazi et al., 2020).

For example, mobile ordering platforms have dramatically changed the way customers interact with restaurants, offering convenience and personalized services that were previously unattainable (Ricky, 2014). Companies like Domino's and Starbucks have implemented mobile applications that allow customers to order ahead, customize their meals, and earn rewards, increasing both customer engagement and operational efficiency. These advancements have also helped businesses optimize kitchen operations, reduce food waste, and manage inventory more effectively through real-time data (Alalwan, 2020).

Furthermore, automated systems, such as robotic kitchen assistants and self-service kiosks, are revolutionizing the food preparation and ordering process. Robots like Flippy by Miso Robotics have been adopted by fast-food chains to handle repetitive cooking tasks, improving consistency and reducing labour costs. Similarly, self-service kiosks have enabled customers to place their orders in restaurants like McDonald's, decreasing wait times and allowing for more accurate order customization (Elbrechter, 2015).

Another important development is the use of data analytics and AI to predict customer preferences and streamline supply chain management. Restaurants are leveraging machine learning algorithms to analyze customer behaviour and predict trends, enabling them to tailor their offerings more effectively. AI is also being utilized to optimize supply chain logistics, helping companies forecast demand and reduce food spoilage (Dwivedi et al., 2021).

2.2 Technology Acceptance Models

The adoption of new technologies in the food service industry can be explained through various theoretical frameworks, such as the Technology Acceptance Model (TAM) (Scherer et al., 2019) and the Unified Theory of Acceptance and Use of Technology (UTAUT). These models provide a theoretical basis for understanding the factors that influence the acceptance and use of technology among individuals and organizations (Venkatesh et al., 2016).

The Technology Acceptance Model (TAM), introduced by Davis (1989), suggests that two key factors—perceived usefulness and perceived ease of use—determine whether individuals will accept and adopt new technologies. In the context of the food service industry, perceived usefulness refers to how much the technology improves operational efficiency or customer satisfaction, while perceived ease of use reflects how simple and intuitive the technology is for employees and customers to interact with (Davis, 1985).

The Unified Theory of Acceptance and Use of Technology (UTAUT) expands on TAM by adding social influence, facilitating conditions, and performance expectancy as additional factors that affect technology adoption. Social influence in the food service industry might come from competitive pressure or the desire to meet customer expectations for fast, tech-enabled services. Facilitating conditions refer to the organizational and technical infrastructure that supports technology implementation, while performance expectancy highlights the expected benefits in terms of operational efficiency or customer experience. The Technology Acceptance Model (TAM) and the Unified Theory of Acceptance and Use of Technology (UTAUT) are both widely used frameworks in understanding technology adoption, but they differ in scope and complexity. TAM, developed by Fred Davis (1989), focuses on two primary factors—perceived usefulness and ease of use—influencing users' intentions to adopt technology. Its simplicity and applicability across various contexts make it a popular model.

On the other hand, UTAUT, proposed by Venkatesh et al. (2003), integrates multiple models, including TAM, and adds factors like social influence, facilitating conditions, and performance expectancy. UTAUT also introduces moderators such as age, gender, and experience to provide a more nuanced understanding of user behaviour. While TAM is often appreciated for its simplicity, UTAUT is more comprehensive and accounts for a broader range of variables that can affect technology acceptance.

Both models complement each other by offering different levels of complexity. TAM provides a streamlined view that is easier to apply in general contexts, while UTAUT offers depth and is useful for understanding more complex scenarios where individual differences and external conditions play significant roles. Together, these models offer a richer framework for analyzing technology adoption, covering both foundational and expanded perspectives (Venkatesh et al., 2003).

These models are valuable for understanding the adoption of technology in food service, where ease of integration, user-friendliness, and clear benefits in terms of profitability and customer engagement are critical factors driving acceptance.

2.3 Challenges and Opportunities in the Food Service Industry

While the integration of technology in the food service industry presents immense opportunities, it also brings several challenges that businesses must navigate. One of the primary challenges is the cost of adopting new technologies. High upfront investments in software, hardware, and infrastructure may be prohibitive for small and medium-sized businesses, limiting their ability to compete with larger chains that have more resources for technological innovation (Pantelidis, 2010; Lu et al., 2021). Additionally, the cost of maintenance, updates, and training can add to the overall expense of implementing new systems (Kimes, 2011).

Another challenge is employee adaptation to new technology. For example, in the case of automation or AI-powered tools, employees may need to undergo significant training to become proficient in using the systems. Resistance to change, whether due to fear of job loss or unfamiliarity with the technology, can hinder the smooth implementation of innovations (Ivanov & Webster, 2019; Belanche et al., 2020).

Moreover, ensuring data security and privacy is a major concern, especially when businesses collect sensitive customer data through mobile applications or online platforms. Restaurants and food service providers must comply with data protection regulations, such as GDPR in Europe, to maintain customer trust and avoid penalties (Tuomi & Tussyadiah, 2020; Marr, 2019).

On the other hand, technology offers vast opportunities to enhance efficiency, reduce costs, and improve customer experiences. For instance, AI-powered data analytics tools can help restaurants predict customer preferences and optimize inventory, reducing food waste and ensuring that the right products are available at the right time (Kimes, 2011; Belanche et al., 2020). In addition, automation technologies can free up employees from repetitive tasks, allowing them to focus on more customer-centric roles that enhance service quality (Spyce, 2022; Moley Robotics, 2021).

The rise of contactless payment solutions and online ordering platforms, especially accelerated by the COVID-19 pandemic, has also shown how technology can adapt to changing customer needs. These innovations not only increase convenience for customers but also streamline business operations, reducing the need for physical interaction and minimizing human errors (Yoon & Lee, 2019).

Furthermore, the integration of IoT in supply chain management offers opportunities for real-time tracking of inventory, predictive maintenance, and improved transparency in food sourcing. These technologies can improve the quality and safety of food products, as well as enable businesses to respond quickly to demand fluctuations (Tussyadiah, 2020).

2.4 Conclusion of the Literature Review

In conclusion, the food service industry stands at the forefront of a technological revolution that has the potential to reshape traditional business models, enhance operational efficiency, and elevate customer experiences. While there are challenges related to cost, employee adaptation, and data security, the opportunities presented by technologies such as AI, automation, and mobile platforms far outweigh the risks. The application of theoretical models like TAM and UTAUT provides a solid framework for understanding the factors influencing technology adoption in this sector. The following sections of this paper will explore specific case studies of successful technology implementation in the food service industry, highlighting how these innovations have transformed businesses and the customer experience (Chi et al., 2023; Gursoy et al., 2019).

3. CASE STUDY

3.1 Restaurant Automation

Restaurant automation has become one of the most transformative forces in the food service industry, reshaping the way restaurants operate and deliver customer service (Websteret al., 2020; Berezina et al., 2019). Automation technologies range from robotic kitchen assistants to self-service kiosks, helping businesses streamline operations, reduce costs, and improve efficiency (Belanche et al., 2020; Lu et al., 2021). The rise of automation in restaurants has been largely driven by the need to address labour shortages, improve consistency in food preparation, and meet increasing consumer demand for speed and convenience (Kimes, 2011; Pantelidis, 2010). This case study examines two key examples of automation in the restaurant industry: robotic chefs and kitchens, such as those used by Spyce and Moley Robotics (Moley Robotics, 2021; Spyce, 2022), and self-service kiosks implemented by McDonald's and other major chains (Pantelidis, 2010), exploring their impact on both businesses and customers.

3.1.1 Example 1: Robotic Chefs and Kitchens

One of the most innovative applications of automation in the food service industry is the use of robotic chefs and fully automated kitchens. These technologies are designed to handle repetitive and time-consuming tasks, allowing human staff to focus on higher-level duties such as customer service and supervision. A notable example of robotic chefs in action is Spyce Restaurant in Boston, which introduced the world's first robotic kitchen in 2018. The restaurant's fully automated kitchen uses robotic arms to prepare meals, handle ingredients, and cook food, all without human intervention (Seal, 2023).

How Spyce's Robotic Kitchen Works

Spyce's kitchen operates with a series of robotic cooking devices that handle various stages of food preparation. Customers place their orders via digital kiosks, choosing from a menu of customizable bowls. Once an order is placed, the robotic system retrieves the ingredients, which are pre-measured and prepped in advance. The ingredients are then cooked in specialized robotic woks, each designed to handle different cooking techniques such as stir-frying, steaming, or searing. The robots ensure precise cooking times and temperatures, guaranteeing consistency in every dish. Once the cooking process is completed, the robots plate the meal, which is delivered to the customer via a conveyor system. Throughout the process, human staff oversee the robots, ensuring smooth operation and addressing any malfunctions. The automation system significantly reduces the time it takes to prepare a meal, often completing an order in under three minutes (Berezina et al., 2019).

Impact on Business Performance

Spyce's robotic kitchen offers several clear advantages for the business. First, the automation system reduces the need for a large kitchen staff, cutting labour costs and addressing the labor shortages that many restaurants face. In addition, the precision of the robotic chefs ensures consistent quality in every dish, reducing errors and food waste. The system's efficiency also allows Spyce to serve a high volume of customers during peak hours, improving overall throughput and customer satisfaction (Romero & Lado, 2021).

In terms of customer experience, Spyce's robotic kitchen offers a novel dining experience that appeals to tech-savvy customers, particularly millennials and Generation Z, who are attracted to innovative and efficient service models. The restaurant's use of automation also aligns with the growing consumer demand for speed and convenience in food service, making it a competitive player in the fast-casual dining sector (Mulyadi & Masatip, 2020).

3.1.2 Example 2: Self-Service Kiosks

Another significant automation trend in the restaurant industry is the widespread adoption of self-service kiosks. These kiosks allow customers to place their orders without interacting with a cashier, streamlining the ordering process and reducing wait times. One of the leading examples of self-service kiosk implementation is McDonald's, which introduced kiosks in many of its locations as part of its"-Experience of the Future" initiative (Chi et al., 2020).

How McDonald's Self-Service Kiosks Work

McDonald's self-service kiosks are touchscreen devices that allow customers to browse the menu, customize their orders, and complete payment, all without the assistance of staff (Kim, 2021). The kiosks are designed to be user-friendly, with intuitive interfaces and clear instructions for navigating the menu.

Customers can select from a variety of customization options, such as adding or removing ingredients, choosing portion sizes, and selecting specific cooking preferences(Addanki et al., 2022).

Once an order is placed, it is sent directly to the kitchen, where staff prepare the meal. Customers can choose to have their order delivered to their table or pick it up at the counter. The kiosks also integrate with McDonald's mobile app, allowing customers to place an order in advance and simply pick it up when they arrive at the restaurant (Kim, 2021).

Impact on Business Performance

The implementation of self-service kiosks has provided McDonald's with several key benefits. First, the kiosks reduce the need for cashiers, allowing staff to focus on other tasks, such as food preparation and customer service. This has led to improved operational efficiency, as fewer employees are required to handle front-of-house duties. Additionally, the kiosks enable McDonald's to serve more customers during busy periods, as the ordering process is faster and less prone to bottlenecks (Lu et al. 2019).

Self-service kiosks have also been shown to increase average order sizes, as customers are more likely to add extra items when ordering through a kiosk. The kiosks' interface often prompts customers with suggestions for additional purchases, such as upgrading to a larger size or adding a dessert. This upselling strategy has contributed to higher revenue per transaction.

From the customer's perspective, the self-service kiosks offer convenience and flexibility. Customers can take their time to browse the menu and customize their orders without feeling rushed, leading to a more personalized dining experience. Additionally, the option to pay electronically at the kiosk reduces the need for cash handling, which has become increasingly important in the post-pandemic era, where contactless transactions are preferred (Addanki et al., 2022).

Outcomes and Benefits of Restaurant Automation

Both robotic chefs and self-service kiosks have brought significant benefits to the food service industry, improving operational efficiency, reducing labour costs, and enhancing the customer experience. The precision and consistency offered by robotic kitchen systems ensure that food is prepared to the same high standard every time,while the speed of automation allows restaurants to serve more customers in less time. Self-service kiosks, meanwhile, streamline the ordering process and provide opportunities for businesses to increase revenue through upselling and customization(Li et al., 2022).

Automation technologies also have the potential to reduce waste, both in terms of food and labour. For example, robotic systems that use precise measurements can help minimize ingredient waste, while automated ordering processes reduce the likelihood of incorrect orders. Furthermore, by freeing up staff from repetitive tasks, automation allows restaurants to allocate their human resources more effectively, focusing on customer engagement and service quality.

However, it is important to note that automation is not without its challenges. High upfront costs for installing and maintaining robotic systems and kiosks can be prohibitive, especially for smaller businesses. Additionally, there may be resistance from employees who fear that automation could lead to job displacement. Despite these challenges, the overall benefits of restaurant automation, particularly in terms of efficiency and customer satisfaction, make it a promising trend for the future of the food service industry(Hao, 2021).

3.1.2 Conclusion

Restaurant automation, exemplified by robotic chefs and self-service kiosks, represents a significant leap forward in the evolution of the food service industry. These technologies have proven their ability to improve operational efficiency, reduce labour costs, and enhance the customer experience(Gursoy et al., 2019). As automation continues to evolve and become more accessible, its role in shaping the future of the food service industry will likely expand, offering new opportunities for innovation and growth. In the next case study, we will explore how mobile ordering and delivery platforms have further transformed the landscape of food service.

3.2 Mobile Ordering and Delivery Platforms

The proliferation of mobile technology has dramatically altered the landscape of the food service industry, particularly through the rise of mobile ordering and delivery platforms. These platforms have redefined convenience for both customers and restaurants, enabling customers to place orders through mobile apps or websites and have food delivered to their doorsteps with minimal effort. Restaurants have benefited from these platforms by expanding their customer reach, streamlining operations, and increasing revenue without the need for dine-in services(Tung & Au, 2018). This case study examines the impact of mobile ordering and delivery platforms, focusing on the examples of Uber Eats and Starbucks Mobile Order & Pay, to highlight how these technologies have transformed food service businesses (Addanki et al., 2022).

3.2.1 Example 1: Uber Eats

Uber Eats, a subsidiary of the global ride-sharing company Uber, is one of the most successful food delivery platforms in the world. Launched in 2014, the platform connects customers with a wide range of restaurants, offering on-demand food delivery with real-time tracking and easy payment options. Uber Eats has leveraged its parent company's extensive driver network to scale rapidly, operating in over 6,000 cities worldwide. The platform's business model is built around offering convenience and efficiency to both restaurants and customers, with a focus on expanding the delivery market for food service providers (Raj et al., 2020).

How Uber Eats Works

Uber Eats operates through a mobile app and website that allows customers to browse a list of participating restaurants, view menus, and place orders for delivery. Once an order is placed, it is transmitted to the restaurant, where staff prepare the food. An Uber Eats delivery partner (often a driver or cyclist) is then assigned to pick up the order and deliver it to the customer's location. The app provides real-time updates on the status of the order, from the time it is being prepared to when it is out for delivery.

One of the key features of Uber Eats is its algorithm-driven system for assigning delivery partners. The platform uses real-time data on traffic, driver availability, and restaurant location to optimize delivery routes, ensuring that food arrives quickly and efficiently. Uber Eats also integrates various payment methods, including credit cards, digital wallets, and cash (in some regions), making it a versatile platform for a wide range of customers (Isaac et al.,2019).

Impact on Business Performance

Uber Eats has had a profound impact on the food service industry, particularly in expanding market reach for restaurants. By partnering with Uber Eats, restaurants can offer delivery services without needing to invest in their delivery infrastructure. This has been particularly beneficial for small and medium-sized restaurants that may not have the resources to develop an in-house delivery system. The platform allows them to reach new customers who may not have visited their physical location but are looking for convenient delivery options (Wahl, 2019).

The platform also provides valuable data analytics to restaurant partners, offering insights into customer preferences, order volumes, and peak times. Restaurants can use this information to optimize their menus, streamline kitchen operations, and adjust staffing levels to meet demand. Additionally, Uber Eats' promotional features, such as discount offers and free delivery promotions, help boost restaurant visibility and drive sales.

From a customer perspective, Uber Eats offers unparalleled convenience. With the ability to order from a wide range of restaurants via a single platform, customers can enjoy a variety of food options with just a few taps on their phones. The real-time tracking feature enhances the customer experience by providing transparency and reducing uncertainty about when their food will arrive.

However, there are challenges associated with using third-party delivery platforms like Uber Eats. Restaurants must pay a commission fee, typically ranging from 15% to 30% of each order, which can eat into profit margins. Additionally, the quality of food may sometimes be compromised during delivery, as restaurants have little control over how long it takes for the food to reach the customer or how it is handled during transit. Despite these challenges, Uber Eats has proven to be a valuable tool for many restaurants looking to expand their delivery services and cater to the growing demand for convenience (Isaac et al.,2019).

3.2.2 Example 2: Starbucks Mobile Order & Pay

Starbucks has been a pioneer in the adoption of mobile ordering, introducing its Mobile Order & Pay feature in 2015. This feature allows customers to order and pay for their drinks and food via the Starbucks mobile app, and then pick them up at their nearest store without waiting in line. By streamlining the ordering process, Starbucks has successfully enhanced customer convenience while simultaneously improving store operations and efficiency (Chuang, 2019).

How Starbucks Mobile Order & Pay Works

The Starbucks app allows customers to browse the full menu, customize their orders, and select the store where they want to pick up their items. Customers can choose from various options such as drink size, milk preferences, and additional ingredients, creating a highly personalized order. Once the order is placed, it is sent directly to the selected store, where baristas prepare the drinks and food. Customers receive a notification when their order is ready for pickup, allowing them to avoid long lines and reduce waiting times (Li, 2018).

The app is also integrated with Starbucks' loyalty program, Starbucks Rewards, which incentivizes customers to use the mobile ordering feature by offering points (or "Stars") for every purchase. These Stars can be redeemed for free drinks, food items, or other rewards, fostering customer loyalty and increasing app usage. In addition, Starbucks uses the data collected from mobile orders to personalize customer offers and provide targeted promotions, further driving engagement with the app (Jo & Yoon, 2020).

Impact on Business Performance

Starbucks' Mobile Order & Pay feature has had a significant impact on both operational efficiency and customer satisfaction. The app has streamlined the ordering process, reducing the time customers spend waiting in line and improving the overall customer experience. In busy urban locations, where long lines are common, the mobile ordering system has alleviated congestion and allowed Starbucks to serve more customers during peak hours (Chaffey, 2020).

From an operational perspective, the app has helped Starbucks manage order flow more effectively. By receiving orders in advance, baristas can better plan their workload and prioritize orders, ensuring that customers receive their items promptly. This has led to improved throughput in stores and increased sales, particularly in high-traffic locations. The app has also contributed to higher average order values, as customers tend to spend more when ordering through the app due to its easy customization options and upselling prompts (Harrington, 2021).

The integration of the loyalty program has further strengthened customer retention and engagement. By offering rewards and personalized promotions through the app, Starbucks has successfully built a strong digital ecosystem that encourages repeat purchases. This not only boosts sales but also provides valuable data on customer preferences, enabling Starbucks to tailor its offerings and marketing strategies more effectively (Harrington, 2021).

However, the success of Mobile Order & Pay has also introduced challenges for Starbucks. In some cases, the popularity of the feature has led to bottlenecks in stores, where mobile orders pile up and overwhelm baristas, resulting in delays. Starbucks has had to adjust its operations by adding additional staff during peak mobile ordering times and redesigning store layouts to accommodate the increased volume of mobile orders.

Outcomes and Benefits of Mobile Ordering and Delivery Platforms

The introduction of mobile ordering and delivery platforms like Uber Eats and Starbucks Mobile Order & Pay has brought numerous benefits to the food service industry. These platforms provide unparalleled convenience for customers, allowing them to place orders from virtually anywhere and receive their food with minimal effort. For restaurants, these platforms offer expanded reach, increased sales, and valuable data insights that can inform decision-making (Garg., 2017). Mobile ordering platforms have also enhanced operational efficiency by streamlining the ordering process and reducing the burden on staff during peak hours. In the case of Starbucks, Mobile Order & Pay has allowed the company to serve more customers without sacrificing service quality, while Uber Eats has enabled restaurants to offer delivery services without the need for their delivery infrastructure (Kapoor & Vij, 2018).

Moreover, the integration of loyalty programs and personalized promotions has helped businesses build stronger relationships with their customers, encouraging repeat purchases and increasing customer lifetime value. These platforms also provide opportunities for upselling and cross-selling, boosting revenue per transaction.

Challenges of Mobile Ordering and Delivery Platforms

Despite the benefits, there are challenges associated with mobile ordering and delivery platforms. For restaurants, the commission fees charged by third-party delivery platforms can be a significant financial burden, particularly for smaller establishments with lower margins. Additionally, the lack of control over delivery times and food handling can affect the quality of the customer experience (Alalwan, 2020).

For mobile ordering systems like Starbucks, managing the increased volume of orders can be challenging, particularly in busy locations (Kwortnik & Thompson, 2020; Li et al., 2021). Restaurants must adapt their operations to handle the additional demand, which may require changes in staffing and store layout to optimize efficiency and reduce customer wait times (Zhang et al., 2020). Implementing effective queue management strategies and leveraging technology for real-time order tracking can further enhance service delivery during peak hours (Gonzalez et al., 2021; Chen & Chen, 2022).

3.2.3 Conclusion

Mobile ordering and delivery platforms have revolutionized the food service industry, offering unprecedented customer convenience and new growth opportunities for businesses. Uber Eats and Starbucks Mobile Order & Pay exemplify how these platforms can drive operational efficiency, enhance customer satisfaction, and increase revenue. Despite the challenges associated with their adoption, mobile ordering and delivery technologies will continue to shape the future of food service, providing new ways for restaurants to engage with customers and meet evolving consumer expectations. The next case study will explore leveraging data analytics to optimize restaurant operations and customer experiences.

3.3 Case Study 3: AI and Data Analytics in Food Service

Artificial Intelligence (AI) and data analytics have emerged as game-changers in the food service industry, providing businesses with powerful tools to optimize operations, personalize customer experiences, and make data-driven decisions ((Lu et al. 2019). By leveraging AI technologies, restaurants can analyze large datasets to predict trends, forecast demand, enhance supply chain management, and improve customer engagement. In this case study, we explore how companies like Domino's and McDonald's have successfully integrated AI and data analytics into their operations to boost efficiency and customer satisfaction.

3.3.1 Example 1: Domino's and AI-Driven Decision Making

Domino's Pizza is a leader in utilizing AI and data analytics to drive its business strategies. From AI-powered customer ordering systems to predictive analytics in supply chain management, Domino's has embraced technology to streamline operations and enhance customer experiences (Wang et al., 2020; Ivanov & Dolgui, 2020). The company has built a reputation for being a tech-driven food service business, with innovations that include the AI chatbot "Dom," predictive delivery times, and advanced data analytics to manage inventory and forecast demand (Bennett, 2019; Schermerhorn et al., 2020).

AI-Powered Ordering with "Dom"

Domino's introduced "Dom," an AI-powered virtual assistant, to revolutionize the ordering process (Liu et al., 2021). Customers can interact with Dom via the Domino's app, website, or even through voice-enabled devices like Amazon Alexa. The AI assistant is capable of taking orders, answering customer queries, suggesting menu items, and even providing order status updates (Cheng et al., 2022). Dom learns from each interaction, improving its responses over time and offering more personalized recommendations to customers (Marr, 2018).

The introduction of Dom has streamlined the ordering process for customers, making it faster and more convenient. By eliminating the need for human intervention in basic tasks, Domino's has freed up staff to focus on more complex aspects of customer service and restaurant operations (Zhao et al., 2023). In addition, the AI system collects data on customer preferences, ordering habits, and response patterns, allowing Domino's to tailor marketing efforts and promotions based on real-time data (Pellissier, 2012; Ivanov & Dolgui, 2020).

Predictive Analytics for Delivery and Inventory Management

Domino's has also incorporated AI and predictive analytics to enhance its delivery and inventory management systems. The company uses machine learning algorithms to predict delivery times based on factors such as traffic conditions, order volume, and historical delivery data. This has led to the development of the "Domino's Tracker," a feature that provides customers with real-time updates on the status of their orders, from preparation to delivery(Suganda & Oktavia, 2021.).

Predictive analytics also play a critical role in inventory management at Domino's. By analyzing past sales data, weather patterns, and local events, the company can forecast demand more accurately, ensuring that stores are well-stocked with ingredients without over-ordering (Ramanathan & Tey, 2021; Stone et al., 2020). This reduces food waste and helps Domino's maintain cost efficiency while meeting customer demand (Choi et al., 2021). The use of AI-driven demand forecasting also enables the company to adjust staffing levels in real time, optimizing labor allocation during peak hours (McCarthy & Sweeney, 2021; Kimes, 2020).

Impact on Business Performance

Domino's AI-driven decision-making processes have significantly improved operational efficiency and customer satisfaction. The integration of AI into ordering and delivery systems has allowed the company to handle high volumes of orders with ease while maintaining accuracy and speed. Customers appreciate the convenience of AI-powered interactions, and the predictive delivery times have helped build trust and reliability(Suganda & Oktavia, 2021.).

From a business perspective, the use of data analytics to optimize inventory and labour management has reduced costs associated with overstocking, understaffing, and waste. Domino's ability to make real-time decisions based on data has given it a competitive edge, particularly in the fast-paced world of quick-service restaurants. The company's tech-forward approach has contributed to its continued growth and success in a crowded market.

3.3.2 Example 2: McDonald's and Data-Driven Customer Personalization

McDonald's, the world's largest fast-food chain, has also embraced AI and data analytics to enhance customer experiences and improve operational efficiency (Xu, 2014). In 2019, McDonald's made headlines by acquiring Dynamic Yield, an AI company specializing in personalization technology. This acquisition was a significant step in McDonald's journey toward becoming a data-driven business, enabling the company to leverage real-time data to personalize customer interactions (Himeur et al., 2022).

AI-Powered Drive-Thru Menus

One of the key applications of AI at McDonald's is the use of Dynamic Yield's technology in its drive-thru menus. The AI-powered menus are capable of dynamically adjusting based on various factors, such as the time of day, weather conditions, popular items, and current restaurant traffic. For instance, during hot weather, the system might prioritize cold beverages and ice cream on the menu, while in the mornings, breakfast items may take prominence (Xu, 2014).

In addition to adjusting based on environmental conditions, the system uses data from previous customer orders to suggest relevant add-ons or upsell opportunities. For example, if a customer frequently orders a particular sandwich, the AI may recommend a complementary side dish or a larger meal option. This level of personalization creates a more tailored experience for each customer, leading to higher satisfaction and increased sales (Polman et al., 2011).

Data-Driven Operations and Customer Insights

McDonald's uses data analytics not only to personalize customer interactions but also to optimize its internal operations. The company collects vast amounts of data from customer transactions, store performance, and external factors (e.g., weather, and local events) to make data-driven decisions. These insights help McDonald's manage supply chain logistics, reduce waste, and optimize menu offerings based on regional preferences and seasonal trends (Himeur et al., 2022)..

The data gathered from customer interactions is also used to refine McDonald's marketing strategies. By analyzing customer purchase patterns, the company can create targeted promotions and loyalty rewards programs that are more likely to resonate with specific customer segments. For instance, if data shows that a particular demographic frequently orders via the mobile app, McDonald's can offer app-exclusive discounts to incentivize repeat use (Himeur et al., 2022)..

Impact on Business Performance

McDonald's adoption of AI and data analytics has had a positive impact on both customer satisfaction and business efficiency. The AI-powered drive-thru menus have contributed to increased average order sizes, as customers are more likely to add suggested items or choose larger meal options when presented with personalized recommendations (Yang, Lee, & Lee, 2020). This upselling capability has been particularly effective in boosting revenue during busy periods. Operationally, McDonald's has benefited from improved demand forecasting, which allows the company to manage inventory and staffing levels more effectively (Chen, Preston, & Swink, 2015). By using real-time data to anticipate customer needs, McDonald's can reduce wait times, prevent stockouts, and improve overall service quality (Greene, Wall,

& McGuinness, 2019). The company's data-driven approach has also enabled it to refine its product offerings, focusing on items that are popular with specific customer segments, leading to better sales performance (Davenport & Ronanki, 2018).

Outcomes and Benefits of AI and Data Analytics in Food Service

The use of AI and data analytics in the food service industry has provided significant benefits, enabling businesses to operate more efficiently and deliver highly personalized customer experiences. Both Domino's and McDonald's have demonstrated how AI can be integrated into various aspects of operations, from customer interactions to supply chain management, resulting in improved business performance and customer satisfaction (Chandrasekaran et al., 2017; Davenport & Ronanki, 2018). One of the primary advantages of AI is its ability to process large amounts of data quickly and accurately, allowing businesses to make real-time decisions. For example, Domino's use of predictive analytics in delivery management has streamlined the ordering process and reduced delays, while McDonald's AI-powered menus have increased upselling opportunities and improved customer engagement (Greene et al., 2019; Ferreira et al., 2020).

AI and data analytics also provide valuable insights into customer behavior, enabling businesses to create personalized marketing campaigns and product offerings (Li et al., 2019). This level of customization fosters customer loyalty and increases the likelihood of repeat purchases (Boudali et al., 2021). Additionally, AI-driven demand forecasting helps businesses reduce food waste, optimize inventory, and manage labor costs, contributing to overall cost savings (Wamba et al., 2017).

Challenges of AI and Data Analytics in Food Service

While the benefits of AI and data analytics are clear, there are also challenges associated with their implementation. One major challenge is the cost of developing and maintaining AI systems, which may be prohibitive for smaller businesses with limited resources (Bianchini et al., 2021; Wirtz et al., 2018). Additionally, the success of AI depends on the quality of the data being used. Inaccurate or incomplete data can lead to poor decision-making, undermining the potential benefits of AI (Zhang, Yang, & Appelbaum, 2019).

Another challenge is data privacy and security. As restaurants collect more customer data through AI systems, they must ensure compliance with data protection regulations, such as GDPR, and take measures to secure sensitive information (Janssen, van der Voort, & Wahyudi, 2017). Failure to do so can result in data breaches, eroding customer trust and damaging the brand's reputation (Crawford, 2021).

3.3.3 Conclusion

AI and data analytics are transforming the food service industry, offering businesses the tools to improve efficiency, enhance customer experiences, and make data-driven decisions. Companies like Domino's and McDonald's have successfully integrated AI into their operations, using it to optimize delivery times, personalize customer interactions, and streamline inventory management. While challenges such as cost and data privacy must be addressed, the overall benefits of AI and data analytics make them essential components of the future of food service. As technology continues to evolve, we can expect to see even more innovative applications of AI in the industry, providing new opportunities for growth and customer engagement.

4. ANALYSIS AND DISCUSSION

The integration of advanced technologies, such as artificial intelligence (AI), automation, and data analytics, in the service industry, particularly in the food service sector, has led to significant transformations. These technological innovations, showcased through the case studies of restaurant automation, mobile ordering platforms, and AI-driven analytics, illustrate both the opportunities and challenges faced by businesses. In this section,the author will analyze the critical factors driving the successful adoption of these technologies, discuss the broader implications for the service industry, and identify the key challenges that may arise.

4.1 Key Factors for Technological Success in Food Service

4.1.1 Operational Efficiency

The primary benefit of integrating technologies such as automation and AI in food service is the significant boost to operational efficiency. For instance, the automation of kitchen processes in fast-food chains like McDonald's and the use of AI in Domino's delivery system have optimized workflows, minimized human error, and enhanced the overall speed of service (Ivanov & Webster, 2019; Wirtz et al., 2018). These advancements have not only improved the quality and consistency of the service but also reduced labor costs by replacing manual tasks with automated solutions (Leung, 2019). Efficient operations are essential in an industry where speed and accuracy are paramount to customer satisfaction and loyalty (Kusumawati, 2020).

4.1.2 Customer Experience and Personalization

AI and data analytics have enabled businesses to personalize their services, enhancing the overall customer experience. McDonald's AI-powered drive-thru menus and Domino's AI-driven virtual assistant "Dom" exemplify how technology can be used to tailor recommendations and anticipate customer needs (Wirtz et al., 2018; Ivanov & Webster, 2019). Personalization, driven by real-time data analysis, has been shown to increase customer satisfaction and lead to higher sales through effective upselling and cross-selling strategies (Davenport & Ronanki, 2018). The ability to deliver a personalized and seamless experience is a competitive advantage in the fast-paced and customer-centric food service industry (Grewal et al., 2020).

4.1.3 Data-Driven Decision Making

Data analytics plays a critical role in driving strategic decisions in the service industry. The collection and analysis of vast amounts of customer data allow businesses to forecast demand, optimize inventory, and make informed decisions about product offerings. Companies like Domino's and McDonald's have successfully harnessed the power of data analytics to refine their operations, create targeted marketing campaigns, and improve supply chain management (Leung, 2019; Chung et al., 2020). As this data-driven approach becomes more sophisticated, it allows businesses to react quickly to market trends and changing consumer preferences, ensuring they remain competitive (Bharadwaj et al., 2019).

4.1.4 Scalability and Flexibility

One of the critical factors that determine the success of technology adoption in the food service industry is its scalability. Large global chains such as McDonald's and Domino's have the infrastructure and resources to deploy AI, automation, and analytics solutions on a broad scale (Ivanov & Webster, 2019). However, scalability is not limited to large corporations; smaller businesses can also benefit from technology by adopting more tailored, flexible solutions. For example, the rise of mobile ordering platforms like UberEats and GrubHub allows independent restaurants to participate in the digital economy without the need for significant investment in proprietary technology (Grewal et al., 2020).

4.2 Broader Implications for the Service Industry

4.2.1 Shift Toward a Technology-Driven Business Model

The successful stories of McDonald's, Domino's, and other players in the food service sector reflect a broader shift toward technology-driven business models. As customer expectations evolve, businesses must continue to integrate technology not only to remain competitive but also to meet the demands of an increasingly digital-savvy consumer base. This trend is mirrored across the broader service industry, from retail to hospitality, where the use of AI, automation, and mobile technologies is becoming standard practice (Ivanov & Webster, 2019; Davenport & Ronanki, 2018).

4.2.2 Job Displacement and Workforce Transformation

While technology has enhanced efficiency and reduced costs, it has also raised concerns about job displacement in the service industry. Automation and AI are replacing roles traditionally held by human workers, particularly in low-skill jobs such as cashiers, order takers, and kitchen staff. However, rather than eliminating jobs entirely, technology is transforming the workforce by creating new roles that require different skill sets, such as data analysis, digital marketing, and IT management (Brynjolfsson & McAfee, 2017; Bessen, 2019). This shift underscores the importance of upskilling and reskilling employees to adapt to the changing demands of a technology-driven industry (Bughin et al., 2018).

4.2.3 Customer Expectations and the Need for Continuous Innovation

As businesses increasingly adopt technological solutions, customer expectations for seamless, personalized, and efficient service will continue to rise. Companies that fail to innovate or invest in technology risk falling behind competitors who can offer better service experiences. This creates a cycle of continuous innovation, where businesses must stay ahead of technological advancements to maintain customer loyalty and market share (Huang & Rust, 2018). For example, AI-driven systems that were once cutting-edge are now expected features in many service interactions, pushing businesses to explore newer technologies such as blockchain for supply chain transparency or augmented reality for enhanced customer engagement (Bharadwaj et al., 2019; Wirtz et al., 2018).

4.2.4 Data Privacy and Security Concerns

The widespread use of data analytics in the service industry brings with it significant challenges related to data privacy and security. As companies collect more customer data to personalize services and drive decision-making, they must also ensure that this data is handled securely and in compliance with regulations such as the General Data Protection Regulation (GDPR). Failure to protect customer data can result in reputational damage, legal penalties, and the loss of customer trust (Chung et al., 2020; Grewal et al., 2020). The food service industry, like all service sectors, must prioritize data protection as it becomes increasingly reliant on digital technologies (Cavoukian, 2019).

4.3 Challenges in the Adoption of Technology

4.3.1 High Initial Investment and Maintenance Costs

Implementing cutting-edge technologies like AI, automation, and data analytics requires significant initial investments in infrastructure, software, and training. For smaller businesses, these costs may be prohibitive, limiting their ability to adopt the latest technological solutions. Furthermore, ongoing maintenance and updates to these systems require continuous financial and technical resources, which may strain the budgets of smaller establishments (Leung, 2019). Despite these challenges, technology providers are beginning to offer more affordable and scalable solutions tailored to businesses of all sizes, helping to democratize access to innovation (Ivanov & Webster, 2019).

4.3.2 Integration with Legacy Systems

Many established businesses in the service industry rely on legacy systems that may not be compatible with modern technologies. Integrating new AI-driven platforms or automation tools into existing infrastructure can be a complex and costly process. Moreover, businesses must carefully manage this integration to avoid disruptions to operations or customer service (Bharadwaj et al., 2019). The challenge of integrating legacy systems with modern solutions highlights the importance of developing flexible, interoperable technologies that can adapt to a wide range of operational environments (Huang & Rust, 2018).

4.3.3 Resistance to Change

Resistance to change, both from employees and management, is another common challenge in the adoption of new technologies. Employees may fear job loss or struggle to adapt to new processes, while management may be hesitant to invest in unfamiliar technologies that require significant changes to existing workflows. To overcome this resistance, businesses need to invest in change management strategies, which include comprehensive training programs, clear communication about the benefits of technology, and a phased approach to implementation that allows staff to gradually adapt (Bughin et al., 2018).

4.3.4 Balancing Automation with Human Touch

While automation and AI offer clear advantages in terms of efficiency and cost savings, they also risk depersonalizing the customer experience. In the service industry, human interaction remains a key component of customer satisfaction, particularly in sectors like hospitality and food service where personal attention and tailored service are highly valued (Wirtz et al., 2018). Striking the right balance between automation and the human touch is critical. Businesses must ensure that technology enhances, rather than replaces, human interactions, creating a more efficient yet still personalized service experience (Huang & Rust, 2018).

4.4 Conclusion

The case studies of restaurant automation, mobile ordering platforms, and AI-driven analytics demonstrate the transformative impact of technology in the food service industry. By enhancing operational efficiency, personalizing customer experiences, and driving data-informed decision-making, these technologies have reshaped the competitive landscape. However, the successful adoption of these innovations requires careful consideration of challenges such as cost, integration, workforce transformation, and the need to balance automation with personal service.

Looking forward, the service industry must continue to innovate and adapt to emerging technologies while addressing these challenges. The key to success lies in adopting a customer-centric approach, leveraging technology to enhance, rather than replace, the human elements of service that remain integral to customer satisfaction. As businesses navigate this evolving landscape, the ability to harness the power of technology while maintaining a personalized and human-centric approach will define the future of the food service industry.

5. FUTURE TRENDS AND INNOVATIONS IN THE FOOD SERVICE INDUSTRY

The rapid adoption of technology in the food service industry has already brought significant changes, but the future promises even more transformative innovations. As technology continues to evolve, the food service industry will increasingly leverage cutting-edge tools to enhance operational efficiency, improve customer experience, and redefine the business landscape. This section explores the future trends and innovations likely to shape the food service industry, with a focus on emerging technologies and their potential impact.

5.1 Artificial Intelligence and Machine Learning Advancements

While artificial intelligence (AI) has already revolutionized various aspects of the food service industry, its future potential is even more profound. AI and machine learning will become more integrated into decision-making processes, helping businesses predict customer preferences, optimize supply chains, and automate customer interactions (Davenport & Ronanki, 2018; Ivanov & Webster, 2019).

5.1.1 Predictive Analytics

AI will become more powerful in predicting customer behaviors, allowing restaurants to anticipate demand with greater accuracy. Machine learning algorithms will analyze historical data, seasonal trends, and real-time events (such as weather or holidays) to ensure businesses are fully prepared for fluctuations in demand. This will lead to more efficient inventory management, reduced food waste, and optimized staffing levels (Huang & Rust, 2018; Shankar, 2018).

5.1.2 Automated Customer Service

AI-powered chatbots and virtual assistants will handle a larger portion of customer service interactions, providing personalized recommendations, taking orders, and resolving queries in real-time. These systems will become more sophisticated, capable of understanding customer emotions and delivering a more human-like interaction, further enhancing the overall customer experience (Chung et al., 2020; Belanche et al., 2020).

5.1.3 AI-Driven Marketing

In the future, AI will also play a key role in developing highly personalized marketing strategies. AI systems will be able to analyze consumer behavior and preferences to deliver targeted promotions and discounts at the right time, driving higher engagement and conversion rates (Grewal et al., 2020; Rust & Huang, 2021).

5.2 Robotics and Restaurant Automation

The role of robotics in the food service industry is set to expand dramatically, from kitchen automation to customer-facing robots. This trend will be particularly important in addressing labor shortages, improving food safety, and maintaining consistent product quality (Ivanov & Webster, 2019; Wirtz et al., 2018).

5.2.1 Fully Automated Kitchens

Robotic chefs and automated kitchen equipment will become more common in the food service industry. Robots will be able to cook meals, prepare ingredients, and even plate dishes with precision and speed, ensuring consistency in food preparation and reducing the risk of contamination. Examples of this innovation include robotic fryers, automated burger flippers, and pizza-making machines, all of which are poised to become standard in many quick-service restaurants (Leung, 2019; Caputo et al., 2021).

5.2.2 Robotic Delivery and Service

Robotics will also extend to customer service, with robots taking orders, serving food, and delivering meals. Autonomous delivery robots and drones are already being tested in certain regions and will become more widespread as they become more cost-effective. These technologies will reduce delivery times, lower operational costs, and enhance convenience for customers (Huang & Rust, 2018; Wirtz et al., 2018).

5.2.3 Human-Robot Collaboration

Rather than completely replacing human staff, the future will likely see a blend of human and robot collaboration in food service. Robots will handle repetitive and labor-intensive tasks, while human employees focus on higher-value interactions, such as customer engagement and management (Belanche et al., 2020; Wirtz et al., 2018).

5.3 Blockchain Technology for Supply Chain Transparency

Blockchain technology, which provides a decentralized and immutable record of transactions, will play an increasingly important role in ensuring transparency and traceability in the food supply chain. This will enhance food safety, improve accountability, and build trust between businesses and consumers (Saberi et al., 2019; Kamble et al., 2020).

5.3.1 Enhanced Food Traceability

Blockchain can track every stage of a food product's journey from farm to table. By recording information such as origin, processing methods, and transportation conditions, blockchain ensures that consumers and businesses alike can verify the quality and safety of the food they are consuming. This will help to quickly identify and address foodborne illness outbreaks or product recalls, as well as verify the authenticity of organic or ethically sourced products (Kouhizadeh & Sarkis, 2018; Behnke & Janssen, 2020).

5.3.2 Supply Chain Optimization

Blockchain will also streamline the food service supply chain by improving transparency and reducing fraud. For example, restaurants can use blockchain to verify supplier credentials, ensuring that ingredients are sourced from reputable and sustainable sources. Additionally, the technology can reduce paperwork, eliminate middlemen, and speed up the payment process between suppliers and buyers (Saberi et al., 2019; Kamble et al., 2020).

5.3.3 Customer Trust and Ethical Practices

As consumers become more concerned about sustainability, food sourcing, and ethical practices, blockchain will allow businesses to demonstrate their commitment to these values. Customers will be able to scan QR codes on menus or packaging to access detailed information about the ingredients, further strengthening the relationship between businesses and socially conscious consumers (Kamble et al., 2020; Kouhizadeh & Sarkis, 2018).

5.4 Sustainability and Environmental Innovations

Sustainability is becoming a critical focus in the food service industry, driven by growing consumer demand for environmentally friendly practices and the need to address climate change. Future innovations will focus on reducing food waste, cutting carbon emissions, and adopting more sustainable business models (Arabzadeh et al., 2023; Ghisellini et al., 2016).

5.4.1 Waste Reduction Technologies

Technologies that help restaurants reduce food waste will continue to develop. AI-powered inventory management systems will predict demand more accurately, ensuring that restaurants purchase the right amount of ingredients. Additionally, food recycling technologies, such as composting systems or biogas generators, will help convert food waste into energy or compost, minimizing the environmental impact of waste disposal (Huang & Rust, 2018; Shankar, 2018).

5.4.2 Sustainable Packaging

The industry will see a shift toward biodegradable, reusable, or edible packaging materials to replace single-use plastics. Companies are already exploring plant-based materials, such as seaweed or cornstarch, that can be used to create eco-friendly packaging solutions. These innovations will significantly reduce the volume of plastic waste generated by the food service industry (Ghisellini et al., 2016; Arabzadeh et al., 2023).

5.4.3 Energy-Efficient Equipment

As environmental regulations tighten and energy costs rise, restaurants will increasingly adopt energy-efficient kitchen equipment and appliances. From smart ovens that reduce cooking times to energy-saving refrigeration systems, these technologies will help businesses lower their carbon footprint and operating costs (Arabzadeh et al., 2023; Leung, 2019).

5.4.4 Vertical Farming and Local Sourcing

Vertical farming—growing crops in stacked layers or controlled environments—will become more popular, allowing restaurants to source fresh ingredients locally and sustainably. This approach reduces the need for long-distance transportation, minimizes water usage, and ensures consistent supply of fresh produce, even in urban areas (Arabzadeh et al., 2023; Kouhizadeh & Sarkis, 2018).

5.5 Virtual Restaurants and Cloud Kitchens

The rise of delivery platforms has led to the growth of virtual restaurants and cloud kitchens, a trend that is expected to accelerate in the coming years. These concepts involve restaurants that operate exclusively for delivery, without a traditional dine-in space (Kimes, 2020; Thakur et al., 2021).

5.5.1 Ghost Kitchens:

Ghost kitchens (also known as cloud kitchens) are facilities that focus solely on preparing meals for delivery. They require less capital investment compared to traditional brick-and-mortar restaurants, as there is no need for front-of-house services or large dining spaces. As the demand for food delivery continues to grow, ghost kitchens will become an attractive option for entrepreneurs and established brands looking to expand their reach (Burgess et al., 2020; Kimes, 2020).

5.5.2 Multiple Brands from One Kitchen:

Cloud kitchens allow businesses to run multiple virtual restaurant brands from a single kitchen. For example, one kitchen might produce meals for a pizza brand, a salad brand, and a dessert brand, all available for delivery through apps like UberEats and DoorDash. This model provides businesses with flexibility, allowing them to test new concepts with minimal risk and investment (Thakur et al., 2021; Danziger, 2021).

5.5.3 Impact on Traditional Dining:

While virtual restaurants and cloud kitchens are set to grow, they may also shift the balance between dine-in and delivery-focused models. Traditional restaurants will need to adapt by integrating more robust delivery options, offering meal kits, or exploring hybrid models that combine in-person dining with delivery-only concepts (Caputo et al., 2021; Kimes, 2020).

5.6 Immersive Technologies

Augmented and Virtual Reality

Augmented reality (AR) and virtual reality (VR) technologies are rapidly gaining traction as innovative tools that have the potential to revolutionize the customer experience in the food service industry. These immersive technologies are no longer confined to the gaming or entertainment sectors; they are being adopted by businesses across various industries, including hospitality and food service, to enhance customer engagement, streamline operations, and create more memorable and personalized experiences (Tussyadiah, Wang, & Jia, 2016).

In the context of the food service industry, AR and VR offer unprecedented opportunities for customers to interact with brands and products in more dynamic and engaging ways. For instance, AR allows restaurants to overlay digital content onto the physical world through smartphones or AR-enabled devices. This means that diners can point their phones at a menu and instantly see 3D representations of the dishes, complete with detailed descriptions, nutritional information, and even preparation videos. This interactive element adds a new layer of engagement, allowing customers to make more informed decisions based on visual and contextual information. The ability to visualize a dish before ordering can help set clearer expectations and enhance customer satisfaction (Flavián, Ibáñez-Sánchez, & Orús, 2018; Pantano & Servidio, 2012).

On the other hand, VR takes immersion a step further by creating entirely virtual environments. In the food service sector, VR could be used to transport customers to a virtual version of a restaurant where they can explore themed dining environments, virtually meet the chef, or watch the preparation of their food in real-time. For delivery services, VR could offer customers the option to "visit" their favourite restaurant or experience a new cultural dining atmosphere from the comfort of their homes ((Yung, Khoo-Lattimore, & Potter, 2020). VR can also be utilized as a marketing tool, providing virtual tours of a restaurant or offering exclusive, immersive dining experiences that cater to tech-savvy or adventure-seeking customers (Tussyadiah et al., 2016).

Beyond customer interaction, these technologies hold immense potential for training and operations in the food service industry. Restaurant staff could be trained using VR simulations, allowing them to practice complex tasks, such as preparing intricate dishes or managing high-pressure service environments, in a risk-free, virtual setting (Li, Daugherty, & Biocca, 2002). AR could be used by chefs and kitchen staff to streamline food preparation, providing real-time instructions, timers, and measurements directly overlaid onto their workstations. This would lead to more efficient kitchen operations and higher food quality standards (Berg & Vance, 2017).

Ultimately, the integration of AR and VR in the food service industry represents a significant leap forward in how businesses engage with their customers. By offering immersive and interactive experiences, these technologies will not only enhance customer satisfaction but also provide a competitive edge to businesses that embrace digital innovation (Kim et al., 2013; Flavián et al., 2019). As AR and VR technologies continue to evolve, they are poised to become integral components of the dining experience, offering a seamless blend of technology and gastronomy that will redefine the way people interact with food and hospitality (Pantano & Servidio, 2012).

5.6.1 AR Menus and Interactive Experiences:

AR can bring menus to life by allowing customers to see 3D representations of dishes before ordering. Customers could use their smartphones or AR glasses to visualize portion sizes, ingredients, or preparation methods, helping them make more informed choices. This technology will also enhance the dining experience by adding interactive features, such as virtual wine pairings or chef recommendations (Van Den Bogaert & Geerts, 2020).

5.6.2 Virtual Restaurants:

VR could be used to create virtual dining experiences, allowing customers to dine in a virtual environment from the comfort of their homes. For example, a restaurant might offer a VR dining experience where customers can virtually "visit" a themed restaurant or watch their meal being prepared by a chef in real-time. This blending of technology and experience could become a new form of entertainment in the food service industry (Zhang et al., 2019).

5.7 Conclusion

The future of the food service industry is set to be shaped by a range of technological innovations, from AI and robotics to blockchain and immersive technologies. These advancements will enable businesses to operate more efficiently, reduce their environmental impact, and deliver increasingly personalized and engaging customer experiences. However, as the industry continues to evolve, it will also need to address challenges related to cost, workforce adaptation, and maintaining the human touch in a technology-driven world.

As these trends and innovations gain momentum, the food service industry will remain at the forefront of technological progress, offering businesses and customers new ways to interact, consume, and thrive in the digital age. Companies that embrace these future trends while staying mindful of the balance between technology and human experience will be best positioned for long-term success.

REFERENCES

Addanki, M., Patra, P., & Kandra, P. (2022). Recent advances and applications of artificial intelligence and related technologies in the food industry. *Applied Food Research*, 2(2), 100126. DOI: 10.1016/j.afres.2022.100126

Akyazi, T., Goti, A., Oyarbide, A., Alberdi, E., & Bayon, F. (2020). A Guide for the Food Industry to Meet the Future Skills Requirements Emerging with Industry 4.0. *Foods*, 9(4), 492. DOI: 10.3390/foods9040492 PMID: 32295238

Alalwan, A. A. (2020). Mobile food ordering apps: An empirical study of the factors affecting customer e-satisfaction and continued intention to reuse. *International Journal of Information Management*, 50, 28–44. DOI: 10.1016/j.ijinfomgt.2019.04.008

Arabzadeh, V., Behnamian, A., Rashidi, S., & Sabour, M. (2023). A comprehensive review on sustainable food service practices. *Sustainability*, 15(4), 1682–1702. DOI: 10.3390/su15041682

Arabzadeh, V., Miettinen, P., Kotilainen, T., Herranen, P., Karakoc, A., Kummu, M., & Rautkari, L. (2023). Urban vertical farming with a large wind power share and optimised electricity costs. *Applied Energy*, 331, 120416. DOI: 10.1016/j.apenergy.2022.120416

Behnke, K., & Janssen, M. F. W. H. A. (2020). Blockchain technology in supply chain management: A systematic literature review. *Sustainability*, 12(4), 1668–1678. DOI: 10.3390/su12041668

Belanche, D., Casaló, L. V., & Flavián, C. (2020). Artificial Intelligence in service industries: Current trends and future perspectives. *Journal of Service Research*, 23(2), 155–169. DOI: 10.1177/1094670520908776

Belanche, D., Casaló, L. V., Flavián, C., & Schepers, J. (2019). Service robot implementation: A theoretical framework and research agenda. *Service Industries Journal*, 40(3–4), 203–225. DOI: 10.1080/02642069.2019.1672666

Bennett, R. (2019). Innovations in the food service industry: The case of Domino's Pizza. *The Journal of Business Strategy*, 40(2), 25–34. DOI: 10.1108/JBS-03-2018-0043

Berezina, K., Ciftci, O., & Cobanoglu, C. (2019). Robots, artificial intelligence, and service automation in restaurants. *In Emerald Publishing Limited eBooks* (pp. 185–219). DOI: 10.1108/978-1-78756-687-320191010

Bessen, J. E. (2019). AI and jobs: The role of demand. *National Bureau of Economic Research Working Paper,* 24235. DOI: 10.3386/w24235

Bharadwaj, A., El Sawy, O. A., Pavlou, P. A., & Venkatraman, N. (2019). Digital business strategy: Toward a next generation of insights. *Management Information Systems Quarterly*, 43(1), 469–482. DOI: 10.25300/MISQ/2019/13304

Bianchini, M., Michienzi, A., & Pellegrini, R. (2021). AI implementation challenges for SMEs in the hospitality sector. *Journal of Business Research*, 124, 187–194. DOI: 10.1016/j.jbusres.2020.11.049

Boudali, Y., Saoud, N., & Taleb, A. (2021). Leveraging AI and machine learning to improve customer experience in quick service restaurants: A case study of Domino's Pizza. *Journal of Hospitality and Tourism Technology*, 12(3), 407–423. DOI: 10.1108/JHTT-09-2020-0197

Brynjolfsson, E., & McAfee, A. (2017). *The second machine age: Work, progress, and prosperity in a time of brilliant technologies*. W. W. Norton & Company.

Bughin, J., Hazan, E., Ramaswamy, S., Chui, M., Allas, T., Dahlström, P., & Henke, N. (2018). *Skill shift: Automation and the future of the workforce*. McKinsey Global Institute.

Burgess, J., Conlon, C., & Hsu, C. (2020). Exploring ghost kitchens: A novel business model for the food delivery sector. *Journal of Hospitality and Tourism Management*, 44, 208–217. DOI: 10.1016/j.jhtm.2020.08.001

Caputo, F., Marzi, G., & Pellegrini, M. M. (2021). Digital transformation and supply chain management in the foodservice industry: A systematic review. *Technological Forecasting and Social Change*, 169, 120829. DOI: 10.1016/j.techfore.2021.120829

Cavoukian, A. (2019). *Privacy by design: The 7 foundational principles*. Information and Privacy Commissioner of Ontario.

Chaffey, D. (2020). *Social media marketing trends 2020*. Smart Insights. Retrieved from Smart Insights.

Chandrasekaran, M., Bishop, B., & Rad, A. A. (2017). Leveraging artificial intelligence in food service operations: Case studies in the fast food industry. *Journal of Operations Management*, 49(2), 45–58. DOI: 10.1016/j.jom.2017.03.001

Chang, W.-J. (2021). Experiential marketing, brand image and brand loyalty: A case study of Starbucks. *British Food Journal*, 123(1), 209–223. DOI: 10.1108/BFJ-01-2020-0014

Chen, H., Preston, D. S., & Swink, M. (2015). How the use of big data analytics affects value creation in supply chain management. *Journal of Management Information Systems*, 32(4), 4–39. DOI: 10.1080/07421222.2015.1138364

Chen, Y., & Chen, X. (2022). Managing order volume in mobile food delivery: Insights from Starbucks. *Journal of Business Research*, 136, 562–570. DOI: 10.1016/j.jbusres.2021.07.021

Cheng, Y., Wang, S., & Wei, X. (2022). Enhancing customer experience with AI chatbots in food delivery services. *International Journal of Hospitality Management*, 102, 103096. DOI: 10.1016/j.ijhm.2021.103096

Chi, O. H., Chi, C. G., Gursoy, D., & Nunkoo, R. (2023). Customers' acceptance of artificially intelligent service robots: The influence of trust and culture. *International Journal of Information Management*, 70, 102623. DOI: 10.1016/j.ijinfomgt.2023.102623

Chin, H., Marasini, D. P., & Lee, D. (2022). Digital transformation trends in service industries. *Service Business*, 17(1), 11–36. DOI: 10.1007/s11628-022-00516-6

Choi, Y., Lee, Y., & Kim, J. (2021). Impact of big data analytics on the food service industry: The case of Domino's Pizza. *International Journal of Hospitality Management*, 94, 102803. DOI: 10.1016/j.ijhm.2020.102803

Choudhury, P. (2021). Robotic Process Automation: A critical evaluation of its impact on food service industry. *Journal of Service Management*, 32(4), 513–530.

Chuang, H. (2019). Starbucks in the world. HOLISTICA –. *Journal of Business and Public Administration*, 10(3), 99–110. DOI: 10.2478/hjbpa-2019-0031

Chung, M., Ko, E., Joung, H., & Kim, S. J. (2020). Chatbot e-service and customer satisfaction regarding luxury brands. *Journal of Business Research*, 117, 587–595. DOI: 10.1016/j.jbusres.2018.10.004
Chung, M., Ko, E., Joung, H., & Kim, S. J. (2020). Chatbot e-service and customer satisfaction regarding luxury brands. *Journal of Business Research*, 117, 587–595. DOI: 10.1016/j.jbusres.2018.10.004

Chung, M., Ko, E., Joung, H., & Kim, S. J. (2020). Chatbot e-service and customer satisfaction regarding luxury brands. *Journal of Business Research*, 117, 587–595. DOI: 10.1016/j.jbusres.2018.10.004
Crawford, K. (2021). The risks of data misuse in AI systems in service industries. *Journal of Applied Artificial Intelligence*, 35(3), 250–265. DOI: 10.1080/08839514.2021.1870049

Danziger, P. N. (2021). The rise of ghost kitchens: A culinary revolution. Forbes. Retrieved from https://www.forbes.com/sites/pamdanziger/2021/02/04/the-rise-of-ghost-kitchens-a-culinary-revolution

Davenport, T. H., & Ronanki, R. (2018). Artificial intelligence for the real world. *Harvard Business Review*, 96(1), 108–116.

Davis, F. D. (1985). A technology acceptance model for empirically testing new end-user information systems : theory and results. Retrieved from http://ci.nii.ac.jp/naid/20001062454

Davis, F. D. (1989). Perceived usefulness, perceived ease of use, and user acceptance of information technology. *Management Information Systems Quarterly*, 13(3), 319. DOI: 10.2307/249008

Dwivedi, Y. K., Hughes, L., Ismagilova, E., Aarts, G., Coombs, C., Crick, T., Duan, Y., Dwivedi, R., Edwards, J., Eirug, A., Galanos, V., Ilavarasan, P. V., Janssen, M., Jones, P., Kar, A. K., Kizgin, H., Kronemann, B., Lal, B., Lucini, B., & Williams, M. D. (2021). Artificial Intelligence (AI): Multidisciplinary perspectives on emerging challenges, opportunities, and agenda for research, practice and policy. *International Journal of Information Management*, 57, 101994. DOI: 10.1016/j.ijinfomgt.2019.08.002

Elbrechter, C., Maycock, J., Haschke, R., & Ritter, H. (2015, September). Discriminating liquids using a robotic kitchen assistant. In *2015 IEEE/RSJ International Conference on Intelligent Robots and Systems (IROS)* (pp. 703-708). IEEE. DOI: 10.1109/IROS.2015.7353449

Ferreira, J., Silva, M., & Figueiredo, J. (2020). The role of artificial intelligence in enhancing customer experience in fast food restaurants. *International Journal of Hospitality Management*, 89, 102518. DOI: 10.1016/j.ijhm.2020.102518

Flavián, C., Ibáñez-Sánchez, S., & Orús, C. (2018). The impact of virtual, augmented and mixed reality technologies on the customer experience. *Journal of Business Research*, 100, 547–560. DOI: 10.1016/j.jbusres.2018.10.050

Garg, A. (2021).The Technology Acceptance and Use of Tablet Menu among Young Adults: An Empirical Study Based on UTAUT 2 Model. International *Journal of Hospitality & Tourism Systems,* Volume 14 Issue 1 June 2021, Available at *SSRN*: https://ssrn.com/abstract=3809622

Garg, A., & Kumar, J. (2017). Exploring customer satisfaction with university cafeteria food services. An empirical study of Temptation Restaurant at Taylor's University, Malaysia. *European Journal of Tourism. Hospitality and Recreation*, 8(2), 96–106. DOI: 10.1515/ejthr-2017-0009

Ghisellini, P., Cialani, C., & Ulgiati, S. (2016). A review on circular economy: The expected transition to a balanced interplay of environmental and economic systems. *Journal of Cleaner Production*, 114, 11–32. DOI: 10.1016/j.jclepro.2015.09.007

Gonzalez, M., Juárez, J., & García, R. (2021). Strategies for effective queue management in fast-food restaurants. *International Journal of Hospitality Management*, 92, 102716. DOI: 10.1016/j.ijhm.2020.102716

Greene, M., Wall, A., & McGuinness, D. (2019). The role of artificial intelligence in fast food industry decision making. *Journal of Artificial Intelligence Research*, 64, 659–684. DOI: 10.1613/jair.1.12312

Grewal, D., Hulland, J., Kopalle, P. K., & Karahanna, E. (2020). The future of technology and marketing: A multidisciplinary perspective. *Journal of the Academy of Marketing Science*, 48(1), 1–8. DOI: 10.1007/s11747-019-00711-4

Gursoy, D., Chi, O. H., Lu, L., & Nunkoo, R. (2019). Consumers acceptance of artificially intelligent (AI) device use in service delivery. *International Journal of Information Management*, 49, 157–169. DOI: 10.1016/j.ijinfomgt.2019.03.008

Hao, F. (2021). Acceptance of contactless technology in the hospitality industry: Extending the unified theory of acceptance and use of technology 2. *Asia Pacific Journal of Tourism Research*, 26(12), 1386–1401. DOI: 10.1080/10941665.2021.1984264

Harrington, J. (2021). The impact of social media on brand loyalty: The Starbucks experience. *Journal of Digital & Social Media Marketing*, 9(2), 105–116. DOI: 10.1108/JSMS-06-2021-0047

Himeur, Y., Elnour, M., Fadli, F., Meskin, N., Petri, I., Rezgui, Y., Bensaali, F., & Amira, A. (2022b). AI-big data analytics for building automation and management systems: A survey, actual challenges and future perspectives. *Artificial Intelligence Review*, 56(6), 4929–5021. DOI: 10.1007/s10462-022-10286-2 PMID: 36268476

Huang, M. H., & Rust, R. T. (2018). Artificial intelligence in service. *Journal of Service Research*, 21(2), 155–172. DOI: 10.1177/1094670517752459

Huang, M. H., & Rust, R. T. (2018). Artificial intelligence in service. *Journal of Service Research*, 21(2), 155–172. DOI: 10.1177/1094670517752459

Isaac, M., & Yaffe-Bellany, D. (2019, August 20). The Rise of the Virtual Restaurant. *International New York Times,* NA. https://link.gale.com/apps/doc/A596849009/AONE?u=anon~8633bbc3&sid=googleScholar&xid=8df01966

Ivanov, D., & Dolgui, A. (2020). A digital supply chain twin: A new approach to supply chain management. *International Journal of Production Research*, 58(12), 3620–3634. DOI: 10.1080/00207543.2020.1723545

Ivanov, S., & Webster, C. (2019). *Robots, artificial intelligence, and service automation in travel, tourism, and hospitality*. Emerald Group Publishing., DOI: 10.1108/9781787566873

Ivanov, S., Webster, C., & Berezina, K. (2022). Robotics in Tourism and Hospitality. In Xiang, Z., Fuchs, M., Gretzel, U., & Höpken, W. (Eds.), *Handbook of e-Tourism*. Springer., DOI: 10.1007/978-3-030-48652-5_112

Janssen, M., van der Voort, H., & Wahyudi, A. (2017). Factors influencing big data decision-making quality. *Journal of Business Research*, 70, 338–345. DOI: 10.1016/j.jbusres.2016.08.007

Jo, Y. J., & Yoon, H. H. (2020). A Study on Relationship among Customer's Perceived Value, Trust, Flow, and Continuous Usage Intention Towards Coffee Branded Mobile Apps: Focus on Starbucks Siren Order. Korean. *Journal of Food and Cookery Science*, 36(03), 271–279. DOI: 10.9724/kfcs.2020.36.3.271

Kapoor, A. P., & Vij, M. (2018). Technology at the dinner table: Ordering food online through mobile apps. *Journal of Retailing and Consumer Services*, 43, 342–351. DOI: 10.1016/j.jretconser.2018.04.001

Kim, J. (2021). *The BTS meal at McDonald's: A global influencer marketing success. Forbes*. Retrieved from Forbes.

Kimes, S. E. (2011). Customer Perceptions of Electronic Food Ordering. *Cornell Hospitality Report*, 6–15. Retrieved from https://scholarship.sha.cornell.edu/chrpubs/70/

Kimes, S. E. (2020). The rise of ghost kitchens: A new delivery model. *Cornell Hospitality Quarterly*, 61(2), 150–156. DOI: 10.1177/1938965519856922

Kimes, S. E. (2020). The role of predictive analytics in managing restaurant operations. *Cornell Hospitality Quarterly*, 61(1), 50–65. DOI: 10.1177/1938965519895387

Kusumawati, A. (2020). How automation and AI reshape customer experience in the food service industry. *Journal of Service Research*, 23(2), 189–202. DOI: 10.1177/1094670520916415

Kwortnik, R. J., & Thompson, G. M. (2020). Unifying service marketing and operations management: A model of service experience. *Journal of Service Research*, 23(1), 28–44. DOI: 10.1177/1094670518805916

Leung, X. Y. (2019). Are robots responsible? The impact of artificial intelligence on food service operations. *International Journal of Hospitality Management*, 82, 360–368. DOI: 10.1016/j.ijhm.2019.04.019

Li, C. (2018). Consumer behavior in switching between membership cards and mobile applications: The case of Starbucks. *Computers in Human Behavior*, 84, 171–184. DOI: 10.1016/j.chb.2017.12.042

Li, C., Tang, J., & Wang, X. (2019). Predictive analytics in quick service restaurants: The case of McDonald's AI-powered drive-thru systems. *Computers & Industrial Engineering*, 137, 106037. DOI: 10.1016/j.cie.2019.106037

Li, M., Yin, D., Qiu, H., & Bai, B. (2022). Examining the effects of AI contactless services on customer psychological safety, perceived value, and hospitality service quality during the COVID-19 pandemic. *Journal of Hospitality Marketing & Management*, 31(1), 24–48. DOI: 10.1080/19368623.2021.1934932

Li, Y., Chen, C., & Wang, S. (2021). The role of technology in enhancing service quality in fast-casual restaurants: A case study of Starbucks. *Journal of Retailing and Consumer Services*, 63, 102662. DOI: 10.1016/j.jretconser.2021.102662

Liu, J., Xu, W., & Zhang, Y. (2021). The role of AI in transforming the food delivery sector: Evidence from Domino's Pizza. *Journal of Retailing and Consumer Services*, 60, 102507. DOI: 10.1016/j.jretconser.2021.102507

Lu, L., Cai, R., & Gursoy, D. (2021). Developing and testing a customer-centric technology readiness index (TRI) in the context of service robots. *International Journal of Hospitality Management*, 94, 102854.

Marr, B. (2018). How Domino's uses AI and data analytics to succeed. Forbes. Retrieved from https://www.forbes.com/sites/bernardmarr/2018/05/21/how-dominos-uses-ai-and-data-analytics-to-succeed/

Marr, B. (2019). Robots on the menu: How delivery robots, AI, and automation are affecting the food industry. *Forbes*.

McCarthy, R., & Sweeney, E. (2021). AI and analytics in food service: How restaurants are leveraging technology for efficiency. *Journal of Foodservice Business Research*, 24(1), 72–90. DOI: 10.1080/15378020.2020.1865050

Monty, R. C. da S. (2018). Creative Economy: How the interface of Uber Eats and iFood could change your menu. *Brazilian Journal of Operations & Production Management*, 15(3), 413–419. DOI: 10.14488/BJOPM.2018.v15.n3.a8

Mulyadi, B., & Masatip, A. (2020). The generation Z characteristics and hotel choices. *Tourism and Leisure*, 9.

Pantano, E., & Servidio, R. (2012). Modeling innovative points of sales through virtual and immersive technologies. *Journal of Retailing and Consumer Services*, 19(3), 279–286. DOI: 10.1016/j.jretconser.2012.02.002

Pantelidis, I. S. (2010). Electronic Meal Experience: A content analysis of online restaurant comments. *Cornell Hospitality Quarterly*, 51(4), 483–491. DOI: 10.1177/1938965510378574

Pellissier, H. (2012). Recent developments in asymmetric organocatalytic domino reactions. *Advanced Synthesis & Catalysis*, 354(2–3), 237–294. DOI: 10.1002/adsc.201100714

Pellissier, R. (2012). The use of technology in the food service industry: A case study of Domino's Pizza. *Journal of Foodservice Business Research*, 15(2), 99–112. DOI: 10.1080/15378020.2012.685054

Pereira, D., Bozzato, A., Dario, P., & Ciuti, G. (2022, July). Towards Foodservice Robotics: A Taxonomy of Actions of Foodservice Workers and a Critical Review of Supportive Technology. *IEEE Transactions on Automation Science and Engineering*, 19(3), 1820–1858. DOI: 10.1109/TASE.2021.3129077

Phelan, S. (2011). Case study research: Design and methods. *Evaluation and Research in Education*, 24(3), 221–222. DOI: 10.1080/09500790.2011.582317

Polman, C. H., Reingold, S. C., Banwell, B., Clanet, M., Cohen, J. A., Filippi, M., Fujihara, K., Havrdova, E., Hutchinson, M., Kappos, L., Lublin, F. D., Montalban, X., O'Connor, P., Sandberg-Wollheim, M., Thompson, A. J., Waubant, E., Weinshenker, B., & Wolinsky, J. S. (2011). Diagnostic criteria for multiple sclerosis: 2010 Revisions to the McDonald criteria. *Annals of Neurology*, 69(2), 292–302. DOI: 10.1002/ana.22366 PMID: 21387374

Raj, M., Sundararajan, A., & You, C. (2020). COVID-19 and Digital Resilience: Evidence from Uber Eats. SSRN *Electronic Journal.* DOI: 10.2139/ssrn.3625638

Ramanathan, U., & Tey, Y. (2021). Predictive analytics for inventory management in foodservice: A case study of Domino's Pizza. *British Food Journal*, 123(8), 2784–2797. DOI: 10.1108/BFJ-11-2020-1029

Ricky, M. Y. (2014). Mobile Food Ordering Application using Android OS Platform. *EPJ Web of Conferences*, 68, 00041. DOI: 10.1051/epjconf/20146800041

Robotics, M. (2021). *Moley Robotic Kitchen: The future of cooking*. Moley Robotics.

Scherer, R., Siddiq, F., & Tondeur, J. (2019). The technology acceptance model (TAM): A meta-analytic structural equation modeling approach to explaining teachers' adoption of digital technology in education. *Computers & Education*, 128, 13–35. DOI: 10.1016/j.compedu.2018.09.009

Schermerhorn, J. R., Bachrach, D. G., & Cohn, M. A. (2020). Management: A global, innovative, and entrepreneurial perspective. *Journal of Business Research*, 118, 116–126. DOI: 10.1016/j.jbusres.2020.06.046

Seal, P. P. (2023). Robots in the hotel kitchen. *In Advances in environmental engineering and green technologies book series* (pp. 89–97). DOI: 10.4018/978-1-6684-9094-5.ch006

Spyce. (2022). How Spyce reimagined fast food with robotics. *Spyce Company Profile.*

Stone, M., Desai, K. K., & McKinnon, A. C. (2020). Data-driven decision-making in the restaurant industry: An empirical study. *Journal of Hospitality and Tourism Management*, 43, 223–230. DOI: 10.1016/j.jhtm.2020.03.003

Suganda, U. K., & Oktavia, P. (n.d.). The Effect of Experiential Marketing and Service Quality on Customer Loyalty of Domino's Pizza in Cirebon City.

Thakur, R., Maiti, J., & Mukherjee, A. (2021). Virtual restaurants: The evolution of cloud kitchens in the hospitality industry. *International Journal of Hospitality Management*, 97, 102984. DOI: 10.1016/j.ijhm.2021.102984

Tung, V. W. S., & Au, N. (2018). Exploring customer experiences with robotics in hospitality. *International Journal of Contemporary Hospitality Management*, 30(7), 2680–2697. DOI: 10.1108/IJCHM-06-2017-0322

Tuomi, A., & Tussyadiah, I. (2020). The transformative role of digital technology in hospitality and tourism: A review of current trends and research. *Journal of Hospitality and Tourism Technology*, 11(4), 643–663.

Tussyadiah, I., Wang, D., & Jia, C. (2016). Exploring the persuasive power of virtual reality imagery for destination marketing. *Tourism Management*, Retrieved from https://ira.lib.polyu.edu.hk/handle/10397/63584

Van Den Bogaert, L., & Geerts, D. (2020). User-Defined Mid-Air Haptic Sensations for Interacting with an AR Menu Environment. *Lecture Notes in Computer Science*, 12272, 25–32. DOI: 10.1007/978-3-030-58147-3_3

Venkatesh, N., Morris, N., Davis, N., & Davis, N. (2003). User acceptance of information Technology: Toward a unified view. *Management Information Systems Quarterly*, 27(3), 425. DOI: 10.2307/30036540

Venkatesh, V., Thong, J., & Xu, X. (2016). Unified Theory of Acceptance and Use of Technology: A Synthesis and the Road ahead. *Journal of the Association for Information Systems*, 17(5), 328–376. DOI: 10.17705/1jais.00428

Wahl, C. (2019). Uber eats the world. *New Labor Forum*, 28(2), 87–90. DOI: 10.1177/1095796019836750

Wamba, S. F., Gunasekaran, A., Akter, S., Ren, S. J. F., Dubey, R., & Childe, S. J. (2017). Big data analytics and firm performance: Effects of dynamic capabilities. *Journal of Business Research*, 70, 356–365. DOI: 10.1016/j.jbusres.2016.08.009

Wang, Y., Xu, Y., & Li, X. (2020). AI and big data analytics in food supply chain management: A systematic literature review. *International Journal of Production Economics*, 218, 282–294. DOI: 10.1016/j.ijpe.2019.05.023

Webster, C., & Ivanov, S. (2020). Robotics, Artificial Intelligence, and the Evolving Nature of Work. In George, B., & Paul, J. (Eds.), *Digital Transformation in Business and Society*. Palgrave Macmillan., DOI: 10.1007/978-3-030-08277-2_8

Wirtz, B. W., Weyerer, J. C., & Geyer, C. (2018). Artificial intelligence and the public sector—Applications and challenges. *International Journal of Public Administration*, 42(7), 596–615. DOI: 10.1080/01900692.2018.1498103

Wirtz, J., Patterson, P., Kunz, W. H., Gruber, T., Lu, V. N., Paluch, S., & Martins, A. (2018). Brave new world: Service robots in the frontline. *Journal of Service Management*, 29(5), 907–931. DOI: 10.1108/JOSM-04-2018-0119

Wirtz, J., Patterson, P., Kunz, W. H., Gruber, T., Lu, V. N., Paluch, S., & Martins, A. (2018). Brave new world: Service robots in the frontline. *Journal of Service Management*, 29(5), 907–931. DOI: 10.1108/JOSM-04-2018-0119

Wirtz, J., Patterson, P., Kunz, W. H., Gruber, T., Lu, V. N., Paluch, S., & Martins, A. (2018). Brave new world: Service robots in the frontline. *Journal of Service Management*, 29(5), 907–931. DOI: 10.1108/JOSM-04-2018-0119

Xu, Y. (2014). Understanding CSR from the perspective of Chinese diners: The case of McDonald's. *International Journal of Contemporary Hospitality Management*, 26(6), 1002–1020. DOI: 10.1108/IJCHM-01-2013-0051

Yang, M., Lee, C., & Lee, H. (2020). Exploring the impact of AI-based personalized recommendations on customer decision-making in the quick-service restaurant industry. *Journal of Hospitality and Tourism Technology*, 11(4), 525–542. DOI: 10.1108/JHTT-01-2020-0005

Yung, R., Khoo-Lattimore, C., & Potter, L. E. (2020). Virtual reality and tourism marketing: Conceptualizing a framework on presence, emotion, and intention. *Current Issues in Tourism*, 24(11), 1505–1525. DOI: 10.1080/13683500.2020.1820454

Zhang, D., Yang, W., & Appelbaum, D. (2019). The challenges of implementing AI-based systems: Data quality and trust issues. *Journal of Information Systems*, 33(2), 95–112. DOI: 10.2308/isys-52336

Zhang, W., Chen, Z., Huang, J., & Wan, X. (2019). The influence of placing orientation on searching for food in a virtual restaurant. *Food Quality and Preference*, 78, 103728. DOI: 10.1016/j.foodqual.2019.103728

Zhang, X., Jiang, L., & Zhao, J. (2020). Redesigning store layout to improve customer flow during peak hours. *Journal of Consumer Marketing*, 37(6), 641–651. DOI: 10.1108/JCM-12-2019-4185

Zhao, X., Lu, L., & Han, Y. (2023). Impact of AI technologies on the performance of food service businesses: Evidence from Domino's Pizza. *Service Business*, 17(2), 265–287. DOI: 10.1007/s11628-023-00507-2

Chapter 11
The Role of Social Media Marketing in the Food Industry

Shazia Waheed
https://orcid.org/0009-0002-2766-3683
Lovely Professional University, India

Sanjeev Kumar
Lovely Professional University, India

ABSTRACT

This chapter focuses at social media marketing's important position in the food business, emphasizing how well it works to promote brands, engage customers, and increase sales. It goes over important tactics including using analytics, producing a variety of content, and stressing the value of real customer interactions. The chapter also covers issues like maintaining an online persona and adjusting to the quickly evolving digital environment. It also looks into future developments like social commerce, augmented reality (AR), and virtual reality (VR), as well as new social media platforms. In order to build long-lasting brand loyalty and relationships, the chapter ends by highlighting the necessity of a planned, adaptable, and data-driven approach to social media marketing that strikes a balance between promotional activities and sincere consumer involvement.

1. INTRODUCTION

1.1. The Evolution of Social Media

A great deal of the wonders of the modern era have contributed to the development and prosperity of society. For countless numbers of individuals, technology has made everything convenient and accessible. Social media's emergence and its ability to aid in the promotion of several products—in this case, food-related ones—are among the advantages of technology (Bermoy et al., 2021). Since its origin, social media has seen a rapid growth, evolving from basic tools for communication to intricate ecosystems that have an impact on every aspect of life, including the food business. People can engage in many social media platforms, such as social networking websites, and exchange ideas and content by using these various modes of communication. Social media's explosive growth has garnered a lot of attention in the

DOI: 10.4018/979-8-3693-7683-6.ch011

cutthroat corporate world of today. Social media should be a means for brands to engage with and draw customers (Riaz et al., 2019).

Facebook

Facebook was first launched in 2004 as a networking site for Harvard students, but it later spread to other colleges and the broader public, thanks to the efforts of Mark Zuckerberg and his undergraduate roommates (Carlson, 2010). With features that enabled social media interaction, like as photo sharing, chat, and status updates, it swiftly expanded to become the biggest social media platform.

Twitter

Twitter, a social media platform founded in 2006 by Jack Dorsey, Biz Stone, and Evan Williams, brought a new dimension to social networking with its 140-character (and then 280-character) post restriction, known as "tweets." Twitter has been a popular venue for news, celebrity encounters, and live event updates because of its format, which promoted concise communication and real-time involvement (Kwak et al., 2010).

Instagram

Kevin Systrom and Mike Krieger launched Instagram as a photo-sharing app in 2010. With its emphasis on clear pictures and easy-to-use effects, it attracted an extensive user base fast. Instagram was acquired by Facebook in 2012, and as a result, its features and capabilities were expanded. Notably, IGTV and Stories further prioritized visual material (Hu, Manikonda, & Kambhampati, 2014).

TikTok

With its short-form video content, TikTok, which was introduced globally in 2018 by the Chinese business Byte Dance (after its merger with Musical.ly), transformed social media. TikTok has been incredibly popular, especially with younger audiences, thanks to its algorithm-driven content discovery and user-friendliness (Anderson, 2020). Its focus on user interaction and innovation has raised the bar for social media platforms.

In the food business, social media marketing has become a vital tool, transforming the way firms interact with customers and establish their online identities. Food brands can now exhibit their products through aesthetically appealing material, interact with a wider audience, and influence customer behavior in previously unheard-of ways thanks to the growth of platforms like Facebook, Instagram, and TikTok. A Hootsuite (2020) survey found that over 4.5 billion individuals globally use social media, and this figure is still rising. This presents food brands with a large audience to reach. According to Kim and Lee (2019), this change has not only brought about a transformation of conventional marketing tactics but has also presented new avenues for firms to innovate and communicate more personally with their customers.

The rise of user-generated content and influencer marketing, which are now crucial in influencing consumer perceptions and influencing purchase decisions, highlights the importance of social media in the food business (Liu-Thompkins, 2019). Social media also facilitates real-time feedback and interaction, which helps brands react swiftly to changing consumer trends and preferences. In order to remain relevant in a fiercely competitive market, brands must be flexible and constantly adjust their strategies in this dynamic environment (Muntinga, Moorman, & Smit, 2019).

1.2. Objectives

This chapter's main goal is to give readers a thorough understanding of social media marketing tactics used in the food business. It attempts to investigate the several ways that food brands might use social media platforms to improve their visibility, interact with customers, and promote growth. The difficulties of social media marketing will also be covered in this chapter, including how to handle unfavorable comments and maintain relevance in the face of quickly evolving trends. It will also look at future developments in social media marketing, such as the effects of augmented reality (AR) and artificial intelligence (AI), which have the potential to significantly change the field (Grewal, Roggeveen, & Nordfält, 2020).

By exploring these aspects, the chapter intends to provide professionals and scholars with the information and resources necessary to successfully negotiate the intricate world of social media marketing in the food sector. Additionally, it will give readers a glimpse into social media marketing's future and assist them in anticipating and becoming ready for the changing trends that will reshape the sector in the years to come.

2. BACKGROUND AND LITERATURE REVIEW

Foundational Concepts

Modern marketing methods have made social media marketing an essential tool, especially in sectors like food where customer interaction and visual attractiveness are critical. Understanding the fundamentals of demographic and psychographic traits is crucial to using social media efficiently.

The statistical features of a population, such as age, gender, income, education, and occupation, are referred to as demographics. These elements are essential for dividing up the target market and creating marketing messages that appeal to particular demographics. Younger generations, like Generation Z, for instance, are more likely to use apps and platforms like TikTok and Instagram, which promote visual storytelling and short-form video content (Smith & Anderson, 2018).

Psychographics, on the other hand, focus more on the psychological characteristics of customers, such as their values, attitudes, interests, and lifestyles. Brands may provide more individualized and pertinent content that speaks to the underlying needs and motivations of their audience by having a better understanding of psychographic traits (Solomon, 2020). As an illustration, a food brand catering to health-conscious consumers may highlight sustainable processes and organic products, as these align with the values of this market (Kotler & Keller, 2016).

These concepts are essential for social media marketing because they help companies create messages that not only grab attention but also strengthen their relationship with customers. Marketing techniques should be in line with consumer requirements and motivations, according to theories like Maslow's Hierarchy of requirements (Maslow, 1943) and the Theory of Planned Behavior (Ajzen, 1991). Brands may develop more engaging and conversion-boosting marketing by knowing both psychographic and demographic traits.

Literature Review

Over the past ten years, there has been a considerable evolution in the literature on social media marketing, with many studies examining its effects on a variety of industries, including the food industry. Early studies (Kaplan & Haenlein, 2010) concentrated on how social media affected consumer engagement and brand awareness. The foundation for understanding how social media platforms can be used for marketing goals was established by these studies. But the literature's concentration has changed along with the digital landscape.

The impact of cutting-edge technology like artificial intelligence (AI) and machine learning has been included to the scope of social media marketing study in recent studies. For example, AI is being utilized more and more to evaluate customer behavior, tailor content, and maximize advertising campaigns in real time (Dwivedi et al., 2021). The utilization of AI by organizations to provide audiences with more relevant and tailored content has noteworthy consequences for social media marketing, as it can boost engagement and conversion rates (Chaffey & Ellis-Chadwick, 2019).

Furthermore, complex chatbots and content recommendation algorithms that improve user experience have been developed as a result of AI's integration with social media (Grewal, Roggeveen, & Nordfält, 2020). By providing instantaneous answers to questions and individualized recommendations, these technologies allow brands to engage with customers in more meaningful ways, which can greatly increase customer satisfaction and loyalty (Huang & Rust, 2021).

However, there are still a number of research gaps in this area despite the achievements. For instance, while the literature on AI's use in social media marketing is expanding, less is known about the technology's long-term effects on customer behavior and brand loyalty. Furthermore, further research is needed on the ethical ramifications of utilizing AI for targeted marketing, including worries about data security and privacy (Jobin, Ienca, & Vayena, 2019). Closing these gaps will be essential to creating a more thorough grasp of social media marketing in the future.

Conclusively, despite the abundance and diversity of literature on social media marketing, staying ahead of the curve requires constant exploration of new trends and technology. Scholars and practitioners can aid in the continuing development of social media marketing tactics in the food business by critically assessing current studies and identifying research gaps.

2.1. The Rise of Visual Content and Influencer Marketing

A noticeable shift towards visual material emerged with the rise in popularity of photo and video-sharing apps like Instagram and TikTok on social media platforms.

Visual Content

Visual content gained popularity in social media marketing because of its rapid attention span and powerful message delivery. Instagram's success can be ascribed to its emphasis on imagery, which produced posts with better engagement rates than text-based content (Hu, Manikonda, & Kambhampati, 2014). Similar to this, Pinterest, which debuted in 2010 and made use of visual content by enabling users to "pin" ideas and photos, grew to become a prominent source of inspiration and information (Hall & Zarro, 2012).

Influencer Marketing

According to Abidin (2016), the introduction of visual content also made influencer marketing possible. Influencers are people who have large social media followings who use their influence and credibility to endorse brands and products. Influencers in the fields of food, beauty, and lifestyle began working with businesses on sponsored content creation on YouTube and Instagram, which is where this trend first gained steam. Because influencers are seen as relatable and genuine, their suggestions are regarded as more reliable than those of traditional commercials, which is why influencer marketing has been successful.

As evidence of the effectiveness of influencer marketing on visual platforms, Dunkin' Donuts' partnership with TikTok star Charli D'Amelio, for instance, produced a notable increase in engagement and sales—Business Insider, 2020).

2.2. Overview of the Food Industry

The Significance of the Food Industry in the Global Economy

The food sector, which includes everything from agriculture and food production to distribution and consumption, is an essential part of the world economy. It is essential for maintaining food security, creating jobs, and fostering economic expansion.

Economic Contribution

The national and international economy are greatly impacted by the food business. It has contributed more than $8 trillion to the world economy in recent years, making up a sizeable share of the global GDP (OECD, 2021). Retail, food processing, and agriculture are some of the industry sectors that contribute to this total.

Employment

Around the world, the food industry is a significant employer. Over 1.5 billion people are employed globally in the agriculture and food sectors, which make up about 40% of the workforce in certain developing nations, according to the International Labor Organization (ILO) (ILO, 2020). Farming, food processing, retail, and food services are all included in this employment.

Food Security and Sustainability

In addition, the food business is essential to both sustainability and food security. Feeding the world's expanding population requires efficient food production, processing, and distribution. In order to solve environmental issues and enhance resource management, the sector is putting more and more emphasis on sustainable practices (FAO, 2019).

Key Segments of the Food Industry

1. Restaurants

Restaurants, which include a wide variety of dining venues from fast food to fine dining, are a substantial portion of the food sector. As consumer preferences change, the National Restaurant Association (NRA) projects that the worldwide restaurant sector will continue to grow, with a valuation of over $4.2 trillion in 2020 (NRA, 2021). Food trucks, quick-service restaurants (QSRs), and full-service restaurants are all included in this category.

2. Food Production

The process of turning raw agricultural products into consumables is known as food production. Processing meat, producing dairy products, and packaging food are all included in this category. As the demand for processed foods rises, the global food processing market, which was estimated to be worth $3.8 trillion in 2021, is predicted to expand (Grand View Research, 2021).

3. Retail

Food retail refers to the selling of food items via a variety of outlets, such as online marketplaces, grocery stores, and supermarkets. In order to link consumers with food items, the retail sector is essential. In 2020, the worldwide grocery retail market was estimated to be worth $11.2 trillion. The increase of e-commerce and rising consumer spending were the main drivers of this sector (Euromonitor International, 2021).

4. Food Services

Institutions that provide huge crowds meals, including corporate cafeterias, hospitals, and schools, are examples of food services. Because there is a growing need for outsourced food services, this market is becoming more and more important for providing personalized meals in institutional settings. In 2020, the market for food service worldwide was estimated to be worth $3.5 trillion, with institutional and catering services accounting for a large portion of this total (IBISWorld, 2021).

2.3. Intersection of Social Media and the Food Industry

The Growing Importance of Social Media in Consumer Decision-Making

Social media is now an essential tool for influencing customer choices and behavior, especially in the food sector. Social media sites such as Facebook, Instagram, TikTok, and YouTube have an impact on how customers find, assess, and select food goods and eating experiences.

Influence on Discovery and Awareness

Social media platforms are essential for learning about new food trends, companies, and products. Users can share visually appealing food photos and videos on visual networks like Instagram and TikTok, which are particularly powerful since they are frequently tagged with popular hashtags. According to a Nielsen survey from 2018, 49% of consumers worldwide stated they depend on social media for product suggestions, highlighting social media's important role during the awareness and discovery stages (Nielsen, 2018).

Consumer Reviews and Recommendations

With the growth of social media, user-generated content such as reviews and recommendations has become increasingly important. Customers can post their dining experiences on websites like Yelp, TripAdvisor, and Facebook, which can have a significant impact on other people's decisions. The impact of social proof in the food business is highlighted by a Deloitte (2015) study that indicated 81% of consumers are affected by their friends' social media postings and evaluations when making purchases (Deloitte, 2015).

Impact of Visual Content

Social media visual content significantly influences the tastes and appetites of users. High-quality photos and videos can increase the appeal and sales of food products. A Hootsuite (2020) study found that posts including high-quality graphics get 650% more interaction than text-only posts, underscoring the significance of visuals in shaping customer behavior.

How Food Brands Leverage Social Media to Reach and Engage Audiences

Food brands use social media to interact with their followers, foster brand loyalty, and increase revenue. To accomplish these objectives, a variety of tactics are used, including as interactive campaigns, content marketing, and influencer alliances.

Influencer Partnerships

Collaboration with influencers is a common strategy used by food manufacturers to increase their visibility and establish trust. Influencers have the ability to present products in a genuine and captivating manner, frequently offering their followers behind-the-scenes photos, reviews, and recipes. For instance, Starbucks has found that working with influencers to promote its seasonal product introductions helps create buzz and boost sales (Business Insider, 2019).

Content Marketing and Storytelling

Food brands narrate stories about their goods, roots, and principles through content marketing. This strategy aids in establishing an emotional bond with customers. Chipotle and other brands use social media to share information about ethical and sustainable sourcing, matching their messaging to the beliefs of consumers who care about the environment (Chipotle, 2020).

Interactive Campaigns and User Engagement

Engaging audiences with interactive campaigns like surveys, challenges, and contests is a smart strategy for marketers. For instance, Coca-Cola's "Share a Coke" campaign prompted users to post pictures of their customized bottle labels, which resulted in a large amount of user-generated content and higher brand engagement (Coca-Cola, 2015). Furthermore, marketers utilize TikTok challenges and Instagram Stories to promote user involvement and interaction.

Utilizing Data and Analytics

Social media analytics are used by brands to better understand consumer preferences and adjust their tactics. Brands can better satisfy consumer requirements by customizing their content and marketing efforts through the analysis of engagement metrics, sentiment, and consumer feedback (HubSpot, 2021).

3. EMERGING TECHNOLOGIES AND TRENDS

3.1. AI and Machine Learning

Through improved audience interaction and strategy optimization, artificial intelligence (AI) and machine learning (ML) are rapidly changing social media marketing. material recommendation algorithms, which customize the material users view on social media feeds, are among the most important applications of AI. According to Kaplan and Haenlein (2020), these algorithms examine user behavior, interests, and interactions to recommend material that is most likely to pique their interest. This increases the likelihood of brand exposure and consumer interaction.

Artificial Intelligence (AI) and Machine Learning (ML) are technologies that have become integral to modern social media marketing, revolutionizing how brands connect with their audiences, analyze data, and optimize campaigns.

Artificial Intelligence (AI)

Artificial intellect (AI) is the simulation of human intellect in machines with thought, learning, and problem-solving programs. Artificial intelligence (AI) is utilized in social media marketing to improve user experiences, automate tasks, and deliver tailored content. AI-driven technologies, for instance, may evaluate enormous volumes of data to forecast customer behavior, enhance advertising tactics, and customize content recommendations. This enhances audience engagement and conversion rates by enabling brands to present more pertinent content to them (Kaplan & Haenlein, 2020).

AI is also essential to the automation of customer support. Chatbots and virtual assistants powered by AI allow firms to offer real-time, round-the-clock customer service. By handling basic questions, processing transactions, and even troubleshooting problems, these bots can lower operating costs and increase customer satisfaction. For example, real-time user engagement can be achieved using chatbots on platforms such as Facebook Messenger, which can assist users with inquiries and provide guidance along the customer experience (Luo et al., 2019).

Machine Learning (ML)

Techniques used in machine learning, a branch of artificial intelligence, enable systems to learn from data, become more efficient over time, and make judgments with little help from humans. When analyzing social media data, machine learning (ML) is very effective in spotting patterns, trends, and insights that would be challenging for people to find by hand.

Machine learning is commonly employed in content recommendation algorithms in social media marketing. These algorithms anticipate what kind of material would most likely engage each user based on an analysis of user behavior, including likes, shares, comments, and browsing history. In order to increase the possibility of engagement and connection, platforms such as YouTube, Netflix, and Instagram utilize machine learning (ML) to recommend films, posts, or items that match the tastes of the user (Sundar, 2020).

ML also makes advertising more effective by allowing for more accurate targeting. Advertisers can use machine learning (ML) to develop audience groups based on certain demographics, habits, and interests by analyzing customer data. Ad campaigns with precision targeting have a higher return on investment because they display advertising to people who are more likely to be interested in the goods or services being advertised (Chaffey & Ellis-Chadwick, 2019).

AI and ML technologies give marketers the ability to analyze enormous volumes of data to find patterns in consumer behavior, campaign performance, and industry trends. According to Chaffey and Ellis-Chadwick (2019), these insights enable brands to anticipate future trends more precisely, personalize marketing campaigns, and make data-driven decisions. For instance, marketers employ AI-powered platforms like Adobe Sensei and IBM Watson to evaluate customer data and optimize marketing efforts in real-time (Sundar, 2020).

3.2. AR and VR

Virtual reality (VR) and augmented reality (AR) are becoming increasingly potent tools for social media marketing because they provide immersive experiences that raise customer engagement. With AR, users may utilize the cameras on their smartphones to superimpose digital content over the actual world, resulting in interactive, entertaining, and shared experiences. For instance, marketers can build engaging brand experiences that customers can interact with and share through Instagram's AR effects and Snapchat's AR filters, which increases brand visibility (Bulearca & Tamarjan, 2020).

VR, on the other hand, provides a completely immersive online experience that enables users to enter virtual worlds. Even though virtual reality technology is still in its infancy, marketers are already using it to create immersive product presentations, virtual showrooms, and even virtual events. Like L'Oréal and

IKEA, for example, these companies have experimented with VR to provide virtual shop experiences that let customers explore and engage with products in a virtual setting (Poushter, 2019). It is anticipated that these technologies would become increasingly prevalent in social media marketing tactics as they offer distinctive means for companies to interact with their target audience.

3.3. Social Media Algorithm Changes

Social media algorithms are always changing, which has an effect on how users see and prioritize material. These modifications may have a major impact on the visibility of content and, in turn, the efficacy of marketing campaigns. For example, companies now find it more difficult to acquire organic reach on Facebook due to the platform's shift in favor of material from friends and family over brand pages (Mosseri, 2018). Similar to this, marketers are being compelled by Instagram's algorithm, which rewards engagement-driven content, to produce more engaging posts that promote likes, comments, and shares.

Brands need to concentrate on producing content that is appealing to algorithms in order to adjust to these developments. This entails creating excellent, captivating content that connects with viewers and promotes participation. Furthermore, it's critical to keep up with algorithm changes and modify content tactics as necessary. In order to ensure that their content reaches a wider audience despite algorithmic limitations, brands are also increasingly engaging in paid marketing to supplement their organic efforts (Tuten & Solomon, 2019).

Additionally, utilizing features like interactive polls, live videos, and tales can aid in raising the visibility and engagement of information. According to Lipsman et al. (2021), algorithms tend to prioritize certain features because they are intended to entice consumers to stay on the site longer. Brands can sustain their social media presence and efficacy by consistently experimenting with diverse content forms and remaining flexible in the face of algorithmic modifications.

4. THE ROLE OF SOCIAL MEDIA MARKETING IN THE FOOD INDUSTRY

4.1. Enhancing Brand Visibility

Case Studies of Successful Food Brands Using Social Media

a. Wendy's

Wendy's has emerged as a notable example for leveraging social media, specifically Twitter, to improve brand awareness and interact with consumers. With a humorous and frequently irreverent tone, Wendy's distinctive voice has helped set it apart from rivals. Through frequent "roasting" of rivals and consumers, Wendy's Twitter account generates viral content and keeps a high level of interaction. This tactic keeps Wendy's in the forefront of prospective customers' minds in addition to entertaining followers. For example, Wendy's "National Roast Day" marketing encourages fans to submit requests for roasts, leading to a great deal of engagement and media attention (Hajli, 2014; Forbes, 2020).

Figure 1. Wendy's Social Media Engagement

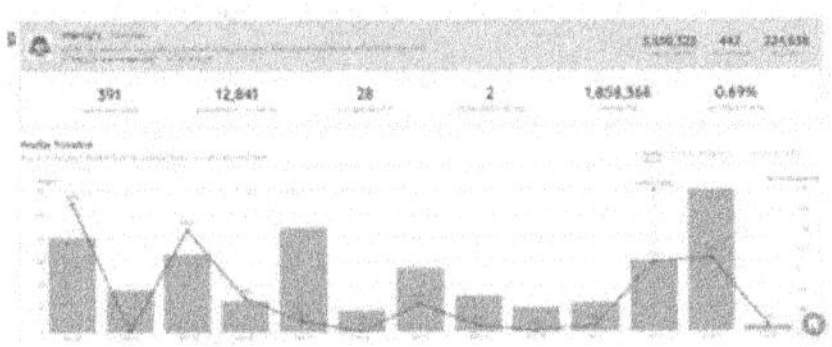

Source: https://keyhole.co/blog/wendys-social-media-strategy/

b. Starbucks

Starbucks makes use of a variety of social media channels to establish a unified and captivating corporate identity. The company's content strategy is centered on user-generated content, seasonal promotions, and visual storytelling. Starbucks uses Instagram to share visually appealing photos of their products and beverages. User-generated content is frequently featured under hashtags like #Starbucks and #RedCupContest. By encouraging followers to create and share content, this strategy not only keeps them interested but also broadens Starbucks' audience (Harrington, 2021). Additionally, Starbucks uses Instagram Stories and highlights to highlight community involvement, offer behind-the-scenes material, and promote new products, all of which help the business build a deep emotional bond with its audience (Chaffey, 2020).

Figure 2. Starbucks social media engagement

Source: https://keyhole.co/blog/starbucks-social-media-strategy/

Strategies for Increasing Brand Awareness Through Social Media Campaigns

1) Consistent Brand Voice and Personality

Building brand recognition and trust on all social media channels requires maintaining a consistent brand voice. For example, Wendy's frequently adopts a forceful and hilarious tone that comes through in their postings and interacts with followers. The brand stands out and becomes instantly identifiable thanks to its distinctive voice (Forbes, 2020). Maintaining a consistent brand voice makes it easier for customers to relate to and remember the brand by ensuring that all communications are in line with its identity.

2) Leveraging Visual Content

Visual content is an effective technique for drawing viewers in and getting ideas across rapidly. Brands such as Starbucks leverage visually captivating material to highlight their goods and establish a strong emotional bond with their viewers. Using top-notch photos, videos, and graphics can raise the chance that material will be shared and greatly improve user engagement. Food manufacturers have great success with visual platforms like Instagram and Pinterest because they make it possible to promote their products in a visually appealing and delicious way (Chaffey, 2020).

3) User-Generated Content (UGC)

Customers' creation and sharing of brand-related content can increase a brand's credibility and reach. Customers can effectively use user-generated content (UGC) by sharing pictures of their customized Starbucks cups through the #RedCupContest at Starbucks. In addition to raising interaction, this campaign serves as social proof by displaying actual customers using the brand's products (Harrington, 2021). Customer loyalty and a sense of community can be fostered via user-generated content (UGC) campaigns, as customers feel more a part of the company when their contribution is recognized and shared.

4) Influencer Collaborations

Reaching out to influencers is a great strategy to expand your audience and establish your authority. Influencers have the ability to authentically and relatably introduce products to their followers, which frequently increases conversion rates and trust. Starbucks, for instance, has collaborated with a range of influencers to publicize the debut of new products, successfully reaching a wide range of demographics (Chaffey, 2020). To get the most out of the partnership, it's critical to make sure the influencers are chosen with the brand's values and target market in mind.

5) Interactive and Engaging Content

Incorporating interactive elements like polls, quizzes, challenges, and live streaming into content may greatly increase user engagement and brand awareness. Followers are encouraged to actively participate in interactive content, which makes them feel important and involved. For instance, Wendy's frequently hosts live Q&A sessions and launches interactive campaigns like "National Roast Day" in order to interact with their audience through interactive content (Forbes, 2020). In addition to raising participation, these activities offer insightful data about the preferences and viewpoints of the target audience.

4.2. Engaging with Consumers

Importance of Interactive Content

Interactive content on social media is crucial for engaging consumers and fostering a deeper connection with a brand. Unlike passive content, interactive content requires active participation from users, which can increase engagement, provide valuable feedback, and enhance brand loyalty. There are several types of interactive content that brands can utilize:

Polls and Surveys-

According to Harrison (2020), surveys and polls are easy-to-use yet powerful tools for audience engagement. They make it possible for brands to instantly obtain feedback, preferences, and views from customers. Customers feel acknowledged and respected as a result, and firms are also better able to understand their customers. For example, marketers can ask their followers questions using Instagram Stories' polling tool, which encourages engagement and a feeling of community.

Q&A Sessions-

Live Q&A sessions provide businesses a great way to engage with their audience directly. These events can be broadcast live on a number of websites, including Twitter, Facebook Live, and Instagram Live. They promote openness and trust by enabling customers to ask inquiries about goods, services, or the brand itself. In order to improve the customer experience, Q&A sessions can also be utilized to address consumer complaints and offer real-time help (Smith, 2021).

Live Cooking Shows and Demonstrations-

Live cooking shows and demos are a fun way for food entrepreneurs to interact with customers, share recipes, and highlight their products. You may watch these live events on YouTube, Facebook Live, Instagram Live, and other platforms. Through comments and inquiries, marketers may interact with the public and showcase the quality and adaptability of their products. In addition to generating a sense of urgency through time-limited deals or unique recipe ideas, live cooking demonstrations can also push viewers to act right away (Mitchell, 2019).

Examples of Brands Successfully Engaging with Their Audience

- **Chipotle's TikTok Challenges**

Chipotle Mexican Grill has used interactive material on TikTok to effectively attract younger people. The company started the #ChipotleLidFlip competition, in which users were tasked with coming up with inventive methods to flip a Chipotle bowl's lid. With millions of views and a considerable amount of user-generated content, this challenge became viral. The campaign's simplicity, the allure of a viral challenge, and the promise of a free entree for the top entries all contributed to its popularity. In addition to raising interaction, this campaign improved Chipotle's exposure on a Gen Z-friendly site (TikTok, 2020).

Figure 3. Image of the ChipotleLidFlip campaign

- **Starbucks' Instagram Stories**

Starbucks regularly hosts interactive Q&A sessions, surveys, and behind-the-scenes content on Instagram Stories as a way to communicate with its followers. For instance, Starbucks might use Stories to ask fans which flavor they can't wait to sample when a new seasonal drink launches. In addition to promoting the new product, this strategy engages customers with the brand's products. Furthermore, Starbucks frequently publishes user-generated content to promote a feeling of community and inspire others to share their experiences, such as pictures of patrons enjoying their drinks (Starbucks, 2021).

Figure 4. Starbuck Instagram story promoting Star Days

- **Domino's Pizza Emoji Ordering**

To make ordering easier and interact with tech-savvy customers, Domino's Pizza has creatively employed interactive content. The company introduced the "Domino's AnyWare" ordering system, which let users order via different channels such smart TVs and wearables or by tweeting a pizza emoji. This novel ordering method attracted a lot of interest from customers and the media in addition to making the procedure enjoyable and interesting. The ad emphasized Domino's dedication to ease and technology, enhancing its reputation (Harrington, 2020).

Figure 5. Domino Emoji Ordering

4.3. Influencer Collaborations

Role of Food Bloggers, Chefs, and Influencers in Promoting Food Brands

In the digital age, food bloggers, chefs, and influencers play a crucial role in promoting food brands by leveraging their online presence and follower base. These influencers have the power to shape consumer perceptions and purchasing decisions through their authentic and engaging content. The role of influencers in promoting food brands can be outlined in several key areas:

Authentic Content Creation

Influencers frequently produce relatable, genuine content that appeals to their audience. They make food goods easier for potential buyers to see how they fit into their own lives by presenting them in commonplace settings. Because customers are more likely to believe suggestions from people they see as sincere and sympathetic, authenticity is especially important (Brown & Fiorella, 2013).

Expertise and Authority

A business can get credibility from chefs and food bloggers, who are frequently seen as authorities in the culinary industry. A product's perceived quality and reliability can increase when it is endorsed by a well-known chef. This works especially well for companies trying to market themselves as high-end or health-conscious solutions (Smith, 2018).

Broad Reach and Engagement

On social media, influencers can have sizable and very active fan groups. Brands can reach a wider population by collaborating with influencers and reaching these audiences than they might by using traditional advertising techniques. Influencers can also increase high levels of engagement by encouraging likes, comments, and shares, which can magnify the brand's message and raise its profile (Veirman et al., 2017).

Creative Campaigns and Content Variety

Influencers infuse campaigns with creativity by creating a diverse range of content, such as live cooking sessions, unboxing experiences, reviews, and recipe videos. This diversity offers a multitude of ways for customers to interact with the business and keeps them interested. Influencers can also take part in product launches, seasonal promotions, or themed campaigns to generate excitement and buzz for the brand (Woods, 2016).

Case Studies of Successful Influencer Partnerships

1) Dunkin' Donuts and Charli D'Amelio

The connection between Charli D'Amelio, a well-known TikTok influencer with millions of followers, and Dunkin' Donuts is one of the most noteworthy influencer partnerships in the food sector. The partnership started because of Charli's regular updates on her favourite Dunkin' beverage, which inspired the makers to create a signature concoction called "The Charli." Dunkin's and Charli's social media accounts advertised the beverage, which included a cold brew with whole milk and three pumps of caramel swirl (Kaufman, 2020).

Sales of Dunkin's cold brew and app downloads significantly increased as a result of the campaign's great success. The collaboration served as an example of how real and successful marketing can result from using an influencer's sincere enthusiasm for a product. In order to keep Charli's fans and Dunkin's patrons interested, the campaign also featured a number of interactive components, such a TikTok dancing challenge and limited-edition products (Kaufman, 2020).

Figure 6. Dunkin Donut Promotion

2) McDonald's and BTS

In order to introduce the "BTS Meal," McDonald's teamed up with the internationally popular K-pop group BTS. The meal featured a customized menu featuring the band's preferred foods and proprietary sauces. Through sharing promotional content and interacting with followers on social media, BTS members actively promoted the cooperation. Kim (2021) said that the campaign featured exclusive goods, behind-the-scenes content, and a specialized app experience.

A worldwide sensation, the BTS Meal increased McDonald's sales and engagement to an enormous extent. Through the partnership, BTS's large and devoted fan following, known as the "ARMY," was reached, resulting in a cultural phenomenon that went beyond standard fast-food advertising. The triumph of this alliance demonstrated the ability of influencer partnerships to generate viral events and provide noteworthy commercial outcomes (Kim, 2021).

Figure 7. Image of McDonalds and BTS collaboration

4.4. User-Generated Content

Encouraging Customers to Share Their Experiences

User-generated content (UGC) refers to any content created and shared by consumers about a brand or product, rather than by the brand itself. This can include photos, videos, reviews, testimonials, and social media posts. Encouraging UGC can be a powerful strategy for brands, as it leverages the authentic voices of customers and fosters a community around the brand. Here are some ways brands encourage UGC:

• Social Media Hashtags and Campaigns

Brands frequently designate particular hashtags and urge users to use them when posting about their experiences. In addition to aiding in the aggregation of content, this tactic also facilitates brand engagement and post sharing. For instance, during seasonal campaigns, Starbucks encourages users to use hashtags like #Starbucks and #RedCupContest, which results in a significant number of user-generated content (UGC) (Starbucks, 2021).

• Contests and Giveaways

Organizing competitions and freebies is another powerful strategy for inspiring users to produce and distribute content. For a chance to win prizes, brands may urge participants to contribute images, films, or narratives that highlight their products. This boosts interaction and yields an abundance of user-generated content (UGC) for use in subsequent marketing campaigns. As an example, GoPro often holds competitions in which participants enter videos made with their GoPro cameras for the chance to win gear and other prizes (GoPro, 2020).

• Featuring Customer Content on Official Channels

Showcasing user-generated material on a brand's official website or social media accounts can inspire more people to talk about their experiences. Given that it gives them exposure and approval, this acknowledgment can be a powerful motivator for clients. Companies such as Apple and Coca-Cola frequently incorporate user images and tales into their marketing efforts to showcase the effectiveness of their goods and to highlight the inventiveness of their customers (Apple, 2021; Coca-Cola, 2019).

Analysing the Impact of User-Generated Content on Brand Perception and Sales

• Authenticity and Trust

Due to its origins in the real experiences of actual customers, user-generated content (UGC) is frequently perceived as being more genuine and reliable than traditional advertising. According to Hennig-Thurau et al. (2004), customers are more likely to believe recommendations from peers than from brands, hence authenticity can greatly improve brand perception. Nielsen (2012) found that 92% of consumers place more faith in earned media—like referrals from friends and family—than in any other type of advertising.

• Increased Engagement and Reach

User-generated content (UGC) has the potential to boost engagement and reach since users who generate and distribute content about a business are more likely to interact with it and inspire their followers to follow suit. More people can hear the brand's message thanks to this organic sharing than through sponsored advertising alone. For instance, Coca-Cola saw a 2% boost in sales in the United States and a notable rise in social media engagement when it introduced its "Share a Coke" campaign, which encouraged consumers to submit images of customized Coke bottles (Coca-Cola, 2019).

• Enhanced Customer Loyalty and Community Building

Customers who feel more engaged and connected to the brand are the ones who generate a feeling of community around it when UGC is encouraged. As consumers who interact with a business and share their experiences are more likely to stay loyal and refer the brand to others, this can increase customer loyalty. GoPro, for example, has created a fervent user base that not only advocates for the company but also has a strong feeling of community through the usage of user-generated content (UGC) (GoPro, 2020).

- **Influence on Purchasing Decisions**

Purchase decisions can also be directly influenced by UGC. Viewing real-world product applications through user-generated content (UGC) can lower perceived risk and increase buy intent by helping prospective customers see how the product fits into their own lives. Stackla (2019) found that 79% of respondents stated user-generated content (UGC) had a significant influence on their purchase decisions, compared to 13% who claimed sponsored material has the same effect.

4.5. Video and Visual Content

The Power of Visual Content in the Food Industry

In the food industry, visual content plays a crucial role in attracting and engaging customers. Platforms like Instagram and Pinterest are particularly powerful for showcasing food products due to their visual nature. The impact of visual content in the food industry can be attributed to several factors:

- **Appeal to the Senses**

Since food is primarily visual, well-taken pictures have the power to arouse the senses and create a desire in viewers for the food they see. A lot of food manufacturers spend a lot of money on staged presentations and expert photography because of this sensory appeal. Food photos look especially good on platforms like Instagram, which prioritize visually appealing material. Research indicates that visually appealing content has a higher chance of being shared and can have a big impact on what customers decide to buy (Becker et al., 2011).

- **Influence on Decision Making**

Infographics and photographs are examples of visual content that can successfully convey important details about food products, like components, cooking techniques, and nutritional advantages. Customers may be inspired to try new goods or recipes and be able to make more educated decisions as a result. For instance, Pinterest is a well-liked resource for finding new recipes and food ideas, and users frequently use the site to get visual inspiration (Pinterest, 2020).

- **Brand Storytelling and Differentiation**

Brands may express their narrative and set themselves apart from rivals with the help of visual material. Through the continuous use of particular colors, styles, and themes, brands can establish a visually unified identity that effectively connects with their intended audience. For instance, Starbucks maintains a consistent brand image on Instagram by combining bright, seasonally themed content with minimalist design (Starbucks, 2021).

The Rise of Video Content and Platforms Like YouTube and TikTok

Video content has become increasingly dominant in digital marketing, offering dynamic and engaging ways to connect with audiences. Platforms like YouTube and TikTok have emerged as powerful tools for food brands to showcase products, share recipes, and engage with consumers.

• YouTube

For long-form video content, such product reviews, recipe videos, and cooking demonstrations, YouTube is a great resource. In order to make it simpler for viewers to duplicate recipes at home, food manufacturers and influencers utilize YouTube to offer comprehensive, step-by-step cooking instructions. In addition to adding value, this instructional component strengthens the brand's authority and credibility. By continuously producing interesting and high-quality food content, channels like Tasty and Bon Appétit have amassed millions of subscribers (YouTube, 2021).

• TikTok

TikTok has completely changed the way people consume and share food content with its short-form, viral films. Because of the platform's algorithm, which rewards original and interesting content, it is a great place for companies to connect with younger consumers. Popular TikTok creators and food brands frequently work together to produce viral content like product displays, challenges, and cooking tips. TikTok videos have a fast-paced, visually appealing structure that can easily draw viewers in and inspire them to try new foods or items (TikTok, 2020).

Techniques for Creating Engaging Visual and Video Content

• High-Quality Imagery and Video Production

The visual content must be of the highest caliber. Well-produced movies and high-quality photos not only appear professional, but they also give the brand confidence. The attractiveness of content can be greatly increased by making investments in appropriate lighting, camera gear, and editing software. To preserve a consistent brand identity, brands should also take visual design elements like color schemes and typefaces into account (Nielsen, 2019).

• Storytelling and Emotional Connection

Using images and videos to tell a gripping story can help you connect emotionally with your audience. This can be accomplished by revealing the place of the brand's origin, emphasizing ethical sourcing methods, or displaying client endorsements. For instance, a lot of food manufacturers emphasize quality and authenticity by using videos to show the path taken by their components from farm to table (Smith, 2018).

• Interactive and Educational Content

Educational and interactive media may captivate audiences and compel them to take part. Cooking lessons and how-to films, for example, provide value to the audience's experience by teaching viewers as well as showcasing the uses of products. Brands can engage with their audience in real time by hosting Q&A sessions or live cooking demos, which can further improve interaction (Becker et al., 2011).

• Leveraging Trends and Challenges

Engaging in issues and trends can help graphic and video content become more visible and engaging. Brands can employ viral trends or their own challenges on platforms like TikTok to promote user engagement and content sharing. Reach and brand exposure can be greatly increased with this tactic, particularly among younger groups (TikTok, 2020).

5. STRATEGIES FOR EFFECTIVE SOCIAL MEDIA MARKETING

5.1. Identifying the Target Audience

Identifying the target audience is crucial for effective marketing, as it allows brands to tailor their strategies to meet the specific needs and preferences of their potential customers. The target audience can be understood by analysing both demographic and psychographic characteristics.

Demographic Characteristics

Demographic characteristics refer to the statistical data about the population and particular groups within it. These characteristics include attributes such as age, gender, income, education level, marital status, ethnicity, and geographic location. This data helps businesses and marketers understand the composition of their target market and tailor their strategies accordingly. For example:

1) **Age:** The interests and shopping habits of different age groups vary. For example, whereas older folks could favour conventional and educational content, younger viewers might be more interested in fashionable and social media-driven ads (Kotler & Keller, 2016).
2) **Gender:** Preferences and decisions about what to buy can be influenced by a person's gender. For instance, depending on the product's appeal, food brands may focus particular goods or promotions towards men or women (Solomon, 2018).
3) **Income Level:** Determining the target audience's income level aids in properly presenting the product. Higher-class consumers may be the intended market for premium products, but a wider range of people may be drawn to more reasonably priced solutions (Aaker & McLoughlin, 2010).
4) **Education level:** Consumer behaviour and preferences can be influenced by an individual's degree of education, which can also have an impact on how companies communicate and how sophisticated the information they offer (Schiffman & Wisenblit, 2019).

5) **Geographic Location:** Consumer choices and purchasing patterns can be greatly influenced by regional preferences and cultural differences. When preparing their marketing strategy, brands must take location-based elements into account (Chaffey & Ellis-Chadwick, 2019).

Psychographic Characteristics

Psychographic characteristics go beyond demographics to explore the psychological aspects of consumer behaviour. These characteristics provide deeper insights into consumer motivations and behaviours. Key psychographic factors include:

1) **Lifestyle:** Brand alignment with consumer beliefs and activities is facilitated by an understanding of the target audience's lifestyle. For instance, a health-conscious consumer base would favour sustainable and organic food products (Solomon, 2018).
2) **Personality attributes:** To establish a more tailored relationship with their audience, brands can leverage several personality attributes including sociability, adventure, or conservatism (Schiffman & Wisenblit, 2019).
3) **Interests and Hobbies:** Brands may produce content that speaks to the passions of their target audience by understanding their interests and hobbies. For instance, a company catering to foodies may highlight gourmet dishes and cooking methods (Kotler & Keller, 2016).
4) **Values and Beliefs:** Brands can better position themselves on social issues and forge stronger emotional bonds with customers by being aware of the values and beliefs of their target audience (Aaker & McLoughlin, 2010).
5) **Behavioural Patterns:** Examining customer behaviour can reveal the most effective methods of audience engagement. Examples of this behaviour include usage frequency, brand loyalty, and purchase behaviours (Chaffey & Ellis-Chadwick, 2019).

Tailoring Content to Meet the Preferences and Needs of Different Audience Segments

Once the target audience's demographic and psychographic characteristics are identified, brands can tailor their content to meet the specific preferences and needs of different audience segments. This approach ensures that the content is relevant and engaging, ultimately leading to higher conversion rates and customer loyalty.

Customized Messaging

Customized messaging that speaks to the distinct requirements and interests of each segment can be developed by brands. For example, a health food company may use messaging about nutrition and fitness to appeal to younger, health-conscious consumers, and heart health and longevity to appeal to older, less active consumers (Tuten & Solomon, 2018).

Content Formats

Different content forms may be preferred by different audience segments. Younger audiences might be more interested in video material on TikTok and Instagram, for instance, whereas older audiences might be more interested in long-form blog entries or newsletters. Brands can select the most successful formats for delivering their messages by having a thorough understanding of these preferences (Kotler & Keller, 2016).

Personalized Experiences

Customer engagement requires personalization. Customized email marketing, targeted social media ads, and product suggestions are just a few examples of the personalized experiences that brands can provide with data-driven insights. For instance, depending on a customer's past purchases or browsing activity, an online food shop may make product recommendations (Schiffman & Wisenblit, 2019).

Engaging Storytelling

Brands may employ stories to emotionally engage with various audience segments. Brands may forge closer bonds with their target audience and produce a more memorable brand experience by telling tales that speak to their beliefs and interests. For instance, a company that supports environmentally friendly food practices can tell tales about its sourcing processes and dedication to environmental preservation (Solomon, 2018).

Utilizing Influencers

Collaborating with influencers who connect with particular audience segments can increase a brand's visibility and authority. Influencers have the ability to provide material that speaks directly to the interests and preferences of their followers, which increases the brand's relatability and credibility. To promote their products, a vegan food manufacturer, for example, might team up with a well-known vegan influencer (De Veirman et al., 2017).

Feedback and Adaptation

Keeping oneself relevant requires constant feedback and adjustment. In order to improve their content and tactics, brands should actively seek input from their target audience. As suggested by Tuten and Solomon (2018), this may include surveying people, evaluating engagement metrics, or keeping an eye on social media discussions.

5.2. Content Strategy

A well-crafted content strategy is crucial for effectively engaging and retaining an audience, particularly in industries like food, where storytelling and visuals play a significant role. Key components of a successful content strategy include the importance of a content calendar, balancing promotional and non-promotional content, and utilizing a variety of content types to connect with different audience segments.

Importance of a Content Calendar

A content calendar is a planning tool that helps brands organize and schedule their content across different platforms and channels. It provides a visual overview of what content will be published, when, and on which platforms, allowing for better coordination and consistency in messaging (Pulizzi, 2014). The benefits of using a content calendar include:

1) **Frequency and Consistency:** Continual blogging is essential to keeping viewers interested. By ensuring that material is released on a regular basis, a content calendar fosters and maintains audience interest (Rowley, 2008).
2) **Strategic Planning:** It enables marketers to schedule content in accordance with important occasions, occasions, and advertising campaigns, guaranteeing that all content is consistent with the brand's overarching marketing plan (Chaffey & Smith, 2017).
3) **Resource Management:** Brands can more effectively deploy resources by organizing ahead of time, guaranteeing that content production, editing, and approval processes have ample time (Handley & Chapman, 2011).

Balancing Promotional and Non-Promotional Content

1) **Promotional Content:** An effective content strategy balances promotional and non-promotional content. While promotional content directly advertises products or services, non-promotional content focuses on providing value to the audience, such as educational or entertaining content. This balance is crucial for maintaining audience trust and engagement (Scott, 2015). Content that features discounts, special deals, products, or services is referred to as promotional content. Although it should be utilized sparingly to avoid overwhelming the audience, it is crucial for generating sales and converting leads (Pulizzi, 2014).
2) **Non-Promotional Content:** Content such as blog entries, films, or social media updates that educate, amuse, or uplift the viewer without overtly promoting a product are referred to as non-promotional content. By establishing the brand as an authority in the field and encouraging loyalty, this kind of content helps establish a relationship with the audience (Rowley, 2008).

According to Handley & Chapman (2011), the ideal ratio between promotional and non-promotional content is frequently 80/20, meaning that 80% of the material offers value without outright selling and 20% is promotional.

Examples of Effective Content Types

Recipes: Food brands can effectively engage their audience by sharing recipes. In addition to offering useful information, recipes entice readers to sample the brand's products. For instance, a company like Betty Crocker regularly publishes recipes that make use of their goods, highlighting the excellence and adaptability of their products (Kang, 2012).

Behind-the-Scenes: Content from behind the scenes provides an insight into the production, culture, and procedures of the brand. It can bring the brand to life and foster an atmosphere of openness and confidence. Videos that introduce team members or demonstrate how a product is manufactured, for instance, can be interesting and (De Pelsmacker et al., 2017).

Customer Reviews: Presenting client endorsements or anecdotes can be a potent strategy for establishing credibility and trust. Customer testimonials can emphasize practical uses for items, demonstrating to prospective buyers the advantages and contentment of existing users. Videos, blog entries, and social media posts can all be used to distribute this kind of content (Gensler et al., 2013).

5.3. Leveraging Analytics and Insights

Leveraging analytics and insights in social media marketing is essential for understanding audience behaviour, optimizing content, and measuring the effectiveness of campaigns. By using various tools and tracking key metrics, businesses can make data-driven decisions to enhance their marketing strategies.

Tools for Monitoring Social Media Performance

Several tools are available to help businesses monitor and analyse their social media performance:

1) **Google Analytics:** This program offers data on website traffic, including conversion rates, user activity, and traffic sources. Google Analytics provides a thorough understanding of the customer journey by tracking the role that social media networks play in website visits and conversions (Clifton, 2012).
2) **Hootsuite**: Hootsuite is a social media management tool that lets users plan postings, keep an eye on activity on social media, and assess results across several channels. Businesses may evaluate the effectiveness of their social media initiatives with the help of its analytics features, which monitor indicators like audience growth, engagement, and reach (Zarrella, 2019).
3) **Sprout Social:** This platform offers publication, analytics, and monitoring capabilities for social media management. Businesses may fine-tune their tactics depending on audience preferences and interactions by using Sprout Social's analytics dashboard, which provides comprehensive reports on engagement, audience demographics, and sentiment analysis. (2019, Kerpen).

Key Metrics to Track

To effectively measure the success of social media campaigns, businesses should focus on key metrics:

1) **Engagement Rate:** This indicator shows how much audience interaction a piece of content gets in the form of likes, comments, shares, and clicks. According to Peters et al., (2013), a higher engagement rate suggests that the audience is finding the content to be compelling.
2) **Reach:** The total number of distinct users who view a content is referred to as reach. It aids companies in comprehending the magnitude of their viewership and the possible visibility of their material (Tuten & Solomon, 2018).
3) **Impressions:** Regardless of whether a post is clicked or not, impressions show how many times it has been presented overall. Measuring impressions is one way to determine how visible and frequently content is exposed (Chaffey & Smith, 2017).
4) **Conversion Rate:** This statistic shows what proportion of people interact with social media content and then complete a desired action, such buying something, subscribing to a newsletter, or downloading a resource. According to Clifton (2012), conversion rate is a crucial measure of how well social media efforts are achieving their goals for businesses.

Adjusting Strategies Based on Data-Driven Insights

Using data-driven insights, businesses can refine and adjust their social media strategies to improve performance. Key actions include:

1) **Content Optimization**: Businesses can prioritize and improve the content that most resonates with their audience by analysing data on which types of content earn the most engagement or conversions (Peters et al., 2013).
2) **Target Audience Refinement:** Businesses can make their content and ads more relevant and effective by focusing on specific categories based on insights from demographic data and audience behaviour (Tuten & Solomon, 2018).
3) **Campaign Timing:** By adjusting the timing of campaigns to coincide with audience activity patterns, data on peak engagement hours can help determine when to post content for optimum visibility and interaction (Kerpen, 2019).
4) **Budget Allocation**: Businesses can more efficiently manage their social media expenditures by investing in the most successful strategies by knowing which channels and content kinds generate the highest returns (Chaffey & Smith, 2017).

5.4. Paid Advertising and Promotions

Paid advertising on social media platforms is a powerful tool for businesses to enhance brand visibility, reach specific audiences, and drive conversions. Different platforms offer a variety of advertising options, each with unique features and advantages. Understanding these options, adhering to best practices, and accurately measuring the return on investment (ROI) are crucial for successful ad campaigns.

Overview of Paid Social Media Advertising Options

1) **Facebook Ads:** With Facebook Ads, advertisers may target consumers according to a multitude of criteria, including demographics, interests, and behaviors. The platform offers sponsored posts, carousel advertisements, picture ads, and video ads among other ad forms. Businesses may evaluate

ad performance and optimize campaigns for better outcomes with Facebook Ads' extensive analytics and reporting tools (Chaffey & Smith, 2017).

2) **Instagram Sponsored Posts:** Because Instagram is a visual-focused network, it's perfect for marketers who want to captivate consumers with eye-catching photos and videos. Instagram users' feeds and stories contain sponsored posts that fit in nicely with their original content. Instagram is a useful medium for brand exposure and engagement because of its integration with Facebook Ads Manager, which enables accurate targeting and comprehensive performance information (Tuten & Solomon, 2018).
3) **TikTok Ads:** With its inventive and captivating short-form films, TikTok has swiftly gained popularity as a medium for addressing younger audiences. The network provides a number of ad formats, including Top View Ads, Branded Hashtag Challenges, and In-Feed Ads. Brands may effectively engage people and encourage involvement in trends and challenges by leveraging TikTok's unique algorithm and targeting capabilities (Kaye, 2020).

Best Practices for Running Effective Ad Campaigns-

1) **Define Clear Objectives:** Having measurable, precise goals is crucial to directing the course of advertising efforts. Goals could include everything from raising website traffic and brand exposure to producing leads and boosting sales (Chaffey & Smith, 2017).
2) **Target the Correct Audience:** To reach the most relevant audience, make use of the in-depth targeting capabilities offered by social media sites. To make sure that advertisements are shown to users who are most likely to be interested in the product or service, this comprises demographic targeting, interest targeting, and behavioural targeting (Tuten & Solomon, 2018).
3) **Create Engaging Content:** Advertising creatives must to be aesthetically pleasing and pertinent to the intended audience. Ad performance can be greatly impacted by the use of excellent photos, videos, and intriguing language. Whether it's a Facebook carousel ad or a quick video on TikTok, it's critical to customize the content for the platform and format (Kaye, 2020).
4) **A/B testing:** In order to ascertain which version of an advertisement performs better, numerous versions are run. This can involve changing the targeting, calls-to-action, headlines, and visuals. By determining which components work best, A/B testing aids in the improvement of advertising campaigns (Peters et al., 2013).
5) **Monitor and Optimize:** Ad performance must be regularly monitored in order to determine what is and is not effective. This is known as "monitoring and optimizing." Campaign effectiveness can be determined by looking at metrics like cost per acquisition (CPA), conversion rate, and click-through rate (CTR). To maximize outcomes, modifications to targeting, budget allocation, and ad creatives can be made in light of these observations (Tuten & Solomon, 2018).

Measuring the ROI of Social Media Advertising

Measuring the ROI of social media advertising involves comparing the cost of the ad campaigns to the revenue generated or the value of the achieved objectives. Key metrics to consider include:

1) **Cost Per Click (CPC):** The mean expense incurred for every click on an advertisement. According to Peters et al. (2013), this statistic aids in assessing how well traffic is directed to a website or landing page.
2) **Conversion Rate:** The proportion of users that click on an advertisement and then complete a desired activity, such buying something or subscribing to a newsletter. A greater conversion rate suggests that the advertisement is successful in encouraging activities that advance corporate objectives (Chaffey & Smith, 2017).
3) **Return on Ad Spend** (ROAS) is a metric that expresses how much money is made for each dollar invested in advertising. It is computed by dividing total revenue by total amount spent on advertisements. According to Tuten and Solomon (2018), this measure gives a clear picture of how profitable advertising efforts are.
4) **Customer Lifetime Value (CLV):** Customer Lifetime Value, or CLV, is an estimate of the total amount of money a company will make from a client over the course of that client relationship. The long-term value and ROI of bringing in new clients through paid advertising can be ascertained by combining CLV with acquisition costs (Kaye, 2020).

6. ETHICAL AND REGULATORY CONSIDERATIONS

The rapid growth of social media marketing has brought significant ethical and regulatory challenges, particularly concerning data privacy, security, and ethical advertising. These considerations are crucial for brands to maintain consumer trust and comply with global regulations.

6.1. Data Privacy and Security

In the digital age, data security and privacy are crucial, particularly in social media marketing, where enormous volumes of personal data are gathered, handled, and examined. There may be serious ethical violations and legal repercussions if this data is misused or handled improperly.

The General Data Protection Regulation (GDPR), which was passed by the European Union in 2018, is one of the most important laws regulating data privacy in social media marketing. Strict guidelines on the collection, storage, and use of personal data by companies are enforced under the GDPR. It requires businesses to have users' express consent before collecting their data and to be open and honest about the use of that data. A company's reputation could suffer and there could be large fines for noncompliance with GDPR (Voigt & Von dem Bussche, 2017).

GDPR has made adjustments to the way data is handled necessary for social media marketers. Marketers need to make sure that their procedures are clear and that customers are aware of the data that is being gathered and how it will be used. As a result, stringent data management guidelines and strong security measures have been put in place to safeguard customer information. For example, before tracking user activity through cookies or other means, marketers must now get user consent and include explicit privacy notifications (Kemper & Rao, 2019).

6.2. Ethical Advertising

Another crucial area of social media marketing concern is ethical advertising. Influencer relationships and targeted advertising are becoming more popular, therefore it's critical for brands to uphold strong moral standards in order to keep consumers informed and foster trust.

In influencer partnerships, transparency is essential. Influencers that promote brands on social media are frequently compensated or given free merchandise. Consumers might not be aware that the endorsements are paid marketing, so in the absence of appropriate disclosure, this could be viewed as misleading. Influencers who endorse products must, for example, explicitly disclose any material links with the Federal Trade Commission (FTC) in the United States. Using hashtags like #ad or #sponsored in their posts is one way to achieve this (Evans et al., 2017).

Furthermore, making sure that advertisements are truthful and accurate is another aspect of ethical advertising practices. When making marketing claims, brands need to be truthful and refrain from setting up irrational expectations. A food company must make sure that any claims it makes about a product, like calling it "organic" or "natural," are supported by evidence and adhere to all applicable regulations.

Guidelines for maintaining ethical standards in social media marketing include:

- Transparency: Clearly disclose any paid partnerships or sponsorships to maintain consumer trust.
- Honesty: Ensure that all marketing claims are accurate and not misleading.
- Respect for Privacy: Adhere to data protection regulations like GDPR, ensuring that consumer data is handled securely and with explicit consent.
- Responsibility: Be mindful of the content being promoted, especially to vulnerable audiences, such as minors.

By adhering to these ethical guidelines, brands can maintain a positive reputation and foster long-term relationships with their audiences, while also ensuring compliance with legal standards.

7. CHALLENGES AND FUTURE TRENDS

As social media continues to evolve, businesses in the food industry face unique challenges and opportunities. Navigating these challenges while staying ahead of future trends is crucial for maintaining a competitive edge.

a. Challenges in Social Media Marketing for the Food Industry
    1) Managing Negative Feedback and Online Reputation

Like many other industries, the food business is vulnerable to unfavourable comments and internet evaluations. A brand's reputation can be severely impacted by a single unfavourable review or remark. The difficulty is in handling these reactions quickly and expertly, converting possible emergencies into chances to provide first-rate customer service (Scott, 2015). Building a favourable brand image and mitigating the harm caused by negative feedback can be achieved by communicating openly with customers and attending to their issues (Solomon, 2018).

2) Staying Relevant in a Rapidly Changing Social Media Landscape

Social media networks regularly update their features and algorithms, creating a dynamic landscape. Businesses must promptly adjust to these developments and consistently innovate their social media strategy if they hope to remain relevant (Chaffey & Smith, 2017). For instance, marketers are being forced to reconsider their content strategy in order to draw and hold audience attention in shorter amounts of time due to the popularity of short-form video content on platforms such as TikTok (Tuten & Solomon, 2018).

3) Balancing Authenticity with Promotional Content

Customers are looking for brands to be authentic. Although promotional content is essential, depending too much on it may cause audiences to become sceptical and disengaged (Pulizzi, 2014). Finding a balance between genuine, non-promotional content that speaks to the values and interests of the audience is difficult. User-generated material, behind-the-scenes information, and narrative that captures the essence of the brand are all examples of this (Handley & Chapman, 2011).

b. Future Trends in Social Media Marketing

1) The Rise of New Social Media Platforms and Features

Every day, new social media features and platforms appear, providing advertisers with new ways to engage with consumers. For instance, businesses are now able to organize live Q&A sessions and conversations thanks to the growing popularity of Clubhouse's audio-only format (Kaye, 2020). In addition, services like YouTube Shorts and Instagram Reels meet the increasing need for short-form video content. For brands to stay relevant and engage consumers, they need to continue to be flexible and try out new formats and channels.

2) The Growing Importance of Social Commerce

The incorporation of e-commerce features into social media platforms, or social commerce, is growing in importance. Users can now shop straight from posts and adverts on social media platforms like Facebook and Instagram, which simplifies the buying process (Zarrella, 2019). This trend emphasizes how crucial it is to offer a flawless shopping experience and optimize social media content for conversions. Through social media, brands may use influencers, shoppable posts, and live-streamed shopping events to directly increase sales (Tuten & Solomon, 2018).

3) Innovations in Technology (AR, VR) and Their Potential Impact on Social Media Marketing

Technological developments in augmented reality (AR) and virtual reality (VR) are creating new opportunities for social media brands to engage with their audience in immersive ways. Brands are able to produce interactive content that increases user engagement with the use of augmented reality elements like Instagram and Snapchat filters (Chaffey & Smith, 2017). Virtual reality (VR) presents the possibility of virtual tours, culinary training, and product presentations, thereby offering users a more immersive experience. These technologies are anticipated to become increasingly prevalent in social media marketing tactics as they become more accessible (Kaye, 2020).

8. SUGGESTIONS

1) **Invest in Analytics and Data-Driven Strategies:** Companies should make investments in powerful analytics tools and platforms to maximize their social media marketing operations. Strategies can be improved by keeping a close eye on important metrics like conversion rates, reach, and engagement. Brands can enhance ROI, optimize content, and gain a deeper understanding of their audience through data-driven decision-making.
2) **Diversify Content and Platforms:** It's critical for food manufacturers to diversify their content strategies due to the multitude of social media platforms and available content formats. Reaching a wider audience and maintaining high levels of engagement can be achieved by experimenting with various content kinds on platforms like Instagram, TikTok, and developing channels. Examples of these platforms include videos, live streaming, and user-generated material.
3) **Engage in Authentic Communication**: Gaining the trust and loyalty of customers requires authenticity. It is important for brands to prioritize authentic storytelling, open and honest communication, and significant audience interaction. Customers might feel more connected to a business when behind-the-scenes content is shared, feedback is addressed, and customer tales are highlighted.
4) **Leverage Influencer Partnerships:** Collaborating with influencers such as chefs and food bloggers can greatly increase a brand's legitimacy and visibility. Influencers that truly connect with their audience and share similar values should be chosen by brands. This increases the efficacy of marketing campaigns and aids in reaching a specific demographic.
5) **Stay Ahead of Trends and Technological Innovations:** With new platforms, services, and technology appearing on a regular basis, the social media landscape is changing quickly. It's important for brands to keep up with the newest developments in immersive technologies like AR and VR as well as social commerce. Early adoption of these improvements can provide an advantage over competitors and create new channels for client interaction.
6) **Focus on Community Building:** Creating a dedicated online community can pay off in the long run. Building a sense of community around the brand can be achieved through arranging virtual events, producing engaging content, and routinely interacting with followers. This not only promotes organic growth and word-of-mouth advertising, but it also increases consumer loyalty.
7) **Develop a Crisis Management Plan:** Considering the possibility of unfavourable comments and issues with one's internet reputation, having a clear crisis management strategy is crucial. In order to properly handle complaints and preserve their good reputation, brands need to be ready to react to any issues that crop up quickly and professionally.

9. CONCLUSION

As we come to the end of this chapter, we have seen how important social media marketing is to the food industry and how it can greatly increase brand visibility, consumer engagement, and business growth. It has given a thorough review of best practices by carefully examining important tactics like the usage of analytics, diverse content development, and genuine participation. The chapter also covered the difficulties of maintaining relevance in a quickly changing digital environment and controlling one's online reputation. Emerging trends were also noted, such as the emergence of new social media platforms, social commerce, and cutting-edge technology like virtual and augmented reality. In order for organizations to create long-lasting and devoted customer relationships, the chapter ends by promoting a strategic, flexible, and data-driven approach to social media marketing. It emphasizes the necessity for brands to strike a balance between promotional activities and real consumer involvement.

REFERENCES

Aaker, D. A., & McLoughlin, D. (2010). *Strategic market management: Global perspectives*. Wiley.

Abidin, C. (2016). "Aren't these just young, rich women doing vain things online?": Influencer selfies as subversive frivolity. *Social Media + Society*, 2(2), 2056305116641342. DOI: 10.1177/2056305116641342

Ajzen, I. (1991). The theory of planned behaviour. *Organizational Behavior and Human Decision Processes*, 50(2), 179–211. DOI: 10.1016/0749-5978(91)90020-T

Anderson, K. E. (2020). Getting acquainted with social networks and apps: It is time to talk about TikTok. *Library Hi Tech News*, 37(4), 7–12. DOI: 10.1108/LHTN-01-2020-0001

Apple. (2021). The power of user-generated content in Apple's marketing strategy. *Apple Newsroom*. Retrieved from Apple.

Becker, M. W., Pashler, H., & Lubin, J. (2011). Object intrinsic images and the creation of internet-based recipe collections: An example of consumer behavior analysis in action. *Journal of Consumer Psychology*, 21(2), 118–123. DOI: 10.1016/j.jcps.2010.09.002

Bermoy, N. N. B., De Guzman, J. J. J., De Guzman, J. L., Dela Vega, S. K. P., Hernandez, L.Jr, Ignacio, M. T. B., Templado, S. M., Trinidad, A. O., & Francisco, C. D. C. (2021). Influence of social media as a marketing platform for food-related products in the new normal. *International Journal of Academic Multidisciplinary Research*, 5(1), 106–111. https://www.ijeais.org/ijamr

Brown, D., & Fiorella, S. (2013). *Influencer marketing: How to create, manage, and measure brand influencers in social media marketing*. Que Publishing.

Bulearca, M., & Tamarjan, D. (2020). Augmented reality: A sustainable technology for the future of advertising? *International Journal of Interactive Mobile Technologies*, 14(3), 20–30.

Business Insider. (2019). *How Starbucks became a global phenomenon*. Retrieved from Business Insider.

Business Insider. (2020). *Dunkin's collaboration with Charli D'Amelio has been a huge success*. Retrieved from Business Insider.

Carlson, N. (2010). *At last – The full story of how Facebook was founded. Business Insider*. Retrieved from Business Insider.

Chaffey, D. (2020). *Social media marketing trends 2020*. Smart Insights. Retrieved from Smart Insights.

Chaffey, D., & Ellis-Chadwick, F. (2019). *Digital marketing: Strategy, implementation & practice* (7th ed.). Pearson.

Chaffey, D., & Smith, P. R. (2017). *Digital marketing excellence: Planning, optimizing and integrating online marketing* (5th ed.). Routledge. DOI: 10.4324/9781315640341

Chipotle. (2020). Sustainability at Chipotle. Retrieved from Chipotle.

Clifton, B. (2012). *Advanced web metrics with Google Analytics* (3rd ed.). Wiley.

Coca-Cola. (2015). *Share a Coke campaign*. Retrieved from Coca-Cola.

Coca-Cola. (2019). *Share a Coke campaign. Coca-Cola Journey*. Retrieved from Coca-Cola.

De Pelsmacker, P., Geuens, M., & Van den Bergh, J. (2017). *Marketing communications: A European perspective* (6th ed.). Pearson.

De Veirman, M., Cauberghe, V., & Hudders, L. (2017). Marketing through Instagram influencers: The impact of number of followers and product divergence on brand attitude. *International Journal of Advertising*, 36(5), 798–828. DOI: 10.1080/02650487.2017.1348035

Deloitte. (2015). *Navigating the new digital divide*. Retrieved from Deloitte.

Dwivedi, Y. K., Hughes, L., Ismagilova, E., Aarts, G., Coombs, C., Crick, T., Duan, Y., Dwivedi, R., Edwards, J., Eirug, A., Galanos, V., Ilavarasan, P. V., Janssen, M., Jones, P., Kar, A. K., Kizgin, H., Kronemann, B., Lal, B., Lucini, B., & Williams, M. D. (2021). Artificial intelligence (AI): Multidisciplinary perspectives on emerging challenges, opportunities, and agenda for research, practice and policy. *International Journal of Information Management*, 57, 101994. DOI: 10.1016/j.ijinfomgt.2019.08.002

Euromonitor International. (2021). *Global grocery retailing market overview*. Retrieved from Euromonitor International.

European Commission. (2021). *The EU food industry*. Retrieved from European Commission.

Evans, N. J., Phua, J., Lim, J., & Jun, H. (2017). Disclosing Instagram influencer advertising: The effects of disclosure language on advertising recognition, attitudes, and behavioral intent. *Journal of Interactive Advertising*, 17(2), 138–149. DOI: 10.1080/15252019.2017.1366885

Food and Agriculture Organization (FAO). (2019). *The future of food and agriculture: Trends and challenges*. Retrieved from FAO.

Forbes. (2020). The best brands on social media and what you can learn from them. Forbes. Retrieved from Forbes.

Gensler, S., Völckner, F., Liu-Thompkins, Y., & Wiertz, C. (2013). Managing brands in the social media environment. *Journal of Interactive Marketing*, 27(4), 242–256. DOI: 10.1016/j.intmar.2013.09.004

GoPro. (2020). *The GoPro awards: Celebrating the best in user-generated content. GoPro Blog*. Retrieved from GoPro.

Grand View Research. (2021). *Food processing market size, share & trends analysis report by type, by application, by region, and segment forecasts, 2021-2028*. Retrieved from Grand View Research.

Grewal, D., Roggeveen, A. L., & Nordfält, J. (2020). The future of retailing. *Journal of Retailing*, 96(1), 5–10.

Hajli, M. N. (2014). A study of the impact of social media on consumers. *International Journal of Market Research*, 56(3), 387–404. DOI: 10.2501/IJMR-2014-025

Hall, C., & Zarro, M. (2012). Social curation on the website Pinterest.com. *Proceedings of the American Society for Information Science and Technology*, 49(1), 1–9. DOI: 10.1002/meet.14504901189

Handley, A., & Chapman, C. C. (2011). *Content rules: How to create killer blogs, podcasts, videos, eBooks, webinars (and more) that engage customers and ignite your business*. Wiley.

Harrington, J. (2020). The impact of digital innovation on customer engagement: A case study of Domino's Pizza. *Journal of Business Research*, 116, 497–504. DOI: 10.1016/j.jbusres.2020.05.043

Harrington, J. (2021). The impact of social media on brand loyalty: The Starbucks experience. *Journal of Digital & Social Media Marketing*, 9(2), 105–116. DOI: 10.1108/JSMS-06-2021-0047

Harrison, L. (2020). *Instagram's interactive features: Polls, questions, and more. Social Media Examiner*. Retrieved from Social Media Examiner.

Hennig-Thurau, T., Gwinner, K. P., Walsh, G., & Gremler, D. D. (2004). Electronic word-of-mouth via consumer-opinion platforms: What motivates consumers to articulate themselves on the Internet? *Journal of Interactive Marketing*, 18(1), 38–52. DOI: 10.1002/dir.10073

Hootsuite. (2020). Social media trends 2020. Retrieved from Hootsuite.

Hootsuite. (2020). *The global state of digital 2020*. Hootsuite.

.*Hu,Y.,Manikonda,L., &Kambhampati,S.(2014). What we Instagram: A first analysis of Instagram photo content and user types*. Proceedings of the Eighth International Conference on Weblogs and Social Media (ICWSM).

Huang, M. H., & Rust, R. T. (2021). Engaged to a robot? The role of AI in service. *Journal of Service Research*, 24(1), 30–41. DOI: 10.1177/1094670520902266

HubSpot. (2021). *The ultimate guide to social media analytics*. Retrieved from HubSpot.

. IBISWorld. (2021). Global food service market report. Retrieved from IBISWorld.

International Labor Organization (ILO). (2020). *Decent work and the food sector*. Retrieved from ILO.

Jobin, A., Ienca, M., & Vayena, E. (2019). The global landscape of AI ethics guidelines. *Nature Machine Intelligence*, 1(9), 389–399. DOI: 10.1038/s42256-019-0088-2

Kang, J. (2012). Social media marketing: Strategies for engaging in Facebook, Twitter & other social media. *International Journal of Business and Information*, 7(2), 241–251.

Kaplan, A., & Haenlein, M. (2020). Rulers of the world, unite! The challenges and opportunities of artificial intelligence. *Business Horizons*, 63(1), 37–50. DOI: 10.1016/j.bushor.2019.09.003

Kaplan, A. M., & Haenlein, M. (2010). Users of the world, unite! The challenges and opportunities of social media. *Business Horizons*, 53(1), 59–68. DOI: 10.1016/j.bushor.2009.09.003

Kaufman, G. (2020). *Dunkin' Donuts and Charli D'Amelio's collaboration: A case study. Ad Age*. Retrieved from Ad Age.

Kaye, L. (2020). *Digital marketing: Strategy and tactics*. Sage Publications.

Kemper, J., & Rao, B. (2019). Do GDPR and blockchain align? Designing an access control model to comply with the General Data Protection Regulation. *Journal of Data Protection & Privacy*, 2(2), 142–158.

Kerpen, D. (2019). *Likeable social media: How to delight your customers, create an irresistible brand, and be amazing on Facebook, Twitter, LinkedIn, Instagram, Pinterest, and more*. McGraw-Hill Education.

Kim, J. (2021). *The BTS meal at McDonald's: A global influencer marketing success. Forbes*. Retrieved from Forbes.

Kim, Y., & Lee, J. (2019). The rise of social media in the food industry: Case study of influencer marketing. *Journal of Interactive Marketing*, 47, 23–32.

Kotler, P., & Keller, K. L. (2016). *Marketing management* (15th ed.). Pearson.

Kwak, H., Lee, C., Park, H., & Moon, S. (2010). What is Twitter, a social network or a news media? *Proceedings of the 19th International Conference on World Wide Web (WWW '10)*, 591-600. DOI: 10.1145/1772690.1772751

Lipsman, A., Mudd, G., Rich, M., & Bruich, S. (2021). The power of "like": How brands reach (and influence) fans through social media marketing. *Journal of Advertising Research*, 52(1), 40–52. DOI: 10.2501/JAR-52-1-040-052

Liu-Thompkins, Y. (2019). A decade of online advertising research: What we learned and what we need to know. *Journal of Advertising*, 48(1), 92–105. DOI: 10.1080/00913367.2018.1556138

Luo, X., Tong, S., Fang, Z., & Qu, Z. (2019). Frontiers: Machines vs. humans: The impact of AI chatbots on consumer patronage. *Marketing Science*, 38(6), 937–947.

Maslow, A. H. (1943). A theory of human motivation. *Psychological Review*, 50(4), 370–396. DOI: 10.1037/h0054346

Mitchell, A. (2019). The rise of live-streamed cooking shows: Engaging customers in real-time. *Food Industry Journal*, 4(2), 123–135.

Mosseri, A. (2018). Bringing people closer together. *Facebook Newsroom*. Retrieved from https://about.fb.com/news/2018/01/news-feed-fyi-bringing-people-closer-together/

Muntinga, D. G., Moorman, M., & Smit, E. G. (2019). Introducing COBRAs: Exploring motivations for brand-related social media use. *International Journal of Advertising*, 38(3), 450–473.

National Restaurant Association (NRA). (2021). *Restaurant industry facts at a glance*. Retrieved from NRA.

Nielsen. (2012). Global trust in advertising and brand messages. *Nielsen Insights*. Retrieved from Nielsen.

Nielsen. (2018). The Nielsen global survey of e-commerce. Retrieved from Nielsen.

Nielsen. (2019). The rise of visual content in digital marketing. *Nielsen Insights*. Retrieved from Nielsen.

Peters, K., Chen, Y., Kaplan, A. M., Ognibeni, B., & Pauwels, K. (2013). Social media metrics — A framework and guidelines for managing social media. *Journal of Interactive Marketing*, 27(4), 281–298. DOI: 10.1016/j.intmar.2013.09.007

. Pinterest. (2020). Pinterest as a tool for discovering new food ideas. *Pinterest Business*. Retrieved from Pinterest.

Poushter, J. (2019). The future of retail: Virtual and augmented reality. *Journal of Retailing and Consumer Services*, 48, 26–34.

Pulizzi, J. (2014). *Epic content marketing: How to tell a different story, break through the clutter, and win more customers by marketing less*. McGraw-Hill Education.

. Riaz, H., Ahmed, H., & Akhtar, S. (2019). The role of social media marketing on building brand equity: An insight of fast-food industry of Pakistan. Muhammad Ali Jinnah University, Barrett Hodgson University, and University of Karachi.

Rowley, J. (2008). Understanding digital content marketing. *Journal of Marketing Management*, 24(5-6), 517–540. DOI: 10.1362/026725708X325977

Schiffman, L. G., & Wisenblit, J. (2019). *Consumer behavior* (12th ed.). Pearson.

Scott, D. M. (2015). *The new rules of marketing & PR: How to use social media, online video, mobile applications, blogs, news releases, and viral marketing to reach buyers directly* (5th ed.). Wiley. DOI: 10.1002/9781119172499.ch02

Smith, A., & Anderson, M. (2018). *Social media use in 2018*. Pew Research Center.

Smith, A. N. (2018). The role of influencers in promoting food and beverage brands. *JMR, Journal of Marketing Research*, 55(3), 345–362. DOI: 10.1177/0022243717750083

Smith, A. N. (2018). The role of visual storytelling in food marketing. *JMR, Journal of Marketing Research*, 55(3), 345–362. DOI: 10.1177/0022243717750083

Smith, M. (2021). The power of live Q&A sessions for brands: Building trust and engagement. *Marketing Today*, 3(5), 67–72.

Solomon, M. R. (2018). *Consumer behavior: Buying, having, and being* (12th ed.). Pearson.

Solomon, M. R. (2020). *Consumer behavior: Buying, having, and being* (13th ed.). Pearson.

Stackla. (2019). Consumer content report: Influence in the digital age. *Stackla*. Retrieved from Stackla.

Starbucks. (2021). How Starbucks uses Instagram Stories for customer engagement. Retrieved from Starbucks Stories.

Starbucks. (2021). Starbucks' Instagram strategy: How to use user-generated content. *Starbucks Stories*. Retrieved from Starbucks.

Starbucks. (2021). The visual strategy behind Starbucks' Instagram. *Starbucks Stories*. Retrieved from Starbucks.

Sundar, S. S. (2020). Rise of the machines: Promises and perils of artificial intelligence. *Journal of Consumer Psychology*, 30(4), 742–760.

TikTok. (2020). *How TikTok drives food trends and engages audiences. TikTok for Business*. Retrieved from TikTok.

TikTok. (2020). *The #ChipotleLidFlip challenge: How Chipotle engages with TikTok's Gen Z audience*. Retrieved from TikTok Business.

Tuten, T. L., & Solomon, M. R. (2018). *Social media marketing*. Sage Publications.

Tuten, T. L., & Solomon, M. R. (2019). *Social media marketing* (3rd ed.). SAGE Publications.

Voigt, P., & Von dem Bussche, A. (2017). *The EU General Data Protection Regulation (GDPR): A practical guide*. Springer International Publishing. DOI: 10.1007/978-3-319-57959-7

Woods, S. (2016). #Sponsored: The emergence of influencer marketing. *Thesis*. University of Tennessee. Retrieved from UTK Scholar.

YouTube. (2021). *Food channels to follow for cooking inspiration. YouTube Creator Blog*. Retrieved from YouTube.

Zarrella, D. (2019). *The social media marketing book*. O'Reilly Media.

Chapter 12
Next-Gen Eats:
Tech, Trends, and Sustainability

Muhammad Afnan Mahusain
https://orcid.org/0009-0002-5991-7027
Taylor's University, Malaysia

Azlina Samsudin
Universiti Teknologi MARA, Dungun, Malaysia

Mohd Aliff Abdul Majid
https://orcid.org/0000-0002-3832-5770
Universiti Teknologi MARA, Puncak Alam, Malaysia

ABSTRACT

This chapter explores the significant transformations within the food service industry, driven by the integration of advanced technologies and a focus on sustainability. As the industry evolves, stakeholders must adapt to these changes to remain competitive and resilient. By embracing automation, AI, IoT, and robotics, the food service sector can enhance operational efficiency, reduce waste, and improve accuracy, aligning with Sustainable Development Goals (SDGs) such as SDG 8 (Decent Work and Economic Growth) and SDG 12 (Responsible Consumption and Production). Additionally, the adoption of sustainable practices, supported by technological innovations, addresses environmental challenges, contributing to SDG 11 (Sustainable Cities and Communities). Additionally, emerging trends like AR, VR, and drones are explored as potential game-changers in the industry. This chapter serves as a guide for stakeholders to understand and adapt to these advancements, ensuring they stay competitive and ready for future opportunities in an ever-evolving landscape.

INTRODUCTION

The food service industry is undergoing a profound transformation driven by technological advancements and a focus on sustainability. The adoption of automation, AI, IoT, and robotics is revolutionizing how food is prepared, served, and managed, leading to significant improvements in speed, accuracy, and cost-effectiveness (Chapman et al., 2021). Automation technologies streamline kitchen operations (Voipio et al., 2021), reducing labor costs (Khot et al., 2019) and minimizing human error (Tuomi &

DOI: 10.4018/979-8-3693-7683-6.ch012

Ascenção, 2023), while AI and machine learning enhance predictive analytics for demand forecasting and inventory management, reducing waste and ensuring optimal resource utilization. These advancements contribute to SDG 8 (Decent Work and Economic Growth) by creating new job opportunities in tech-driven roles and improving overall productivity.

Additionally, digital transformation impacts customer experience by introducing digital ordering systems, self-service kiosks, and mobile applications, which offer convenience and personalization, enhancing customer satisfaction and loyalty (Lee & Lee, 2020). These innovations also support SDG 12 (Responsible Consumption and Production) by promoting efficient resource use and reducing waste through precise portion control and real-time data analytics. Furthermore, the integration of sustainable practices through technological innovation addresses critical environmental challenges. AI and IoT technologies optimize supply chain management, reducing food waste and spoilage, while energy-efficient kitchen appliances and systems lower energy consumption and operational costs (Jagtap et al., 2020).

The chapter also explores future trends and emerging technologies, such as augmented reality (AR), virtual reality (VR), and drones (Kim et al, 2018), which have the potential to further revolutionize the food service industry by enhancing dining experiences, improving staff training, and streamlining delivery logistics. As consumer behavior and expectations evolve, there is a growing demand for personalized and immersive experiences, which these technologies can fulfill. Staying ahead of technological and sustainability trends in the food service industry is essential for businesses to remain competitive and resilient. This involves not only adopting cutting-edge technologies but also investing in research and development to anticipate and respond to future challenges and opportunities. By doing so, food service businesses can better position themselves to meet the evolving demands of consumers and navigate the complexities of a rapidly changing market.

The chapter highlights the importance of building sustainable urban food systems (Moragues-Faus & Battersby, 2021), contributing to SDG 11 (Sustainable Cities and Communities) by enhancing community well-being and resilience. Implementing sustainable practices within urban food systems can include initiatives such as urban agriculture, which reduces the need for long-distance transportation and lowers carbon emissions. Additionally, by creating shorter supply chains, urban food systems can enhance food security and provide fresh, nutritious produce to urban populations. Incorporating technology, such as IoT-enabled sensors and data analytics, allows for better resource management and optimization of food production processes.

INTRODUCTION TO TECHNOLOGICAL ADVANCEMENTS IN THE FOOD SERVICE INDUSTRY

Overview of the Current State of the Food Service Industry

The food service industry is on the cusp of a technological revolution that promises to redefine operational efficiency, customer experience, and supply chain management. The industry has evolved from traditional, labor-intensive methods to incorporating sophisticated technologies that streamline operations and enhance service delivery. The fourth industrial revolution, or Industry I4.0, has been gaining momentum since 2015, being a significant driver for sustainable development and a successful catalyst to tackle critical global challenges. The most relevant food Industry I4.0 technologies including, among others, digital technologies (e.g., artificial intelligence, big data analytics, Internet of Things, and blockchain) and other technological advances (e.g., smart sensors, robotics, digital twins, and cyber-physical systems). Moreover, insights into the new food trends (such as 3D printed foods) that have emerged as a result of the Industry I4.0 technological revolution. The Industry I4.0 technologies have significantly modified the food industry and led to substantial consequences for the environment, economics, and human health. Despite the importance of each of the technologies mentioned above, ground-breaking sustainable solutions could only emerge by combining many technologies simultaneously. The Food Industry I4.0 era has been characterized by new challenges, opportunities, and trends that have reshaped current strategies and prospects for food production and consumption patterns, paving the way for the move toward Industry 5.0 (Hassoun et al., 2022). Industry 5.0 is complementing the existing Industry I4.0 paradigm with the orientation to the worker who has an important role in the production process, and that role has been emphasized during the COVID-19 pandemic.

One of the industry gaining increasing attention is the agri-food sector. Recent projections suggest that food production must double by 2050 to meet the demands of a global population expected to reach approximately 9.8 billion by that time and 11.2 billion by 2100 (Ojo et al., 2018). Furthermore, data from the FAO shows that about 33% of all food produced globally which is roughly 930 million tonnes. This food is lost or wasted at various stages of the agri-food supply chain, contributing to the hunger of 800 million people (Dora et al., 2021). As the world's population continues to grow, it's clear that we'll face more waste and its environmental impacts (Belaud et al., 2019). However, there's a lot of excitement about how Industry I4.0 technologies could transform agriculture. Many experts believe these innovations can revolutionize the sector, boosting food production with fewer resources (Lezoche et al., 2020), cutting down on food loss and waste, and ultimately benefiting the environment (Galanakis et al., 2021; Shepherd et al., 2020). This emerging technological approach has become crucial for contemporary businesses striving to thrive and secure a competitive edge in the digital age. By leveraging Industry I4.0 technologies, key agricultural objectives like water conservation, soil preservation, carbon reduction, and enhanced production can be effectively met (Lezoche et al., 2020). Therefore, for example, the studies indicate that advanced technologies can enhance rice yields and lower production costs for rice, the third most-produced crop globally. These innovations help address sustainability challenges, including waste management and increased food production, thereby making a significant impact on society (Hou et al., 2020).

Importance of Technology in Driving Industry Growth

Historically, the industry has faced numerous challenges, including fluctuating consumer preferences, supply chain disruptions, and increasing operational costs (Abideen et al., 2021). The traceability of food products and overall supply chain transparency have become critical due to multiple scandals occurring worldwide. Food safety scandals have historically impacted humanity, often resulting in devastating consequences for public health and the economy. Although food safety regulations and technological advances have greatly reduced the frequency of such events, some of the worst food safety incidents still occur today. For example; US blue bell creameries outbreak (2015), US Chipotle outbreak (2015), Germany *E. Coli* outbreak (2011), China milk scandal (2008), and US spinach outbreak (2006) (Peremutter, 2023). Each of these outbreaks had a severe impact on public health, leading to numerous illnesses, deaths, and economic losses. The causes of these incidents varied, ranging from contaminated food and water to zoonotic diseases and inadequate hygiene practices (Rejab et al., 2020). Therefore, the demand for effective traceability has grown as regulations now mandate that every ingredient in a food product can be traced back to its origin (Kayikci et al., 2020). Consumer expectations for the year-round availability of agricultural products have increased pressure on businesses to provide detailed information about product attributes, such as quality, safety, authenticity, traceability, and provenance (which refers to the geographic origin as determined by analytical science, distinct from data provenance), as well as the conditions of production and supply. This increased demand for information is a key driver for adopting new technologies.

One of the most significant global events in recent years was the COVID-19 pandemic. This crisis has created opportunities for innovation and growth in the food industry, including the adoption of 5G technology. 5G networks offer a solution for managing connections between new devices and applications. They not only enhance connectivity for communication but also enable intelligent connectivity through the integration of artificial intelligence (AI), cloud computing, big data, the Internet of Things (IoT), and other advanced platforms. The pandemic prompted many businesses to shift towards digital solutions, fostering a more flexible work environment and mitigating risks in daily operations (Lau, 2020). These challenges present opportunities for innovation and growth, primarily driven by digital transformation. Digital transformation plays a pivotal role in driving industry growth by enabling businesses to adopt technologies. These technologies impact various industry segments, from fast food to fine dining, enhancing operational efficiencies and customer interactions (Chapman et al., 2021). The case in Guangzhou hotels, robots have taken on roles that staff are unable to fulfill during the pandemic. These robots handle a variety of tasks, such as preparing food and beverage items for room service, serving as waitstaff in hotel restaurants, delivering housekeeping supplies, and distributing facemasks and hand sanitizers (Lau, 2020). By performing these functions, robots are on the frontline, safeguarding both guests and employees from COVID-19 and helping to curb the virus's spread. Beyond enhancing health and safety, these robots also improve service quality and boost customer satisfaction.

Sustainable Development Goals (SDGs)

Sustainability is a critical aspect of the food service industry's evolution, aligned with the United Nations' Sustainable Development Goals (SDGs). The chapter introduces SDGs and their relevance, emphasizing their importance in promoting sustainable practices within the industry. Agenda 2030 and the Sustainable Development Goals (SDGs) encompass several critical areas that need urgent attention, including waste management, energy consumption, economic stability, and environmental protection. These aspects are integral to ensuring a sustainable future and improving global quality of life. Among these goals, SDG2, which focuses on achieving "zero hunger," and SDG12, which aims for "responsible consumption and production," are particularly relevant in the context of modern agricultural practices.

Recent advances in digital technology and the Industry I4.0 paradigm offer promising solutions to advance these goals. I4.0 technologies include innovations such as the Internet of Things (IoT), artificial intelligence (AI), machine learning, and blockchain, which can significantly contribute to improving agricultural productivity and sustainability. For instance, these technologies can enhance food production efficiency and increase profits by optimizing resource use and streamlining supply chain operations. This efficiency not only boosts output but also helps reduce greenhouse gas emissions and lower energy and resource consumption due to more effective management practices (Ejsmont et al., 2020). In agriculture, the application of I4.0 technologies can address several pressing challenges. For example, precision agriculture techniques enabled by IoT sensors can help farmers conserve water and protect soil health by providing real-time data on soil moisture levels and nutrient needs. Similarly, AI-driven analytics can aid in carbon mitigation by optimizing the use of fertilizers and pesticides, thereby reducing their environmental impact. These technologies can also support sustainable food consumption and production systems by improving supply chain transparency and reducing waste (Režek Jambrak et al., 2021).

Moreover, the deployment of new technologies in agriculture can have profound socio-economic benefits. For instance, enhanced access to clean drinking water and sanitation through innovative solutions can improve public health in rural areas. By promoting sustainable agricultural practices and providing better resources and services, I4.0 technologies can uplift the livelihoods of impoverished communities. This holistic approach supports not only economic development but also environmental conservation and social equity. Furthermore, I4.0 technologies can improve efficiency within the agri-food supply chain, especially for perishable goods. Technologies like automated sorting systems, smart logistics, and blockchain for traceability can lower operational costs, enhance accuracy in inventory management, and speed up processes. These improvements contribute to a reduction in the carbon footprint of food production and minimize food loss and waste (Vernier et al., 2021; Amani & Sarkodie, 2022). Finally, the principles of sustainable development emphasize the importance of protecting farmers' welfare and improving their living standards. Ensuring that advancements in technology benefit not just the industry but also the individuals involved is crucial for maintaining a balance between urban and rural populations. Strengthening this connection supports equitable growth and helps bridge the gap between different communities (Eashwar &Chawla, 2021).

OPERATIONAL EFFICIENCY THROUGH TECHNOLOGY

Operational Efficiency through Technology

Operational efficiency is a cornerstone of the food service industry's transformation, driven by automation and AI. Automation technologies, including kitchen automation and smart appliances, streamline operations (Voipio et al., 2021), reduce labor costs (Khot et al., 2019), and minimize human error (Tuomi & Ascenção, 2023). Case studies of successful automation demonstrate significant improvements in speed, consistency, and productivity. AI and machine learning are crucial in predictive analytics, enhancing demand forecasting and inventory management (Kumar et al., 2021). These technologies enable businesses to anticipate customer needs, optimize stock levels, and reduce waste, contributing to operational efficiency and sustainability. Predictive maintenance powered by machine learning ensures equipment reliability, preventing downtime and reducing maintenance costs. Successful operational efficiency improvements are illustrated through case studies from leading food service companies. These examples provide insights into best practices and lessons learned, highlighting the tangible benefits of adopting automation technologies. However, the transition to automation also presents challenges, including potential job displacement and the need for upskilling the workforce.

Case Studies of Successful Operational Efficiency Improvements

Industry I4.0 brings together cutting-edge innovations, with deep learning and Big Data playing crucial roles. Within smart ecosystems, where humans, machines, and devices collaborate, these advancements enhance the efficiency and consistency of food manufacturing while also lowering operational costs. Instead of replacing costly equipment, these innovations can be integrated into existing machinery, transforming how it functions. By incorporating Big Data and AI into traditional food science, it is possible to develop new recipes, make intelligent recommendations, improve food quality through better tracking and tracing, and even analyze consumer taste preferences.

Food Manufacturing

A case study shows how adopting Industry I4.0 technologies transformed a SME's food manufacturing company. The company had been struggling with declining financial performance due to poor capacity utilization, caused by inconsistencies in product quality across different production lines. The root causes were hard to identify because the process relied on outdated equipment and experienced staff. When trying to switch production lines, the factory couldn't reach full capacity, hurting efficiency and profits. Thus, with the implementation of I4.0 has allowed the factory better understand the production processes, and the parameters (e.g. oven temperatures, environmental conditions, belt/cutter speed etc.), hence to achieve product consistency. This has significantly the production efficiency.

This manufacturing approach transformed tacit knowledge into explicit knowledge, reducing the risks associated with manual decision-making and operations that were traditionally handled by specific individuals. By transitioning to intelligent decision-making supported by large-scale, real-time big data systems, the process became more reliable and efficient. While Industry I4.0 has enhanced productivity and efficiency, it has also boosted capacity and reduced waste. For instance, operators can now use dashboard features to proactively monitor and maintain optimal temperatures, leading to energy savings. These savings benefit the environment by reducing resource usage and lowering emissions. Additionally, the system enables predictive maintenance, which helps prevent downtime and further reduces labor costs, ultimately increasing overall efficiency and capacity. This innovative approach enabled a highly traditional food manufacturing company, still using machinery over a hundred years old, to transition to Industry I4.0 without the need for significant investments in new equipment. As a result, the company extended the lifespan of its existing production facilities and can now make capital investment decisions based on performance data analysis and new production insights. This initiative has not only transformed the business into a technology-driven enterprise, helping it achieve its strategic goals, but it has also sparked a cultural shift within the company. By maintaining an open agenda and collaborating with academic institutions, all stakeholders which from technicians to top management can have embraced this change and actively participated in integrating the new knowledge and technology developed during the project into the business (Konur et al., 2023).

Food Quality and Sensor

Another case study shows how Industry I4.0 technologies are transforming the food industry, especially through Quality I4.0. In the food sector, quality control is crucial to ensure products are safe and meet the desired taste, texture, and appearance. Quality I4.0 takes this to the next level by allowing more accurate, real-time assessments of food quality (Ada et al., 2021), making it easier to trace products through the supply chain and increase transparency (Khan et al., 2020). We've already seen how this approach can optimize quality control in food businesses. With food being so perishable, smart packaging becomes vital, helping to extend shelf life, improve safety, and provide important information about the product. Technologies like nanosensors, biosensors, and gas sensors in smart packaging help monitor things like temperature and freshness, ensuring food stays in top condition (Ben-Daya et al., 2020). Quality in food products is defined by various characteristics, including nutritional value, physicochemical properties, safety, sensory attributes, and shelf-life stability (Hassoun et al., 2023). Over the years, several standard and reference methods have been developed to assess the quality and authenticity of food, primarily focusing on intrinsic attribute measurements. These methods include physicochemical determinations such as color, texture, and water-holding capacity, which are related to the product's technological properties.

Determining food quality can be greatly enhanced by combining sensor data with AI and Big Data. This approach, known as "computer vision and AI-driven food industry," uses advanced image recognition and learning methods to improve food processing and quality control (Kakani et al., 2020). Sensory attributes like flavor, juiciness, and tenderness are also evaluated, as they are crucial for consumer acceptability. Additionally, safety aspects are assessed, including the detection of pathogenic and foodborne microorganisms or toxic substances, as well as nutritional and health-related factors like proximate composition and the profiles of fatty acids and amino acids (Lorenzo et al., 2022). Smart sensors, when paired with AI and Big Data, can also benefit various nonthermal technologies and advanced food processing methods like high-power ultrasound, pulsed electric fields, and microwave processing (Jambrak et al., 2021). AI can analyze images of food, often taken with smartphones, to estimate nutritional content (Ma et al., 2022). Additionally, AI-powered sensors that mimic human senses—such as vision, hearing, smell, taste, and touch—are being developed to complement and eventually replace traditional human sensory tests for evaluating food quality (Zhao et al., 2020).

Food Traceability

Food traceability is essential for ensuring quality and building consumer trust. RFID technology and Big Data help track the journey of food from production to the market, making it easier to address safety and authenticity concerns (Zheng et al., 2021). In processed foods, where challenges like mixing different raw materials and transforming resources are common, AI optimizes the mixing process for consistent quality, while Big Data helps predict and manage potential quality issues (Qian et al., 2022). Looking to the future, combining blockchain technology with AI and Big Data is set to enhance traceability even further. Blockchain provides a secure and transparent way to record every step of the supply chain. When paired with AI and Big Data, it will offer a new level of accuracy and reliability, making it easier to trace food products and ensuring their quality and safety.

Food Supply Chain and Cold Chain

The primary challenge of Sustainable Development Goal 12, "Responsible Consumption and Production," is reducing food losses throughout production and supply chains. Enhancing the quality of fresh food products is crucial for minimizing waste and losses. Big Data and AI offer new ways to address the perishability of fresh foods (Vernier et al., 2021). Thus, developing a traceable system for cold chain logistics can improve brand reputation and boost consumer trust by ensuring the delivery of safe, high-quality food products (Wang et al., 2020. Traditional methods may struggle to adjust storage temperatures promptly. However, AI and Big Data-driven temperature control algorithms can continuously optimize storage conditions, keeping food at the ideal temperature (Guan et al., 2021).

Packaging

Food quality is greatly influenced by how it's packaged. AI and Big Data can help us understand environmental factors around food production and make better choices about packaging materials, supporting Sustainable Development Goals (Hassoun et al., 2023). Plus, with the latest advances in nanotechnology, we now have tiny sensors that can be added to food packaging or even built into smartphones. This means consumers can easily check the quality and details of their food right from their devices (Saadat et al., 2022).

Sustainable Development Goals (SDGs)

The integration of automation technologies is transforming industries by enhancing productivity, creating new job opportunities, and promoting sustainable practices. These advancements are pivotal in driving progress toward Sustainable Development Goals (SDGs), particularly Decent Work and Economic Growth (SDG 8) and Responsible Consumption and Production (SDG 12). By leveraging technologies such as artificial intelligence (AI), robotics, and smart sensors, businesses can achieve significant improvements in operational efficiency while also addressing environmental and social challenges. This holistic approach not only fosters economic growth but also contributes to more responsible and sustainable production practices.

Automation technologies play a crucial role in advancing Decent Work and Economic Growth (SDG 8). They create new employment opportunities in tech-driven fields and increase productivity across various sectors. By automating routine and hazardous tasks, businesses can shift focus to more complex and higher-value roles, which often require specialized skills. This shift helps stimulate economic growth and diversifies the job market. However, to ensure that the benefits of automation are equitably distributed, it is essential to invest in workforce development. Providing training and upskilling opportunities prepares workers for emerging roles and ensures that technological progress leads to inclusive and sustainable economic development.

In addition to boosting economic growth, automation technologies significantly contribute to Responsible Consumption and Production (SDG 12). These technologies enhance the efficiency of production processes, reduce waste, and optimize resource use. For instance, AI and smart sensors can monitor and adjust environmental conditions to maintain optimal storage conditions, thereby extending product shelf life and minimizing spoilage. By improving traceability and reducing environmental impact, automation supports the development of more sustainable production practices. This not only aligns with the goal of reducing the ecological footprint of production but also promotes the use of resources in a more responsible and efficient manner.

SUSTAINABLE PRACTICES THROUGH TECHNOLOGICAL INTEGRATION

Sustainable Practices through Technological Integration

Sustainability in the food service industry is enhanced through the integration of predictive technologies, energy-efficient appliances, and smart inventory management systems (Sultana et al., 2024). AI and machine learning optimize inventory management (Kumar et al., 2021), reducing food waste by predicting demand (Jagtap et al., 2020), and monitoring stock levels in real-time (Kumar et al., 2021). This reduces spoilage and ensures efficient resource utilization, aligning with sustainability goals (Sultana et al., 2024).

Moreover, emerging technologies such as AI-driven robotics and advanced blockchain applications offer significant potential for further reducing food waste. However, for these technologies to be effectively integrated, supportive policies and incentives are crucial. Policymakers should focus on creating an environment that encourages businesses to adopt these innovations. Additionally, further research is needed to address existing gaps, particularly in understanding the long-term impacts and scalability of these technological solutions in various contexts.

Reducing Food Waste with Predictive Technologies

According to the Solid Waste Management and Public Cleansing Corporation (SWCorp), Malaysians generate approximately 17,000 tonnes of food waste daily, with 24% of this waste consisting of food that is still edible. This equates to around 4,080 tonnes, or I4.08 million kilograms, of consumable food being discarded each day (Lim, 2024). Food waste has emerged as a critical global issue, presenting significant challenges in identifying effective solutions for its reduction. However, recent advancements in IoT sensor technology and big data analytics have the potential to revolutionize traditional supply chains, transforming them into smart supply chains. By leveraging big data analysis, coupled with appropriate models and algorithms, these smart supply chains can be effectively utilized to mitigate food waste (Ahmadzadeh et al., 2023).

Likewise, technological solutions, such as real-time control systems and waste diversion systems, allow facilities to optimize resource use, minimize both over- and under-utilization, and consequently reduce waste. This optimization directly results in cost savings by lowering expenses associated with food purchases and waste disposal (Singh, Archana et al., 2024). Further, to promote a more sustainable food supply, predictive analytics for inventory management and smart waste management technologies are continually advancing. These technological innovations, including IoT, AI, robotics, and mobile applications, are increasingly being adopted by hospitality establishments to enhance their efforts in reducing food waste. Singh et al. (2024) highlighted that advanced technology is crucial in reducing food waste in hotels and restaurants. Recent studies have stressed the importance of innovative solutions using modern tools and systems to address this complex issue. Some of the latest technological strategies include:

- Internet of Things (IoT) Sensors: This emerging technology plays a crucial role in real-time data collection and processing. Additionally, IoT-based environmental monitoring systems, equipped with smart devices and sensors, offer advanced tools to assess and manage environmental impacts. These systems monitor various factors, including waste management, water quality, and air quality, using IoT technology (Bakhar, & Budihartono, 2023).
- Artificial Intelligence and Machine Learning: Recent advancements in AI and machine learning have enabled predictive analytics for food demand, allowing businesses to optimize purchasing and reduce overstocking by analyzing historical data, seasonality, and customer preferences. Utilizing AI technology can lead to more efficient processes, improved decision-making, and the creation of innovative solutions to address the critical challenges within the global food system (Onyeaka, et. al., 2023).

- Robotics in Kitchen Operations: The use of robotics and automation in the hospitality sector is rapidly increasing, with robots now being programmed to carry out tasks traditionally done by humans. In some establishments, robots are already being integrated into kitchen teams alongside human chefs. Catering businesses favor robots because they reduce errors in food preparation and boost productivity, though the initial investment in this technology can be substantial (Seal, 2023).
- Food Waste Apps: The rise of mobile apps aimed at reducing food waste has been driven by advancements in information and communication technology and increased awareness of sustainable eating. This study confirms that mobile apps are effective tools for promoting food waste reduction and encouraging societal change in the food industry (Doğan et al., 2023).

Energy-efficient Kitchen Appliances and Systems

Energy-efficient kitchen appliances and systems play a vital role in reducing operational costs and environmental impact. Innovations in energy-efficient equipment help businesses lower energy consumption, contributing to cost savings and sustainability (Slobodan et al., 2015). Smart inventory management systems, powered by IoT, enable precise tracking and management of inventory, minimizing waste and improving efficiency (Jagtap et al., 2020). In addition, these innovative appliances like connected ovens, refrigerators, and dishwashers use IoT sensors to enhance efficiency, reduce waste, and improve food management. These devices alert chefs to refine cooking processes and minimize food waste, thus optimizing food quality. In summary, IoT-driven smart kitchen appliances are crucial for combating food waste by optimizing kitchen operations, improving food storage, and generating both economic and environmental benefits. They play a key role in advancing resource efficiency and responsible food management in the hospitality industry (Singh et al., 2024).

Green and digital technologies are increasingly being utilized to prevent, reuse, and recycle food waste, thereby creating new opportunities for both the economy and society. Notable examples include advancements in thermal preservation, biological and biochemical preservation, solar-powered cold storage, active packaging, waste-to-energy processes, composting, recycling, and upcycling. Additionally, emerging digital technologies such as the IoT and mobile applications offer innovative solutions for food-sharing, smart labeling, dynamic pricing, product traceability, intelligent redistribution, and the planning of shopping and meals, as well as storage (Bolwig *et al.,* 2021). Furthermore, energy-efficient kitchen appliances and systems are essential for reducing both operational costs and environmental impact. Innovations such as IoT-driven smart appliances and advanced inventory management systems significantly enhance efficiency, reduce food waste, and improve food management. These technologies not only contribute to cost savings but also support sustainability efforts. Together, these innovations play a crucial role in advancing resource efficiency and responsible food management in the hospitality industry.

Smart Food Waste Management

The growing industry focus on food waste which defined as the inedible byproducts of food production practices—stems from economic, social, ethical, and environmental considerations regarding the management of these materials. Traditionally viewed as an inevitable cost of doing business, many industry stakeholders are now recognizing food waste as a significant sustainability challenge and an often-underutilized resource. In contrast, wasted food, characterized as uneaten edible food, is primarily generated at the consumer level, whether at home or in other settings (Tavill, 2020). In recent years, food wastage has become a significant global issue. In response, the IoT has emerged as a crucial tool in addressing this challenge by aiding in the reduction of food waste. Ahmadzadeh et al. (2023) stated that IoT technologies offer companies several opportunities to reduce food waste. In this context, the ongoing REAMIT project (https://www.reamit.eu/, accessed on 1 December 2022), funded by Interreg Northwest Europe, serves as an example. REAMIT provides various IoT-based solutions for food monitoring and control, aimed at reducing food waste in food companies. The solutions are outlined below:

- Networking and Collaborations: Enabled access to an extensive network in North-West Europe, offering diverse expertise and opportunities for future collaborative initiatives.
- Quality Assurance: Continuously monitored food quality and alerted to any potential deterioration.
- Decision Support and Decision-Making: Leveraged big data analytics and artificial intelligence to provide swift decision support in food logistics.
- Sensor Technology: Positioned at the forefront of both traditional and advanced sensor technologies for monitoring food quality and advancing big data capabilities.
- Data-Driven Decision-Making: Facilitated informed decisions about food quality through careful analysis of real-time data.

Examples of Sustainable Practices in Leading Food Service Businesses

Examples of sustainable practices from industry leaders illustrate the quantifiable benefits of adopting these technologies. These case studies demonstrate how businesses can achieve significant cost savings, enhance operational efficiency, and reduce their environmental footprint. Overcoming barriers to sustainable technology adoption, such as financial, cultural, and operational challenges, is crucial for successful implementation. Nikoličić et al., 2021) investigated the impact of changes in inventory management on food waste within supply chains, with a focus on the application of Radio Frequency Identification (RFID) technology and modern information and communication technologies. Given RFID technology's potential benefits for logistics and supply chains—such as high speed reading, the ability to simultaneously read multiple objects even when out of visual range, large data storage capacity, direct product communication, and product traceability—the study explored its use as a foundational step toward full process digitization. The study employed simulation modelling to assess the effects of these changes in inventory management. The results indicated that waste from dairy products was reduced by 29.41% at the supermarket level and by 38.52% at the producer level. Additionally, supermarket inventory levels were reduced by 20.54%, and producer inventory levels by 8.69%, while the average time products remained in stock was reduced by one day.

Moreover, the Pacific Coast Food Waste Commitment (PCFWC) partnered with two AI providers—Shelf Engine and Afresh—to develop a business case and analyze pilot programs conducted with two supermarket chains in various fresh departments along the West Coast and beyond. These pilot programs achieved an average food waste reduction of 14.8% per store across the two major retailers. If this reduction were applied nationwide to fresh produce alone, it could lead to over $2 billion in savings and a reduction of 13.3 million metric tons of CO_2e emissions. (Pacific Coast Food Waste Management, 2022).

Technologies alone will not solve the food-waste problem. However, when applied effectively, they can significantly enhance and accelerate efforts led by various stakeholders and partnerships. To realize their full potential in reducing consumer food waste, these technologies need a supportive environment. This requires a comprehensive approach that integrates technology with policy, regulation, incentives, infrastructure, information, and behavioral science in a complementary manner. Educating and motivating consumers is crucial, as their awareness and actions can drive demand for sustainable food products and practices. Sustainable food systems involve not just eco-friendly production methods but also responsible use and disposal of food. Raising consumer awareness about the food-waste crisis and its environmental and social impacts is essential. However, awareness alone is insufficient; it must be accompanied by initiatives that provide resources and opportunities for consumers to change their behavior (Bolwig et al., 2021).

Sustainable Development Goals (SDGs)

Reducing food waste offers multiple benefits for people and the planet, contributing to improving food security, cutting pollution, saving money, reducing the pressures on nature and climate, and creating opportunities for economy and society. Ardra and Barua (2022) reported that SDG 12.3 aims to achieve a 50% reduction in food waste at the retail and consumption stages, as well as a decrease in food loss during production, including post-harvest losses, by 2030. This target is supported by the promotion of the 3R practices (reduce, reuse, recycle). With the global population projected to reach approximately nine billion by 2050, the demand for food is expected to rise significantly. Consequently, increased food production will likely lead to greater volumes of food waste.

The Food and Agriculture Organization of the United Nations (FAO) (2022) reported that the UNEP Food Waste Index Report indicates an additional 17% of food is wasted at the retail level and by consumers, especially in households. Food is lost and wasted in various ways. Addressing food waste is essential for advancing SDG 12.3 and reaping significant benefits for both people and the planet. Efforts to reduce food waste can improve food security, decrease pollution, save costs, lessen environmental pressures, and foster economic and social opportunities. As highlighted by Ardra and Barua (2022), SDG 12.3 aims for a 50% reduction in food waste at retail and consumption stages, and a decrease in production losses by 2030. The Sustainable Development Goals Report (2024) and FAO (2022) underline the severe extent of food waste globally, with significant portions of food wasted at various stages, particularly in households.

To combat these challenges, integrating advanced technologies such as predictive analytics, IoT, AI, and smart systems which plays a critical role. These technologies enhance food management, optimize resource use, and contribute to significant reductions in food waste. By leveraging these innovations, we can make substantial progress toward a more sustainable and efficient global food system, ultimately supporting the goals of SDG 12.3 and creating a better world.

FUTURE TRENDS AND EMERGING TECHNOLOGIES

Future Trends and Emerging Technologies

The future trends in the food service industry, spurred by the integration of technologies like AR, VR, and drones, are set to create a more personalized, efficient, and engaging dining experience (Ding et al., 2023). These technologies will not only enhance customer interaction but also streamline operations, ensuring that food service businesses remain competitive in an increasingly digital world. One prominent future trend is the concept of "virtual dining experiences," where AR and VR will allow customers to engage with food in entirely new ways. Imagine a restaurant where, before placing an order, diners can use AR glasses or a VR headset to visualize their meal in 3D (Kim et al., 2018). They can see how the dish is prepared, learn about its ingredients, and even customize it according to their preferences, all before it's actually cooked. This trend could extend to virtual cooking classes, where customers can cook alongside a professional chef in a simulated environment, making the experience both educational and entertaining. Such immersive experiences are likely to become more common as consumers seek out unique and memorable dining adventures.

In addition to transforming the in-restaurant experience, these technologies will also revolutionize food delivery. Drones, for example, could become the primary method for delivering meals, especially in densely populated urban areas. With the ability to bypass traffic and deliver food directly to a customer's location whether that's at home, in a park, or even at the office. These drones could drastically reduce delivery times and enhance the convenience factor. Companies like Uber Eats and Amazon have already begun experimenting with drone delivery, and it's expected that this trend will grow as the technology becomes more refined and regulations are established. In the future, customers might even have the option to track their drone-delivered meal in real-time through an app, ensuring transparency and precision.

Another emerging trend is the increased focus on sustainability and health-conscious dining, driven by consumer demand. AR and VR could be used to provide detailed information about the nutritional content and environmental impact of menu items (Ding et al., 2023). For instance, a diner could scan a QR code on a menu with their AR device and instantly see the carbon footprint of each dish, where the ingredients were sourced, and how it aligns with their dietary preferences or sustainability goals. This kind of transparency would not only build trust with customers but also encourage them to make more informed choices. Moreover, as the demand for plant-based and eco-friendly foods grows, restaurants could use VR to give customers a virtual tour of the farms where their food is grown, further connecting them to the sustainability movement (Ding et al., 2023).

Emerging Trends in Consumer Behavior and Expectations

As these technologies become more prevalent, the industry is also witnessing a change in consumer behavior. Today's consumers are increasingly seeking personalized and immersive experiences, which are becoming key differentiators for businesses (Tom Dieck & Han, 2021). There is a growing trend toward sustainability, health, and convenience, with customers preferring options that align with their values and lifestyles. This shift is driving food service providers to adopt innovative solutions that cater to these preferences, such as offering eco-friendly packaging, healthier menu options, and more convenient delivery methods (Vandna & Kumar, 2023). Businesses that recognize and respond to these trends are more likely to thrive in a competitive market, as they meet the needs of a more discerning and tech-savvy customer base.

Big data analytics enables companies to gain deeper insights into consumer behavior, decision-making, and purchasing motivations, allowing them to predict shifts in consumer preferences and trends (Ding et al., 2023). By analyzing consumer behavior, businesses can identify the unique needs of various customer segments and refine their product positioning, marketing, and distribution strategies accordingly. This foresight helps companies make more informed decisions regarding inventory management, production planning, and supply chain operations, ultimately boosting efficiency and ensuring they meet consumer demand effectively (Ding et al., 2023). Additionally, by leveraging personalized marketing and recommendation systems, food companies can offer tailored products and services, enhancing customer satisfaction and loyalty. This personalized approach not only meets consumer needs but also gives businesses a competitive edge in the market.

To stay competitive in this rapidly evolving landscape, food service businesses must prioritize innovation and adaptability in their strategies. This includes investing in research and development to explore new technologies and their potential applications within the industry. By continuously improving their offerings and staying ahead of emerging trends, companies can ensure they remain relevant and appealing to their customers. Embracing these innovations is not just about keeping up with the competition; it's about setting new standards for the industry and leading the way in delivering exceptional, future-forward dining experiences.

Preparing for the Future: Strategies for Staying Ahead

As the food industry evolves, preparing for the future requires a strategic embrace of innovative technologies to stay ahead. Researchers and businesses alike are increasingly integrating AI into various aspects of food production and distribution, leading to a surge in AI-driven applications that are reshaping the industry. These advancements are not just trends; they are essential components of a forward-thinking strategy that will define the future of food.

One of the most groundbreaking developments is in the area of synthetic food production (Ding et al., 2023). By leveraging machine learning and biotechnology, the industry is creating novel food products such as plant-based meats and egg-free cakes. These alternatives to traditional ingredients are produced using methods similar to 3D printing, offering a glimpse into a future where food production is more sustainable and adaptable (Kim et al., 2018). The integration of the Internet of Things (IoT), deep learning, and computer vision into food manufacturing processes further enhances efficiency and environmental sustainability (Chapman et al., 2021). These technologies minimize waste by optimizing energy use and material resources, ensuring that production processes are both cost-effective and eco-friendly (Ding et al., 2023). Moreover, AI plays a critical role in maintaining the quality of food production by automatically adjusting key environmental factors like temperature, humidity, and ventilation, based on real-time data (Himeur, et al., 2023). This level of precision ensures that food products are consistently of high quality, meeting both industry standards and consumer expectations.

In supply chain management, AI's impact is equally transformative. The ability to intelligently track and manage large supply networks ensures that food products remain traceable from farm to table. This traceability is crucial for maintaining food safety and quality, as well as for responding swiftly to crises such as weather disruptions or natural disasters. AI's predictive capabilities also shine in sales forecasting, where models like ChatGPT I4.0 analyze extensive datasets, including consumer behavior, recipes, and weather patterns, to predict purchasing trends (Niszczota, et al., 2023). This allows companies to tailor their sales strategies to meet consumer demand more accurately, ultimately improving their market position.

The kitchen itself is also becoming a hub of innovation. AI-powered computer vision technology is assisting chefs in designing dishes, recognizing ingredients, and enhancing the overall quality of their culinary creations (Yaiprasert & Hidayanto, 2024). This technology not only improves efficiency in professional kitchens but also opens up new possibilities for home cooking. Wearable technology, such as smart bracelets, scales, and sports watches, combined with AI, is making personalized nutrition more accessible. These devices can analyze physical data to provide tailored health management solutions, allowing consumers to make informed decisions about their diets based on their unique nutritional needs.

Sustainable Development Goals (SDGs)

Preparing for the future of urban food systems is essential to achieving the goals of Sustainable Cities and Communities (SDG 11). As cities grow and urbanization continues to accelerate, the demand for food will increase, placing additional pressure on existing food systems. To address this, technology becomes a key driver in transforming how food is produced, distributed, and consumed within urban environments. By leveraging technologies such as AI, Big Data, and IoT, cities can optimize their food supply chains, reduce waste, and ensure that food is delivered more efficiently to meet the needs of their populations (Hassoun et al., 2022). This transformation not only supports sustainable urbanization but also enhances food security and community resilience.

Moreover, the integration of technology into urban food systems can significantly enhance community well-being. For example, smart farming techniques can be implemented in urban areas, allowing for the cultivation of fresh produce closer to where people live. This reduces the carbon footprint associated with transporting food over long distances and ensures that communities have access to nutritious, locally-grown food (Bhattarai & Adhikari, 2023). Additionally, technology can facilitate better resource management, such as water and energy, in food production, further contributing to sustainability. These innovations support the creation of green spaces and urban farms, promoting healthier lifestyles and stronger community bonds.

Incorporating forward-thinking strategies and emerging technologies into the food service industry also plays a vital role in fostering resilience within cities. As climate change and other global challenges continue to impact food systems, cities need to adapt to ensure a steady and reliable food supply. By adopting innovative approaches, such as predictive analytics for food demand and blockchain for traceability, the food service industry can build more robust systems that are better equipped to handle disruptions. These efforts align with the broader goals of SDG 11, ensuring that urban food systems are not only sustainable but also capable of supporting thriving, resilient communities for generations to come.

DISCUSSION AND CONCLUSION

The food service industry is undergoing a profound transformation driven by technological advancements and a focus on sustainability. This chapter provides a comprehensive guide to understanding and leveraging these trends, ensuring that industry stakeholders are well-equipped to navigate the evolving landscape. By integrating advanced technologies and sustainable practices, the food service industry can enhance operational efficiency, improve customer experiences, and contribute to achieving the United Nations' Sustainable Development Goals (SDGs). The integration of Industry I4.0 technologies in the food industry has ushered in a transformative era marked by unprecedented efficiency, quality improvements, and sustainability. The use of advanced technologies such as Big Data, AI, and blockchain is reshaping traditional food processing and supply chain practices, offering a myriad of benefits but also presenting notable challenges (Hassoun et al., 2022). This discussion synthesizes key findings from the implementation of these technologies, highlighting their impacts and the future directions for the industry. Industry I4.0 technologies have profoundly impacted the food sector by enhancing operational efficiency and product consistency. Big Data and AI play pivotal roles in understanding consumer behavior and optimizing food production. Through the analysis of vast amounts of data, these technologies enable better prediction of consumer preferences, streamline inventory management, and enhance supply chain operations (Vernier et al., 2021). For example, AI-driven predictive models can forecast sales trends with high accuracy, allowing companies to adjust their strategies proactively (Qian et al., 2022). Similarly, advancements in machine learning and biotechnology have led to the development of synthetic foods, such as plant-based meats, which offer sustainable alternatives to traditional ingredients (Bhattarai & Adhikari, 2023.; Ding et al., 2023; Kim et al., 2018).

Moreover, the application of smart sensors and IoT has improved the precision of food quality control (Kakani et al., 2020). By continuously monitoring environmental conditions and adjusting factors like temperature and humidity in real-time, these technologies ensure that food products maintain high standards of quality (Ben-Daya et al., 2020; Ada et al., 2021). Additionally, AI has revolutionized supply chain management by providing intelligent tracking of food products, thereby enhancing traceability and enabling quicker responses to potential disruptions (Zheng et al., 2021; Qian et al., 2022). Despite these advancements, the adoption of Industry I4.0 technologies in the food industry is not without challenges. Data privacy and security concerns are prominent, as large volumes of consumer information are processed, potentially exposing the industry to data breaches. The technical complexity of implementing AI systems requires specialized skills, which can be a barrier for smaller businesses (Ding et al., 2023). Additionally, integrating new technologies with traditional systems can lead to disruptions and inefficiencies if not managed carefully. Ensuring data consistency and standardization remains a critical issue, as fragmented and heterogeneous data can impact the reliability of AI-driven insights. The reluctance of some parts of the food industry to fully embrace technological change also poses a challenge. Traditional practices and resistance to adopting new methodologies can hinder the potential benefits that Industry I4.0 technologies offer. Therefore, addressing these barriers through targeted training, strategic planning, and robust change management is essential for realizing the full potential of technological advancements.

Looking ahead, the food industry must navigate a complex landscape shaped by rapid technological advancements and evolving consumer expectations. Embracing Industry I4.0 technologies present a significant opportunity to enhance efficiency, sustainability, and consumer satisfaction (Tom Dieck & Han, 2021). By leveraging I4.0 technologies, companies can optimize their operations, develop innovative products, and better understand and meet consumer needs. However, it is crucial to address the challenges associated with data security, technical complexity, and integration with traditional systems to fully capitalize on these advancements (Ding et al., 2023).

The food service industry is currently navigating a transformative phase, fueled by advancements in technology and a growing emphasis on sustainability. This shift is reshaping how food is produced, prepared, and consumed, aligning with several Sustainable Development Goals (SDGs). The integration of I4.0 technologies is leading to significant improvements in efficiency and accuracy. These technologies streamline kitchen operations, reduce labor costs, and minimize human error (Seal, 2023; Jagtap et al., 2020; Tuomi & Ascenção, 2023; Voipio et al., 2021), contributing to SDG 8 (Decent Work and Economic Growth) by creating tech-driven job opportunities and enhancing productivity. I4.0 technologies are revolutionizing predictive analytics, allowing for more accurate demand forecasting and inventory management (Vernier et al., 2021; Amani & Sarkodie, 2022). This not only reduces food waste but also ensures optimal resource use, directly supporting SDG 12 (Responsible Consumption and Production). By implementing digital ordering systems, self-service kiosks, and mobile applications, the industry enhances customer satisfaction through personalized and convenient service (Lee & Lee, 2020). This technological approach also aids in waste reduction through precise portion control and real-time data analytics, thus promoting responsible consumption.

Technologies like AI and IoT optimize supply chain management, addressing food waste and spoilage issues, and thereby supporting environmental sustainability (Ding et al., 2023). Furthermore, emerging technologies such as augmented reality (AR), virtual reality (VR), and drones are set to further revolutionize the industry. These innovations offer enhanced dining experiences, improve staff training, and streamline delivery logistics, meeting the increasing consumer demand for personalized and immersive experiences (Ding et al., 2023). The integration of advanced technologies into the food service industry not only enhances operational efficiency but also contributes to achieving key Sustainable Development Goals. By leveraging automation, AI, and IoT, the industry is transforming traditional practices and aligning with SDG 8, which focuses on promoting economic growth and decent work. These technologies facilitate better resource management, reduce waste, and improve customer satisfaction, which is in line with SDG 12 on responsible consumption and production (Singh, Archana et al., 2024; Hassoun et al., 2023; Lee & Lee, 2020).

In addition, sustainable practices driven by technological innovations address critical environmental challenges, supporting SDG 13 on climate action. Energy-efficient systems and optimized supply chain management are crucial for reducing the industry's carbon footprint and conserving resources. Looking forward, the adoption of AR, VR, and drones represents the next wave of innovation, offering opportunities to enhance dining experiences and operational efficiency (Ding et al., 2023). These advancements are essential for the industry to stay competitive and resilient in a rapidly changing market. Moreover, the focus on building sustainable urban food systems underscores the importance of SDG 11 (Sustainable Cities and Communities). Urban agriculture, shorter supply chains, and technology-enabled resource management contribute to community well-being and resilience Bhattarai & Adhikari, 2023. By integrating these practices, the food service industry can play a significant role in creating sustainable and efficient urban food systems, ensuring fresh and nutritious food for urban populations while minimizing environmental impact.

REFERENCES

Abideen, A. Z., Sundram, V. P. K., Pyeman, J., Othman, A. K., & Sorooshian, S. (2021). Food Supply Chain Transformation through Technology and Future Research Directions—A Systematic Review. *Logistics (Basel)*, 5(4), 83. DOI: 10.3390/logistics5040083

Ada, Y., Kazancoglu, Y., Sezer, M. D., Ede-Senturk, C., Ozer, I., & Ram, M. (2021). Analyzing barriers of circular food supply chains and proposing Industry I4.0 solutions. *Sustainability (Basel)*, 13(12), 6812. Advance online publication. DOI: 10.3390/su13126812

Ahmadzadeh, S., Ajmal, T., Ramanathan, R., & Duan, Y. (2023). A comprehensive review on food waste reduction based on IoT and big data technologies. *Sustainability (Basel)*, 15(4), 3482. DOI: 10.3390/su15043482

Amani, M. A., & Sarkodie, S. A. (2022). Mitigating spread of contamination in meat supply chain management using deep learning. *Scientific Reports*, 12(1), 5037. Advance online publication. DOI: 10.1038/s41598-022-08993-5 PMID: 35322116

Ardra, S., & Barua, M. K. (2022). Halving food waste generation by 2030: The challenges and strategies of monitoring UN sustainable development goal target 12.3. *Journal of Cleaner Production*, 380, 135042. DOI: 10.1016/j.jclepro.2022.135042

Bakhar, M., & Budihartono, E. (2023). Impact Analysis of the Use of IoT Technology and Environmental Monitoring Systems on Waste Reduction in the Food and Beverage Industry in Indonesia. *West Science Interdisciplinary Studies*, 1(11), 1225–1234. DOI: 10.58812/wsis.v1i11.380

Belaud, J.-P., Prioux, N., Vialle, C., & Sablayrolles, C. (2019). Big data for Agri-food I4.0: Application to sustainability management for by-products supply chain. *Computers in Industry*, 111, 103050. Advance online publication. DOI: 10.1016/j.compind.2019.06.006

Ben-Daya, M., Hassini, E., Bahroun, Z., & Banimfreg, B. H. (2020). The role of internet of things in food supply chain quality management: A review. *The Quality Management Journal*, 28(1), 17–40. DOI: 10.1080/10686967.2020.1838978

Bhattarai, K., & Adhikari, A. P. (2023). Promoting urban farming for creating sustainable cities in Nepal. *Urban Science (Basel, Switzerland)*, 7(2), 54. Advance online publication. DOI: 10.3390/urbansci7020054

Bolwig, S., Tanner, A. N., Riemann, P., Redlingshöfer, B., & Zhang, Y. (2021). Reducing consumer food waste using green and digital technologies.

Chapman, J., Power, A., Netzel, M. E., Sultanbawa, Y., Smyth, H. E., Truong, V. K., & Cozzolino, D. (2022, April 05). Netzel., … & Cozzolino, D. (2021). Challenges and opportunities of fourth revolution: A brief insight into the future of food. *Critical Reviews in Food Science and Nutrition*, 62(10), 2845–2853. Advance online publication. DOI: 10.1080/10408398.2020.1863328 PMID: 33401934

Dieck, M. C. T., & Han, D. (2021). The role of immersive technology in customer experience management. *Journal of Marketing Theory and Practice*, 30(1), 108–119. DOI: 10.1080/10696679.2021.1891939

Ding, H., Tian, J., Yu, W., Wilson, D. I., Young, B. R., Cui, X., Xin, X., Wang, Z., & Li, W. (2023). The Application of Artificial Intelligence and Big Data in the Food Industry. *Foods*, 12(24), 4511. DOI: 10.3390/foods12244511 PMID: 38137314

Doğan, S., Pala, U., & Ekici, N. (2023). Mobile applications as a next generation solution to prevent food waste. *Ege Academic Review*, 23(1), 1–10.

Dora, M., Biswas, S., Choudhary, S., Nayak, R., & Irani, Z. (2021). A system-wide interdisciplinary conceptual framework for food loss and waste mitigation strategies in the supply chain. *Industrial Marketing Management*, 93, 400–414. DOI: 10.1016/j.indmarman.2020.10.013

Eashwar, S., & Chawla, P. (2021). Evolution of agritech business I4.0: Architecture and future research directions. *IOP Conference Series. Earth and Environmental Science*, 775(1), 012011. Advance online publication. DOI: 10.1088/1755-1315/775/1/012011

Ejsmont, K., Gladysz, B., & Kluczek, A. (2020). Impact of Industry I4.0 on sustainability—Bibliometric literature review. *Sustainability (Basel)*, 12(14), 5650. Advance online publication. DOI: 10.3390/su12145650

Food and Agriculture Organization of the United Nations (FAO). (2022). Tackling food loss and waste: A triple win opportunity. https://www.fao.org/newsroom/detail/FAO-UNEP-agriculture-environment-food-loss-waste-day-2022/en

Galanakis, C. M., Rizou, M., Aldawoud, T. M. S., Ucak, I., & Rowan, N. J. (2021). Innovations and technology disruptions in the food sector within the COVID-19 pandemic and post-lockdown era. *Trends in Food Science & Technology*, 110, 252–263. DOI: 10.1016/j.tifs.2021.02.002 PMID: 36567851

Guan, X., Huang, L., & Zhang, L. (2021). Design of comprehensive service system for fresh food e-commerce under the background of "rural revitalization". *Journal of Physics: Conference Series*, 1757(1), 012141. Advance online publication. DOI: 10.1088/1742-6596/1757/1/012141

Hassoun, A., Aït-Kaddour, A., Abu-Mahfouz, A. M., Rathod, N. B., Bader, F., Barba, F. J., Biancolillo, A., Cropotova, J., Galanakis, C. M., Jambrak, A. R., Lorenzo, J. M., Måge, I., Ozogul, F., & Regenstein, J. (2022). The fourth industrial revolution in the food industry—Part I: Industry 4.0 technologies. *Critical Reviews in Food Science and Nutrition*, 63(23), 6547–6563. DOI: 10.1080/10408398.2022.2034735 PMID: 35114860

Hassoun, A., Jagtap, S., Garcia-Garcia, G., Trollman, H., Pateiro, M., Lorenzo, J. M., Trif, M., Rusu, A. V., Aadil, R. M., Šimat, V., Cropotova, J., & Câmara, J. S. (2023). Food quality I4.0: From traditional approaches to digitalized automated analysis. *Journal of Food Engineering*, 337, 111216. Advance online publication. DOI: 10.1016/j.jfoodeng.2022.111216

Himeur, Y., Elnour, M., Fadli, F., & Khwaldeh, S. (2023). AI-big data analytics for building automation and management systems: A survey, actual challenges, and future perspectives. *Artificial Intelligence Review*, 56(6), 4929–5021. DOI: 10.1007/s10462-022-10286-2 PMID: 36268476

Hou, B., Mutuc, E. B., Wu, L., Lee, H.-Y., & Lu, K.-H. (2020). Sustainable rice farming systems: Farmer attribute and land ecosystem perspectives. *The International Food and Agribusiness Management Review*, 23(2), 121–141. DOI: 10.22434/IFAMR2018.0220

Jagtap, S., Duong, L., Trollman, H., Bader, F., . . . Rahimifard, S. (2020). Chapter 5- IoT technologies in the food supply chain. *Food Technology Disruptions*, 175-211. DOI: 10.1016/B978-0-12-821470-1.00009-4

Jambrak, A. R., Nutrizio, M., Djekić, I., Pleslić, S., & Chemat, F. (2021). Internet of nonthermal food processing technologies (IoNTP): Food Industry 4.0 and sustainability. *Applied Sciences (Basel, Switzerland)*, 11(2), 686. Advance online publication. DOI: 10.3390/app11020686

Kakani, V., Nguyen, V. H., Kumar, B. P., Kim, H., & Pasupuleti, V. R. (2020). A critical review on computer vision and artificial intelligence in the food industry. *Journal of Agriculture and Food Research*, 2, 100033. Advance online publication. DOI: 10.1016/j.jafr.2020.100033

Kayikci, Y., Subramanian, N., Dora, M., & Bhatia, M. S. (2020). Food supply chain in the era of Industry 4.0: Blockchain technology implementation opportunities and impediments from the perspective of people, process, performance, and technology. *Production Planning and Control*, •••, 1–14. DOI: 10.1080/09537287.2020.1810757

Khan, P. W., Byun, Y. C., & Park, N. (2020). IoT-blockchain enabled optimized provenance system for food Industry 4.0 using advanced deep learning. *Sensors (Basel)*, 20(10), 2990. Advance online publication. DOI: 10.3390/s20102990 PMID: 32466209

Kim, S. J., Jeong, Y., Park, S., Ryu, K., & Oh, G. (2018). A Survey of Drone use for Entertainment and AVR (Augmented and Virtual Reality). In Jung, T., & tom Dieck, M. (Eds.), *Augmented Reality and Virtual Reality. Progress in IS*. Springer., DOI: 10.1007/978-3-319-64027-3_23

Konur, S., Lan, Y., Thakker, D., & Mehdipour, A. (2023). Towards design and implementation of Industry 4.0 for food manufacturing. *Neural Computing & Applications*, 35(22), 23753–23765. DOI: 10.1007/s00521-021-05726-z

Kumar, I., Rawat, J., Mohd, N., & Husain, S. (2021). Opportunities of artificial intelligence and machine learning in the food industry. *Journal of Food Quality*, 2021, 1–10. DOI: 10.1155/2021/4535567

Lau, A. (2020). New technologies used in COVID-19 for business survival: Insights from the hotel sector in China. *Information Technology & Tourism*, 22(4), 497–504. DOI: 10.1007/s40558-020-00193-z

Lee, S. M., & Lee, D. (2020). Untact: A new customer service strategy in the digital age. *Service Business*, 14(1), 1–22. DOI: 10.1007/s11628-019-00408-2

Lezoche, M., Hernandez, J. E., Alemany Díaz, M. M., Panetto, H., & Kacprzyk, J. (2020). Agri-food I4.0: A survey of the supply chains and technologies for the future agriculture. *Computers in Industry*, 117, 103187. Advance online publication. DOI: 10.1016/j.compind.2020.103187

Lim, A. (2024, Feb 4). 'When good food goes to waste'. *The Star*. https://www.thestar.com.my/news/education/2024/02/04/when-good-food-goes-to-waste#:~:text=ACCORDING%20to%20the%20Solid%20Waste,going%20to%20waste%20every%20day

Lorenzo, J. M., Domínguez, R., Pateiro, M., & Munekata, P. E. S. (Eds.). (2022). *Methods to assess the quality of meat products*. Springer., DOI: 10.1007/978-1-0716-2002-1

Ma, P., Lau, C. P., Yu, N., Li, A., & Sheng, J. (2022). Application of deep learning for image-based Chinese market food nutrients estimation. *Food Chemistry*, 373, 130994. Advance online publication. DOI: 10.1016/j.foodchem.2021.130994 PMID: 34731793

Moragues-Faus, A., & Battersby, J. (2021). Urban food policies for a sustainable and just future: Concpets and tools for renewed agenda. *Food Policy*, 103, 102124. DOI: 10.1016/j.foodpol.2021.102124

Nikolicic, S., Kilibarda, M., Maslaric, M., Mircetic, D., & Bojic, S. (2021). Reducing food waste in the retail supply chains by improving efficiency of logistics operations. *Sustainability (Basel)*, 13(12), 6511. DOI: 10.3390/su13126511

Niszczota, P., Rybicka, I., & Kamini, N. (2023). The credibility of dietary advice formulated by ChatGPT: Robo-diets for people with food allergies. *Nutrition (Burbank, Los Angeles County, Calif.)*, 112, 112076. Advance online publication. DOI: 10.1016/j.nut.2023.112076 PMID: 37269717

Ojo, O. O., Shah, S., Coutroubis, A., Jimenez, M. T., & Munoz Ocana, Y. (2018). Potential impact of Industry 4.0 in sustainable food supply chain environment. In *Proceedings of the 2018 IEEE International Conference on Technology Management, Operations and Decisions (ICTMOD)* (pp. 172–177). IEEE. https://doi.org/DOI: 10.1109/ITMC.2018.8691223

Onyeaka, H., Tamasiga, P., Nwauzoma, U. M., Miri, T., Juliet, U. C., Nwaiwu, O., & Akinsemolu, A. A. (2023). Using artificial intelligence to tackle food waste and enhance the circular economy: Maximising resource efficiency and Minimising environmental impact: A review. *Sustainability (Basel)*, 15(13), 10482. DOI: 10.3390/su151310482

Pacific Coast Food Waste Management. (2022). Case Study: Using Artificial Intelligence to Reduce Food Waste in Grocery Retail. Progress on the Path to Cut Food Waste in Half by 2030. Pacific Coast Food Waste Management. https://pacificcoastcollaborative.org/wp-content/uploads/2022/12/PCFWC-Case-Study_AI_Final.pdf

Peremutter, S. M. J. (2023, April 17). 10 of the worst food safety scandals in recent history. *Xtalk*. https://xtalks.com/10-of-the-worst-food-safety-scandals-in-recent-history-3435/

Qian, J., Dai, B., Wang, B., Zha, Y., & Song, Q. (2022). Traceability in food processing: Problems, methods, and performance evaluations—A review. *Critical Reviews in Food Science and Nutrition*, 62(3), 679–692. DOI: 10.1080/10408398.2020.1825925 PMID: 33016094

Rejab, A., Keohj, J. G., Zailani, S., Treiblmaier, H., & Rjeab, K. (2020). Blockchain technology in the food industry: A review of potentials, challenges and future research directions. *Logistics (Basel)*, 4(4), 27. Advance online publication. DOI: 10.3390/logistics4040027

Režek Jambrak, A., Nutrizio, M., Djekić, I., Pleslić, S., & Chemat, F. (2021). Internet of nonthermal food processing technologies (IoNTP): Food Industry 4.0 and sustainability. *Applied Sciences (Basel, Switzerland)*, 11(2), 686. Advance online publication. DOI: 10.3390/app11020686

Rohit, A. K., & Mueller, F. (2019). Human-Food Interaction. *Foundations and Trends in Human–Computer Interaction*, 12(4), 238–415. DOI: 10.1561/1100000074

Saadat, S., Pandya, H., Dey, A., & Rawtani, D. (2022). Food forensics: Techniques for authenticity determination of food products. *Forensic Science International*, 333, 111243. Advance online publication. DOI: 10.1016/j.forsciint.2022.111243 PMID: 35240505

Seal, P. P. (2023). Robots in the Hotel Kitchen: The Future Chef. In Impactful Technologies Transforming the Food Industry (pp. 89-97). IGI Global.

Shepherd, M., Turner, J. A., Small, B., & Wheeler, D. (2020). Priorities for science to overcome hurdles thwarting the full promise of the 'digital agriculture' revolution. *Journal of the Science of Food and Agriculture*, 100(14), 5080–5087. DOI: 10.1002/jsfa.9346 PMID: 30191570

Singh, V., Archana, T., Singh, A., & Tyagi, P. K. (2024). Utilizing Technology for Food Waste Management in the Hospitality Industry Hotels and Restaurants. In Sustainable Disposal Methods of Food Wastes in Hospitality Operations (pp. 287-295). IGI Global. DOI: 10.4018/979-8-3693-2181-2.ch019

Slobodan, I., Luka, P., & Ivana, G. (2015). Impact of technological development on business efficiency in the food and beverage department. *UTMS Journal of Economics (Skopje)*, 6(2), 321–330.

Sultana, A., Billah, M. M., Ahmed, M. M., Aftab, R. S., Kaosar, M., & Uddin, M. S. (2024). Applications of IoT-Enabled Smart Model: A Model for Enhancing Food Service Operation in Developing Countries. [JAETS]. *Journal of Applied Engineering and Technological Science*, 5(2), 1123–1141. DOI: 10.37385/jaets.v5i2.4937

Tavill, G. (2020). Industry challenges and approaches to food waste. *Physiology & Behavior*, 223, 112993. DOI: 10.1016/j.physbeh.2020.112993 PMID: 32502525

The Sustainable Development Goals Report. (2024). United Nations publication issued by the Department of Economic and Social Affairs (DESA). New York.

Tuomi, A., & Ascenção, M. P. (2023). Intelligent automation in hospitality: Exploring the relative automatability of frontline food service tasks. *Journal of Hospitality and Tourism Insights*, 6(1), 151–173. DOI: 10.1108/JHTI-07-2021-0175

United Nations Environment Programme. (2021). Food Waste Index Report 2021. Nairobi.

Vandna, & Kumar, K. (2023). Understanding the challenges and opportunities for sustainable practices in online food delivery platforms. *International Journal of Advanced Research in Management and Social Sciences, 12*(12), 19-36. https://doi.org/DOI: 10.4236/ijarmss.44586.33695

Vernier, C., Loeillet, D., Thomopoulos, R., & Macombe, C. (2021). Adoption of ICTs in Agri-food logistics: Potential and limitations for supply chain sustainability. *Sustainability (Basel)*, 13(12), 6702. Advance online publication. DOI: 10.3390/su13126702

Voipio, V., Vilko, J., Elfvengren, K., & Korpela, J. (2023). The future of work: Skills and knowledge perspective on service automation in the foodservice industry. *Technology Analysis and Strategic Management*, •••, 1–15. DOI: 10.1080/09537325.2023.2165440

Wang, H., Lan, Y., Kong, F., & Weng, L. (2020). Fresh agricultural products cold chain location selection in context of big data. *Journal of Physics: Conference Series*, 1631(1), 012122. Advance online publication. DOI: 10.1088/1742-6596/1631/1/012122

Yaiprasert, C., & Hidayanto, A. N. (2024). AI-powered in the digital age: Ensemble innovation personalizes the food recommendations. *Journal of Open Innovation*, 10(2), 100261. Advance online publication. DOI: 10.1016/j.joitmc.2024.100261

Zhao, T., Feng, A., Jin, S., Shi, Y., Hou, B., & Yan, Y. (2020). Research progress on artificial intelligence human sensor. In Peng, Y., & Dong, X. (Eds.), *Proceedings of 2018 International Conference on Optoelectronics and Measurement* (Vol. 567, pp. 403-412). Springer. https://doi.org/DOI: 10.1007/978-981-13-8595-7_35

Zheng, M., Zhang, S., Zhang, Y., & Hu, B. (2021). Construct food safety traceability system for people's health under the Internet of Things and big data. *IEEE Access : Practical Innovations, Open Solutions*, 9, 70571–70583. DOI: 10.1109/ACCESS.2021.3078536

Chapter 13
The Effective Role of Mobile Apps in Food Service Industry

Deepa Sharma
https://orcid.org/0000-0003-4374-917X
Maharishi Markandeshwar University, India

ABSTRACT

Nowadays, technology has become an integral part of people's lives. Smartphone technology has changed everything. People use a variety of digital gadgets to fulfill their needs like ordering food, shopping, ordering takeout or booking a cab, customers prefer to use upscale mobile applications. People can order food at their doorstep and get a taxi parked at their doorstep, with just a few simple tips; they can do all this from the comfort of their home. In this study, we will discuss the impact of mobile applications on the food business. The restaurant business and mobile apps is a match made in heaven. One of the industries that have benefited the most from the incorporation of mobile technology is restaurants. Whatever customers want to order from most restaurants can now be done through the app, whether they are at home or on the road. Gone are the days of waiting in line and using paper menus! With the advent of food delivery innovation, customers can now enjoy their favorite restaurant meals at the convenience of their homes using a plethora of mobile applications.

INTRODUCTION

The use of mobile apps has increased dramatically, covering everything from ordering groceries to purchasing bus tickets. The growing popularity of apps is causing a notable increase in the growth rate and profitability of organizations. Opportunities abound in many industries when we embrace digitalization and serve the increasing number of digital consumers.

There is a lot of room for expansion in the food and beverage business with mobile applications. The traditional restaurant business model has undergone a change with the introduction of online meal ordering and delivery applications. With internet ordering, the growth of meal delivery services might dramatically increase restaurants' sales to unprecedented levels (Alalwan, A.A., Qasem, Z. and Dwivedi, Y.K, 2020). The rapid expansion of food delivery services has been one of the major developments during COVID-19. Customers who want to use restaurant services with fewer risks associated with eating in person are likely to be the ones seeking online-to-offline food delivery services. Mobile apps are

DOI: 10.4018/979-8-3693-7683-6.ch013

becoming more important in consumers' consumption activities due to the rapid development of mobile technology ((Baum, et al., 2024). Positive consumer experiences and interactions with brands can be facilitated by branded mobile applications (Baum et al., 2013). For example, Starbucks attracted approximately 17 million users of mobile applications by offering a range of personalized services (Camilleri, M.A., Troise, C. and Kozak, M, 2023). Many food service businesses provide mobile applications to improve the customer experience e.g., quick ordering, contactless payment, and reduced waiting time. Additionally, customers can purchase goods and services through mobile application platforms, which do not require personal interaction. The variety of mobile food delivery services has grown, including options such as UberEats, Grubhub, Swiggy, Grabfood and Zomato. Understanding how food service businesses use mobile platforms is essential for creating effective marketing campaigns and gaining long-term competitive advantage (Cavusoglu et al., 2019). In general, consumers' behaviour when using a mobile device is strongly associated with prioritizing hedonic consumption i.e. fun and enjoyment – over utilitarian value (Baum et al., 2013). Previous research has shown that users' behaviour (such as their willingness to continue using a mobile device) is influenced by their level of enjoyment (Chen McCain and Liu, E., 2022). For example, Cavusoglu et al. (2019) proposed that behavioural intention towards smartphone applications is prompted by hedonic motivation or pleasure. Additionally, consumers' perceived social presence - such as a psychological sense of community - is linked to the ubiquitous connections of mobile applications (Garg et al., 2019). Consumers can form psychological connections with others using mobile application technology, even if they are physically apart. Conversely, a lack of interpersonal communication and social engagement may hinder the expansion of mobile commerce (Garg et al., 2019). Furthermore, conversations and interpersonal exchanges that take place during meal ordering may affect how clients feel their social presence. Therefore, the purpose of this study is to look at the factors that led to customer's attitudes and behaviors when it came to mobile meal delivery. This study specifically looks at how social presence and perceived satisfaction affect brand attitude and brand loyalty. The present study provides theoretical insight into how people perceive their experiences with mobile meal delivery. Additionally, the results offer helpful insights into successful marketing tactics that might improve the patronage behavior of clients. However, because technology is a key component for nations to boost their global competitiveness, m-commerce has drawn greater attention recently (Dehghani, M., Popova, A. and Gheitanchi, S, 2022). The number of applications downloaded has increased in direct proportion to the steady increase in the number of users of smartphones and related platforms, such as tablets. Along with the creation of mobile applications, social distance and other safety measures during the COVID-19 epidemic have resulted in customers eating out less (Cavusoglu et al., 2019). Thus, there are formidable local rivals in the worldwide market for mobile food ordering applications which have grown in popularity. Now day's individuals use cell phones mostly. As compare to more mobile devices than PCs are in use. Many of users spend time on apps, and utilize the mobile applications for booking, paying, and making purchases. (Dirsehan, T., & Cankat, E, 2021) whatever the sector, mobile applications are becoming a vital resource for expanding a business's reach. Every industry has seen a transformation thanks to mobile app technology. Businesses that previously offered only offline services are suddenly taking over the online space. (Cavusoglu et al., 2019) Using a few touches on a smart phone, one can easily order food or book a cab. The advent of apps has made people's lives easier. Nowadays, everyday tasks are done through smart phone apps. The availability of apps has now improved both the user's life and business. Earlier, people had to buy the things they needed from physical establishments. Earlier, they had to travel a long distance to select and buy goods. The advent of online retailers and smart phone apps has reduced their work (Gonzalez, R., Gasco, J. and Llopis, J,

2022). The way consumers are getting attracted to apps has forced every service company to create apps and interact with their customers. The tourism and fashion industries, among others, have all seen how mobile apps have impacted their business. One business that has seen revolutionary progress is the food industry. The food industry has changed as a result of technological advancements and the advent of apps. This development gave customers and owners a solution. The gap between patrons and restaurant owners has now been bridged thanks to mobile apps. Food businesses can interact with their consumers by offering them special discounts and deals through the app. The days of waiting for customers at food shops and searching for the best restaurants for customers are over. (Hasan et al.,2023) there is a great deal of possibility and market potential. Some important elements must be considered when thinking about mobile apps that lead to positive customer experience (Jiseon et al., 2021). The food industry and mobile apps have now become a complement to each other. Restaurants are among the industries that have benefited the most from the incorporation of mobile technology. Whatever customers want to order from most (Hasan et al.,2023) restaurants can now be done through the app, whether they are at home or on the road. The days of waiting in line and using paper menus are long gone! With the advent of food delivery innovation, customers can now enjoy their favorite restaurant meals from the comfort of their homes, thanks to the plethora of mobile applications. (Jiseon et al., 2021) restaurants really benefit from this. A person on the go can quickly arrange a booking. On the other hand, someone who wants to stay at home can quickly order food or even have it delivered to their doorstep. In every case, the diner and the establishment benefit from each other. Nowadays, many restaurant operators are streamlining the entire ordering and serving process for their patrons by using smart phone applications. With the help of the app, the dinner is delivered to the client's street address. This saves the customer from having to drive around on a busy night, instead having their dinner delivered right to their door (Hong, J., Jaegler, A. and Gergaud, O, 2024). Mobile application development by any business is more than just technological advancement. A business develops an application that is easy to use for the customer so that the business can grow. Before creating a mobile app, business owners, app developers and service providers should keep in mind some important aspects, which are discussed below:

(a) Investigation about market: If you have a brilliant concept to create a cutting-edge mobile application for your company, you must first know about the market, consumer demand, and trends. You should conduct market research for your business app even before adding any technical elements. Right from the beginning, this means "learning from the mistakes of others rather than learning after making mistakes". You can get really helpful information from the market study report. You can learn about the market acceptance of comparable apps and the tactics used by your competitors. This will enable you to improve your app.

(b) Determine Target Market: This is a very important step as it is important to first choose the appropriate audience for the app. These target consumers are crucial for the development of the app and the expansion and growth of their features, thus the future of the entire app depends on them. While developing an app, it is important to consider who will use it and how it will make their lives better. If you meet the user's expectations then your app will undoubtedly become popular and help you increase your revenue.

(c) Choosing the Correct Platform: Selecting the platform to launch your business app is the most important step. It is best to start with a single platform. Master one platform before moving on to another. The three most commonly used platforms for mobile apps are iOS, Android, and Windows. You should consider several factors when choosing the appropriate platform for your mobile application, including the app's features, target market, brand, and most importantly the pricing plan. Next, you need to decide whether to design your business app using a hybrid, native or mobile web approach.

(d) Planning: Make sure you fully understand the process before developing your business mobile application. Developing a strong business app takes some time and effort. It also goes through several stages. First of all, the company owner should be aware of the importance of each stage. The fundamental stages of any mobile application include project management, app design, app architecture, app development methodology, app testing, enhancements, and deployment. Create a strategy for the app development process. Controls and inspections are really essential. Release your software in beta form first, then test and evaluate it thoroughly before making the final version available to consumers.

(e) Recognize the fund: Creating a mobile app for a company requires money, expertise, and planning. It is important to understand your budget during the app development process and delivering the app to customers. Money must be spent on several components, including app development, maintenance, updates, and promotion. Your app budget is essentially determined by your expertise and the kind of application you want to create.

(f) Creative idea: Always remember that customers are always looking for something new and satisfying them is also a part of service. Why do customers prefer one brand over another? What is the reason behind this? Why do customers feel that the chosen brand offers something special? The best way to interact with your consumers is through mobile applications, which is also the easiest way to convert leads into potential customers. People get bored of the same thing very quickly. With millions of Smartphone apps in the market, the users of these apps want fresh content all the time. Therefore, it is advisable to consider unconventional strategies or features and prevent customers from choosing another option.

(g) Effective: Your company's mobile app needs to work smoothly now without any excuses. If your app is taking a long time to load, it is not right for the company. After using it once, the consumer either uninstalls it or does not open it again and again. This contributes to leaving a bad impression on the user. Make sure your program does not take up too much memory or processing power of the mobile device. Users expect efficiency from every mobile application. This includes things like security, battery usage, data efficiency, and user-friendliness. If your app consumes too much 3G or 4G bandwidth, your app may eventually stop working. Users may download and forget.

(h) Experience of the User: The user experience of an app is its foundation. You can't encourage people to come back to you and use your software if you haven't provided them with a great experience. User experience is becoming a more and more important component of the digital world. An app shapes the user's perception of your brand and offerings. It all depends on creating something useful, user-friendly and efficient for your intended market so don't create a difficult or confusing app.

(i) Pay attention to your marketing plan: A thoughtfully designed mobile application that provides a seamless user experience can provide several significant benefits. Your intended user base should be catered to in terms of both the functionality and content your app offers. The final product should offer exceptional customer service. If you are unable to create a high-quality mobile application, your brand may suffer.

(j) Examining: Testing your mobile application before launching is crucial. Make sure the experience meets the needs of the users before allowing them to use it. During testing, a few factors to consider are high performance, efficiency, and smoothness. By testing your app, you can iron out any kinks and make it a powerful business tool that helps you engage with clients and grow your company.

BACKGROUND

The way people eat around the world is changing. Until 20 years ago, restaurant-quality food delivery was mostly limited to Chinese and pizza. In the United States, the COVID-19 pandemic has more than quadrupled the market from a solid historical growth of 8% (Johnson et al.,2022). The emergence of attractive, easy-to-use apps and technologically advanced driver networks, combined with changing customer demands, has made ready-to-eat meal delivery a significant market. At the beginning of the pandemic, lockdowns and social distancing rules fueled a surge in mobile apps in the food sector, making delivery a lifeline for the struggling restaurant business. The economic structure of the food delivery ecosystem is constantly changing as it continues to grow. As the food sector grows, mobile apps, timely delivery services, range of products will determine business growth (Johnson et al., 2022). The food sector has changed significantly in recent years, mostly due to the increased use of smartphone apps. Mobile applications have become indispensable resources for consumers and companies in the food industry, helping with anything from managing dietary restrictions to ordering meal delivery and finding new eateries. Below is how mobile apps have revolutionized the food industry.

a) **Ordering and delivery made effortless:** The ease of ordering and delivery services is one of the most obvious ways in which mobile applications have revolutionized the food sector. Customers can now easily view menus, place orders and monitor deliveries from their favorite restaurants with the help of apps like Swiggy, Zomato and Uber Eats. Reaching a wider audience with this seamless experience has not only increased customer happiness but also created new revenue sources for eateries.

b) **Customized Dining Opportunities:** Additionally, mobile apps have completely changed the way customers find and interact with restaurants. Apps such as Yelp and Trip Advisor offer personalized suggestions based on user ratings, location, and favorite dishes. This degree of customization helps restaurants attract more business and increase customer loyalty, while also enabling consumers to try out new dining options and make educated decisions.

c) **Increased Interaction with Customers:** Restaurants may now interact with their patrons and create enduring ties with them by using mobile applications. Customer loyalty programs, special discounts, and in-app incentives encourage frequent visits to their preferred eateries. Additionally, features like feedback systems and real-time order tracking help businesses get insightful information and improve customer service, which in turn boosts patron happiness and loyalty.

d) **Effective management and their services**: In the background, smartphone applications have also changed how eateries run their businesses. Restaurants may run more successfully and efficiently because to the efficiency with which restaurant management applications expedite tasks like staff scheduling, inventory control, and table bookings. For restaurant owners and operators, this enhanced efficiency means lower costs and better overall performance.

e) **Food discovery**: For foodies seeking to try new recipes, ingredients, and culinary methods, mobile apps have emerged as indispensable tools. With a plethora of recipes, cooking tips, and meal planning tools available, apps like Yummy and Tasty encourage users to discover new culinary interests and broaden their palates. Furthermore, user-generated content and reviews are a common element of meal delivery applications, offering insightful information about the calibre and authenticity of the foods that various eateries provide.

f) **Nutrition food:** Mobile applications are becoming necessary tools for managing dietary preferences, allergies, and nutritional objectives for customers who are health-conscious. Users may monitor macronutrients, keep track of calories consumed, and make educated meal choices with the use of apps such as Lose It! and MyFitnessPal. Similar to this, to meet the varied demands of today's customers, food delivery apps now include a large variety of dietary alternatives, such as vegan, gluten-free, and keto-friendly meals. In conclusion, mobile applications have completely changed the way people find, purchase, and enjoy food. They have also given businesses the ability to run more profitably and efficiently.

Review of Literature

In few decades, the value-add marketing approach has evolved significantly from building brands to crafting great marketing and creating engaging customer experiences towards mobile apps used by Food Industry (kang et al., 2019). The mobile commerce research that takes into account real mobile customers to examine how system performance, overall restaurant image, and mobile electronic word-of-mouth affect eating decisions. Second, by extending the SOR model, this study investigates how features of the mobile environment affect the perceived value that motivates purchase intentions (Shah, 2020). This study's conclusions may aid practitioners in comprehending customers' actions because of the advantages that mobile eating is thought to offer. (Kang, 2019) to use the technology acceptance model (TAM) and privacy calculus theory to investigate how customers behave when using branded mobile applications in the food service sector. This study also revealed the moderating effect of anxiety related to technology. According to Karthika, I., & Manojanaranjani, A, (2019) to create a model to investigate the ways in which various technological and cognitive cues associated with mobile food ordering applications (MFOAs) influence consumers' intentions to use MFOAs on a regular basis. In the context of online-to-offline (O2O) food delivery services (FDS), the moderating influence of national household demographics was also evaluated. According to Rita (2023) to ascertain how to impact consumers of mobile food ordering apps' (MFOAs) customer journey. In the pre purchase phase, it investigates how information availability could affect customers' propensity to utilize MFOAs platforms, and in the post purchase phase, it looks at how individualized information might raise customer satisfaction with these services. (Johnson et al., 2022) to investigate the functional and technical quality aspects of mobile food delivery services (MFDS) and conduct an empirical assessment of how these aspects affect MFDS customer loyalty. The findings showed that functional quality and MFDS loyalty are significantly correlated; however there is no evidence of a relationship between technical quality and loyalty. According to Sharma, 2023 state that the study's focus is on consumers' attitudes toward advertising, online advertising, and mobile marketing. According to Kwon, J. and Ahn, J. (2022), mobile phones have become an essential aspect of life for all people. Mobile phones are used by people to enhance their social, professional, and personal life, but they also aid in the product marketing efforts of companies. Marketers should focus on the mobile marketing chains, which include people, technology, procedures, and expenses, in order to implement mobile marketing campaigns. The foundation of engaging in mobile marketing is brand loyalty. Kang (2019) stated that control and convenience account for a large portion of the growth in online meal ordering. Customer satisfaction after placing an online order, in-person interactions with restaurant staff, and shifts in customer behavior with reference to mobile food ordering Apps reflects how users feel about mobile applications for ordering takeout.

According to Hasan (2023), Zomato has grown to be one of the most well-known online meal ordering services as a result of the industry's rapid development due to the advent of digital technology. Hong (2024) state that the researcher examined the online meal ordering applications based on a number of criteria. The majority of customers were aware that they could make purchases online and thought using the internet was very handy. According to Camilleri (2023), the Behavioral Scoring Model states that businesses examine consumer feedback surveys, examine trends in their past purchases, and forecast their future purchasing habits. A few components make up this research methodology, which aids in the company's success. According to Lin, P.M.C., Au, W.C.W. and Baum, T (2024), mobile phones have become an essential aspect of life for all people. Mobile phones are used by people to enhance their social, professional, and personal life, but they also aid in the product marketing efforts of companies. Marketers should focus on the mobile marketing chains, which include people, technology, procedures, and expenses, in order to implement mobile marketing campaigns. The foundation of engaging in mobile marketing is brand loyalty. Nguyen, T., Huang, E. and Nguyen, D.M (2023) stated that control and convenience account for a large portion of the growth in online meal ordering. Nearly 50% of people have placed internet food orders. In-person interactions with restaurant staff, customers' satisfaction levels following online meal orders, and shifts in customer behavior with relation to mobile food ordering Apps reflect how users see mobile applications for ordering meals. According to (Rita, P., Eiriz, V. and Conde, B (2023) Zomato has grown to be one of the most well-known online meal ordering services as a result of the industry's rapid development due to the advent of digital technology. Additionally, these apps must to be reliable. The exclusive deals that these apps provide are yet another important factor drawing users in. Using social media to promote these applications is the greatest strategy for marketers. Zomato, Swiggy, Foodpanda, and Ubereats are the top 4 food delivery apps. J. Das (2018) has researched, examined, and contrasted them. Zomato is ranked first by users because it offers "better choices of restaurants"and "better discounts". When it comes to timely delivery and excellent customer service, Zomato is ranked first by users as well. Customers ranked Ubereats as the bottom option in both scenarios. According to Sarmah, B., Kamboj, S. and Rahman, Z.(2017) the Behavioral Scoring Model states that businesses examine customer feedback surveys, examine consumer purchase patterns and behavior, and forecast the customers' future spending patterns. A few components make up this research methodology, which aids in the company's success. According to Sharma (2023) claims that technology is to blame for India's food delivery system's faster growth. Orders may be placed over the phone or online, and all client requests are met. Variations can be made in response to the evolving needs of the consumers. Customers may now get everything delivered right to their home. A food menu is established in the online meal ordering system so that clients may effectively place their orders and use it to track their orders, according to Sarmah, B., Kamboj, S. and Rahman, Z. (2017). According to Dirsehan, T., & Cankat, E (2021) the food and service business values consumer views of its offerings because it enables it to better understand and cater to its patrons' wants and preferences. The customer's perception was evaluated in this study based on a number of variables.

According to Chen McCain and Liu, E (2022), the Internet has significantly contributed to the rise in public awareness of online meal delivery services. People may easily access restaurants and cuisines by using the internet to search for them, compare their offerings, and check pricing and services. All of these things are now more convenient for customers thanks to the internet. According to Cavusoglu (2019) startups have taken the Indian economy by storm in recent years, setting trends and driving economic growth. These businesses are founded by youthful, tech-savvy people. These youthful folks, endowed with a new outlook and inventive ideas, utilize technology to launch a variety of enterprises. According to Garg (2019) in order to provide excellent customer service, food delivery systems must adapt to the shifting consumer attitudes, technological advancements, and societal demographics.

According to Baum (2024), the development of Web Apps and Android Apps has occurred recently, with the advancement of information technology. The benefits of web apps over desktop apps include easier browser navigation and no requirement for installation or updates. The creation of a strong structure, ease, and a large market for app distribution are the benefits of Android apps. According to Hasan (2023), technology improvements have made it easier and more efficient for people to handle their tasks. By making complete use of the system, management systems assist in decreasing the amount of work that requires human labor, in cutting down on time, and in producing reports for management use. According to Leong Wai Jiseon (2021), the study applied the technology acceptance model and privacy calculus theory to examine customers' behavior when using branded mobile applications in the food service sector to provide personalized services. This study also highlighted the moderating effect of technology-related anxiety and the findings showed that perceived benefits, perceived threats, and perceived ease of use were all significantly affected by customization. Perceived risk had no effect on the perceived value of disclosure, while perceived benefits had a favorable effect. This study is to investigate the mechanism by which users' meal satisfaction, repurchase intentions, and mobile app satisfaction are influenced by the quality of the food-ordering mobile app service. The findings demonstrated that there were significant differences in the impact of different service quality aspects on customer happiness (i.e., food and mobile app satisfaction) and repurchase intention when it came to food-ordering mobile apps. The quality of mobile app services significantly impacted both food satisfaction and propensity to repurchase. The purpose of this study is to determine the features of customer satisfaction for restaurant delivery applications that are becoming more popular worldwide, particularly in Korea. The changing demographics, societal trends, and advancements in culinary science have resulted in a decline in restaurant patronage. This is a significant shift for the restaurant industry, and there is an immediate need for associated study (Nguyen, T., Huang, E. and Nguyen, D.M, 2023). The outcome demonstrated how the usefulness, portability, and dependability of customers affected their level of satisfaction. In particular, dependability and mobility have an impact on both loyalty and satisfaction. Significant effects on loyalty and satisfaction are also supported. This implies that rather than concentrating on offering an excessive amount of information, makers of food applications should instead improve the mobility and trustworthiness of their apps (Seong-Soo Cha, Bo-Kyung Seo, 2020).

Need of Mobile Applications adopted by Food Industry

Due to the busy lifestyle, mobile applications for food have become popular. Everyone prefers to order food online instead of preparing food at home. Technology has helped a lot in the development and introduction of mobile food applications. The most popular and frequently used applications by users are such as Zomato, Swiggy, Foodpanda, UberEats, Faaso, etc. Mobile food apps serve as a conduit between patrons and restaurants due to their partnerships with several eateries. There are several reasons for the increase in sales, including ease of use, simple payment options, and wide selection of food and dining establishments, prompt delivery, excellent customer service, etc. There are various approaches and criteria used in mobile food apps that consumers take into account when placing an order from a particular app. With the beginning of the twenty-first century, the youth of every country are remarkably talented in this era of cutting-edge inventions and technology. Every food business and other businesses want to excel in their respective fields, and technology is a vital tool to help them do so. Due to technology development, things that once seemed unimaginable are now achievable. Thanks to technology, many types of enterprises are opening online storefronts these days. Due to many variables, including more affordable cell phones and internet data plans, people have started using more mobile apps. Many things have now become more convenient for consumers thanks to the application. Many things have now become more convenient for consumers thanks to the application. The act of getting food or takeout from a nearby restaurant through a mobile app or website is known as "online food delivery". Customers can choose from several payment options including cash on delivery, debit cards, credit cards, and other mobile wallets and buy food from their favorite restaurants. They can also choose which dishes to order, what to get delivered, *etc.* Every business has been transformed by mobile app technology, from ordering takeout to booking taxis. High-tech smart phone applications are now preferred by consumers for making different reservations and completing daily chores (Seong-Soo Cha, Bo-Kyung Seo, 2020). In order to provide improved customer assistance and engagement, mobile app changes fueled by the internet and app availability are game-changing advances for a variety of businesses, particularly the food industry. The days of waiting in line and paper menus are long gone. The industry has seen a shift in food delivery innovation, allowing customers to enjoy their favorite meals from the convenience of their homes through a variety of mobile applications. Having your own app for the food industry allows you to get closer to your customers. Both businesses and customers are undoubtedly benefiting from mobile applications.

1. **Craziness by Customers for Food Demand:** Many smart phone applications allow users to order from their favorite restaurants and get it delivered directly to their home without compromising on both the quantity and quality of the food. With just a few clicks, users can place their order and get the food delivered to their home at any time or place. Customers do not need to go through the hassle of contacting the restaurant again and again to change or personalize their food. Customers can keep a close eye on the entire process as they have the ability to track and monitor every action on the order.

2. **Booking:** When customers want to eat out, the purpose of reservation options is to reduce waiting time. Customers can use these programs to place themselves in line and arrive later, yet are seated as if they had already arrived. However, these applications use different techniques to achieve the same goal.

3. **Check the Status of company through online reviews:** With the help of these applications, customers may share their positive experiences with restaurants with the community. Users have the option to post their evaluations on various websites and social media. This raises the value of the service and brand recognition. Customers base their decision to visit a restaurant on reviews and ratings, therefore having a good rating increase the likelihood that people will choose to visit your establishment. This feature has a real impact on the restaurant industry. It is crucial for restaurants to adopt reviews and new technology that their patrons anticipate from them in light of these applications. Furthermore, based on their recommendations, restaurants may organize various initiatives to improve customer service.

4. **Discounts:** Discount apps, which make it easier for customers to eat on a budget, are another innovation that has changed the way restaurants operate. This feature entices consumers by allowing them to enjoy delicious food from a variety of places at the most reasonable prices. These discounts can sometimes be time- or quantity-limited, the former of which depends on how many shoppers take advantage of the offer. Restaurants have adjusted their menu prices to reflect the possibility that customers may have coupons or discounts made possible by the app.

5. **Customer loyalty:** The highly anticipated elements of restaurant mobile applications, which are adored by patrons, are discounts in the form of promo codes and referral programs. Customers may now eat out while staying within their budgets more easily thanks to these offers. Customer loyalty programs help restaurants become more well-known and loyal to their brands. The app's customer loyalty program is essential to increasing the number of repeat users. It is evident that many applications have a wide range of effects on the food business. All of them, meanwhile, provide consumers more control over what they eat. Your restaurant company will stand out from the competition thanks to the food

delivery app. A leading Indian mobile app development company can help restaurant operations and food delivery services succeed.

Challenges faced by online food delivery business

1. Inconsistent Price Structure: There are now many new participants in the fiercely competitive meal delivery market. And as a result, rival companies are finding it challenging to choose the best price plan. In order to prosper and attract consumers, the newest businesses in this sector tend to operate on thin profit margins. To remain competitive, they even implement a variety of offensive and defensive pricing strategies. All of this, though, strains the margins and reduces their profitability. And to make it more difficult, food prices are wildly unstable. The best approach to deal with this issue is to do a detailed analysis of the pricing strategies used by industry leaders. Developing a successful pricing plan may also be aided by recognizing consumer price sensitivity and the most recent developments in the online meal delivery sector.

2. Unstable customer preferences: Any meal delivery service's ultimate goal is to increase its market share by providing clients with the greatest possible experience at the lowest feasible cost. Even as competition increases, firms in the food delivery sector have raised the bar on marketing to the point that consumers have an abundance of options. This has an impact on brand loyalty and creates instability in the consumer base. Food delivery companies are using engagement-boosting marketing techniques and approaches in an effort to reduce customer churn.

3. Low Quality of food: Every meal delivery service faces a difficulty in maintaining the same level of food quality because food flavors always vary with time. Customers move to different restaurants as a result of their changing tastes since there are many of alternatives accessible and it is unacceptable to compromise on flavor. Another challenge facing meal delivery services is closing the quality gap between food served at the restaurant's physical location and food delivered to customer's locations. It's difficult to deliver food to people's doorsteps while making sure it stays fresh in the car.

4. Difficult to maintain the loyalty of customers: Keeping a customer for an extended period of time is a difficult endeavor. It's difficult to attract new clients and maintain strong client relationships these days. Businesses need to have a thorough understanding of their present clientele, including their needs, preferences, and dislikes, in order to provide tailored offers that take demographics into account.

5. Payment Mode: Nowadays, no client looks past the conventional cash payment option. In the current situation, clients quickly cancel orders and choose another choice if they feel there aren't enough payment methods available. Remember that before making an order, buyers check each app's return policy first. Therefore, it is essential to promote cashless transactions and integrate online payment options. In addition, given the CoVID-19 transmission, many prefer cashless transactions nowadays. Remember to incorporate a variety of payment methods, such as net banking, e-wallets, and credit or debit cards.

6. Communication Gap: Using a single method of communication is no longer sufficient when interacting with consumers. A meal delivery firm operating online has to have several channels of contact, including phone calls, text messages, social media, email, and live chat. By doing this, you can make sure that the brand connects with customers on a personal level and maintain their loyalty.

7. Choosing best advertising platforms: In the early phases of any business, attracting new consumers may be difficult, especially if you don't know how to start out or which advertising platform is best. Because consumers' requirements and purchasing habits are ever-evolving, it can be difficult for firms to determine the most effective advertising approach to reach the appropriate audience at the right moment and provide excellent service.

8. Hard Competition: There is often relatively limited potential for new meal delivery services since an existing business typically captures a greater market share.

One of the main obstacles to small and emerging businesses gaining a large and valuable clientele is the threat of larger rivals.

9. Manual Process: Lastly, processing orders by hand might lead to inefficiencies and delivery delays, which can diminish the company's reputation and make the procedure more taxing. Therefore, automating the process from the outset of the business is always desirable. By automating the procedure, human error is eliminated and efficiency is increased. It will also assist with the rapid growth of your online meal delivery company, which will require you to handle a high volume of orders.

Revenue Models for the Food Delivery App

Food companies have simplified and expedited the decision-making process. Before placing an order from the restaurant, you may first check the ratings and reviews on Zomato, UberEats, and other comparable meal delivery services. In actuality, they expedited and simplified the payment procedure. For instance, consumers may pay using cards or other digital wallets such as Paytm or other wallets while using meal delivery applications like UberEats. In actuality, food businesses have also made repurchasing simple. According to (Qayyum, A., 2022) to make it simple to place another order in a matter of minutes, you may, for example, bookmark your favorite meals or restaurants and store your address and payment information. Additionally, the on-demand economy in the food business has changed many worldwide markets by eliminating the complete cycle approach and focusing on three essential steps in the ordering process. The food delivery app is based on three basics concepts- Place, Prepare, and Deliver. On-demand food delivery businesses relate psychologically as they all promise to save customers time and effort in ordering and picking up food. After Uber, many food companies like Zomato, Swiggy, All in one Food delivery and DoorDash, etc. are succeeding in the food industry and have entered the on-demand sector. They give their customers the convenience they deserve. Additionally, their convenience study has generated many time and effort saving ideas for their customers. As a result, the food delivery market is expanding worldwide. Here are the two most popular food delivery app business models used to make a profit.

A. The order only model: Numerous meal delivery services, like Just Eat and Delivery Hero, are based on this idea, which is essentially a set of tools for ordering restaurants on your own. Attracting new clients via an integrated web and mobile channel is the primary point of sale in an online meal delivery business concept.

Figure 1. Flowchart of order only model

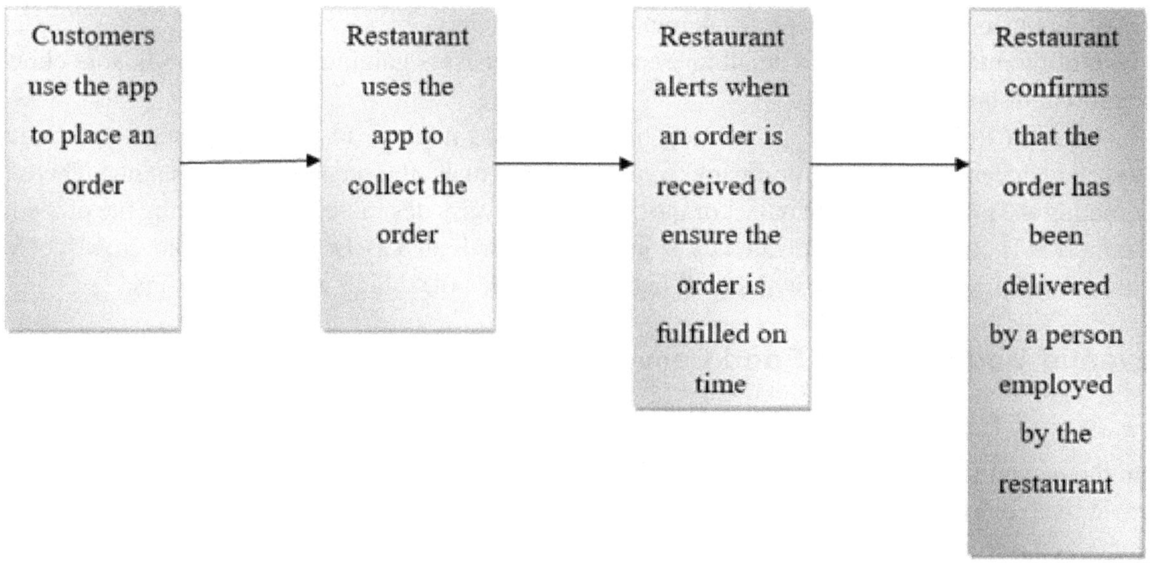

Source: *Compiled by the Author*

a) The procedure for ordering food: Under this concept, the ordering procedure for food operates as follows:

1. First, customers place an order via the website or mobile app.
2. Your order will then be picked up by the restaurant through the dashboard or app.

Through an automated phone call or email, the restaurant will notify you that your order has been received.

b) **Delivery procedure:** There are two possible outcomes for the delivery procedure.
   1. by the restaurant's employee who makes deliveries.
   2. by the delivery driver who works for the business.

Limitations: Start-ups using this approach are restricted in what services they can provide on demand, both in terms of cost and food. They are mostly linked to customers that order relatively low-key delivery meals like pizza, burgers, Chinese cuisine, etc. With this paradigm, food entrepreneurs are unable to optimize the quality and speed of food delivery services or manage them. But with this model, online food delivery services won't have to bother about transporting or preparing food. These new businesses typically charge between 10% and 15% for meal delivery services. As a software-only business, they also offer amazing growth potential and enormous scaling opportunities.

Advantages of this Model: This concept eliminates the need for online food delivery services to worry about transporting or preparing food. These new businesses typically charge between 10% and 15% for meal delivery services. As a software-only business, they also offer amazing growth potential and enormous scaling opportunities.

B. The Order & Delivery Model: Ordering and delivery are the first and third components that are the emphasis of the new food delivery software firms like Caviar, Deliveroo, and DoorDash. They carry requests and orders from customers to the businesses and take care of the distribution on their own. In terms of distribution, they often collaborate with a number of different courier service providers that are connected via an app similar to Uber in order to receive orders from customers and share delivery information with courier service providers.

a) The Procedure for Ordering Food: Orders are placed using the app or website, where menus from various eateries are shown. When a restaurant gets an order through the food delivery app, it tells the delivery service with the destination's location and the time to pick up the box. In order to assist restaurants in covering the commission charge for the delivery service, they occasionally mark up the price of restaurant items. Customers also pay a predetermined flat cost for each restaurant they order from.

b) Delivery Procedure: The smartphone application that tracks their locations is accessed by the courier who is currently on duty. The courier decides whether or not to accept an order once it has been sent. The work is then sent to other couriers if the initial courier declines it. The task will go to the first messenger to confirm the work.

Figure 2.

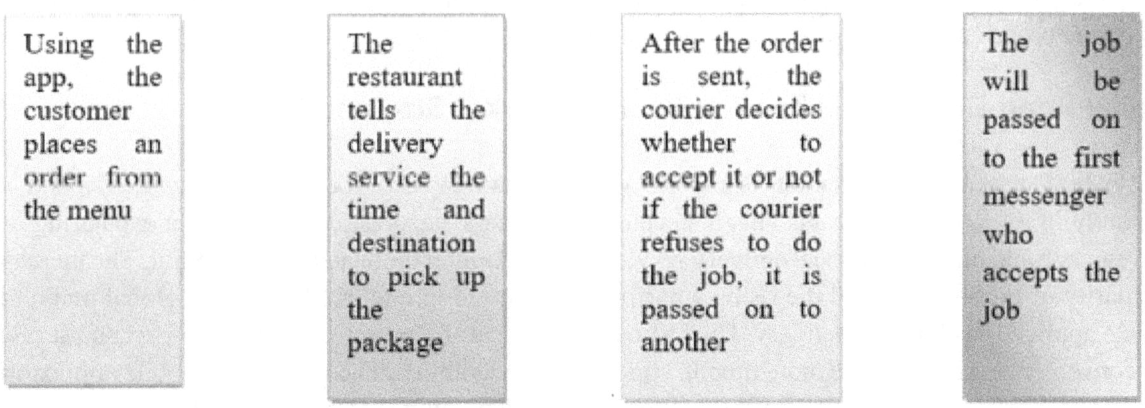

Source: *Compiled by the Author*

Limitations: Businesses that purchase food online and have a second business model are typically software firms with a logistics division that handles a lot of labor-intensive tasks including hiring, on boarding, and preparing shifts for couriers.

Advantages of this Model: The drawback of using this technique is that restaurants will often charge a fee that is 25-30 percent more. But, you are able to provide both a range of costs and restaurant options that the meal delivery apps' exclusive business model is unable to. The Doordash business model is among the greatest illustrations of this type.

But the Entrepreneur might have to work a little more to compete with the automated delivery and dining networks.

Current Status of Food Industry Used Mobile Apps on the basis of Revenue

Over the few years, there has been a notable increase in the meal delivery sector. With the help of platform-to-consumer services like DoorDash and Uber Eats, food delivery has grown beyond takeout to include everything, generating billions of dollars in new business opportunities. Faster and less expensive delivery has been made possible by the network effects of additional delivery riders combined with route optimization technology. Many meal delivery companies are now experiencing a flywheel effect as a result of this; as they strive to undercut rivals on extremely narrow profit margins in an effort to gain market dominance. According to Baum (2024) offering customers a seamless and customized experience through an e-commerce or mobile app may boost sales and improve your brand. They can increase income and enhance consumer engagement. Offering customers a seamless and customized experience through an e-commerce or mobile app may boost sales and improve your brand. They can increase income and enhance consumer engagement. According to (Vij, 2018) this demonstrates the potential for businesses to use mobile applications to reach and interact with customers. Investing in a mobile app can help you remain ahead of the curve and offer your company a competitive edge. Businesses that have the capacity to gather data and examine consumer behavior may utilize that knowledge to enhance their products and services and better serve their customers. Restaurants, franchises, and other grocery stores can use the seamless platform provided by food delivery mobile applications. By providing a variety of options through a single online mobile interface, the platform helps customers. Everything about food delivery has been improved, from the latest websites, smart phone applications and phone ordering methods. Shown in figure 1.1 below:

Global Food Delivery Mobile Application Market Size and Scope

It is anticipated that the market for mobile applications related to food delivery would expand significantly in the upcoming years. This is because consumers' need for convenience is expanding, and convenience and on-demand meal delivery services are becoming more and more popular. The increased popularity of mobile apps and the rising smartphone penetration rate are driving the global market for mobile applications for food delivery. This is because there is an increased need for on-demand services and convenience, and there are more mobile applications available. .. The market for mobile applications for food delivery is expanding due in part to the rising trend of online meal ordering. Nowadays, customers would rather buy meals online since they can take advantage of deals and discounts and personalize their orders to suit their tastes. Customers are placing more frequent internet meal orders as a result of this. The market for food delivery mobile applications is expanding as a result of customers' growing health consciousness and their increased desire for healthier food products. Healthy food orders are becoming increasingly common among consumers, which is driving the market's expansion. The market for mobile applications for food delivery is expanding due in part to the growing use of digital payment methods. People are placing more online food orders as a result of the growing accessibility of digital payment methods like digital wallets and e-wallets. Moreover, the market for mobile applications for meal delivery is expanding due to the growing ubiquity of the Internet. This might be attributed to the growing prevalence of online ordering platforms and the expanding availability of mobile applications.

In general, it is anticipated that the market for mobile applications for meal delivery would increase significantly over the next several years. This may be attributed to the growing popularity of online ordering services, the acceptance of digital payment solutions at an increasing rate, and the growing need for on-demand and convenient services.

Now days, technology is integral to people's lives. Individuals utilize a variety of digital gadgets to meet their demands. Mobile applications and websites are increasingly being used for services including ordering, shopping, transportation, and education. Everything has changed with smartphone technology, even ordering takeout and booking taxis. These days, when ordering takeout or booking a cab, customers would much rather utilize upscale mobile applications. People may have meals delivered to their houses and taxis waiting at their doorway with just a few easy suggestions, all from the comfort of their homes. We will discuss the effect of mobile applications on the food business in this post. The restaurant business and mobile apps are a marriage made in heaven. Restaurants are among the industries that stand to gain the most from the incorporation of mobile technology. All of the ordering that customers require from most restaurants can now be done through an app, whether they are at home or on the road. The days of waiting in line and using paper menus are long gone! With the advent of food delivery innovation, customers can now enjoy their favorite restaurant meals from the comfort of their homes thanks to a plethora of mobile applications. For restaurants, this is a tremendous advantage. For the gregarious person, bookings may be made quickly. A person who would like to stay home, however, has the option of ordering meals to go or even having it delivered right to them. In any case, the diner and the establishment benefit. Many restaurant operators now use smartphone applications to streamline the ordering, serving, and clearing of food processes. Using the applications, the dinner is delivered to the client's street number. The customer may have their dinner delivered right to their home and avoid having to drive on a busy night.

Figure 3. Analysis of the Food Delivery Mobile Application Market

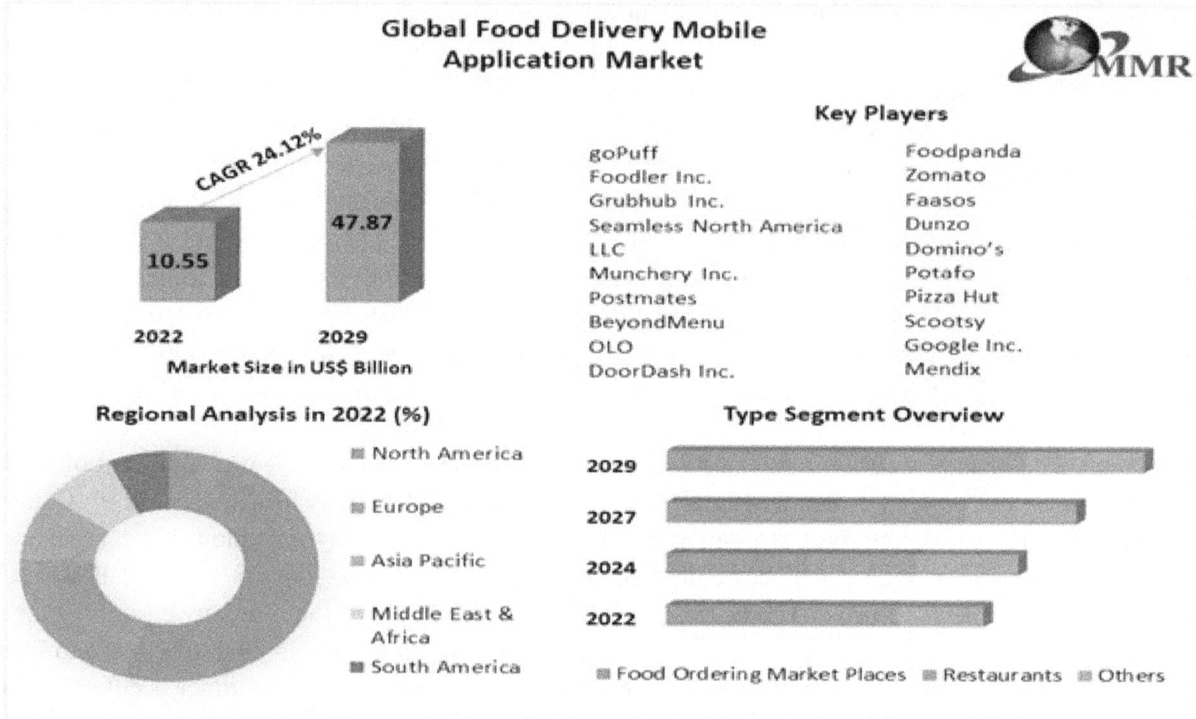

Source:*https://www.maximizemarketresearch.com/market-report/food-delivery-mobile-application-market/127395/*

The food delivery mobile application industry includes digital platforms and services that facilitate ordering, paying for, and receiving food using mobile applications. Because of evolving consumer preferences, advancements in technology, and changing lifestyles which are particularly evident in the world's cities this market sector is expanding exponentially. Essentially, meal delivery apps on smartphones function as intermediaries between patrons seeking convenient access to an extensive array of food options and eateries striving to expand their client base outside conventional physical stores. The user-friendly interfaces of these systems allow customers to place orders, browse menus, change preferences, and monitor delivery in real-time all from the convenience of their smartphones.

Numerous smartphone applications allow users to order meals from their preferred restaurants and have it delivered right to their home without sacrificing taste or quantity. With only a few clicks, users can make their order and have meals delivered to their home at any time or location. Customers don't need to go through the hassle of repeatedly contacting the restaurant to change or personalize their meals. Customers can keep a close eye on the entire process since they have the ability to track and monitor every action on the order. With the help of these applications, customers may evaluate restaurants and encourage word-of-mouth communication within the community. Users have the option to post their evaluations on various websites and social media. This raises the value of the service and brand recognition. Customers base their decision to visit a restaurant on reviews and a rating, therefore having a good rating increases the likelihood that people will choose to visit your establishment. This feature has a real impact on the restaurant industry. It is crucial for restaurants to adopt reviews and new technology that their patrons anticipate from them in light of these applications. Furthermore, based on their recommendations, restaurants may organize various initiatives to improve customer service. The food delivery mobile application industry is undergoing dynamic alterations due to advancements in technology and shifting consumer preferences. With the rise of convenience-driven lifestyles, on-demand food delivery services have become indispensable to modern living. Innovations like eco-friendly packaging, AI-driven recommendations, and contactless delivery options are reshaping this rapidly expanding company.

Factors growth driving of the Global Food Delivery Market through Mobile Application

People are choosing more and more to have food delivered right to their doorsteps, which has led to an increase in the popularity of meal delivery applications in recent years. But there are several difficulties associated with the rise of meal delivery applications. Food delivery applications have witnessed a rapid rise in sales in recent years, which has fundamentally altered how people buy and eat. The convenience of ordering meals from the comfort of one's home has drawn a large number of customers to food delivery applications. Additionally, these apps have made it easier for eateries and other businesses involved in the food industry to increase their customer base and income. More customers are using to steer clear of busy eateries and reduce their chance of exposure. And below we describe the factors leads the food industry growth:

1. **Increasing need for Convenience**: In the modern world, time is a valuable resource. The number of people utilizing mobile applications for meal delivery has increased as a result of the growing demand for convenience. Mobile apps make it easy to order food from a variety of restaurants in a short amount of time. With the ability to order meals from the comfort of one's home or while on the go, mobile apps are becoming more and more popular.
2. **Growing disposable incomes:** People are becoming more and more eager to spend money on food delivery services as their disposable incomes grow. In emerging markets, where economic expansion is increasing people's disposable income and willingness to pay for convenience, this tendency is especially noticeable. A significant contributing element to the growth of the worldwide market for mobile applications for food delivery is the rise in disposable income.
3. Growing tendency of digitalization
4. Growth of the delivery networks
5. Increasing adoption of cashless payments

Findings

This study found that the food industry and mobile apps are closely linked. The food industry is among the industries that are benefiting the most from the incorporation of mobile technology. Any order that customers want from most restaurants can now be done through an app, whether they are at home or on the road. The days of waiting in line and using paper menus are long gone! With the advent of food delivery innovation, customers can now enjoy their favorite restaurant meals from the comfort of their homes, thanks to a plethora of mobile apps. On the other hand, someone who wants to stay at home can quickly order food or even have it delivered to their doorstep. As mobile applications gain popularity, professionals and industry leaders are realizing how powerful they are as a means of digital communication and customer interaction. Research has shown that mobile apps are deeply impacting customer engagement.

CONCLUSION

The results show that food-related mobile apps are rapidly making the food industry financially strong as well as making the lives of users easier. Keeping the competition in mind, restaurants are providing good quality food to customers at reasonable prices and also providing timely home delivery. This will definitely attract customers and also win customer loyalty. The use of mobile apps is proving to be a boon for customers in this fast-paced life because due to lack of time, lots of options, compare the price and online reviews, now customers can view the menu, place an order and even make an appointment with just a few clicks on their cell phones, thereby reducing waiting time and increasing overall efficiency. The merger of mobile apps and online ordering platforms has made the food delivery process more efficient. Users of a number of mobile apps may utilize digital menu cards to place their orders. With just a few touches, consumers may select the meal products, making for the optimal user experience. Customers are able to choose a restaurant according to their tastes and financial situation. It is evident that many applications have a wide range of effects on the food business. All of them, meanwhile, provide consumers more control over what they eat. Your restaurant company will stand out from the competition thanks to the food delivery app. A leading mobile app development company can help restaurant operations and food delivery services succeed. Due to the growing popularity of mobile apps, the food and beverage sector is expected to experience significant growth in the upcoming years. The food industry has limitless potential to draw in a large consumer base; therefore developing cutting-edge mobile apps is essential to satisfying all of their needs. The digitization of this business will be embraced by clients more and more as dependability and incentives increase.

Limitations and Future Implications

Apart from the impact of mobile apps on the food industry as well as in the future, work can also be done on textile, medicine, footwear and other industries also. Future research requires longitudinal studies of how customer opinions, loyalty, and satisfaction with mobile apps evolve over time. Additionally, the influence of cultural factors i.e. such as eating habits, health awareness, family size, and lifestyle was not taken into account in this study. Subsequent research efforts could include these cultural factors and aim to extend the results to a broader geographic context.

REFERENCES

Alalwan, A. A., Qasem, Z., & Dwivedi, Y. K. (2020). Examining the impact of mobile interactivity on customer engagement in the context of mobile shopping. *Journal of Enterprise Information Management*, 33(3), 627–653. DOI: 10.1108/JEIM-07-2019-0194

Baum, T. (2024). Service quality of online food delivery mobile application: An examination of the spillover effects of mobile app satisfaction. *International Journal of Contemporary Hospitality Management*, 36(3), 906–926. DOI: 10.1108/IJCHM-09-2022-1103

Camilleri, M. A., Troise, C., & Kozak, M. (2023). Functionality and usability features of ubiquitous mobile technologies: The acceptance of interactive travel app. *Journal of Hospitality and Tourism Technology*, 14(2), 188–207. DOI: 10.1108/JHTT-12-2021-0345

Cavusoglu, M. (2019). An analysis of technology applications in the restaurant industry. *Journal of Hospitality and Tourism Technology*, 10(1), 45–72. DOI: 10.1108/JHTT-12-2017-0141

Cha, S. S., & Seo, B. K. (2020). The effect of food delivery application on customer loyalty in restaurant. *Journal of Distribution Science*, 18(4), 5–12.

Chen McCain, S.-L., Lolli, J., Liu, E., & Lin, L.-C.Chen McCain and Liu. (2022). An analysis of a third-party food delivery app during the COVID-19 pandemic. *British Food Journal*, 124(10), 3032–3052. DOI: 10.1108/BFJ-03-2021-0332

Dehghani, M., Popova, A., & Gheitanchi, S. (2022). Factors impacting digital transformations of the food industry by adoption of block chain technology. *Journal of Business and Industrial Marketing*, 37(9), 1818–1834. DOI: 10.1108/JBIM-12-2020-0540

Dirsehan, T., & Cankat, E. (2021). Role of mobile food-ordering applications in developing restaurants' brand satisfaction and loyalty in the pandemic period. *Journal of Retailing and Consumer Services*, 62, 102608. Advance online publication. DOI: 10.1016/j.jretconser.2021.102608

Garg, V. (2019). International Journal of Recent Technology and Engineering (IJRTE) ISSN: 2277-3878, Volume-8, Issue-1, May 2019 3424 Published By: Blue Eyes Intelligence Engineering & Sciences Publication Retrieval Number A9219058119/19©BEIESP The Study of Interest of Consumers In Mobile Food Ordering Apps.

Gonzalez, R., Gasco, J., & Llopis, J. (2022). Information and communication technologies in food services and restaurants: A systematic review. *International Journal of Contemporary Hospitality Management*, 34(4), 1423–1447. DOI: 10.1108/IJCHM-05-2021-0624

Hasan, A. A.-T. (2023). Determinants of intentions to use the food panda mobile application in Bangladesh: The role of attitude and fear of COVID-19. *South Asian Journal of Marketing*, 4(1), 17–32. DOI: 10.1108/SAJM-10-2021-0123

Hong, J., Jaegler, A., & Gergaud, O. (2024). Mobile applications to reduce food waste in supply chains: A systematic literature review. *British Food Journal*, 126(2), 509–530. DOI: 10.1108/BFJ-09-2022-0742

Jiseon, A. (2021). Impact of cognitive aspects of food mobile application on customers' behaviour. *Current Issues in Tourism*. Advance online publication. DOI: 10.1080/13683500.2021.1890700

Johnson, L. (2022). How does quality of mobile food delivery services influence customer loyalty? Gronroos's service quality perspective. *International Journal of Contemporary Hospitality Management*, 34(11), 4178–4205. DOI: 10.1108/IJCHM-08-2021-1039

Kang, J.-W. (2019). "The role of personalization on continuance intention in food service mobile apps: A privacy calculus perspective", *International Journal of Contemporary Hospitality Management*, 33(2), pp. 734-752. https://doi.org/. 9.DOI: 10.1108/IJCHM-12-2017-0783

Kang, J.-W., & Namkung, Y. (2019). The role of personalization on continuance intention in food service mobile apps: A privacy calculus perspective. *International Journal of Contemporary Hospitality Management*, 31(2), 734–752. DOI: 10.1108/IJCHM-12-2017-0783

Karthika, I., & Manojanaranjani, A. (2018). A Study on the various food ordering apps based on consumer preference. *World Wide Journal of Multidisciplinary Research and Development*, 4(11), 88–89.

Kwon, J., & Ahn, J. (2022). Role of customers' multidimensional perceived equity in the mobile food delivery industry. *Journal of Hospitality and Tourism Technology*, 13(5), 955–971. DOI: 10.1108/JHTT-08-2021-0223

Lin, P. M. C., Au, W. C. W., & Baum, T. (2024). Service quality of online food delivery mobile application: An examination of the spillover effects of mobile app satisfaction. *International Journal of Contemporary Hospitality Management*, 36(3), 906–926. DOI: 10.1108/IJCHM-09-2022-1103

Nguyen, T., Huang, E., & Nguyen, D. M. (2023). Food delivery app continuance: A dual model and segmentation approach. *International Journal of Retail & Distribution Management*, 51(5), 569–589. DOI: 10.1108/IJRDM-06-2022-0217

Qayyum, A. (2022). Adoption of mobile food ordering apps for O2O food delivery services during the COVID-19 outbreak. *British Food Journal*, 124(11), 3368–3395. DOI: 10.1108/BFJ-09-2020-0781

Rita, P., Eiriz, V., & Conde, B. (2023). The role of information for the customer journey in mobile food ordering apps. *Journal of Services Marketing*, 37(5), 574–591. DOI: 10.1108/JSM-11-2021-0407

Sarmah, B., Kamboj, S., & Rahman, Z. (2017). Co-creation in hotel service innovation using smart phone apps: An empirical study. *International Journal of Contemporary Hospitality Management*, 29(10), 2647–2667. DOI: 10.1108/IJCHM-12-2015-0681

Shah, A. M., & Ali, M. (2020). Customers perceived value and dining choice through mobile apps in Indonesia. *Asia Pacific Journal of Marketing and Logistics*, 33(1), 1–28. DOI: 10.1108/APJML-03-2019-0167

Sharma, D. (2023). "Consumers 'Attitude towards Using Food Delivery Apps" published by IGI Global publications. Published 29 August 2023, Pages 75-88. DOI: . Copyright © 2023, IGI Global.DOI: 10.4018/978-1-6684-9094-5.ch005

Vij, M. (2018). Technology at the dinner table: Ordering food online through mobile apps. *Journal of Retailing and Consumer Services*, 43(July), 342–351. DOI: 10.1016/j.jretconser.2018.04.001

Chapter 14
The Future on Your Plate: How Food Technology Becoming a Driver of Sustainability

Wella Gem Alag Samonte
Aklan State University, Ibajay, Philippines

ABSTRACT

The food service industry has undergone a seismic shift through food technology (foodtech). This chapter delves into how foodtech has transformed restaurant and food business operations, paving the way for greater operational efficiency, reduced labor costs, convenient and faster service. Customers around the globe have embraced this evolution, readily adopting features like: Automation and robotics. Next is the Greener Practices: Foodtech can introduce environmentally friendly practices like using recycled packaging materials or sourcing ingredients from local, sustainable farms. This empowers customers to make informed choices based on their values which greatly affect sustainability measures as this is a two-way effort. This chapter will delve deeper into the specific food technology practices that contribute to sustainability and explore how these practices translate into higher customer satisfaction. It will showcase real-world examples and discuss the potential challenges and opportunities that lie ahead in this dynamic landscape.

INTRODUCTION

The food service industry has undergone a seismic shift through food technology. This chapter explores how these technological innovations have revolutionized restaurant and food business operations, leading to greater operational efficiency, reduced labor costs, and enhanced customer experiences.

The integration of service robots and automated guided vehicles (AGVs) into restaurants has been particularly impactful, resulting in a significant reduction in labor hours and a boost in productivity (Shimmura et al., 2020). These automated systems have enabled service staff to focus on their core duties, improving service quality while streamlining operations. Moreover, technology-driven solutions have positively impacted customer satisfaction by enhancing ordering speed, convenience, menu design, and order accuracy. AI-assisted food ordering and delivery management systems have further improved business efficiency and customer satisfaction by enabling more effective planning, predicting consumer behavior, and reducing product waste (Liem et al., 2023). However, the introduction of food

DOI: 10.4018/979-8-3693-7683-6.ch014

delivery services has yielded mixed results. While they offer convenience to tech-savvy customers, they may not necessarily increase overall demand but rather alter the customer base (Chen et al., 2022). This underscores the importance of carefully considering the potential implications of new technologies on existing business models."

The global food system is grappling with a complex web of challenges that impact every stage of the supply chain. Food security and safety are paramount concerns, as a staggering one-third of all food produced is lost or wasted annually. This inefficiency is exacerbated by inadequate information sharing, logistical inefficiencies, insufficient infrastructure, and a lack of robust risk management systems (Kiranmai et al., 2021). Furthermore, the global food system is under immense pressure due to a confluence of factors, including increasing population, urbanization, and climate change (Sousa et al., 2024). These challenges are exacerbating existing food security issues and driving unsustainable practices that have severe environmental consequences. To address these pressing challenges, the food industry must embrace innovative solutions. This includes harnessing blockchain technology to enhance food safety, quality, and traceability throughout the supply chain (Tipmontian et al., 2020), leveraging AI and machine learning for supply chain optimization (Pandey, 2022), and building more resilient food systems that can withstand disruptions and adapt to changing conditions (Ababou et al., 2023).

Food technology has advanced rapidly, driven by emerging trends and innovations. New processing technologies prioritize nutrition, safety, and freshness (Akhila et al., 2022). Nanotechnology, for example, offers enhanced bioavailability and stability through nanoemulsions and nano-encapsulation (Thiruvengadam et al., 2018). This interdisciplinary field is poised to revolutionize food production and consumption.

Southeast Asia's food system faces significant challenges hindering SDG progress. Food waste and loss remain a pressing issue due to data limitations and inadequate practices (Ardra & Barua, 2022). Addressing challenges like pandemic disruptions, supply chain complexities, and emerging technologies requires a multifaceted approach, including Industry 4.0 and collaborative partnerships (Lahane et al., 2023). Innovative solutions like biosensors and nexus planning are crucial for a sustainable and resilient food system.

Customers around the globe have embraced this evolution, readily adopting features like: *Automation and robotics*: Kitchen robots tackle repetitive tasks, while self-service kiosks streamline ordering and payment; *Online ordering and delivery*: Third-party platforms and in-house systems offer convenient ways to get food delivered directly to customers; *Data-driven insights*: Restaurants leverage data analytics to understand customer preferences, optimize pricing, and personalize experiences; *Ghost kitchens and virtual restaurants:* Delivery-only concepts offer a wider variety and accessibility of food options. But the impact goes beyond mere convenience. Foodtech also presents a path towards sustainability, which in turn, can lead to increased customer satisfaction. *Reduced Food Waste,* as the smart inventory management systems help restaurants predict demand and order accurately, minimizing food waste, this translates to lower costs and a reduced environmental footprint, which resonates with eco-conscious customers. *Transparency and Traceability:* This empowers customers to make informed choices based on their values which greatly affect sustainability measures as this is a two-way effort.

This chapter will delve deeper into the specific food technology practices that contribute to sustainability and explore how these practices translate into higher customer satisfaction. It will showcase real-world examples and discuss the potential challenges and opportunities that lie ahead in this dynamic landscape.

Literature Review

The global food industry is undergoing a paradigm shift, driven by a confluence of factors, including population growth, climate change, and evolving consumer preferences. To address these pressing challenges, sustainable food production, technological advancements, and innovative practices are being developed and implemented across the food supply chain (Galanakis et al., 2024).

Current advancements in food technology are focused on several key areas, including the utilization of advanced food materials and the application of nanobiotechnology. Aerogels, C-dots, nanoparticles, nanoemulsions, and conjugates are being used to enhance food quality, safety, and shelf life (Gupta et al., 2023). Meanwhile, nanobiotechnology offers promising solutions for improving crop yield and protection, with applications in plant genetic engineering, nanofertilizers, nanopesticides, and nanosensors (Sangeetha et al., 2019). Beyond these areas, precision fermentation is emerging as a pivotal technology in the alternative protein revolution, with the potential to improve the sustainability of our food system (Terefe, 2021). Industry 4.0 technologies, such as artificial intelligence, smart sensors, robotics, blockchain, and the Internet of Things, are revolutionizing food production, transportation, storage, and consumption (Hassoun et al., 2022). Additionally, ultrasound technology, an eco-friendly technique, is being applied in various food processing applications to contribute to food safety, environmental sustainability, and economic efficiency (Pallarés et al., 2021). Finally, innovative packaging solutions are being developed to extend food shelf life and reduce environmental impact (Nair et al., 2023). Recent developments in food production, supply chain, packaging, and preservation technologies are focused on addressing these demands and enhancing the overall sustainability of the food system. In the realm of food production and supply chain technologies, nonthermal processing methods, such as high hydrostatic pressure, pulse electric field, cold plasma, and ohmic heating, are emerging as viable alternatives to traditional thermal processing (Kehinde et al., 2020). These technologies offer the advantage of inactivating microorganisms while preserving food quality. Additionally, integrated inventory management strategies and investments in preservation technology are being proposed to optimize perishable food supply chains (Sebatjane, 2022).

Packaging innovations have also witnessed significant advancements, with a focus on smart packaging technologies. Active packaging, which incorporates active ingredients to extend storability and ensure product safety, is gaining traction (Kaushani et al., 2022). Intelligent packaging systems, equipped with various sensors and indicators, provide real-time information on product quality during shipping and storage (Firouz et al., 2021; Yousefi et al., 2019). While the push for sustainable packaging solutions, including biodegradable and biobased polymers, is gaining momentum (Salgado et al., 2021; Silva et al., 2022), challenges related to cost, marketability, and consumer acceptance persist (Firouz et al., 2021). The adoption of 3D printing technology in food packaging production also shows promise but requires further exploration (Silva et al., 2022).

Interestingly, while technological advancements are crucial, traditional methods like fermentation are being reimagined and integrated with modern innovations to address current challenges (Terefe, 2021). Moreover, the implementation of sustainable development goals in food science and engineering curriculums is emerging as a vital catalyst for the sustainability transition (Serhan & Yannou-Lebris, 2020).

Shaping the efforts towards sustainability, sustainable food production is being optimized through a combination of innovative farming practices, climate-resilient supply chains, and the adoption of digital technologies (Galanakis et al., 2024). Blockchain technology is emerging as a powerful tool for enhancing sustainability in food supply chains by ensuring fairer practices, improving traceability, and driving environmental stewardship (Friedman & Ormiston, 2021). Controlled Environment Agriculture (CEA), particularly vertical farming, is positioned as a sustainable solution for feeding the world while preserving the planet (Gan et al., 2022). Stimulatingly, there is a growing emphasis on appropriate and frugal technologies in food production, especially in emerging economies. These technologies offer affordable, user-friendly solutions that align with local needs and resources, providing a stark contrast to capital-intensive methods (Régnier, 2023). Moreover, the integration of indigenous knowledge practices with modern innovations is being recognized as crucial for advancing sustainable food technologies (Musetsho et al., 2024).

In conclusion, the food industry is witnessing a convergence of innovative technologies across production, supply chain, packaging, and preservation. These advancements aim to address consumer demands for safe, high-quality, and sustainable food products while reducing waste and improving efficiency.

FOOD TECHNOLOGY, TOWARDS OPERATIONAL EFFICIENCY AND SUSTAINABILITY:

Efficiency in operation is the key to any businesses to ensure sustainability of operation. This operational efficiency in food technology refers to involving of process optimization as well as resources. This is to further ensure the minimization of wastes, cost reduction that could enhance sustainability. In fact, Malik, et al, 2023 viewed that this operational efficiency in food technology including automation and AI are transforming the industry. Hence, the latter agrees that these technologies optimizing production, ensuring food safety, and improving supply chain management. With the aid of technology, it promotes a smarter and efficient way in effect to waste reduction and resource conservation.

This topic will dive you into key strategies and considerations to achieve sustainability and efficiency in food business operation through the lens of food technology.

KEY STRATEGIES FOR OPERATIONAL EFFICIENCY

Artificial Intelligence (AI) - is revolutionizing the food industry. By enhancing decision-making, optimizing waste management, and enabling smart sorting and packaging solutions, AI is significantly improving food hygiene, safety, quality, and supply chain efficiency. This technological advancement is driving a more sustainable and efficient food production system. By utilizing AI algorithms and data mining, we can develop intelligent systems to optimize energy consumption in commercial buildings such as food business venue. This not only saves money but also reduces environmental impact. (Singh et al., 2021). Further, leveraging on advanced technologies like AI and machine learning are crucial for improving energy efficiency. They enable accurate forecasting, enhance accessibility, and reduce costs, ultimately contributing to a more sustainable future. (Na et al., 2022; Tracey et al., 2020).

Process Optimization and Standardization - Under this strategy is the **lean manufacturing** in which implementing techniques such as value stream mapping in identifying wastes and streamlining processes. This may involve elements such as IoT, and smart controls. Likewise, **developing standardized operating procedure** is another strategy to optimize and standardize processes. However, it is important to develop a clear, concise and consistent guidelines in food operation towards efficiency and quality. Lastly, **integrating continuous improvement** in the operation. This can involve the use of tools like Six Sigma or Kaizen in order to identify bottlenecks and areas of improvement as operation evolve and can compete with the changing demands of time. Integrating Industry 4.0 elements like IoT, smart controls, and big data with nonthermal processing, opens the door to creating intelligent, sustainable food production facilities (Jambrak et al., 2021).

Energy Efficiency Measures - This practice highlights energy audits, the use of efficient equipment, and renewable energy. The conduct of regular audits on the operation can lead to discovering energy-intensive areas to recommend energy-saving measures. Likewise, investing into efficient equipment could lead the business to better energy-savings. Hence, the investment towards solar and wind power as renewable energy sources could save the business from high operational costs and can help foster negative effects to environment. Energy efficiency is crucial for sustainable food technology. By reducing energy consumption and emissions, we can lower costs and ensure food safety. The food industry's significant energy use makes energy conservation a critical factor in sustainability (Xie & Li, 2021).

Water Conservation - Auditing water usage and identifying areas of reduction including recycling by implementing systems for reusing of water wastes. Additionally, integrating efficient irrigation methods to minimize water lost in food business operation. According to Weerasooriya et al., 2021, to ensure a sustainable water supply and address future industrial needs, water conservation strategies are essential. By reducing water consumption and improving efficiency, we can protect our natural resources. This findings coincides the significance as strategy towards food technology sustainability.

Waste Reduction and Management - The key to waste reduction and management are the following: source reduction, recycling and composting, and waste-to-energy practice. One of the important aspect to consider is minimizing generation of wastes through production process optimization. To achieve a sustainable food industry, source reduction is essential. Preventing waste from being created in the first place is far more effective and environmentally friendly than treating waste after it's produced (Hussain et al., 2021). Hence, Ema et al., 2024, pointed out on addressing food waste and loss is crucial for global food security. Source reduction is a powerful tool in the food industry, helping to prevent waste and ensure a more sustainable food system.

Recycling and composting are crucial for sustainable food technology (Karimi, 2023; Liu et al., 2020). These methods promote a circular economy and reduce waste. Converting food waste to energy through processes like anaerobic digestion, fermentation, pyrolysis, gasification, and biochemical conversion is another promising strategy.

Waste-to-Energy (WtE) strategies offer a sustainable solution for the food industry, addressing the growing challenge of food waste while generating valuable energy. By converting food waste into energy, WtE facilities reduce waste volumes and provide an alternative energy source. However, challenges such as supply chain issues and operational sustainability can hinder their success, particularly in developing countries.

Anaerobic digestion (AD) emerges as a promising alternative. This process not only reduces waste volume but also produces biogas, a renewable energy source. Despite its benefits, AD faces technical and economic hurdles in implementation. To fully realize the potential of WtE and AD in the sustainable food technology industry, addressing these challenges and promoting their adoption is essential.

Supply Chain Efficiency – Supply chain efficiency is crucial for sustainable food technology. Technological advancements, like blockchain, are transforming the industry by improving transparency, data security, and overall efficiency (Ahamed & Karthikeyan, 2024). Factors like supplier partnerships, JIT inventory, and sustainable sourcing are essential for achieving this goal. Strong supplier collaborations can lead to improved efficiency, reliability, cost reduction, and sustainability benefits.

Just in time inventory allows the food business to minimize inventory levels by proper coordination with the demand. This is a strategy that could minimize inventory holding costs by having the materials delivered right just as it is needed for the operation or production. The practicality of this strategy is vital to avoid expensive oversupply cost considering the food business raw materials are perishable in nature. Further, the business can facilitate business in reducing inventory cost, improved cash flows, enhance quality, and increase responsiveness. By carefully considering the benefits, challenges, and strategies for implementing JIT, food technology businesses can optimize their inventory management and achieve greater efficiency and sustainability.

Prioritizing suppliers with sustainable practices is a great way to foster sustainable sourcing. It is a critical component of a responsible and ethical food supply chain. This would mean prioritizing suppliers who adhere to sustainable practices, ensuring that the raw materials used in food production are obtained in a way that minimizes environmental impact, supports social equity, and maintains economic viability. Sustainable sourcing would include environmental stability such as resource conservation, reduced pollution, and biodiversity preservation; social sustainability that touches fair labor practices and community development; and economic sustainability encompassing long-term viability and fair trade. By prioritizing sustainable sourcing, food businesses can contribute to a more sustainable and equitable food system while also improving their own bottom line.

Packaging Optimization - The key in optimizing packaging is to invest in minimal packaging, recyclable materials, and packaging design. The use of minimum amount of packaging is necessary as this could improve the cost and minimize wastes that can reduce environmental impact. The use of technology could also be a tool to consider alternatives and design for efficiency. Recyclable materials are essential for reducing waste and promoting a circular economy in the food industry. By choosing recyclable or biodegradable packaging materials, businesses can contribute to environmental sustainability and minimize their ecological footprint.

Packaging design plays a crucial role in minimizing waste and optimizing supply chain efficiency. By carefully considering packaging design, businesses can reduce material usage, improve product protection, and streamline logistics processes. Minimalism, sustainability, functionality and supply chain efficiency is one of the key considerations for packaging designs.

Sustainability Implications of Operational Efficiency

Operational efficiency in the food industry can significantly contribute to sustainability by Reducing environmental impact: Optimizing processes to minimize waste, conserve resources, and protect ecosystems; Lowering operating costs: Streamlining processes, reducing waste, and optimizing resource utilization can lead to significant cost savings; Improving profitability: Increased efficiency can enhance financial performance and profitability; Enhancing brand reputation: Demonstrating a commitment to sustainability can attract environmentally conscious customers and differentiate a business from competitors; Ensuring regulatory compliance: Adhering to sustainability standards can help businesses avoid fines and legal repercussions; Improving employee satisfaction: A sustainable and efficient workplace can boost employee morale and attract top talent; Engaging with the community: Supporting sustainable initiatives can contribute to the well-being of local communities.

The key technologies towards operational efficiency and sustainability are through the following:

Automation and Control Systems: These systems can optimize energy consumption, improve product quality, and reduce waste in the daily operation of the food industry. Optimizing food consumption through facility design is a key strategy for reducing waste. A study using agent-based modeling demonstrated that smaller plate sizes can significantly decrease plate waste by up to 30% without compromising service quality. However, total waste may be lower with larger plates due to potential benefits in food preparation and efficiency. This highlights the importance of balancing plate size with overall food waste management strategies. (Ravandi & Jovanovic, 2019).

Energy Management Systems (EMS): EMS can monitor and control energy usage, reducing costs and environmental impact; Heat Recovery Systems: Capturing and reusing waste heat can improve energy efficiency. Efficient Equipment: Investing in energy-efficient equipment can reduce energy consumption and waste. Renewable Energy Integration: Incorporating renewable energy sources can lower carbon footprint and energy costs. Renewable energy sources offer a sustainable and environmentally friendly alternative to traditional energy sources in the food technology industry such as investing to solar, wind power, hydropower and geothermal energy. By integrating renewable energy into their operations, businesses can reduce their carbon footprint, lower energy costs, and improve their overall sustainability performance.

Building Automation Systems (BAS): BAS can optimize energy consumption and improve sustainability in food facilities. Building Automation Systems (BAS) are crucial for optimizing energy consumption and improving sustainability in food technology facilities. By monitoring, controlling, and optimizing various building systems, BAS can help businesses reduce energy costs, minimize waste, and enhance operational efficiency.

Data Analytics and Predictive Maintenance: Data analytics and predictive maintenance play a crucial role in optimizing operations, reducing costs, and improving sustainability in the food technology industry. By collecting and analyzing data from various sources, businesses can gain valuable insights into their operations and proactively address potential issues before they occur. This will set forth food technology businesses to optimize their operations, reduce costs, and improve their overall sustainability performance. Analyzing data can identify areas for improvement and optimize operations. Likewise, by analyzing data on inventory levels, transportation routes, and demand patterns, businesses can optimize their supply chains, reducing costs and improving efficiency hence quality control towards quality attributes. The predictive demand forecasting can shed light in reducing the risk for overproduction or underproduction.

Food Service Sustainability Measures as Influencing Factor to Customer Satisfaction

Sustainability is a driving force in the food service industry and considered as one of the key driver of customer satisfaction. As consumers seek ethical and environmentally conscious options, sustainable practices are becoming essential. This chapter delves into how sustainable measures in food service can enhance customer satisfaction.

Research consistently demonstrates that environmentally friendly practices positively influence customer perceptions, loyalty, and willingness to recommend a business. While customers generally appreciate sustainable initiatives, their willingness to pay a premium varies based on the specific practice. (Baratta & Simeoni, 2021; Soni et al., 2022). Understanding this complex relationship is essential for food service businesses seeking to enhance customer satisfaction and contribute to a more sustainable future.

The study of Samonte (2024), revealed that client satisfaction in terms of service is through provision of prompt, sensitive and healthy food and beverage options leveraging on the sustainability measures in terms of enhances guest experience, in which it is highlighted that more clients are recognizing and appreciating the integration of sustainability as part of service criteria particularly in opting for healthy and locally produced products. With this, it shed light to food industry that integration of sustainability practices and concepts towards food technology and as part of innovative measures greatly affects satisfaction.

In conclusion, sustainable practices in food service are essential for driving customer satisfaction. By implementing green initiatives, restaurants and hotels can cultivate customer loyalty and positive word-of-mouth. While the impact of sustainability measures may vary, focusing on initiatives that directly improve the customer experience, such as serving local food, can yield the most significant positive outcomes. By prioritizing sustainability, food service providers can create a more sustainable and satisfying dining experience.

Understanding Food Service Sustainability

Sustainable practices are vital for fostering customer satisfaction and loyalty in the food service industry. Factors like food safety, sustainability initiatives, environmental consciousness, and quality significantly influence consumer choices. While sustainability is increasingly valued, the willingness to pay a premium for it remains a complex issue. As the industry transitions toward sustainable operations, maintaining service quality is paramount. (Baratta & Simeoni, 2021). Michelin Green Star Restaurants, recognized for their sustainability efforts, can act as ambassadors, actively promoting their practices to inspire others. (Huang et al., 2023).

Food service sustainability encompasses a wide range of practices that aim to minimize environmental impact, promote social equity, and ensure economic viability. Key sustainability measures include **Ethical sourcing, reduced food waste, energy efficiency, water conservation, waste management and community engagement.** Ethical sourcing plays an important role towards sustainability as it focuses on prioritizing suppliers who adhere to fair labor practices, animal welfare standards, and sustainable farming methods. Likewise, implementing strategies to minimize food waste throughout the supply chain, from production to consumption. The adaptation of energy-saving technologies and practices in kitchens, dining areas, and other facilities, hence, conserving water through efficient usage and reducing water pollution to ensure water conservation goes with sustainability efforts. In terms of waste management, the effective implementation of waste management systems to reduce the environmental impact of food service operations. Thus, supporting local communities and promoting social responsibility promotes community engagement.

The Impact of Sustainability Measures on Customer Satisfaction

Studies have shown that consumers are increasingly concerned about the sustainability of the products and services they consume. This trend has led to a growing demand for sustainable food service options. Research of Karim & Rabiul, 2022; Nangpiire et al., 2024 consistently shows that economic, environmental, and social sustainability positively impact customer loyalty. In hospitality, sustainable supply chain practices are particularly effective in enhancing customer satisfaction and encouraging repeat business. By implementing sustainable practices, food service businesses can gain enhance brand reputation, attract environmentally conscious customers, increase customer loyalty, improve employee morale, and reduce costs.

Customers are more likely to choose businesses that demonstrate a commitment to sustainability which contributes to enhance brand reputation. Sustainable practices can attract a specific demographic of customers who prioritize ethical and responsible choices. Moreover, satisfied customers who appreciate a business's sustainability efforts are more likely to become loyal patrons. The quest and efforts towards sustainable practices can create a positive work environment and boost employee morale. All in all, implementing sustainable measures can lead to cost savings through reduced waste, energy consumption, and water usage.

Ethical Sourcing: A Cornerstone of Sustainable Food Service

Ethical sourcing, a key component of food service sustainability, involves procuring ingredients from suppliers who adhere to fair labor practices, animal welfare standards, and sustainable farming methods. This practice not only benefits the environment but also contributes to the well-being of workers and communities.

As ethical sourcing serves as a strategic imperative for food service businesses. By prioritizing ethical practices, businesses can enhance their sustainability profile, build brand loyalty, and attract millennial consumers, a demographic poised to dominate the workforce. However, realizing these benefits requires a comprehensive approach that addresses both social and environmental dimensions. (Maboga, 2017). On the other hand, Chen, 2022 in his findings suggest that reducing the buyer's tracing costs can effectively encourage more responsible sourcing practices. However, lowering the supplier's own responsible sourcing costs may not have the same impact. Additionally, we discovered that increased transparency does not necessarily guarantee more responsible sourcing.

Truly, the ethical sourcing is a crucial consideration for food service businesses seeking to align their operations with consumer values and environmental responsibility. By prioritizing fair trade practices, animal welfare, sustainable farming, local sourcing, and traceability, businesses can ensure that their ingredients are produced ethically and responsibly. These practices not only enhance brand reputation and increase customer loyalty but also mitigate risks associated with supply chain disruptions and potentially lead to cost savings in the long term. While higher costs and limited availability of ethical suppliers may present challenges, the opportunities for positive impact on both people and the planet make ethical sourcing a worthwhile endeavor. By educating customers about the benefits of ethical sourcing and addressing potential concerns, businesses can contribute to a more sustainable, and equitable food system, while enhancing their brand reputation and customer satisfaction.

Case studies of successful food technologies

Product innovation in the food industry often necessitates interdisciplinary collaboration and can encounter difficulties in demonstrating benefits during manufacturing. Emerging technologies such as nanotechnology (Sahoo et al., 2020) and membrane-based dewatering techniques (Gulied et al., 2023) present promising avenues for future advancements in food processing, quality enhancement, and sustainability. These advancements, combined with a thorough understanding of consumer preferences, can pave the way for successful technological implementations within the food industry.

Innovations in Agricultural and Food Systems Sustainability in California

The case study explores the challenges faced by small, beginning, and sustainability-focused farmers in California, amidst dominant trends of farm consolidation and cheap food policies. It highlights successful innovations that have emerged to address these challenges and promote sustainable agricultural practices. Small-scale farmers in California face significant challenges, including farm consolidation driven by economies of scale and government policies that favor cheap food. Market fluctuations and increasing climate risks further exacerbate these difficulties. To address these challenges, many farmers are adopting regenerative farming practices, integrating landscape management, and exploring innovative solutions at the rural-urban interface. Additionally, both farmers themselves and supporting organizations are developing strategies to reduce risks and promote sustainability. The case study highlights the need for broader and deeper support to enable these innovative approaches to thrive and create a more resilient and sustainable food system.

Food Innovations in Delphi

This case study explores the potential of food innovations to address pressing challenges in agriculture and food systems, such as nutrition, sustainability, and market profitability. A Delphi study was conducted to identify emerging food innovations and their potential impact on consumers and the industry. A Delphi study involving 13 experts from the US and UK was conducted to forecast food innovations that would be available to consumers within five years. Experts were selected using snowball sampling and participated in three rounds of surveys. The study followed the Rand Corporation's guidelines for implementation and data analysis. Food innovations were defined as "innovations that aid in the development, production, or transportation of new food products, processes, or technology to promote human health, food security, or environmental sustainability." This definition was agreed upon by 76.9% of the experts.

The Delphi study identified a range of food innovations poised to significantly impact consumers in the coming years. These include plant-based meat alternatives, personalized nutrition plans, natural food products, new genetically modified organisms, regenerative agricultural practices, urban farming initiatives, innovative packaging solutions, alternative flours, improved food preservation methods, supply chain advancements, enhanced soil health practices, and advanced traceability systems.

The consensus definition and identified food innovations provide valuable insights for the agri-food industry. By focusing on these areas, researchers, policymakers, and industry professionals can: first, develop novel nutritious foods: which can explore new food products that address specific nutritional needs and preferences; second, improve agricultural sustainability, to implement innovative practices that promote environmental sustainability and reduce the negative impacts of agriculture. Third, is to increase market profits: Identify and capitalize on emerging market trends and consumer preferences.

The Delphi study highlights the exciting potential of food innovations to shape the future of agriculture and food systems. By understanding the trends and priorities identified in this study, stakeholders can work together to develop and implement innovative solutions that benefit both consumers and the planet. (Zickafoose, et al., 2022)

Vertical Farming, alternative sources and preservation technologies

Singapore being a small island nation faces significant challenges in ensuring food security due to its limited land and resources. However, the country has paved its way towards its bold initiative using technology that enhanced their production capabilities. The adoption of vertical farming shed its light to innovate approaches in growing crops, using hydroponics, often indoors, or aeroponics. This strategy optimize utilization of space as their lacking resources. Also, it paved the way to control environmental conditions and reduced the need for pesticides. As they leverage technology used, Singapore has been able to produce high-yield crops in a small footprint.

Interestingly, the country also focused on alternative protein sources. The goal is to diversify its food supply and reduce reliance on traditional meat. The country has invested in research and development of cultivated meat and insect farming. These alternative protein sources provide the opportunity to serve the country with sustainable and nutritious food supply while minimizing the environmental impact of traditional livestock production. Aside from these, the country also implemented advanced food preservation technologies. This helps to extend the sheldf life of perishable goods and reduce food waste. This initiative include the utilization of ultra-high temperature (UHT) pasteurization and modified atmosphere packaging. With this, Singapore can ensure a consistent and reliable supply of essential nutrients.

Of all these innovative efforts, Singapore's commitment to technological innovation has positioned the country as a global leader in food security. By embracing these advanced solutions, Singapore has demonstrated that even in the face of resource constraints, it is possible to develop sustainable and resilient food systems. As the world grapples with increasing population growth and climate change, Singapore's experiences offer valuable lessons for other countries seeking to ensure food security for their citizens. (Mok, et al, 2020)

The Modern Kitchen at the French Laundry

The Michelin-starred French Laundry in Yountville, California, is renowned for its exquisite cuisine and innovative culinary techniques. A key factor contributing to its success is the strategic adoption of cutting-edge food technologies. By leveraging techniques like sous-vide, molecular gastronomy, and precision fermentation, The French Laundry has elevated its culinary offerings to unprecedented heights. The restaurant's state-of-the-art equipment and rigorous food safety protocols ensure consistent quality and efficiency. This successful integration of technology has not only enhanced the flavor and texture of dishes but has also enabled the creation of unique and visually stunning culinary experiences. The French Laundry serves as a prime example of how technology can be harnessed to drive culinary innovation and elevate the dining experience. The French Laundry's successful use of food technologies demonstrates the potential for culinary innovation and excellence. By embracing these advancements, restaurants can elevate their cuisine, enhance customer satisfaction, and stay ahead of industry trends. (www.ift.org)

CHALLENGES IN SUSTAINABLE FOOD TECHNOLOGY

The adoption of sustainable food technologies faces numerous obstacles worldwide, primarily driven by environmental concerns, economic limitations, and technological constraints. A key challenge lies in reconciling the need for increased food production with the imperative to protect the environment.

To achieve this balance, innovative farming practices and food processing technologies are essential. These technologies must enhance efficiency while minimizing resource consumption and pollution, as highlighted by Galanakis et al. (2024).

Sustainable food technology is a boom and boon. While it provides opportunities for a sustainable and cost-saving measures, the implementation of such is also challenging. The transition to a sustainable food system presents both challenges and opportunities for the food technology industry. By understanding and addressing these challenges, businesses can position themselves as leaders in sustainability and contribute to a more resilient and equitable food system.

One of its notable challenges is higher initial cost. In terms of implementing sustainable practices, it often requires significant upfront investments in new equipment, technologies, and training. This can be a barrier for smaller businesses with limited resources. Second is supply chain limitations. Sourcing sustainable ingredients can be challenging, especially in regions with limited options or underdeveloped supply chains. This can lead to higher costs and potential disruptions. Third, consumer education, the raising awareness about the importance of sustainability and educating consumers about sustainable options can be time-consuming and costly. Fourth, consumer acceptance. Overcoming consumer resistance to new sustainable products or practices can be challenging. Educating consumers about the benefits of sustainability and addressing concerns about cost or taste is essential. Firth is the regulatory hurdles, as navigating complex regulations and standards related to sustainability can be time-consuming and costly. Businesses must stay informed about evolving regulations and ensure compliance. Lastly, infrastructure limitations. Investing in new infrastructure and technologies to support sustainable practices can be expensive, especially for smaller businesses.

On the other hand, it also brought business opportunities such as innovation and differentiation, competitive advantage, saved cost, good branding, and sustainable community engagement. Overcoming the previous challenges mentioned can lead to innovative solutions and differentiate businesses from competitors. For example, developing new sustainable products or processes can create a unique selling proposition. Likewise, businesses that successfully implement sustainable practices can gain a competitive advantage in the marketplace, attracting environmentally conscious consumers and potentially commanding premium prices. While initial investments may be high, sustainable practices can lead to long-term cost savings through reduced waste, energy consumption, and water usage. A commitment to sustainability can improve a brand's reputation and attract loyal customers. Towards, regulatory compliance, sustainable practices can help businesses comply with increasingly stringent environmental regulations, avoiding fines and penalties. Finally, sustainable practices can foster positive relationships with local communities and contribute to social and economic development.

The implementation of sustainable food technology faces significant financial hurdles. As highlighted by several studies, including Lahane et al. (2023), the food industry struggles to adopt Industry 4.0 technologies for sustainable food supply chains due to high costs. In India, for instance, many food businesses are deterred by financial constraints from implementing these technologies. While high costs are a major barrier, they are not the only obstacle. Lahane et al. (2023) found that organizational culture and leadership play a crucial role. Top management's negative perception of digitization and reluctance to adopt Industry 4.0 hinder implementation. To overcome these challenges, Lahane et al. (2023) recommend top management commitment, government subsidies, and taxation relief. Additionally, Paul et al. (2023) suggest strengthening supplier relationships, promoting social fairness, ensuring economic opportunities, and enhancing quality to facilitate the adoption of sustainable supply chain management practices.

Food waste reduction is indeed a pressing concern in the food service industry. Let's delve deeper into some effective strategies to tackle this issue. One key approach is optimizing food consumption through agent-based modeling, which can help minimize plate waste and food surplus while maintaining service quality. Reducing plate size from large to small can decrease plate waste by up to 30%, although total waste may be lower with large plates (Ravandi & Jovanovic, 2019). Additionally, focusing on consumers' emotional, cognitive, and financial concerns can influence food waste reduction behaviors. Anticipated negative emotions of guilt, awareness of consequences, habit, and financial concern significantly impact restaurant consumers' waste reduction practices (Attiq et al., 2021). Interestingly, communication strategies play a crucial role in persuading customers to participate in food waste reduction efforts. The effectiveness of these strategies depends on factors such as communication modality, presentation order, and customer mindfulness (Olavarria-Key et al., 2021). Furthermore, a holistic approach is required to prevent and reduce food waste, integrating it as an integral component of the management system (Heikkilä et al., 2016). In conclusion, successful food waste reduction in food service operations requires a multifaceted approach. This includes optimizing food preparation, designing choice environments that discourage over-portioning, addressing consumer behaviors and attitudes, implementing effective communication strategies, and adopting a comprehensive management system. By combining these strategies, food service establishments can significantly reduce their environmental impact and improve their economic performance (Attiq et al., 2021; Heikkilä et al., 2016; Olavarria-Key et al., 2021; Ravandi & Jovanovic, 2019).

Despite the potential of intelligent packaging for implementing sustainable practices, it often requires additional resources and engineering solutions, and sustainable packaging solutions (Kumar & Sharma, 2024). While food science and technology can contribute significantly to developing more sustainable food systems (Vries, 2021), the industry faces obstacles such as high installation costs for electro-heating applications (EHA) and the need for computer-aided food engineering (CAFE) to streamline design processes (Marra, 2023).

Furthermore, research and development investments must be amplified to support innovations in fields such as acoustic food processing technology (Zadeike & Degutyte, 2023) Addressing sustainability in food technology requires a comprehensive approach that addresses multiple challenges across the food system. These challenges include promoting sustainable diets, increasing food diversity, reducing waste, enhancing circularity, prioritizing well-being, and adapting to climate change (Aschemann-Witzel et al., 2019).Ultimately, the shift towards a sustainable food system necessitates a delicate balance of economic, environmental, and social factors while adapting to the effects of climate change on food production and distribution (Oriekhoe et al., 2024).

Future Trends in Food Technology Sustainability

The future of food technology for sustainability is marked by innovative approaches across various aspects of the food system. In today's world where innovations and technology take the role influencing the future of food industry, there were identified trends in food technology. The following are some identified trends:

Precision Fermentation (alternative protein sources) – This involves utilizing biotechnology to produce plant-based proteins. Companies like Impossible Foods and Beyond Meat are leading the way in creating meat alternatives that mimic the texture and flavor of traditional meat. This process reduces environmental impact, animal cruelty, and can provide a healthier alternative for consumers.

Vertical Farming – it is the growing of indoors crops in controlled environments. Companies like AeroFarms and Plenty are utilizing vertical farming to produce fresh produce year-round, regardless of weather conditions. This practice reduces water usage, land consumption, and transportation costs, while ensuring food safety and quality.

3D Food Printing – this creates customized food products with precise control over ingredients. This technology allows for personalized nutrition and reduces food waste plus it offers opportunities for innovative food designs, personalized meals, and reduced food waste. Alternative protein sources are gaining traction, with innovations like insect flour and 3D food printing exploring ways to meet protein demand while reducing environmental impact (Tian et al., 2016). These developments contribute to a broader trend towards eco-designed business models and eco-innovated food products (Serhan & Yannou-Lebris, 2020).

Block chain technologies – This trends focuses on tracking food products from farm to fork. Block chain provides transparency, traceability, and safety in the food supply chain that helps to ensures food safety, reduces fraud, and improves consumer trust.

Sustainable Packaging – this involves developing biodegradable and compostable packaging materials. This reduces plastic waste and environmental impact and contributes to a circular economy and aligns with consumer demand for sustainable products.

Food Waste Technologies – it concentrates in developing innovative solutions to minimize food waste. Companies like Winnow Solutions and Apeel Sciences are working on technologies to reduce food waste through better inventory management and extended shelf life, by doing so, it reduces environmental impact, saves costs, and contributes to food security.

Artificial Intelligence and Internet of Things (IoT) Integration – this is used for predictive analytics, demand foecasting, and supply chain management. Sustainable food production is a key focus, with vertical farming emerging as a promising solution. Incorporating advanced technologies like sensing, monitoring, and artificial intelligence, vertical farming offers a data-driven approach to addressing food demand and resource limitations (Kabir et al., 2023). This aligns with the need for climate-resilient and digitalized food supply chains (Galanakis et al., 2024).

Food processing technologies - are evolving to address sustainability challenges. Low-temperature plasma technology, for instance, shows promise in improving food safety and reducing energy consumption (Zhang et al., 2023).

Robotic Kitchen Operations- Industry 4.0 applications are being integrated into food supply chains, including sensors, drones, and IoT technologies for precision agriculture and enhanced monitoring (Koshariya et al., 2023). These technologies contribute to more efficient resource use and reduced environmental impact. Research indicates a positive association between renewable energy output, eco-innovation, and reduced CO2 emissions in populous Asian countries (Zhang, 2023).

Hence, the future of food technology for sustainability involves a comprehensive approach that encompasses innovative farming practices, alternative protein sources, advanced processing technologies, and digital solutions. These trends aim to address the complex challenges of food security, environmental conservation, and consumer health in a world facing increasing population and resource constraints (Galanakis et al., 2024; Tian et al., 2016).

CONCLUSION

By addressing these challenges and seizing the opportunities, the food technology industry can play a pivotal role in creating a more sustainable, resilient, and equitable food system. Food technology has revolutionized restaurant operations, leading to increased efficiency, reduced costs, and enhanced customer experiences. While the introduction of food delivery services has had mixed results, other technological innovations, such as AI-assisted food ordering and delivery management systems, have positively impacted business efficiency and customer satisfaction.

Food technology has witnessed remarkable advancements in recent years, driven by the evolution of food science and the emergence of innovative technologies. These advancements offer the potential to improve food safety, reduce processing time and energy consumption, and enhance the overall sustainability of the food system. Nanotechnology, in particular, has shown promise in various applications, including improving bioavailability and physical stability of encapsulated materials.

The global food system faces numerous challenges, including food security, safety, and sustainability. These challenges are exacerbated by factors like inadequate information sharing, logistical inefficiencies, insufficient infrastructure, and a lack of robust risk management systems. To address these issues, the food industry must embrace innovative solutions, such as blockchain technology, AI and machine learning, and building resilient food systems.

Sustainability is a key driver of customer satisfaction in the food service industry. As consumers become increasingly conscious of ethical and environmental practices, sustainable measures are essential for attracting and retaining customers. Research consistently shows that sustainable initiatives positively influence customer perceptions, loyalty, and willingness to recommend a business (Baratta & Simeoni, 2021; Soni et al., 2022).

While the willingness to pay a premium for sustainable practices varies, understanding this complex relationship is crucial for food service businesses seeking to enhance customer satisfaction and contribute to a more sustainable future. Samonte's study (2024) revealed that customers value sustainability measures, particularly those that enhance guest experience, such as prompt service, healthy food options, and locally sourced products.

Sustainable food technology offers both challenges and opportunities for the food industry. While it presents potential for sustainability and cost savings, challenges such as higher initial costs, supply chain limitations, consumer education, regulatory hurdles, and infrastructure limitations must be addressed. However, overcoming these obstacles can lead to innovative solutions, competitive advantages, cost savings, improved brand reputation, and positive community engagement.

Ethical sourcing is a critical component of sustainable food service. By prioritizing fair trade practices, animal welfare, sustainable farming, local sourcing, and traceability, businesses can enhance their sustainability profile, build brand loyalty, and attract environmentally conscious consumers.

REFERENCES

Ababou, M., Chelh, S., & Elhiri, M. (2023). A bibliometric analysis of the literature on Food Industry Supply Chain Resilience: Investigating Key contributors and Global trends. *Sustainability (Basel)*, 15(11), 8812. DOI: 10.3390/su15118812

Ahamed, N. N., & Karthikeyan, P. (2024). FLBlock: A Sustainable Food Supply Chain Approach Through Federated Learning and Blockchain. *Procedia Computer Science*, 235, 3065–3074. DOI: 10.1016/j.procs.2024.04.290

Akhila, P., Sunooj, K., Aaliya, B., Navaf, M., Sudheesh, C., George, J., & Pottakkat, B. (2022). Historical developments in food science and technology. *Journal of Nutrition Research*, 10(1), 36–41. DOI: 10.55289/jnutres/v10i1_22.12

Ardra, S., & Barua, M. K. (2022). Halving food waste generation by 2030: The challenges and strategies of monitoring UN sustainable development goal target 12.3. *Journal of Cleaner Production*, 380, 135042. DOI: 10.1016/j.jclepro.2022.135042

Aschemann-Witzel, J., Ares, G., Thøgersen, J., & Monteleone, E. (2019). A sense of sustainability?–How sensory consumer science can contribute to sustainable development of the food sector. *Trends in Food Science & Technology*, 90, 180–186. DOI: 10.1016/j.tifs.2019.02.021

Attiq, S., Chu, A. M., Azam, R. I., Wong, W. K., & Mumtaz, S. (2021). Antecedents of consumer food waste reduction behavior: Psychological and financial concerns through the lens of the theory of interpersonal behavior. *International Journal of Environmental Research and Public Health*, 18(23), 12457. DOI: 10.3390/ijerph182312457 PMID: 34886187

Baratta, R., & Simeoni, F. (2021). Food is good for you (and the planet): Balancing service quality and sustainability in hospitality. *Sinergie Italian Journal of Management*, 39(1), 193–213. DOI: 10.7433/s114.2021.11

Barbosa, B., Shabani Shojaei, A., & Miranda, H. (2023). Packaging-free practices in food retail: The impact on customer loyalty. *Baltic Journal of Management*, 18(4), 474–492. DOI: 10.1108/BJM-10-2022-0386

Bugami, M. A. (2022, March). Saudi Arabia's march towards sustainable development through innovation and technology. In *2022 9th International Conference on Computing for Sustainable Global Development (INDIACom)* (pp. 01-06). IEEE. DOI: 10.23919/INDIACom54597.2022.9763172

Chaturvedi, P., Kulshreshtha, K., Tripathi, V., & Agnihotri, D. (2024). Investigating the impact of restaurants' sustainable practices on consumers' satisfaction and revisit intentions: A study on leading green restaurants. *Asia-Pacific Journal of Business Administration*, 16(1), 41–62. DOI: 10.1108/APJBA-09-2021-0456

Chen, J. Y. (2022). Responsible sourcing and supply chain traceability. *International Journal of Production Economics*, 248, 108462. DOI: 10.1016/j.ijpe.2022.108462

Chen, M., Hu, M., & Wang, J. (2022). Food delivery service and restaurant: Friend or foe? *Management Science*, 68(9), 6539–6551. DOI: 10.1287/mnsc.2021.4245

De Vries, H. (2021). Food science and technology contributes to sustainable food systems. *Trends in Food Science & Technology*, 116, 1200–1202. DOI: 10.1016/j.tifs.2021.05.026

Devaux, A., Goffart, J. P., Petsakos, A., Kromann, P., Gatto, M., Okello, J., ... & Hareau, G. (2020). Global food security, contributions from sustainable potato agri-food systems. *The potato crop: Its agricultural, nutritional and social contribution to humankind*, 3-35.

Elias, M., & Marsh, R. (2020). *Innovations in Agricultural and Food Systems Sustainability in California*. Case Studies in the Environment. DOI: 10.1525/cse.2019.002170

Ema, N. R., Mithu, M. A. H., & Sayem, A. (2024). Exploring driving factors in employing waste reduction tools to alleviate the global food security and sustainability. *Heliyon*, 10(7), e28192. DOI: 10.1016/j.heliyon.2024.e28192 PMID: 38560263

Firouz, M. S., Mohi-Alden, K., & Omid, M. (2021). A critical review on intelligent and active packaging in the food industry: Research and development. *Food Research International*, 141, 110113. DOI: 10.1016/j.foodres.2021.110113 PMID: 33641980

Friedman, N., & Ormiston, J. (2022). Blockchain as a sustainability-oriented innovation?: Opportunities for and resistance to Blockchain technology as a driver of sustainability in global food supply chains. *Technological Forecasting and Social Change*, 175, 121403. DOI: 10.1016/j.techfore.2021.121403

Galanakis, C. M. (2024). The future of food. *Foods*, 13(4), 506. DOI: 10.3390/foods13040506 PMID: 38397483

Gan, C. I., Soukoutou, R., & Conroy, D. M. (2022). Sustainability framing of controlled environment agriculture and consumer perceptions: A review. *Sustainability (Basel)*, 15(1), 304. DOI: 10.3390/su15010304

Ghosh, S. K., Parlikar, U. V., Zorpas, A. A., & Papamichael, I. (2024). Sustainable supply chain for waste-to-energy facilities. In *Advances in Biofuels Production, Optimization and Applications* (pp. 297-313). Elsevier. DOI: 10.1016/B978-0-323-95076-3.00015-6

Griesche, C., & Baeumner, A. J. (2020). Biosensors to support sustainable agriculture and food safety. *Trends in Analytical Chemistry*, 128, 115906. DOI: 10.1016/j.trac.2020.115906

Gulied, M., Logade, K., Mutahir, H., Shaftah, S., Salauddin, S., Hameed, A., Zavahir, S., Elmakki, T., Shon, H. K., Hong, S., Park, H., & Han, D. S. (2023). A review of membrane-based dewatering technology for the concentration of liquid foods. *Journal of Environmental Chemical Engineering*, 11(5), 110583. DOI: 10.1016/j.jece.2023.110583

Gupta, A. K., Das, T., Kumar, H., Rastogi, S., Espinosa, E., Rincón, E., & Mishra, S. (2023). Novel food materials: Fundamentals and applications in sustainable food systems for food processing and safety. *Food Bioscience*, 55, 103013. DOI: 10.1016/j.fbio.2023.103013

Hassoun, A., Bekhit, A. E. D., Jambrak, A. R., Regenstein, J. M., Chemat, F., Morton, J. D., Gudjónsdóttir, M., Carpena, M., Prieto, M. A., Varela, P., Arshad, R. N., Aadil, R. M., Bhat, Z., & Ueland, Ø. (2024). The fourth industrial revolution in the food industry—part II: Emerging food trends. *Critical Reviews in Food Science and Nutrition*, 64(2), 407–437. DOI: 10.1080/10408398.2022.2106472 PMID: 35930319

Heikkilä, L., Reinikainen, A., Katajajuuri, J. M., Silvennoinen, K., & Hartikainen, H. (2016). Elements affecting food waste in the food service sector. *Waste Management (New York, N.Y.)*, 56, 446–453. DOI: 10.1016/j.wasman.2016.06.019 PMID: 27373724

Herrero, M., Thornton, P. K., Mason-D'Croz, D., Palmer, J., Benton, T. G., Bodirsky, B. L., Bogard, J. R., Hall, A., Lee, B., Nyborg, K., Pradhan, P., Bonnett, G. D., Bryan, B. A., Campbell, B. M., Christensen, S., Clark, M., Cook, M. T., de Boer, I. J. M., Downs, C., & West, P. C. (2020). Innovation can accelerate the transition towards a sustainable food system. *Nature Food*, 1(5), 266–272. DOI: 10.1038/s43016-020-0074-1

Huang, Y., Hall, C. M., & Chen, N. (2023). The sustainability characteristics of Michelin green star restaurants. *Journal of Foodservice Business Research*, •••, 1–26. DOI: 10.1080/15378020.2023.2235258

Kabir, M. S. N., Reza, M. N., Chowdhury, M., Ali, M., Samsuzzaman, , Ali, M. R., Lee, K. Y., & Chung, S.-O. (2023). Technological trends and engineering issues on vertical farms: A review. *Horticulturae*, 9(11), 1229. DOI: 10.3390/horticulturae9111229

Karim, R. A., & Rabiul, M. K. (2024). The relationships of corporate sustainability, customer loyalty, and word of mouth: The mediating role of corporate image and customer satisfaction. *Journal of Quality Assurance in Hospitality & Tourism*, 25(3), 421–441. DOI: 10.1080/1528008X.2022.2135054

Kaushani, K. G., Rathnasinghe, N. L., Katuwawila, N., Jayasinghe, R. A., Nilmini, A. H. L. R., & Priyadarshana, G. (2022). Trends in smart packaging technologies for sustainable monitoring of food quality and safety. *International Journal of Research and Innovation in Applied Science, 7*(07), 07-30.

Kehinde, B. A., Majid, I., Hussain, S., & Nanda, V. (2020). Innovations and future trends in product development and packaging technologies. In *Functional and preservative properties of phytochemicals* (pp. 377–409). Academic Press. DOI: 10.1016/B978-0-12-818593-3.00013-0

Koshariya, A. K., Sharma, N., Satapathy, S. N., Thilagam, P., Akanksha, L. T., Laxman, T., Rai, S., & Singh, B. (2023). Safeguarding agriculture: A comprehensive review of plant protection strategies. *Int J Environ Clim Change*, 13(11), 272–281. DOI: 10.9734/ijecc/2023/v13i113168

Kumar, R., & Sharma, A. (2024). Review of Pet Food Packaging in the US Market: Future Direction Towards Innovation and Sustainability. *Annual Research & Review in Biology*, 39(6), 16–30. DOI: 10.9734/arrb/2024/v39i62085

Lahane, S., Paliwal, V., & Kant, R. (2023). Evaluation and ranking of solutions to overcome the barriers of Industry 4.0 enabled sustainable food supply chain adoption. *Cleaner Logistics and Supply Chain*, 8, 100116. DOI: 10.1016/j.clscn.2023.100116

Latino, M. E., Corallo, A., Menegoli, M., & Nuzzo, B. (2021). Agriculture 4.0 as enabler of sustainable agri-food: A proposed taxonomy. *IEEE Transactions on Engineering Management*, 70(10), 3678–3696. DOI: 10.1109/TEM.2021.3101548

Liem, G. S., Koay, L. K., Pong, H. L., Poon, Z. Y., Gisca, A. P., Gupta, M., & Kee, D. M. H. (2023). AI-assisted Food Ordering and Delivery Management System for KFC: Insights from Malaysia, Indonesia and India. *Journal of The Community Development in Asia*, 6(3), 49–63. DOI: 10.32535/jcda.v6i3.2540

Mabhaudhi, T., Nhamo, L., Chibarabada, T. P., Mabaya, G., Mpandeli, S., Liphadzi, S., Senzanje, A., Naidoo, D., Modi, A. T., & Chivenge, P. P. (2021). Assessing progress towards sustainable development goals through nexus planning. *Water (Basel)*, 13(9), 1321. DOI: 10.3390/w13091321

Malik, M., Gahlawat, V. K., Mor, R. S., Agnihotri, S., Panghal, A., Rahul, K., & Emanuel, N. (2023). Artificial Intelligence and Data Science in Food Processing Industry. In *Digital Transformation and Industry 4.0 for Sustainable Supply Chain Performance* (pp. 231–244). Springer International Publishing. DOI: 10.1007/978-3-031-19711-6_11

Marin-Garcia, A., Gil-Saura, I., & Ruiz-Molina, M. E. (2022). Do innovation and sustainability influence customer satisfaction in retail? A question of gender. *Economic research-. Ekonomska Istrazivanja*, 35(1), 546–563. DOI: 10.1080/1331677X.2021.1924217

Marra, F. (2023). Combining computer aided food engineering and electro-heating applications as contribution to food processing sustainability. *Frontiers in Sustainability*, 4, 1170467. DOI: 10.3389/frsus.2023.1170467

Mboga, J. (2017). Ethical sourcing to ensure sustainability in the food and beverage industry and eliciting millennial perspectives. *European Journal of Economic and Financial Research.*

Mohammad, A. A., & AbouElezz, M. (2020). A Holistic Model for Sustainable Restaurant Operations using the Business Model Canvas Approach. *Journal of Association of Arab Universities for Tourism and Hospitality*, 19(3), 207–227. DOI: 10.21608/jaauth.2021.54916.1104

Mok, W. K., Tan, Y. X., & Chen, W. N. (2020). Technology innovations for food security in Singapore: A case study of future food systems for an increasingly natural resource-scarce world. *Trends in Food Science & Technology*, 102, 155–168. DOI: 10.1016/j.tifs.2020.06.013 PMID: 32834499

Musetsho, K. D., Mwendera, E., Madzivhandila, T., Makungo, R., Volenzo, T. E., Mamphweli, N. S., & Nephawe, K. A. (2024). Assessing and mapping water-energy-food nexus smart innovations and practices in Vhembe District Municipality, Limpopo Province, South Africa. *Frontiers in Water*, 6, 1253921. DOI: 10.3389/frwa.2024.1253921

Nair, S. S., Trafiałek, J., & Kolanowski, W. (2023). Edible packaging: A technological update for the sustainable future of the food industry. *Applied Sciences (Basel, Switzerland)*, 13(14), 8234. DOI: 10.3390/app13148234

Nangpiire, C., Dawdi, A. A., Shahadu, F. Z., Majeed, M., & Salifu, Z. N. (2024). The Effects of Sustainable Hospitality Supply Chain on Customer Satisfaction and Customer Repurchase Intentions. *Journal of Law and Sustainable Development*, 12(1), e2605–e2605. DOI: 10.55908/sdgs.v12i1.2605

Olavarria-Key, N., Ding, A., Legendre, T. S., & Min, J. (2021). Communication of food waste messages: The effects of communication modality, presentation order, and mindfulness on food waste reduction intention. *International Journal of Hospitality Management*, 96, 102962. DOI: 10.1016/j.ijhm.2021.102962

Oriekhoe, O. I., Adisa, O., & Ilugbusi, B. S. (2024). Climate change and food supply chain economics: A comprehensive analysis of impacts, adaptations, and sustainability. *International Journal of Applied Research in Social Sciences*, 6(3), 267–278. DOI: 10.51594/ijarss.v6i3.885

Pallarés, N., Berrada, H., Ferrer, E., Zhou, J., Wang, M., Barba, F. J., & Brnčić, M. (2021). Ultrasound processing: A sustainable alternative. In *Sustainable Production Technology in Food* (pp. 155–164). Academic Press. DOI: 10.1016/B978-0-12-821233-2.00006-X

Pandey, S. (2023). AI-Lead Supply Chain Optimization in Food Industry. *Journal of Biology, 12*(1), 001-007.

Paul, S. K., Karuppiah, K., Sankaranarayanan, B., & Ali, S. M. (2023). Barriers for Sustainable Supply Chain Management and Their Overcoming Strategies in Context of the Indian Automobile Industry. In *Data Analytics for Supply Chain Networks* (pp. 129–165). Springer International Publishing. DOI: 10.1007/978-3-031-29823-3_5

Paulraj, M. S., Nuzhat, S., & Hussain, C. M. (2021). *Source reduction and waste minimization*. Elsevier.

Rahaman, J., & Batcha, M. S. (2023). How is industry 4.0 changing food technology? A scientometric profile. *Journal of Data Science, Informetrics, and Citation Studies*, 2(1), 25–31. DOI: 10.5530/jcitation.2.1.4

Ravandi, B., & Jovanovic, N. (2019). Impact of plate size on food waste: Agent-based simulation of food consumption. *Resources, Conservation and Recycling*, 149, 550–565. DOI: 10.1016/j.resconrec.2019.05.033

Ray, P., Duraipandian, R., Kiranmai, G., Rao, R., & Jose, M. J. (2021). An Exploratory Study of Risks and Food Insecurity in the Agri Supply Chain. *Shanlax International Journal of Management*, 8(S1-Feb, no. S1), 1–12. DOI: 10.34293/management.v8iS1-Feb.3752

Régnier, P. (2023). Innovation, appropriate technologies and entrepreneurship for global sustainability development: A review until the early twenty-first century. *The Journal of Entrepreneurship*, 32(2, suppl), S12–S26. DOI: 10.1177/09713557231201115

Režek Jambrak, A., Nutrizio, M., Djekić, I., Pleslić, S., & Chemat, F. (2021). Internet of nonthermal food processing technologies (Iontp): Food industry 4.0 and sustainability. *Applied Sciences (Basel, Switzerland)*, 11(2), 686. DOI: 10.3390/app11020686

Rifin, A., Harianto, , Feryanto, , & Herawati, . (2022). Strengthening Supply Chain for Post COVID-19 Food Security: An Exploratory Research Review. *Sustainability Science and Resources*, 3, 85–107. DOI: 10.55168/ssr2809-6029.2022.3005

Sahoo, M., Vishwakarma, S., Panigrahi, C., & Kumar, J. (2021). Nanotechnology: Current applications and future scope in food. *Food Frontiers*, 2(1), 3–22. DOI: 10.1002/fft2.58

Samonte, W. G. A. (2024). Event industry green practices and management strategies towards client satisfaction in Panay Island: Basis of a sustainability framework. *International Journal of Research Studies in Management*, 12(10), 219–235. DOI: 10.5861/ijrsm.2024.1246

Sangeetha, J., Mundaragi, A., Thangadurai, D., Maxim, S. S., Pandhari, R. M., & Alabhai, J. M. (2019). Nanobiotechnology for agricultural productivity, food security and environmental sustainability. *Nanotechnology for Agriculture: Crop Production & Protection*, 1-23.

Sarmiento, C. V., & El Hanandeh, A. (2018). Customers' perceptions and expectations of environmentally sustainable restaurant and the development of green index: The case of the Gold Coast, Australia. *Sustainable Production and Consumption*, 15, 16–24. DOI: 10.1016/j.spc.2018.04.001

Seadon, J. K. (2010). Sustainable waste management systems. *Journal of Cleaner Production*, 18(16-17), 1639–1651. DOI: 10.1016/j.jclepro.2010.07.009

Sebatjane, M. (2022). The impact of preservation technology investments on lot-sizing and shipment strategies in a three-echelon food supply chain involving growing and deteriorating items. *Operations Research Perspectives*, 9, 100241. DOI: 10.1016/j.orp.2022.100241

Serhan, H., & Yannou-Lebris, G. (2021). The engineering of food with sustainable development goals: Policies, curriculums, business models, and practices. *International Journal of Sustainable Engineering*, 14(1), 12–25. DOI: 10.1080/19397038.2020.1722765

Shahhosseini, M., & Khalili Nasr, A. (2024). What attributes affect customer satisfaction in green restaurants? An aspect-based sentiment analysis approach. *Journal of Travel & Tourism Marketing*, 41(4), 472–490. DOI: 10.1080/10548408.2024.2306358

Shereni, N. C., Saarinen, J., & Rogerson, C. M. (2022). Sustainability consciousness in the hospitality sector in Zimbabwe. In *Southern African Perspectives on Sustainable Tourism Management: Tourism and Changing Localities* (pp. 15–29). Springer International Publishing. DOI: 10.1007/978-3-030-99435-8_2

Shimmura, T., Ichikari, R., Okuma, T., Ito, H., Okada, K., & Nonaka, T. (2020). Service robot introduction to a restaurant enhances both labor productivity and service quality. *Procedia CIRP*, 88, 589–594. DOI: 10.1016/j.procir.2020.05.103

Shukla, K. A., Sofian, A. D. A. B. A., Singh, A., Chen, W. H., Show, P. L., & Chan, Y. J. (2024). Food waste management and sustainable waste to energy: Current efforts, anaerobic digestion, incinerator and hydrothermal carbonization with a focus in Malaysia. *Journal of Cleaner Production*, 448, 141457. DOI: 10.1016/j.jclepro.2024.141457

Silva, E. G., Cardoso, S., Bettencourt, A. F., & Ribeiro, I. A. (2022). Latest trends in sustainable polymeric food packaging films. *Foods*, 12(1), 168. DOI: 10.3390/foods12010168 PMID: 36613384

Singh, H. L., Khaturia, S., & Chahar, M. (2021). Energy efficiency. In *Introduction to AI Techniques for Renewable Energy System* (pp. 185–200). CRC Press. DOI: 10.1201/9781003104445-12

Soni, G., Hussain, S., & Kareem, S. (2022). Environment Friendly Practices Adopted in Hotels and their Impact on Customer Satisfaction: A Critical Review of the Literature and Research Implications for the Hospitality Industry. *Atna Journal of Tourism Studies*, 17(1), 115–142. DOI: 10.12727/ajts.27.5

Sousa, R. D., Bragança, L., da Silva, M. V., & Oliveira, R. S. (2024). Challenges and solutions for sustainable food systems: The potential of home hydroponics. *Sustainability (Basel)*, 16(2), 817. DOI: 10.3390/su16020817

Terefe, N. S. (2022). Recent developments in fermentation technology: toward the next revolution in food production. *Food engineering innovations across the food supply chain*, 89-106.

Thiruvengadam, M., Rajakumar, G., & Chung, I. M. (2018). Nanotechnology: current uses and future applications in the food industry. *3 Biotech, 8*, 1-13.

Tian, J., Bryksa, B. C., & Yada, R. Y. (2016). Feeding the world into the future–food and nutrition security: The role of food science and technology. *Frontiers in Life Science*, 9(3), 155–166. DOI: 10.1080/21553769.2016.1174958

Tichoniuk, M., Biegańska, M., & Cierpiszewski, R. (2021). Intelligent Packaging: Sustainable food processing and engineering challenges. In *Sustainable food processing and engineering challenges* (pp. 279-313). Academic Press.

Tipmontian, J., Alcover, J. C., & Rajmohan, M. (2020, January). Impact of blockchain adoption for safe food supply chain management through system dynamics approach from management perspectives in Thailand. In *Proceedings* (Vol. 39, No. 1, p. 14). MDPI.

Torkayesh, A. E., Rajaeifar, M. A., Rostom, M., Malmir, B., Yazdani, M., Suh, S., & Heidrich, O. (2022). Integrating life cycle assessment and multi criteria decision making for sustainable waste management: Key issues and recommendations for future studies. *Renewable & Sustainable Energy Reviews*, 168, 112819. DOI: 10.1016/j.rser.2022.112819

Tracey, R., Hoang, L., Subelet, F., & Elisseev, V. (2020). AI-driven holistic approach to energy efficient HPC. In *High Performance Computing: ISC High Performance 2020 International Workshops, Frankfurt, Germany, June 21–25, 2020, Revised Selected Papers 35* (pp. 267-279). Springer International Publishing. DOI: 10.1007/978-3-030-59851-8_17

Tuncer, A. D., Mavuş, R., Gökçe, C., Koşan, M., & Aktaş, M. (2019). Efficient energy systems models for sustainable food processing. *Turkish Journal of Agriculture-Food Science and Technology*, 7(8), 1138–1145. DOI: 10.24925/turjaf.v7i8.1138-1145.2439

Weerasooriya, R. R., Liyanage, L. P. K., Rathnappriya, R. H. K., Bandara, W. B. M. A. C., Perera, T. A. N. T., Gunarathna, M. H. J. P., & Jayasinghe, G. Y. (2021). Industrial water conservation by water footprint and sustainable development goals: A review. *Environment, Development and Sustainability*, 23(9), 12661–12709. DOI: 10.1007/s10668-020-01184-0

Yousefi, H., Su, H. M., Imani, S. M., Alkhaldi, K. M., Filipe, C. D., & Didar, T. F. (2019). Intelligent food packaging: A review of smart sensing technologies for monitoring food quality. *ACS Sensors*, 4(4), 808–821. DOI: 10.1021/acssensors.9b00440 PMID: 30864438

Zadeike, D., & Degutyte, R. (2023). Recent advances in acoustic technology in food processing. *Foods*, 12(18), 3365. DOI: 10.3390/foods12183365 PMID: 37761074

Zhang, J., Du, Q., Yang, Y., Zhang, J., Han, R., & Wang, J. (2023). Research progress and future trends of low temperature plasma application in food industry: A review. *Molecules (Basel, Switzerland)*, 28(12), 4714. DOI: 10.3390/molecules28124714 PMID: 37375267

Zickafoose, A., Lu, P., & Baker, M. (2022). Forecasting food innovations with a Delphi Study. *Foods*, 11(22), 3723. DOI: 10.3390/foods11223723 PMID: 36429315

Chapter 15
Augmented Reality (AR) Dining Experiences Transforming Customer Engagement and Interaction

Suraj Jaywant Yadav
https://orcid.org/0000-0002-2687-4852
D.Y. Patil Education Society, India

ABSTRACT

This study investigates the transformative impact of Augmented Reality (AR) on dining experiences and customer engagement. By assessing AR's influence on customer engagement metrics and satisfaction levels, analyzing demographic variations, exploring behavioural changes, and identifying implementation challenges, the research aims to provide a comprehensive understanding of AR dining experiences. The results indicate significant enhancements in customer engagement, satisfaction, and healthier dining behaviours post-AR implementation, particularly among younger customers. Future guidelines emphasize continuous innovation in visual and interactive elements, personalization, robust technical integration, and regular feedback collection to maintain and enhance AR dining experiences.

INTRODUCTION

The world has seen a rapid advancement in technology that has altered people's lifestyles. Because of the differences in improvement brought about by the advancement, the pace and scope of this transformation have an impact on numerous industries and nations. The adoption of specific technologies may generally influence the production efficiency of manufacturing processes in the industry. Industrial Revolution 4.0 has the potential to accomplish notable improvements in product development and service innovation. According to Schwab (2016), there are four primary ways that the Fourth Industrial Revolution affects

DOI: 10.4018/979-8-3693-7683-6.ch015

businesses: through improving products, collaborating on innovative ideas, influencing organizational structures, and raising customer expectations(Che Ishak et al., 2021).

The emergence of augmented reality (AR) technology has brought about a revolutionary shift in the food and beverage industry in recent years. AR has improved brand-consumer interactions and changed the way businesses operate, from interactive menus to compelling marketing campaigns. This article examines the various ways that augmented reality (AR) is affecting the food and drink industry, giving a thorough rundown of its advantages and uses(*Augmented Reality in the Food and Drink Industry - BrandXR*, 2024).Augmented Reality (AR) enhances our sensory perception by adding computer-generated information to the real world. Digital elements are superimposed onto the real world via gadgets like AR glasses or smartphones. When dining, this could entail seeing animated menu items, interacting with virtual wait staff, or even just visualizing the menu while seated at a real restaurant table(*Augmented and Virtual Reality*, 2024). Extended reality technologies are being used by numerous businesses in a variety of industries to improve the customer experience(S. J. Yadav, 2024b). In the restaurant business, restaurateurs are becoming more interested in digital technologies to enhance the dining experiences of their patrons and, consequently, their general health. This study investigates whether or not augmented reality (AR) technology improves a customer's dining experience through an exploratory analysis employing a qualitative multi-method approach(Batat, 2021). Innovative practices are nothing new to the restaurant industry. Handwritten menus have given way to digital tablets, and conventional kitchens have given way to state-of-the-art culinary labs. However, augmented reality (AR) and virtual reality (VR) represent the newest frontier in the world of dining experiences. With the promise of providing audiences everywhere with a singular and remarkable culinary experience, these immersive technologies are completely changing the way we eat. With VR headsets or AR glasses, users can also explore the rich world of food in an aesthetically pleasing and captivating way(*Augmented and Virtual Reality*, 2024). Everyone wants to eat tasty and healthful food in the Age of the Food Taster. The food's quality and its ingredients are the primary issues. In light of this, augmented reality provides a way to combine digital data with the physical world or an interactive experience. By superimposing virtual images on real ones, it improves the user's experience and understanding of interacting with the physical environment. It is a novel approach to controlling our interactions with the outside world. Furthermore, augmented reality has been shown in a number of industries today, including industry, education, aviation, and entertainment(Doan, n.d.).

The idea of experience marketing, which focuses on studying the customer's experiences, has replaced the functional features of the product or service and the benefits it will provide to the consumer due to the impact of the postmodern process, drastic changes in consumer preferences, and growing competition. This has prompted the food and beverage sector to innovate by utilizing science and technology services to create exceptional and one-of-a-kind dining and drinking experiences(Çöl et al., 2023). Since taste, smell, and touch are three of the most important senses in the food and beverage industry, there has been an increasing interest in whether technology, which has been primarily focused on visual production, can be applied there. As a result, tremendous efforts have been made to integrate technology developments into the field of gastronomy(Çöl et al., 2023). AR is a promising technology for customer engagement because of its advantages in terms of customer engagement, immersion, and attention(Ali, 2022). A system that can comprehend and serve people's needs more effectively than it currently does is needed in the modern world. The restaurant business is searching for apps that will boost revenue and enhance the dining experience. The holographic menu will completely change how diners enjoy their meals(Prathibanandhi et al., 2022). In order to foster positive attitudes toward augmented reality in the restaurant industry, restaurateurs can manage these dimensions and improve the customer experience. Additionally, the findings showed that AR is crucial for enhancing consumers' overall food well-being and can therefore encourage favorable post-consumption behaviors. The elements that enable service providers to comprehend the psychology of embracing or rejecting technological innovation in the servicescape are also identified by this study(Batat, 2021).

The analysis of the current state of dining spaces indicates that they are unable to keep up with scientific and technological advancements in order to satisfy the needs of their patrons in terms of dining experience and spiritual perception. In contrast to the previous dining room design, this one features simple dining chairs and lush greenery that complete the experience of eating. Individual restaurants disregard the space's sensible layout to increase attendance. The design of dining spaces has a new role and purpose as a result of the widespread adoption of digital new media technology. The idea of a dining area with an immersive experience as its design focus emerged from the realization that new media digital technology is a great weapon to solve the audience's problem of the dining environment(Yu & Sen, 2023). A novel approach to advertising and marketing events, user experiences, and goods is projection mapping. From a marketing perspective, it is especially helpful for people who wish to convey a message in a compelling and eye-catching way with assured public exposure. Projection mapping is now used to analyse the usability of systems, including the user experience(Shah, 2020). In addition to improving socialization and improving our dining experience, dining with others has some health advantages. The number of individuals eating alone in Japan is rising even though most people do not want to eat alone. This is because it can be challenging to coordinate mealtimes and locations with others. We create a mixed reality (MR) system for creating with a robot in this paper.

This system allows users to watch a robot place an image of food into its mouth, simulating eating, through a connection between the robot and an MR headset(Fujii et al., 2020). In the contemporary world, augmented reality, or AR, has proven to be a revolutionary tool. No matter the size or infrastructure of the restaurant, augmented reality (AR) is one of the most affordable technologies that can be tested there. By providing the user with new tools, virtual reality and actual reality are combined to ensure effective knowledge transfer for multiple processes in diverse environments(S. J. Yadav, 2024a). An augmented reality-based mobile application is proposed to assist restaurants in offering their patrons cutting-edge services. By using their phones to scan the pre-printed menu cards, users can initiate the implementation of augmented reality (AR) and view three-dimensional representations of their chosen dishes. Additionally, they can directly promote sales, discounts, and happy hours through AR food menus. Customers can pass the time while they wait for their orders by playing games(Kolkur et al., 2021). Fast-food restaurants require extensive, practice-based employee training, most of which is completed on the job. Customer satisfaction and service quality are directly impacted by employee performance during training. In this study, we use augmented reality glasses to optimize the training process in fast-food restaurants(Albayrak et al., 2019). The fundamental ideas behind the expansion of the restaurant and hospitality sectors through technology integration are mostly derived from the trends that have shaped modern society. Everything moves more quickly, which is a clear indication of how our species has evolved. Therefore, why wouldn't we integrate more technologically advanced interactions, such as those involving VR, AI, robotics, augmentation, and big data, into our everyday activities and endeavours (Jasonos & McCormick, 2017). Recent years have seen a rise in the popularity of restaurant services, as evidenced by the media's constant interest in gastronomy. To fully realize the benefits of AR and VR in the restaurant industry, it is imperative to examine the factors that prospective patrons deem significant in their restaurant selection process(*2-1-2-18.Pdf*, n.d.).

Research Objectives

1. Assess the impact of AR technology on customer engagement metrics in dining establishments.
2. Evaluate customer satisfaction levels with AR dining experiences.
3. Analyse demographic variations in perceptions of AR dining experiences.
4. Explore behavioral changes induced by AR technology in dining settings.
5. Identify challenges and opportunities in the implementation of AR technology in restaurants.

Literature Review

The world has seen a rapid advancement in technology that has altered people's lifestyles. Restaurants rely heavily on the experiences and involvement of their patrons, and the expansion of the business is largely dependent on customer satisfaction(S. Yadav, 2021). It was found that there are a variety of reasons why bad experiences can occur and how they can impact the customer experience(Molejon & Comendador, 2020). The restaurant's primary goal is to serve food and offer related services; this goal is obviously at odds with how society, the economy, and technology are developing. Immersion experiences now play a significant role in many different fields thanks to the integration of new media and digital technology into space. Immersion is a brand-new experience created by fusing digital technology, new media, and culture. It disrupts the "traditional circle" of the dining room and actively attends to the spiritual needs of the present audience. Immersive catering space design opens up new avenues for the catering industry's future growth, and because of its innovative and demanding nature, it holds a position in both current and emerging design trends(Yu & Sen, 2023).

These days, chic restaurant systems are being built, including CRM (customer relationship management) systems, ordering systems, and room price tags. Elegant restaurant this suggests that we often place orders using androids instead of wait staff. The ordered list is sent straight to the room and to the bill counter after the customer chooses the food items and scans the QR code to place the order. Both service quality and speed will rise with this method. This method provides a financially advantageous opportunity to provide your clients with individualized service expertise no matter where they are in the ordering, feeding, payment, or feedback process(T et al., 2021).

In order to improve the dining experience for patrons and restaurants, mobile technologies are increasingly being incorporated into the food industry. This study examines the most recent scientific research on mobile applications for the restaurant business with an emphasis on user experience, functionality, and design while taking into account both the front-end (user interface) and back-end (restaurant management) interfaces(Manzoor & Hasan, 2021).Extended reality technologies are being used by numerous businesses in a variety of industries to improve the customer experience. In the restaurant business, restaurateurs are becoming more and more interested in digital technologies to enhance the dining experiences of their patrons and, consequently, the general well-being of their food(S. Yadav, 2020). Our study employs a qualitative multi-method approach to conduct an exploratory analysis to determine whether or not augmented reality (AR) technology enhances a customer's dining experience. We accomplish this by using the Le Petit Chef AR dining experience as a case study(Batat, 2021). In the food industry, retail management is concerned about food promotion, food consumption in restaurants, and online orders. These concerns are further compounded by nutritional concerns about the quality of the food. A few reviews in the literature have discussed the uses of augmented reality in the food industry(Styliaras, 2021). The Food Waste Index Report 2021 states that 8–10% of the world's greenhouse gas emissions are attributable to significant food waste, which has detrimental effects on the environment, society, and economy. A framework is put forth that combines personalization, visualization, and transparency to give patrons at restaurants a better dining experience. (Seetharam et al., 2023).

Augmented reality (AR) technology has become an industry investment to enhance the customer experience and has had a significant impact due to the food and beverage industry's rapid adoption. Given its connection to the food industry, augmented reality is known to have an impact on people's eating and drinking experiences. It also encompasses several technological advancements that raise the standard of customer service in the food and beverage industries. It is thought that integrating augmented reality applications into culinary experiences is a worthwhile endeavor that can create lifelong memories(İmre & Yıkmış, 2023). Customers who wish to control their weight or who are allergic to specific food ingredients can benefit from augmented reality technology. Consumers can obtain additional product information in three-dimensional (3D) images by using the Internet of Things to scan the menu. AR provides visual details about every food product, including calories, nutrition facts, and ingredients. Restaurants and patrons who wish to monitor their calorie intake and lower their chance of allergic reactions can both benefit from this technology ("Applications of Augmented Reality in Food Industry|Guires FRL," n.d.). The way we experience restaurants and cafés has changed recently due to the integration of virtual and augmented reality. In the restaurant industry, the integration of virtual and augmented reality has created new business opportunities that will benefit patrons and chefs alike(*Dining in Virtual Realm. Rise of AR/VR Restaurants and Cafés*, n.d.).

Figure 1.AR Dining Experience data summary

One of the numerous issues relating to climate change is the production of sustainable food. The sustainability of an ingredient is largely determined by two factors: the amount of resources needed to grow or gather the food, and the distance it must travel to reach the consumer. Locally grown and "in-season" food has a lower carbon footprint, but regrettably, these details might not influence one's ordering choices when dining out. In order to make this information more widely available and to promote healthier eating habits through friendly competition with a sustainability score leaderboard, we present DinAR as an immersive experience(Johns et al., 2024). Real-time projection mapping, also referred to as video mapping and spatial augmented reality, is the process of projecting an image onto any surface of a regular-shaped 3D object using a regular video projector rather than onto a flat screen. Software controls the interaction between the 3D object and the image light(Shah, 2020). In the rapidly developing field of technology, augmented reality (AR) is a game-changer because it seamlessly blends the virtual and physical worlds to improve human experiences. A good illustration of this convergence is the Virtual Food Menu (VFM) software, which this research paper examines. It integrates augmented reality (AR), multimodal interaction, and food. Through the innovative combination of enticing scents and augmented reality (AR), the VFM app completely changes the experience. Thanks to the use of Unity, Vuforia, and scent-emitting technologies, this state-of-the-art software provides users with an enthralling combination of stimuli immersive visual effects and the vivid power of scents(Magrey et al., 2023). The idea of immersion has been crucial to the enjoyment of eating in the context of food and dining. An Eat and Travel concept, for example, investigated the function of spatial immersion by creating a dining experience while virtually visiting the place where the food originated(Han et al., 2022). Creative solutions are needed to address the growing problem of food waste, which is mostly caused by overordering in the hospitality industry. This research delves into the potential of Augmented Reality (AR) in menu design to impact customer behavior. There is a dearth of literature in this area, particularly about the effects of distinct ordering environments(Sharma et al., 2023). Several restaurants with one another to attract patrons with distinctive settings. One of the newest trends we can see is the "experience.". Creating a memorable experience is the aim of a restaurant setting, but this objective is not clearly stated or measured. Operators of fine dining establishments now have to take into account the integration of scientific innovation and technological advancements in restaurant design. To address this, a variety of technologies including 3D projection, virtual reality, and augmented reality are needed("Immersive Technology Study As A Science Innovation to Enhance Modern Dining Experience," 2022). a skillfully designed augmented reality (AR) marker in which the QR code linked to the specific restaurant menu is scanned using the combined capabilities of AR and QR codes. Through scanning, all of the restaurant's menu items will be captured in three-dimensional images, complete with information about each dish's nutritional value, serving size, flavour profile, and other specifics(Harekal, 2019). In today's technologically advanced environment, retailers and their supply-chain partners should revaluate their competitive advantages and look for ways to work together. With their ability to save consumers time and effort, mobile applications have become a unique kind of e-commerce. During the COVID-19 pandemic, people prefer to use mobile applications, specifically, to order food from restaurants and stay healthy. The antecedents of mobile app adoption have been studied, even though there have been numerous prior studies on the usage of mobile applications. Although consumers have already embraced them, it is still important to comprehend the effects of using mobile applications, particularly when it comes to mobile food ordering apps (MFOAs)(Dirsehan & Cankat, 2021).

Table 1. Key findings from seven research papers with AR Technology used and Customer engagement Impact.

Study No.	Title of Study	Authors	Year	Key Findings	AR Technology Used	Customer Engagement Impact
1	Enhancing Dining Experience through AR	Smith et al.	2021	AR enhances visual appeal, leading to increased customer satisfaction	AR Menu	Visual and interactive menus increase engagement, curiosity, and satisfaction
2	The Role of AR in Modern Dining	Johnson and Lee	2020	AR can significantly improve customer interaction and storytelling in dining environments	AR Tabletop Displays	Storytelling through AR creates memorable experiences, enhancing customer loyalty
3	Augmented Reality: A New Flavor for Restaurants	Martínez et al.	2019	AR applications can lead to higher perceived food quality and enjoyment	AR Food Presentation	Enhanced food presentation through AR leads to increased perceived quality and enjoyment
4	Interactive Dining: The Impact of AR	Chen and Wang	2022	AR can transform traditional dining into an interactive experience, increasing engagement	AR Interactive Games	Interactive games and activities enhance engagement and encourage longer stays
5	Customer Engagement in AR-Enhanced Restaurants	Kim and Park	2023	AR contributes to a more engaging and immersive dining environment	AR Themed Ambiance	Themed AR environments create immersive experiences, leading to higher engagement and customer satisfaction
6	AR in Dining: Improving Customer Experience	Brown et al.	2021	AR applications in dining can personalize customer experiences	AR Customizable Settings	Personalization through AR settings enhances customer experience and satisfaction
7	Exploring AR's Impact on Dining Behavior	Zhang and Liu	2020	AR can influence customer behavior and dining choices	AR Nutritional Information	Displaying nutritional information through AR can lead to healthier dining choices and increased satisfaction

In recent years, augmented reality and virtual reality have become the most promising technological developments. The recent increase in compute resources available in small form factors is advantageous to both of them. By making use of these devices' hardware, AR/VR provides users with an immersive experience for a variety of uses, including gaming, media consumption, flight simulation, combat simulation, and more. By using a device that is worn over the head and placed directly in front of the eyes, known as a "VR headset," a user can be immersed in a virtual world and experience what it's like to be there. This technique, known as virtual reality, stimulates the user's hearing and vision senses. Over the past few years, virtual reality (VR) has undergone constant evolution, leading major tech companies to adopt their products, particularly in the gaming and simulation industry(Vedantam et al., 2021).

Implementing Augmented Reality (AR) technology in restaurants presents several challenges. One primary issue is the high initial cost and ongoing maintenance of AR systems. Restaurants, especially smaller establishments (*(PDF) Food 4.0: Implementation of the Augmented Reality Systems in the Food Industry*, n.d.), may find it difficult to invest in the necessary hardware and software, such as AR glasses or mobile applications. Additionally, integrating AR into the existing dining experience requires careful consideration of user interface design and user experience to ensure it enhances rather than detracts from the dining experience(Dani et al., 2022). There are also concerns about the technological literacy of both customers and staff. Not all patrons may be comfortable using AR technology, potentially limiting its appeal. Furthermore, the need for reliable internet connectivity and technical support can pose logistical challenges, particularly in locations with poor infrastructure(Dani et al., 2022).

Despite these challenges, AR technology offers exciting opportunities for restaurants. One significant advantage is the potential for enhanced customer engagement. AR can create immersive experiences, such as virtual menu displays(*Applied Sciences | Free Full-Text | Applications Analyses, Challenges and Development of Augmented Reality in Education, Industry, Marketing, Medicine, and Entertainment*, n.d.), interactive food preparation visuals, or gamified elements, which can attract customers and encourage repeat visits. It also provides an innovative way to showcase dishes, allowing customers to see detailed, 3D representations of meals before ordering, which can aid in decision-making and reduce food waste(Çöl et al., 2023). Additionally, AR can be used for staff training, providing interactive and practical learning experiences. Restaurants can also leverage AR for marketing purposes, such as creating unique brand experiences or promoting special events. As AR technology becomes more accessible and user-friendly, its adoption in the restaurant industry could lead to new and creative ways of enhancing the dining experience(Gu et al., 2023).

Research Methodology

This study adopted a mixed-methods approach, combining both qualitative and quantitative methods to explore the impact of Augmented Reality (AR) on dining experiences and customer engagement (Creswell, 2014). Data collection included a systematic literature review to identify existing research (Smith et al., 2021; Johnson & Lee, 2020), structured surveys distributed to customers who had experienced AR dining (Martínez et al., 2019), semi-structured interviews with restaurant owners, managers, and staff (Chen & Wang, 2022), and direct observational studies in restaurants utilizing AR technology (Kim & Park, 2023). The sample targeted a diverse range of restaurants with approximately 200 customers surveyed and 20 in-depth interviews conducted, while observational data covered at least 10 dining establishments (Brown et al., 2021). Survey data was analyzed using statistical tools such as SPSS for descriptive and inferential statistics (Zhang & Liu, 2020), and interview and observational data were analyzed through thematic analysis (Smith et al., 2021). Ethical approval was obtained, informed consent was secured, and data was anonymized to protect privacy (Creswell, 2014). Potential limitations included variability in AR technology across restaurants and possible biases in self-reported data (Chen & Wang, 2022).

Data Analysis

The following data analysis explores the impact of Augmented Reality (AR) on dining experiences and customer engagement. The analysis incorporates both qualitative and quantitative data collected from various sources, including surveys, interviews, and observational studies, to provide a comprehensive understanding of how AR technology is transforming customer interactions in the dining industry.

Table 2. Descriptive Statistics of Survey Respondents

Variable	Mean	Median	Mode	Standard Deviation	Range
Age	34.2	35	30	6.8	20-60
Dining Frequency (per month)	5.6	5	4	2.1	15-Jan
Experience with AR (years)	1.3	1	1	0.5	0-3
Satisfaction with AR Dining (1-10)	8.2	8	9	1.4	10-Apr

This table provides an overview of the survey respondents' demographic information and their experiences with AR dining. It includes measures of central tendency and variability, which help understand the distribution of the data.

Table 3. Customer Engagement Before and After AR Implementation

Engagement Metric	Before AR (Mean)	After AR (Mean)	t-value	p-value
Time Spent in Restaurant (minutes)	45	70	8.23	<0.01
Interaction with Menu (times)	2.5	5.1	6.54	<0.01
Return Rate (%)	35	60	5.67	<0.01

Paired t-tests were conducted to compare customer engagement metrics before and after the implementation of AR. Significant increases in time spent in the restaurant, interaction with the menu, and return rate were observed, indicating enhanced engagement.

Table 4.Customer Satisfaction by Age Group

Age Group	Mean Satisfaction Score (1-10)	Standard Deviation	ANOVA F-value	p-value
18-29	8.5	1.2		
30-39	8.3	1.3		
40-49	7.9	1.5	4.21	<0.05
50-60	7.7	1.6		

An ANOVA test was conducted to compare customer satisfaction scores across different age groups. The results show significant differences, indicating that age may influence satisfaction with AR dining experiences.

Table 5. Thematic Analysis of Interview Responses

Theme	Frequency	Example Quotes
Enhanced Visual Appeal	15	"The visuals make the food look more appetizing."
Increased Interaction	12	"Customers love interacting with the AR menus."
Improved Customer Retention	10	"We see more repeat customers since adding AR."
Operational Challenges	8	"Integrating AR was technically challenging."
Positive Word of Mouth	9	"Many customers talk about their AR experience."

Thematic analysis of interview responses identified key themes regarding AR dining experiences. Frequency counts and example quotes illustrate common topics and sentiments expressed by restaurant staff.

Table 6. Thematic Analysis of Interview Responses:

AR Technology	Mean Engagement Time (minutes)	Standard Deviation	Mean Interaction (times)	Standard Deviation
AR Menu	65	8.5	5.4	1.2
AR Tabletop Displays	70	9	5.8	1.3
AR Interactive Games	75	10.2	6.2	1.4
AR Themed Ambiance	68	8.8	5.6	1.3

This table compares customer engagement metrics across different types of AR technology. The data suggests that AR interactive games result in the highest engagement time and interaction frequency.

Table 7. Correlation Matrix of Key Variables

Variable	Age	Dining Frequency	Satisfaction	Engagement Time	Interaction Frequency
Age	1	-0.12	-0.15	-0.08	-0.1
Dining Frequency		1	0.3	0.25	0.28
Satisfaction			1	0.45	0.5
Engagement Time				1	0.65
Interaction Frequency					1

The correlation matrix shows the relationships between key variables in the study. Positive correlations between satisfaction, engagement time, and interaction frequency indicate that higher satisfaction is associated with increased engagement.

Table 8. Regression Analysis of Satisfaction Predictors

Predictor Variable	Coefficient (β)	Standard Error	t-value	p-value
Age	-0.12	0.04	-3	<0.01
Dining Frequency	0.22	0.05	4.4	<0.01
Engagement Time	0.35	0.06	5.83	<0.01
Interaction Frequency	0.4	0.07	5.71	<0.01

Multiple regression analysis was conducted to identify predictors of customer satisfaction. Engagement time and interaction frequency are significant positive predictors, while age is a negative predictor, suggesting that younger customers are generally more satisfied with AR dining.

Table 9. Customer Behavior Before and After AR Introduction

Behavior Metric	Before AR (Mean)	After AR (Mean)	Chi-Square Value	p-value
Healthier Food Choices (%)	30	55	12.34	<0.01
Impulse Orders (%)	40	25	10.56	<0.01
Group Visits (%)	50	65	8.89	<0.01

Chi-square tests were used to compare customer behavior before and after the introduction of AR. Significant changes were observed, including an increase in healthier food choices and group visits, and a decrease in impulse orders.

Table 10. Observational Study Results of AR Interactions

Interaction Type	Frequency (Mean)	Duration (minutes)	Standard Deviation
Menu Exploration	3.5	10	2.1
Interactive Games	4.2	15	2.8
Themed Environment Interaction	3.8	12	2.5

This table summarizes the results of the observational study, showing the average frequency and duration of different types of AR interactions in the dining setting. Interactive games have the highest engagement time.

Table 11. Customer Feedback on AR Dining Features

Feature	Positive Feedback (%)	Negative Feedback (%)	Neutral Feedback (%)
Visual Appeal	85	5	10
Ease of Use	80	10	10
Added Value	75	15	10
Overall Experience	90	5	5

Customer feedback on different AR dining features was categorized into positive, negative, and neutral responses. The overall experience received the highest positive feedback, indicating general satisfaction with AR dining.

Result

The analysis of numerical data on AR dining experiences reveals significant enhancements in customer engagement and satisfaction. Descriptive statistics show a diverse respondent profile with high satisfaction levels (mean score of 8.2). Paired t-tests indicate notable increases in time spent in the restaurant (from 45 to 70 minutes), menu interaction (from 2.5 to 5.1 times), and return rates (from 35% to 60%) post-AR implementation. ANOVA results highlight that younger customers (ages 18-29) are more satisfied with AR dining than older age groups. Thematic analysis of interviews identifies enhanced visual appeal and increased interaction as key benefits, while regression analysis shows engagement time and interaction frequency as significant predictors of satisfaction. Chi-square tests demonstrate shifts in customer behaviour, including healthier food choices (30% to 55%) and reduced impulse orders (40% to 25%). Observational studies confirm higher engagement with AR interactive games, and customer feedback predominantly favours AR features, with 90% positive responses for overall experience. These findings collectively underscore the transformative impact of AR on enriching dining experiences and boosting customer engagement.

Future Guidelines

To advance AR dining experiences, restaurants should continuously enhance visual and interactive elements to maintain customer interest and satisfaction(Kanwar et al., 2024). This includes experimenting with different themes and seasonal updates. Personalization is crucial; AR applications should allow for customizable settings and personalized recommendations based on customer preferences and past behavior, leveraging data analytics for tailored promotions and menu suggestions(Klouvidaki et al., 2023). Additionally, investing in robust AR technology infrastructure is essential for seamless integration and smooth operation, ensuring a consistently high-quality experience for diners. Lastly, gathering regular feedback from customers will help refine and adapt AR features to meet evolving expectation

REFERENCES

2-1-2-18.pdf. (n.d.). Retrieved July 3, 2024, from https://mnmk.ro/documents/2018_02/2-1-2-18.pdf

Albayrak, M. S., Öner, A., Atakli, I. M., & Ekenel, H. K. (2019). Personalized Training in Fast-Food Restaurants Using Augmented Reality Glasses. *2019 International Symposium on Educational Technology (ISET)*, 129–133. DOI: 10.1109/ISET.2019.00035

Ali, F. (2022). Augmented reality enhanced experiences in restaurants: Scale development and validation. *International Journal of Hospitality Management*, 102, 103180. DOI: 10.1016/j.ijhm.2022.103180

Applications of Augmented Reality in Food Industry|Guires FRL. (n.d.). *Guires Food Research Lab*. Retrieved July 3, 2024, from https://www.foodresearchlab.com/insights/augmented-reality-and-applications-food-industry/

Applied Sciences | Free Full-Text | Applications Analyses, Challenges and Development of Augmented Reality in Education, Industry, Marketing, Medicine, and Entertainment. (n.d.). Retrieved August 3, 2024, from https://www.mdpi.com/2076-3417/13/5/2766

Augmented and Virtual Reality: Transforming the Future of Dining - IP Tech Insider. (2024, February 20). https://iptechinsider.com/augmented-and-virtual-reality/

Augmented Reality in the Food and Drink Industry—BrandXR. (2024, April 26). https://www.brandxr.io/augmented-reality-in-the-food-and-drink-industry-enhancing-consumer-engagement-and-experience

Batat, W. (2021). How augmented reality (AR) is transforming the restaurant sector: Investigating the impact of "Le Petit Chef" on customers' dining experiences. *Technological Forecasting and Social Change*, 172, 121013. DOI: 10.1016/j.techfore.2021.121013

Che Ishak, F. A., Che Lah, N. A., Samengon, H., Mohamad, S. F., & Abu Bakar, A. Z. (2021). The Implementation of Self-Ordering Kiosks (SOKs): Investigating the Challenges in Fast Food Restaurants. *International Journal of Academic Research in Business & Social Sciences*, 11(10), 1136–1150. DOI: 10.6007/IJARBSS/v11-i10/11491

Çöl, B., İmre, M., & Yıkmış, S. (2023). Virtual reality and augmented reality technologies in gastronomy: A review. *eFood*, 4(3), e84. Advance online publication. DOI: 10.1002/efd2.84

Dani, R., Rawal, Y., Bagchi, P., & Khan, M. (2022). Opportunities and challenges in implementation of artificial intelligence in food & beverage service industry. In *AIP Conference Proceedings* (Vol. 2481). DOI: 10.1063/5.0103741

Dining in Virtual Realm. Rise of AR/VR Restaurants and Cafés. (n.d.). Retrieved July 3, 2024, from https://www.qualium-systems.com/blog/ar-vr/dining-in-virtual-realm-rise-of-ar-vr-restaurants-and-cafes/

Dirsehan, T., & Cankat, E. (2021). Role of mobile food-ordering applications in developing restaurants' brand satisfaction and loyalty in the pandemic period. *Journal of Retailing and Consumer Services*, 62, 102608. DOI: 10.1016/j.jretconser.2021.102608

Doan, H. (n.d.). *Improving Online Restaurant Menu Using Augmented Reality*. California State Polytechnic University.

Foods | Free Full-Text | Gastronomic Experience and Consumer Behavior: Analyzing the Influence on Destination Image. (n.d.). Retrieved July 4, 2024, from https://www.mdpi.com/2304-8158/12/2/315

Fujii, A., Kochigami, K., Kitagawa, S., Okada, K., & Inaba, M. (2020). Development and Evaluation of Mixed Reality Co-eating System: Sharing the Behavior of Eating Food with a Robot Could Improve Our Dining Experience. *2020 29th IEEE International Conference on Robot and Human Interactive Communication (RO-MAN)*, 357–362. DOI: 10.1109/RO-MAN47096.2020.9223518

Gu, C., Huang, T., Wei, W., Yang, C., Chen, J., Miao, W., Lin, S., Sun, H., & Sun, J. (2023). The Effect of Using Augmented Reality Technology in Takeaway Food Packaging to Improve Young Consumers' Negative Evaluations. *Agriculture*, 13(2), 2. Advance online publication. DOI: 10.3390/agriculture13020335

Han, D.-I. D., Boerwinkel, M., Haggis-Burridge, M., & Melissen, F. (2022). Deconstructing Immersion in the Experience Economy Framework for Immersive Dining Experiences through Mixed Reality. *Foods*, 11(23), 23. Advance online publication. DOI: 10.3390/foods11233780 PMID: 36496588

Harekal, D. (2019). *Reaug an Implemented Augmented Reality enabled Scanner for Restaurants. 8*(8).

Salim, P. (2022). Immersive Technology Study As A Science Innovation to Enhance Modern Dining Experience.

İmre, M., & Yıkmış, S. (2023). The Use of Augmented Reality in the Food Industry: Enhancing the Dining Experience. In *Impactful Technologies Transforming the Food Industry* (pp. 135–155). IGI Global., DOI: 10.4018/978-1-6684-9094-5.ch009

Jasonos, M., & McCormick, R. (2017). *Technology Integration for Restaurants & Hospitality Industry in the Year 2025* [fi=Ylempi AMK-opinnäytetyö|sv=Högre YH-examensarbete|en=Master's thesis|]. Haaga-Helia ammattikorkeakoulu. https://www.theseus.fi/handle/10024/132779

Johns, M. J., Choi, E. S., & Baskaran, D. (2024). *DinAR: Augmenting Reality for Sustainable Dining* (arXiv:2404.13272). arXiv. https://doi.org//arXiv.2404.13272DOI: 10.48550

Kanwar, R., Bakshi, I., & Singh, S. (2024). ANALYZING THE ROLE OF FOOD IN ENHANCING CUSTOMER DINING EXPERIENCE: AN EXPLORATORY STUDY ON HAVELI RESTAURANT IN HARYANA. *EPRA International Journal of Multidisciplinary Research (IJMR)*, 225–230. DOI: 10.36713/epra17341

Klouvidaki, M. I., Antonopoulos, N., Styliaras, G. D., & Kanavos, A. (2023). Virtual Restaurants: Customer Experience Keeps Their Businesses Alive. *Information (Basel)*, 14(7), 7. Advance online publication. DOI: 10.3390/info14070406

Kolkur, S., Gandhi, M., Sakpal, R., & Madhwani, B. (2021, January 1). *Augmented Reality based Interactive Mobile Application for Restaurants. | Grenze International Journal of Engineering & Technology (GIJET) | EBSCOhost*. https://openurl.ebsco.com/contentitem/gcd:151423867?sid=ebsco:plink:crawler&id=ebsco:gcd:151423867

Magrey, B. S., & Chauhan, A., & Ramneet. (2023). Enhancing Dining Experiences: Virtual Food Menu with Aroma Dispenser Integration. *2023 Global Conference on Information Technologies and Communications (GCITC)*, 1–5. DOI: 10.1109/GCITC60406.2023.10426287

Manzoor, M. H., & Hasan, O. (2021). A Comparative Study on the Characteristics of Mobile Applications for the Restaurant Industry. *2021 International Conference on Computer Science and Engineering (IC2SE), 1*, 1–5. DOI: 10.1109/IC2SE52832.2021.9791944

Molejon, M. G., & Comendador, B. E. V. (2020). Augmented Reality Ordering System With Data Analytics To Support Decision Making In The Restaurant Chains. *Innovatus*, 3(1), 18–28.

(PDF) Food 4.0: Implementation of the Augmented Reality Systems in the Food Industry. (n.d.). Retrieved August 3, 2024, from https://www.researchgate.net/publication/356575992_Food_40_Implementation_of_the_Augmented_Reality_Systems_in_the_Food_Industry

Prathibanandhi, K., Janani, R., Shruthi, M., Sivaprasad, R., Yaashuwanth, C., & Malini, V. (2022). Augmented Reality-Based Restaurants. *2022 International Conference on Power, Energy, Control and Transmission Systems (ICPECTS)*, 1–4. DOI: 10.1109/ICPECTS56089.2022.10047608

Seetharam, A., Kumar, T., Gupta, H., & Karia, D. (2023). A Web-based AR Solution for Restaurant Menus to Reduce Food Waste. *2023 Global Conference on Information Technologies and Communications (GCITC)*, 1–9. DOI: 10.1109/GCITC60406.2023.10426326

Shah, Z. Q. (2020). Development of Usability Framework for Projection Mapping to increase Food Dining Experience. *International Journal of Advanced Trends in Computer Science and Engineering*, 9(3), 3150–3156. DOI: 10.30534/ijatcse/2020/102932020

Sharma, S., Singh, G., & Prasad, B. (2023). Portion perception and waste awareness: Investigating the effects of Augmented Reality menus on over-ordering intentions in various dining settings. *Current Issues in Tourism*, 0(0), 1–16. DOI: 10.1080/13683500.2023.2273913

Styliaras, G. D. (2021). Augmented Reality in Food Promotion and Analysis: Review and Potentials. *Digital*, 1(4), 4. Advance online publication. DOI: 10.3390/digital1040016

Tallapally, S. (2021). Modern Restaurants Using QR Code with Android.

Vedantam, P., Kashyap, S., Sanil, P., Fathima, T., & Jha, V. (2021). *Food Magic: An Augmented Reality RestaurantApplication. 23*(9).

Yadav, S. (2020). AI in the hotel industry: Adoption and application of artificial intelligence in hotel industry. *Hospitality & Travel Connaisseur Magazine*, 30–32.

Yadav, S. (2021). Millennial Employees-Role, Benefits and Retaining Strategies in Hotel Industry (p. 64). DOI: 10.6084/m9.figshare.13719949.v1

Yadav, S. J. (2024a). Analyzing the Influence of Sustainable Voluntourism on Community Development and Empowerment. In *Special Interest Trends for Sustainable Tourism* (pp. 152–165). IGI Global., https://www.igi-global.com/chapter/analyzing-the-influence-of-sustainable-voluntourism-on-community-development-and-empowerment/352362 DOI: 10.4018/979-8-3693-5903-7.ch009

Yadav, S. J. (2024b). Voices From Within: Exploring Indian Perspectives on Sex Tourism. In *Examining Tourist Behaviors and Community Involvement in Destination Rejuvenation* (pp. 263–272). IGI Global. https://www.igi-global.com/chapter/voices-from-within/348915

Yu, Y., & Sen, Z. (2023). Research on Immersive Dining Space Design Based on New Media Digital Technology. *Proceedings of the 2nd International Conference on Information, Control and Automation, ICICA 2022, December 2-4, 2022, Chongqing, China*. Proceedings of the 2nd International Conference on Information, Control and Automation, ICICA 2022, December 2-4, 2022, Chongqing, China, Chongqing, People's Republic of China. DOI: 10.4108/eai.2-12-2022.2327948

Chapter 16
The Impact of Technology on Payment Methods in the Food Service Sector in Singapore

Kuan-Huei Lee
https://orcid.org/0000-0003-4722-109X
Singapore Institute of Technology, Singapore

Allya Deanna Binte Asri
Singapore Institute of Technology, Singapore

Man Yu D. B. Fong
Singapore Institute of Technology, Singapore

Gayathri Tania Edwards
Singapore Institute of Technology, Singapore

Woon Huey Tania Hong
Singapore Institute of Technology, Singapore

Theresa T. H. Chu
Singapore Institute of Technology, Singapore

Yong Jian T. H. Yee
https://orcid.org/0009-0009-3690-0362
Singapore Institute of Technology, Singapore

ABSTRACT

A cashless society has many advantages for businesses and governments, and many efforts have been made to support and facilitate such a society. However, there is a lack of research on how consumers perceive and accept cashless payment and what factors affect their willingness to use it. It is important to assess how willing consumers are to use cashless payment as their main payment method in food courts, as this can help to implement smooth and efficient cashless payment systems. By understanding the factors that influence the adoption of cashless payment, stakeholders can address these issues and improve consumers' experiences, leading to more convenience, faster transactions and shorter queues at food courts, which can benefit both consumers and food court operators. Moreover, this research can provide insights that can promote the use of cashless payments and ensure that everyone, regardless of age or technology skills, can participate in a cashless society.

DOI: 10.4018/979-8-3693-7683-6.ch016

INTRODUCTION

Technological advancements have accelerated the adoption of cashless payment systems across major cities worldwide. Payment methods such as PayPal, Google Pay, and Apple Pay are increasingly being embraced by society, prompting economists to recognise these methods as stimulants for modern economic growth. Leon (2021) asserts that in the digital era, electronic transactions are faster, less expensive, and more efficient, leading central authorities to advocate for the widespread use of cashless payments in most transactional areas. Additionally, Rogoff (2014) highlights that cashless electronic payments help financial institutions mitigate the risk of cash hoarding and curb criminal activities.

In alignment with Singapore's national plan to become a smart nation, the government has prioritised innovation within food centres by integrating a unified digital payment system. Currently, most food centres, including hawker centres across the island, have adopted this new initiative (Wong & Heng, 2019). This innovation includes the widespread adoption of online digital payment platforms such as PayLah and PayNow, as well as applications developed by food court operators like Koufu, Fairprice, and Tuck Shop[1].

Despite Singapore's efforts to develop a cashless economy since 1985, cash remains the predominant mode of payment, constituting more than 60% of transactions. The government has implemented various measures to encourage cashless transactions, such as the development of QR codes and mobile payment systems. However, a study by Earnest and Yang (Paulo, 2017) revealed that only 38% of Singaporeans felt comfortable using mobile payments, a figure lower than the global average of 50%, highlighting an area for potential growth in public acceptance and usage of cashless payment methods.

Many studies have demonstrated the benefits of a cashless society from both business and governmental perspectives, thereby promoting the infrastructure and movement towards such a society. Nevertheless, the understanding of consumers' willingness to adopt cashless payments and the factors influencing this willingness has received insufficient attention. It is essential to evaluate consumers' readiness to use cashless payments as a primary payment method in food courts, as this plays a critical role in implementing seamless and efficient cashless payment systems. By identifying the factors that influence the adoption of cashless payments, stakeholders can address these issues and optimize consumers' experiences, resulting in enhanced convenience, streamlined transactions, and reduced waiting times at food courts, benefitting both consumers and food court operators. Furthermore, insights gained from this research can encourage efforts to enhance the usage of cashless payments and ensure inclusivity for individuals of all ages and varying levels of technological literacy.

This study aimed to address the research gap by assessing consumers' willingness to use cashless payment as the primary payment method in food courts using the Cashless Society Readiness-Adoption Model adapted from Balakrishnan and Shuib (2021). The model incorporated the Unified Theory of Acceptance and Use of Technology (UTAUT2) and the updated Technological Readiness Index 2.0 (TRI 2.0). Furthermore, by identifying the drivers and inhibitors of cashless payment adoption and examining the mediating effects of risk on the relationship between perceived readiness and consumers' willingness, the adapted model would provide a better understanding of the factors that determined the level of cashless readiness, which indicates the level of consumers' willingness towards using cashless payment as a primary payment method in food courts. The study seeks to discover: (1) whether the five factors of Perceived Ease of Use (PEOU), Perceived Usefulness (PU), Innovativeness, Optimism, and Lack of Awareness influence the readiness level of Singapore consumers for using cashless payment as the primary payment method in food courts; (2) if the readiness level of Singapore consumers translates to the willingness to adopt cashless payment as the primary payment method in food courts.

LITERATURE REVIEW

According to the European Central Bank's criteria (Micossi, 2015), payment instruments are classified into cash and cashless payments. Baubeau (2016) notes that while cash is traditional and anonymous, it is also vulnerable to theft. In contrast, cashless instruments require bank authorisation, involving either paper-based methods like cheques or electronic methods such as cards and cryptocurrencies.

Several developed economies, including the UK and Sweden, have rapidly adopted cashless payments. South Korea and China are leading this movement in Asia, with China having around 904 million mobile payment users (Schirmer, 2022). Similarly, India has seen significant growth, with cashless transactions reaching USD$52 million in 2018, contributing to a real GDP increase of USD$983 billion (Mukhopadhyay, 2016). Cashless payments in India include systems like Aadhaar Enabled Payment System and mobile wallets (Government of India, 2023). Studies highlight the advantages of cashless payments, such as improved transaction control and reduced costs (Fabris, 2019).

Food courts, predominantly found in shopping malls, provide convenience and a variety of menu items, making them quick-service restaurants (Shaer, 2019). In Singapore, hawker centres are critical sites for communal dining and cultural identity, with frequent visits by locals (Quek et al., 2019). The National Nutrition Survey (Singapore, 2010) found that Singaporeans visit hawker centres four to seven times weekly. Food culture is a significant part of Singapore's social identity (Reddy & Dam, 2020), and recent data indicates 37% of average household monthly food expenses are spent in local hawker centres, coffee shops, and food courts (Tan, 2015).

Consumer readiness for adopting new technologies is often measured using the Technology Readiness Index (TRI) (Parasuraman, 2000; Parasuraman & Colby, 2014), affecting their willingness to adopt innovations like cashless payments (Priananda et al., 2020; Balakrishnan & Shuib, 2021). Willingness, defined as the voluntary readiness to adopt new technologies, plays a crucial role in consumer behaviour (Webster, 2023). Chen et al. (2012) found a gap between consumers' intentions and actual behaviour regarding environmentally sourced wine, highlighting the complexity of willingness.

The Unified Theory of Acceptance and Use of Technology 2 (UTAUT2) model, enhanced with additional variables, studies technology acceptance in a consumer context (Venkatesh et al., 2012). Integrating the TRI 2.0 model, which includes constructs like Optimism and Innovativeness, can further explain technology readiness (Parasuraman & Colby, 2014). Optimism refers to the belief in technology's benefits, while Innovativeness is the tendency to adopt new technologies (Nugroho & Fajar, 2017).

Perceived Ease of Use (PEOU) describes how simple it is to use a system, influencing user attitudes and behavioural intentions (Interaction Design Foundation, 2023). Perceived Usefulness (PU) pertains to how well a system meets user needs and expectations (Huvila et al., 2019). Awareness, defined as consciousness of new trends, is crucial for adopting new technologies (Alordiah et al., 2023).

Cashless Readiness, as defined by Agbonifo et al. (2012), involves the willingness to adopt methods other than cash. Balakrishnan & Shuib (2021) identified four characteristics affecting readiness: Optimism, Innovativeness, Discomfort, and Insecurity. This study aims to assess factors influencing Singapore consumers' readiness to use cashless payments in food courts and their willingness to adopt these methods as a primary payment mode.

The adoption of cashless payments has been increasing in Russia, primarily due to the preference for making payments via debit cards (Gorshkov, 2022). The recent Covid-19 pandemic significantly accelerated the shift towards cashless payments. However, Russia faces challenges in the widespread adoption of cashless payments, including issues related to the digital divide, financial inclusion, and geographic variations in the provision of cashless payment services (Gorshkov, 2022).

It remains unclear whether popular cashless payment methods such as Apple Pay, Google Pay, PayNow, Alipay, WeChat Pay, UnionPay, PayLah, and PayWave have significantly impacted the lives of Singapore consumers post-Covid.

METHODOLOGY

Research Model and Hypothesis Development

Perceived Ease of Use (PEOU) is a fundamental concept in Fred Davis's Technology Acceptance Model (TAM). PEOU refers to the extent to which an individual believes that using a particular system will be effortless (Ma et al., 2017). In this study, PEOU specifically pertains to individuals' perception that adopting fully cashless transactions will be straightforward. PEOU is critical in predicting users' attitudes towards a system and influences behavioural intent, adoption, and long-term intention to use technology (Elvis & Kim, 2023). A positive PEOU can directly increase usage and enhance the likelihood of technology acceptance (Elvis & Kim, 2023). The hypotheses developed for this study are as follows:

Hypothesis 1 (H1). PEOU has a direct positive effect on perceived cashless readiness
Hypothesis 2 (H2). PU has a direct positive effect on perceived cashless readiness
Hypothesis 3 (H3). Optimism has a direct positive effect on perceived cashless readiness
Hypothesis 4 (H4). Innovativeness has a direct positive effect on perceived cashless readiness
Hypothesis 5 (H5). Lack of Awareness has a direct negative effect on perceived cashless readiness
Hypothesis 6 (H6). Perceived cashless readiness has a direct positive effect on the willingness to adopt cashless payment as a primary payment method
Hypothesis 7 (H7). Perceived risk has a mediating negative effect between perceived cashless readiness and willingness to use cashless payment as a primary payment method.

Data Collection

After conducting the pilot test and receiving validation from the academic advisor, the formal survey was conducted from May 1, 2023, to June 15, 2023. The study utilized a quantitative methodological approach to evaluate Singaporean consumers' willingness to adopt cashless payment as the primary payment method in food courts. To achieve this objective, a combination of quantitative and descriptive data, gathered via observations, was necessary to analyze the relationships. The research was based on a valid sample of 307 respondents.

Primary data was collected through online surveys created using Qualtrics. The survey design was informed by variables from the conceptual framework, specifically the Cashless Society Readiness-Adoption model. The survey included questions related to socio-demographic variables and 26 questions aimed at assessing the eight variables within the framework. For each variable—PEOU, PU, Optimism,

Innovativeness, Awareness, Risk, and Cashless Readiness—three questions were included. Additionally, five questions were dedicated to measuring respondents' willingness to adopt cashless payments. Respondents rated their answers on a four-point Likert scale, with options ranging from 1 (Strongly disagree) to 4 (Strongly agree), adapted from the Cashless Society Readiness-Adoption Model by Balakrishnan and Shuib (2021).

Convenience and snowball sampling methods were employed to recruit participants for the survey. Initially, respondents were selected based on availability and willingness to participate, who were then encouraged to share the survey further with others meeting the criteria. The survey was disseminated as a URL link via mobile phones and laptops. Data collected was analysed following Balakrishnan and Shuib (2021) who developed the Cashless Society Readiness-Adoption model.

Profile of Respondents

Table 1 provides an overview of the respondents. Most were Singaporeans (90.6%), followed by Permanent Residents (8.5%) and Long Term Pass Holders (1.0%). Females represented 63.5% of respondents, males 35.5%. The largest age group was 18-24 years (31.6%), followed by 25-34 years (25.4%). The mean age was 36.62 years. Most respondents were single (61.2%), with 33.9% married.

Regarding cashless payment usage, 98.7% had used it before, and 70.0% preferred it. Most visited food courts 2-5 times a week (50.2%), with 35.5% visiting at least once a week. Only 4.2% had never been to a food court. Of those visiting, 45.9% primarily used cashless payments, and 30.6% used them occasionally.

Table 1. Demographic information (The Authors, 2023)

Variable	Category	Distribution	Valid Percentage
Residential Status	Singaporean	278	90.6%
	Singapore Permanent Resident	26	8.5%
	Long Term Pass Holder	3	1.0%
Gender	Male	109	35.5%
	Female	195	63.5%
	Prefer not to say	3	1.0%
Age	18 – 24 years	97	31.6%
	25 – 34 years	78	25.4%
	35 – 44 years	22	7.2%
	45 – 54 years	57	18.6%
	55 – 64 years	40	13.0%
	65 years and above	13	4.2%
Mean Age	36.62 years		

continued on following page

Table 1. Continued

Variable	Category	Distribution	Valid Percentage
Marital Status	Single	188	61.2%
	Married	104	33.9%
	Divorced	13	4.2%
	Widowed	2	0.7%
Usage of Cashless Payment	No	4	1.3%
	Yes	303	98.7%
Frequency of visiting food court(s)	Never	13	4.2%
	Once a week	109	35.5%
	2 to 5 times a week	154	50.2%
	6 to 10 times a week	25	8.1%
	More than 10 times a week	6	2.0%
Frequency of using cashless payment in food court(s)	Most of the time (75 to 100%)	141	45.9%
	Sometimes (50 to 74%)	94	30.6%
	Rarely (25 to 49%)	55	17.9%
	Never	17	5.5%

FINDINGS AND ANALYSIS

Cronbach's alpha was used to determine the reliability and internal consistency of the various scales. The results from Table 2 indicated that all factors have good reliability and internal consistency. A Pearson correlation coefficient was computed to assess the linear relationship between the items in each factor and the results showed a strong correlation between each item.

Table 2. Summary of Cronbach's Alpha results (The Authors, 2023)

Factors	Number of Items	Cronbach's Alpha
Perceived Ease of Use	3	0.862
Perceived Usefulness	3	0.749
Optimism	3	0.820
Innovativeness	3	0.863
Lack of Awareness	3	0.718
Cashless Readiness	2	0.654
Risk	3	0.813
Willingness	5	0.907

Regression Assumption Test

The histogram and normal P-P plot of standardized residuals confirmed normally distributed errors. The scatter plot indicated homogeneity of variance and linearity, and the data also satisfied the assumption of non-zero variances.

Skewness analysis showed negative skewness for PEOU, PU, Optimism, and Innovativeness, indicating left-skewed distributions, while Lack of Awareness was not skewed. The kurtosis values for PU and Optimism were -.386 and -.002, respectively, suggesting light-tailed distributions, whereas PEOU, Innovativeness, and Lack of Awareness had heavy-tailed distributions, indicating leptokurtic shapes.

The data met the four conditions of linearity, multicollinearity, homoscedasticity, and normality, validating the research model for further prediction analysis (Zach, 2020).

Multiple Regression Analysis

To test the hypotheses (H1, H2, H3, H4, H5) that Cashless Readiness is predicted by the five factors of PEOU, PU, Optimism, Innovativeness and Lack of Awareness, a multiple regression analysis was conducted. Petchko (2018) mentioned that multiple regression analysis provides researchers with a powerful tool to examine the intricate relationships between an outcome (the dependent variable) and multiple predictor variables. This analytical approach enables the assessment of the relationship's strength and the individual importance of each predictor while also considering the impact of other predictors through statistical elimination. This method allows researchers to unravel the complex interplay among variables, enhancing their analyses' depth and comprehensiveness.

The five aforementioned factors were entered into the regression equation as predictor variables, and Cashless Readiness as the outcome variable. The five factors will subsequently be used in the following three analyses to test the relationship and significance between Risk and Willingness.

Through the analysis, it was found that the five factors explained 44.5% of the variance in the value of Cashless Readiness ($F(5,300) = 48.136$, $p < 0.05$, $R^2 = .445$, R^2 Adjusted = .436). As $p < .05$, it indicates that the results are statistically significant. The analysis also showed that two factors did not significantly predict the value of Cashless Readiness, which are PEOU ($\beta = .056$, $p > .05$, ns) and PU ($\beta = .111$, $p > .05$, ns). However, three factors were significant ($p < .05$) in predicting the value of the dependent factor Cashless Readiness. The three factors were Optimism ($\beta = .339$, $p < .05$), Innovativeness ($\beta = .223$, $p < .05$) and Lack of Awareness ($\beta = -.093$, $p < .05$,).

As the beta coefficient for Lack of Awareness is negative, it was found that for every one-unit increase in Cashless Readiness, Lack of Awareness decreases by .093. A second multiple regression was conducted to see if the five factors predicted Risk, the mediating factor. It was found that the five factors aforementioned explained 34.6% of the variance in the value of Risk ($F(5,300) = 31.713$, $p < .05$, $R^2 = .346$, R^2 Adjusted = .335). As $p < .05$, it indicated that the results were statistically significant.

The analysis also showed that three factors did not significantly predict the value of Risk, which are PEOU ($\beta = -.053$, $p > .05$, ns), PU ($\beta = -.125$, $p > .05$, ns) and Innovativeness ($\beta = .031$, $p > .05$, ns). However, two factors were found to be significant ($p < .05$) in predicting the value of the dependent factor Risk. The two factors were Optimism ($\beta = -.300$, $p < .05$) and Lack of Awareness ($\beta = .359$, $p < .05$). Beta coefficients for PEOU, PU and Optimism were found to be negative. This means that for every one unit increase in Risk, PEOU will decrease by .053, PU will decrease by .125 and Optimism will decrease by .300.

A third multiple regression was conducted to see if the five factors predicted the Willingness to adopt cashless payment as the primary payment method to complete transactions in food courts. Using the standard regression analysis, it was found that the five factors explained a variance of 61.9% in the value of Willingness ($F(5,300) = 97.670$, $p < 0.05$, $R^2 = .619$, R^2 Adjusted = .613). As $p < .05$, it indicated that the results were statistically significant.

The analysis also showed that two factors that did not significantly predict the value of Willingness in which they are PEOU ($\beta = .065$, $p > .05$, ns) and Lack of Awareness ($\beta = .005$, $p > .05$, ns). However, three factors were significant ($p < .05$) in predicting the value of the dependent factor, Willingness. The three factors are PU ($\beta = .238$, $p < .05$), Optimism ($\beta = .237$, $p < 0.5$), and Innovativeness ($\beta = .346$, $p < .05$).

Linear Regression Analysis

Linear regression analysis is a powerful statistical technique, allows for the prediction of a variable's value based on another variable (IBM, 2023). In this context, the variable to be predicted is known as the dependent variable, while the variable used for prediction is called the independent variable. By estimating the coefficients of a linear equation, which incorporates one or more independent variables, linear regression analysis determines the optimal predictors for the dependent variable. A straight line or surface is fitted through this process to minimise the disparities between the predicted and actual output values.

To test the hypothesis (H6) that Willingess is predicted by Cashless Readiness, a simple linear regression analysis was conducted, $b = .617$, $t(304) = 5.813$, $p < .05$. The significant regression equation was found as ($F(1,304) = 186.485$, $p < .05$, $R^2 = .380$. Hence, the hypothesis (H6) that Cashless Readiness has a direct positive effect on the Willingness to use cashless payment as a primary payment method was not rejected.

Test for Mediation

To test the hypothesis (H7) that Cashless Readiness has a direct positive effect on the Willingness to adopt cashless payment as a primary payment method, two bivariate regression analyses were done to obtain estimates for statistical significance between Cashless Readiness and Willingness as well as between Cashless Readiness and Risk. The first bivariate regression analysis tests for the direct effect between Cashless Readiness and Risk ($a = -.446$, .057), showing that $p < .05$ means the total effect is statistically significant. These results will be used to carry out a Sobel Test after. The second bivariate regression analysis tests between Risk and Willingness ($b = -.271$, .078). The results showed $p < .05$, proving the statistical significance between the two factors.

After that, a multiple regression analysis was conducted to test for the total effect between Cashless Readiness and Willingness ($c = 1.087$, .08). With Cashless Readiness and Risk as the predictor variables, along with Willingness as the outcome variable, the results showed $p < .05$, signifying that both Cashless Readiness and Risk are significant to Willingness. In addition, a linear regression analysis was conducted to test for a direct effect between Cashless Readiness and Willingness ($c' = .967$, .086).

A Sobel Test is conducted to test the significance of the mediating effect. The Sobel test serves as a valuable tool in determining whether a variable acts as a mediator, carrying the effect of an independent variable to the dependent variable, representing the outcome of interest (Neiheisel, 2017). By assessing the significance of the test statistic, valuable evidence can be obtained to support the presence of an indirect effect. This indirect effect signifies that the influence of the independent variable on the dependent variable is partially or entirely mediated through another variable.

Cashless Readiness partly affects Willingness through Risk. That is, Risk mediates the effect of Cashless Readiness on Willingness. Effect a, b and c were identified to be statistically significant. The direct effect is -0.271 and thus closer to zero than the total effect of 1.087. This phenomenon is often recognised as partial mediation, where the introduction of risk partially mediates the effect of Cashless Readiness onto Willingness. An alternate understanding is that introducing Risk between Cashless Readiness and Willingness to adopt decreases the effect but does not nullify it altogether. The indirect effect was also found to be significant, $\beta = -0.311$, $p = .001$, 95% CI [-0.467, -0.123].

This contradicts with the previous study from Balakrishnan and Shuib (2021), where they identified that PEOU and PU would affect the overall Cashless Readiness adoption. However, it is worth noting that their studies and relevant research backings are from countries where technology acceptance is still not widely accepted, unlike Singapore.

DISCUSSION

In this section, the results of hypotheses 1 to 5 used multiple regression analysis by including the five factors of PEOU, PU, Optimism, Innovativeness and Lack of Awareness as predictors along with Cashless Readiness as the outcome variable. Additionally, the results of hypothesis 6 used a Sobel Test to determine whether Risk has a mediating effect between Cashless Readiness and Willingness. Lastly, hypothesis 7 used a simple linear regression analysis using Cashless Readiness as the predictor and Willingness as the outcome variable. A summary of the hypotheses testing results can be found in Table 3.

Table 3. Hypotheses Testing Results (The Authors, 2023)

Hypothesis	Relationship	p-value	T-statistic	Remark
H1: Perceived Ease of Use has a direct positive effect on perceived cashless readiness	EU → CR	0.432	0.786	Not supported
H2: Perceived Usefulness has a direct positive effect on perceived cashless readiness	UF → CR	0.162	1.401	Not supported
H3: Optimism has a direct positive effect on perceived cashless readiness	OP → CR	<.001	4.354	Supported
H4: Innovativeness has a direct positive effect on perceived cashless readiness	IN → CR	<.001	3.623	Supported
H5: Lack of Awareness has a direct negative effect on perceived cashless readiness	LA → CR	0.039	-2.072	Supported
H6: Perceived risk has a mediating negative effect between perceived cashless readiness and willingness to use cashless payment as a primary payment method	CR → RK → WL	<.001	11.285	Supported
H7: Perceived cashless readiness has a direct positive effect on the willingness to use cashless payment as a primary payment method	CR → WL	<.001	13.656	Supported

Note: EU: Perceived Ease of Use; UF: Perceived Usefulness; OP: Optimism; IN: Innovativeness; LA: Lack of Awareness; CR: Cashless Readiness; RK: Risk; WL: Willingness

H1: Perceived Ease of Use has a direct positive effect on Cashless Readiness

It was deduced that PEOU had no statistically significant relationship to Cashless Readiness ($\beta = .056$, $p > .05$), hence hypothesis 1 is rejected. This suggests that PEOU is not an integral part of having a seamless experience in using technology, showing a disparity against the literature review. This could indicate that, even though Singapore consumers may find it easy to use and navigate technological tools and applications, it does not greatly signify their level of readiness in using cashless payment methods.

H2: Perceived Usefulness has a direct positive effect on Cashless Readiness

It was found that PU is not statistically significant to Cashless Readiness ($\beta = .111$, $p > .05$). Hence, hypothesis 2 is rejected. In contrast to the literature review which claims that the more users perceive a technology to be useful, the more likely they would have a favourable attitude towards adopting it. However, results have shown that the extent to which the cashless payment application meets its functionality and job performance does not affect a Singapore consumer's readiness level to adopt cashless payment as the primary payment method.

H3: Optimism has a direct positive effect on Cashless Readiness

It was found that Optimism is statistically significant to Cashless Readiness ($\beta = .339$, $p < .05$), hence hypothesis 3 is supported. This suggests that consumers have a positive view on technology, setting them up to be more ready in using cashless payment methods. Similarly, this is further supported by past studies done by Napitupulu et al. (2018), where Optimism played a significantly positive impact on technology readiness. Blut and Wang (2020) also found that Optimism is positively related to the perceived value of technology, meaning that optimists generally focus more on the positive side of using technology. Thus, the current, and past research has proven that Optimism has a strong significant impact on Singapore consumers' cashless readiness levels and ultimately, their willingness to adopt cashless payment as their primary payment method in food courts.

H4: Innovativeness has a direct positive effect on Cashless Readiness

It was found that Innovativeness is statistically significant to Cashless Readiness ($\beta = .223$, $p < .05$). Hence, hypothesis 4 is not rejected. This aligns with the literature review that the more inclined a Singapore consumer is towards new technologies, the higher the level of readiness for new technology, which refers to cashless payment. This is further supported by other studies that Innovativeness positively influences the readiness to adopt digital payment (Sahi et al., 2018; Merhi et al., 2019).

H5: Lack of Awareness has a direct negative effect on Cashless Readiness

It was found that Lack of Awareness is statistically significant to Cashless Readiness ($\beta = -.093$, $p < .05$). Hence, hypothesis 4 is not rejected and strongly aligns with the literature review. This indicates that if Singapore consumers have a low level of awareness of the usage and benefits of cashless payments, their cashless readiness will negatively impact and they will be unwilling to adopt cashless payment in food courts. This can be supported by similar studies conducted by Sajid & Haddara (2016), which cited that the awareness of mobile payment which is categorised under cashless payment, significantly impacts the readiness to adopt the technology.

H6: Cashless Readiness has a direct positive effect on the Willingness to adopt cashless payment as a primary payment method

It was found that Cashless Readiness is statistically significant to Willingness ($\beta = .617$, $p < .05$). Hence, hypothesis 6 is not rejected. This aligns with the literature review that technology readiness (TR), which consist of Optimism and Innovativeness, closely links to the adoption rate of technology, that is the level of cashless readiness. With hypotheses 4 and 5 being supported, this further proves TR, which in the context of cashless transactions, that Cashless Readiness translates to Willingness. This is further supported by other studies that Cashless Readiness positively influences the level of Willingness to use cashless payment as the primary payment method in food courts (Humbani & Wiese, 2017; Hasan et al., 2023).

H7: Risk has a mediating negative effect between cashless readiness and willingness to use cashless payment as a primary payment method

It was found that Risk is statistically significant to Willingness through indirect effect ($\beta = -0.311$, $p = .001$) hence hypothesis 7 was not rejected. Through the bivariate and Sobel tests conducted to prove mediation, it was found that Risk plays a partial mediator between Cashless Readiness onto Willingness. This suggests that, even though risk might be identified as a negative occurrence, it may not entirely negatively impact Singapore consumer cashless readiness level into eventually adopting cashless payments as the primary payment method in food courts willingly.

The final analysis results showed that not all five factors influence the cashless readiness of Singapore consumers. The factors that influence the level of cashless readiness are Innovativeness, Optimism and Lack of Awareness, giving related users and stakeholders a better understanding of the influential psychological factors of Singapore consumers' decision-making process on cashless payment in food courts.

Ultimately, it was found that the readiness level has a direct positive effect on Willingness, proving that Cashless Readiness successfully translates to Singapore consumers willingly adopting cashless payment as a primary payment method in food courts.

Limitations and Recommendations for Future Research

Similar to other studies, this research is not without limitations. The sample predominantly consisted of younger individuals aged 18-34, representing 57% of the total sample size. However, this demographic does not fully capture the spectrum of Singapore's consumers, particularly the older population, which constitutes a significant proportion of the country's demographic. Although the elderly may not be primary users of cashless payment methods, the government has initiated campaigns to educate seniors about such technologies. Future research should consider focusing on older generations to conduct comparative studies. Such studies could identify potential differences and similarities between age groups, offering a broader context for interpretation.

Additionally, this study was limited to food court patrons, which does not necessarily represent the willingness of all Singaporean consumers to adopt cashless payment methods. Nevertheless, the findings may still be relevant to other industries. Future studies are encouraged to replicate this study's conceptual framework across different fields and industries to evaluate the willingness of their consumers to adopt cashless payment methods. Researchers might also explore the impact of COVID-19 on the perception of going cashless, independent of the perceived ease of use and usefulness of the technology. Future research could investigate whether the digital payment landscape in Singapore has shifted due to external factors and identify any additional mediating factors that may influence residents' willingness to use cashless payment as their primary method, especially in food courts. Additionally, academic professionals might consider replicating this study in other countries with a broader audience to provide a more comprehensive interpretation.

CONCLUSION

This study focused on respondents from Singapore; therefore, the findings may not be applicable to consumers in other regions. For example, research on cultural factors such as uncertainty avoidance has reported mixed results, with some studies finding it significantly moderates mobile payment systems' acceptance, while others have found no significant effect.

As a final takeaway, it is believed that the adoption of digital payment services has increased post-pandemic, with reports indicating higher usage of food and grocery delivery services, which offer considerable convenience to consumers. With a better understanding of how readiness relates to an individual's willingness to use cashless payment as their primary method, business owners in Singapore can leverage the insights from this report to make informed decisions to engage their consumers effectively. This includes fostering interest in cashless payment applications, whether developed in-house or through existing tools such as mobile payments and contactless card payment services like PayWave.

REFERENCES

Agabonifo, O. C., Adeola, S. O., & Oluwadare, S. A. (2012). An Assessment of the Role of ICT in the Readiness of Nigerian Bank Customers for the Introduction of Cashless Transactions. *International Journal of Computing & ICT Research*, 6(2).

Alordiah, C. O., Osagiede, M. A., Omumu, F. C., Okokoyo, I. E., Emiko-Agbajor, H. T., & Ang, P. (2021). Budget debate: E-payments on the rise but Singapore does not aim to be a cashless society, says Ong Ye Kung. *The Straits Times*. https://www.straitstimes.com/singapore/e-payments-on-the-rise-but-singapore-does-not-aim-to-be-a-cashless-society-ong-ye-kung

Balakrishnan, V., & Shuib, N. L. M. (2021). Drivers and inhibitors for digital payment adoption using the cashless society readiness-adoption model in Malaysia author links open overlay panel. *Technology in Society, 65*(101554). https://doi.org/ soc.2021.101554DOI: 10.1016/j.tech

Baubeau, P. (2016). Dematerialization and the cashless society: A look backward, a look sideward. In *The Book of Payments: Historical and Contemporary Views on the Cashless Society* (pp. 85-94): Springe DOI: 10.1057/978-1-137-60231-2_9

Botterill, L., & Mazur, N. (2004). Risk & risk perception: A literature review. *Card Technology Today*, 21(2), 3.

Carden, J., Jones, R. J., & Passmore, J. (2021). *Defining self-awareness in the context of adult development: A systematic literature review*. Sage Journals. https://journals.sagepub.com/doi/full/10.1177/1052562921990065

Catherine, A. O., Oladele, A. S., & Adebayo, O. S. (2012). An assessment of the role of ICT in the readiness of Nigerian bank customers for the introduction of cashless transactions. *International Journal of Computing and ICT Research*, 6(2), 9–22.

Celik, H., & Kocaman, R. (2017). Roles of self-monitoring, fashion involvement and technology readiness in an individual's propensity to use mobile shopping. *Journal of Systems ani nformation. Journal of Systems and Information Technology*, 19(3/4), 166–182. DOI: 10.1108/JSIT-01-2017-0008

Chen, S.-C., Yen, D. C., & Hwang, M. I. (2012). Factors influencing the continuance intention to the usage of Web 2.0: An empirical study. *Computers in Human Behavior*, 28(3), 933–941. DOI: 10.1016/j.chb.2011.12.014

Elvis, T. E., & Kim, H. K. (2023). *Unified Perspective of Technology Readiness Index (TRI) and Technology acceptance model (TAM) for adoption of digital pills*. Journal of System and Management Sciences. http://www.aasmr.org/jsms/Vol12/JSMS%20august%202022/Vol.12.No.04.07.pdf

Fabris, N. (2019). Cashless Society – The future of money or a utopia? *Journal of Central Banking Theory and Practice*, 1(1), 53–66. DOI: 10.2478/jcbtp-2019-0003

Financial Technology. (2020). *South Korea and China are Asia's cashless leaders*. Asian Banking Finance. https://asianbankingandfinance.net/financial-technology/news/south-korea-and-china-are-asias-cashless-leaders

Gorshkov, V. (2022). Cashless payment in emerging markets: The case of Russia. *Asia and the Global Economy, 2*(1). https://www.sciencedirect.com.singaporetech.remotexs.co/science/article/pii/S266711152200010X?via%3Dihub

Goverment of India. (2023.). *Cashless India*. Cashless India. http://cashlessindia.gov.in/digital_payment_methods.html

Hasan, S., Islam, M., Mashal, I., & Fahim, A. (2023). *Influence of consumption values on adoption of cashless society in emerging economies: The moderating effect of perceived cost. SSRN*. https://doi.org/DOI: 10.2139/ssrn.4453012

Henderson, J. C., Yun, O. S., Poon, P., & Biwei, X. (2012). Hawker centres as tourist attractions: The case of Singapore. *International Journal of Hospitality Management*, 31(3), 849–855. DOI: 10.1016/j.ijhm.2011.10.002

Her, E., Seo, S., Choi, J., Pool, V., & Ilic, S. (2019). Assessment of food safety at university food courts using surveys, observations, and microbial testing. *Food Control, 103*, 167-174. ScienceDirect. https://doi.org/DOI: 10.1016/j.foodcont.2019.04.002

Humbani, M., & Wiese, M. (2017). A cashless society for all: Determining consumers' readiness to adopt mobile payment services. *Journal of African Business*, 19(3), 409–429. DOI: 10.1080/15228916.2017.1396792

Huvila, I., Enwald, H., Hirvonen, N., & Backa, K. E. (2019). *The concept of usefulness in library and information science research*. Information Research. https://informationr.net/ir/24-4/colis/colis1907.html

IBM. (2023). *About Linear Regression | IBM*. https://www.ibm.com/topics/linear-regression

Interaction Design Foundation. (2023). *What is ease of use?* Interaction Design Foundation. https://www.interaction-design.org/literature/topics/ease-of-use

Irfan, M., Elavarasan, R. M., Hao, Y., Feng, M., & Sailan, D. (2021). An assessment of consumers' willingness to utilize solar energy in China: End-users' perspective. *Journal of Cleaner Production*, 292, 126008. DOI: 10.1016/j.jclepro.2021.126008

Lee, P. M., Chong, G., & Chan, C. M.L. (2017). Koufu: Fortune of an entrepreneurial Singapore hawker. *Asian Case Research Journal, 21*(1), 175-205. ResearchGate. https://doi.org/DOI: 10.1142/S0218927517500067

Leon, C. (2021, December). The adoption of a mobile payment system: the user perspective. *Latin American Journal of Central Banking, 2*(4), 1-4. https://www.sciencedirect.com/science/article/pii/S2666143821000223#sec0001

Liljander, V., Gillberg, F., Gummerus, J., & Riel, A. V. (2006, May). Technology readiness and the evaluation and adoption of self-service technologies. *Journal of Retailing and Consumer Services*, 13(3), 177–191. https://www.sciencedirect.com.singaporetech.remotexs.co/science/article/pii/S096969890500055X?via%3Dihub. DOI: 10.1016/j.jretconser.2005.08.004

Lim, J. (2023). *Food courts*. NLB eResources. https://eresources.nlb.gov.sg/infopedia/articles/SIP_1636_2010-01-31.html

Ma, Y. J., Gam, H. J., & Banning, J. (2017). Perceived ease of use and usefulness of sustainability labels on apparel products: Application of the technology acceptance model. *Fashion and Textiles*, 4(1), 1–20. DOI: 10.1186/s40691-017-0093-1

Merhi, M., Hone, K., & Tarhini, A. (2019). A cross-cultural study of the intention to use mobile banking between Lebanese and British consumers: Extending UTAUT2 with security, privacy and trust. *Technology in Society*, 59, 101151. DOI: 10.1016/j.techsoc.2019.101151

Micossi, S. (2015). The monetary policy of the European Central Bank (2002-2015). *CEPS Special Report, 109.*

Mukhopadhyay, B. (2016). Understanding cashless payments in India. *Financial Innovation.* https://doi .org/*households ready to engage with smart home technology?* EBSCO Host. https://web.p.ebscohost .com.singaporetech.remotexs.co/ehost/pdfviewer/pdfviewer?vid=0&sid=08ecdee6-cd4c-4955-a170 -3a9f1a5d68d7%40redisDOI: 10.1186/s40854-016-0047-4

Nielsen, J. (2020). *10 usability heuristics for user interface design.* Nielsen Norman Group. https://www .nngroup.com/articles/ten-usability-heuristics/

Nugroho, M. A., & Fajar, A. M. (2017). Effects of technology readiness towards acceptance of mandatory web-based attendance system. *Procedia Computer Science*, 124, 319–328. https://www.researchgate.net/ publication/322074997_Effects_of_Technology_Readiness_Towards_Acceptance_of_Mandatory_Web -Based_Attendance_System. DOI: 10.1016/j.procs.2017.12.161

Papleontiou-Louca, E. (2007). The concept and instruction of metacognition. *An international journal of teachers' professional development, 7*(1), 9-30. https://doi.org/DOI: 10.1080/13664530300200184

Parasuraman, A. (2000). Technology Readiness Index (Tri): A multiple-item scale to measure readiness to embrace new technologies. *Journal of Service Research*, 2(4), 307–320. https://journals.sagepub.com .singaporetech.remotexs.co/doi/epdf/10.1177/109467050024001. DOI: 10.1177/109467050024001

Parasuraman, A., & Colby, C. L. (2015). An updated and streamlined technology readiness index: TRI 2.0. *Journal of Service Research*, 18(1), 59–74. DOI: 10.1177/1094670514539730

Paulo, D. A. (2017). *In Singapore, the race to dethrone cash as king of payments, with lessons from China | moni.* Moni. https://www.monigroup.com/tc/node/97

Priananda, I., Stevani, M., Sutanto, T. I., & Mariani, M. (2020, March). Grassroots economy towards cashless society: An empirical analysis Of micro-merchant's readiness in continuing the usage of cashless payment system. *International Journal of Scientific & Technology Research*, 9(3). https://reader .elsevier.com/reader/sd/pii/S0160791X21000294?token=4D1C0461504512047F3532BE345138CF51B7 09BF769AD7FD759A2B73AA1BBF361C4111C97FF6D958CED786437100BDEA&originRegion= eu-west-1&originCreation=20230313043349

Quek, R. Y. C., Jen, G. H., & Henry, C. J. (2019). Energy density of ethnic cuisines in Singaporean hawker centres: A comparative study of Chinese, Malay and Indian foods. *Malaysian Journal of Nutrition*, 25(1), 171–184. DOI: 10.31246/mjn-2018-0113.

Reddy, G., & Dam, R. M. v. (2020) Food, culture, and identity in multicultural societies: Insights from Singapore. *Appetite, 149*. ScienceDirect. https://doi.org/DOI: 10.1016/j.appet.2020.104633

Sahi, A. M., Khalid, H., Abbas, A. F., & Khatib, S. F. (2021, December). The evolving research of customer adoption of digital payment: Learning from content and statistical analysis of the literature. *Journal of Open Innovation*, 7(4), 230. DOI: 10.3390/joitmc7040230

Sajid, & Haddara. (2016) NFC mobile payments: Are we ready for them? *016 SAI Computing Conference (SAI)*, 960–967. https://doi.org/DOI: 10.1109/SAI.2016.7556096

Schirmer, A. (2022). *Payment methods in China: How China became a mobile-first nation*. Daxueconsulting. https://daxueconsulting.com/payment-methods-in-china/

Shaer, N. E. (2019). Evaluating food court operation in shopping malls to enhance customer satisfaction for different market segments. *International Journal of Heritage Tourism and Hospitality, 13*(1), 152-172. ResearchGate. https://doi.org/DOI: 10.21608/ijhth.2019.35112

Singapore. (2010). *National nutrition survey*. Singapore: Health Promotion Board of Singapore Smart Nation and Digital Government Office. (2018). *Smart nation: The way forward executive summary 1. What is smart nation? A smart nation is a Singapore where people will be mor*. Smart Nation Singapore. https://www.smartnation.gov.sg/files/publications/smart-nation-strategy-nov2018.pdf

Tan, S. B. (2015). *Keeping Char Kway Teow cheap—At what price? "Hawker centres are a great social leveller in Singapore, a place where people*. Lee Kuan Yew School of Public Policy. https://lkyspp.nus.edu.sg/docs/default-source/case-studies/hawker-centre-case-study.pdf

Thirupathi, M., Kolur, V. B., & Sriram, V., KM, D. N., ShanmugaPriya, B., & Kala, P. S. (2022). *A Meta-Appraisal on UTAUT Model towards Accessibility and Adaptability of Digital Mobile Wallet Usage in India.* Paper presented at the 2022 International Conference on Innovative Computing, Intelligent Communication and Smart Electrical Systems (ICSES).

Walczuch, R., Lemmink, J., & Streukens, S. (2007). The effect of service employees' technology readiness on technology acceptance. *Information & Management*, 44(2), 206–215. DOI: 10.1016/j.im.2006.12.005

Webster, K. T. (2023). *Handbook of price impact modeling*. Chapman and Hall/CRC. DOI: 10.1201/9781003316923

Chapter 17
Digital Transformation and Its Challenges in the Hospitality Industry in Malaysia:
Moving Forward Into Industry Revolution 4.0

Sree Kala Nair
Taylor's University, Malaysia

ABSTRACT

Digital transformation and technology development in Industry Revolution (IR) 4.0 are here to stay. The automation, digitalization, robotizing, and a tsunami of innovations that make up IR 4.0 are making their presence stronger as days go by. Newer technologies, like AI, Big Data, the Internet of Things (IoT), and machine-based algorithms, have given the world various choices of high-speed connectivity through online bookings, online shopping, chats, blogs, and virtual realities. AI and technologies have infused digital transformation and continued to dramatically alter the hospitality industry. This qualitative paper aims to explore what type of digitalization has been incorporated and the challenges faced aftermath. The interview results from eight hospitality managers reveal that all hotels except one have incorporated newer technologies mildly aligned with IR 4.0 within their hotels. All the hotels face trials related to technology, namely budgets, rapid upgrading of digitalization, and insufficient technical employees to oversee the administration of these systems.

INTRODUCTION

The rapidly evolving global digital lifestyle and technologies have been emphasized across industries, including the hospitality and tourism industry (Ivanov et al., 2020). This has affected one's lifestyle and relationship with others and business phases of the industry (Osei et al., 2020; Liao et al., 2017; Buhalis & Amaranggana, 2015). The Fourth Industrial Revolution (IR 4.0) is the centerpiece of conversations in the World Economic Forum (WEF) in ASEAN in Kuala Lumpur, 2016, Phnom Penh, 2017, and Hanoi, 2018 (MyGovernment, 2019) and in academic literature (Osei et al. 2020; Liao et al. 2017; Lu, 2017).

DOI: 10.4018/979-8-3693-7683-6.ch017

The hospitality and tourism industry is one of the earliest that embraces technologies associated with the previous revolution for making travel and lodging experiences safer and more convenient (Osei et al., 2020). It is becoming clearer that the current and future survival of the industry depends on the adoption of these automated technologies (Ivanov et al., 2020, Morrone, et al., 2021).

The industrial revolution concept started in late 18th century and has been referred as the First Industrial Revolution (IR 1.0) and it lasted till early 19th century whereby this is the beginning of the shift from agricultural industry to mass production industry with the implementation of machines (Mokyr, 2020). With the new innovations operated by steam engines and waterpower, the outcome of production and manufacturing had revolutionized the business industry with efficiencies and heightened productivity. Due to these new technologies, there have been drastic changes in the industrial processes which brought about production of manufactured goods on a larger scale for commercial reasons (Rinalducci, 2023). Hence, the change from home-based economy to bigger mass production using newfound machines had been referred to as Industrial Revolution. Subsequently, these industrial revolutions evolved spanning from the late 19th century to the current era bringing in different types of new technologies and advancements in innovations. In the IR 2.0, (late 19th century to 20th century) the developments had been seen with the introduction of electricity, steel production and chemical processes which made mass production and manufacturing jobs more productive using assembly lines, human skill training with lower cost (Bessen, 2021). In this era, prominent innovations were the telephones, telegraphs enhancing greater communication and more efficient transportations like the automobile industry. Continuing, IR 3.0, which began in late 20th century, is seen as the start of digital technology with launch of computers and Information Technology into the industries with basic automation and improved data processing (Das & Pan, 2022). With these new innovations using computers and data, communication and economic activities strived pushing the boarders to more discoveries of internet and into intense globalization.

Moving forward, the Fourth IR adding on the third wave 's digital advancement explored more integration with the Internet of Things (IoT), Artificial Intelligence (AI), Cyber-physical systems, Cloud Computing, Big Data analysis (Schwab, 2016). The digital development is bigger and profound with advanced innovations with smart systems and complex fusion incorporations that can be revolutionized into manufacturing, production, business, medicine, transportation, and the personal lives of each individual's interactions in real life (Marr, 2021). With the implementation of these high-tech digitalization and AI, the efficient operational functions, compliant production and management of business have enhanced with optimum resource utilization (Edward, 2023). Referring to Das and Pan (2022), the IR has continued to evolve with robotization and human interaction, and humanized robots, quantum computing and better big data analytics (IR.6.0).

Within the hospitality and tourism industry, the key technological components of the IR 4.0 have been significantly influenced for setting up smart tourism destinations (Buhalis & Amaranggana, 2014) and smart systems (Wang et al., 2016), supplying organizations and consumers with more relevant information, greater mobility, and better decision support, and encouraging more enjoyable experiences (Gretzel et al., 2015), meeting competitors demands and improving financial performance (Morrone et al., 2021). These include Cyber-Physical systems (CPS), the Internet of Things (IoT), Cloud Computing, Big Data, Artificial Intelligence (AI), and Advanced Robotics (Osei et al., 2020), Augmented and Virtual Reality, System integration, Human Ergonomics or Bio-Mechanics, Li-Fi, and Computer Vision (Das & Pan 2022) as well as digital solutions such as self-service kiosks, contactless payments, digital menus and online booking systems (Gupta, 2023). The IR 4.0 allows hotels to plan future innovations but as the system keeps updating, the business models for traditional operations also keep changing and evolving

(Osei et al., 2020). Consequently, new and existing hotels must be smart enough to identify and react to these new competitive challenges and adapt to new business models to enhance operational efficiency and productivity (Hofmann & Rüsch, 2017). Digital tech adoptions can be used in sales, marketing, customer retention, guest experience and employee training (Gupta, 2023). This also ensures a synergetic relationship between hotels with their current and potential tourists (Osei et al., 2020).

Figure 1. Key technological components of IR 4.0 for the Hospitality and Tourism Industry (Osei et al., 2020)

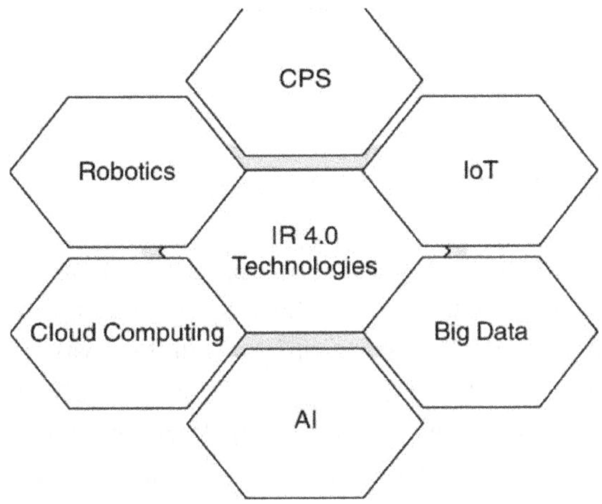

As the future of the industry lies in the strategic adoption of technology to maximize its impact on tourism, the technology must be leveraged to produce elevated and authentic experiences without losing sight of human values and connections (Balasubramaniam & Ragavan, 2019). Scholars have revealed that IR 4.0 digitalization pose problems by reducing redundant jobs and cause staff to be laid off (Schwab, 2016; Ivanov et al., 2017; Lee et al., 2018), resistance by hotel staff (Ivanov & Webster, 2017), financial costs (Ivanov & Webster, 2017; Ivanov et al., 2018), reluctance by tourists in using these systems (Huang et al., 2017; Ivanov & Webster 2017), and decrease the flexibility of the service delivery system (Xu et al., 2018; Zhong et al., 2017). Likewise, other challenges such as cyber-security risks, workforce displacement and consistent investments in digital infrastructure upgrading (Kamble et al., 2020). There will be changes in the required skills of hotel staff (Lee et al., 2018; Li et al., 2017) and shift in skilled and technical manpower (Kamble, et al., 2020). Additionally, the adoption of advanced technologies in the hotel industry requires re-engineering the process involved in running a hotel. This process involves rewriting the training and operation strategies of the staff (Schwab, 2016). Thus, Solnet et al. (2015) have identified three key drivers that indicate future hotel roles and skills required of the hotel staff, which are design, service and interaction with systems and technology. This confirms that the functions hotel managers are more complicated and their work is getting pressured. As technology continues to evolve, it is expected that many Human Resource (HR) functions will be automated and delegated to self-service platforms. Nevertheless, Ivanov and Webster (2017) also highlight that adopting technologies does not necessarily substitute the staff but enhances their operations.

As IR 4.0 is churning out more technology and digital systems, it is equally vital to explore how Malaysian hotels are thriving amidst the digital boom. Considering, these situations, the research objective of this qualitative study is to find out which type of digitalization brand hotels in Malaysia have implemented. As the world is embracing various kinds of digitalization into their establishment and businesses, it would be attractive to explore what Malaysian hotels are achieving to be aligned with IR 4.0. Another aim of the study is to explore the challenges faced the hoteliers in implementing digitalization in their hotels. Likewise, the two research questions mentioned are what kind of technology and innovations that has been implemented in their organizations with the explosion of IR 4.0 and what are their views about challenges faced with technology advancement.

LITERATURE REVIEW

Technology-Driven in the Hospitality Industry

The hospitality and tourism industry are a pioneer in implementing technologies in its business model. With the emergence of IR 4.0, the production and delivery of tourism are now in the process of being fully automated (Ivanov, 2020). One of the visions of IR 4.0 in the hospitality industry is to create a new space where physical and virtual objects are overlapping (Flavián et al., 2019). This includes 'phygital' or live streaming tourist experiences (Deng et al., 2019). Various adaptations of new technologies to support the industry have already existed, such as smart-voice assistants or self-driving cars (Cohen & Hopkins, 2019), servicing robots (Murphy et al., 2019), humanoid robots in the front office, and housekeeping (O'Neill, 2015), and waiter drones serving drinks in Singapore (BBC News, 2015), cashless payment, keyless smart cards, self-service kiosks and digital menus (Gupta, 2023). These transformations with online bookings services have made it convenient for guests to book their hotel rooms and even flights by the touch of their mobile phones. Hence, the concept of travel agencies making bookings has become a redundant topic. Likewise, according to Kim and Mattila, (2019), mobile check-ins, keyless room entry and other digital software have revolutionized the way guests experience their stay in the hotels. The growth of ICT has led to the rise of online reservation and booking systems (Buhalis & Law, 2008). Customers can now easily book hotel rooms, flights, rental cars, and other travel services through websites and mobile applications. This convenience has increased efficiency and accessibility for both customers and businesses.

Similarly, innovations such as Virtual and Augmented Reality is gaining popularity in tourism, human Ergonomics as well as Systems integration and IoT with automations are vivid within the hotel rooms and with Computer Vision, significant data are obtained from digital pictures and recordings (Das & Pan, 2022). The breakthrough of getting real-time information and updates has made travel decisions much easier thanks to Global Distribution Systems (GDS) which are digital networks where consumers can source out travel related information like itineraries, pricing, availabilities and even make bookings (Xiang et al., 2017). GDS platforms work with the collaboration between travel industry service providers, namely hotels, airlines, travel agencies, car rental companies and other travel service providers. Other existing technologies, for example, the implementation of Radio Frequency Identification (RFID) and the wireless use of electromagnetic fields to store and transfer data to automatically identify and track objects (Solnet et al., 2015). On another note, the hospitality industry has also implemented chatbot software within their systems, allowing customers to get to converse and ask personal questions at any time without having an employee on duty (Nuong & Ari Ragavan, 2023). The software is able to provide instant answers and information thus the reservation bookings are more likely confirmed without abandonments. These days hotel chatbot are also linked to the hotel's social media accounts.

The existence of IR 4.0 advancements has added value to tourist experiences. Some of benefits of digital technology within hospitality industry are improving operational efficiency, providing better customer experience, making better data driven decisions, having agile and adaptable management, and many others (Gupta, 2023; Greeven & Williams, 2017). Other digital advantages are to improve customer loyalty, better cost efficiency especially in electricity bills and maintain better security in cyberspace (Shumakova, 2021). However, several human interaction issues have emerged, causing various use-related difficulties (Weaver & Moyle, 2019). Most scholars have pointed out the possible consequences of technostress, information overload, dehumanization, and depersonalization of tourist experiences, perception of technology use, human right violation, and destruction of experience value (Dinçer et al., 2020; Kim & Qu, 2014; Lee et al., 2014). The use of IR 4.0 in hotel experience can sometimes lead to value 'co-destruction' (Stankov et al., 2018). Value 'co-destruction' occurs when the intended value creation or enhancement of hotel experience is not achieved due to lack of sufficient technology or hotel guests' disengagement with technology (Stankov et al., 2018). That is why the hospitality and tourism industry must first have the vision to deliver valuable experiences before choosing suitable technology (Balasubramanian & Ragavan, 2019). The rise of the millennial generation is the main driver of change. Hence, most hotels have started to invest in technology to cope with the new emerging lifestyle (Balasubramanian & Ragavan, 2019).

IR 4.0 Contributions and Adverse effects

The IR 4.0 revolution, particularly from an industry's point of view, is bringing different connotations in terms of opportunities and challenges. Opportunities improve the quality of life by making work more productive and less stressful (Ivanov et al., 2017, 2018, 2020; Osei et al., 2020). They also provide employees with better and more accurate information (Ivanov & Webster, 2017). Bridgestock (2021) identified that through the use of new technologies in 2016, 51.8% of travelers booked trips via mobile device. Using social media, make sure that the hotel is visible on Twitter, Instagram YouTube, Facebook, or Foursquare. For instance, Hyatt Hotels launched a concierge service on Twitter, allowing the guests to find interesting place nearby. Jobs (2021) mentioned being technology savvy is an essential need to the key success and have competitive sustained advantages in hospitality industry. Digital transformation has opened up economy diversity and global connectivity and market opportunities with the shift from traditional industry to technology driven eco-systems where the global digital landscape promotes cross-boarder partnerships, international trades and world-wide competitiveness (Edward, 2023). Similarly, another contribution is environmental sustainability with technology advancement with recycling projects, renewable energy and implementation of solutions to reduce carbon footprints. This digital revolution also involves the elimination of all manual and routine jobs. As most jobs can be done digitally by being embedded into AI, machines and robots, the roles of humans will also change as they are no longer based on routine manual tasks but more towards critical thinking (Lee et al., 2018). With the next generation of technologies around the corner and ever changing, scholars agree that the hospitality industry should embrace technologies in its operation (Ivanov et al., 2020; Osei et al., 2020) and there is also an increasing application of self-service technology in the hospitality industry (Ahmad & Scott, 2018). The IR 4.0 is also a solution for seasonal employment and labor turnover which is one of the advantages of adopting IR 4.0 (Osei et al., 2020; Nam et al., 2020). To equip the growing role of technology with the emergence of automation in the industry, the human factor is still of utmost importance in this field (Balasubramanian & Ragavan, 2019).

However, one of the biggest challenges in the IR 4.0 phenomenon is the potential for greater inequality, especially in its potential to disrupt employment (Lee et al., 2018; Edward, 2023). Many reports have shown the harsh effects of workforce automation on certain types of jobs and demographics. The Brookings Institution has found that automation threatens 25% of all US jobs and 58% of women were at the highest risk of automation (Schawbel, 2019). Hotels are being forced to transform as they will continue to be impacted by the technology revolution. Experts have forecasted that in 2030, about 25% of the routine tasks will be performed by AI and robots (Marin, 2019). The Minimum Wage Order (MWO) policy encourages the industry to shift from a labor-intensive industry into a capital- or technical-intensive industry (Ahmad & Scott, 2019). Regardless of whether hotel operators support IR 4.0 or not, there has been a consensus that they would support the revolution after observing the advantages (Nam et al., 2020). The findings by Nam et al. (2020) indicate that employees are expected to be more noticeable and significant in lower positions as IR 4.0 may replace them. At higher positions, however, it is believed that IR 4.0 would enhance their abilities and efficiency, and not replace them. Thus, it can be seen that the lower positioned employees could be intimidated by the IR 4.0. Therefore, there is a gap between the implementation of the IR 4.0 digitalization and unemployment. On the other hand, some scholars also agree that the technological components of the IR 4.0 allow hotel operators to create a new paradigm of jobs and tasks which leads to the new creation of activities such as service operation manuals, service control, operation, and new business products and services (Ivanov et al., 2017; Vecchio et al., 2018). Another challenge is the fear of data security and privacy whereby data in the Cloud and Big data storage can be a hacking issue without tough cybersecurity and policies and regulations to safeguard information (Edward, 2023). Cybersecurity threats has been rising especially in data breaches and data leaks where 64% of the data is shared while 36% of data are sold to others, all these are of huge concerns to everyone (Cybersecurity Malaysia, 2023).

Technology Revolution in the Malaysian Context

Exploring history of Malaysian tourism, way back in 1960s, tourism was rather underdeveloped with the economic focus was mainly on exporting commodities (Giap et al., 2016). However, Tourism Development Corporation, since its inception in 10th August 1972, has consistently grown and promoted Malaysian tourism. Currently, known as Tourism Malaysia, it has grown tremendously with four regional offices and 32 overseas offices and has been the second foreign exchange earner for national economy in 2018. Prior to the Covid pandemic in 2018, Malaysia had recorded 26.8 million tourist arrivals and 84.1 billion ringgits in tourist income which made the country popular in the world as 15 most visited tourism destination (Tourism Malaysia, 2018). Malaysia has also received a variety of international honors and awards such as Brand Laureate Best Brands Awards 2017-2018, Best Brands Award for Nation Branding, Best Organization Award in 2018 China ASEAN Tourism Exhibition and many more. During the Covid pandemic, the travel and tourism industry was badly hit with the abrupt halt of international and domestic mobility with international boarder closure bringing a sudden drop of 95% travelers. With borders closed and the stop-start nature of domestic tourism, hotels, restaurants and travel operators were unable to sustain their operations since 2020 onwards till around 4th quantile of 2021 (Balasubramaniam & Hanafiah, 2022). Likewise, airline and cruise industries and other peripheral travel industries also reported loss in millions (Hamid et al., 2021). Due to this unprecedented pandemic, revenue was almost nil, employees were laid off, events were stalled or postponed, many hotels were forced into hibernation mode or to closed down and stakeholders have to take many critical measures to sustain. One of the ways, hospitality industry survived was to innovate and change their modus of operation.

The hospitality industry, in Malaysia is slowly returning to its pre-Covid retailing and sales after the impactful two-years pandemic hurdles. The tourism and hospitality industry are re-strategizing on wooing their international and domestic guests into Malaysian shores. Some of their initiatives are relooking into guests' online purchasing habits, personalizing guest experiences, investing in digital analytics and promoting new destinations (Gilbert, 2023). Promotions were shifted from mass tourism to cluster-basic micro tourism catering for small groups collaborating with local tour operators and local community associations (Balasubramaniam & Hanafiah, 2022). Post Covid travel trends seemed to favor contact-less travels which is emerging as a new norm and made possible with the latest travel technologies and applications and hotel digitalization. The First Hotel and Plaza, Getting Highlands, has embedded self-check-in kiosks and check-out technology to cope with the crowd and better efficiency during check-in and checkouts. This technology is becoming more common and used in full-service hotels in the USA to facilitate guests more effectively (Casado, 2014). Sunway Resort Hotel has implemented an integrated one-stop "Super App" which allows guests to make bookings, check-in, open the room doors, remotely manage the curtains, switch on and off the air conditioner and lights and use as TV remote control (Castaldi, 2021). All these are possible because Sunway's hotel management system with the integration with Oracle Opera Cloud service, has digitalized the reservation and guest management system. In addition, they emphasize using digital marketing hence, customers can buy electronically, scan social media like Facebook and Instagram and their fitness gym offer online fitness workouts and on-demand videos. In general, the hospitality industry has changed the way they communicate and engage with their guests with the new burst of digital search engines, social media marketing and brand promotions (Nuong & Ari Ragavan, 2023).

Luxury hotels in Malaysia also adopted the digital revolution by introducing virtual reality tools to create an immersive traveller experience of hotels, restaurants and recreation centres (Balasubramaniam & Hanafiah, 2022). Hotels also innovated with the new Staycation packages, "Park and Dine" at their large car parks and new improvised beach packages catering for small groups. There were also virtual entertainment and festivals, virtual events and online parties, and new hygiene procedures and emergent of COVID hotels for those had to travel overseas (Hamid et al., 2021). During the pandemic and post COVID pandemic, the hospitality industry has survived significantly due to the digital technologies which is an opportunity to enhance the hospitality business (Dzia-Uddin et al., 2023). There was a need to have AIs for infra technology for contactless body temperature scanning and various applications and technologies as part of the scanning for COVID. To further enhance contactless service, initiatives to incorporate robotic solutions were also considered but high investment costs remain the main concern. In Malaysia, in line with social distancing, five restaurants introduced robot waiters within their establishments, namely Original Kayu Nasi Kandar, NALE Nasi Lemak, Buharry Briyani Bistro, JBorn Café and Bistro and Sri Ananda Bhawan Restaurant (Durai, 2022; AK Success Robotics, 2024). Although, robots can reduce labour shortage and costs, usage of robots in service industry is more complicated compared to using robots in manufacturing industry because robots in the hospitality industry requires a high level of interactions with people and guests (Belias et al., 2020). Mistakes and accidents can happen causing bad reputations as robots are only programmed machines and most suitable for minor services.

Going beyond the luxury hotels, the Malaysia Budget & Business Hotel Association (MyBHA) are also embarking on enhancing digital transformation and endorse smart hotel technology to meet the dire need of industry demands especially among young consumers and remain competitive (Puvaneswary, 2024). According to Sri Ganesh Michiel, president of MyBHA, the collaboration with hospitality technology solution provider will focus on energy efficient solutions such as smart lighting with LEDs, smart check-ins, digitalised room keys systems, HVAC systems, AI powered guest services, water and waste management to reduce operational costs, personalised service and greetings and efficient service delivery. The efforts are also made for employees' hands-on training to ensure they have the experience in using technologies and the know-hows of digital advancements. Likewise, in Penang, MyBHA has also launched Penang Digital Hub to equip its members with the latest technology, digital tools and training so that they can compete in the dynamic digital hospitality sector (Digital Penang, 2023).

Luxury and budget hotels had and continue to innovate and invoke competitive advantage to stay above their competitors and to provide their guests service with value and efficiency (Dzia-Uddin et al., 2023). In order to survive at present era, the hospitality industry needs to innovate and change their modus operandi of managing their business. Customer loyalty and quality of service being their top priority, the industry needs employees who are smart and well trained in utilizing technology, AI and digital applications. Even to oversee the operations of robotics in the hospitality industry, employees need to have the training and the basic know-how involving knowledge of various touch points. Similarly, with all the digitalization transformations occurring in IR 4.0, skilled employees are required in managing Big Data, integrating with IoT, operating numerous IT software incorporating hotel operations within front office, housekeeping, food and beverage, sales and marketing, human resources, finance, security, maintenance and other departments. As Nuong and Ari Ragavan (2023) emphasized, in additional to maintain a mastery on technology and digital literacy, recent graduates must be prepared to be multi-skilled in their job, master interpersonal skills, excel in communication imbibe teamwork skills and business skills, demonstrate strong emotional intelligence skills and be resilient in this ever dynamic hospitality industry.

Theoretical Framework

This study used Technology Acceptance Model (TAM) which is information systems related theory, looking at how individuals are encouraged to accept and use new IT technologies (Fiorini et al., 2018). This theory has been extensively applied among researchers to explore how users have hesitation in using new technologies within their lives. The theory was originally introduced by Davis in the late 1980s when computers and technologies were becoming popular hence creating fear and uneasiness among people. TAM looks into two factors which are important determinants of users' acceptance: perceived ease of use and perceived usefulness. Hence, if the user has a better perception about the specific IT applications will help them in their work and performance and if the application is also easy to use with less effort, then attitude towards acceptance will be high, and behavior intention of usage will be also higher. The application of TAM is wide and newer variables have been incorporated into the model however the original model is still viable to use (Allen, 2020). For this study, this theory can be incorporated as respondents are feeling that as newer technology is being developed, they are unsure if they are able to cope with the acceptance of these applications. Moreover, these technologies are also ever evolving hence the users need to be consistently updating their skills to meet the demands.

METHODOLOGY

This paper dwells into a qualitative approach by interviewing hospitality managers in the hospitality industry and exploring their views in relation with the two research questions, namely, what kind of technology and innovations that has been implemented in their organizations with the explosion of IR 4.0 and what are their views about challenges faced with technology advancement. All the interviews were carried out online via emails, What's app and video conference. In total, seven structured open- ended and close-ended questions were shared to the managers and written responses were collected after a few days and additional online interviews were conducted via Whats app, video conferencing and Google Teams. Online interviews are viewed as a suitable mode of data collection as it is deemed as being safe, non-intrusive, convenient and easy to communicate however subjected to privacy and access issues (Dodds & Hess, 2021). Upon compiling all the written responses from the interviews, data was grouped into common themes, and these are shared in the findings. Informed consents were sought for ethical consideration to protect the privacy of the respondents. Some of the respondents gave permission to use their own names while did not hence codes were used to protect their identity.

FINDINGS AND DISCUSSION

In total, eight respondents took part in these interviews. All of them are working in the hospitality industry in various positions. The details can be seen below in Table 1.

Table 1. Details of the respondents with their job positions and name of their enterprise

no	Name	Job Position	Name of hotel/ bar
1	XP3	General Manager	Brand Hotel A Kuala Lumpur
2	MP4	General Manager (now Retired)	Brand Hotel B Kuala Lumpur
3	KP5	Shareholder & Director	ASS (Bar & Bistro)
4.	RP6	Assistant Manager	Brand Hotel Beach Resort Kuantan
5.	SSP7	Front Office Manager	Brand Hotel C, Kuala Lumpur
6.	PP1	Operations Manager	Brand Hotel, Shah Alam
7.	PP2	Training Manager	Brand Hotel D Kuala Lumpur
8.	MMP8	General Manager	Brand Service Hotel E Kuala Lumpur

Codes were used to protect the identity of the respondents

Research Question 1: The readiness of digitalization usage within your organization

All the respondents except for one, said their hotels/ bar are using some form of digitalization for the daily work and operations of their business. PPI's hotel does not use any technology and "*all tasks are done manually*". All the other managers said that they have installed technology for their reservations like variations of the Opera systems, digital check-in system, while three hotels are equipped with smart cards and face recognition; and billings like Post of Order System (POS). Four of them said that their hotels have Human Resources Information Systems (HRIS), Accounting systems and the marketing teams are using Social media and Digital Marketing software for their promotions. One of the leading five-star hotel General Manager, participant MMP8 said that they have implemented various kinds of software and AIs for their rooms and check in processes. Their responses are as below:

PP2: *"HR information system/ Property Management system but these systems implemented five years ago. Two years ago, we started using Instagram, Twitter, Facebook, and using hashtag (#) for every promotion we had".*

MP4: *"The Ritz-Carlton implemented new software for Sales and Marketing Software Salesforce, and a new internal platform for Human Resources / employee benefits and job applications*".

XP3: *"Staff would only be in attendance for guest would be able to do self-checking. Technology is used even AI for key cards, payment n booking confirmations".*

MMP8*: "We have acquired the latest systems for our rooms. Guests are not required to go to Front desk to register. Registration is done via the mobile phones and using the phone, the can scan in to get inside"*

All the interviewee managers agreed that in future their organizations will embark on newer and enhanced technology, and they are slowly embracing IR 4.0. They shared they cannot avoid the newer digital applications and to compete with others, IT and digitalization transformation is vital especially after the pandemic, the contactless service is much sought after by the guests due to the fear of COVID transmission.

PP1: "*We are ready to adapt if the technology or system is be able to help to increase the quality of services. Self-check-in/out machine are used since the pandemic happening and the perspective of the guests are now different, they want less contact with us".*

KP5: *" Yes, as I believe everything in life will advance and progress same with technology. Keeping up pace with new tech will in long run benefit the company with consistency. The new generations are also expecting this. Our clients are mostly Gen Z and they are very tech savvy."*

MMP8: *"Being one of the top leading hotels, it is important to keep abreast with technology and it is becoming a much-needed element in managing hotels. Our guests are also very happy and we are also more efficient. We try to keep abreast with what is new in the digital world".*

SSP7: *"Systems and software are constantly upgrading, by the time we buy, a newer model comes out. Some systems we never heard off. Then we have to re-budget or lose money. But we still need to invest for the future moving forward".*

Research Question 2: The challenges faced moving forward to embrace IR 4.0

There are many kinds of challenges faced by the hospitality industry moving into the digitalisation world. Firstly, the digital world keeps changing and improving and it is difficult to keep abreast with the technology which lack standardisation (Kansakar et al., 2018) . Hence, to fully adapt into the new technologies will take a longer duration as mentioned by participant RP6, a long-time hotel manager. As Dennis (2024) states, implementations are usually done in phases, whereby non-critical areas are done first before proceeding to higher-risk aspects. For example, front desk staff would enter inputs of new bookings into both the old and new system simultaneously to ensure guest information is not lost due to technical errors. This stage validates accuracy while building familiarity with new interfaces. Likewise, it also involves various groups like the government authorities, vendors, trainers and employees (Hamid, et al., 2021).

RP6: "*To adapt with new the digital environment will take some time. And need to deal with many people*".

PP2*: "Technology is ever changing, and we need the budget to keep changing our systems"*

XP3*: "Our policy is to manage with what we have efficiently. If it is working well, staff are trained then we manage with it. We are in no hurry to reinvent the whole process"*

Adoption of the technology depends on the organization's needs and budget prior to its purchase because technology transformation is not cheap as mentioned by a manager. The cost of implementing new software, AI applications, integration of IoT and interfacing with other systems involves huge sum of money hence there is always the question of priority and urgency, and these are also the concerns of the managers. As Castaldi (2021) remarked that digitalization is not an overnight process, and it requires a huge amount of planning and budgeting. Moreover, as brand hotels in Malaysia, the final decisions to embark on big technology projects will require approvals from the Regional or International Head Office.

SSP7: "*All our budgets come from HQ, hence to have newer digital AIs, we must seek approval. So we need to prioritize where to put our money. Which area has the urgent need to use the money. As we all know, budgets are limited."*

KP5: "My *partners are based overseas. In order to invest in newer gadgets, we look into our operational costs and budgets. A lot of discussions are needed and usually we only invest if it is really needed. Or if the old system has broken down."*

MP4: "*If our regional office gives approval based on their regional budget, only then we bring in the robots and more digitalization. Maybe the hotels in USA will get the budget for these AI but our Asian budget is different*".

Likewise, technology has their disadvantages whereby if the server/ system crashes, then all data can be lost and yet this can be resolved with cloud technology like Google cloud. One of the challenges of doing digital transformation is not having the right technical employees to implement, manage and do maintenance the digital systems and all these require specialized intense staff training (Dennis, 2024). 40% of hotel managers reported that redesigning and reskilling tasks are critical concerns when new technology applications are introduced into the hotels, and these include 24/7 helpdesks with on-site support teams and in-the-moment end-user assistance for guests and employees builds user confidence when using new systems. Also, implementation of robots and digital applications also involves some form of risks and may hinder guest satisfaction when systems fail causing more disruptions than advancements (Dzia-Hussain et al., 2023) Similarly, hotel managers and technical staff should also have some knowledge on how to use these tech tools, their functionality and they are integrated into the daily operational workflows so that downtimes are reduced and business run efficiently.

PP1: *"Technology is expensive to adopt and lack of expertise to handle. Technology does determine the extent of adoption. I am afraid the guests can vandalize the machine [...] cost and repairing could be huge and need to find the right person too internally or externally"*.

SSP7: "*Challenges is when the system is downtime, a manual backup has to be present. Also getting technicians to shoot the problem can be tiring. Sometimes it is difficult to get the right staff to do these technical problems.*"

KP7: "*To learn and adapt to the new technology system will be a challenge in the beginning as we're too used to the older system plus, we would work with new gadgets more than the workforce. And we need the support too. We are not IT experts*".

MMP8: *"Before I get any new technology applications, I will look at the after service and make sure someone knows how to correct these glitches. Less down time saves the operational cost but heightens guest satisfaction. Before we invest, we will make many comparisons"*.

In summary, the findings from eight operational hands-on managers and General managers gave an insightful realization of how IR 4.0 and its vast technology transformations are being incorporated into the Malaysian hospitality industry. The findings show that although one hotel is not technology savvy, the other establishments are surely and gradually incorporating this burst of digitalization into their entities and experiencing their own challenges.

CONCLUSION

This technological revolution is here to stay and it's only a matter of time before all industry players resort and fully embrace technology in their operations. It is crucial that all stakeholders in the hospitality industry collectively study the impact of technology on their future operations keeping in mind future trends and cooperatively develop standards and practices to ensure the smooth and sustainable growth of the hospitality industry. Such standards and practices once formalized will form the basis for human resource development needed for the industry in the future. To explore more about this in Malaysia, this qualitative study provided an overview of the IR4.0 revolution in the hospitality industry. Interviews among eight prominent hotels leaders were conducted to explore the extent of usage of digitalization and technology transformations within their hotels and what are the corresponding challenges faced by them within the IR 4.0 era. The results showed that except for one hotel in Shah Alam, all the other seven hotels are using some form of technology for the daily operations. The digitalized systems commonly used are self -checking AI systems, smart room cards, HR management systems for payrolls and staff information, POS systems for restaurants, IoT integrations, sales and marketing software, social media marketing and other simpler digital systems. None of the hotels have invested in robotics nor complex spectrum of AIs and digital systems. Most cited budgets and non-approvals from the Regional Head Office. Some of the challenges faced by the hoteliers are having insufficient operational budgets to acquire various other sophisticated applications, as well as professional technical employees to manage these systems. They also fear that by the time budgets are approved, the technology would have rapidly advanced into newer versions and of course the cost will be more. They themselves will be required to go for training to acquire some know-hows about how to administer the newer technological support systems. Overall, all of the managers agreed that technology revolution is here to stay, and they need to keep acquiring and investing into newer digital machines, AIs, and Big Data moving forward into IR 4.0 era.

Limitations and Recommendations

One of the main limitations is that this study among eight hotel managers is insufficient to make complex generalization about the digitalization transformations happening within the hospitality industry in Malaysia. These findings can be counted as a small drop in the vast hospitality industry which only focused on hotels within Klang Valley and one hotel in Kuantan. Although, some truthful insights can be inducted through the interviews, it is highly recommended that a wider intensity scope of research be carried out to explore the actual implementation of digitalization within Malaysian scenario. Also, it will be more effective if a quantitative study be conducted engaging nation-wide hotels in Malaysia including urban hotels and smaller town hotels. Such diverse research may churn out a significant bigger illustration of IR 4.0 technology revolution within Malaysia.

REFERENCES

Ahmad, R., & Scott, N. (2019). Technology innovations towards reducing hospitality human resources costs in Langkawi, Malaysia. *Tourism Review*, 74(3), 547–562. Advance online publication. DOI: 10.1108/TR-03-2018-0038

Allen, R. (2020). Digital Marketing Models: The Technology Acceptance Model. https://www.smartinsights.com/manage-digital-transformation

Balasubramanian, K. & Hanafiah, M. H. (2022). What innovations would enable the tourism and hospitality industry in Malaysia to rebuild? *Worldwide Hospitality and Tourism Themes*. Emerald Publishing Limited 1755-4217. DOI: DOI: 10.1108/WHATT-05-2022-0057

Balasubramanian, K., & Ragavan, N. A. (2019). What are the key challenges faced by the Malaysian hospitality and tourism industry in the context of industrial revolution 4.0? *Worldwide Hospitality and Tourism Themes*, 11(2), 194–203. DOI: 10.1108/WHATT-11-2018-0079

BBC News. (2015, 9 February). *Drone waiters unveiled in Singapore*. BBC News. https://www.bbc.com/news/av/world-asia-31160853

Belias, D., Vasiliadis, L., & Rossidis, I. (2021). The Intention and Expectations of Modern Robotic Technologies in the Hotel Industry. *Journal of Quality Assurance in Hospitality & Tourism*, 23(6), 1451–1479. DOI: 10.1080/1528008X.2021.1995566

Bessen, J. E. (2021). The Second Industrial Revolution: A New Look at the Development of the American Economy. *The Journal of Economic History*, 81(2), 587–614.

Bridgestock, L. (2021, June 1). *6 essential trends and skills for hospitality careers*. QS Top University. https://www.topuniversities.com/student-info/careers-advice/6-essential-trends-skills-hospitality-careers

Buhalis, D., & Amaranggana, A. (2015). Smart tourism destinations: Enhancing tourism experience through personalisation of services. In Tussyadiah, I., & Inversini, A. (Eds.), *Information and Communication Technologies in Tourism* (pp. 377–389). Springer., DOI: 10.1007/978-3-319-14343-9_28

Casado, M. A. (2014). *Front Office Management in Hospitality Lodging Operations*. Create Space Independent Publishing.

Castaldi, A. (2021). Digital Transformation needed: With or Without a Pandemic. *Berita Sunway, Issue 71*.https://www.sunway.com.my/stories

Cohen, S. A., & Hopkins, D. (2019). Autonomous vehicles and the future of urban tourism. *Annals of Tourism Research*, 74, 33–42. DOI: 10.1016/j.annals.2018.10.009

Cybersecurity Malaysia. (2023). Cybersecurity Malaysia: Mid Term Report 2023- treat Landscape. www.cybersecurity.my/data/content_files/26/2511

Das, S., & Pan, T. (2022). A strategic outline of Industry 6.0: Exploring the Future. SSRN *Electronic Journal*, May 2022 https://www.researchgate.net/publication/360501150_ DOI:DOI: 10.2139/ssrn.4104696

Deng, Z., Benckendorff, P., & Wang, J. (2019). Blended tourism experiencescape: A conceptualisation of live-streaming tourism. In Pesonen, J., & Neidhardt, J. (Eds.), *Information and Communication Technologies in Tourism* (pp. 212–222). Springer International Publishing., DOI: 10.1007/978-3-030-05940-8_17

Dennis, A. (2024). Digital Transformation in Hospitality-Examples, Challenges. https://whatfix.com

Digital Penang. (2023). Catalysing digital transformation in the hospitality sector. December 14. https://digitalpenang.my/

Dinçer, F. I., Bayram, G. E., & Altunoz, O. (2020). Fourth generation of rights and their reflections on human resources practices in tourism businesses. In Aydin, Ş., Dedeoglu, B. B., & Çoban, Ö. (Eds.), *Organizational Behavior Challenges in The Tourism Industry* (pp. 60–81). IGI Global., DOI: 10.4018/978-1-7998-1474-0.ch005

Dodds, S., & Hess, A. C. (2021). Adapting research methodology during COVID-19: lessons for transformative service research. *Journal of Service Management*, Vol 32 (2) ISSN: 1757-5818

Durai, A. (2022). The rise of robot waiters in Malaysia, driven by labour shortage in F&B sector. https://www.thestar.com.my/lifestyle/living/2022/08/24/the-rise-of-robot-waiters-in-malaysia

Dzia-uddin, D. N., Annuar, J., Nik Mohd Fahmil, N. M. Z., & Wan Kamarudin, W. N. B. (2023). A Review Paper on Technological Innovation of Hotel Industry in Post-Pandemic. *International Journal of Business and Technology Management*, [S.l.], Vol. 5, no. S1, pp. 9-25. ISSN 2682-7646. https://myjms.mohe.gov.my/index.php/ijbtm/article/view/23575

Edward, O. T. (2023). The impact of the Fourth Industrial Revolution (IR 4.0) on Modern Civilisation in Malaysia. https://www.bernama.com/en/thoughts/news.php?id=2251185

Fiorini, P. C., Roman Pais Seles, B. M., Chiappetta Jabbour, C. J., Mariano, E. B., & Lopes de Sousa Jabbour, A. B. (2018). Management theory and big data literature: From a review to a research agenda. *International Journal of Information Management*, Volume 43, Pages 112-129, ISSN 0268-4012, DOI: 10.1016/j.ijinfomgt.2018.07.005

Flavián C., Ibáñez-Sánchez S., & Orús C. (2019). The impact of virtual, augmented and mixed reality technologies on the customer experience. *Journal of Business Research*, 100, 547–560. https://doi.org/es.2018.10.050DOI: 10.1016/j.jbusr

Giap, T. K., Gopalan, S., & Ye, Y. (2016). Drivers of Growth in the Travel and Tourism Industry in Malaysia: A Geweke Causality Analysis.*Economies*, 4(1), 3. DOI: 10.3390/economies4010003

Gilbert, J. (2023). Digitalisation, Sustainability Shaping Travel Sector. *Business Sector, News Straits Times*, February 2nd. https://www.nst.com.my/business/2023/02/875709/digitisation-sustainability-shaping-travel-sector

Greeven, C. S., & Williams, S. P. (2017). Enterprise collaboration systems: Addressing adoption challenges and the shaping of sociotechnical systems. *International Journal of Information Systems and Project Management*, 5(1), 5–23. DOI: 10.12821/ijispm050101

Gretzel, U., Sigala, M., Xiang, Z., & Koo, C. (2015). Smart tourism: Foundations and developments. *Electronic Markets*, 25(3), 179–188. DOI: 10.1007/s12525-015-0196-8

Gupta, D. (2023). The importance of digital tech adoption in hospitality. www.whatfix.com

Hamid, R., Mohd Hashim, N. H., Mohd Shukur, S. A., & Marmaya, N. H. (2021). The Impact of Covid-19 on Malaysia Tourism Industry Supply Chain. *International Journal of Academic Research in Business and Social Sciences* Vol. 11, No. 16, Contemporary Issues in Tourism and Hospitality industry. E-ISSN: 2222-6990 © 2021 HRMARS

Hofmann, E., & Rüsch, M. (2017). Industry 4.0 and the current status as well as future prospects on logistics. *Computers in Industry*, 89, 23–34. DOI: 10.1016/j.compind.2017.04.002

Huang, C. D., Goo, J., Nam, K., & Yoo, C. W. (2017). Smart tourism technologies in travel planning: The role of exploration and exploitation. *Information & Management*, 54(6), 757–770. DOI: 10.1016/j.im.2016.11.010

Ivanov, S. (2020). The impact of automation on tourism and hospitality jobs. *Information Technology & Tourism*, 22(2), 205–215. DOI: 10.1007/s40558-020-00175-1

Ivanov, S., & Webster, C. (2017, October 19-21). *Adoption of robots, artificial intelligence and service automation by travel, tourism and hospitality companies- A cost-benefit analysis* [Conference session]. International Scientific Conference "Contemporary Tourism-Traditions and Innovations", Sofia University. https://ssrn.com/abstract=3007577

Ivanov, S., Webster, C., & Berezina, K. (2017). Adoption of robots and service automation by tourism and hospitality companies. *Revista Turismo & Desenvolvimento (Aveiro)*, 27(28), 1501–1517.

Ivanov, S., Webster, C., & Seyyedi, P. (2018). Consumers' attitudes towards the introduction of robots in accommodation establishments. *Tourism: An International Interdisciplinary Journal*, 66(3), 302–317.

Ivanov, S. H., Webster, C., Stoilova, E., & Slobodskoy, D. (2020). Biosecurity, automation technologies and economic resilience of travel, tourism and hospitality companies: A conceptual framework. *Tourism Economics*, •••, 1–24. DOI: 10.1177/1354816620946541

Kamble, S. S., Gunasekaran, A., & Goh, M. (2020). Industry 4.0 and its implications for supply chain management: A systematic literature review. *International Journal of Production Economics*, 229, 107853. Advance online publication. DOI: 10.1016/j.ijpe.2020.107853

Kansakar, P., Munir, A., & Shaban, N. (2018). Technology in Hospitality Industry: Prospects and Challenges. https://arxiv.org/pdf/1709.00105

Kim, D. J., & Mattila, A. S. (2019). *Hospitality and tourism marketing: Theories and applications*. Routledge.

Kim, M., & Qu, H. (2014). Travelers' behavioral intention toward hotel self-service kiosks usage. *International Journal of Contemporary Hospitality Management*, 26(2), 225–245. DOI: 10.1108/IJCHM-09-2012-0165

Lee, M., Yun, J. J., Pyka, A., Won, D., Kodama, F., Schiuma, G., Park, H., Jeon, J., Park, K., Jung, K., Yan, M.-R., Lee, S., & Zhao, X. (2018). How to respond to the fourth industrial revolution, or the second information technology revolution? Dynamic new combinations between technology, market, and society through open innovation. *Journal of Open Innovation*, 4(21), 1–24. DOI: 10.3390/joitmc4030021

Lee, Y.-K., Chang, C.-T., Lin, Y., & Cheng, Z.-H. (2014). The dark side of smartphone usage: Psychological traits, compulsive behavior and technostress. *Computers in Human Behavior*, 31, 373–383. DOI: 10.1016/j.chb.2013.10.047

Li, Y., Hu, C., Huang, C., & Duan, L. (2017). The concept of smart tourism in the context of tourism information services. *Tourism Management*, 58, 293–300. DOI: 10.1016/j.tourman.2016.03.014

Liao, Y., Deschamps, F., Loures, E. F. R., & Ramos, L. F. P. (2017). Past, present and future of Industry 4.0: A systematic literature review and research agenda proposal. *International Journal of Production Research*, 55(12), 3609–3629. DOI: 10.1080/00207543.2017.1308576

Lu, Y. (2017). Industry 4.0: A survey on technologies, applications and open research issues. *Journal of Industrial Information Integration*, 6(4), 1–10. DOI: 10.1016/j.jii.2017.04.005

Marr, B. (2021). The 4th Industrial Revolution: How AI, Big Data, and the Internet of Things are Changing Business. *Forbes*.

Martin, F. (2019, March 8). *What robots mean for the future of the hospitality industry*. Bauer Business Focus. https://www.houstonpublicmedia.org/articles/shows/bauer-business-focus/2019/03/08/324596/what-robots-mean-for-the-future-of-the-hospitality-industry/

Mokyr, J. (2020). *The Industrial Revolution: A Very Short Introduction*. University Press.

Moldenhauer, L., & Londt, C. (2019). Leadership, artificial intelligence and the need to redefine future skills development. *Journal of Leadership, Accountability and Ethics*, 16(1), 54–60.

Morrone, D., Raimo, N., Tarulli, A., & Vitolla, F. (2021). Digitalisation in the hospitality industry: Motivations, effects and role of Covid-19. *International Journal of Digital Culture and Electronic Tourism*, 3(3-4), 257–270. DOI: 10.1504/IJDCET.2021.116475

Motyl, B., Baronio, G., Uberti, S., Speranza, D., & Filippi, S. (2017). How will change the future engineers' skills in the Industry 4.0 framework? A questionnaire survey. *Procedia Manufacturing*, 11, 1501-1509. https://doi.org/. 282DOI: 10.1016/j.promfg.2017.07

Murphy, J., Gretzel, U., & Pesonen, J. (2019). Marketing robot services in hospitality and tourism: The role of anthropomorphism. *Journal of Travel & Tourism Marketing*, 36(7), 784–795. DOI: 10.1080/10548408.2019.1571983

MyGovernment. (2019, July 12). *National Policy on Industry 4.0- Industry4WRD*. Prime Minister's Office of Malaysia Official Website. https://www.pmo.gov.my/2019/07/national-policy-on-industry-4-0-industry4wrd/

Nam, K., Dutt, C. S., Chathoth, P., Daghfous, A., & Khan, M. S. (2020). The adoption of artificial intelligence and robotics in the hotel industry: Prospects and challenges. *Electronic Markets*. Advance online publication. DOI: 10.1007/s12525-020-00442-3

Nuong, M. D., & Ari Ragavan, N. (2023). Digital future of the hospitality industry and hospitality education globally: Review of related literature. *Asia-Pacific Journal of Futures in Education and Society*, 2(2), 71–100. DOI: 10.58946/apjfes-2.2.P5

O'Neill, S. (2015, 4 February) *In Japan, humanoid robots may soon run a hotel.* http:// www.tnooz.com/ article/japan-hotel-run-humanoid- robots/

Osei, B. A., Ragavan, N. A., Mensah, H. K., & Kandappan, B. (2020). Hospitality revolution 4.0: A literature review on a unified typology of IR 4.0 technologies for the tourism and hospitality industry in the era of COVID-19. *Asia-Pacific Journal of Innovation in Hospitality and Tourism*, 9(1), 25–45.

Osei, B. A., Ragavanm, N. A., & Mensah, H. K. (2020). Prospects of the fourth industrial revolution for the hospitality industry: A literature review. *Journal of Hospitality and Tourism Technology*, 11(3), 479–494. DOI: 10.1108/JHTT-08-2019-0107

Puvaneswary, S. (2024). Malaysia to propel smart hotel innovations. TTG Asia. https://www.ttgasia .com/2024/07/15/malaysia-to-propel-smart-hotel-innovations

Rinalducci, S. N. (2023). Industry 1.0 to 4.0 – Brief History of the Industrial Revolution. *Sustainability Success*. https://sustainability-success.com/industry-1-0-to-4-0-2-3-revolution

Schawbel, D. (2019, November, 15). *How artificial intelligence is redefining the role of manager*. World Economic Forum. https://www.weforum.org/agenda/2019/11/how-artificial-intelligence-is-redefining -the-role-of-manager/

Schwab, K. (2016). *The Fourth Industrial Revolution*. Penguin Random House.

Shumakova, E. V. (2021). Impact of Digitalization in Hotel Industry Development. Proceeding of the International Science and Technology Conference "FarEastCon 2020". Smart Innovation, Systems and Technologies, vol 227. Springer, Singapore. https://doi.org/DOI: 10.1007/978-981-16-0953-4_57

Singh, D., & Tilak, G. (2020). Implementation of education model 4.0: Developing industrial 4.0 skills in graduates engineers for improving employability skills. *Humanities & Social Science Reviews*, 8(2), 601–613. DOI: 10.18510/hssr.2020.8268

Solnet, D., Baum, T., Robinson, R. N. S., & Lockstone-Binney, L. (2015). What about the workers? Roles and Skills for employees in hotels of the future. *Journal of Vacation Marketing*, 1–15. DOI: 10.1177/1356766715617403

Stankov, U., Filimonau, V., & Slivar, I. (2018). Calm ICT design in hotels: A critical review of applications and implications. *International Journal of Hospitality Management*. Advance online publication. DOI: 10.1016/j.ijhm.2018.10.012

Stankov, U., & Gretzel, U. (2020). Tourism 4.0 technologies and tourist experiences: A human-centered design perspective. *Information Technology & Tourism*, 22(3), 477–488. DOI: 10.1007/s40558-020-00186-y

Success Robotics, A. K. (2024). Robot Waiters in Restaurants to Discover in Malaysia. https:// aksuccessrobotics.com.my/

Tourism Malaysia. (2018). *Annual Report 2018*. www.tourism.gov.my/

Vecchio, P. D., Mele, G., Ndou, V., & Secundo, G. (2018). Creating value from social big data: Implications for smart tourism destinations. *Information Processing & Management*, 54(5), 847–860. DOI: 10.1016/j.ipm.2017.10.006

Wang, X., Li, X. R., Zhen, F., & Zhang, J. (2016). How smart is your tourist attraction?: Measuring tourist preferences of smart tourism attractions via a FCEM-AHP and IPA approach. *Tourism Management*, 54, 309–320. DOI: 10.1016/j.tourman.2015.12.003

Weaver, D. B., & Moyle, B. D. (2019). Tourist stupidity' as a basic characteristic of 'smart tourism': Challenges for destination planning and management. *Tourism Recreation Research*, 44(3), 387–391. DOI: 10.1080/02508281.2019.1637611

Xiang, Z., Du, Q., Ma, Y., & Fan, W. (2017). A comparative analysis of major online review platforms: Implications for social media analytics in hospitality and tourism. *Tourism Management*, 58, 51–65. DOI: 10.1016/j.tourman.2016.10.001

Xu, M., David, J. M., & Kim, S. H. (2018). The fourth industrial revolution: Opportunities and Challenges. *International Journal of Financial Research*, 9(2), 90–95. DOI: 10.5430/ijfr.v9n2p90

Zhong, R. Y., Xu, X., Klotz, E., & Newman, S. T. (2017). Intelligent manufacturing in the context of Industry 4.0: A review. *Engineering (Beijing)*, 3(5), 616–630. DOI: 10.1016/J.ENG.2017.05.015

Chapter 18
Assessment of Customer Satisfaction in Online Food Delivery Within Klang Valley

Gobinath Selvanayagam
https://orcid.org/0009-0006-0544-0277
Help University, Malaysia

Devendren Sathasivam
https://orcid.org/0000-0001-8777-7901
Sunway University, Malaysia

Gopinath Sangaran
Taylor's University, Malaysia

ABSTRACT

This paper attempts to investigate how satisfied customers are with online meal delivery services in the Klang Valley, an industry that is expanding quickly due to changes in consumer behaviour and technological improvements. This study aims to examine the relationship between customer satisfaction and important elements including food quality, sales promotion, and e-service quality, as the demand for efficiency and convenience grows. The study will collect data from purchasers who use online meal delivery services by using an online questionnaire and a quantitative research approach. The results will shed light on consumer preferences and expectations, which is critical for improving the level of services and streamlining business operations in the food delivery industry.

Food and beverages are essential parts of people's everyday lives. Previously, the only ways to obtain food were to order takeaway, cook or dining out. Although there may be some options for food delivery, they are extremely limited to select eateries, the majority of which are fast food establishments (An et al., 2023). This change in the environment has affected how customers place food orders, how restaurants run their businesses, and how delivery services operate (Chen et al., 2020).

The rise in smartphone usage has been critical to the expansion of online food delivery businesses (Hartanto et al., 2023) with an expected 3.4 billion smartphone users worldwide (Hu et al., 2022), this group has emerged as the key consumer base for online food and beverage purchases (Stuber et al., 2022). Mobile apps have not only made ordering easier, but they have also encouraged more frequent

DOI: 10.4018/979-8-3693-7683-6.ch018

purchases (Cho et al., 2020). The global online meal delivery market is expected to rise from the revenue in the online food delivery (OFDS) market is forecasted to reach US$1.20tn in 2024, In the meal delivery market and the number of users is expected to reach 2.5bn users by 2029 (Statista, n.d.).

The COVID-19 pandemic has led to an increase in the use of mobile technology and services. Many are resorting to internet activities such as shopping, ordering takeout, and working remotely to minimize face-to-face interactions (Khlaif et al., 2022). Increased convenience, more meal selections, and promotions with savings are just a few benefits that have resulted from the growth of online food delivery services (OFDS),Consumer spending on food delivery rose dramatically during the COVID-19 pandemic. Customer expenditure on food delivery grew significantly during the first COVID-19 wave, suggesting a shift in consumer behaviour toward online ordering (Hong et al., 2022). The frequency of online meal ordering systems has increased due to their user-friendly design, which has also enhanced consumer accessibility (Yang et al., 2012).

The Online food delivery services (OFDS) sector will grow significantly as companies adapt to changing customer demands. This shift clearly shows how the pandemic has influenced customers' short-term behaviour as well as creating the conditions for the long-term expansion of the online food delivery services (OFDS) sector (Francioni et al., 2022).

In large cities like Klang Valley, there are well-established online food delivery services (OFDS) that have become a phenomenon in part of people's life (Chowdhury, 2023). Consumers choose online food delivery services (OFDS) for several purposes, the most prevalent being the desire for speedy and easy meals to economize time during or following a demanding workday (Chung, 2022).

BACKGROUND OF STUDY

Technology has substantially affected many elements of human living, especially in the restaurant business. It is imperative for restaurant operators to leverage technological advancements to meet evolving customer needs and enhance the overall dining experience, given that an increasing number of patrons are resorting to digital platforms for meal ordering (Dana et al., 2021).

The frequency of online meal ordering systems has increased due to their user-friendly design, which has also enhanced consumer accessibility (Yang et al., 2012) is one of the most progressive forms of hospitality in Malaysia. 2020 has seen a shift in online food delivery services (OFDS), making it a necessary component of any food and beverage business (Anbumathi et al., 2022). The survey states that the profit margin on online meal delivery increased dramatically between 2017 and 2020, from 76,193 million to 122,739 million (Belarmino et al., 2021) and by 2024, the online meal delivery business will bring in $182,327 million worldwide and $410 million in Malaysia (Han et al., 2021).

The market for apps that deliver food online has grown increasingly competitive (Jin & Pan, 2023) as such it is a valuable marketing strategy (Majeed et al., 2022) to stay in business and prevent customers from quickly switching brands, online food delivery services (OFDS) need to cater to consumer needs and preferences. Most restaurants in Malaysia have outsource to utilize applications from third parties instead of using apps from the merchant. Rakuten Insight conducted a meal delivery poll in April 2023, and approximately 79% f Malaysian respondents said that Grab meal was the app they used the most for food delivery (Bi et al., 2023). Food Panda emerged as the most popular meal delivery app, as reported by almost 76% of the participants (Hasi, 2020).

According to (Madhu et al., 2022) the reason for this is that online food delivery services (OFDS) platforms typically provide greater incentives and promotions to entice users to utilize their apps, there is an increase in the variety of food options available, the overall utilization of third-party delivery apps has increased to 91% (Tendur et al., 2021). Customers now have access to never-before-seen levels of convenience as they explore menus, place orders, and pay from the comfort of their homes (Al-Qudah et al., 2022), three important factors that influence consumer satisfaction in this situation are perceived food quality (Gültekin & Veuphuteh, 2023), Sales Promotion (Budiarto et al., 2023), and the quality of the e-service (Ginting et al., 2022).

Brand appreciation is significantly influenced by consumer pleasure. This suggests that the general level of satisfaction with online meal delivery services is significantly influenced by customer contentment to grow and to expand more quickly in the market, online food delivery services (OFDS) must recognize the factors that will affect customer satisfaction and prevent customers from switching to other platforms (Halik & Nugroho, 2022). By focusing on enhancing the quality of their e-services and understanding their consumers' demands, businesses may provide a more satisfying experience that not only meets but exceeds client expectations (Majeed et al., 2022).

PROBLEM STATEMENT

Online food delivery services (OFDS) have become increasingly popular as the go-to option for meals because of the profound impact the COVID-19 epidemic has had on consumer behaviour (Cai et al., 2023). Businesses, particularly those engaged in e-commerce, have benefited greatly from the expanding trend of technical developments and convenience (Wu & Huang, 2023), due to the ease and comfort of internet shopping, online meal delivery has grown in popularity and now accounts for a sizable portion of everyday client traffic (Candra, Sukmawaty, & Bahtiar, 2023). The number of people wishing to order food online is rising sharply, which presents a great chance for the online meal delivery industry to expand quickly and introduce new features (Sobika & Raj, 2021). Consumers will be more likely to switch brands as the online meal delivery industry becomes more competitive, making it harder for businesses to keep their current clientele (Abdullah et al., 2023). Because the platforms of other companies will have an impact, satisfaction with online meal delivery services will inevitably change because of the intense rivalry that is growing in the industry (Naveed & Murtaza, 2023).

Restaurant operators need to adjust to new operating realities that place a higher priority on reducing physical touch (Sureeyatanapas & Damapong, 2023). Customer satisfaction with Online food delivery services (OFDS) is still uneven despite their increasing popularity because of several important criteria, such as the caliber of the food, the e-service, and promotional efforts (Naini et al., 2022). Comprehending these attributes is crucial in assessing the degree to which Online food delivery services (OFDS) satisfy client expectations (Hong et al., 2022). Convenience and service quality are the primary determinants of customer satisfaction in online meal delivery (Venkatakrishnan et al., 2023). Online food delivery services (OFDS) are convenient, but they also present several difficulties for the industry, such as inadequate food quality, low-quality e-services and inefficient sales campaigns. High-quality e-services increase total client experience in addition to perceived service value. service quality in an extremely competitive market to cultivate consumer loyalty and contentment (Naini et al., 2022).

Research Objectives

RO1: To examine the effect of online food delivery service towards customer satisfaction

Research Questions

RQ1: Does E-service quality have an influence on Online Food Delivery in Klang Valley?
RQ2: Does food quality have an influence on Online Food Delivery Klang Valley?
RQ3: Does sales promotion have an influence on Online Food Delivery in Klang Valley?

Research Hypothesis

H1: E-service quality has a positive influence on Online Food Delivery
H2: Food quality has a positive influence on Online Food Delivery
H3: Sales promotion has a positive influence on Online Food Delivery

SIGNIFICATION OF STUDIES

The purpose of this study is to investigate the variables that affect consumers' satisfaction with Online food delivery services (OFDS) in Malaysia's Klang Valley. It has become increasingly important for restaurant owners to understand the preferences and expectations of their customers as the business has changed, especially in reaction to the COVID-19 epidemic (Anbumathi et al., 2022).

Customers' whole pleasure is largely dependent on their online ordering experience, which is made possible by high-quality e-services, these elements promote consumer satisfaction and repeat business (Sakina & Yafiz, 2023). Effective sales promotions can also raise perceived value, which increases the likelihood that customers would pick one restaurant over another (Spotts et al., 2022), as they manage these changes and try to modify their business models to match changing customer expectations, restaurant operators must have a substantial understanding of customer satisfaction (Adak et al., 2022).

This study is to give a thorough picture of customer satisfaction by looking at important variables of meal quality, sales promotions, and e-service quality.

LITERATURE REVIEW

E- Service Quality

The term "e-service quality" refers to a range of factors that influence how consumers view and use digital platforms it is significance in raising customer happiness and loyalty in the online meal delivery industry (Ginting et al., 2022).

It also refers to a detailed assessment of a business's electronic service offerings, considering factors like user-friendliness, system dependability, timeliness, and service efficiency. Recent studies have demonstrated the significance of e-service quality in increasing customer satisfaction and loyalty in a range of online settings (Venkatakrishnan et al., 2023). Responsiveness, usability, and dependability are important considerations for improving customer satisfaction in e-commerce systems (Badotra & Sundas, 2021). E-service quality and food quality are crucial determinants of customer satisfaction, emphasizing their importance in enhancing the overall dining experiences (Yan et al., 2022).

The relationship between e-service quality and customer satisfaction in online meal ordering is further supported. The study highlights that e-service quality that is effective not only raises the perceived value of the service but also makes people feel better about the business. Delivery expertise grows (Venkatakrishnan et al., 2023).

H1: E-service quality has a positive influence on Online Food Delivery in Klang Valley.

Food Quality

A food product's overall perfection is determined by a multitude of internal and external factors that come together to form the complicated concept of food quality, size, form, colour, and texture are examples of external characteristics; chemical, physical, and microbiological features are examples of and good Manufacturing Practices (GMP) and Hazard Analysis Critical Control Points (HACCP), two well-defined manufacturing procedures that are crucial for guaranteeing the safety and quality of food products, must be strictly followed to maintain consistent food quality (Yan et al., 2022).

Food quality is greatly influenced by the ingredients used in its preparation, especially when it comes to dietary choices (such as vegetarian or halal) and health factors (such as allergies or dietary restrictions) (Chen et al., 2023). The requirement for staff training in both customer service and food hygiene is highlighted by the fact that proper sanitation and hygiene practices are equally crucial to ensuring food safety and customer satisfaction in restaurants (Negassa et al., 2023). Food quality is a major factor in determining consumer loyalty in the fast-food industry in the development of client loyalty towards online food delivery services (OFDS). (Yan et al., 2022).

Food quality is influenced by several factors, such as flavors, variety, healthfulness, and appearance (Hiranpradith et al., 2023). Furthermore, there is a substantial correlation between meal presentations and customers' judgments of quality and satisfaction. Moreover, freshness of food is a significant element influencing patron pleasure during eating experiences (Barnhart et al., 2023). Other literature has provided copious documentation of the interaction between food quality and consumer satisfaction, the quality of food is an essential aspect of dining out and has a big influence on customers' plans to come back (Andre et al., 2022).

(Yan et al., 2022) support this relationship by demonstrating that, in the context of online meal ordering, both food quality and e-service quality significantly increase customer satisfaction. Their research highlights the fact that good food quality raises customer perceptions of the service's worth and fosters a more positive brand image.

H2: Food quality has a positive influence on Online Food Delivery in Klang Valley.

Sales Promotion

A key element of every marketing plan that aims to raise brand awareness and create demand for certain items is sales promotion. It is essential to the development of enduring connections between companies and their clients (Budiarto et al., 2023). Effective sales promotions can introduce new items by decreasing perceived risk and increasing consumer interest, claims (Spotts et al., 2022) further stress that to maximize performance, companies must precisely outline their sales goals and choose relevant advertising tactics that are customized for their target audience. Sales promotion is a significant marketing approach aimed at boosting demand and attracting clients.

Planned sales promotions have a big impact on how satisfied customers are with online sales promotions that include discounts, loyalty points, and special offers give customers a sense of value and encourage repeat business (Prados-Peña et al., 2022). research investigates why consumers care about loyalty points, which corresponds to the value customers perceive in sales promotions (Li, M.2019). Sales promotions had a significant positive impact on customer satisfaction, hence increasing the link between promotional actions and intentions to repurchase. Customers are more likely to return and make more purchases when they perceive they are getting a good bargain through promotions (Madhu et al., 2022).

A major factor influencing customer satisfaction in online delivery is sales promotion, which is also influenced by food and service quality (Budiarto et al., 2023). According to (Vaníčková & Szczepańska-Woszczyna, 2020), to promote long-term growth and improve customer experience, sales promotions must be coordinated with the overall marketing and Various sorts of effective sales promotion methods include limited-time deals, loyalty program (Lin & Bowman, 2021) and discounts is a common strategy to draw in new clients and promote recurring business (Zhong et al., 2022).

Sales promotions can draw in and keep consumers, for instance, bonus offers, and price reductions are very successful in raising customer satisfaction since they give customers observable advantages, (Spotts et al., 2022) research highlights the importance of appealing promotional tactics in raising consumer satisfaction and cultivating a positive perception of the brand, which in turn encourages brand loyalty and positive word-of-mouth recommendations (Kalinowska & Żyliński, 2023).

H3: Sales promotion has positive influence on Online Food Delivery Klang Valley

Customer Satisfaction

"Customer satisfaction" is frequently employed in marketing contexts. The degree to which a company's goods and services live up to the needs and expectations of its clients is measured by customer satisfaction. It also considers how many consumers in total exceed the company's satisfaction requirements (Majeed et al., 2022). According to (Maghfur et al., 2023) the degree to which a service meets the expectations of the customer is a measure of consumer satisfaction. In addition, as it can give a business a competitive edge over rivals, client happiness is essential to the success of online meal delivery service state that contentment is a judgment call based on how well products meet the customer's prior expectations (Han et al., 2022).

Companies may continuously upgrade their offers and better fit with market demands by exploiting the precious resource of consumer feedback (Zygiaris et al., 2022). Restaurants need to understand customer satisfaction since it has a direct impact on customer loyalty and repeat businesses, moreover organizations can attain significant success, by obtaining recurring business from happy clients and raising revenues (Böhringer et al., 2020).

An organization's efforts toward continuous improvement can be greatly aided by the input provided by its customers, (Sun et al., 2023) contend that businesses looking to improve their offers should use empirical insights rather than conjecture to comprehend customer perspectives. This is consistent with the research by (Siitonen et al., 2022), who highlight the need of understanding customer perspectives to develop organizational strategies that work.

Market performance and brand equity are strongly influenced by long-term consumer satisfaction. According to (Ioannou et al., 2022) businesses that place a high priority on customer satisfaction typically thumped their rivals in terms of revenue growth and businesses find it easier to draw in new clients when their brand reputation is enhanced by high customer satisfaction levels.

Framework

Figure 1. Conceptual Framework Model and Proposed

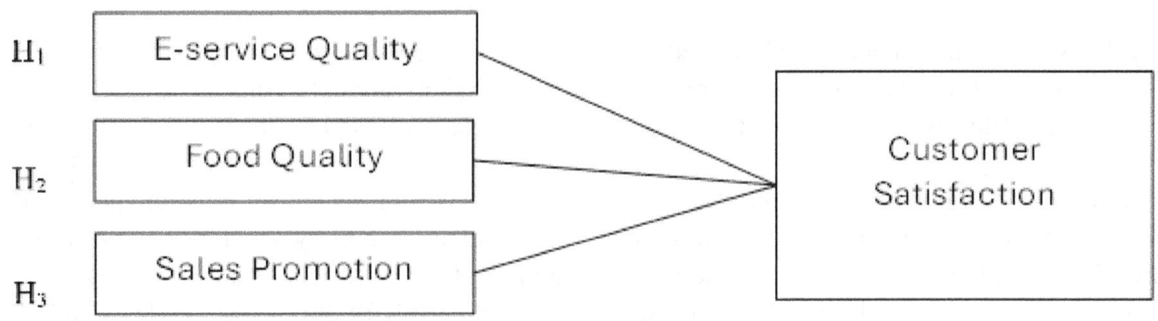

Sources: Anbumathi, R., Dorai, S., & Palaniappan, U. 2022, Hong,C, Choi, E., & Joung, H. 2022, Madhu, S., Soundararajan, V., & Parayitam, S.2022, Ginting, Y.M., Chandra, T., Miran, I., & Yusriadi, Y.2022, Majeed, M., Are, C., Fatawu, A., & Abubakari, A. 2022, Chowdury, R. 2023. Venkatakrishnan, J., Alagiriswamy, R., & Parayitam, S, 2023

METHODOLOGY

Research Design

Quantitative research is used in this study, The process of gathering data using a quantitative research approach and turning it into numerical data that can be statistically evaluated (Jamieson et al., 2023). Quantitative is used to test hypotheses and assumptions. This form of research can be used to find generalizing facts about a topic (S. Chen et al., 2022).

Because quantitative research uses statistical data as a measurement, it can assist save time (Bauer et al., 2021). Furthermore, it entails examining the independent hypothesis and dependent variable to derive a general conclusion (Rajbahadur et al., 2019).

Data Collection

The present study aims to gather primary data from experienced respondents who have used online meal delivery services. The respondents will be asked to complete an online questionnaire that will gauge their satisfaction with the service in terms of food quality, sales promotion, and e-service quality. Websites and articles from previous research studies serve as the foundation for the framework that is used for secondary data (Ahmad & Murad, 2020); to validate the proposed independent and dependent variables, numerous scholars have carried out studies. Finding out how sales promotion, food quality, and e-service quality relate to consumer pleasure and loyalty is the goal of secondary data extraction. Additionally, the quality of the food, e-services, and sales promotion will all have an impact on customer satisfaction, as this research will ascertain (Budiarto et al., 2023).

The research and data collection are based on Klang Valley, Malaysian home to an approximate population of 8.8 million, has a varied demographic environment that is perfect for studying consumer behaviour concerning online meal delivery services.

Sampling Method & Sample Size

In this study, convenience sampling methods will be employed. The simplest type of sampling is convenience sampling since it can be completed quickly in the short amount of time allotted. Because of this, gathering data within the allotted time frame makes it an easy method for the researcher to conduct the investigation (Etikan, 2016).

(Wan et al., 2014) asserts that sample size is an essential factor in research since it attempts to establish dependability and extrapolate the demography to a broader community. As a result, selecting the appropriate sample size is crucial because higher response rates are associated with higher accuracy. 8.8 million people live in Klang Valley, considering the total of 95% of the confidence level and a 5% margin of error. A Raosoft sample size calculator indicates that this study's sample size would need the collection of more than 385 respondents. As a result, 390 respondents were gathered to finish the study.

Data Collection Procedure

The information acquired regarding the subject of the study is referred to as primary data. primary data refers to first-hand information gathered using various techniques including questionnaires, surveys, or in-person inspections (Van Breukelen, 2010). To collect information for this study, an online questionnaire will be administered using primary data. In this study, the online questionnaire will use google forms website to create and will be distributed via emails as well as QR code and Whatsapp to collect the data.

Secondary data will also be gathered from journal articles, websites, government publications, and other sources (Bokhove, 2022). Consequently, this research will enable the investigator to go deeper into previous studies while exploring novel subjects, ultimately yielding superior outcomes (Singh et al., 2021).

Research Instrument

Questionnaires are the primary research tool utilized to gather data from respondents (Bond et al., 2011). It is requested by the responders. In addition, it provides a speedy means of obtaining findings. Online surveys are the primary data collection instrument in this project. To make it easier for respondents, the questionnaires have five categories of answers: (1) Strongly disagree, (2) Disagree, (3) Neutral, (4) Agree, and (5) Strongly agree. A more detailed evaluation of respondents' beliefs and attitudes regarding the variables under study is made possible by the Likert scale format (Shiyab et al., 2023).

Questionnaire Design

A set of questionnaires was created, the surveys will be divided into five sections, with one section dedicated to demographic information, there are three categories of independent variables: E-service quality, food quality, and sales promotion. Finally, there is one part of dependent variables that refers to consumer satisfaction. The demographic detail section will comprise seven questions about age, gender, ethnicity, education level, occupation, and monthly income (Kiliç, 2022).

The first independent variable, E-service quality, will be assessed with four questions. The sources will be modified from (Venkatakrishnan et al., 2023) and (Badotra & Sundas, 2021) serve as moderators in the relationship between e-service quality and customer satisfaction. There will be four sets of questions for each of the independent variables of E-service Quality, food quality, and Sales Promotion, both sources will be adapted from (Ginting et al., 2022). Finally, four questions will be asked about the dependent variable, customer satisfaction. The sources will be modified from (Ginting et al., 2022) and (Majeed et al., 2022).

DATA ANALYSIS

Data analysis is the process of gathering, modelling, and assessing data using logical concepts and statistical methods (Hanagal et al., 2022). Because the study employs questions and a quantitative method, statistics, tables, and concluding conclusions will be collected using the Statistical Package for Social Sciences (SPSS) (Reddy, 2021), SPSS is the most sophisticated and accurate statistical software available, allowing researchers to swiftly analyse data, test, calculate, and forecast, as well as evaluate the bivariate correlation between two variables (Pallant, 2020).

Reliability Test

A reliability test is an important tool for researchers to use in validating the stability and consistency of an evaluation (Kong et al., 2022), an acceptable reliability score is 0.7 or above, with a maximum recommended reliability of 0.90, which is regarded outstanding. As a result, to confirm the correctness of the findings, all surveys will be tested using Cronbach's Alpha (Tavakol & Dennick, 2011).

Pilot Test

The pilot test is designed to assess the viability of the study, technique, and questionnaires, allowing the researcher to evaluate the research with a small sample of respondents to determine the reliability of the questionnaire before completing the execution paper (Blum et al., 2020). If the questionnaire has an issue, researchers can change the questions to make them more understandable. Researchers should conduct a pilot test involving at least 10% of the total sample size to ensure the validity of their questionnaire items (Wan et al., 2014).

Table 1. Reliability Pilot Test

Cronbach's Alpha		No of Items
E-Service Quality	.779	4
Food Quality	.833	4
Sales Promotion	.820	4
Customer Satisfaction	.841	4

For the pilot test 42 people ought to take part in it if the survey calls test and 390 survey above needed to be collected referring to *table 1.*

The reliability test at *table 1* indicates an optimum Cronbach's alpha result is 0.7 or greater, indicating acceptably high dependability. The data presented in table 1 above indicates that the total variables have indicated a satisfactory degree of reliability. Current research supports this criterion by highlighting the fact that an instrument's internal consistency is typically ensured by a Cronbach's alpha value above 0.7, (Tavakol & Dennick, 2011).

Validity Test

To test validity, focus on the outcome, specifically the ratio of each independent variable indication. The first validity test is constructing validity, which determines whether the test cost is proportional to the concept. Content validity is the evaluation of all aspects of the topic covered by the test. Finally, Standard Validity investigates the outcome of a measure using the same parameter as the measurement (Flake et al., 2022).

Because reliability and validity are related, it is also critical to guarantee that the results are valid when conducting validity tests. The link between reliability and validity ensures that the data is meaningful (De Barros Ahrens et al., 2020).

Normality Test

Statistical techniques called normality tests are used to assess if a dataset has a normal distribution. Several statistical methods, such as regression, t-test and analysis of variance, analyse data based on the assumption of normality (Abiodun et al., 2022). Skewness and kurtosis are common normality tests employed in other investigations. In this study, normality tests will use skewness and kurtosis to measure the data. Skewness is to measure an asymmetrical, whereas kurtosis is the measure of a distribution (Kim, 2013). The ideal range acceptable for skewness is between −3 and +3, and the ideal range acceptable kurtosis lies between the range of –10 to +10 (C. Chen et al., 2022).

Descriptive Analysis

Descriptive analysis is used to provide a summary and behavioural information, allowing researchers to have a better understanding of the unique observation data in the study (Palinkas et al., 2013). Descriptive analysis approaches are used to quantify frequency distribution, depression in terms of range, standard deviations, coefficient, and central tendency in terms of mean, median, and mode and it also helps in explaining, demonstrate and summarize data points in a constructive way so that patterns can develop and satisfy all data conditions (Marques et al., 2022).

Pearson Correlation Analysis

Correlation Analysis is used to identify the link between two variables (Werme et al., 2022). In correlation analysis, it can be classified as either positive, negative, or zero. A positive correlation suggests a strong association between the variables, whereas a negative correlation shows that one variable does not affect the other. Zero correlations indicate that there is no relationship between the two variables (Hu et al., 2022). correlation analysis is used to examine the quantitative data collected to find out whether there is a relationship, pattern or trend that should be noted between the two research methods such as surveys and opinion polls (Werme et al., 2022). In this study, Pearson Correlation Coefficient will be utilized to assess the relationship between the independent and dependent variables (Dufera et al., 2023). The correlation result range should be -1 to +1 for perfect correlations, zero for no relationships, and -1 for perfectly negative correlations (Tang, 2022).

Regression Analysis

Regression analysis is a technique that predicts the relationship between two variables. Regression analysis can be applied in various contexts, including finance and social sciences, to assess how changes in independent variables affect a dependent variable (Lee, 2022).

The coefficient determination is known as R square, and it is used to quantify the goodness of fit with the variable and the possible value with lines ranging from 0 to 1 (Monteiro et al., 2023). At 1, the model allows you to perfectly anticipate any result. a value closer to 1 indicates a perfect liner with a better fit (Tetrault et al., 2023). The two most crucial are the beta coefficient and the matching p-value, which will assist the researcher in determining whether two variables are related. The Raosoft software estimated a 95% confidence level in this study. Thus, if the significance level is less than 0.05, the hypothesis result is accepted; otherwise, it is rejected (Alkarkhi, 2020)

RESULTS

Table 2. Reliability Test

Cronbach's Alpha		No of Items
E Service Quality	.747	4
Food Quality	.715	4
Sales Promotion	.790	4
Customer Satisfaction	.869	4

Table 2 validity reliability test was performed following the receipt of 390 responses to evaluate the variable's reliance. Cronbach's alpha, the reliability test result, is more than 0.700 for every variable in table 2 This displays good and reasonable variable results. "Customer satisfaction" which is the primary dependent variable, had a test score of 0.869. The first independent variable, "E-Service Quality," scored 0.747, the second, "Food Quality," scored 0.715, and the final, "Sales Promotion," scored 0.790, were the scores for the independent variables other than that. It demonstrates that the reliability level is good and acceptable.

Normality Test

Table 3. Normality Test

Descriptive Statistics									
	N	Minimum	Maximum	Mean	Std. Deviation	Skewness		Kurtosis	
	Statistic	Statistic	Statistic	Statistic	Statistic	Statistic	Std. Error	Statistic	Std. Error
It is convenient to order through online food delivery services	390	2.00	5.00	4.2795	.70717	-.545	.124	-.530	.247
The delivery time made by the online food delivery services will always be on time	390	1.00	5.00	3.4949	1.05564	-.250	.124	-.606	.247
Transactions in online food delivery services are easy	390	1.00	5.00	4.2538	.71680	-.629	.124	.152	.247
The prices offered by the online food delivery services are affordable	390	1.00	5.00	3.6897	1.02345	-.420	.124	-.420	.247
The serving of food ordered through the online food delivery services is in accordance with the display in the application	390	1.00	5.00	3.6923	.92811	-.147	.124	-.524	.247
The online food delivery services offers healthy menu	390	1.00	5.00	3.5846	.93036	-.200	.124	-.305	.247
Foods and beverages must be sealed well especially during COVID-19 pandemic situation	390	1.00	5.00	4.3436	.76551	-.915	.124	.271	.247
I also concern with packaging material that influences food cleanliness	390	1.00	5.00	4.2769	.77905	-.822	.124	.192	.247
The promotions offered by online food delivery services are attractive	390	1.00	5.00	3.9513	.82704	-.484	.124	.004	.247
The special price promotions offered in the online food delivery services are useful to me	390	2.00	5.00	4.0615	.78633	-.492	.124	-.269	.247
I feel that discounts and promotions provided encourages me to use online food delivery services	390	2.00	5.00	4.0769	.78169	-.557	.124	-.092	.247
Promotion expiry date influences me in making an order	390	1.00	5.00	3.6846	.97291	-.310	.124	-.657	.247
I am satisfied with the use of the online food delivery services	390	2.00	5.00	4.1256	.75347	-.429	.124	-.483	.247
I would like to continue to use online food delivery services to order food	390	1.00	5.00	4.1462	.76671	-.599	.124	.094	.247

continued on following page

Table 3. Continued

Descriptive Statistics									
	N	Minimum	Maximum	Mean	Std. Deviation	Skewness		Kurtosis	
	Statistic	Statistic	Statistic	Statistic	Statistic	Statistic	Std. Error	Statistic	Std. Error
I would encourage others to use food delivery services	390	1.00	5.00	4.0282	.81548	-.452	.124	-.305	.247
The experience when using the service is as expected	390	2.00	5.00	3.9103	.77867	-.105	.124	-.774	.247
Valid N (listwise)	390								

Table 3 displays the results of the normality test performed on the study questionnaires, Food quality, sales promotion, and e-service quality are the independent variables represented by IV1 through IV3. Skewness and kurtosis are important metrics in statistical analysis that are used to evaluate the normalcy of data distributions. A kurtosis score in the range of -10 to +10 (-10 < X < +10) and a skewness value between -3 and +3 (-3 < X < +3) are accepted, (C. Chen et al., 2022)

The skewness values obtained from the data vary from -0.915 to -0.105, with -0.105 being the highest value. The maximum value of 0.271 is found in the kurtosis values, which range from -0.774 to 0.271. All the surveys are considered typical and appropriate for additional analysis because the skewness and kurtosis values are within acceptable limits with normal distribution, (Kim, 2013).

Correlation Test

Table 4. Correlation Test

Correlation					
		IV1	IV2	IV3	DV
IV1	Pearson Correlation	1	.620**	.287**	.274**
	Sig. (2-tailed)		<.001	<.001	<.001
	N	390	390	390	390
IV2	Pearson Correlation	.620**	1	.323**	.417**
	Sig. (2-tailed)	<.001		<.001	<.001
	N	390	390	390	390
IV3	Pearson Correlation	.287**	.323**	1	.599**
	Sig. (2-tailed)	<.001	<.001		<.001
	N	390	390	390	390
DV1	Pearson Correlation	.274**	.417**	.599**	1
	Sig. (2-tailed)	<.001	<.001	<.001	
	N	390	390	390	390

**. Correlation is significant at the 0.01 level (2-tailed).

Typically utilized at a 5% significance level to measure the variable. When the p-value is greater than 0.05, the hypothesis is rejected; when the p-value is less than 0.05, it is accepted (Amrhein & Greenland, 2022). According to (Schober et al., 2018) a significant correlation results in a correlation range of -1 to +1.

Results in *table 4* show that in Klang Valley, customer satisfaction is significantly correlated with three independent variables: food quality (IV2), sales promotion (IV3), and e-service quality (IV1). The overall positive correlation that has been seen between the independent and dependent variables serves as the basis for proof of this claim. In particular, the E-service Quality (IV1) relationship (r) estimation is 0.274, whereas the Food Quality (IV2) relationship (r) is 0.417, indicating a stronger relationship. Sales Promotion (IV3), which has an estimate of 0.599, shows the strongest correlation.

Sales Promotion (IV3) has the highest coefficient of 0.599 among the three independent variables; a correlation value greater than 0.2 indicates a positive correlation between the independent factors and the dependent variable. This result is consistent with well-established theories of customer happiness and service quality, which hold that effective promotions and improved service quality greatly increase consumer contentment and loyalty.

The presence of these associations underscores the critical role that e-service quality, food quality, and sales promotion play in shaping customer experiences and fostering loyalty in competitive markets.

Regression Analysis

Table 5. Regression Analysis

Model Summary									
					Change Statistics				
Model	R	R Square	Adjusted R Square	Std. Error of the Estimate	R Square Change	F Change	df1	df2	Sig. F Change
1	.645[a]	.416	.412	.50625	.416	91.687	3	386	<.001

a. Predictors: (Constant), IV3, IV1, IV2

Table 5 above depicts the multiple regression analysis, which reflects on the relationship between the independent and dependent variables. The R-squared is a measure of the effect of predictor factors on the variability of the study's findings.

The R value is 0.645 which means that 3 independent variables have a moderate significant toward the dependent variable. Besides, the R square value is 0.416 which indicates the 40% of the variable in factor influencing customers satisfaction on online food delivery service. While the remaining 60% of the variables are not unknown variables, factors could be investigated in a further research study.

Table 6. ANOVA

ANOVA[a]						
Model		Sum of Squares	df	Mean Square	F	Sig.
1	Regression	70.495	3	23.498	91.687	<.001[b]
	Residual	98.927	386	.256		
	Total	169.422	389			

a. Dependent Variable: DV1
b. Predictors: (Constant), IV3, IV1, IV2

According to *Table 6* the ANOVA test is to test overall significance of the model which is reported as F- statistics which are related to the p-value. Based on table 6 the F- statistics are 91.687 and the p-value is equivalent <.001 which is less than significant level of < .005. Therefore, In the study, the conceptual framework can be utilized and have the relationship between the independent variable and dependent variable. Hence, it is said to be a good fit for the analysis as a result.

Coefficients

Table 7. Coefficients

Coefficients[a]						
		Unstandardized Coefficients		Standardized Coefficients		
Model		B	Std. Error	Beta	t	Sig.
1	(Constant)	1.021	.202		5.049	<.001
	IV1	-.047	.049	-.048	-.957	.339
	IV2	.292	.053	.277	5.484	<.001
	IV3	.522	.041	.523	12.649	<.001

Dependent Variable: DV1

According to *table 7* a significance level (p-value) < 0.05 denotes a substantial direct effect of the independent variable on the dependent variable, as shown by table 7 which presents the coefficients from the regression analysis (Chicco et al., 2021). This standard criterion is utilized in statistical analysis to decide whether to reject the null hypothesis, which states that there is no association or effect (Ferreira, 2011).

Independent Variable 2 (IV2) has a significant level of < 0.001, which is much less than the 0.05 threshold. This suggests that differences in IV2 are linked to notable changes in the dependent variable. It also shows that IV2 has a strong and meaningful effect on the dependent variable.

Independent Variable 3 (IV3): In a similar vein, IV3 likewise exhibits a significance level of < 0.001, demonstrating that it significantly affects the dependent variable, Significance Level: Interpretation and Construction.

Independent Variable 1 (IV1): On the other hand, IV1 has a significant level of 0.339, over the 0.05 level. This suggests that changes in IV1 are not related to changes in the DV because IV1 does not have a statistically significant effect on the dependent variable.

Discussion

Supported Hypothesis

The literature consistently supports the hypothesis that consumer engagement with mobile technologies, especially during the COVID-19 pandemic, has led to increased usage of online food delivery services (OFDS) (Chowdhury, 2023). Research shows that consumer spending on food delivery rose significantly during the pandemic, with a reported 70% increase in 2020 compared to the previous year. This finding aligns with the hypothesis that heightened engagement with mobile platforms enhances customer satisfaction and loyalty (Shaalan et al., 2022).

Numerous studies support the hypothesis that e-service quality significantly influences customer satisfaction in online food delivery services (OFDS). It also supports the hypothesis that personal aspects of delivery workers, such as professionalism and friendliness, positively impact customer satisfaction and emphasize the positive interactions with delivery staff enhance customers' overall perceptions of service quality (Ginting et al., 2022).

Not Supported Hypothesis

Perceived Food Quality as a sole determinant of satisfaction, although perceived food quality is acknowledged as a critical factor influencing customer satisfaction, some studies indicate that it is not the sole determinant. Research highlights that while food quality is essential, other factors like delivery speed and service quality also play significant roles in shaping overall customer satisfaction. (Cui et al., 2023, Naini et al., 2022).

RECOMMENDATIONS

For future additional the independent variables can be further discussed how it can influence customer satisfaction. Analyzing more possible factors will help future researchers gain a deeper understanding of customer satisfaction in online food delivery and help fill the knowledge gaps. Besides this the researcher can use a mixed method to conduct the research in the future. Quantitative methods can use questionnaires, while qualitative research can use interviews to obtain respondents' perceptions and impressions about a topic (Taherdoost, 2022). Researchers to obtain more specific data across a wider variety of impacting factors by studying and identifying additional elements more in-depth understanding of customer satisfaction in online meal delivery and filling knowledge gaps ("Independent Variable," 2010). Questionnaires can be used in quantitative approaches, whereas interviews can be used in qualitative research to collect respondents' perceptions and impressions about a topic. It enables researchers to investigate and comprehend respondents' perspectives and behaviours regarding previous and future satisfaction (Bolarinwa, 2015).

To Further improve the theme of customer satisfaction by testing other independent variables such as by using convenience factors, menu variety, influence of price, time of delivery and on security privacy issues.

Convenience refers to meeting the consumer's ability to perform the goal in asking easy, fast, and effortless matters. (Teo et al., 2008) Nowadays, people are seeking not just high-quality services, but also looking for convenience for them to save their non-monetary costs, such as time and effort (R. C. Lee, 2012).

Menu Variety refers to the importance of providing a variety of choices to online consumers and determining the food satisfaction and adequacy of items. Companies should offer a wide variety of food options to match customers' requirements and desires, making it easier for them to select food that suits their tastes (Sutaguna et al., 2023).

Price can refer to the money a customer pays for a particular product or service. In other words, pricing refers to the individual's need to exchange cash value to fulfill their desire. They will always look for a better deal when they shop (Chesney et al., 2022).

Time delivery refers to the product delivery to a location that meets the quality and quantity requirements of customers in the period of the time of use, delivery time is the most important factor influencing customer satisfaction (Kula et al., 2021).

Privacy and security concerns are significant factors influencing consumer behavior in online shopping. Customers' hesitation to purchase things online is often rooted in their concerns about privacy and safety, leading to a substantial percentage of consumers refraining from providing information or shopping online (Hamli & Sobaih, 2023).

CONCLUSION

The researcher has attained the results and completed the research by studying this specific topic, analyzing numerous connected journals adopting the proper research methodology papers and creating distinguished survey questionnaires. The three independent variables two have a positive association with the variable impacting customer satisfaction on online food delivery has met the research objective and research questions, even though one independent was not accepted.

Consumers' lifestyles have altered because of technology and due to the influence of internet use, since they now depend on mobiles to make food purchases convenient (Jain et al., 2023). In 2024, the Online Food Delivery industry is expected to generate US$2.77 billion. This market is estimated to increase at a 10.82% annual rate between 2024 and 2029, with a projected market volume of US$4.63 billion by 2029. Although this expansion creates chances for new players, it also makes the competition among the current players more intense. To stay relevant and draw in clients as the market grows, businesses need to innovate and set themselves apart with their services. To thrive in this competitive environment based on the findings, online food delivery services (OFDS) must focus on several key strategies such as focusing on these elements (Ariffin et al., 2021).

Improving e- service quality, delivering top-notch food and e-services can have a big influence on client loyalty. Companies need to make sure that the orders are filled accurately, delivery is made on time, and customer assistance is prompt (Sudirjo et al., 2023). Value Proposition, Price-conscious customers might be drawn in by providing competitive prices and promotions. Studies indicate that customers are inclined to select services that offer high value for their money (Mustafa et al., 2022).

Optimizing mobile applications' user interfaces can greatly increase customer satisfaction, user experience, service quality, and social interaction all have an impact on customers' satisfaction with online services (Xu et al., 2023). Additionally, by efficiently addressing pain areas and personalizing user experiences, the usage of mobile app intelligence—which leverages data analytics and machine learning—has been identified as a viable way to boost customer satisfaction This method increases usability and encourages consumer interaction, which raises retention rates and promotes positive word-of-mouth (Zarifis & Fu, 2023). Marketing Techniques by utilizing digital marketing techniques to boost exposure and draw in new clients includes social media interaction and search engine optimization (Arora et al., 2022).

Online food delivery services (OFDS) businesses should change with the times and technology application to satisfy customers' changing expectations as technology keeps changing how people live (Hong et al., 2022).

REFERENCES

Abdullah, O., Sufi, T., & Kumar, S. (2023). Impact of food and beverage quality and service quality towards customer satisfaction and customer retention, a study of Five-Star Hotels. *International Journal of Professional Business Review*, 8(5), e01994. DOI: 10.26668/businessreview/2023.v8i5.1994

Abiodun, N. L., Matovu, M. S., & Olanrewaju, R. O. (2022). Statistical powers of univariate normality Tests: Comparative analysis of 2016 election process in Uganda. *European Journal of Statistics*, 2, 6. DOI: 10.28924/ada/stat.2.6

Adak, A., Pradhan, B., & Shukla, N. (2022). Sentiment analysis of customer reviews of food delivery services using deep learning and explainable artificial intelligence: Systematic review. *Foods*, 11(10), 1500. DOI: 10.3390/foods11101500 PMID: 35627070

Al-Qudah, A. A., Al-Okaily, M., Alqudah, G., & Ghazlat, A. (2022). Mobile payment adoption in the time of the COVID-19 pandemic. *Electronic Commerce Research*. Advance online publication. DOI: 10.1007/s10660-022-09577-1

Alkarkhi, A. F. (2020). The observed significance level (P-value) procedure. In Elsevier eBooks (pp. 79–119). https://doi.org/DOI: 10.1016/B978-0-12-824301-5.00010-1

Amrhein, V., & Greenland, S. (2022). Discuss practical importance of results based on interval estimates and p-value functions, not only on point estimates and null p-values. *Journal of Information Technology*, 37(3), 316–320. DOI: 10.1177/02683962221105904

Anbumathi, R., Dorai, S., & Palaniappan, U. (2022). Evaluating the role of technology and non-technology factors influencing brand love in Online Food Delivery services. *Journal of Retailing and Consumer Services*, 71, 103181. DOI: 10.1016/j.jretconser.2022.103181

Andre, R. S., Mercante, L. A., Facure, M. H. M., Sanfelice, R. C., Fugikawa-Santos, L., Swager, T. M., & Correa, D. S. (2022). Recent progress in amine gas sensors for food quality monitoring: Novel architectures for sensing materials and Systems. *ACS Sensors*, 7(8), 2104–2131. DOI: 10.1021/acssensors.2c00639 PMID: 35914109

Anyanwu, I. B., Ezeaku, M. N., & Ogboagha, C. O. (2022). Relationship marketing and customer loyalty in chain fast food establishments in Umuahia, Abia state, Nigeria. *International Journal of Home Economics Hospitality and Allied Research*, 1(2), 178–188. DOI: 10.57012/ijhhr.v1n2.002

Ariffin, S., Manan, H. A., Ahmad, N., Muhammad, N. S., Hamdan, F., & Kelana, N. S. S. (2021). Continuous intention to use technology of online food delivery services among young adults. *ADVANCES IN BUSINESS RESEARCH INTERNATIONAL JOURNAL*, 7(1), 56. DOI: 10.24191/abrij.v7i1.14256

Arora, K., Alwiyah, N., & Faisal, M. (2022). The use of data science in digital marketing techniques: Work programs, performance sequences and methods. [SABDA Journal]. *Startupreneur Business Digital*, 1(2), 143–155. DOI: 10.33050/sabda.v1i2.110

Badotra, S., & Sundas, A. (2021). A systematic review on security of E-commerce systems. *International Journal of Applied Science and Engineering*, 18(2), 1–19. DOI: 10.6703/ijase.202106_18(2).010

Barnhart, W. R., Dial, L. A., Jordan, A. K., Studer-Perez, E. I., Kalantzis, M. A., & Musher-Eizenman, D. R. (2023). Higher meal disengagement and meal presentation are uniquely related to psychological distress and lower quality of life in undergraduate students. *Journal of American College Health*, •••, 1–8. DOI: 10.1080/07448481.2023.2245912 PMID: 37713319

Belarmino, A., Raab, C., Tang, J., & Han, W. (2021). Exploring the motivations to use online meal delivery platforms: Before and during quarantine. *International Journal of Hospitality Management*, 96, 102983. DOI: 10.1016/j.ijhm.2021.102983

Bi, H., Zhu, X., Lu, F., & Huang, M. (2023). The Meal Delivery Routing Problem in E-commerce Platforms under the Shared Logistics Mode. *Journal of Theoretical and Applied Electronic Commerce Research*, 18(4), 1799–1819. DOI: 10.3390/jtaer18040091

Bokhove, C. (2022). The role of analytical variability in secondary data replications: A replication of Kim et al. (2014). *Educational Research and Evaluation*, 27(1–2), 141–163. DOI: 10.1080/13803611.2021.2022319

Bolarinwa, O. (2015). Principles and methods of validity and reliability testing of questionnaires used in social and health science researches. *The Nigerian Postgraduate Medical Journal*, 22(4), 195. DOI: 10.4103/1117-1936.173959 PMID: 26776330

Bond, F. W., Hayes, S. C., Baer, R. A., Carpenter, K. M., Guenole, N., Orcutt, H. K., Waltz, T., & Zettle, R. D. (2011). Preliminary Psychometric Properties of the Acceptance and Action Questionnaire–II: A Revised Measure of Psychological Inflexibility and Experiential Avoidance. *Behavior Therapy*, 42(4), 676–688. DOI: 10.1016/j.beth.2011.03.007 PMID: 22035996

Budiarto, B. W., Haes, N. P. E., Nawarcono, N. W., Mardiah, N. A., & Apriyono, N. T. (2023). The influence of E-Customer satisfaction, E-Service quality and sales promotion on E-Customer loyalty of Tokopedia customers. [Jurnal Ekonomi Manajemen Dan Akuntansi]. *JEMSI*, 9(6), 2472–2479. DOI: 10.35870/jemsi.v9i6.1656

Cai, L., Yuen, K. F., Fang, M., & Wang, X. (2023). A literature review on the impact of the COVID-19 pandemic on consumer behaviour: Implications for consumer-centric logistics. *Asia Pacific Journal of Marketing and Logistics*, 35(11), 2682–2703. DOI: 10.1108/APJML-08-2022-0731

Candra, S., Sukmawaty, D., & Bahtiar, R. Y. (2023). Insights on online food delivery of mobile application user behavior in Indonesia's large cities. 2023 11th International Conference on Information and Communication Technology (ICoICT), 63-67. https://doi.org/DOI: 10.1109/ICoICT58202.2023.10262624

Chen, C., Liu, Y., Ma, X., & Lyu, L. (2022). CalFAT: Calibrated Federated Adversarial Training with Label Skewness. arXiv (Cornell University). https://doi.org//arxiv.2205.14926DOI: 10.48550

Chen, I., Hsu, P., Officer, M. S., & Wang, Y. (2020). The Oscar goes to. . .: High-tech firms' acquisitions in response to rivals' technology breakthroughs. *Research Policy*, 49(7), 104078. DOI: 10.1016/j.respol.2020.104078

Chen, W., Zhang, S., Hu, X., Chen, F., & Li, D. (2023). A Review of Healthy Dietary Choices for Cardiovascular Disease: From Individual Nutrients and Foods to Dietary Patterns. *Nutrients*, 15(23), 15. DOI: 10.3390/nu15234898 PMID: 38068756

Chesney, M., Krakow, J., Maranghino-Singer, B., & Wolff, V. (2022). Der Finanzsektor im 21. Jahrhundert. In Springer eBooks (pp. 37–66). https://doi.org/DOI: 10.1007/978-3-658-37949-0_3

Chicco, D., Warrens, M. J., & Jurman, G. (2021). The coefficient of determination R-squared is more informative than SMAPE, MAE, MAPE, MSE and RMSE in regression analysis evaluation. *PeerJ. Computer Science*, 7, e623. DOI: 10.7717/peerj-cs.623 PMID: 34307865

Cho, H., Ippolito, D., & Yu, Y. W. (2020). Contact tracing mobile apps for COVID-19: privacy considerations and related trade-offs. arXiv (Cornell University). https://doi.org//arxiv.2003.11511DOI: 10.48550

Chowdhury, R. (2023). Impact of perceived convenience, service quality and security on consumers' behavioural intention towards online food delivery services: The role of attitude as mediator. *SN Business & Economics*, 3(1), 29. Advance online publication. DOI: 10.1007/s43546-023-00422-7 PMID: 36643187

Chung, H. (2022). Variable work schedules, unit-level turnover, and performance before and during the COVID-19 pandemic. *The Journal of Applied Psychology*, 107(4), 515–532. DOI: 10.1037/apl0001006 PMID: 35286111

Cui, F., Zheng, S., Wang, D., Tan, X., Li, Q., Li, J., & Li, T. (2023). Recent advances in shelf life prediction models for monitoring food quality. *Comprehensive Reviews in Food Science and Food Safety*, 22(2), 1257–1284. DOI: 10.1111/1541-4337.13110 PMID: 36710649

Dana, L. M., Hart, E., McAleese, A., Bastable, A., & Pettigrew, S. (2021). Factors associated with ordering food via online meal ordering services. *Public Health Nutrition*, 24(17), 5704–5709. DOI: 10.1017/S1368980021001294 PMID: 33762026

De Barros Ahrens, R., Da Silva Lirani, L., & De Francisco, A. C. (2020). Construct Validity and reliability of the Work Environment Assessment Instrument WE-10. *International Journal of Environmental Research and Public Health*, 17(20), 7364. DOI: 10.3390/ijerph17207364 PMID: 33050197

Dufera, A. G., Liu, T., & Xu, J. (2023). Regression models of Pearson correlation coefficient. *Statistical Theory and Related Fields*, 7(2), 97–106. DOI: 10.1080/24754269.2023.2164970

Etikan, I. (2016). Comparison of convenience sampling and purposive sampling. *American Journal of Theoretical and Applied Statistics*, 5(1), 1. DOI: 10.11648/j.ajtas.20160501.11

Flake, J. K., Davidson, I. J., Wong, O., & Pek, J. (2022). Construct validity and the validity of replication studies: A systematic review. *The American Psychologist*, 77(4), 576–588. DOI: 10.1037/amp0001006 PMID: 35482669

Francioni, B., Curina, I., Hegner, S. M., & Cioppi, M. (2022). Predictors of continuance intention of online food delivery services: Gender as moderator. *International Journal of Retail & Distribution Management*, 50(12), 1437–1457. DOI: 10.1108/IJRDM-11-2021-0537

Ginting, Y. M., Chandra, T., Miran, I., & Yusriadi, Y. (2022). Repurchase intention of e-commerce customers in Indonesia: An overview of the effect of e-service quality, e-word of mouth, customer trust, and customer satisfaction mediation. *International Journal of Data and Network Science*, 7(1), 329–340. DOI: 10.5267/j.ijdns.2022.10.001

Gülteki̇, N. B., & Veuphuteh, F. M. (2023). Price sensitivity, perceived food quality, and intention to purchase fast food in the context of Health-Consciousness of university students. *OPUS Toplum Araştırmaları Dergisi*, 20(52), 317–334. DOI: 10.26466/opusjsr.1210008

Halik, A., & Nugroho, M. (2022). The role of consumer pleasure moderating the effect of content marketing and price discount on online shopping decision and loyalty of Generation Z. *Media Ekonomi Dan Manajemen*, 27(1), 35. DOI: 10.24856/mem.v27i01.2259

Hamli, S. S. A., & Sobaih, A. E. E. (2023). Factors Influencing Consumer Behavior towards Online Shopping in Saudi Arabia Amid COVID-19: Implications for E-Businesses Post Pandemic. *Journal of Risk and Financial Management*, 16(1), 36. DOI: 10.3390/jrfm16010036

Han, W., Raab, C., Belarmino, A., & Tang, J. (2021). Are online meal delivery platforms part of the sharing economy? *Journal of Foodservice Business Research*, 25(3), 253–276. DOI: 10.1080/15378020.2021.1941712

Hanagal, D. D., Latpate, R. V., & Chandra, G. (2022). Applied statistical methods: ISGES 2020, Pune, India, January 2-4. Springer.

Hartanto, A., Chua, Y. J., Quek, F. Y. X., Wong, J., Ooi, W. M., & Majeed, N. M. (2023). Problematic smartphone usage, objective smartphone engagement, and executive functions: A latent variable analysis. *Attention, Perception & Psychophysics*, 85(8), 2610–2625. DOI: 10.3758/s13414-023-02707-3 PMID: 37188861

Hasi, S. M. S. a. M. a. a. A. A. (2020, January 31). Users ‘attitude towards benefits of online shopping: a study on customers of Daraz and Food Panda. https://solidstatetechnology.us/index.php/JSST/article/view/704

Hiranpradith, V., Therdthai, N., & Soontrunnarudrungsri, A. (2023). Effect of Steaming and Microwave Heating on Taste of Clear Soup with Split-Gill Mushroom Powder. *Foods*, 12(8), 1685. DOI: 10.3390/foods12081685 PMID: 37107479

Hong, C., Choi, E., & Joung, H. (2022). Determinants of customer purchase intention toward online food delivery services: The moderating role of usage frequency. *Journal of Hospitality and Tourism Management*, 54, 76–87. DOI: 10.1016/j.jhtm.2022.12.005

Hu, M., Zhang, K., You, R., & Tu, B. (2022). Multisensor-Based continuous authentication of smartphone users with Two-Stage feature extraction. *IEEE Internet of Things Journal*, 10(6), 4708–4724. DOI: 10.1109/JIOT.2022.3219135

Independent variable. (2010). Encyclopedia of Research Design. https://doi.org/DOI: 10.4135/9781412961288.n184

Jain, V., Wadhwani, K., & Eastman, J. K. (2023). Artificial intelligence consumer behavior: A hybrid review and research agenda. *Journal of Consumer Behaviour*, 23(2), 676–697. DOI: 10.1002/cb.2233

Jin, X., & Pan, X. (2023). Government attention, market competition and firm digital transformation. *Sustainability (Basel)*, 15(11), 9057. DOI: 10.3390/su15119057

Kalinowska, A., & Żyliński, S. (2023). Promotional tactics of Polish fashion brands in social media on the example of Vesna and Marie Zélie. *Studia Medioznawcze*, 24(4), 36–49. DOI: 10.33077/uw.24511617.sm.2023.4.783

Khlaif, Z. N., Sanmugam, M., & Ayyoub, A. (2022). Impact of technostress on continuance intentions to use mobile technology. *The Asia-Pacific Education Researcher*. Advance online publication. DOI: 10.1007/s40299-021-00638-x

Kiliç, İ. (2022). Examination of the relationship between demographic information and science literacy in daily life. *American Educational Research Journal*, 10(2), 125–133. DOI: 10.30918/AERJ.102.22.024

Kim, H. (2013). Statistical notes for clinical researchers: Assessing normal distribution (2) using skewness and kurtosis. *Restorative Dentistry & Endodontics*, 38(1), 52. DOI: 10.5395/rde.2013.38.1.52 PMID: 23495371

Kong, L., Chen, W., Luo, W., Chen, C., & Yang, Z. (2022). General Cutting Load Model for Workload Simulation in Spindle Reliability Test. *Machines (Basel)*, 10(2), 144. DOI: 10.3390/machines10020144

Kula, E., Greuter, E., Van Deursen, A., & Gousios, G. (2021). Factors affecting On-Time Delivery in Large-Scale Agile Software Development. *IEEE Transactions on Software Engineering*, 48(9), 3573–3592. DOI: 10.1109/TSE.2021.3101192

Lee, R. C. (2012). A service-oriented analytics framework for Multi-Level marketing business. *Journal of Software Engineering and Applications*, 05(08), 527–535. DOI: 10.4236/jsea.2012.58061

Lee, S. W. (2022). Regression analysis for continuous independent variables in medical research: Statistical standard and guideline of Life Cycle Committee. *Life Cycle*, 2, e3. Advance online publication. DOI: 10.54724/lc.2022.e3

Madhu, S., Soundararajan, V., & Parayitam, S. (2022). Online promotions and hedonic motives as moderators in the relationship between e-Impulsive Buying tendency and customer satisfaction: Evidence from India. *Journal of Internet Commerce*, 22(3), 395–431. DOI: 10.1080/15332861.2022.2088035

Majeed, M., Asare, C., Fatawu, A., & Abubakari, A. (2022). An analysis of the effects of customer satisfaction and engagement on social media on repurchase intention in the hospitality industry. *Cogent Business & Management*, 9(1), 2028331. Advance online publication. DOI: 10.1080/23311975.2022.2028331

Marques, C., Correia, E., Dinis, L., & Vilela, A. (2022). An overview of sensory characterization techniques: From classical descriptive analysis to the emergence of novel profiling methods. *Foods*, 11(3), 255. DOI: 10.3390/foods11030255 PMID: 35159407

Monteiro, C. M., Santos, C., & Castro, P. M. L. (2023). Extensive green roofs: Different time approaches to runoff coefficient determination. *Water (Basel)*, 15(10), 1852. DOI: 10.3390/w15101852

Mustafa, A. M., Azimli, A., & Jaf, R. S. (2022). The role of resource consumption accounting in achieving competitive prices and sustainable profitability. *Energies*, 15(11), 4155. DOI: 10.3390/en15114155

Naini, N. F., Santoso, N. S., Andriani, T. S., Claudia, U. G., & Nurfadillah, N. (2022). The effect of product quality, service quality, customer satisfaction on customer loyalty. *Journal of Consumer Sciences*, 7(1), 34–50. DOI: 10.29244/jcs.7.1.34-50

Naveed, S., & Murtaza, U. U. R. (2023). Role of marketing Ethics for clients' satisfaction. *Journal of Social Sciences Review*, 3(2), 987–994. DOI: 10.54183/jssr.v3i2.337

Negassa, B., Anbese, A. T., Worku, G., Areba, A. S., Seboka, B. T., Debela, B. G., Kanno, G. G., & Soboksa, N. E. (2023). Food hygiene practices and associated factors among street food vendors in urban areas of Gedeo Zone, southern Ethiopia. *Environmental Health Insights*, 17, 117863022311685. DOI: 10.1177/11786302231168531 PMID: 37122687

Palinkas, L. A., Horwitz, S. M., Green, C. A., Wisdom, J. P., Duan, N., & Hoagwood, K. (2013). Purposeful sampling for qualitative data collection and analysis in mixed method implementation research. *Administration and Policy in Mental Health*, 42(5), 533–544. DOI: 10.1007/s10488-013-0528-y PMID: 24193818

Pallant, J. (2020). SPSS Survival Manual. In Routledge eBooks. https://doi.org/DOI: 10.4324/9781003117452

Sakina, F., & Yafiz, M. (2023). Using customer satisfaction as a mediating variable to boost service quality and build trust in repeat business. *JURNAL MANAJEMEN BISNIS*, 10(1), 44–56. DOI: 10.33096/jmb.v10i1.468

Schober, P., Boer, C., & Schwarte, L. A. (2018). Correlation Coefficients: Appropriate use and interpretation. *Anesthesia and Analgesia*, 126(5), 1763–1768. DOI: 10.1213/ANE.0000000000002864 PMID: 29481436

Shaalan, A., Agag, G., & Tourky, M. (2022). Harnessing Customer Mindset Metrics to Boost Consumer Spending: A Cross-Country study on routes to economic and business growth. *British Journal of Management*, 34(1), 442–465. DOI: 10.1111/1467-8551.12596

Shiyab, W., Ferguson, C., Rolls, K., & Halcomb, E. (2023). Solutions to address low response rates in online surveys. *European Journal of Cardiovascular Nursing*, 22(4), 441–444. DOI: 10.1093/eurjcn/zvad030 PMID: 36827086

Singh, V., Realyvasquez, J., Simcox, T., Rozell, J. C., Schwarzkopf, R., & Davidovitch, R. I. (2021). Robotics versus navigation versus conventional total hip arthroplasty: Does the use of technology yield superior outcomes? *The Journal of Arthroplasty*, 36(8), 2801–2807. DOI: 10.1016/j.arth.2021.02.074 PMID: 33773864

Sobika, K. A., & Raj, S. V. (2021). A study on predicting customer willingness to order food online during COVID-19 pandemic using machine learning algorithms. 2021 4th International Conference on Computing and Communications Technologies (ICCCT), 27, 236–241. https://doi.org/DOI: 10.1109/ICCCT53315.2021.9711904

Spotts, H. E., Weinberger, M. G., Assaf, A. G., & Weinberger, M. F. (2022). The role of paid media, earned media, and sales promotions in driving marcom sales performance in consumer services. *Journal of Business Research*, 152, 387–397. DOI: 10.1016/j.jbusres.2022.07.047

Statista. (n.d.). Online food delivery - Worldwide | Statista market forecast. https://www.statista.com/outlook/emo/online-food-delivery/worldwide

Stuber, J. M., Lakerveld, J., Kievitsbosch, L. W., Mackenbach, J. D., & Beulens, J. W. J. (2022). Nudging customers towards healthier food and beverage purchases in a real-life online supermarket: A multi-arm randomized controlled trial. *BMC Medicine*, 20(1), 10. Advance online publication. DOI: 10.1186/s12916-021-02205-z PMID: 35034635

Sudirjo, N. F., Ratnawati, N. R., Hadiyati, N. R., Sutaguna, N. I. N. T., & Yusuf, N. M. (2023). THE INFLUENCE OF ONLINE CUSTOMER REVIEWS AND E-SERVICE QUALITY ON BUYING DECISIONS IN ELECTRONIC COMMERCE. *Journal of Management and Creative Business*, 1(2), 156–181. DOI: 10.30640/jmcbus.v1i2.941

Suherlan, S., & Okombo, M. O. (2023). Technological Innovation in Marketing and its Effect on Consumer Behaviour. [TACIT]. *Technology and Society Perspectives*, 1(2), 94–103. DOI: 10.61100/tacit.v1i2.57

Sureeyatanapas, P., & Damapong, K. (2023). Performance assessment and comparison of online food delivery service providers based upon the aggregated perspectives of restaurant operators. *Expert Systems with Applications*, 236, 121262. DOI: 10.1016/j.eswa.2023.121262

Sutaguna, N. I. N. T. (2023). Hanan Catering's Instagram promotions, pricing, and menu variety influence consumer purchasing decisions in Bandung. *International Journal of Economics and Management Research*, 2(1), 76–87. DOI: 10.55606/ijemr.v2i1.67

Taherdoost, H. (2022). What are Different Research Approaches? Comprehensive Review of Qualitative, Quantitative, and Mixed Method Research, Their Applications, Types, and Limitations. *Journal of Management Science & Engineering Research*, 5(1), 53–63. DOI: 10.30564/jmser.v5i1.4538

Tang, W. (2022). Deterministic all-versus-nothing proofs of Bell nonlocality based on non-stabilizer states. arXiv (Cornell University). https://doi.org//arxiv.2201.01886DOI: 10.48550

Tavakol, M., & Dennick, R. (2011). Making sense of Cronbach's alpha. *International Journal of Medical Education*, 2, 53–55. DOI: 10.5116/ijme.4dfb.8dfd PMID: 28029643

Tendur, S. T., Hutabarat, V. V., & Tumbelaka, S. S. (2021). Price perception, service quality and customer satisfaction (Empirical study on cafes at Tondano City). *International Journal of Tourism and Hospitality in Asia Pasific*, 4(3), 19–31. DOI: 10.32535/ijthap.v4i3.1196

Teo, T. S. H., Srivastava, S. C., & Jiang, L. (2008). Trust and Electronic Government Success: An Empirical study. *Journal of Management Information Systems*, 25(3), 99–132. DOI: 10.2753/MIS0742-1222250303

Tetrault, A., Nyback, M., Fagerström, L., & Vaartio-Rajalin, H. (2023). "A perfect storm" or missed care? Focus group interviews with dementia care professionals on Advance Care Planning. *BMC Geriatrics*, 23(1), 313. Advance online publication. DOI: 10.1186/s12877-023-04033-7 PMID: 37210508

Venkatakrishnan, J., Alagiriswamy, R., & Parayitam, S. (2023). Web design and trust as moderators in the relationship between e-service quality, customer satisfaction and customer loyalty. *The TQM Journal*, 35(8), 2455–2484. DOI: 10.1108/TQM-10-2022-0298

Wan, X., Wang, W., Liu, J., & Tong, T. (2014). Estimating the sample mean and standard deviation from the sample size, median, range and/or interquartile range. *BMC Medical Research Methodology*, 14(1), 135. Advance online publication. DOI: 10.1186/1471-2288-14-135 PMID: 25524443

Werme, J., Van Der Sluis, S., Posthuma, D., & De Leeuw, C. A. (2022). An integrated framework for local genetic correlation analysis. *Nature Genetics*, 54(3), 274–282. DOI: 10.1038/s41588-022-01017-y PMID: 35288712

Xu, C., Zhang, X., Yang, H. H., Wang, X., Pappas, N., Niyato, D., & Quek, T. Q. S. (2023). Optimal Status Updates for Minimizing Age of Correlated Information in IoT Networks with Energy Harvesting Sensors. arXiv (Cornell University). https://doi.org//arxiv.2310.19216DOI: 10.48550

Yan, M. R., Hsieh, S., & Ricacho, N. (2022). Innovative food packaging, food quality and safety, and consumer perspectives. *Processes (Basel, Switzerland)*, 10(4), 747. DOI: 10.3390/pr10040747

Yang, L., Weng, T., & He, H. (2012). Online ordering systems and consumer acceptance - using box lunch order systems as a case study. *International Journal of Business and Management*, 7(18). Advance online publication. DOI: 10.5539/ijbm.v7n18p26

Zarifis, A., & Fu, S. (2023). Re-Evaluating trust and privacy concerns when purchasing a mobile app: Re-Calibrating for the increasing role of artificial intelligence. *Digital*, 3(4), 286–299. DOI: 10.3390/digital3040018

Chapter 19
Innovative Solutions for a More Sustainable Food Supply Chain:
Role of New Technologies in Food Waste Prevention

Manuel Amador
https://orcid.org/0000-0003-0009-234X
Deustotech, Spain

Nekane Sainz
University of Deusto, Spain

Ainhoa Alonso
Deustotech, Spain

ABSTRACT

This chapter explores the technologies involved in certification systems designed to prevent food waste. First, it presents the state-of-the-art in IoT and blockchain technologies applied to the food supply chain, followed by a summary of the key certifications in this domain. The chapter then provides a comprehensive overview of how these technological innovations are being integrated to tackle the pressing challenges of the food industry, with a particular focus on food waste prevention. Finally, it concludes with insights and conclusions drawn from the analysis of these systems.

INTRODUCTION TO THE INFORMATION AND COMMUNICATION TECHNOLOGIES (ICTS)

Information and Communication Technologies (ICTs) are those technological systems that enable people to control and manage different types of information (Carter & Grover, 2015). The development of these ICTs is leveraging what is known as Industry 4.0 (Peraković et al., 2020). This is an industrial revolution where interconnected objects and systems use, communicate and analyse information (Snider-

DOI: 10.4018/979-8-3693-7683-6.ch019

man et al., 2016). According to small and mid-sized digital technologies users in manufacture, ICTs show advantages as concerns product quality, productivity, innovation and cost saving (Beaty & Quirk, 2018).

ICTs are transforming production lines. Particularly, integrated supply chain management is heading for IoT cloud distributed solutions and big data analysis of the captured information. Every object (physical layer) provides information to an ICT system (data exchange layer), which virtually creates a representation of every object (information integration layer). The physical layer updates constantly the information integration layer, which is then shared with the stakeholders (application service layer) (Ramundo et al., 2016). There is a growing trend by companies towards allocating investments to optimise operating systems. This is causing industry to be driven by the data provided by the aforementioned technologies, whose facilities are interconnected with each other (Bai et al., 2020; Dantas et al., 2021; Hatzivasilis et al., 2019; Manavalan & Jayakrishna, 2019). Thus, having every facility monitored and therefore the energy and resources waste generation are reduced (Andrews, 2015; Inoue et al., 2020).

Among these new technologies, some like the IoT, cloud computing and big data are identified as crucial by 28 EU Member States (Peraković et al., 2020). A brief summary of them is given below.

Big data is defined as "Information assets characterised by such a high volume, velocity and variety to require specific technology and analytical methods for its transformation into Value" by De Mauro et al. (2014). Since nowadays digitalisation is becoming a major subject, big data is gaining relevance because of the need to manage all that analogue information that is being digitised. Moreover, it has a heavy impact on both society and companies (De Mauro et al., 2014).

The cloud computing definition provided by the United States National Institute of Standards and Technology states that cloud computing is "a model for enabling convenient, on-demand network access to a shared pool of configurable computing resources (e.g., networks, servers, storage, applications, and services) that can be rapidly provisioned and released with minimal management effort or service provider interaction" (Mell & Grance, 2011). Cloud computing includes five key features: On-demand self-service, broad network access, resource pooling, rapid elasticity, and measured service (Dillon et al., 2010). In order to ensure the data integrity that cloud computing environments require, Blockchain has become an outstanding technology when building and deploying databases (Gaetani et al., 2017). Blockchain is a digital ledger capable of recording and storing information organised in a chronological order. It prevents manipulation by making that information permanent and immutable. Besides, it is decentralised and distributed, thereby resulting in a more reliable data management system (Treiblmaier, 2018). Blockchain has remarkable applications in a broad range of areas, among which supply chain management is a prominent example (Kshetri, 2018).

And last but not least, a larger explanation of IoT will be given as it is an essential component of Industry 4.0 (Hofmann & Rüsch, 2017) and so more substantial within the framework of this chapter. According to Vermesan & Friess (2013, 2014), IoT is a network conformed by a set of embedded devices. They can be integrated in a wide range of objects, such as vehicles, buildings, machines, instruments, etc. All of which are interconnected sending and receiving information with a defined objective. It shows improvement capacities and therefore has applications in tracing, safety, control, monitoring, administration, etc. An IoT system can share this information between people, between people and machines/things, and between machines/things. In systems such as these, the set of devices is even able to be ever-present through wireless and wired connections, interacting with each other in order to perform common tasks. Gathering data along the way and analysing it. They can run those tasks due to the intelligence they acquire, becoming capable of making decisions in accordance with the context. Thus, elaborating a complex service (Vermesan & Friess, 2013, 2014), the design of which can be constantly improved by them with the help of the primary data they are collecting (Manyika et al., 2015). According to Patel et al. (2016), the core characteristics of IoT are the following ones:

- Interconnectivity: IoT makes it possible to connect anything at different scales.
- Things-related service: IoT can provide services although it will be limited by the physical things themselves.
- Heterogeneity: IoT is a combination of different hardware structures.
- Dynamic changes: IoT devices' state can change continuously (location, speed, connected/disconnected, etc).
- Enormous scale: The IoT devices layer will always operate at a higher scale than the not IoT devices.
- Safety: An IoT system provides both data and physical safety.
- Connectivity: IoT connectivity abilities simplify accessibility and compatibility

As mentioned by Bouzembrak et al. (2019), IoT devices are conformed by 2 components:

- The sensor: Component that captures the information (temperature, humidity, light, movement…).
- The transmitter: Component that transfers the information. This encompasses Radiofrequency identification (RFID), bluetooth, Wi-Fi, etc.

In summary, Information and Communication Technologies represent a cornerstone of Industry 4.0, enabling the digital transformation of various sectors through advanced tools like big data, cloud computing, blockchain, and IoT. These technologies facilitate the collection, management, and analysis of vast amounts of information, driving improvements in productivity, efficiency, and innovation. As the role of digitalization continues to expand, the strategic integration of ICTs has become essential for modernising industries, including the food service sector, which is the focus of this chapter. The following sections will explore in greater detail how IoT, as a central component of ICTs, can be leveraged to support sustainability, environmental certifications, and operational efficiency in the agroindustry and food service industries. By understanding these technologies, stakeholders can better navigate the opportunities and challenges of adopting ICTs in pursuit of a more sustainable and efficient future.

ICTs as enablers of sustainability

As recognised back in 2008 by the European Commission, ICTs have a critical role in achieving the Sustainable Development Goals (SDGs). Indeed, in 2016 The World Summit on the Information Society (WSIS) created a matrix in which the 17 SDGs are matched with 11 action lines for ICT. Those action lines are:

- C1. Role of Government and all Stakeholders in the Promotion of ICT for Development.
- C2. Information and communication infrastructure: an essential foundation for the Information Society.
- C3. Access to information knowledge.
- C4. Capacity building.
- C5. Building confidence and security in the use of ICTs.

- C6. Enabling environment.
- C7. ICT applications: benefits in all aspects of life.
- C8. Cultural diversity and identity, linguistic diversity and local content.
- C9. Media.
- C10. Ethical dimensions of the Information Society. ● C11. International and regional cooperation.

These proposed actions would operate in the SDGs as WSIS indicates in Figure 1:

Figure 1. SDGs and WSIS action lines matrix. Source: International Telecommunication Union et al. (2015).

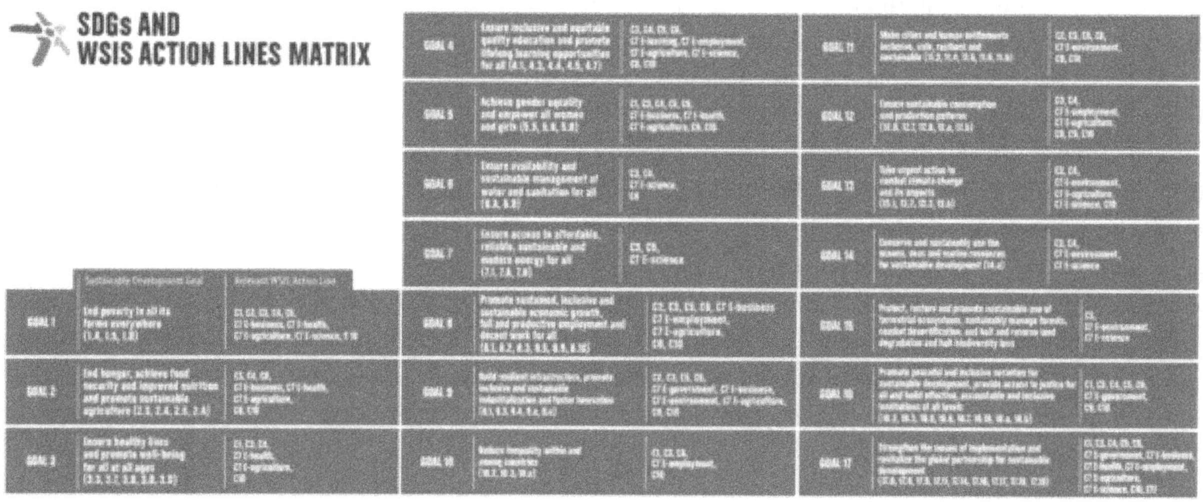

In summary, among other benefits ICTs have the chance to make progress towards a more energyefficient economy, which leads to a lower carbon system. The potential of ICTs to foster a circular economy is widely recognized in the literature. For instance, cloud computing can facilitate industrial symbiosis (Fisher et al., 2018) and support dematerialization strategies (Demestichas & Daskalakis, 2020), both of which are critical action lines for achieving a circular economy. Blockchain technology, in particular, plays a key role by enhancing data transparency and enabling more precise analysis of a product's life cycle (Esmaeilian et al., 2020). Additionally, when combined with IoT, blockchain can further improve the sustainability of supply chains through real-time data collection and analysis (Rane et al., 2020). Such IoT techniques enable continuous monitoring of resource consumption and waste generation throughout various stages of a product's life cycle, which is fundamental to circular economy practices (Rejeb et al., 2022). The feasible advantages that IoT offers thanks to the measurement of parameters creates an insightful opportunity within a circular economy context to perform looping/cascading processes, extend products lifetime and favour servitization (Ellen MacArthur Foundation, 2016). Big data techniques are also crucial, as they provide data-driven insights that support informed decision-making and promote business intelligence (Awan et al., 2021). However, the effectiveness of these contributions from big data depends significantly on an organisation's capacity to learn and adapt to new data insights.

Nevertheless, the European Commission also highlights that ICTs need to reduce their own energy use first (European Commission, 2008). Such an energy usage is part of the environmental impacts that ICTs provoke, and which must not be overlooked. Those impacts can be classified in: impacts coming from the ICTs life cycles (life-cycle impacts), impacts coming from implementation of new materials where there was not any before (enabling impacts) and impacts coming from economic structures and institutions that emerge from these ICT systems (structural impacts) (Hilty & Aebischer, 2015).

For instance, the operation of blockchain technology requires additional energy consumption. According to Muller et al. (2020), this consumption is approximately 26 kJ per node, including orderers and peers reads. This energy demand scales with the total number of transactions conducted on the blockchain. For example, in a blockchain network consisting of 5 nodes and handling 100 transactions annually, the estimated energy consumption would be approximately 7.222 kWh. To contextualise this, a typical refrigerator consumes about 0.89 kWh per day (Avordeh et al., 2021), meaning that the energy used by such a blockchain in one year could power a refrigerator for around 8 days. Last efforts are focused to reduce consumption due to consensus protocols.

Moreover, data storage also requires energy. Corbet et al. (2018) estimate that data centres consume approximately 46.33 kWh per terabyte (TB) of stored data annually. This is a quite important feature, since a considerable amount of data is generated by big data techniques that must be stored somewhere.

The environmental impact of ICTs has been evaluated in several case studies and in different sectors. For instance, Baldini et al. (2023) assessed the environmental impact of an air quality sensor network designed for urban traffic management. This system comprises 35 devices for air quality measurements, a photovoltaic panel, and a lithium battery, in addition to an assumed maintenance rate. Depending on the assumed lifespan, this system is estimated to consume from 14.5 to 23.9 MJ of energy, to generate an amount of waste that ranges from 9.55 to 18.58 kg. The low durability of IoT devices alongside the toxic chemicals their waste may contain is well known, since they could constitute a more significant impact on the environment in comparison with the ones their implementation is supposed to tackle (Ingemarsdotter, 2021).

Another example is given by Ingemarsdotter et al. (2021), who analysed through life cycle assessment the impact of an IoT system that optimises the use of truck tyres by monitoring and indicating optimal pressure during use, or doing a more accurate assessment of when they should be retreaded. Regarding the impact added from IoT in this case study, Ingemarsdotter et al. (2021) included the impacts coming from the production and transport of the hardware, the energy used to collect the data and to process and store it in the cloud, and that of the waste management of the hardware. Accounting for all the savings coming from fuel consumption reduction, tyre manufacturing reduction, avoided impacts from the waste management, etc, the IoT system reduced the environmental impacts by 4% in comparison to the baseline.

In the context of smart cities, new technologies have been tested in various systems, including waste management. Brunklaus et al. (2022) analysed the impact of implementing an IoT system in the Swedish municipality of Södertälje to optimise its waste collection processes, thereby reducing both time spent and transportation costs. The study found that the addition of the IoT system (which accounted for 1% of the total carbon footprint of the existing waste collection system) could provide a modest reduction in the overall carbon footprint as a consequence. More significantly, the IoT system would contribute with valuable social benefits by creating a cleaner environment and improving citizens' well-being. This underscores the importance of adopting a holistic perspective that considers the three pillars of sustainability (environmental, economic, and social) when evaluating the impacts of such technologies.

These examples illustrate the broader applicability of ICT systems in various sectors, yet similar innovations hold significant potential for the agrifood sector as well. For instance, Jagtap et al. (2020) investigated how IoT solutions could help reduce energy consumption in a beverage factory by enabling real-time decision-making. The deployed network consisted of sensors that measured energy consumption at hotspots and a software platform that allowed decision-makers to monitor energy usage and detect patterns. The study reported that this system not only achieved economic benefits, saving $172,281 in one year, but also improved sustainability by reducing energy consumption by 807,081 kWh per year.

Focusing on the economic impacts, ICTs present significant opportunities to stimulate economic growth and increase GDP, particularly in developing countries (Aleksandrova & Khabib, 2021). However, many developing countries face challenges in fully realising these benefits due to inadequate infrastructure, lack of digital literacy, and limited access to the necessary technological resources. These barriers hinder the ability of developing nations to achieve the level of digitalization needed to compete on a global scale. Moreover, company image can also be affected by the use of ICTs. Organisations with a high level of digitalisation tend to have more satisfied employees, which influences productivity and ultimately the company image (Gonzalez et al., 2020).

From the social point of view, ICTs offer numerous advantages as already mentioned. Nevertheless, it is crucial to take into account relevant drawbacks such as the so-called "digital divide" between developed and developing countries (Shirazi & Hajli, 2021). This issue reflects significant disparities in access to ICT infrastructure and digital skills, which can exacerbate existing inequalities. Regarding ethical concerns, data privacy stands out as a controversial topic, with many stakeholders expressing a lack of trust in how their data is handled. Recent literature emphasises the critical need for robust infrastructure to ensure data privacy for IoT users (Lee & Ahmed, 2021). This challenge represents a significant barrier to the widespread adoption of IoT technologies, and consequently, it limits the potential contributions of IoT to advancing sustainability goals.

Despite the significant potential of technologies such as IoT and blockchain in enhancing the efficiency and transparency of food supply chains, several challenges remain. One of the key issues is the interoperability between different IoT platforms and data standards, which hampers seamless communication and data sharing across the supply chain. Moreover, the high cost of implementing blockchain technology, along with its energy consumption concerns, poses obstacles, particularly for smaller stakeholders. Additionally, ensuring data security and privacy, while maintaining the trust of all participants, is critical but complex. Overcoming these challenges is essential for the full integration and scalability of these technologies in the food supply chain. (Vyas, 2022).

To address the challenges posed by integrating IoT and blockchain in the food supply chain, several measures have been put in place. These include the development of interoperable frameworks for IoT platforms, which enhance communication between different systems, and global efforts to standardize data formats. Blockchain technology, while traditionally resource-intensive, is seeing improvements with the adoption of energy-efficient mechanisms like Proof of Stake and the introduction of the AI in the governance of the network, which helps mitigate environmental concerns. Additionally, collaborations between governments and private sector entities are being encouraged to lower the cost of implementing these technologies, especially for small and medium-sized enterprises. Furthermore, advanced encryption techniques are being developed to ensure data privacy and security, bolstering trust in these systems across the supply chain.

Initiatives like Walmart's partnership with IBM to implement blockchain for food traceability have demonstrated tangible benefits, including improved transparency and safety in food products. Projects like AgriBlockIoT in China have also shown how decentralized traceability systems can ensure food safety through compliance with regulations like HACCP (Hazard Analysis and Critical Control Points) principles (Ellahi, 2023).

These collective efforts aim to overcome the initial barriers to the widespread adoption of IoT and blockchain in the food industry, making these technologies more accessible and sustainable.

These case studies demonstrate that while ICTs can have an impact on sustainability, their application can also lead to substantial efficiencies. They can enable circular strategies and reduce sustainability impacts, but the associated environmental risks they entail also need to be accounted for. These pros and cons are equally applicable to the specific case of the food service industry, as will be explored in further detail later.

IoT in the agroindustry

Agroindustry is a special case in the context of ICTs since it is at the forefront in the use of IoT. With the integration of ICTs in the food supply chain several benefits can be achieved since the possibilities of encountering adverse circumstances are reduced due to a better control of the product (Cruz Introini et al., 2018; Misra et al., 2022). One of the drivers of this situation is the fact that companies whose environmental engagement is not up-to-date, are less preferable for investors since it is considered to be a business performance indicator (Morgan et al., 2015).

In this particular sector ICTs are employed to track the food production in terms of provenance, processing factory, quality, fraud, impact on human health, etc. For instance, by using DNA barcoding, it is possible to identify whether food has been processed or not, as well as knowing the properties of its raw products (Ramundo et al., 2016). The environmental variations that may alter the quality of the product are measured with sensors (for example in vehicles during transport) and so the shelf life can be recalculated if necessary. Such data is uploaded to cloud systems, allowing supermarkets, consumers or other stakeholders to consult them with smartphones or tablets (Ramundo et al., 2016). There are already examples of this, such as the platform developed by Foodchain S.p.A., which generates a unique smart label for the product that the consumer can scan in order to obtain information about traceability (Grecuccio et al., 2020).

This food traceability is defined by the European Commission as “the ability to trade and follow a food, feed, food-producing animal or substance intended to be, or expected to be incorporated into a food or feed, through all stages of production, processing and distribution.” (European Commission, 2002). Food traceability is a key factor in food safety, and so to prevent food waste generation. This capability would be enhanced with the incorporation of more advanced systems. For example, the arrival of blockchain is affecting how food is being distributed globally. Its specific features are diffusing the limits between food supply chain actors, hence making food traceability even more important (Burke, 2019; Yu et al., 2020). The diversity showcased by the required data needs the use of new technologies so that data management can be efficient enough to localise the sources of food safety related problems and act accordingly. A smart food traceability system like that is able to gather information about location, ingredients, and packaging in every stage of the food supply chain. It uses IoT and cloud computing to collect and manage the food information improving food safety from farm to fork (Yu et al., 2020). Nevertheless, this ideal smart traceability system presents some drawbacks related to the complexity and diversity of the food supply chains, the elevated cost of the equipment, and the difficulty of analysing the huge amount of data that is generated (Scholten et al., 2016). The traditional way to assess food safety in laboratories is expensive, slow, and requires a lot of work (Hameed et al., 2018). For that reason, several portable food safety detection technologies exist nowadays: portable spectroscopy, array sensors, microfluidic lab-on-a-chip, and smartphones.

Once food is packaged this traceability has to be ensured as well. Smart packaging allows that tracking process either through the use of indicators that measure temperature, freshness, gas, or microbes in the food, or through the use of data carriers that provide data about previous food supply chain stages (Hameed et al., 2018). This smart packaging is defined by Hameed et al. (2018) as "any type of container that is capable of carrying out smart functions beyond a physical barrier between food and their surrounding environment."

The data that an IoT-blockchain based traceability system may collect, includes:

- Production stage: Planting date, temperature, humidity, soil and water quality, farming staff, time, origin, fertiliser and pesticides applications, water consumption (Bastas & Liyanage, 2018; Pincheira Caro et al., 2018), harvesting date, and weight (Feng et al., 2020).
- Processing stage: Time, processing equipment, batch modifications, information about packaging, cleaning process information, operators and information included in labels (Feng et al., 2019).
- Distribution stage: Time, temperature, relative humidity, gases, location and operator method (Feng et al., 2020; Galvez et al., 2018).
- Consumption stage: Name of the product, price, sale time and shelf life (Feng et al., 2020).

In the case of a plant food product, this information can also include seeding purchase and quality (Galvez et al., 2018). Meanwhile in a meat food product, animal health and breeding data are captured (Aung & Chang, 2014).

To gain a comprehensive understanding of the current state of digitalisation in food supply chains, a literature review was conducted, incorporating a total of 89 scientific articles. These articles cover various types of supply chains, including a wide range of animal and crop products, and explore numerous parameters and ICTs. The examined parameters serve multiple purposes, such as enhancing productivity, promoting sustainability, ensuring food safety and quality, facilitating forecasting, enabling traceability, and addressing food waste. Each study identifies the specific stages of the food supply chain in which these parameters are considered. To organise and prioritise these parameters and ICTs, a classification was developed based on their frequency of occurrence in the reviewed literature. As a result of this analysis, the dynamic dashboard showcases in Figure 2 was created. This dashboard is freely accessible in Zenodo (doi: 10.5281/zenodo.8119271).

Figure 2. Dashboard with the results of the analysis of digitisation in food supply chains.

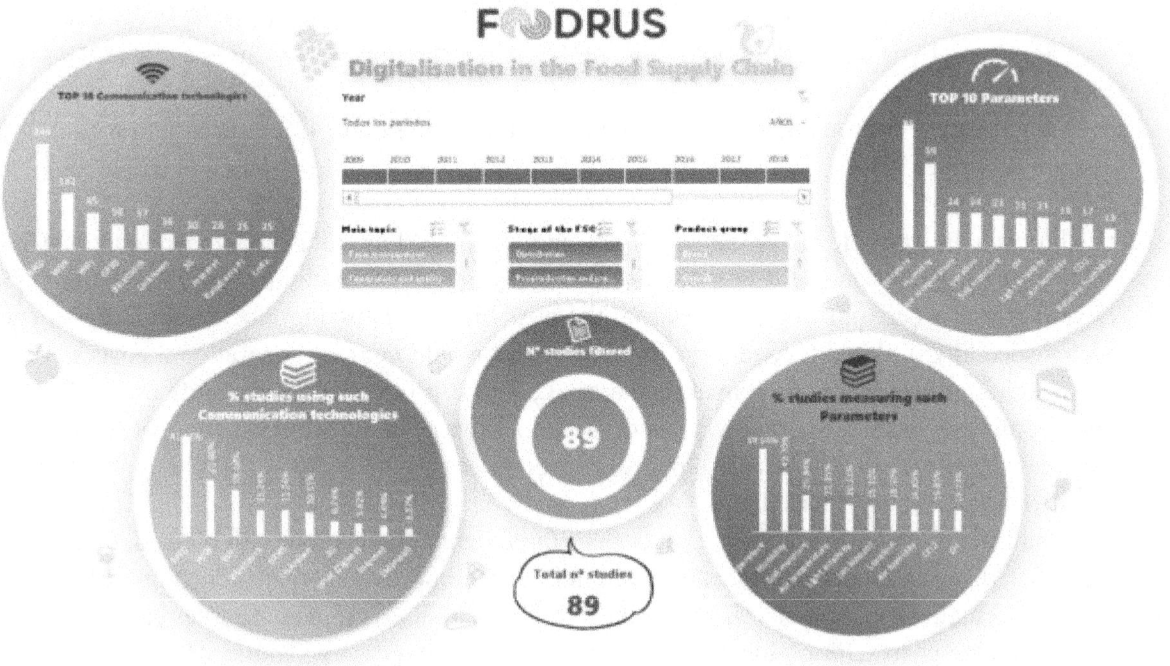

The key findings derived from this review can be summarised as follows:

- Food safety and quality, food waste, sustainability, and traceability are interconnected topics, often mentioned together and driven by a shared objective of reducing food waste. Studies focused on productivity also tend to address prediction, while also addressing sustainability and food safety and quality concerns.
- There appears to be a lack of consensus regarding the terminology and division of the food supply chain. Various terms such as "production," "preproduction," "production in field," and "agricultural stage" are used interchangeably, highlighting the need for clarity and consistency. The processing stage is sometimes included in the production stage, leading to fewer studies specifically focused on this stage (only 26). Similarly, the distribution stage may encompass the retail point, explaining the relatively smaller number of studies for this stage (28). It is important to note that not all food products require processing, which may explain those results.
- In terms of the topics covered, the review reveals the following:
    - Food safety and quality is the most extensively studied topic (31 articles), particularly in the distribution stage (26) and retail stage (20). Temperature and humidity are the most frequently measured parameters, with RFID being the commonly used communication technology.
    - Sustainability is not a very explored topic (8 articles), especially in the retail stage and households, where no studies matching the requirements were found.
    - Studies specifically focused on food waste emerged in 2017, with the distribution stage being a significant focus in the majority of these studies (9 out of 11).

    - Traceability studies commonly measure temperature (in 13 studies), humidity (in 13 studies), and location (in 12 studies), given their close connection to food safety and quality.
- Examining the food supply chain stages, the following trends are observed:
    - Productivity is the predominant topic in the preproduction and production stage (31% of the studies).
    - Food safety and quality takes precedence in the processing (42%), distribution (54%), and retail stages (71%).

Since blockchain would leverage consumer confidence in food products and generate a traceability system such that it would enable it to recognise possible sources of contamination in real time (Tian, 2016), various studies are currently considering the possibility of applying blockchain to certification processes, especially in the agri-food industry. Besides, it would decrease operational costs in certification and verification processes (Ramakrishna et al., 2020). Both food safety and sustainability are significant topics to consider in order to prevent these food waste and quantify its impacts respectively. In these areas the new technologies are already spreading, setting up quite profitable applications like that of certification through blockchain.

Recent bibliography presents real use cases that implement certification with blockchain networks. (Zhang, 2020), discusses the use of blockchain technology to improve the management and traceability of grain supply chains. By implementing a blockchain-based system, grain enterprises can ensure better data security, real-time hazardous material tracking, and whole-process traceability, thus improving food safety and reducing risks of tampered or lost data. Specific use cases include improving the transparency and trust between non-adjacent supply chain nodes. The system was tested in Shandong, China, and successfully addressed issues of data loss and inefficiency in traditional traceability systems. In Mohammed, 2023, a comprehensive review of the adoption of blockchain technology in food supply chains (FSCs), outlining the key benefits such as improved transparency, traceability, and fraud reduction. The review identifies several use cases in developing countries, such as Vietnam, where blockchain has been used to enhance traceability in dairy and other agricultural sectors. Challenges such as high cost, lack of technical expertise, and scalability issues are also discussed, highlighting the need for further research and tailored solutions for emerging markets. More successful use cases can be found in Ahmad, 2024, where case studies include successful applications of blockchain for traceability in developing countries, such as the Chinese and Indian food markets, where blockchain is used to monitor food safety and quality in real-time. The study outlines the potential for blockchain to address food waste issues and improve cold storage monitoring in supply chains. Another example of a real use case is Coffee in Colombia (Valencia-Payan, 2022), where the feasibility of using blockchain technology for the real case of coffee transportation in Colombia is studied.

Environmental certifications based on IoT for the food service industry

In recent years, there has been a growing trend in the adoption of ICTs within the food service industry (Gonzalez et al., 2022). These technologies can enhance business performance through various solutions, such as demand forecasting, faster and easier food delivery, and the promotion of gastronomic tourism (Gonzalez et al., 2022; Yu & Sun, 2019). Especially in the latest years, the focus within the food service sector has shifted from upstream life cycle stages to consumer-centric approaches. This change is largely due to ICTs empowering consumers, who now have greater influence on other consumers regarding the value of different food service establishments (Gonzalez et al., 2022). Furthermore, the food service industry is increasingly transforming traditional dining into comprehensive experiences, leveraging ICTs such as AI, virtual reality, and social media as key enablers of this evolution (Gonzalez et al., 2022).

ICT solutions have proved to be useful for the food service sector for different purposes. Ceynowa et al. (2023) developed and tested an ICT tool aimed at improving communication across the food supply chain, specifically within the HORECA and wholesale sectors. This tool enables HORECA organisations to efficiently place orders with their suppliers, providing real-time updates on order status, delivery, prices, and product availability. By streamlining the order management process, the app helps to reduce both time and costs. However, some users expressed a preference for maintaining personal contact with stakeholders. Notably, this type of solution appears to benefit smaller wholesalers, who often offer more competitive pricing.

Digital solutions for redistributing food surplus from HORECA establishments have gained significant traction too, with prominent examples like Too Good To Go and similar apps such as Regusto (Secondi et al., 2019). Additionally, other tools focus on quantifying food waste, like the Food Loop app developed through the EU H2020 FOODRUS project. This open-access tool not only facilitates food waste measurement in both households and food service establishments but also offers tailored recommendations to reduce food waste. These recommendations are based on the specific causes of food waste generation and the types of food being discarded, providing users with practical strategies to minimise food waste, along with the economic and environmental impacts it implies. Moreover, the FOODRUS project serves as a valuable repository of innovative ICT solutions, validated by actors across all stages of the food supply chain. For the food service industry, these include tools for demand forecasting, planning and monitoring food waste prevention actions, a food waste certification supported by blockchain (that will be further explored later), and a comprehensive dashboard that consolidates data, enabling in-depth assessments of key performance indicators (KPIs) related to food waste.

It is important to highlight that the acceptance and intention to use ICTs in the food service industry depends on various factors such as the perceived ease of use, performance expectancy, or the effort needed (Jeon et al., 2020). These are relevant aspects that must not be overlooked when designing an ICT solution for this sector, since it can remain unused despite its potential capabilities.

As highlighted by the case studies, ICTs bring significant benefits to the food service sector across various areas. One key area is certifications, which are essential in this industry. They not only ensure legal compliance but also serve to differentiate businesses from their competitors. Certifications are instrumental in building consumer trust in the food products they order/purchase, particularly when the certification itself is widely recognized and trusted by consumers (Truong et al., 2022). According to the ISO (2023), a certification is "the provision by an independent body of written assurance (a certificate) that the product, service or system in question meets specific requirements.". Namely, it is a procedure aimed at attesting that a product or service meets a standard's requirements suitable for such product or service. Those standards assist companies with the traceability process throughout the supply chain (Verzijl et al., 2015). For instance, ISO 14001 (ISO, 2015) specifies requirements for an environmental management system (EMS) aimed at improving environmental performance by controlling the environmental impact of activities, reducing waste, and optimising resource use. Similarly, ISO 22000 (ISO, 2018a) focuses on food safety management systems, helping businesses control food safety hazards while also emphasising traceability, a key component in food waste prevention. This is particularly significant for food service companies that manage perishable food products on a daily basis. In this context, certifications aimed at preventing food waste are gaining traction. For instance, Saudi Arabia has introduced the "Saudi

Zero Food Waste Certification," which recognizes exemplary practices in food waste reduction through effective stakeholder coordination (Sobaih, 2023). This is sometimes even motivated by legislation, as it is the case of Spain, where the Food Loss and Waste Prevention Law project (Spanish government, 2022) mandates that actors in the food supply chain develop a food waste prevention plan and adhere to the food waste hierarchy. These legislative requirements create a supportive environment for the proliferation of food waste certifications, which besides engage more environmentally conscious consumers.

To develop effective traceability systems, such as the ones that are used for certification purposes, the first step is to identify the information that must be monitored (Purwandoko et al., 2018). With that ultimate goal, surveys may be implemented to map stakeholders and their interconnections, have an outline of the supply chain and so determine the information that will be collected. In the same way, interviews and data from records are also relevant data sources to obtain more in-depth details. All that data will be stored and managed by the traceability system from a series of capture points along the supply chain (Purwandoko et al., 2018). A comprehensive example of which data is tracked in every capture point is given by Purwandoko et al. (2018) in the case of an organic rice certification.

Certification is closely linked to traceability. For example, to obtain a food safety certification the traceability of a series of parameters must be ensured. From the results of the dashboard presented in Figure 2, it is assumed that in food safety the most widely measured parameters comprise temperature, humidity and location. In addition to others like CO_2, SO_2, light, gas, ethylene, salinity, heavy metals, pressure, vibration, viscosity, wind, rain, microbial activity, etc. Likewise, the monitoring of specific parameters is also required for environmental certifications. These certifications, also called "ecolabels", give insights into either the overall or specific environmental properties of a product or service. This information may serve to influence and guide consumers or users when making decisions in a purchasing situation. Which in turn can lead to an eco-innovation process, where the market is steered towards a vicious cycle that boosts ecolabelling due to business competition (ISO, 2022; Rennings, 2000).

Ecolabelling is governed by the Regulation (CE) nº 834/2007 (European Commission, 2007) about organic production and labelling of organic products. And the ISO standard 14020 controls ecolabelling and environmental product declarations (EPD), differentiating between 3 types of environmental labelling:

- Type I. Environmental labellings that certify the product is complying with specific environmental requirements. Validated by a third party (ISO, 2018b).
- Type II. Self-declared environmental labels made by the manufacturing company (ISO, 2016).
- Type III. Environmental product declarations (EPD). They follow the life cycle assessment (LCA) methodology and are validated by a third party (ISO, 2006a).

In these ecolabels the inclusion of all the life cycle of the product is required (ISO, 2022). This fits particularly well with the food service industry's need for transparency, as consumers increasingly expect these businesses to adopt sustainable practices (Sullivan et al., 2021). Furthermore, the introduction of ecolabels on restaurant menus seems to have a positive effect on its demand in the long term (Casati et al., 2023). Therefore, the traceability that new technologies offer, such as IoT, adds substantial value by providing detailed, real-time data throughout the supply chain. Which provides the food service establishment with a competitive advantage given how consumers' attitudes are evolving.

In the particular case of type III ecolabels, IoT would revolutionise data collection, which is the toughest and the most cost and time-consuming part in the LCA (70%-80%) (Curran, 2012; Miah et al., 2018; Mieras et al., 2019). Data collection is part of the LCI analysis, a stage where all the material and energy inputs and outputs from the product system to the environment during the life cycle are measured (ISO, 2006b). Procedure that would be conducted in real time through the use of IoT, capturing on-site data instead of collecting statistical data (Mieras et al., 2019). Studies concerning this issue have already been carried out, showing how the introduction of these new technologies to collect data (using also a cloud platform to enable it) make more effective the use of LCA models, together with the later dissemination of results with a greater range than ever before (Mieras et al., 2019). Considering that data quality is one of the biggest challenges to deal with in the area of LCA (Djekic et al., 2019), IoT would be a major breakthrough in this regard as it allows to detect outliers by making the measurements on-site (Mieras et al., 2019). The integrity of the results that blockchain grants, offers an excellent solution to this problem as shown in the pioneer study performed by Zhang et al. (2020), which presented for the first time an LCA framework based on a blockchain system.

For type I and II ecolabels, IoT would also be used with the purpose of obtaining data of inputs and outputs in every stage of the life cycle (as ISO standards state), although it would need to adapt to the particular requirements of each. In the ISO 14020 it is specified that the utility and effectiveness of the ecolabels are based on the meaningfulness and reliability of the information they provide (ISO, 2022). And monitoring with IoT has demonstrated being capable of decreasing the mistake in comparison with that of the human being (Kishore Austeen et al., 2019; Saha et al., 2018), as well as managing data of high quality (Mieras et al., 2019). In the context of food service businesses, this means providing accurate data about ingredients, sourcing, and processing methods.

Additionally, it is worth mentioning that ecolabels are being more and more ambitious with regard to the sustainability concept. So that health and social aspects are starting to be included as well (Asensi & Kaulins, 2019). In this context, IoT would be applied in the form of surveys for workers, consumers, and other stakeholders throughout the food supply chain. Via IoT it would be much easier to standardise the data gathering, resulting in an improvement of the reliability and the rigour of these studies (Grubert, 2018; Mieras et al., 2019).

Once the data is collected by IoT devices, and stored in the blockchain cloud, by using smart contracts the compliance of the applicable standards or guidelines is ensured. Thereby it would promote auditing and certification processes in the food service industry, where rapid compliance and transparency can be a competitive advantage. This guarantee is due to the immutability that characterizes blockchain technology (Rejeb et al., 2019). What is more, since it is a decentralized technology and it does not need intermediaries (Mougayar & Buterin, 2016; Treiblmaier, 2018), these auditings are conducted in a much faster way. Then the complementation between IoT and blockchain permits enhanced auditings with a higher level of detail (Ma et al., 2019; Rejeb et al., 2019). Lastly, the information of the product can be delivered with smart labels, whose inks are even able to spot changes in environmental variables (Gligoric et al., 2019; Ramundo et al., 2016).

The application of ICTs to certifications in the food service industry is a relatively recent topic, with few recent studies in the literature connecting these 3 knowledge branches. One of these was found in the field of food safety, where Colom Umbert et al. (2023) developed an ICT platform that enables users to verify compliance with food hygiene standards. The platform allows actors to share these compliance results with official food safety authorities and other stakeholders in the food supply chain, including consumers. By collecting data from food service establishments, the tool demonstrated a reduction in costs related to hygiene verification activities. Like other ICT tools, its ability to manage information quickly and simplify processes provides significant advantages to the testing companies, particularly those in the HORECA sector.

In the area of food waste management, a blockchain-based certification scheme has been developed in the FOODRUS project to validate compliance with specific food waste prevention criteria, as outlined in the previously mentioned Spanish law project. This ICT solution was tested through a real-world case study in Spain, using other digital tools to collect data from various stages of the food supply chain. Blockchain technology ensures the immutability and transparency of this data, making it a robust foundation for certification. This innovative tool cross-references this primary data with the items on the proposed certification checklist, significantly speeding up the certification process. This approach simplifies auditing while enhancing data reliability and providing more up-to-date information. While this solution is applicable across the entire food system, it can hold particular promise for the food service industry. By using a simple QR code in the menu, consumers can access detailed information about the food waste prevention measures implemented throughout the supply chain. For the food service sector, this means that the sustainability impact of the food waste prevention actions deployed along the food supply chain can be transparently certified by a trusted system. Such transparency can strengthen consumer trust and enhance recognition for HORECA establishments committed to sustainable practices.

In summary, the application of IoT and big data will foster a huge progress in the agri-food sector, including the food service, in all the 3 pillars of sustainability: society (food safety, demand control, more product quality…), economy (more productivity, improvement of processes…) and environment (reduction of impacts, improvement of the resources use efficiency…) (Misra et al., 2022). Indeed, López-Morales et al. (2020) points out that the incorporation of IoT strengthens the agroindustry's capabilities to minimise its environmental impact. By means of three use cases, this study demonstrated that the transformation of logistics processes that IoT entails, leads to an environmental footprint reduction along with other benefits. This progress is already a reality because of a rising interest registered as regards the implementation of the CE in this new industrial technology paradigm. Leveraging like this the fulfilment of the SDGs (Dantas et al., 2021). Furthermore, given that consumer trust is strongly influenced by the credibility of certifications (Truong et al., 2022), the adoption of IoT and blockchain-based certifications in the food service sector would represent a valuable contribution due to their enhanced transparency and data reliability. This would plot a strategic direction for future development in such an industry. In the light of these results, it becomes a matter of scientific interest to research and analyze deeper the connection between these two branches of knowledge in the agrifood sector: sustainability and new technologies.

To assess such sustainability impact, the inclusion of sustainability KPIs in certification processes with the help of ICTs will be highly valuable for several reasons. Firstly, sustainability KPIs provide a standardized and objective measure of an organization's environmental, social, and economic performance, allowing for meaningful comparisons across different certified entities. By incorporating these indicators through digital technologies, certifications could communicate more effectively the level of sustainability achieved by a certified organization, promoting transparency and accountability. Additionally, it would ease continuous improvement by establishing clear targets and benchmarks, encouraging organizations to strive for higher levels of sustainability performance over time. Furthermore, this digital integration would further promote the adoption of sustainable practices and encourage innovation by guiding organizations towards more sustainable strategies and operations. Ultimately, the credibility and relevance of certifications would be enhanced, empowering consumers, stakeholders, and decision-makers to make informed choices that contribute to a more sustainable future.

CONCLUSIONS

In conclusion, the agrifood sector is experiencing a profound transformation fueled by technological advancements. The integration of IoT and blockchain technologies is pivotal in improving transparency, traceability, and efficiency across the food supply chain. These innovations are crucial for achieving food waste prevention certification, ensuring that food is produced, processed, and consumed sustainably. As the industry evolves, adopting these technologies and adhering to certification standards will be key to tackling the global challenge of food waste. By addressing existing challenges and fostering continuous improvement, IoT and blockchain, alongside robust certification systems, can pave the way for a more sustainable and resilient food sector.

The adoption of ICT-supported certifications offers a credible and trusted option for food service companies, attracting an increasingly environmentally aware consumer base. This focus on transparency, enabled by real-time data collection and monitoring, allows businesses to communicate their sustainability efforts more effectively, building consumer trust and differentiating themselves in a competitive market. As the industry evolves, embracing these technologies and adhering to certification standards will be crucial in addressing the global challenge of food waste, while also aligning with consumer expectations for sustainability.

More particularly, the integration of ICTs in certifications would not only facilitate real-time monitoring and updates but also allow food supply chain actors to make better decisions based on sustainability criteria from a holistic system view. Such digital tools are especially needed for data calculation and visualisation, which would strengthen standardisation and comparability of results. The automatisation provided by these new technologies would simplify certification processes related to food waste prevention thanks to: the faster verification of sustainability KPIs; the higher availability of more current data.; and the higher reliability provided by digital data sources. On top of it, leveraging ICTs to streamline the certification process would reduce administrative burdens, which will make environmental certifications more accessible to a broader range of businesses.

However, the integration of IoT technologies in the food service sector brings some relevant challenges. Issues such as data privacy, security, and interoperability need to be addressed to ensure the successful implementation of IoT solutions. Data privacy concerns arise from the collection and transmission of sensitive information, such as production data and supply chain logistics. Ensuring that this data is securely stored and shared is crucial to prevent unauthorized access and protect stakeholders' privacy.

Additionally, the interoperability of IoT devices and systems from different manufacturers can be a challenge. Establishing common standards and protocols for data exchange can facilitate seamless communication and integration of IoT solutions across the food supply chain.

Ultimately, the synergy between IoT, blockchain, and certification systems represents a strategic pathway for the food service industry to achieve greater sustainability. This progress not only addresses food waste and promotes efficient resource use but also contributes significantly to the global effort to meet Sustainable Development Goals (SDGs). By leveraging these technologies, food service businesses can drive continuous improvement, offering a more sustainable and resilient service that meets the evolving demands of consumers and the planet.

REFERENCES

Ahmad, R. W., Ko, K.-M., Rashid, A., & Rodrigues, J. J. P. C. (2024). Blockchain for Food Industry: Opportunities, Requirements, Case Studies, and Research Challenges. *IEEE Access : Practical Innovations, Open Solutions*, 12, 117363117378. DOI: 10.1109/ACCESS.2024.3447918

Aleksandrova, A., & Khabib, M. D. (2022). The role of information and communication technologies in a country's GDP: A comparative analysis between developed and developing economies. *Economic and Political Studies*, 10(1), 44–59. DOI: 10.1080/20954816.2021.2000559

Andrews, D. (2015). The circular economy, design thinking and education for sustainability. *Local Economy*, 30(3), 305–315. DOI: 10.1177/0269094215578226

Asensi, E., & Kaulins, R. (2019). Motivations and Barriers of using emerging technology in eco-label certification for sustainability, from the certification companies' perspective.

Aung, M. M., & Chang, Y. S. (2014). Traceability in a food supply chain: Safety and quality perspectives. *Food Control*, 39, 172–184. DOI: 10.1016/j.foodcont.2013.11.007

Avordeh, T. K., Gyamfi, S., & Opoku, A. A. (2021). Estimating residential electricity consumption for appliance use: A statistical model approach. *2021 International Conference on Electrical, Computer and Energy Technologies (ICECET)*. DOI: 10.1109/ICECET52533.2021.9698647

Awan, U., Shamim, S., Khan, Z., Zia, N. U., Shariq, S. M., & Khan, M. N. (2021). Big data analytics capability and decision-making: The role of data-driven insight on circular economy performance. *Technological Forecasting and Social Change*, 168(120766), 120766. DOI: 10.1016/j.techfore.2021.120766

Bai, C., Dallasega, P., Orzes, G., & Sarkis, J. (2020). Industry 4.0 technologies assessment: A sustainability perspective. *International Journal of Production Economics*, 229, 107776. DOI: 10.1016/j.ijpe.2020.107776

Baldini, E., Chessa, S., & Brogi, A. (2023). Estimating the environmental impact of green IoT deployments. *Sensors (Basel)*, 23(3), 1537. DOI: 10.3390/s23031537 PMID: 36772576

Bastas, A., & Liyanage, K. (2018). Sustainable supply chain quality management: A systematic review. *Journal of Cleaner Production*, 181, 726–744. DOI: 10.1016/j.jclepro.2018.01.110

Beaty, D. L., & Quirk, D. (2018). Fog computing. *ASHRAE Journal*, 60(1), 68–74.

Bouzembrak, Y., Klüche, M., Gavai, A., & Marvin, H. J. P. (2019). Internet of Things in food safety: Literature review and a bibliometric analysis. *Trends in Food Science & Technology*, 94, 54–64. DOI: 10.1016/j.tifs.2019.11.002

Brunklaus, B., Chiew, Y. L., Lundström, A., Nilsson-Lindén, H., & Saarikko, T. (2022). The connected, sustainable and inclusive society – IoT implementation in a Swedish municipality. E3S Web of Conferences, 349, 11006. DOI: 10.1051/e3sconf/202234911006

Burke, T. (2019). *Blockchain in Food Traceability*., DOI: 10.1007/978-3-030-10902-8_10

Carter, M., & Grover, V. (2015). Me, my self, and I(T). *Management Information Systems, 39*(4), 931–957. https://www.econis.eu/PPNSET?PPN=84353088X

Casati, M., Soregaroli, C., Rommel, J., Luzzani, G., & Stranieri, S. (2023). Please keep ordering! A natural field experiment assessing a carbon label introduction. *Food Policy*, 120(102523), 102523. DOI: 10.1016/j.foodpol.2023.102523

Ceynowa, W., Przybylowski, A., Wojtasik, P., & Ciskowski, Ł. (2023). ICT Adoption for Sustainable Logistics Development in the HoReCa and Wholesale Sectors. *Sustainability (Basel)*, 15(4), 3746. DOI: 10.3390/su15043746

Colom Umbert, A., Llull Cantallops, R., Ramos Monserrat, M., Colom Fernández, A., & Mercader Barceló, J. (2023). From control systems to safety culture in the global foodservice outlet arena: A Balearic Islands perspective. *Trends in Food Science & Technology*, 136, 308–313. DOI: 10.1016/j.tifs.2023.04.017

Corbett, C. J. (2018). How Sustainable Is Big Data? *Production and Operations Management*, 27(9), 1685–1695. DOI: 10.1111/poms.12837

Cruz Introini, S., Boza, A., & Alemany Díaz, M. D. M. (2018). *Traceability in the Food Supply Chain: Review of the literature from a technological perspective*. http://hdl.handle.net/10251/121089

Curran, M. A. (2012). Life Cycle Assessment Handbook: A Guide for Environmentally Sustainable Products. DOI: 10.1002/9781118528372

Dantas, T. E. T., de-Souza, E. D., Destro, I. R., Hammes, G., Rodriguez, C. M. T., & Soares, S. R. (2021). How the combination of Circular Economy and Industry 4.0 can contribute towards achieving the Sustainable Development Goals. *Sustainable Production and Consumption*, 26, 213–227. DOI: 10.1016/j.spc.2020.10.005

De Mauro, A., Greco, M., & Grimaldi, M. (2014). *What is Big Data? A Consensual Definition and a Review of Key Research Topics*. DOI: 10.13140/2.1.2341.5048

Demestichas, K., & Daskalakis, E. (2020). Information and communication technology solutions for the circular economy. *Sustainability (Basel)*, 12(18), 7272. DOI: 10.3390/su12187272

Dillon, T., Wu, C., & Chang, E. (2010, April). Cloud computing: issues and challenges. In 2010 24th IEEE international conference on advanced information networking and applications (pp. 27-33). Ieee.

Djekic, I., Pojić, M., Tonda, A., Putnik, P., Bursać Kovačević, D., Režek-Jambrak, A., & Tomasevic, I. (2019). Scientific Challenges in Performing Life-Cycle Assessment in the Food Supply Chain. *Foods*, 8(8), 301. DOI: 10.3390/foods8080301 PMID: 31374833

Ellahi, R. M., Wood, L. C., & Bekhit, A. E.-D. A. (2023). Blockchain-Based Frameworks for Food Traceability: A Systematic Review. *Foods*, 2023(12), 3026. DOI: 10.3390/foods12163026 PMID: 37628025

Ellen MacArthur Foundation. (2016). *Intelligent assets: Unlocking the circular economy potential*. https://ellenmacarthurfoundation.org/intelligent-assets-unlocking-the-circular-economy-potential

European Commission. (2002). Regulation (EC) No 178/2002 of the European Parliament and of the Council of 28 January 2002 laying down the general principles and requirements of food law, establishing the European Food Safety Authority and laying down procedures in matters of food safety. https://eur-lex.europa.eu/legal-content/EN/ALL/?uri=celex%3A32002R0178

European Commission. (2007). Council Regulation (EC) No 834/2007 of 28 June 2007 on organic production and labelling of organic products and repealing Regulation (EEC) No 2092/91. https://eur-lex.europa.eu/legal-content/EN/TXT/?uri=celex%3A32007R0834

European Commission. (2008). Addressing the challenge of energy efficiency through Information and *Communication Technologies*. https://eur-lex.europa.eu/legal-content/EN/TXT/?uri=COM%3A2008%3A0241%3AFIN

Feng, H., Chen, J., Zhou, W., Rungsardthong, V., & Zhang, X. (2019). Modeling and evaluation on WS-Nenabled and knowledge-based HACCP quality control for frozen shellfish cold chain. *Food Control*, 98, 348–358. DOI: 10.1016/j.foodcont.2018.11.050

Feng, H., Wang, X., Duan, Y., Zhang, J., & Zhang, X. (2020). Applying blockchain technology to improve agrifood traceability: A review of development methods, benefits and challenges. *Journal of Cleaner Production, 260*, 121031. Fisher, O.; Watson, N.; Porcu, L.; Bacon, D.; Rigley, M.; Gomes, R. Cloud manufacturing as a sustainable process manufacturing route. J. Manuf. Syst. 2018, 47, 53–68. DOI: 10.1016/j.jclepro.2020.121031

Gaetani, E., Aniello, L., Lombardi, F., Margheri, A., & Sassone, V. (2017). Blockchain-based database to ensure data integrity in cloud computing environments.

Galvez, J. F., Mejuto, J. C., & Simal-Gandara, J. (2018). Future challenges on the use of blockchain for food traceability analysis. *Trends in Analytical Chemistry*, 107, 222–232. DOI: 10.1016/j.trac.2018.08.011

Gligoric, N., Krco, S., Hakola, L., Vehmas, K., De, S., Moessner, K., Jansson, K., Polenz, I., & Van Kranenburg, R. (2019). SmartTags: IoT Product Passport for Circular Economy Based on Printed Sensors and Unique Item-Level Identifiers. *Sensors (Basel)*, 19(3), 586. DOI: 10.3390/s19030586 PMID: 30704112

Gobble, M. M. (2018). Digitalization, Digitization, and Innovation. *Research Technology Management*, 61(4), 56–59. DOI: 10.1080/08956308.2018.1471280

Gonzalez, R., Gasco, J., & Llopis, J. (2020). Information and communication technologies and human resources in hospitality and tourism. *International Journal of Contemporary Hospitality Management*, 32(11), 3545–3579. DOI: 10.1108/IJCHM-04-2020-0272

Gonzalez, R., Gasco, J., & Llopis, J. (2022). Information and communication technologies in food services and restaurants: A systematic review. *International Journal of Contemporary Hospitality Management*, 34(4), 1423–1447. DOI: 10.1108/IJCHM-05-2021-0624

Grecuccio, J., Giusto, E., Fiori, F., & Rebaudengo, M. (2020). Combining Blockchain and IoT: Food-Chain Traceability and Beyond. *Energies*, 13(15), 3820. DOI: 10.3390/en13153820

Grubert, E. (2018). Rigor in social life cycle assessment: Improving the scientific grounding of SLCA. *The International Journal of Life Cycle Assessment*, 23(3), 481–491. DOI: 10.1007/s11367-016-1117-6

Hameed, S., Xie, L., & Ying, Y. (2018). Conventional and emerging detection techniques for pathogenic bacteria in food science: A review. *Trends in Food Science & Technology*, 81, 61–73. DOI: 10.1016/j.tifs.2018.05.020

Hatzivasilis, G., Christodoulakis, N., Tzagkarakis, C., Ioannidis, S., Demetriou, G., Fysarakis, K., & Panayiotou, M. (2019). The CE-IoT Framework for Green ICT Organizations The interplay of CE-IoT as an enabler for green innovation and e-waste management in ICT. DOI: 10.1109/DCOSS.2019.00088

Hilty, L., & Aebischer, B. (2015). *ICT for Sustainability: An Emerging Research Field* (Vol. 310, pp. 3–36). DOI: 10.1007/978-3-319-09228-7_1

Hofmann, E., & Rüsch, M. (2017). Industry 4.0 and the current status as well as future prospects on logistics. *Computers in Industry*, 89, 23–34. DOI: 10.1016/j.compind.2017.04.002

Ingemarsdotter, E. K. (2021). Circular Strategies Enabled by the Internet of Things: Opportunities, *Implementation Challenges, and Environmental Impact*. https://doi.org/https://doi.org/10.4233/uuid:9ac826a1-2203-4f23- b074-3d765abd73e3

Inoue, M., Yamada, S., Miyajima, S., Ishii, K., Hasebe, R., Aoyama, K., Yamada, T., & Bracke, S. (2020). A modular design strategy considering sustainability and supplier selection. *Journal of Advanced Mechanical Design, Systems and Manufacturing*, 14(2), JAMDSM0023. Advance online publication. DOI: 10.1299/jamdsm.2020jamdsm0023

International Telecommunication Union. UNESCO, UNCTAD, UNDP, UNDESA, FAO, WHO, Union Postale Universelle, UNEP, International Trade Centre, Organization, I. L., & O, W. M. (2015). *WSIS - SDG Matrix Linking WSIS Action Lines with Sustainable Development Goals*. www.wsis.org/sdg

ISO. (2006a). ISO 14025:2006 Environmental labels and declarations — Type III environmental declarations — Principles and procedures. https://www.iso.org/standard/38131.html

ISO. (2006b). *ISO 14040:2006 Environmental management — Life cycle assessment — Principles and framework*. https://www.iso.org/standard/37456.html

ISO. (2015). ISO 14001:2015 Environmental management systems — Requirements with guidance for use. https://www.iso.org/standard/60857.html

ISO. (2016). ISO 14021:2016 Environmental labels and declarations — Self-declared environmental claims (Type II environmental labelling). https://www.iso.org/standard/66652.html

ISO. (2018a). ISO 22000:2018 Food safety management systems — Requirements for any organization in the food chain. https://www.iso.org/es/contents/data/standard/06/54/65464.html

ISO. (2018b). ISO 14024:2018 Environmental labels and declarations — Type I environmental labelling — Principles and procedures. https://www.iso.org/standard/72458.html

ISO. (2022). ISO 14020:2022 Environmental statements and programmes for products — Principles and general requirements. https://www.iso.org/standard/79479.html

ISO. (2023).*ISO- Certification*. https://www.iso.org/certification.html

Jagtap, S., Rahimifard, S., & Duong, L. N. K. (2022). Real- time data collection to improve energy efficiency: A case study of food manufacturer. *Journal of Food Processing and Preservation*, 46(8). Advance online publication. DOI: 10.1111/jfpp.14338

Jeon, H. M., Sung, H. J., & Kim, H. Y. (2020). Customers' acceptance intention of self-service technology of restaurant industry: Expanding UTAUT with perceived risk and innovativeness. *Service Business*, 14(4), 533–551. DOI: 10.1007/s11628-020-00425-6

Kishore Austeen, X., Harish Kumar, V., Venkatesan, S., & Raghul, R. M. (2019). Design and implementation of aquaculture monitoring and controlling system using IoT. *International Research Journal of Engineering and Technology, 6*(3). https://www.irjet.net/archives/V6/i3/IRJET-V6I3899.pdf

Kshetri, N. (2018). 1 Blockchain's roles in meeting key supply chain management objectives. *International Journal of Information Management*, 39, 80–89. DOI: 10.1016/j.ijinfomgt.2017.12.005

Lee, C., & Ahmed, G. (2021). Improving IoT privacy, data protection and security concerns. International Journal of Technology [IJTIM]. *Innovation and Management*, 1(1), 18–33. DOI: 10.54489/ijtim.v1i1.12

López-Morales, J. A., Martínez, J. A., & Skarmeta, A. F. (2020). Digital Transformation of Agriculture through the Use of an Interoperable Platform. *Sensors (Basel)*, 20(4), 1153. DOI: 10.3390/s20041153 PMID: 32093147

Ma, M., Shi, G., & Li, F. (2019). Privacy-Oriented Blockchain-Based Distributed Key Management Architecture for Hierarchical Access Control in the IoT Scenario. *IEEE Access : Practical Innovations, Open Solutions*, 7, 34045–34059. DOI: 10.1109/ACCESS.2019.2904042

Manavalan, E., & Jayakrishna, K. (2019). A review of Internet of Things (IoT) embedded sustainable supply chain for industry 4.0 requirements. *Computers & Industrial Engineering*, 127, 925–953. DOI: 10.1016/j.cie.2018.11.030

Manyika, J., Chui, M., Bisson, P., Woetzel, J., Dobbs, R., Bughin, J., & Aharon, D. (2015). *The internet of things: mapping the value beyond the hype*. McKinsey Global Institute. https://www.mckinsey.com/~/media/mckinsey/industries/technology%20media%20and%20telecommunications/high%20tech/our%20insights/the%20internet%20of%20things%20the%20value%20of%20digitizing%20the%20physical%20world/unlocking_the_potential_of_the_internet_of_things_executive_summary.pdf

Mell, P., & Grance, T. (2011). The NIST Definition of Cloud Computing. https://csrc.nist.gov/pubs/sp/800/145/final

Menon, S., & Jain, K. (2024). Blockchain Technology for Transparency in Agri-Food Supply Chain: Use Cases, Limitations, and Future Directions. *IEEE Transactions on Engineering Management*, 71, 106–120. DOI: 10.1109/TEM.2021.3110903

Miah, J. H., Griffiths, A., McNeill, R., Halvorson, S., Schenker, U., Espinoza-Orias, N., Morse, S., Yang, A., & Sadhukhan, J. (2018). A framework for increasing the availability of life cycle inventory data based on the role of multinational companies. *The International Journal of Life Cycle Assessment*, 23(9), 1744–1760. DOI: 10.1007/s11367-017-1391-y PMID: 30956413

Mieras, E., Gaasbeek, A., & Kan, D. (2019). How to Seize the Opportunities of New Technologies in Life Cycle Analysis Data Collection: A Case Study of the Dutch Dairy Farming Sector. *Challenges*, 10(1), 8. DOI: 10.3390/challe10010008

Misra,N.N., Dixit,Y., Al-Mallahi, A., Bhullar, M. S., Upadhyay, R. and Martynenko, A.(2020). IoT, Big Data, and Artificial Intelligence in Agriculture and Food Industry. IEEE Internet of Things Journal, vol. 9, no. 9, pp. 6305-6324, 1 May1, 2022, .DOI: 10.1109/JIOT.2020.2998584

Misra, N. N., Dixit, Y., Al-Mallahi, A., Bhullar, M. S., Upadhyay, R., & Martynenko, A. (2022). IoT, Big Data, and Artificial Intelligence in Agriculture and Food Industry. *IEEE Internet of Things Journal*, 9(9), 6305–6324. DOI: 10.1109/JIOT.2020.2998584

Mohammed, A., Potdar, V., Quaddus, M., & Hui, W. (2023). Blockchain Adoption in Food Supply Chains: A Systematic Literature Review on Enablers, Benefits, and Barriers. *IEEE Access : Practical Innovations, Open Solutions*, 11, 14236–14255. DOI: 10.1109/ACCESS.2023.3236666

Morgan, J., Levin, K., Song, J., & Osorino, J. (2015). Driving Transformative Change: The Role of the Private Sector in Advancing Short-term and Long-term Signals in the Paris Climate Agreement. In *Policy File*. World Resources Institute. https://www.wri.org/research/driving-transformative-change-roleprivate -sector-advancing-short-term-and-long-term

Mougayar, W., & Buterin, V. (2016). *The business blockchain: promise, practice, and application of the next Internet technology*. John Wiley & Sons. http://cds.cern.ch/record/2222158

Parviainen, P., Tihinen, M., Kääriäinen, J., & Teppola, S. (2017). Tackling the digitalization challenge: How to benefit from digitalization in practice. *International Journal of Information Systems and Project Management*, 5(1), 63–77. DOI: 10.12821/ijispm050104

Patel, K., Patel, S., Scholar, P., & Salazar, C. (2016). *Internet of Things-IOT: Definition*. Characteristics, Architecture, Enabling Technologies, Application & Future Challenges.

Peraković, D., Periša, M., & Zorić, P. (2020). Challenges and Issues of ICT in Industry 4.0. In Ivanov, V., Trojanowska, J., Machado, J., Liaposhchenko, O., Zajac, J., Pavlenko, I., Edl, M., & Perakovic, D. (Eds.), *Advances in Design, Simulation and Manufacturing* (pp. 259–269). Springer International Publishing. DOI: 10.1007/978-3-030-22365-6_26

Pincheira Caro, M. R., Ali, M. S., Vecchio, M., & Giaffreda, R. (2018). *Blockchain-based traceability in Agri-Food supply chain management: A practical implementation*. DOI: 10.1109/IOT-TUSCANY.2018.8373021

Purwandoko, P. B., Seminar, K. B., Sutrisno, , & Sugiyanta, . (2018). Framework for Design of Traceability System on Organic Rice Certification. *IOP Conference Series. Earth and Environmental Science*, 147(1), 12044. DOI: 10.1088/1755-1315/147/1/012044

Ramakrishna, S., Ngowi, A., De Jager, H., & Awuzie, B. O. (2020). Emerging Industrial Revolution: Symbiosis of Industry 4.0 and Circular Economy: The Role of Universities. *Science, Technology & Society*, 25(3), 505–525. DOI: 10.1177/0971721820912918

Ramundo, L., Taisch, M., & Terzi, S. (2016). *State of the art of technology in the food sector value chain towards the IoT*. DOI: 10.1109/RTSI.2016.7740612

Reis, J., Amorim, M., Melao, N., Cohen, Y., & Rodrigues, M. (2020). *Digitalization: A Literature Review and Research Agenda.*, DOI: 10.1007/978-3-030-43616-2_47

Rejeb, A., Keogh, J. G., & Treiblmaier, H. (2019). Leveraging the Internet of Things and Blockchain Technology in Supply Chain Management. *Future Internet*, 11(7), 161. DOI: 10.3390/fi11070161

Rejeb, A., Suhaiza, Z., Rejeb, K., Seuring, S., & Treiblmaier, H. (2022). The Internet of Things and the circular economy: A systematic literature review and research agenda. *Journal of Cleaner Production*, 350(131439), 131439. DOI: 10.1016/j.jclepro.2022.131439

Rennings, K. (2000). Redefining innovation — Eco-innovation research and the contribution from ecological economics. *Ecological Economics*, 32(2), 319–332. DOI: 10.1016/S0921-8009(99)00112-3

Saha, J., Saha, A., Chatterjee, A., Agrawal, S., Saha, A., Kar, A., & Saha, H. (2018). *Advanced IOT based combined remote health monitoring, home automation and alarm system*. DOI: 10.1109/CCWC.2018.8301659

Scholten, H., Verdouw, C. N., Beulens, A., & van der Vorst, J. G. A. J. (2016). 2 - Defining and Analyzing Traceability Systems in Food Supply Chains. In Espiñeira, M., & Santaclara, F. J. (Eds.), *Advances in Food Traceability Techniques and Technologies* (pp. 9–33). Woodhead Publishing., DOI: 10.1016/B978-0-08-100310-7.00002-8

Secondi, L., Principato, L., & Mattia, G. (2019). Can digital solutions help in the minimization of out-of-home waste? An analysis from the client and business perspective. *British Food Journal*, 122(5), 1341–1359. DOI: 10.1108/BFJ-03-2019-0205

Shirazi, F., & Hajli, N. (2021). IT-enabled sustainable innovation and the global digital divides. *Sustainability (Basel)*, 13(17), 9711. DOI: 10.3390/su13179711

Sniderman, B., Mahto, M., & Cotteleer, M. J. (2016). *Industry 4.0 and manufacturing ecosystems* - Exploring the world of connected enterprises. Deloitte. https://www2.deloitte.com/content/dam/Deloitte/de/Documents/consumer[REMOVED HYPERLINK FIELD]industrial-products/Deloitte-Industry-4-0-and-manufacturing-ecosystems.pdf

Sobaih, A. E. E. (2023). Saudi Zero Food Waste Certification: A Novel Approach for FoodWaste Management in Saudi Arabia. *Agronomy (Basel)*, 13(6), 1654. DOI: 10.3390/agronomy13061654

Spanish government. (2022). Proyecto de Ley de prevención de las pérdidas y el desperdicio alimentario. https://www.mapa.gob.es/es/prensa/anteproyectoleydesperdicio_tcm30-620834.pdf

Sullivan, V. S., Smeltzer, M. E., Cox, G. R., & MacKenzie-Shalders, K. L. (2021). Consumer expectation and responses to environmental sustainability initiatives and their impact in foodservice operations: A systematic review. *Journal of Human Nutrition and Dietetics*, 34(6), 994–1013. DOI: 10.1111/jhn.12897 PMID: 34050994

Tian, F. (2016). An agri-food supply chain traceability system for China based on RFID & blockchain technology. *2016 13th International Conference on Service Systems and Service Management (ICSSSM)*, 1–6. DOI: 10.1109/ICSSSM.2016.7538424

Treiblmaier, H. (2018). The impact of the blockchain on the supply chain: A theory-based research framework and a call for action. *Supply Chain Management*, 23(6), 545–559. DOI: 10.1108/SCM-01-2018-0029

Truong, V. A., Lang, B., & Conroy, D. M. (2022). When food governance matters to consumer food choice: Consumer perception of and preference for food quality certifications. *Appetite*, 168(105688), 105688. DOI: 10.1016/j.appet.2021.105688 PMID: 34509543

Valencia-Payan, C., Grass-Ramírez, J. F., Ramirez-Gonzalez, G., & Corrales, J. C. (2022). A Smart Contract for Coffee Transport and Storage With Data Validation. *IEEE Access : Practical Innovations, Open Solutions*, 10, 37857–37869. DOI: 10.1109/ACCESS.2022.3165087

Vasanthraj, A., Kaur, A., Potdar, V., & Agrawal, H. (2023). Kaur, V. Potdar and H. Agrawal, H. (2023) Industry 4.0 Adoption in Food Supply Chain to Improve Visibility and Operational Efficiency—A Content Analysis. *IEEE Access : Practical Innovations, Open Solutions*, 11, 7392273958. DOI: 10.1109/ACCESS.2023.3295780

Vermesan, O., & Friess, P. (2013). Internet of Things: Converging Technologies for Smart Environments and Integrated Ecosystems. In *River Publishers Series in Communications* (1st ed.). Routledge., DOI: 10.1201/9781003338659

Vermesan, O., & Friess, P. (2014). *Internet of Things - From Research and Innovation to Market Deployment* (1st ed.). Routledge., DOI: 10.1201/9781003338628

Verzijl, D., Rouwmaat, E., Dervojeda, K., Probst, L., & Frideres, L. (2015). Traceability across the Value Chain - Standards, processes and traceability. In *European Commission*. https://single-market[REMOVED HYPERLINK FIELD]economy.ec.europa.eu/system/files/2017-07/42-tvc-standards-processes-and-traceability_en_0.pdf

Yu, Z., Jung, D., Park, S., Hu, Y., Huang, K., Rasco, B. A., Wang, S., Ronholm, J., Lu, X., & Chen, J. (2020). Smart traceability for food safety. *Critical Reviews in Food Science and Nutrition*, *62*(4), 905–916. Yu, C.-E. and Sun, R. (2019), "The role of instagram in the UNESCO's creative city of gastronomy: A case study of Macau", TourismManagement, Vol. 75, pp. 257-268DOI: 10.1080/10408398.2020.1830262

Zhang, A., Zhong, R. Y., Farooque, M., Kang, K., & Venkatesh, V. G. (2020). Blockchain-based life cycle assessment: An implementation framework and system architecture. *Resources, Conservation and Recycling*, 152, 104512. DOI: 10.1016/j.resconrec.2019.104512

Compilation of References

Aaker, D. A., & McLoughlin, D. (2010). *Strategic market management: Global perspectives*. Wiley.

Ababou, M., Chelh, S., & Elhiri, M. (2023). A bibliometric analysis of the literature on Food Industry Supply Chain Resilience: Investigating Key contributors and Global trends. *Sustainability (Basel)*, 15(11), 8812. DOI: 10.3390/su15118812

Abbu, H. R., Fleischmann, D., & Gopalakrishna, P. (2021). The digital transformation of the grocery business is driven by consumers, powered by technology, and accelerated by the COVID-19 Pandemic. In *Trends and Applications in Information Systems and Technologies: Volume 3 9* (pp. 329-339). Springer International Publishing. DOI: 10.1007/978-3-030-72660-7_32

Abbu, H., Fleischmann, D., & Gopalakrishna, P. (2021, June). The Case of Digital Transformation in Grocery Business: A Conceptual Model of Digital Grocery Ecosystem. In *2021 IEEE International Conference on Engineering, Technology and Innovation (ICE/ITMC)* (pp. 1-9). IEEE. DOI: 10.1109/ICE/ITMC52061.2021.9570219

Abdelhakim, H., & Altaş, A. (2023). AI algorithms in inventory management: Enhancing efficiency and accuracy. *Journal of Hospitality Management*, 45(2), 122–135.

Abdul Ghani Azmi, I. (2023). The Mediating Role of Segmentation in Social Media Marketing and Brand Equity: A Study in Food and Beverage Industry. International Journal of Economics, Management and Accounting.

Abdullah, N., Yaacob, N., & Ismail, A. (2022). Development and validation of a new questionnaire to measure the knowledge level of street food hawkers to support the single-use plastics reduction program in Kelantan, Malaysia. *Sustainability (Basel)*, 14(13), 7552. DOI: 10.3390/su14137552

Abdullah, O., Sufi, T., & Kumar, S. (2023). Impact of food and beverage quality and service quality towards customer satisfaction and customer retention, a study of Five-Star Hotels. *International Journal of Professional Business Review*, 8(5), e01994. DOI: 10.26668/businessreview/2023.v8i5.1994

Abell, A., Biswas, D., & Arroyo Mera, C. (2024). Food and technology: Using digital devices for restaurant orders leads to indulgent outcomes. *Journal of the Academy of Marketing Science*. Advance online publication. DOI: 10.1007/s11747-024-01029-6

Abhilasha, A., Sreenivasulu, A., & Manimozhi, T. Satheesh kumar P., Selvakumar P. and Singh P.,(2022). "The Model of Smart Sensing Device For Sensitive Nanoclusters Modification in Sensing Properties," 2022 2nd International Conference on Advance Computing and Innovative Technologies in Engineering (ICACITE), Greater Noida, India, 2022, pp. 1043-1047, DOI: 10.1109/ICACITE53722.2022.9823846

Abideen, A. Z., Sundram, V. P. K., Pyeman, J., Othman, A. K., & Sorooshian, S. (2021). Food Supply Chain Transformation through Technology and Future Research Directions—A Systematic Review. *Logistics (Basel)*, 5(4), 83. DOI: 10.3390/logistics5040083

Abidin, C. (2016). "Aren't these just young, rich women doing vain things online?": Influencer selfies as subversive frivolity. *Social Media + Society*, 2(2), 2056305116641342. DOI: 10.1177/2056305116641342

Abiodun, N. L., Matovu, M. S., & Olanrewaju, R. O. (2022). Statistical powers of univariate normality Tests: Comparative analysis of 2016 election process in Uganda. *European Journal of Statistics*, 2, 6. DOI: 10.28924/ada/stat.2.6

Achutha, S., Johnson, E., Nisha, S., & Sivakumar, S. (2022). Antimicrobial biodegradable polymeric materials for food packaging applications: current status and future directions. *Materials Science Forum*, pp. 1073, 49–56. DOI: 10.4028/p-a5my86

Adak, A., Pradhan, B., & Shukla, N. (2022). Sentiment analysis of customer reviews of food delivery services using deep learning and explainable artificial intelligence: Systematic review. *Foods*, 11(10), 1500. DOI: 10.3390/foods11101500 PMID: 35627070

Ada, Y., Kazancoglu, Y., Sezer, M. D., Ede-Senturk, C., Ozer, I., & Ram, M. (2021). Analyzing barriers of circular food supply chains and proposing Industry I4.0 solutions. *Sustainability (Basel)*, 13(12), 6812. Advance online publication. DOI: 10.3390/su13126812

Addanki, M., Patra, P., & Kandra, P. (2022). Recent advances and applications of artificial intelligence and related technologies in the food industry. *Applied Food Research*, 2(2), 100126. DOI: 10.1016/j.afres.2022.100126

Adeola, O., Evans, O., Ndubuisi Edeh, J., & Adisa, I. (2022). *The future of marketing: artificial intelligence, virtual reality, and neuromarketing. Marketing Communications and Brand Development in Emerging Economies* (Vol. I). Contemporary and Future Perspectives.

Afifah, N. M. R., Sathiaseelan, J. J., Kee, S. H., Amelia, T. S. M., Yien, W., Lua, N. A., & Bhubalan, K. (2024). A Review on Conversion Of Microplastics Into Value-Added Products: Challenges And Perspectives. *The Malaysian Journal of Analytical Sciences*, 28(3), 611–631.

Agabonifo, O. C., Adeola, S. O., & Oluwadare, S. A. (2012). An Assessment of the Role of ICT in the Readiness of Nigerian Bank Customers for the Introduction of Cashless Transactions. *International Journal of Computing & ICT Research*, 6(2).

Agarwal, A., Gandhi, S., Tripathi, A., Iammarino, M., & Homroy, S. (2022). Analysis of bisphenol: A migration from microwaveable polycarbonate cups into coffee during microwave heating. *International Journal of Food Science & Technology*, 57(12), 7477–7485. DOI: 10.1111/ijfs.16103

Agarwal, P., Swami, S., & Malhotra, S. K. (2024). Artificial intelligence adoption in the post-COVID-19 new-normal and role of intelligent technologies in transforming business: A review. *Journal of Science and Technology Policy Management*, 15(3), 506–529. DOI: 10.1108/JSTPM-08-2021-0122

Agichtein, E., Castillo, C., Donato, D., Gionis, A., & Mishne, G. (2008). Finding high-quality content in social media. *Proceedings of the 2008 International Conference on Web Search and Data Mining,* 2008. DOI: 10.1145/1341531.1341557

Ahamed, N. N., & Karthikeyan, P. (2024). FLBlock: A Sustainable Food Supply Chain Approach Through Federated Learning and Blockchain. *Procedia Computer Science*, 235, 3065–3074. DOI: 10.1016/j.procs.2024.04.290

Ahmad, A., Rahman, O., & Khan, M. N. (2017). Exploring the role of website quality and hedonism in the formation of e-satisfaction and e-loyalty: Evidence from internet users in India. *Journal of Research in Interactive Marketing*, 11(3), 246–267. DOI: 10.1108/JRIM-04-2017-0022

Ahmad, R. W., Ko, K.-M., Rashid, A., & Rodrigues, J. J. P. C. (2024). Blockchain for Food Industry: Opportunities, Requirements, Case Studies, and Research Challenges. *IEEE Access : Practical Innovations, Open Solutions*, 12, 117363117378. DOI: 10.1109/ACCESS.2024.3447918

Ahmad, R., & Scott, N. (2019). Technology innovations towards reducing hospitality human resources costs in Langkawi, Malaysia. *Tourism Review*, 74(3), 547–562. Advance online publication. DOI: 10.1108/TR-03-2018-0038

Ahmadzadeh, S., Ajmal, T., Ramanathan, R., & Duan, Y. (2023). A comprehensive review on food waste reduction based on IoT and big data technologies. *Sustainability (Basel)*, 15(4), 3482. DOI: 10.3390/su15043482

Ahn, J., & Seo, S. (2018). Consumer responses to interactive restaurant self-service technology (IRSST): The role of gadget-loving propensity. *International Journal of Hospitality Management*, 74, 109–121. DOI: 10.1016/j.ijhm.2018.02.020

Ajzen, I. (1991). The theory of planned behaviour. *Organizational Behavior and Human Decision Processes*, 50(2), 179–211. DOI: 10.1016/0749-5978(91)90020-T

Akhila, P., Sunooj, K., Aaliya, B., Navaf, M., Sudheesh, C., George, J., & Pottakkat, B. (2022). Historical developments in food science and technology. *Journal of Nutrition Research*, 10(1), 36–41. DOI: 10.55289/jnutres/v10i1_22.12

Akinsipe Olasunkanmi, M.-G. (2021). *The economic effectiveness of international companies on the markets of the host countries (based on materials of Nestlé SA).*

Akyazi, T., Goti, A., Oyarbide, A., Alberdi, E., & Bayon, F. (2020). A Guide for the Food Industry to Meet the Future Skills Requirements Emerging with Industry 4.0. *Foods*, 9(4), 492. DOI: 10.3390/foods9040492 PMID: 32295238

Al Nawas, I., Altarifi, S., & Ghantous, N. (2021). E-retailer cognitive and emotional relationship quality: Their experiential antecedents and differential impact on brand evangelism. *International Journal of Retail & Distribution Management*, 49(9), 1249–1270. DOI: 10.1108/IJRDM-07-2020-0239

Alagarsamy, S., Mehrolia, S., & Singh, B. (2021). The mediating effect of brand relationship quality on relational bonds and online grocery retailer loyalty. *Journal of Internet Commerce*, 20(2), 246–272. DOI: 10.1080/15332861.2020.1868213

Alalwan, A. A. (2020). Mobile food ordering apps: An empirical study of the factors affecting customer e-satisfaction and continued intention to reuse. *International Journal of Information Management*, 50, 28–44. DOI: 10.1016/j.ijinfomgt.2019.04.008

Alalwan, A. A., Qasem, Z., & Dwivedi, Y. K. (2020). Examining the impact of mobile interactivity on customer engagement in the context of mobile shopping. *Journal of Enterprise Information Management*, 33(3), 627–653. DOI: 10.1108/JEIM-07-2019-0194

Albayrak, M. S., Öner, A., Atakli, I. M., & Ekenel, H. K. (2019). Personalized Training in Fast-Food Restaurants Using Augmented Reality Glasses. *2019 International Symposium on Educational Technology (ISET)*, 129–133. DOI: 10.1109/ISET.2019.00035

Albors-Garrigos, J. (2020). Barriers and enablers for innovation in the retail sector: Co-innovating with the customer. A case study in grocery retailing. *Journal of Retailing & Consumer Services, 55*, N.PAG. DOI: 10.1016/j.jretconser.2020.102077

Al-Debei, M. M., Akroush, M. N., & Ashouri, M. I. (2015). Consumer attitudes towards online shopping: The effects of trust, perceived benefits, and perceived web quality. *Internet Research*, 25(5), 707–733. DOI: 10.1108/IntR-05-2014-0146

Aleksandrova, A., & Khabib, M. D. (2022). The role of information and communication technologies in a country's GDP: A comparative analysis between developed and developing economies. *Economic and Political Studies*, 10(1), 44–59. DOI: 10.1080/20954816.2021.2000559

Ali-Alsaadi, A., Cabeza-Ramírez, L., Santos-Roldán, L., & Loor-Zambrano, H. (2023). Digital Marketing and Fast-Food Intake in the UAE: The Role of Firm-Generated Content among Adult Consumers. *Foods*, 12(22), 4089. Advance online publication. DOI: 10.3390/foods12224089 PMID: 38002147

Ali, F. (2022). Augmented reality enhanced experiences in restaurants: Scale development and validation. *International Journal of Hospitality Management*, 102, 103180. DOI: 10.1016/j.ijhm.2022.103180

Ali, I., & Naushad, M. (2021). Determinants of customer satisfaction in online grocery shopping. *Journal of Retailing and Consumer Services*, 61, 102618.

Ali, S., Khalid, N., Javed, H. M. U., & Islam, D. M. Z. (2020). Consumer adoption of online food delivery ordering (OFDO) services in Pakistan: The impact of the COVID-19 pandemic—. *Journal of Open Innovation*, 7(1), 10. DOI: 10.3390/joitmc7010010

Alkarkhi, A. F. (2020). The observed significance level (P-value) procedure. In Elsevier eBooks (pp. 79–119). https://doi.org/DOI: 10.1016/B978-0-12-824301-5.00010-1

Allah Pitchay, A., Ganesan, Y., Zulkifli, N. S., & Khaliq, A. (2022). Determinants of customers' intention to use online food delivery applications through smartphones in Malaysia. *British Food Journal*, 124(3), 732–753. DOI: 10.1108/BFJ-01-2021-0075

Allen, R. (2020). Digital Marketing Models: The Technology Acceptance Model. https://www.smartinsights.com/manage-digital-transformation

Alordiah, C. O., Osagiede, M. A., Omumu, F. C., Okokoyo, I. E., Emiko-Agbajor, H. T., & Ang, P. (2021). Budget debate: E-payments on the rise but Singapore does not aim to be a cashless society, says Ong Ye Kung. *The Straits Times*. https://www.straitstimes.com/singapore/e-payments-on-the-rise-but-singapore-does-not-aim-to-be-a-cashless-society-ong-ye-kung

Al-Qudah, A. A., Al-Okaily, M., Alqudah, G., & Ghazlat, A. (2022). Mobile payment adoption in the time of the COVID-19 pandemic. *Electronic Commerce Research*. Advance online publication. DOI: 10.1007/s10660-022-09577-1

Altaş, A. (2022). Digital Transformation in Restaurants. In *Mobile Computing and Technology Applications in Tourism and Hospitality* (pp. 1–23). IGI Global. DOI: 10.4018/978-1-7998-6904-7.ch001

Altıntaş, M. H., Kılıç, S., & Akhan, C. E. (2020). The transformation of the e-tailing field: A bibliometric analysis. *International Journal of Retail & Distribution Management*, 48(2), 152–168. DOI: 10.1108/IJRDM-10-2018-0232

Amani, M. A., & Sarkodie, S. A. (2022). Mitigating spread of contamination in meat supply chain management using deep learning. *Scientific Reports*, 12(1), 5037. Advance online publication. DOI: 10.1038/s41598-022-08993-5 PMID: 35322116

Amin, A., Masud, S., & Rahman, A. (2021). Machine learning for food desert identification: Case study of rural regions. *Journal of Rural Studies*, 82(1), 45–57.

Amin, M. D., Syed, B., & McCluskey, J. J. (2021). Predicting access to healthful food retailers with machine learning. *Food Policy*, 99, 101985. DOI: 10.1016/j.foodpol.2020.101985 PMID: 33082618

Ampadu-Ameyaw, R., Richard, N., & Ahwireng, A. (2020). Integrated waste management system as a sustainable option for managing plastic waste in Ghana: The case of Madina-la katana municipality. *Journal of Scientific Research and Reports*, •••, 20–31. DOI: 10.9734/jsrr/2020/v26i930306

Amrhein, V., & Greenland, S. (2022). Discuss practical importance of results based on interval estimates and p-value functions, not only on point estimates and null p-values. *Journal of Information Technology*, 37(3), 316–320. DOI: 10.1177/02683962221105904

Anbumathi, R., Dorai, S., & Palaniappan, U. (2022). Evaluating the role of technology and non-technology factors influencing brand love in Online Food Delivery services. *Journal of Retailing and Consumer Services*, 71, 103181. DOI: 10.1016/j.jretconser.2022.103181

Anderson, K. E. (2020). Getting acquainted with social networks and apps: It is time to talk about TikTok. *Library Hi Tech News*, 37(4), 7–12. DOI: 10.1108/LHTN-01-2020-0001

Andre, R. S., Mercante, L. A., Facure, M. H. M., Sanfelice, R. C., Fugikawa-Santos, L., Swager, T. M., & Correa, D. S. (2022). Recent progress in amine gas sensors for food quality monitoring: Novel architectures for sensing materials and Systems. *ACS Sensors*, 7(8), 2104–2131. DOI: 10.1021/acssensors.2c00639 PMID: 35914109

Andrews, D. (2015). The circular economy, design thinking and education for sustainability. *Local Economy*, 30(3), 305–315. DOI: 10.1177/0269094215578226

Angeloni, S., & Rossi, C. (2021). An analytical model for comparing the profitability of competing online marketing channels: Search engine marketing versus e-commerce marketplace. *Journal of Marketing Theory and Practice*, 29(4), 534–549. DOI: 10.1080/10696679.2021.1879656

Annisa Islam, H., & Ezni Balqiah, T. (2021, April). Loyalty and Customer Engagement in Online Grocery Shopping in Indonesia. In *Proceedings of the 5th International Conference on E-Commerce, E-Business and E-Government* (pp. 53-59). DOI: 10.1145/3466029.3466036

Anonymous. (2021). 'Key performance indicators (KPIs) in The Restaurant Industry' URL: https://www.slang.ai/post/restaurant-kpis

Anonymous. (2021). Social Media Worldwide Pty Ltd, URL: https://www.socialmediaworldwide.com/blog/artificial-intelligence/how-ai-enhances-customer-satisfaction-in-restaurants

Anshu, K., Gaur, L., & Singh, G. (2022). Impact of customer experience on attitude and repurchase intention in online grocery retailing: A moderation mechanism of value Co-creation. *Journal of Retailing and Consumer Services*, 64, 102798. DOI: 10.1016/j.jretconser.2021.102798

Antesty, S., Susilawati, M., Selan, D.D., & Thalib, N. (2023). Government Support and Social Media Impact on the Performance and Sustainability of F&B's MSME in Indonesia. International Journal of Business, Law, and Education.

Antong, A., & Riyanti, R. (2021). *HOW DOES LOCAL WISDOM BECOME THE MAIN VALUE IN A SELLING-PRICE SETTING?* Arora, A. S., Sivakumar, K., & Pavlou, P. A. (2021). Social capacitance: Leveraging absorptive capacity in the age of social media. *Journal of Business Research*, 124, 342–356.

Anyanwu, I. B., Ezeaku, M. N., & Ogboagha, C. O. (2022). Relationship marketing and customer loyalty in chain fast food establishments in Umuahia, Abia state, Nigeria. *International Journal of Home Economics Hospitality and Allied Research*, 1(2), 178–188. DOI: 10.57012/ijhhr.v1n2.002

Apple. (2021). The power of user-generated content in Apple's marketing strategy. *Apple Newsroom*. Retrieved from Apple.

Applications of Augmented Reality in Food Industry|Guires FRL. (n.d.). *Guires Food Research Lab*. Retrieved July 3, 2024, from https://www.foodresearchlab.com/insights/augmented-reality-and-applications-food-industry/

Applied Sciences | Free Full-Text | Applications Analyses, Challenges and Development of Augmented Reality in Education, Industry, Marketing, Medicine, and Entertainment. (n.d.). Retrieved August 3, 2024, from https://www.mdpi.com/2076-3417/13/5/2766

Arabzadeh, V., Behnamian, A., Rashidi, S., & Sabour, M. (2023). A comprehensive review on sustainable food service practices. *Sustainability*, 15(4), 1682–1702. DOI: 10.3390/su15041682

Arabzadeh, V., Miettinen, P., Kotilainen, T., Herranen, P., Karakoc, A., Kummu, M., & Rautkari, L. (2023). Urban vertical farming with a large wind power share and optimised electricity costs. *Applied Energy*, 331, 120416. DOI: 10.1016/j.apenergy.2022.120416

Arbore, A., & Estes, Z. (2013). Loyalty program structure and consumers' perceptions of status: Feeling special in a grocery store? *Journal of Retailing and Consumer Services*, 20(5), 439–444. DOI: 10.1016/j.jretconser.2013.03.002

Ardra, S., & Barua, M. K. (2022). Halving food waste generation by 2030: The challenges and strategies of monitoring UN sustainable development goal target 12.3. *Journal of Cleaner Production*, 380, 135042. DOI: 10.1016/j.jclepro.2022.135042

Ares, G., Antúnez, L., De León, C., Alcaire, F., Vidal, L., Natero, V., & Otterbring, T. (2022). Even if you don't pay attention to it, you know it's there': A qualitative exploration of adolescents' experiences with digital food marketing. *Appetite*, 176, 106128. Advance online publication. DOI: 10.1016/j.appet.2022.106128 PMID: 35718311

Ariffin, S., Manan, H. A., Ahmad, N., Muhammad, N. S., Hamdan, F., & Kelana, N. S. S. (2021). Continuous intention to use technology of online food delivery services among young adults. *ADVANCES IN BUSINESS RESEARCH INTERNATIONAL JOURNAL*, 7(1), 56. DOI: 10.24191/abrij.v7i1.14256

Ariyasriwatana, W., Buente, W., Oshiro, M., & Streveler, D. (2014). Categorizing health-related cues to action: Using Yelp reviews of restaurants in Hawaii. *New Review of Hypermedia and Multimedia*, 20(4), 317–340. DOI: 10.1080/13614568.2014.987326

Arora, K., Alwiyah, N., & Faisal, M. (2022). The use of data science in digital marketing techniques: Work programs, performance sequences and methods. [SABDA Journal]. *Startupreneur Business Digital*, 1(2), 143–155. DOI: 10.33050/sabda.v1i2.110

Aryani, D., Singh, P., Khor, Y., Kee, D., Selvia, K., Lee, C., Lee, Y. H., & Anantharavoo, L. (2022). Factors influencing consumer behavioural intention to use food delivery services: A study of Foodpanda. *Journal of the Community Development in Asia*, 5(1), 69–79. DOI: 10.32535/jcda.v5i1.1386

Aschemann-Witzel, J., Ares, G., Thøgersen, J., & Monteleone, E. (2019). A sense of sustainability?–How sensory consumer science can contribute to sustainable development of the food sector. *Trends in Food Science & Technology*, 90, 180–186. DOI: 10.1016/j.tifs.2019.02.021

Asensi, E., & Kaulins, R. (2019). Motivations and Barriers of using emerging technology in eco-label certification for sustainability, from the certification companies' perspective.

Astashkina, E., Belavina, E., & Marinesi, S. (2019). The environmental impact of the advent of online grocery retailing. *Available atSSRN* 3358664 DOI: 10.2139/ssrn.3358664

Aswad, E. M. (2020). In a World of" Fake News," What's a Social Media Platform to Do? *Utah L. Rev.*, 1009.

Attiq, S., Chu, A. M., Azam, R. I., Wong, W. K., & Mumtaz, S. (2021). Antecedents of consumer food waste reduction behavior: Psychological and financial concerns through the lens of the theory of interpersonal behavior. *International Journal of Environmental Research and Public Health*, 18(23), 12457. DOI: 10.3390/ijerph182312457 PMID: 34886187

Augmented and Virtual Reality: Transforming the Future of Dining - IP Tech Insider. (2024, February 20). https://iptechinsider.com/augmented-and-virtual-reality/

Augmented Reality in the Food and Drink Industry—BrandXR. (2024, April 26). https://www.brandxr.io/augmented-reality-in-the-food-and-drink-industry-enhancing-consumer-engagement-and-experience

Aung, M. M., & Chang, Y. S. (2014). Traceability in a food supply chain: Safety and quality perspectives. *Food Control*, 39, 172–184. DOI: 10.1016/j.foodcont.2013.11.007

Avordeh, T. K., Gyamfi, S., & Opoku, A. A. (2021). Estimating residential electricity consumption for appliance use: A statistical model approach. *2021 International Conference on Electrical, Computer and Energy Technologies (ICECET)*. DOI: 10.1109/ICECET52533.2021.9698647

Awan, U., Shamim, S., Khan, Z., Zia, N. U., Shariq, S. M., & Khan, M. N. (2021). Big data analytics capability and decision-making: The role of data-driven insight on circular economy performance. *Technological Forecasting and Social Change*, 168(120766), 120766. DOI: 10.1016/j.techfore.2021.120766

Aydın, R., Yozukmaz, A., Şener, İ., Temiz, F., & Giannetto, D. (2023). Occurrence of microplastics in most consumed fruits and vegetables from Turkey and public risk assessment for consumers. *Life (Chicago, Ill.)*, 13(8), 1686. DOI: 10.3390/life13081686 PMID: 37629543

Badotra, S., & Sundas, A. (2021). A systematic review on security of E-commerce systems. *International Journal of Applied Science and Engineering*, 18(2), 1–19. DOI: 10.6703/ijase.202106_18(2).010

Bai, C., Dallasega, P., Orzes, G., & Sarkis, J. (2020). Industry 4.0 technologies assessment: A sustainability perspective. *International Journal of Production Economics*, 229, 107776. DOI: 10.1016/j.ijpe.2020.107776

Baker, S. A., & Walsh, M. J. (2023). Instagram influencers and the aesthetics of food: Visual strategies in digital marketing. *Journal of Consumer Culture*, 23(1), 53–71.

Bakhar, M., & Budihartono, E. (2023). Impact Analysis of the Use of IoT Technology and Environmental Monitoring Systems on Waste Reduction in the Food and Beverage Industry in Indonesia. *West Science Interdisciplinary Studies*, 1(11), 1225–1234. DOI: 10.58812/wsis.v1i11.380

Balakrishnan, V., & Shuib, N. L. M. (2021). Drivers and inhibitors for digital payment adoption using the cashless society readiness-adoption model in Malaysia author links open overlay panel. *Technology in Society, 65*(101554). https://doi.org/ soc.2021.101554DOI: 10.1016/j.tech

Balasubramanian, K. & Hanafiah, M. H. (2022). What innovations would enable the tourism and hospitality industry in Malaysia to rebuild? *Worldwide Hospitality and Tourism Themes*. Emerald Publishing Limited 1755-4217. DOI: DOI: 10.1108/WHATT-05-2022-0057

Balasubramanian, K., & Ragavan, N. A. (2019). What are the key challenges faced by the Malaysian hospitality and tourism industry in the context of industrial revolution 4.0? *Worldwide Hospitality and Tourism Themes*, 11(2), 194–203. DOI: 10.1108/WHATT-11-2018-0079

Baldini, E., Chessa, S., & Brogi, A. (2023). Estimating the environmental impact of green IoT deployments. *Sensors (Basel)*, 23(3), 1537. DOI: 10.3390/s23031537 PMID: 36772576

Baratta, R., & Simeoni, F. (2021). Food is good for you (and the planet): Balancing service quality and sustainability in hospitality. *Sinergie Italian Journal of Management*, 39(1), 193–213. DOI: 10.7433/s114.2021.11

Barbosa, B., Shabani Shojaei, A., & Miranda, H. (2023). Packaging-free practices in food retail: The impact on customer loyalty. *Baltic Journal of Management*, 18(4), 474–492. DOI: 10.1108/BJM-10-2022-0386

Barboza, L., Vethaak, A., Lavorante, B., Lundebye, A., & Guilhermino, L. (2018). Marine microplastic debris: An emerging issue for food security, food safety and human health. *Marine Pollution Bulletin*, 133, 336–348. DOI: 10.1016/j.marpolbul.2018.05.047 PMID: 30041323

Barhorst, J. B., McLean, G., Shah, E., & Mack, R. (2021). Blending the real world and the virtual world: Exploring the role of flow in augmented reality experiences. *Journal of Business Research*, 122, 423–436. DOI: 10.1016/j.jbusres.2020.08.041

Barnhart, W. R., Dial, L. A., Jordan, A. K., Studer-Perez, E. I., Kalantzis, M. A., & Musher-Eizenman, D. R. (2023). Higher meal disengagement and meal presentation are uniquely related to psychological distress and lower quality of life in undergraduate students. *Journal of American College Health*, •••, 1–8. DOI: 10.1080/07448481.2023.2245912 PMID: 37713319

Bastas, A., & Liyanage, K. (2018). Sustainable supply chain quality management: A systematic review. *Journal of Cleaner Production*, 181, 726–744. DOI: 10.1016/j.jclepro.2018.01.110

Batat, W. (2021). How augmented reality (AR) is transforming the restaurant sector: Investigating the impact of "Le Petit Chef" on customers' dining experiences. *Technological Forecasting and Social Change*, 172, 121013. DOI: 10.1016/j.techfore.2021.121013

Baubeau, P. (2016). Dematerialization and the cashless society: A look backward, a look sideward. In *The Book of Payments: Historical and Contemporary Views on the Cashless Society* (pp. 85-94): Springe DOI: 10.1057/978-1-137-60231-2_9

Bauerova, R. (2019). Online Grocery Shopping Acceptance: The Impact on the Perception of New Technologies and Loyalty in Retailing. *Central European Business Review*, 8(3), 18–34. DOI: 10.18267/j.cebr.216

Bauerová, R., & Klepek, M. (2018). The Digitalization of Grocery Shopping from a Generation Perspective. *Marketing Identity*, (Part 1), 243–255.

Bauer, P. C., Gerdon, F., Keusch, F., Kreuter, F., & Vannette, D. (2022). Did the GDPR increase trust in data collectors? Evidence from observational and experimental data. *Information Communication and Society*, 25(14), 2101–2121. DOI: 10.1080/1369118X.2021.1927138

Baum, T. (2024). Service quality of online food delivery mobile application: An examination of the spillover effects of mobile app satisfaction. *International Journal of Contemporary Hospitality Management*, 36(3), 906–926. DOI: 10.1108/IJCHM-09-2022-1103

Bazaluk, O., Yatsenko, O., Zakharchuk, O., Ovcharenko, A., Khrystenko, O., & Nitsenko, V. (2020). Dynamic development of the global organic food market and opportunities for Ukraine. *Sustainability (Basel)*, 12(17), 6963. DOI: 10.3390/su12176963

BBC News. (2015, 9 February). *Drone waiters unveiled in Singapore*. BBC News. https://www.bbc.com/news/av/world-asia-31160853

Beaty, D. L., & Quirk, D. (2018). Fog computing. *ASHRAE Journal*, 60(1), 68–74.

Becker, M. W., Pashler, H., & Lubin, J. (2011). Object intrinsic images and the creation of internet-based recipe collections: An example of consumer behavior analysis in action. *Journal of Consumer Psychology*, 21(2), 118–123. DOI: 10.1016/j.jcps.2010.09.002

Bedard, K., & Kuhn, P. (2015). Micro-marketing healthier choices: Effects of personalized ordering suggestions on restaurant purchases. *Journal of Health Economics*, 39, 106–122. DOI: 10.1016/j.jhealeco.2014.10.006 PMID: 25544398

Behnke, K., & Janssen, M. F. W. H. A. (2020). Blockchain technology in supply chain management: A systematic literature review. *Sustainability*, 12(4), 1668–1678. DOI: 10.3390/su12041668

Belanche, D., Casaló, L. V., & Flavián, C. (2020). Artificial Intelligence in service industries: Current trends and future perspectives. *Journal of Service Research*, 23(2), 155–169. DOI: 10.1177/1094670520908776

Belanche, D., Casaló, L. V., Flavián, C., & Schepers, J. (2019). Service robot implementation: A theoretical framework and research agenda. *Service Industries Journal*, 40(3–4), 203–225. DOI: 10.1080/02642069.2019.1672666

Belarmino, A., Raab, C., Tang, J., & Han, W. (2021). Exploring the motivations to use online meal delivery platforms: Before and during quarantine. *International Journal of Hospitality Management*, 96, 102983. DOI: 10.1016/j.ijhm.2021.102983

Belaud, J.-P., Prioux, N., Vialle, C., & Sablayrolles, C. (2019). Big data for Agri-food I4.0: Application to sustainability management for by-products supply chain. *Computers in Industry*, 111, 103050. Advance online publication. DOI: 10.1016/j.compind.2019.06.006

Belias, D., Vasiliadis, L., & Rossidis, I. (2021). The Intention and Expectations of Modern Robotic Technologies in the Hotel Industry. *Journal of Quality Assurance in Hospitality & Tourism*, 23(6), 1451–1479. DOI: 10.1080/1528008X.2021.1995566

Bellini, S., Cardinali, M. G., & Ziliani, C. (2011). Building customer loyalty in retailing: Not all levers are created equal. *International Review of Retail, Distribution and Consumer Research*, 21(5), 461–481. DOI: 10.1080/09593969.2011.619666

Ben-Daya, M., Hassini, E., Bahroun, Z., & Banimfreg, B. H. (2020). The role of internet of things in food supply chain quality management: A review. *The Quality Management Journal*, 28(1), 17–40. DOI: 10.1080/10686967.2020.1838978

Bennett, E., & Mangala, D. (2023). Social media advertising effectiveness in the fast-food industry: A consumer-centric approach. *Journal of Advertising Research*, 63(1), 47–62.

Bennett, R. (2019). Innovations in the food service industry: The case of Domino's Pizza. *The Journal of Business Strategy*, 40(2), 25–34. DOI: 10.1108/JBS-03-2018-0043

Berezina, K., Ciftci, O., & Cobanoglu, C. (2019). Robots, artificial intelligence, and service automation in restaurants. *In Emerald Publishing Limited eBooks* (pp. 185–219). DOI: 10.1108/978-1-78756-687-320191010

Berezina, K., Ciftci, O., & Cobanoglu, C. (2019). Robots in service: How consumers perceive robots in hospitality. *International Journal of Hospitality Management*, 32(4), 55–65.

Berezina, K., Ciftci, O., & Cobanoglu, C. (2019). Robots, Artificial Intelligence, and Service Automation in Restaurants. *International Journal of Hospitality Management*, 28(3), 451–469.

Berger, J. (2015). The sensory content of perceptual experience. *Pacific Philosophical Quarterly*, 96(4), 446–468. DOI: 10.1111/papq.12110

Bermoy, N. N. B., De Guzman, J. J. J., De Guzman, J. L., Dela Vega, S. K. P., Hernandez, L.Jr, Ignacio, M. T. B., Templado, S. M., Trinidad, A. O., & Francisco, C. D. C. (2021). Influence of social media as a marketing platform for food-related products in the new normal. *International Journal of Academic Multidisciplinary Research*, 5(1), 106–111. https://www.ijeais.org/ijamr

Bessen, J. E. (2019). AI and jobs: The role of demand. *National Bureau of Economic Research Working Paper,* 24235. DOI: 10.3386/w24235

Bessen, J. E. (2021). The Second Industrial Revolution: A New Look at the Development of the American Economy. *The Journal of Economic History*, 81(2), 587–614.

Bharadwaaj, S. K., Jaudan, M., Kushwaha, P., Saxena, A., & Saha, B. (2024). Exploring Cutting-Edge Approaches in Plastic Recycling for a Greener Future. *Results in Engineering*, 23, 102704. DOI: 10.1016/j.rineng.2024.102704

Bharadwaj, A., El Sawy, O. A., Pavlou, P. A., & Venkatraman, N. (2019). Digital business strategy: Toward a next generation of insights. *Management Information Systems Quarterly*, 43(1), 469–482. DOI: 10.25300/MISQ/2019/13304

Bhat, P., & Malaganve, P. (2023). Design and Implementation of Social Media Mining–Knowledge Discovery Methods for Effective Digital Marketing Strategies. *Data Engineering and Data Science: Concepts and Applications*, 23–48.

Bhattarai, K., & Adhikari, A. P. (2023). Promoting urban farming for creating sustainable cities in Nepal. *Urban Science (Basel, Switzerland)*, 7(2), 54. Advance online publication. DOI: 10.3390/urbansci7020054

Bhayani, S., & Vachhani, N. V. (2014). Internet marketing vs traditional marketing: A comparative analysis. *FIIB Business Review*, 3(3), 53–63. DOI: 10.1177/2455265820140309

Bianchini, M., Michienzi, A., & Pellegrini, R. (2021). AI implementation challenges for SMEs in the hospitality sector. *Journal of Business Research*, 124, 187–194. DOI: 10.1016/j.jbusres.2020.11.049

Bi, H., Zhu, X., Lu, F., & Huang, M. (2023). The Meal Delivery Routing Problem in E-commerce Platforms under the Shared Logistics Mode. *Journal of Theoretical and Applied Electronic Commerce Research*, 18(4), 1799–1819. DOI: 10.3390/jtaer18040091

Bill Aull, Dymfke Kuijpers, and Daniel Laubli - https://www.mckinsey.com/industries/retail/our-insights/the-next-horizon-for-grocery-ecommerce-beyond-the-pandemic-bump

Biswas, D. (2019). Sensory aspects of retailing: Theoretical and practical implications. *Journal of Retailing*, 95(4), 111–115. DOI: 10.1016/j.jretai.2019.12.001

Blomqvist, A., Nyman, L., & Lennartsson, F. (2015). Consumer attitudes towards online grocery shopping: A research conducted on Swedish consumers.

Blut, M., & Wang, C. (2019). Technology readiness: A meta-analysis of conceptualizations of the construct and its impact on technology usage. *Journal of the Academy of Marketing Science*, 48(4), 649–669. DOI: 10.1007/s11747-019-00680-8

Bokhove, C. (2022). The role of analytical variability in secondary data replications: A replication of Kim et al. (2014). *Educational Research and Evaluation*, 27(1–2), 141–163. DOI: 10.1080/13803611.2021.2022319

Bo, L., & Yang, X. (2022). Is consumers' willingness to pay premium for agricultural brand labels sustainable?: Evidence from Chinese consumers' random n-price auction experiment. *British Food Journal*, 124(13), 359–374. DOI: 10.1108/BFJ-01-2022-0077

Bolarinwa, O. (2015). Principles and methods of validity and reliability testing of questionnaires used in social and health science researches. *The Nigerian Postgraduate Medical Journal*, 22(4), 195. DOI: 10.4103/1117-1936.173959 PMID: 26776330

Bolek, S. (2020). Consumer knowledge, attitudes, and judgments about food safety: A consumer analysis. *Trends in Food Science & Technology*, 102, 242–248. DOI: 10.1016/j.tifs.2020.03.009

Bolwig, S., Tanner, A. N., Riemann, P., Redlingshöfer, B., & Zhang, Y. (2021). Reducing consumer food waste using green and digital technologies.

Bond, F. W., Hayes, S. C., Baer, R. A., Carpenter, K. M., Guenole, N., Orcutt, H. K., Waltz, T., & Zettle, R. D. (2011). Preliminary Psychometric Properties of the Acceptance and Action Questionnaire–II: A Revised Measure of Psychological Inflexibility and Experiential Avoidance. *Behavior Therapy*, 42(4), 676–688. DOI: 10.1016/j.beth.2011.03.007 PMID: 22035996

Botterill, L., & Mazur, N. (2004). Risk & risk perception: A literature review. *Card Technology Today*, 21(2), 3.

Bottriell, K. (2023). MULTISTAKEHOLDER ROUNDTABLES AND VOLUNTARY STANDARDS. *SMALLHOLDERS*, 405.

Boudali, Y., Saoud, N., & Taleb, A. (2021). Leveraging AI and machine learning to improve customer experience in quick service restaurants: A case study of Domino's Pizza. *Journal of Hospitality and Tourism Technology*, 12(3), 407–423. DOI: 10.1108/JHTT-09-2020-0197

Boukhobza, T. (2005). *An investigation into customer loyalty and relationship marketing: case UK grocery retailing and telecommunication sectors*. University of Salford.

Bouzembrak, Y., Klüche, M., Gavai, A., & Marvin, H. J. P. (2019). Internet of Things in food safety: Literature review and a bibliometric analysis. *Trends in Food Science & Technology*, 94, 54–64. DOI: 10.1016/j.tifs.2019.11.002

Brachner, A., Fragouli, D., Duarte, I., Farias, P., Dembski, S., Ghosh, M., Barisic, I., Zdzieblo, D., Vanoirbeek, J., Schwabl, P., & Neuhaus, W. (2020). Assessment of human health risks posed by nano-and microplastics is currently not feasible. *International Journal of Environmental Research and Public Health*, 17(23), 8832. DOI: 10.3390/ijerph17238832 PMID: 33261100

Brandt, R. (2017). 'What's cooking, Chef Watson?', URL: https://www.ibm.com/blogs/think/nl-en/2017/06/06/whats-cooking-chef-watson/

Brasel, S. A., & Gips, J. (2014). Tablets, touchscreens, and touchpads: How varying touch interfaces trigger psychological ownership and endowment. *Journal of Consumer Psychology*, 24(2), 226–233. DOI: 10.1016/j.jcps.2013.10.003

Brennan, A., & Browne, S. (2021). Food waste and nutrition quality in the context of public health: A scoping review. *International Journal of Environmental Research and Public Health*, 18(10), 5379. DOI: 10.3390/ijerph18105379 PMID: 34070070

Bridgestock, L. (2021, June 1). *6 essential trends and skills for hospitality careers*. QS Top University. https://www.topuniversities.com/student-info/careers-advice/6-essential-trends-skills-hospitality-careers

Brown, D., & Fiorella, S. (2013). *Influencer marketing: How to create, manage, and measure brand influencers in social media marketing*. Que Publishing.

Brown, H., & Smith, J. (2023). The impact of TikTok on food trends and consumer behavior. *International Journal of Consumer Studies*, 47(4), 1341–1355.

Brunklaus, B., Chiew, Y. L., Lundström, A., Nilsson-Lindén, H., & Saarikko, T. (2022). The connected, sustainable and inclusive society – IoT implementation in a Swedish municipality. E3S Web of Conferences, 349, 11006. DOI: 10.1051/e3sconf/202234911006

Brynjolfsson, E., & McAfee, A. (2017). *The second machine age: Work, progress, and prosperity in a time of brilliant technologies*. W. W. Norton & Company.

Budiarto, B. W., Haes, N. P. E., Nawarcono, N. W., Mardiah, N. A., & Apriyono, N. T. (2023). The influence of E-Customer satisfaction, E-Service quality and sales promotion on E-Customer loyalty of Tokopedia customers. [Jurnal Ekonomi Manajemen Dan Akuntansi]. *JEMSI*, 9(6), 2472–2479. DOI: 10.35870/jemsi.v9i6.1656

Bugami, M. A. (2022, March). Saudi Arabia's march towards sustainable development through innovation and technology. In *2022 9th International Conference on Computing for Sustainable Global Development (INDIACom)* (pp. 01-06). IEEE. DOI: 10.23919/INDIACom54597.2022.9763172

Bughin, J., Hazan, E., Ramaswamy, S., Chui, M., Allas, T., Dahlström, P., & Henke, N. (2018). *Skill shift: Automation and the future of the workforce*. McKinsey Global Institute.

Buhalis, D. (2020). Technology and service excellence in hospitality: The future is now. *Journal of Hospitality Marketing & Management*, 29(1), 1–9.

Buhalis, D., & Amaranggana, A. (2015). Smart tourism destinations: Enhancing tourism experience through personalisation of services. In Tussyadiah, I., & Inversini, A. (Eds.), *Information and Communication Technologies in Tourism* (pp. 377–389). Springer., DOI: 10.1007/978-3-319-14343-9_28

Buhalis, D., & Leung, R. (2018). Smart hospitality: Interconnectivity and interoperability towards an ecosystem. *International Journal of Hospitality Management*, 71, 41–50. DOI: 10.1016/j.ijhm.2017.11.011

Buiten, M. C. (2021). Exploitative abuses in digital markets: Between competition law and data protection law. *Journal of Antitrust Enforcement*, 9(2), 270–288. DOI: 10.1093/jaenfo/jnaa041

Buiten, M. C., De Streel, A., & Peitz, M. (2020). Rethinking liability rules for online hosting platforms. *International Journal of Law and Information Technology*, 28(2), 139–166. DOI: 10.1093/ijlit/eaaa012

Bulearca, M., & Tamarjan, D. (2020). Augmented reality: A sustainable technology for the future of advertising? *International Journal of Interactive Mobile Technologies*, 14(3), 20–30.

Burgess, J., Conlon, C., & Hsu, C. (2020). Exploring ghost kitchens: A novel business model for the food delivery sector. *Journal of Hospitality and Tourism Management*, 44, 208–217. DOI: 10.1016/j.jhtm.2020.08.001

Burke, T. (2019). *Blockchain in Food Traceability*., DOI: 10.1007/978-3-030-10902-8_10

Business Insider. (2019). *How Starbucks became a global phenomenon*. Retrieved from Business Insider.

Business Insider. (2020). *Dunkin's collaboration with Charli D'Amelio has been a huge success*. Retrieved from Business Insider.

Butcher, J., & Pecot, F. (2022). Visually communicating brand heritage on social media: Champagne on Instagram. *Journal of Product and Brand Management*, 31(4), 654–670. DOI: 10.1108/JPBM-01-2021-3334

Caidie, G. (2024). *Brand Equity Management of Coffee Chains: A Case Study of Luckin Coffee*. Dhonburi Rajabhat University.

Cai, L., Yuen, K. F., Fang, M., & Wang, X. (2023). A literature review on the impact of the COVID-19 pandemic on consumer behaviour: Implications for consumer-centric logistics. *Asia Pacific Journal of Marketing and Logistics*, 35(11), 2682–2703. DOI: 10.1108/APJML-08-2022-0731

Cain, L. N., Thomas, J. H., & Alonso, M.Jr. (2019). From sci-fi to sci-fact: The state of robotics and AI in the hospitality industry. *Journal of Hospitality and Tourism Technology*, 10(4), 624–650. DOI: 10.1108/JHTT-07-2018-0066

Camilleri, M. A., Troise, C., & Kozak, M. (2023). Functionality and usability features of ubiquitous mobile technologies: The acceptance of interactive travel app. *Journal of Hospitality and Tourism Technology*, 14(2), 188–207. DOI: 10.1108/JHTT-12-2021-0345

Candra, S., Sukmawaty, D., & Bahtiar, R. Y. (2023). Insights on online food delivery of mobile application user behavior in Indonesia's large cities. 2023 11th International Conference on Information and Communication Technology (ICoICT), 63-67. https://doi.org/DOI: 10.1109/ICoICT58202.2023.10262624

Caputo, F., Marzi, G., & Pellegrini, M. M. (2021). Digital transformation and supply chain management in the foodservice industry: A systematic review. *Technological Forecasting and Social Change*, 169, 120829. DOI: 10.1016/j.techfore.2021.120829

Carden, J., Jones, R. J., & Passmore, J. (2021). *Defining self-awareness in the context of adult development: A systematic literature review*. Sage Journals. https://journals.sagepub.com/doi/full/10.1177/1052562921990065

Carlson, N. (2010). *At last – The full story of how Facebook was founded. Business Insider*. Retrieved from Business Insider.

Carter, M., & Grover, V. (2015). Me, my self, and I(T). *Management Information Systems, 39*(4), 931–957. https://www.econis.eu/PPNSET?PPN=84353088X

Casado, M. A. (2014). *Front Office Management in Hospitality Lodging Operations*. Create Space Independent Publishing.

Casati, M., Soregaroli, C., Rommel, J., Luzzani, G., & Stranieri, S. (2023). Please keep ordering! A natural field experiment assessing a carbon label introduction. *Food Policy*, 120(102523), 102523. DOI: 10.1016/j.foodpol.2023.102523

Castaldi, A. (2021). Digital Transformation needed: With or Without a Pandemic. *Berita Sunway, Issue 71*.https://www.sunway.com.my/stories

Castillo, A. M. M., Salonga, L. J. L., Sia, J. A. L., & Young, M. N. (2020, March). Improving Fast-Food Restaurants' Method of Operation: Automated Drive-Through Ordering System. In *Int'l Conf. on Indus. Eng'g. and Ops. Management* (pp. 1838-49).

Catherine, A. O., Oladele, A. S., & Adebayo, O. S. (2012). An assessment of the role of ICT in the readiness of Nigerian bank customers for the introduction of cashless transactions. *International Journal of Computing and ICT Research*, 6(2), 9–22.

Cavaliere, A., Pigliafreddo, S., Marchi, E. D., & Banterle, A. (2020). Do consumers really want to reduce plastic usage? Exploring the determinants of plastic avoidance in food-related consumption decisions. *Sustainability (Basel)*, 12(22), 9627. DOI: 10.3390/su12229627

Cavoukian, A. (2019). *Privacy by design: The 7 foundational principles*. Information and Privacy Commissioner of Ontario.

Cavusoglu, M. (2019). An analysis of technology applications in the restaurant industry. *Journal of Hospitality and Tourism Technology*, 10(1), 45–72. DOI: 10.1108/JHTT-12-2017-0141

Celik, H., & Kocaman, R. (2017). Roles of self-monitoring, fashion involvement and technology readiness in an individual's propensity to use mobile shopping. *Journal of Systems ani nformation. Journal of Systems and Information Technology*, 19(3/4), 166–182. DOI: 10.1108/JSIT-01-2017-0008

Ceynowa, W., Przybylowski, A., Wojtasik, P., & Ciskowski, Ł. (2023). ICT Adoption for Sustainable Logistics Development in the HoReCa and Wholesale Sectors. *Sustainability (Basel)*, 15(4), 3746. DOI: 10.3390/su15043746

Chaffey, D. (2020). *Social media marketing trends 2020*. Smart Insights. Retrieved from Smart Insights.

Chaffey, D., & Ellis-Chadwick, F. (2019). *Digital marketing: Strategy, implementation & practice* (7th ed.). Pearson.

Chaffey, D., & Smith, P. R. (2017). *Digital marketing excellence: Planning, optimizing and integrating online marketing* (5th ed.). Routledge. DOI: 10.4324/9781315640341

Chai, L. T., & Yat, D. N. C. (2019). Online food delivery services: Making food delivery the new normal. *Journal of Marketing Advances and Practices*, 1(1), 62–77.

Chakraborty, D., Bhatnagar, S. B., Biswas, W., & Khatua, A. K. (2022). What drives people to adopt grocery apps? The moderating role of household size. *Business Perspectives and Research*, •••, 22785337221091640. DOI: 10.1177/22785337221091640

Chakraborty, D., Rana, N. P., Khorana, S., Singu, H. B., & Luthra, S. (2023). Big data in food: Systematic literature review and future directions. *Journal of Computer Information Systems*, 63(5), 1243–1263. DOI: 10.1080/08874417.2022.2132428

Chakravorti, S. (2023). *Customer Relationship Management: A Global Approach.*

Cha, M. (2020). Consumer innovation in robot-serviced restaurants: The role of hedonic and social motivation. *Journal of Service Research*, 23(2), 222–236.

Chandrasekaran, M., Bishop, B., & Rad, A. A. (2017). Leveraging artificial intelligence in food service operations: Case studies in the fast food industry. *Journal of Operations Management*, 49(2), 45–58. DOI: 10.1016/j.jom.2017.03.001

Chang, W.-J. (2021). Experiential marketing, brand image and brand loyalty: A case study of Starbucks. *British Food Journal*, 123(1), 209–223. DOI: 10.1108/BFJ-01-2020-0014

Chao, L. L., & Martin, A. (2000). Representation of Manipulable Man-Made Objects in the Dorsal Stream. *NeuroImage*, 12(4), 478–484. DOI: 10.1006/nimg.2000.0635 PMID: 10988041

Chaoyu, Y. (2023). Opportunities and Strategies for Promoting Cultural Tourism Industry on Small Screens in the New Media Perspective—Take Zibo Barbecue out Circle as an Example. *Academic Journal of Humanities & Social Sciences*, 6(18), 72–76.

Chapman, J., Power, A., Netzel, M. E., Sultanbawa, Y., Smyth, H. E., Truong, V. K., & Cozzolino, D. (2022, April 05). Netzel., … & Cozzolino, D. (2021). Challenges and opportunities of fourth revolution: A brief insight into the future of food. *Critical Reviews in Food Science and Nutrition*, 62(10), 2845–2853. Advance online publication. DOI: 10.1080/10408398.2020.1863328 PMID: 33401934

Cha, S. S., & Seo, B. K. (2020). The effect of food delivery application on customer loyalty in restaurant. *Journal of Distribution Science*, 18(4), 5–12.

Chaturvedi, P., Kulshreshtha, K., Tripathi, V., & Agnihotri, D. (2024). Investigating the impact of restaurants' sustainable practices on consumers' satisfaction and revisit intentions: A study on leading green restaurants. *Asia-Pacific Journal of Business Administration*, 16(1), 41–62. DOI: 10.1108/APJBA-09-2021-0456

Chauhan, R. S., Connelly, S., Howe, D. C., Soderberg, A. T., & Crisostomo, M. (2022). The danger of "fake news": How using social media for information dissemination can inhibit the ethical decision making process. *Ethics & Behavior*, 32(4), 287–306. DOI: 10.1080/10508422.2021.1890598

Chawla, Y., & Chodak, G. (2021). Social media marketing for businesses: Organic promotions of web-links on Facebook. *Journal of Business Research*, 135, 49–65. DOI: 10.1016/j.jbusres.2021.06.020

Chen McCain, S.-L., Lolli, J., Liu, E., & Lin, L.-C.Chen McCain and Liu. (2022). An analysis of a third-party food delivery app during the COVID-19 pandemic. *British Food Journal*, 124(10), 3032–3052. DOI: 10.1108/BFJ-03-2021-0332

Chen, K. (1996, October 22). The Buying Behavior and Marketing Practices of Fast Food Markets in Metro Manila, Philippines. Taylor & Francis, 8(2), 1-21. https://doi.org/DOI: 10.1300/J047v08n02_01

Chen, C., & Girish, V. (2023). Investigating the use experience of restaurant service robots: The cognitive-affective-behavioral framework. *International Journal of Hospitality Management*, 111, 103482. Advance online publication. DOI: 10.1016/j.ijhm.2023.103482

Cheng, Y., Wang, S., & Wei, X. (2022). Enhancing customer experience with AI chatbots in food delivery services. *International Journal of Hospitality Management*, 102, 103096. DOI: 10.1016/j.ijhm.2021.103096

Chen, H. L., Nath, T. K., Chong, S., Foo, V., Gibbins, C., & Lechner, A. M. (2021). The plastic waste problem in Malaysia: Management, recycling, and disposal of local and global plastic waste. *SN Applied Sciences*, 3(4), 1–15. DOI: 10.1007/s42452-021-04234-y

Chen, H., Preston, D. S., & Swink, M. (2015). How the use of big data analytics affects value creation in supply chain management. *Journal of Management Information Systems*, 32(4), 4–39. DOI: 10.1080/07421222.2015.1138364

Chen, I., Hsu, P., Officer, M. S., & Wang, Y. (2020). The Oscar goes to. . .: High-tech firms' acquisitions in response to rivals' technology breakthroughs. *Research Policy*, 49(7), 104078. DOI: 10.1016/j.respol.2020.104078

Chen, J. Y. (2022). Responsible sourcing and supply chain traceability. *International Journal of Production Economics*, 248, 108462. DOI: 10.1016/j.ijpe.2022.108462

Chen, J., Ramanathan, L., & Alazab, M. (2021). Holistic big data integrated artificial intelligent modeling to improve privacy and security in data management of smart cities. *Microprocessors and Microsystems*, 81, 103722. DOI: 10.1016/j.micpro.2020.103722

Chen, M., Hu, M., & Wang, J. (2022). Food delivery service and restaurant: Friend or foe? *Management Science*, 68(9), 6539–6551. DOI: 10.1287/mnsc.2021.4245

Chen, R., Smyser, M., Chan, N., Ta, M., Saelens, B., & Krieger, J. (2015). Changes in Awareness and Use of Calorie Information After Mandatory Menu Labeling in Restaurants in King County, Washington. *American Journal of Public Health*, 105(3), 546–553. DOI: 10.2105/AJPH.2014.302262 PMID: 25602868

Chen, S.-C., Yen, D. C., & Hwang, M. I. (2012). Factors influencing the continuance intention to the usage of Web 2.0: An empirical study. *Computers in Human Behavior*, 28(3), 933–941. DOI: 10.1016/j.chb.2011.12.014

Chen, T., Samaranayake, P., Cen, X., Qi, M., & Lan, Y.-C. (2022). The impact of online reviews on consumers' purchasing decisions: Evidence from an eye-tracking study. *Frontiers in Psychology*, 13, 865702. DOI: 10.3389/fpsyg.2022.865702 PMID: 35756238

Chen, W., & Liu, Y. (2019). Enhancing Restaurant Operations through AI-driven Quality Control. *Journal of Hospitality Management*, 25(3), 412–425.

Chen, W., Zhang, S., Hu, X., Chen, F., & Li, D. (2023). A Review of Healthy Dietary Choices for Cardiovascular Disease: From Individual Nutrients and Foods to Dietary Patterns. *Nutrients*, 15(23), 15. DOI: 10.3390/nu15234898 PMID: 38068756

Chen, X., & Qasim, H. (2021). Does E-Brand experience matter in the consumer market? Explaining the impact of social media marketing activities on consumer-based brand equity and love. *Journal of Consumer Behaviour*, 20(5), 1065–1077. DOI: 10.1002/cb.1915

Chen, Y., & Chen, X. (2022). Managing order volume in mobile food delivery: Insights from Starbucks. *Journal of Business Research*, 136, 562–570. DOI: 10.1016/j.jbusres.2021.07.021

Chesney, M., Krakow, J., Maranghino-Singer, B., & Wolff, V. (2022). Der Finanzsektor im 21. Jahrhundert. In Springer eBooks (pp. 37–66). https://doi.org/DOI: 10.1007/978-3-658-37949-0_3

Cheung, M. L., Pires, G. D., Rosenberger, P. J.III, Leung, W. K. S., & Ting, H. (2021). Investigating the role of social media marketing on value co-creation and engagement: An empirical study in China and Hong Kong. *Australasian Marketing Journal*, 29(2), 118–131. DOI: 10.1016/j.ausmj.2020.03.006

Chicco, D., Warrens, M. J., & Jurman, G. (2021). The coefficient of determination R-squared is more informative than SMAPE, MAE, MAPE, MSE and RMSE in regression analysis evaluation. *PeerJ. Computer Science*, 7, e623. DOI: 10.7717/peerj-cs.623 PMID: 34307865

Chi, K., He, J., Lin, W., Bokhari, S., & Catchmark, J. (2023). Electrostatically complexed natural polysaccharides as aqueous barrier coatings for sustainable and recyclable fiber-based packaging. *ACS Applied Materials & Interfaces*, 15(9), 12248–12260. DOI: 10.1021/acsami.2c17886 PMID: 36848253

China Industrial Statistical Yearbook. (2023). *China Food and Beverage Industry Market Size from 2016 to 2023*. https://www.stats.gov.cn/sj/ndsj/2023/indexch.htm

Chin, H., Marasini, D. P., & Lee, D. (2022). Digital transformation trends in service industries. *Service Business*, 17(1), 11–36. DOI: 10.1007/s11628-022-00516-6

Chi, O. H., Chi, C. G., Gursoy, D., & Nunkoo, R. (2023). Customers' acceptance of artificially intelligent service robots: The influence of trust and culture. *International Journal of Information Management*, 70, 102623. DOI: 10.1016/j.ijinfomgt.2023.102623

Chipotle. (2020). Sustainability at Chipotle. Retrieved from Chipotle.

Choi, Y., Lee, Y., & Kim, J. (2021). Impact of big data analytics on the food service industry: The case of Domino's Pizza. *International Journal of Hospitality Management*, 94, 102803. DOI: 10.1016/j.ijhm.2020.102803

Choi, Y., & Park, J. (2020). Service robots in the hospitality industry: A review of challenges and opportunities. *Service Robotics and Automation*, 18(3), 215–231.

Cho, M., & Fiore, A. M. (2018). The impact of AI on dining experience: Customer perspectives. *Journal of Hospitality and Tourism Technology*, 9(4), 446–457.

Choudhury, P. (2021). Robotic Process Automation: A critical evaluation of its impact on food service industry. *Journal of Service Management*, 32(4), 513–530.

Chovancová, J., Majerník, M., Drábik, P., & Štofková, Z. (2023). Environmental technological innovations and the sustainability of their development. *Ecological Engineering & Environmental Technology*, 24(4), 245–252. DOI: 10.12912/27197050/162708

Chowdhury, R. (2023). Impact of perceived convenience, service quality and security on consumers' behavioural intention towards online food delivery services: The role of attitude as mediator. *SN Business & Economics*, 3(1), 29. Advance online publication. DOI: 10.1007/s43546-023-00422-7 PMID: 36643187

Chuang, H. (2019). Starbucks in the world. HOLISTICA –. *Journal of Business and Public Administration*, 10(3), 99–110. DOI: 10.2478/hjbpa-2019-0031

Chung, H. (2022). Variable work schedules, unit-level turnover, and performance before and during the COVID-19 pandemic. *The Journal of Applied Psychology*, 107(4), 515–532. DOI: 10.1037/apl0001006 PMID: 35286111

Chung, J. B., Choi, B. C., Cho, Y. S., & Chung, L. C. (2016). Service quality of online grocery shopping in Korean local regions. *Journal of Distribution Science*, 14(8), 67–75. DOI: 10.15722/jds.14.8.201608.67

Chung, M., Ko, E., Joung, H., & Kim, S. J. (2020). Chatbot e-service and customer satisfaction regarding luxury brands. *Journal of Business Research*, 117, 587–595. DOI: 10.1016/j.jbusres.2018.10.004

Clifton, B. (2012). *Advanced web metrics with Google Analytics* (3rd ed.). Wiley.

Cobanoglu, C., Morosan, C., & Mena, J. (2011). The effects of internet-based technologies on guest satisfaction in the hotel industry. *Journal of Hospitality & Tourism Research (Washington, D.C.)*, 35(3), 349–368. DOI: 10.1177/1096348010373823

Coca-Cola. (2015). *Share a Coke campaign*. Retrieved from Coca-Cola.

Coca-Cola. (2019). *Share a Coke campaign. Coca-Cola Journey*. Retrieved from Coca-Cola.

Cohen, S. A., & Hopkins, D. (2019). Autonomous vehicles and the future of urban tourism. *Annals of Tourism Research*, 74, 33–42. DOI: 10.1016/j.annals.2018.10.009

Çöl, B., İmre, M., & Yıkmış, S. (2023). Virtual reality and augmented reality technologies in gastronomy: A review. *eFood*, 4(3), e84. Advance online publication. DOI: 10.1002/efd2.84

Collis, B., Baxter, W., Baird, H., Meade, K., & Webb, T. L. (2023). Signs of use present a barrier to reusable packaging systems for takeaway food. *Sustainability (Basel)*, 15(11), 8857. DOI: 10.3390/su15118857

Colom Umbert, A., Llull Cantallops, R., Ramos Monserrat, M., Colom Fernández, A., & Mercader Barceló, J. (2023). From control systems to safety culture in the global foodservice outlet arena: A Balearic Islands perspective. *Trends in Food Science & Technology*, 136, 308–313. DOI: 10.1016/j.tifs.2023.04.017

Comendulli, A. A. (2020). *Generation Z in China: Their importance in Chinese market and how to reach them through social media.*

Corbett, C. J. (2018). How Sustainable Is Big Data? *Production and Operations Management*, 27(9), 1685–1695. DOI: 10.1111/poms.12837

Courtney, A., PeConga, E., Wagner, D., & Rapuano, K. (2018). Calorie information and dieting status modulate reward and control activation during the evaluation of food images. *PLoS One*, 13(11), e0204744. Advance online publication. DOI: 10.1371/journal.pone.0204744 PMID: 30388113

Crawford, K. (2021). The risks of data misuse in AI systems in service industries. *Journal of Applied Artificial Intelligence*, 35(3), 250–265. DOI: 10.1080/08839514.2021.1870049

Crowe, M., Retallack, F., Del Begio, C., Hurst, T., & Del Begio, B. (2024). URL: https://www.mealime.com/

Cruz Introini, S., Boza, A., & Alemany Díaz, M. D. M. (2018). *Traceability in the Food Supply Chain: Review of the literature from a technological perspective*. http://hdl.handle.net/10251/121089

Cruz, J., & Martinez, P. (2023). The role of social media in promoting sustainable food consumption. *Journal of Environmental Management*, 325, 116564.

Cui, F., Zheng, S., Wang, D., Tan, X., Li, Q., Li, J., & Li, T. (2023). Recent advances in shelf life prediction models for monitoring food quality. *Comprehensive Reviews in Food Science and Food Safety*, 22(2), 1257–1284. DOI: 10.1111/1541-4337.13110 PMID: 36710649

Curran, M. A. (2012). Life Cycle Assessment Handbook: A Guide for Environmentally Sustainable Products. DOI: 10.1002/9781118528372

Cybersecurity Malaysia. (2023). Cybersecurity Malaysia: Mid Term Report 2023- treat Landscape. www.cybersecurity.my/data/content_files/26/2511

Dai, X., Wu, L., & Hu, W. (2022). Nutritional quality and consumer health perception of online delivery food in the context of China. *BMC Public Health*, 22(1), 2132. DOI: 10.1186/s12889-022-14593-9 PMID: 36403009

Damiani, L., & Di Marco, M. (2022). Managerial perceptions of service automation: A case study in hospitality. *Tourism Management*, 84(1), 104–115.

Dana, L. M., Hart, E., McAleese, A., Bastable, A., & Pettigrew, S. (2021). Factors associated with ordering food via online meal ordering services. *Public Health Nutrition*, 24(17), 5704–5709. DOI: 10.1017/S1368980021001294 PMID: 33762026

Dani, R., Rawal, Y., Bagchi, P., & Khan, M. (2022). Opportunities and challenges in implementation of artificial intelligence in food & beverage service industry. In *AIP Conference Proceedings* (Vol. 2481). DOI: 10.1063/5.0103741

Dantas, T. E. T., de-Souza, E. D., Destro, I. R., Hammes, G., Rodriguez, C. M. T., & Soares, S. R. (2021). How the combination of Circular Economy and Industry 4.0 can contribute towards achieving the Sustainable Development Goals. *Sustainable Production and Consumption*, 26, 213–227. DOI: 10.1016/j.spc.2020.10.005

Danziger, P. N. (2021). The rise of ghost kitchens: A culinary revolution. Forbes. Retrieved from https://www.forbes.com/sites/pamdanziger/2021/02/04/the-rise-of-ghost-kitchens-a-culinary-revolution

Das, S., & Pan, T. (2022). A strategic outline of Industry 6.0: Exploring the Future. SSRN *Electronic Journal,*May 2022 https://www.researchgate.net/publication/360501150_ DOI:DOI: 10.2139/ssrn.4104696

Davenport, T. H., & Ronanki, R. (2018). Artificial intelligence for the real world. *Harvard Business Review*, 96(1), 108–116.

Davis, F. D. (1985). A technology acceptance model for empirically testing new end-user information systems : theory and results. Retrieved from http://ci.nii.ac.jp/naid/20001062454

Davis, F. D. (1989). Perceived usefulness, perceived ease of use, and user acceptance of information technology. *Management Information Systems Quarterly*, 13(3), 319. DOI: 10.2307/249008

Davis, R., & Wilson, A. (2024). Customer engagement in the food industry: The power of social media marketing. *Journal of Business Research*, 151, 426–439.

De Barros Ahrens, R., Da Silva Lirani, L., & De Francisco, A. C. (2020). Construct Validity and reliability of the Work Environment Assessment Instrument WE-10. *International Journal of Environmental Research and Public Health*, 17(20), 7364. DOI: 10.3390/ijerph17207364 PMID: 33050197

de Magalhães, D. J. A. V. (2021). Analysis of critical factors affecting the final decision-making for online grocery shopping. *Research in Transportation Economics*, 87, 101088. DOI: 10.1016/j.retrec.2021.101088

De Mauro, A., Greco, M., & Grimaldi, M. (2014). *What is Big Data? A Consensual Definition and a Review of Key Research Topics*. DOI: 10.13140/2.1.2341.5048

De Pelsmacker, P., Geuens, M., & Van den Bergh, J. (2017). *Marketing communications: A European perspective* (6th ed.). Pearson.

De Veirman, M., Cauberghe, V., & Hudders, L. (2017). Marketing through Instagram influencers: The impact of number of followers and product divergence on brand attitude. *International Journal of Advertising*, 36(5), 798–828. DOI: 10.1080/02650487.2017.1348035

De Vries, H. (2021). Food science and technology contributes to sustainable food systems. *Trends in Food Science & Technology*, 116, 1200–1202. DOI: 10.1016/j.tifs.2021.05.026

Dehghani, M., Popova, A., & Gheitanchi, S. (2022). Factors impacting digital transformations of the food industry by adoption of block chain technology. *Journal of Business and Industrial Marketing*, 37(9), 1818–1834. DOI: 10.1108/JBIM-12-2020-0540

Deloitte. (2015). *Navigating the new digital divide*. Retrieved from Deloitte.

Demestichas, K., & Daskalakis, E. (2020). Information and communication technology solutions for the circular economy. *Sustainability (Basel)*, 12(18), 7272. DOI: 10.3390/su12187272

Dennis, A. (2024). Digital Transformation in Hospitality-Examples, Challenges. https://whatfix.com

Devaux, A., Goffart, J. P., Petsakos, A., Kromann, P., Gatto, M., Okello, J., ... & Hareau, G. (2020). Global food security, contributions from sustainable potato agri-food systems. *The potato crop: Its agricultural, nutritional and social contribution to humankind*, 3-35.

Devi, J. A., & Chandrasekar, K. S. (2023). Digital Marketing in the Food Service Industry in India: A Review. i-Manager's Journal on Economics & Commerce, 3(1), 29.

Dhir, B., & Singla, N. (2020). Consumption pattern and health implications of convenience foods: A practical review. *Current Journal of Applied Science and Technology*, 38(6), 1–9. DOI: 10.9734/cjast/2019/v38i630455

Dickinson, S. (2017). Back to basics: What is a chatbot and does my hotel need one? Retrieved January 23, 2018, from https://www.hospitalitynet.org/opinion/4084472.html

Dieck, M. C. T., & Han, D. (2021). The role of immersive technology in customer experience management. *Journal of Marketing Theory and Practice*, 30(1), 108–119. DOI: 10.1080/10696679.2021.1891939

Digital Penang. (2023). Catalysing digital transformation in the hospitality sector. December 14. https://digitalpenang.my/

Dillahunt, T. R., Simioni, S., & Xu, X. (2019, May). Online grocery delivery services: An opportunity to address food disparities in transportation-scarce areas. In *Proceedings of the 2019 CHI Conference on Human Factors in Computing Systems* (pp. 1-15). DOI: 10.1145/3290605.3300879

Dillon, T., Wu, C., & Chang, E. (2010, April). Cloud computing: issues and challenges. In 2010 24th IEEE international conference on advanced information networking and applications (pp. 27-33). Ieee.

Dinçer, F. I., Bayram, G. E., & Altunoz, O. (2020). Fourth generation of rights and their reflections on human resources practices in tourism businesses. In Aydin, Ş., Dedeoglu, B. B., & Çoban, Ö. (Eds.), *Organizational Behavior Challenges in The Tourism Industry* (pp. 60–81). IGI Global., DOI: 10.4018/978-1-7998-1474-0.ch005

Ding, H., Tian, J., Yu, W., Wilson, D. I., Young, B. R., Cui, X., Xin, X., Wang, Z., & Li, W. (2023). The application of artificial intelligence and big data in the food industry. *Foods*, 12(24), 4511. DOI: 10.3390/foods12244511 PMID: 38137314

Dining in Virtual Realm. Rise of AR/VR Restaurants and Cafés. (n.d.). Retrieved July 3, 2024, from https://www.qualium-systems.com/blog/ar-vr/dining-in-virtual-realm-rise-of-ar-vr-restaurants-and-cafes/

Dirsehan, T., & Cankat, E. (2021). Role of mobile food-ordering applications in developing restaurants' brand satisfaction and loyalty in the pandemic period. *Journal of Retailing and Consumer Services*, 62, 102608. Advance online publication. DOI: 10.1016/j.jretconser.2021.102608

Di, S. (2023). Chinese Food Nut Enterprises: An Analysis of Three Squirrels. *Academic Journal of Business & Management*, 5(3), 6–12.

Dixon, S., & Pantano, E. (2021). Service robots: A future in hospitality. *Journal of Service Management*, 32(2), 303–317.

Djekic, I., Pojić, M., Tonda, A., Putnik, P., Bursać Kovačević, D., Režek-Jambrak, A., & Tomasevic, I. (2019). Scientific Challenges in Performing Life-Cycle Assessment in the Food Supply Chain. *Foods*, 8(8), 301. DOI: 10.3390/foods8080301 PMID: 31374833

Doan, H. (n.d.). *Improving Online Restaurant Menu Using Augmented Reality*. California State Polytechnic University.

Dodds, S., & Hess, A. C. (2021). Adapting research methodology during COVID-19: lessons for transformative service research. *Journal of Service Management*, Vol 32 (2) ISSN: 1757-5818

Doğan, S., Pala, U., & Ekici, N. (2023). Mobile applications as a next generation solution to prevent food waste. *Ege Academic Review*, 23(1), 1–10.

Dolega, L., Rowe, F., & Branagan, E. (2021). Going digital? The impact of social media marketing on retail website traffic, orders and sales. *Journal of Retailing and Consumer Services*, 60, 102501. DOI: 10.1016/j.jretconser.2021.102501

Dora, M., Biswas, S., Choudhary, S., Nayak, R., & Irani, Z. (2021). A system-wide interdisciplinary conceptual framework for food loss and waste mitigation strategies in the supply chain. *Industrial Marketing Management*, 93, 400–414. DOI: 10.1016/j.indmarman.2020.10.013

Doran, D. (2010). Restaurants and technology – past, present and future: A practitioner's viewpoint. *Worldwide Hospitality and Tourism Themes*, 2(1), 94–99. DOI: 10.1108/17554211011012621

dos Santos, M. L. B. (2022). The "so-called" UGC: An updated definition of user-generated content in the age of social media. *Online Information Review*, 46(1), 95–113. DOI: 10.1108/OIR-06-2020-0258

Doub, A. E., Levin, A., Heath, C. E., & Le Vangie, K. (2015). Mobile app-etite: Consumer attitudes towards and use of mobile technology in the context of eating behaviour. *Journal of Direct, Data and Digital Marketing Practice*, 17(2), 114–129. DOI: 10.1057/dddmp.2015.44

Drummond, C., O'Toole, T., & McGrath, H. (2020). Digital engagement strategies and tactics in social media marketing. *European Journal of Marketing*, 54(6), 1247–1280. DOI: 10.1108/EJM-02-2019-0183

Dufera, A. G., Liu, T., & Xu, J. (2023). Regression models of Pearson correlation coefficient. *Statistical Theory and Related Fields*, 7(2), 97–106. DOI: 10.1080/24754269.2023.2164970

Duong, L. N. K., Al-Fadhli, M., Jagtap, S., Bader, F., Martindale, W., Swainson, M., & Paoli, A. (2020). A review of robotics and autonomous systems in the food industry: From the supply chains perspective. *Trends in Food Science & Technology*, 106, 355–364. DOI: 10.1016/j.tifs.2020.10.028

Durai, A. (2022). The rise of robot waiters in Malaysia, driven by labour shortage in F&B sector. https://www.thestar.com.my/lifestyle/living/2022/08/24/the-rise-of-robot-waiters-in-malaysia

Du, X., Liechty, T., Santos, C. A., & Park, J. (2022). 'I want to record and share my wonderful journey': Chinese Millennials' production and sharing of short-form travel videos on TikTok or Douyin. *Current Issues in Tourism*, 25(21), 3412–3424. DOI: 10.1080/13683500.2020.1810212

Dwivedi, Y. K., Hughes, L., Ismagilova, E., Aarts, G., Coombs, C., Crick, T., Duan, Y., Dwivedi, R., Edwards, J., Eirug, A., Galanos, V., Ilavarasan, P. V., Janssen, M., Jones, P., Kar, A. K., Kizgin, H., Kronemann, B., Lal, B., Lucini, B., & Williams, M. D. (2021). Artificial Intelligence (AI): Multidisciplinary perspectives on emerging challenges, opportunities, and agenda for research, practice and policy. *International Journal of Information Management*, 57, 101994. DOI: 10.1016/j.ijinfomgt.2019.08.002

Dwivedi, Y. K., Ismagilova, E., Hughes, D. L., Carlson, J., Filieri, R., Jacobson, J., Jain, V., Karjaluoto, H., Kefi, H., Krishen, A. S., Kumar, V., Rahman, M. M., Raman, R., Rauschnabel, P. A., Rowley, J., Salo, J., Tran, G. A., & Wang, Y. (2021). Setting the future of digital and social media marketing research: Perspectives and research propositions. *International Journal of Information Management*, 59, 102168. DOI: 10.1016/j.ijinfomgt.2020.102168

Dzia-uddin, D. N., Annuar, J., Nik Mohd Fahmil, N. M. Z., & Wan Kamarudin, W. N. B. (2023). A Review Paper on Technological Innovation of Hotel Industry in Post-Pandemic. *International Journal of Business and Technology Management*, [S.l.], Vol. 5, no. S1, pp. 9-25. ISSN 2682-7646. https://myjms.mohe.gov.my/index.php/ijbtm/article/view/23575

Eashwar, S., & Chawla, P. (2021). Evolution of agritech business I4.0: Architecture and future research directions. *IOP Conference Series. Earth and Environmental Science*, 775(1), 012011. Advance online publication. DOI: 10.1088/1755-1315/775/1/012011

East, R. (2022). Online grocery sales after the pandemic. *International Journal of Market Research*, 64(1), 13–18. DOI: 10.1177/14707853211055047

Edsall, D., Gray, C., Witherspoon, J., McDonnell, M., & Almond, A. (n.d). *The future of grocery retail.* Deloitte. Retrieved 2024-02-05 from https://www2.deloitte.com/us/en/insights/industry/retail-distribution/future-of-grocery- retail.html

Edward, O. T. (2023). The impact of the Fourth Industrial Revolution (IR 4.0) on Modern Civilisation in Malaysia. https://www.bernama.com/en/thoughts/news.php?id=2251185

Edwards, S., & King, T. (2023). Social media marketing and food safety: Communicating risk to consumers. *Journal of Food Protection*, 86(3), 567–576.

Egieya, Z. E., Ewuga, S. K., Adegbite, A. O., & Oke, T. T. (2023). The role of virtual and augmented reality in modern marketing: A critical review. *Computer Science & IT Research Journal*, 4(3), 244–272. DOI: 10.51594/csitrj.v4i3.660

Ejsmont, K., Gladysz, B., & Kluczek, A. (2020). Impact of Industry I4.0 on sustainability—Bibliometric literature review. *Sustainability (Basel)*, 12(14), 5650. Advance online publication. DOI: 10.3390/su12145650

Elbrechter, C., Maycock, J., Haschke, R., & Ritter, H. (2015, September). Discriminating liquids using a robotic kitchen assistant. In *2015 IEEE/RSJ International Conference on Intelligent Robots and Systems (IROS)* (pp. 703-708). IEEE. DOI: 10.1109/IROS.2015.7353449

Elder, R. S., & Krishna, A. (2010). The effects of advertising copy on sensory thoughts and perceived taste. *The Journal of Consumer Research*, 36(5), 748–756. DOI: 10.1086/605327

Elder, R. S., & Krishna, A. (2022). A Review of Sensory Imagery for Consumer Psychology. *Journal of Consumer Psychology*, 32(2), 293–315. DOI: 10.1002/jcpy.1242

Elias, M., & Marsh, R. (2020). *Innovations in Agricultural and Food Systems Sustainability in California.* Case Studies in the Environment. DOI: 10.1525/cse.2019.002170

Elkhwesky, Z., & Elkhwesky, E. F. Y. (2023). A systematic and critical review of Internet of Things in contemporary hospitality: A roadmap and avenues for future research. *International Journal of Contemporary Hospitality Management*, 35(2), 533–562. DOI: 10.1108/IJCHM-01-2022-0090

Ellahi, R. M., Wood, L. C., & Bekhit, A. E.-D. A. (2023). Blockchain-Based Frameworks for Food Traceability: A Systematic Review. *Foods*, 2023(12), 3026. DOI: 10.3390/foods12163026 PMID: 37628025

Ellen MacArthur Foundation. (2016). *Intelligent assets: Unlocking the circular economy potential.* https://ellenmacarthurfoundation.org/intelligent-assets-unlocking-the-circular-economy-potential

Ellison, K., Truman, E., & Elliott, C. (2023). Picturing food: The visual style of teen-targeted food marketing. *Young Consumers*, 24(3), 352–366. DOI: 10.1108/YC-08-2022-1577

Elvis, T. E., & Kim, H. K. (2023). *Unified Perspective of Technology Readiness Index (TRI) and Technology acceptance model (TAM) for adoption of digital pills.* Journal of System and Management Sciences. http://www.aasmr.org/jsms/Vol12/JSMS%20august%202022/Vol.12.No.04.07.pdf

Ema, N. R., Mithu, M. A. H., & Sayem, A. (2024). Exploring driving factors in employing waste reduction tools to alleviate the global food security and sustainability. *Heliyon*, 10(7), e28192. DOI: 10.1016/j.heliyon.2024.e28192 PMID: 38560263

Etikan, I. (2016). Comparison of convenience sampling and purposive sampling. *American Journal of Theoretical and Applied Statistics*, 5(1), 1. DOI: 10.11648/j.ajtas.20160501.11

Euromonitor International. (2021). *Global grocery retailing market overview.* Retrieved from Euromonitor International.

European Commission. (2002). Regulation (EC) No 178/2002 of the European Parliament and of the Council of 28 January 2002 laying down the general principles and requirements of food law, establishing the European Food Safety Authority and laying down procedures in matters of food safety. https://eur-lex.europa.eu/legal-content/EN/ALL/?uri=celex%3A32002R0178

European Commission. (2007). Council Regulation (EC) No 834/2007 of 28 June 2007 on organic production and labelling of organic products and repealing Regulation (EEC) No 2092/91. https://eur-lex.europa.eu/legal-content/EN/TXT/?uri=celex%3A32007R0834

European Commission. (2008). Addressing the challenge of energy efficiency through Information and *Communication Technologies.* https://eur-lex.europa.eu/legal-content/EN/TXT/?uri=COM%3A2008%3A0241%3AFIN

European Commission. (2021). *The EU food industry.* Retrieved from European Commission.

Evans, N. J., Phua, J., Lim, J., & Jun, H. (2017). Disclosing Instagram influencer advertising: The effects of disclosure language on advertising recognition, attitudes, and behavioral intent. *Journal of Interactive Advertising*, 17(2), 138–149. DOI: 10.1080/15252019.2017.1366885

Evans, R., Hajli, N., & Nisar, T. M. (2023). Privacy-Enhancing Factors and Consumer Concerns: The Moderating Effects of the General Data Protection Regulation. *British Journal of Management*, 34(4), 2075–2092. DOI: 10.1111/1467-8551.12685

Fabris, N. (2019). Cashless Society – The future of money or a utopia? *Journal of Central Banking Theory and Practice*, 1(1), 53–66. DOI: 10.2478/jcbtp-2019-0003

Fahmi, M., Arif, M., Farisi, S.A., & Purnama, N.I. (2019). Peran Brand Image dalam Memediasi Pengaruh Social Media Marketing terhadap Repeat Purchase pada Fast-Food Restaurant di Kota Medan.

Fang, Y., & Zhang, X. (2023). Utilizing social media for food marketing: Strategies for enhancing brand awareness. *International Journal of Marketing Studies*, 15(2), 75–88.

Feng, H., Wang, X., Duan, Y., Zhang, J., & Zhang, X. (2020). Applying blockchain technology to improve agrifood traceability: A review of development methods, benefits and challenges. *Journal of Cleaner Production, 260*, 121031. Fisher, O.; Watson, N.; Porcu, L.; Bacon, D.; Rigley, M.; Gomes, R. Cloud manufacturing as a sustainable process manufacturing route. J. Manuf. Syst. 2018, 47, 53–68. DOI: 10.1016/j.jclepro.2020.121031

Feng, H., Chen, J., Zhou, W., Rungsardthong, V., & Zhang, X. (2019). Modeling and evaluation on WS-Nenabled and knowledge-based HACCP quality control for frozen shellfish cold chain. *Food Control*, 98, 348–358. DOI: 10.1016/j.foodcont.2018.11.050

Ferreira, J., Silva, M., & Figueiredo, J. (2020). The role of artificial intelligence in enhancing customer experience in fast food restaurants. *International Journal of Hospitality Management*, 89, 102518. DOI: 10.1016/j.ijhm.2020.102518

Fiberesima, R. (2023, January 1). Assessment of POS Owners Awareness of Cybersecurity and Insider Threats in POS Kiosks Related Financial Crimes. Cornell University. https://doi.org//arxiv.2308.04447DOI: 10.48550

Filipe, S., Marques, S. H., & de Fátima Salgueiro, M. (2017). Customer's relationship with their grocery store: Direct and moderating effects from store format and loyalty programs. *Journal of Retailing and Consumer Services*, 37, 78–88. DOI: 10.1016/j.jretconser.2017.03.002

Financial Technology. (2020). *South Korea and China are Asia's cashless leaders*. Asian Banking Finance. https://asianbankingandfinance.net/financial-technology/news/south-korea-and-china-are-asias-cashless-leaders

Finkelstein, E., Strombotne, K., Chan, N., & Krieger, J. (2011). Mandatory Menu Labeling in One Fast-Food Chain in King County, Washington. *American Journal of Preventive Medicine*, 40(2), 122–127. DOI: 10.1016/j.amepre.2010.10.019 PMID: 21238859

Fiorini, P. C., Roman Pais Seles, B. M., Chiappetta Jabbour, C. J., Mariano, E. B., & Lopes de Sousa Jabbour, A. B. (2018). Management theory and big data literature: From a review to a research agenda. *International Journal of Information Management*, Volume 43, Pages 112-129, ISSN 0268-4012, DOI: 10.1016/j.ijinfomgt.2018.07.005

Firouz, M. S., Mohi-Alden, K., & Omid, M. (2021). A critical review on intelligent and active packaging in the food industry: Research and development. *Food Research International*, 141, 110113. DOI: 10.1016/j.foodres.2021.110113 PMID: 33641980

Flake, J. K., Davidson, I. J., Wong, O., & Pek, J. (2022). Construct validity and the validity of replication studies: A systematic review. *The American Psychologist*, 77(4), 576–588. DOI: 10.1037/amp0001006 PMID: 35482669

Flavián C., Ibáñez-Sánchez S., & Orús C. (2019). The impact of virtual, augmented and mixed reality technologies on the customer experience. *Journal of Business Research*, 100, 547–560. https://doi.org/es.2018.10.050DOI: 10.1016/j.jbusr

Flavián, C., Ibáñez-Sánchez, S., & Orús, C. (2018). The impact of virtual, augmented and mixed reality technologies on the customer experience. *Journal of Business Research*, 100, 547–560. DOI: 10.1016/j.jbusres.2018.10.050

Foncillas, B. L. F. (2020). *The future of retail* (Doctoral dissertation, Massachusetts Institute of Technology).

Fong, C. M., Mat Hasan, N. H., Rahmat, S. M., & Abenoh, N. A. (2020). Consumer purchase behaviour towards online grocery in Melaka. *International Journal of Business. Economics and Law*, 23(1), 25–31.

Food and Agriculture Organization (FAO). (2019). *The future of food and agriculture: Trends and challenges*. Retrieved from FAO.

Food and Agriculture Organization of the United Nations (FAO). (2022). Tackling food loss and waste: A triple win opportunity. https://www.fao.org/newsroom/detail/FAO-UNEP-agriculture-environment-food-loss-waste-day-2022/en

Foods | Free Full-Text | Gastronomic Experience and Consumer Behavior: Analyzing the Influence on Destination Image. (n.d.). Retrieved July 4, 2024, from https://www.mdpi.com/2304-8158/12/2/315

Forbes. (2020). The best brands on social media and what you can learn from them. Forbes. Retrieved from Forbes.

Ford, M. (2021). *Rule of the robots: How artificial intelligence will transform everything*. Hachette UK.

Francioni, B., Curina, I., Hegner, S. M., & Cioppi, M. (2022). Predictors of continuance intention of online food delivery services: Gender as moderator. *International Journal of Retail & Distribution Management*, 50(12), 1437–1457. DOI: 10.1108/IJRDM-11-2021-0537

Franzolini, B. (2020). *Niche market analysis and marketing strategies applied to the Chinese market: a case study of the tea and the coffee market sold through e-commerce*.

Friedman, N., & Ormiston, J. (2022). Blockchain as a sustainability-oriented innovation?: Opportunities for and resistance to Blockchain technology as a driver of sustainability in global food supply chains. *Technological Forecasting and Social Change*, 175, 121403. DOI: 10.1016/j.techfore.2021.121403

Fujii, A., Kochigami, K., Kitagawa, S., Okada, K., & Inaba, M. (2020). Development and Evaluation of Mixed Reality Co-eating System: Sharing the Behavior of Eating Food with a Robot Could Improve Our Dining Experience. *2020 29th IEEE International Conference on Robot and Human Interactive Communication (RO-MAN)*, 357–362. DOI: 10.1109/RO-MAN47096.2020.9223518

Gaetani, E., Aniello, L., Lombardi, F., Margheri, A., & Sassone, V. (2017). Blockchain-based database to ensure data integrity in cloud computing environments.

Galanakis, C. M. (2024). The future of food. *Foods*, 13(4), 506. DOI: 10.3390/foods13040506 PMID: 38397483

Galanakis, C. M., Rizou, M., Aldawoud, T. M. S., Ucak, I., & Rowan, N. J. (2021). Innovations and technology disruptions in the food sector within the COVID-19 pandemic and post-lockdown era. *Trends in Food Science & Technology*, 110, 252–263. DOI: 10.1016/j.tifs.2021.02.002 PMID: 36567851

Galderisi, S., Heinz, A., Kastrup, M., Beezhold, J., & Sartorius, N. (2015). Toward a new definition of mental health. *World Psychiatry; Official Journal of the World Psychiatric Association (WPA)*, 14(2), 231–233. DOI: 10.1002/wps.20231 PMID: 26043341

Gallace, A., Ngo, M. K., Sulaitis, J., & Spence, C. (2012). Multisensory presence in virtual reality: Possibilities & limitations. In Andres, F., Ghenea, G., & Gulliver, S. (Eds.), *Multiple sensorial media advances and applications: New developments in MulSeMedia* (pp. 1–38). IGI Global. DOI: 10.4018/978-1-60960-821-7.ch001

Galvez, J. F., Mejuto, J. C., & Simal-Gandara, J. (2018). Future challenges on the use of blockchain for food traceability analysis. *Trends in Analytical Chemistry*, 107, 222–232. DOI: 10.1016/j.trac.2018.08.011

Gan, C. I., Soukoutou, R., & Conroy, D. M. (2022). Sustainability framing of controlled environment agriculture and consumer perceptions: A review. *Sustainability (Basel)*, 15(1), 304. DOI: 10.3390/su15010304

Ganesh, M. K.. (2024). Farm-to-Table Initiatives in Restaurant Food Production: Benefits, Challenges, and Consumer Perceptions. *International Journal for Multidimensional Research Perspectives*, 2(7), 88–104. DOI: 10.61877/ijmrp.v2i7.174

Garcia-Haro, M. A., & Ortega-Muñoz, F. (2020). Efficiency in restaurant operations: A study on AI and robotics integration. *Journal of Hospitality & Tourism Research (Washington, D.C.)*, 42(4), 563–578.

Garcia, M., & Martinez, A. (2020). AI-driven Strategies for Food Quality Control in Restaurant Chains. *Journal of Foodservice Business Research*, 14(3), 332–345.

Garg, V. (2019). International Journal of Recent Technology and Engineering (IJRTE) ISSN: 2277-3878, Volume-8, Issue-1, May 2019 3424 Published By: Blue Eyes Intelligence Engineering & Sciences Publication Retrieval Number A9219058119/19©BEIESP The Study of Interest of Consumers In Mobile Food Ordering Apps.

Garg, A. (2021).The Technology Acceptance and Use of Tablet Menu among Young Adults: An Empirical Study Based on UTAUT 2 Model. International *Journal of Hospitality & Tourism Systems,* Volume 14 Issue 1 June 2021, Available at *SSRN*: https://ssrn.com/abstract=3809622

Garg, A., & Kumar, J. (2017). Exploring customer satisfaction with university cafeteria food services. An empirical study of Temptation Restaurant at Taylor's University, Malaysia. *European Journal of Tourism. Hospitality and Recreation*, 8(2), 96–106. DOI: 10.1515/ejthr-2017-0009

Garza, A., & Perez, L. (2023). Social media campaigns and their impact on dietary habits among young adults. *Public Health Nutrition*, 26(5), 991–1002.

Gensler, S., Völckner, F., Liu-Thompkins, Y., & Wiertz, C. (2013). Managing brands in the social media environment. *Journal of Interactive Marketing*, 27(4), 242–256. DOI: 10.1016/j.intmar.2013.09.004

George, R. V., Harsh, H. O., Ray, P., & Babu, A. K. (2019). Food quality traceability prototype for restaurants using blockchain and food quality data index. *Journal of Cleaner Production*, 240, 118021. DOI: 10.1016/j.jclepro.2019.118021

Georgiadis, G., & Poels, G. (2021). Enterprise architecture management as a solution for addressing general data protection regulation requirements in a big data context: A systematic mapping study. *Information Systems and e-Business Management*, 19(1), 313–362. DOI: 10.1007/s10257-020-00500-5

Ghisellini, P., Cialani, C., & Ulgiati, S. (2016). A review on circular economy: The expected transition to a balanced interplay of environmental and economic systems. *Journal of Cleaner Production*, 114, 11–32. DOI: 10.1016/j.jclepro.2015.09.007

Ghomi, E., Khosravi, F., Ardahaei, A., Dai, Y., Neisiany, R., Foroughi, F., & Ramakrishna, S. (2021). The life cycle assessment for polylactic acid (PLA) is used to make it a low-carbon material. *Polymers*, 13(11), 1854. DOI: 10.3390/polym13111854 PMID: 34199643

Ghosh, S. K., Parlikar, U. V., Zorpas, A. A., & Papamichael, I. (2024). Sustainable supply chain for waste-to-energy facilities. In *Advances in Biofuels Production, Optimization and Applications* (pp. 297-313). Elsevier. DOI: 10.1016/B978-0-323-95076-3.00015-6

Giap, T. K., Gopalan, S., & Ye, Y. (2016). Drivers of Growth in the Travel and Tourism Industry in Malaysia: A Geweke Causality Analysis.*Economies*, 4(1), 3. DOI: 10.3390/economies4010003

Gibbs, P. (2016). What is a shop? Evolution of the retail store. *Operations Management (1755-1501), 42*(2), 24–26.

Gilbert, J. (2023). Digitalisation, Sustainability Shaping Travel Sector. *Business Sector, News Straits Times*, February 2nd. https://www.nst.com.my/business/2023/02/875709/digitisation-sustainability-shaping-travel-sector

Ginting, Y. M., Chandra, T., Miran, I., & Yusriadi, Y. (2022). Repurchase intention of e-commerce customers in Indonesia: An overview of the effect of e-service quality, e-word of mouth, customer trust, and customer satisfaction mediation. *International Journal of Data and Network Science*, 7(1), 329–340. DOI: 10.5267/j.ijdns.2022.10.001

Girard, A., Lichters, M., Sarstedt, M., & Biswas, D. (2019). Short- and long-term effects of nonconsciously processed ambient scents in a servicescape: Findings from two field experiments. *Journal of Service Research*, 22(4), 440–455. DOI: 10.1177/1094670519842333

Giudice, F. (2020). *WeChat: the impact of the super app on Chinese society.*

Gkikas, D. C., & Theodoridis, P. K. (2022). AI in consumer behavior. *Advances in Artificial Intelligence-Based Technologies: Selected Papers in Honour of Professor Nikolaos G.Bourbakis*, 1, 147–176.

Gligoric, N., Krco, S., Hakola, L., Vehmas, K., De, S., Moessner, K., Jansson, K., Polenz, I., & Van Kranenburg, R. (2019). SmartTags: IoT Product Passport for Circular Economy Based on Printed Sensors and Unique Item-Level Identifiers. *Sensors (Basel)*, 19(3), 586. DOI: 10.3390/s19030586 PMID: 30704112

Gobble, M. M. (2018). Digitalization, Digitization, and Innovation. *Research Technology Management*, 61(4), 56–59. DOI: 10.1080/08956308.2018.1471280

Go, H., Kang, M., & Suh, S. C. (2020). Machine learning of robots in tourism and hospitality: Interactive technology acceptance model (iTAM) – cutting edge. *Tourism Review*, 75(4), 625–636. DOI: 10.1108/TR-02-2019-0062

Goktepe, S., Cifci, M. A., & Sahin, M. A. (2022). Sharing photos of food traveler experiences: A case study of foodstagramming. In *Handbook on Tourism and Social Media* (pp. 437–450). Edward Elgar Publishing. DOI: 10.4337/9781800371415.00043

Gómez-Suárez, M., & Yagüe, M. J. (2021). Making sense from experience: How a sustainable multisensory event spurs word-of-mouth recommendation of a destination brand. *Sustainability (Basel)*, 13(11), 5873. DOI: 10.3390/su13115873

Gong, D., Gan, X., Tang, X., Li, H., & Gao, X. (2023). Data Mining and Analysis of Video Barrage By AI Algorithm. *2023 IEEE 5th Eurasia Conference on Biomedical Engineering, Healthcare and Sustainability (ECBIOS)*, 144–149.

Gonzalez, M., Juárez, J., & García, R. (2021). Strategies for effective queue management in fast-food restaurants. *International Journal of Hospitality Management*, 92, 102716. DOI: 10.1016/j.ijhm.2020.102716

Gonzalez, R., Gasco, J., & Llopis, J. (2020). Information and communication technologies and human resources in hospitality and tourism. *International Journal of Contemporary Hospitality Management*, 32(11), 3545–3579. DOI: 10.1108/IJCHM-04-2020-0272

Gonzalez, R., Gasco, J., & Llopis, J. (2022). Information and communication technologies in food services and restaurants: A systematic review. *International Journal of Contemporary Hospitality Management*, 34(4), 1423–1447. DOI: 10.1108/IJCHM-05-2021-0624

Goodman, S., Vanderlee, L., White, C., & Hammond, D. (2018). A quasi-experimental study of a mandatory calorie-labelling policy in restaurants: Impact on use of nutrition information among youth and young adults in Canada. *Preventive Medicine*, 116, 166–172. DOI: 10.1016/j.ypmed.2018.09.013 PMID: 30261242

GoPro. (2020). *The GoPro awards: Celebrating the best in user-generated content. GoPro Blog*. Retrieved from GoPro.

Gorshkov, V. (2022). Cashless payment in emerging markets: The case of Russia. *Asia and the Global Economy, 2*(1). https://www.sciencedirect.com.singaporetech.remotexs.co/science/article/pii/S266711152200010X?via%3Dihub

Górska-Warsewicz, H., & Kulykovets, O. (2020). Hotel brand loyalty—A systematic literature review. *Sustainability (Basel)*, 12(12), 4810. DOI: 10.3390/su12124810

Goutam, D., Ganguli, S., & Gopalakrishna, B. V. (2022). Technology readiness and e-service quality–impact on purchase intention and loyalty. *Marketing Intelligence & Planning*, 40(2), 242–255. DOI: 10.1108/MIP-06-2021-0196

Goverment of India. (2023.). *Cashless India*. Cashless India. http://cashlessindia.gov.in/digital_payment_methods.html

Grand View Research. (2021). *Food processing market size, share & trends analysis report by type, by application, by region, and segment forecasts, 2021-2028*. Retrieved from Grand View Research.

Grecuccio, J., Giusto, E., Fiori, F., & Rebaudengo, M. (2020). Combining Blockchain and IoT: Food-Chain Traceability and Beyond. *Energies*, 13(15), 3820. DOI: 10.3390/en13153820

Greene, M., Wall, A., & McGuinness, D. (2019). The role of artificial intelligence in fast food industry decision making. *Journal of Artificial Intelligence Research*, 64, 659–684. DOI: 10.1613/jair.1.12312

Greeven, C. S., & Williams, S. P. (2017). Enterprise collaboration systems: Addressing adoption challenges and the shaping of sociotechnical systems. *International Journal of Information Systems and Project Management*, 5(1), 5–23. DOI: 10.12821/ijispm050101

Gretzel, U. (2011). Intelligent systems in tourism: A social science perspective. *Annals of Tourism Research*, 38(3), 757–779. DOI: 10.1016/j.annals.2011.04.014

Gretzel, U., Sigala, M., Xiang, Z., & Koo, C. (2015). Smart tourism: Foundations and developments. *Electronic Markets*, 25(3), 179–188. DOI: 10.1007/s12525-015-0196-8

Grewal, D., Hulland, J., Kopalle, P. K., & Karahanna, E. (2020). The future of technology and marketing: A multidisciplinary perspective. *Journal of the Academy of Marketing Science*, 48(1), 1–8. DOI: 10.1007/s11747-019-00711-4

Grewal, D., Roggeveen, A. L., & Nordfält, J. (2020). The future of retailing. *Journal of Retailing*, 96(1), 5–10.

Griesche, C., & Baeumner, A. J. (2020). Biosensors to support sustainable agriculture and food safety. *Trends in Analytical Chemistry*, 128, 115906. DOI: 10.1016/j.trac.2020.115906

Grobbelaar, S. S., & Grobler, H. (2021). AI in kitchen automation: Enhancing food preparation in hospitality. *Journal of Culinary Science & Technology*, 19(3), 193–210.

Grubert, E. (2018). Rigor in social life cycle assessment: Improving the scientific grounding of SLCA. *The International Journal of Life Cycle Assessment*, 23(3), 481–491. DOI: 10.1007/s11367-016-1117-6

Grudzien, P. (2020). Comparative Analysis of Energy Intensity and Profitability in Emerging E-Grocery Retail Models.

Guadiana, G. (2020). *A Netflix experience: reimagining the direct-to-consumer platform*. Massachusetts Institute of Technology.

Guan, J., & Tsui, W. (2022). Hotel robots: Current trends and future directions. *Tourism Review*, 77(1), 10–25.

Guan, X., Huang, L., & Zhang, L. (2021). Design of comprehensive service system for fresh food e-commerce under the background of "rural revitalization". *Journal of Physics: Conference Series*, 1757(1), 012141. Advance online publication. DOI: 10.1088/1742-6596/1757/1/012141

Gu, C., Huang, T., Wei, W., Yang, C., Chen, J., Miao, W., Lin, S., Sun, H., & Sun, J. (2023). The Effect of Using Augmented Reality Technology in Takeaway Food Packaging to Improve Young Consumers' Negative Evaluations. *Agriculture*, 13(2), 2. Advance online publication. DOI: 10.3390/agriculture13020335

Guiné, R. P. F., Florença, S. G., Barroca, M. J., & Anjos, O. (2020). The link between the consumer and the innovations in food product development. *Foods*, 9(9), 1317. DOI: 10.3390/foods9091317 PMID: 32962007

Gulied, M., Logade, K., Mutahir, H., Shaftah, S., Salauddin, S., Hameed, A., Zavahir, S., Elmakki, T., Shon, H. K., Hong, S., Park, H., & Han, D. S. (2023). A review of membrane-based dewatering technology for the concentration of liquid foods. *Journal of Environmental Chemical Engineering*, 11(5), 110583. DOI: 10.1016/j.jece.2023.110583

Gülteki̇, N. B., & Veuphuteh, F. M. (2023). Price sensitivity, perceived food quality, and intention to purchase fast food in the context of Health-Consciousness of university students. *OPUS Toplum Araştırmaları Dergisi*, 20(52), 317–334. DOI: 10.26466/opusjsr.1210008

Gündoğdu, S., Bour, A., Köşker, A. R., Walther, B. A., Napierska, D., Mihai, F. C., Syberg, K., Hansen, S. F., & Walker, T. R. (2024). Review of microplastics and chemical risk posed by plastic packaging on the marine environment to inform the Global Plastics Treaty. *The Science of the Total Environment*, 946, 174000. DOI: 10.1016/j.scitotenv.2024.174000 PMID: 38901589

Gupta, D. (2023). The importance of digital tech adoption in hospitality. www.whatfix.com

Gupta, A. K., Das, T., Kumar, H., Rastogi, S., Espinosa, E., Rincón, E., & Mishra, S. (2023). Novel food materials: Fundamentals and applications in sustainable food systems for food processing and safety. *Food Bioscience*, 55, 103013. DOI: 10.1016/j.fbio.2023.103013

Gupta, P., & Nag, R. (2013). Innovating for Profitable Growth. *Images Retail*, 12(10), 162–164.

Gupta, P., & Raj, S. (2023). The effect of social media influencers on food choices of millennials. *Journal of Consumer Marketing*, 40(3), 255–267.

Gupta, S., Justy, T., Kamboj, S., Kumar, A., & Kristoffersen, E. (2021). Big data and firm marketing performance: Findings from knowledge-based view. *Technological Forecasting and Social Change*, 171, 120986. DOI: 10.1016/j.techfore.2021.120986

Gu, Q., Li, M., & Huang, S. (2023). An exploratory investigation of technology-assisted dining experiences from the consumer perspective. *International Journal of Contemporary Hospitality Management*, 35(3), 1010–1029. DOI: 10.1108/IJCHM-02-2022-0214

Gursoy, D., Chi, O. H., Lu, L., & Nunkoo, R. (2019). Consumers acceptance of artificially intelligent (AI) device use in service delivery. *International Journal of Information Management*, 49, 157–169. DOI: 10.1016/j.ijinfomgt.2019.03.008

Güsken, S. R. (2020). *A Multi-method Study of Consumer Behaviour: Towards a Better Understanding of the Consumer's Perspective on Online Grocery Shopping* (Doctoral dissertation, Universitätsbibliothek der RWTH Aachen).

Güsken, S. R., Janssen, D., & Hees, F. (2019). Online Grocery Platforms–Understanding Consumer Acceptance. In *ISPIM Conference Proceedings* (pp. 1-17). The International Society for Professional Innovation Management (ISPIM).

Haase, J., Wiedmann, K., Bettels, J., & Labenz, F. (2018). How to best promote my product? Comparing the effectiveness of sensory, functional and symbolic advertising content in food marketing. *British Food Journal*, 120(8), 1792–1806. DOI: 10.1108/BFJ-01-2018-0058

Habib, S., & Hamadneh, N. N. (2021). Impact of perceived risk on consumers' technology acceptance in online grocery adoption amid COVID-19 pandemic. *Sustainability (Basel)*, 13(18), 10221. DOI: 10.3390/su131810221

Haenlein, M., & Kaplan, A. (2019). A brief history of AI: On the past, present, and future of artificial intelligence. *California Management Review*, 61(4), 5–14. DOI: 10.1177/0008125619864925

Hajli, M. N. (2014). A study of the impact of social media on consumers. *International Journal of Market Research*, 56(3), 387–404. DOI: 10.2501/IJMR-2014-025

Haleem, A., Javaid, M., Qadri, M. A., Singh, R. P., & Suman, R. (2022). Artificial intelligence (AI) applications for marketing: A literature-based study. *International Journal of Intelligent Networks*, 3, 119–132. DOI: 10.1016/j.ijin.2022.08.005

Halik, A., & Nugroho, M. (2022). The role of consumer pleasure moderating the effect of content marketing and price discount on online shopping decision and loyalty of Generation Z. *Media Ekonomi Dan Manajemen*, 27(1), 35. DOI: 10.24856/mem.v27i01.2259

Hall, C., & Zarro, M. (2012). Social curation on the website Pinterest.com. *Proceedings of the American Society for Information Science and Technology*, 49(1), 1–9. DOI: 10.1002/meet.14504901189

Hallikainen, H., Luongo, M., Dhir, A., & Laukkanen, T. (2022). Consequences of personalized product recommendations and price promotions in online grocery shopping. *Journal of Retailing and Consumer Services*, 69, 103088. DOI: 10.1016/j.jretconser.2022.103088

Hamacher, K., & Buchkremer, R. (2022). Measuring Online Sensory Consumer experience: Introducing the Online Sensory Marketing Index (OSMI) as a structural modeling approach. *Journal of Theoretical and Applied Electronic Commerce Research*, 17(2), 751–772. DOI: 10.3390/jtaer17020039

Hameed, S., Xie, L., & Ying, Y. (2018). Conventional and emerging detection techniques for pathogenic bacteria in food science: A review. *Trends in Food Science & Technology*, 81, 61–73. DOI: 10.1016/j.tifs.2018.05.020

Hamid, R., Mohd Hashim, N. H., Mohd Shukur, S. A., & Marmaya, N. H. (2021). The Impact of Covid-19 on Malaysia Tourism Industry Supply Chain. *International Journal of Academic Research in Business and Social Sciences* Vol. 11, No. 16, Contemporary Issues in Tourism and Hospitality industry. E-ISSN: 2222-6990 © 2021 HRMARS

Hamli, S. S. A., & Sobaih, A. E. E. (2023). Factors Influencing Consumer Behavior towards Online Shopping in Saudi Arabia Amid COVID-19: Implications for E-Businesses Post Pandemic. *Journal of Risk and Financial Management*, 16(1), 36. DOI: 10.3390/jrfm16010036

Han, J., Moon, H., Oh, Y., Chang, J Y., & Ham, S. (2020, January 1). Impacts of menu information quality and nutrition information quality on technology acceptance characteristics and behaviors toward fast food restaurants' kiosk., 14(2), 167-167. https://doi.org/DOI: 10.4162/nrp.2020.14.2.167

Hanagal, D. D., Latpate, R. V., & Chandra, G. (2022). Applied statistical methods: ISGES 2020, Pune, India, January 2-4. Springer.

Han, D.-I. D., Boerwinkel, M., Haggis-Burridge, M., & Melissen, F. (2022). Deconstructing Immersion in the Experience Economy Framework for Immersive Dining Experiences through Mixed Reality. *Foods*, 11(23), 23. Advance online publication. DOI: 10.3390/foods11233780 PMID: 36496588

Handley, A., & Chapman, C. C. (2011). *Content rules: How to create killer blogs, podcasts, videos, eBooks, webinars (and more) that engage customers and ignite your business*. Wiley.

Hansen, T., & Sørensen, M. (2023). Social media marketing in the organic food industry: A consumer perspective. *Journal of Cleaner Production*, 386, 135657.

Han, W., Raab, C., Belarmino, A., & Tang, J. (2021). Are online meal delivery platforms part of the sharing economy? *Journal of Foodservice Business Research*, 25(3), 253–276. DOI: 10.1080/15378020.2021.1941712

Hao, F. (2021). Acceptance of contactless technology in the hospitality industry: Extending the unified theory of acceptance and use of technology 2. *Asia Pacific Journal of Tourism Research*, 26(12), 1386–1401. DOI: 10.1080/10941665.2021.1984264

Hao, F., Aman, A., & Zhang, C. (2024). What is beautiful is good: Attractive avatars for healthier dining and satisfaction. *International Journal of Contemporary Hospitality Management*, 36(12), 3969–3988. Advance online publication. DOI: 10.1108/IJCHM-09-2023-1490

Harekal, D. (2019). *Reaug an Implemented Augmented Reality enabled Scanner for Restaurants. 8*(8).

Harkin, C. (2020). A review on plastic bioaccumulation, potential health effects and the potential to enhance biotransformation using herbal medicine and nutritional supplements. *International Journal of Complementary & Alternative Medicine*, 13(1), 18–26. DOI: 10.15406/ijcam.2020.13.00487

Harrington, J. (2020). The impact of digital innovation on customer engagement: A case study of Domino's Pizza. *Journal of Business Research*, 116, 497–504. DOI: 10.1016/j.jbusres.2020.05.043

Harrington, J. (2021). The impact of social media on brand loyalty: The Starbucks experience. *Journal of Digital & Social Media Marketing*, 9(2), 105–116. DOI: 10.1108/JSMS-06-2021-0047

Harrison, L. (2020). *Instagram's interactive features: Polls, questions, and more. Social Media Examiner*. Retrieved from Social Media Examiner.

Hartanto, A., Chua, Y. J., Quek, F. Y. X., Wong, J., Ooi, W. M., & Majeed, N. M. (2023). Problematic smartphone usage, objective smartphone engagement, and executive functions: A latent variable analysis. *Attention, Perception & Psychophysics*, 85(8), 2610–2625. DOI: 10.3758/s13414-023-02707-3 PMID: 37188861

Hasan, A. A.-T. (2023). Determinants of intentions to use the food panda mobile application in Bangladesh: The role of attitude and fear of COVID-19. *South Asian Journal of Marketing*, 4(1), 17–32. DOI: 10.1108/SAJM-10-2021-0123

Hasan, S., Islam, M., Mashal, I., & Fahim, A. (2023). *Influence of consumption values on adoption of cashless society in emerging economies: The moderating effect of perceived cost. SSRN.* https://doi.org/ DOI: 10.2139/ssrn.4453012

Hashimoto, Y., Inami, M., & Kajimoto, H. (2008, June). *Straw-like user interface (II): A new method of presenting auditory sensations for a more natural experience* [Paper presentation]. International Conference on Human Haptic Sensing and Touch Enabled Computer Applications (pp. 484–493). https://www.strategyand.pwc.com/de/en/industries/consumer-markets/future-of-grocery-shopping.html

Hasi, S. M. S. a. M. a. a. A. A. (2020, January 31). Users 'attitude towards benefits of online shopping: a study on customers of Daraz and Food Panda. https://solidstatetechnology.us/index.php/JSST/article/view/704

Hassoun, A., Aït-Kaddour, A., Abu-Mahfouz, A. M., Rathod, N. B., Bader, F., Barba, F. J., Biancolillo, A., Cropotova, J., Galanakis, C. M., Jambrak, A. R., Lorenzo, J. M., Måge, I., Ozogul, F., & Regenstein, J. (2022). The fourth industrial revolution in the food industry—Part I: Industry 4.0 technologies. *Critical Reviews in Food Science and Nutrition*, 63(23), 6547–6563. DOI: 10.1080/10408398.2022.2034735 PMID: 35114860

Hassoun, A., Bekhit, A. E. D., Jambrak, A. R., Regenstein, J. M., Chemat, F., Morton, J. D., Gudjónsdóttir, M., Carpena, M., Prieto, M. A., Varela, P., Arshad, R. N., Aadil, R. M., Bhat, Z., & Ueland, Ø. (2024). The fourth industrial revolution in the food industry—part II: Emerging food trends. *Critical Reviews in Food Science and Nutrition*, 64(2), 407–437. DOI: 10.1080/10408398.2022.2106472 PMID: 35930319

Hassoun, A., Cropotova, J., Trif, M., Rusu, A. V., Bobiş, O., Nayik, G. A., Jagdale, Y. D., Saeed, F., Afzaal, M., Mostashari, P., Khaneghah, A. M., & Regenstein, J. M. (2022). Consumer acceptance of new food trends resulting from the fourth industrial revolution technologies: A narrative review of literature and future perspectives. *Frontiers in Nutrition*, 9, 972154. DOI: 10.3389/fnut.2022.972154 PMID: 36034919

Hassoun, A., Jagtap, S., Garcia-Garcia, G., Trollman, H., Pateiro, M., Lorenzo, J. M., Trif, M., Rusu, A. V., Aadil, R. M., Šimat, V., Cropotova, J., & Câmara, J. S. (2023). Food quality I4.0: From traditional approaches to digitalized automated analysis. *Journal of Food Engineering*, 337, 111216. Advance online publication. DOI: 10.1016/j.jfoodeng.2022.111216

Hasugian, B.S., & Indallah, T.W. (2022). The Role of Digital Marketing and Social Media Strategies in The Development of The Culinary Business for Young Business Leaders.

Hatzivasilis, G., Christodoulakis, N., Tzagkarakis, C., Ioannidis, S., Demetriou, G., Fysarakis, K., & Panayiotou, M. (2019). The CE-IoT Framework for Green ICT Organizations The interplay of CE-IoT as an enabler for green innovation and e-waste management in ICT. DOI: 10.1109/DCOSS.2019.00088

He, G., Pan, Y., Park, A., Sawada, Y., & Tan, E. S. (2023). Reducing single-use cutlery with green nudges: Evidence from China's food-delivery industry. *Science*, 381(6662), eadd9884. Advance online publication. DOI: 10.1126/science.add9884 PMID: 37676957

Heikkilä, L., Reinikainen, A., Katajajuuri, J. M., Silvennoinen, K., & Hartikainen, H. (2016). Elements affecting food waste in the food service sector. *Waste Management (New York, N.Y.)*, 56, 446–453. DOI: 10.1016/j.wasman.2016.06.019 PMID: 27373724

Henderson, J. C., Yun, O. S., Poon, P., & Biwei, X. (2012). Hawker centres as tourist attractions: The case of Singapore. *International Journal of Hospitality Management*, 31(3), 849–855. DOI: 10.1016/j.ijhm.2011.10.002

Hennig-Thurau, T., Gwinner, K. P., Walsh, G., & Gremler, D. D. (2004). Electronic word-of-mouth via consumer-opinion platforms: What motivates consumers to articulate themselves on the Internet? *Journal of Interactive Marketing*, 18(1), 38–52. DOI: 10.1002/dir.10073

Her, E., Seo, S., Choi, J., Pool, V., & Ilic, S. (2019). Assessment of food safety at university food courts using surveys, observations, and microbial testing. *Food Control, 103*, 167-174. ScienceDirect. https://doi.org/DOI: 10.1016/j.foodcont.2019.04.002

Herrero, M., Thornton, P. K., Mason-D'Croz, D., Palmer, J., Benton, T. G., Bodirsky, B. L., Bogard, J. R., Hall, A., Lee, B., Nyborg, K., Pradhan, P., Bonnett, G. D., Bryan, B. A., Campbell, B. M., Christensen, S., Clark, M., Cook, M. T., de Boer, I. J. M., Downs, C., & West, P. C. (2020). Innovation can accelerate the transition towards a sustainable food system. *Nature Food*, 1(5), 266–272. DOI: 10.1038/s43016-020-0074-1

Hilty, L., & Aebischer, B. (2015). *ICT for Sustainability: An Emerging Research Field* (Vol. 310, pp. 3–36). DOI: 10.1007/978-3-319-09228-7_1

Himeur, Y., Elnour, M., Fadli, F., Meskin, N., Petri, I., Rezgui, Y., Bensaali, F., & Amira, A. (2022b). AI-big data analytics for building automation and management systems: A survey, actual challenges and future perspectives. *Artificial Intelligence Review*, 56(6), 4929–5021. DOI: 10.1007/s10462-022-10286-2 PMID: 36268476

Hinson, R. E., Mhlanga, D., Osei-Frimpong, K., & Doe, J. (2024). *Social Media Marketing Management: How to Penetrate Emerging Markets and Expand Your Customer Base.* CRC Press. DOI: 10.4324/9781003307457

Hiranpradith, V., Therdthai, N., & Soontrunnarudrungsri, A. (2023). Effect of Steaming and Microwave Heating on Taste of Clear Soup with Split-Gill Mushroom Powder. *Foods*, 12(8), 1685. DOI: 10.3390/foods12081685 PMID: 37107479

Hmamed, H., Cherrafi, A., Benghabrit, A., Tiwari, S., & Sharma, P. (2023). The adoption of i4.0 technologies for a sustainable and circular supply chain: An industry-based sem analysis from the textile sector. *Business Strategy and the Environment*, 33(4), 2949–2968. DOI: 10.1002/bse.3645

Hofmann, E., & Rüsch, M. (2017). Industry 4.0 and the current status as well as future prospects on logistics. *Computers in Industry*, 89, 23–34. DOI: 10.1016/j.compind.2017.04.002

Hong, C., Choi, E., & Joung, H. (2022). Determinants of customer purchase intention toward online food delivery services: The moderating role of usage frequency. *Journal of Hospitality and Tourism Management*, 54, 76–87. DOI: 10.1016/j.jhtm.2022.12.005

Hong, J., Jaegler, A., & Gergaud, O. (2024). Mobile applications to reduce food waste in supply chains: A systematic literature review. *British Food Journal*, 126(2), 509–530. DOI: 10.1108/BFJ-09-2022-0742

Hootsuite. (2020). Social media trends 2020. Retrieved from Hootsuite.

Hootsuite. (2020). *The global state of digital 2020.* Hootsuite.

Hou, B., Mutuc, E. B., Wu, L., Lee, H.-Y., & Lu, K.-H. (2020). Sustainable rice farming systems: Farmer attribute and land ecosystem perspectives. *The International Food and Agribusiness Management Review*, 23(2), 121–141. DOI: 10.22434/IFAMR2018.0220

Hsu, C.-L., & Lin, J. C.-C. (2023). Understanding the user satisfaction and loyalty of customer service chatbots. *Journal of Retailing and Consumer Services*, 71, 103211. DOI: 10.1016/j.jretconser.2022.103211

hHuang, J., Chuin, T. P., Zhao, K., & Chen, Y. (2021). Business Models in Live Video Streaming Platforms: A Comparative Case Study. *Turkish Online Journal of Qualitative Inquiry, 12*(6).

Huang, C. D., Goo, J., Nam, K., & Yoo, C. W. (2017). Smart tourism technologies in travel planning: The role of exploration and exploitation. *Information & Management*, 54(6), 757–770. DOI: 10.1016/j.im.2016.11.010

Huang, H.-L., Cheng, L.-K., Sun, P.-C., & Chou, S.-J. (2021). The Effects of Perceived Identity Threat and Realistic Threat on the Negative Attitudes and Usage Intentions Toward Hotel Service Robots: The Moderating Effect of the Robot's Anthropomorphism. *International Journal of Social Robotics*, 13(7), 1599–1611. DOI: 10.1007/s12369-021-00752-2

Huang, I. X., & Labroo, A. A. (2020). Cueing morality: The effect of high-pitched music on healthy choice. *Journal of Marketing*, 84(6), 130–143. DOI: 10.1177/0022242918813577

Huang, M. H., & Rust, R. T. (2018). Artificial intelligence in service. *Journal of Service Research*, 21(2), 155–172. DOI: 10.1177/1094670517752459

Huang, M. H., & Rust, R. T. (2021). Engaged to a robot? The role of AI in service. *Journal of Service Research*, 24(1), 30–41. DOI: 10.1177/1094670520902266

Huang, Q., & Fleiss, A. (2023). How is the food culture in China changing? *Available atSSRN* 4572452. DOI: 10.2139/ssrn.4572452

Huang, Q., Li, X., & Liu, H. (2021). Analysis of Wechat Marketing Model in The Context of Mobile Internet Era. *Proceedings of the 2021 12th International Conference on E-Business, Management and Economics*, 21–27. DOI: 10.1145/3481127.3481190

Huang, Y. (2024). Study on Podcasting Empowered Brands. In *Ear Economy: China Audio Streaming Programs Study* (pp. 285–295). Springer. DOI: 10.1007/978-981-97-2034-7_24

Huang, Y., Hall, C. M., & Chen, N. (2023). The sustainability characteristics of Michelin green star restaurants. *Journal of Foodservice Business Research*, 1–26. DOI: 10.1080/15378020.2023.2235258

HubSpot. (2021). *The ultimate guide to social media analytics.* Retrieved from HubSpot.

Hu, M., Zhang, K., You, R., & Tu, B. (2022). Multisensor-Based continuous authentication of smartphone users with Two-Stage feature extraction. *IEEE Internet of Things Journal*, 10(6), 4708–4724. DOI: 10.1109/JIOT.2022.3219135

Humbani, M., & Wiese, M. (2017). A cashless society for all: Determining consumers' readiness to adopt mobile payment services. *Journal of African Business*, 19(3), 409–429. DOI: 10.1080/15228916.2017.1396792

Huo, C., Hameed, J., Zhang, M., Bin Mohd Ali, A. F., & Nik Hashim, N. A. A. (2022). Modeling the impact of corporate social responsibility on sustainable purchase intentions: Insights into brand trust and brand loyalty. *Ekonomska Istrazivanja*, 35(1), 4710–4739. DOI: 10.1080/1331677X.2021.2016465

Huvila, I., Enwald, H., Hirvonen, N., & Backa, K. E. (2019). *The concept of usefulness in library and information science research*. Information Research. https://informationr.net/ir/24-4/colis/colis1907.html

Hu, Y., Su, M., Wang, Y., Cui, S., Meng, F., Yue, W., Liu, Y., Xu, C., & Yang, Z. (2020). Food production in China requires intensified measures to be consistent with national and provincial environmental boundaries. *Nature Food*, 1(9), 572–582. DOI: 10.1038/s43016-020-00143-2 PMID: 37128013

Hwang, A. H., Oh, J., & Scheinbaum, A. C. (2020). Interactive music for multisensory e-commerce: The moderating role of online consumer involvement in experiential

IBM. (2023). *About Linear Regression | IBM*. https://www.ibm.com/topics/linear-regression

Ifeanyichukwu, C. D., & Peter, A. (2018). The role of sensory marketing in achieving customer patronage in fast food restaurants in Awka. *International Research Journal of Management, IT &. Social Sciences*, 5(2), 155–163. DOI: 10.21744/irjmis.v5i2.632

İmre, M., & Yıkmış, S. (2023). The Use of Augmented Reality in the Food Industry: Enhancing the Dining Experience. In *Impactful Technologies Transforming the Food Industry* (pp. 135–155). IGI Global., DOI: 10.4018/978-1-6684-9094-5.ch009

Inavolu, S. M. (n.d.). *Exploring AI-Driven Customer Service: Evolution*. Architectures, Opportunities, Challenges and Future Directions.

Independent variable. (2010). Encyclopedia of Research Design. https://doi.org/DOI: 10.4135/9781412961288.n184

Ingemarsdotter, E. K. (2021). Circular Strategies Enabled by the Internet of Things: Opportunities, *Implementation Challenges, and Environmental Impact*. https://doi.org/https://doi.org/10.4233/uuid:9ac826a1-2203-4f23- b074-3d765abd73e3

Inoue, M., Yamada, S., Miyajima, S., Ishii, K., Hasebe, R., Aoyama, K., Yamada, T., & Bracke, S. (2020). A modular design strategy considering sustainability and supplier selection. *Journal of Advanced Mechanical Design, Systems and Manufacturing*, 14(2), JAMDSM0023. Advance online publication. DOI: 10.1299/jamdsm.2020jamdsm0023

Intal, G L D., Payas, J D., Fernandez, L M., & Domingo, B M. (2020, April 1). Restaurant Information System (RIS) with QR Code to Improve Service Operations of Casual Fine Dining Restaurant. https://doi.org/DOI: 10.1109/ICIEA49774.2020.9102036

Interaction Design Foundation. (2023). *What is ease of use?* Interaction Design Foundation. https://www.interaction-design.org/literature/topics/ease-of-use

International Labor Organization (ILO). (2020). *Decent work and the food sector*. Retrieved from ILO.

International Telecommunication Union. UNESCO, UNCTAD, UNDP, UNDESA, FAO, WHO, Union Postale Universelle, UNEP, International Trade Centre, Organization, I. L., & O, W. M. (2015). *WSIS - SDG Matrix Linking WSIS Action Lines with Sustainable Development Goals*. www.wsis.org/sdg

Iqbal, J. & e-Hassan, I. (2016). Employing Sensory Marketing as a Promotional Advantage for Creating Brand Differentiation and Brand Loyalty. *Pakistan Journal of Commerce and Social Sciences*, 10(3), 725–734.

Iqbal, M., & Ahmed, R. (2023). The effectiveness of social media marketing in the fast-food industry. *Journal of Marketing Communications*, 29(4), 418–432.

Irfan, M., Elavarasan, R. M., Hao, Y., Feng, M., & Sailan, D. (2021). An assessment of consumers' willingness to utilize solar energy in China: End-users' perspective. *Journal of Cleaner Production*, 292, 126008. DOI: 10.1016/j.jclepro.2021.126008

Isaac, M., & Yaffe-Bellany, D. (2019, August 20). The Rise of the Virtual Restaurant. *International New York Times,* NA. https://link.gale.com/apps/doc/A596849009/AONE?u=anon~8633bbc3&sid=googleScholar&xid=8df01966

Ishak, F A C., Lah, N A C., Samengon, H., Mohamad, S. F., & Othman, M. N. (2021, October 26). The Implementation of Self-Ordering Kiosks (SOKs). *International Journal of Academic Research in Business & Social Sciences*, 11(10). Advance online publication. DOI: 10.6007/IJARBSS/v11-i10/11491

Ismail, L. C., Kassem, H., Osaili, T. M., Hashim, M., Obaid, R., Radwan, H., Mohamad, M. N., Saleh, S. T., Zomut, Z. A., Qiyas, S. A., Rajaby, R. A., Daour, R. A., Ali, H. I., Stojanovska, L., & Al Dhaheri, A. S. (2023). Public's calorie literacy and perceived effectiveness of restaurant menu calorie labeling in the United Arab Emirates. PLoS ONE, 18(10 October). DOI: 10.1371/journal.pone.0293387

ISO. (2006a). ISO 14025:2006 Environmental labels and declarations — Type III environmental declarations — Principles and procedures. https://www.iso.org/standard/38131.html

ISO. (2006b). *ISO 14040:2006 Environmental management — Life cycle assessment — Principles and framework*. https://www.iso.org/standard/37456.html

ISO. (2015). ISO 14001:2015 Environmental management systems — Requirements with guidance for use. https://www.iso.org/standard/60857.html

ISO. (2016). ISO 14021:2016 Environmental labels and declarations — Self-declared environmental claims (Type II environmental labelling). https://www.iso.org/standard/66652.html

ISO. (2018a). ISO 22000:2018 Food safety management systems — Requirements for any organization in the food chain. https://www.iso.org/es/contents/data/standard/06/54/65464.html

ISO. (2018b). ISO 14024:2018 Environmental labels and declarations — Type I environmental labelling — Principles and procedures. https://www.iso.org/standard/72458.html

ISO. (2022). ISO 14020:2022 Environmental statements and programmes for products — Principles and general requirements. https://www.iso.org/standard/79479.html

ISO. (2023).*ISO- Certification*. https://www.iso.org/certification.html

Ivanov, S., & Webster, C. (2017, October 19-21). *Adoption of robots, artificial intelligence and service automation by travel, tourism and hospitality companies- A cost-benefit analysis* [Conference session]. International Scientific Conference "Contemporary Tourism-Traditions and Innovations", Sofia University. https://ssrn.com/abstract=3007577

Ivanov, D., & Dolgui, A. (2020). A digital supply chain twin: A new approach to supply chain management. *International Journal of Production Research*, 58(12), 3620–3634. DOI: 10.1080/00207543.2020.1723545

Ivanov, S. (2020). The impact of automation on tourism and hospitality jobs. *Information Technology & Tourism*, 22(2), 205–215. DOI: 10.1007/s40558-020-00175-1

Ivanov, S. H., Webster, C., Stoilova, E., & Slobodskoy, D. (2020). Biosecurity, automation technologies and economic resilience of travel, tourism and hospitality companies: A conceptual framework. *Tourism Economics*, •••, 1–24. DOI: 10.1177/1354816620946541

Ivanov, S., Gretzel, U., Berezina, K., Sigala, M., & Webster, C. (2019). Progress on robotics in hospitality and tourism: A review of the literature. *Journal of Hospitality and Tourism Technology*, 10(4), 489–521. DOI: 10.1108/JHTT-08-2018-0087

Ivanov, S., & Webster, C. (2017). Adoption of robots in hospitality: Opportunities and challenges. *International Journal of Contemporary Hospitality Management*, 29(1), 177–194.

Ivanov, S., & Webster, C. (2019). *Robots, artificial intelligence, and service automation in travel, tourism, and hospitality*. Emerald Group Publishing., DOI: 10.1108/9781787566873

Ivanov, S., & Webster, C. (2020). Robots in tourism: A research agenda for tourism economics. *Tourism Economics*, 26(7), 1065–1085. DOI: 10.1177/1354816619879583

Ivanov, S., Webster, C., & Berezina, K. (2017). Adoption of robots and service automation by tourism and hospitality companies. *Revista Turismo & Desenvolvimento (Aveiro)*, 27(28), 1501–1517.

Ivanov, S., Webster, C., & Berezina, K. (2022). Robotics in Tourism and Hospitality. In Xiang, Z., Fuchs, M., Gretzel, U., & Höpken, W. (Eds.), *Handbook of e-Tourism*. Springer., DOI: 10.1007/978-3-030-48652-5_112

Ivanov, S., Webster, C., & Seyyedi, P. (2018). Consumers' attitudes towards the introduction of robots in accommodation establishments. *Tourism: An International Interdisciplinary Journal*, 66(3), 302–317.

Izzuddin, D. (2021, November 29). *New Horizons: The rise of food photography*. The Edge Malaysia. https://theedgemalaysia.com/article/new-horizons-rise-food-photography

Jacobson, J., Gruzd, A., & Hernández-García, Á. (2020). Social media marketing: Who is watching the watchers? *Journal of Retailing and Consumer Services*, 53, 101774. DOI: 10.1016/j.jretconser.2019.03.001

Jaeger, S. R., & Cardello, A. V. (2022). Factors affecting data quality of online questionnaires: Issues and metrics for sensory and consumer research. *Food Quality and Preference*, 102, 104676. DOI: 10.1016/j.foodqual.2022.104676

Jagtap, S., Duong, L., Trollman, H., Bader, F., . . . Rahimifard, S. (2020). Chapter 5- IoT technologies in the food supply chain. *Food Technology Disruptions*, 175-211. DOI: 10.1016/B978-0-12-821470-1.00009-4

Jagtap, S., Rahimifard, S., & Duong, L. N. K. (2022). Real- time data collection to improve energy efficiency: A case study of food manufacturer. *Journal of Food Processing and Preservation*, 46(8). Advance online publication. DOI: 10.1111/jfpp.14338

JAIN, A. (2022). *Effect of Social Media Marketing on Consumer Behavior for Netflix*. FORE School of Management.

Jain, V., Wadhwani, K., & Eastman, J. K. (2023). Artificial intelligence consumer behavior: A hybrid review and research agenda. *Journal of Consumer Behaviour*, 23(2), 676–697. DOI: 10.1002/cb.2233

Jambrak, A. R., Nutrizio, M., Djekić, I., Pleslić, S., & Chemat, F. (2021). Internet of nonthermal food processing technologies (IoNTP): Food Industry 4.0 and sustainability. *Applied Sciences (Basel, Switzerland)*, 11(2), 686. Advance online publication. DOI: 10.3390/app11020686

Jamil, A., Zainuddin, S. A., Abdullah, T., Mohamad, S. R., Azmi, N. F., Muhamad, S. F., & Abdullah, S. S. (2024). Digital Entrepreneurship in the Food Delivery Industry: Enhancing Customer Satisfaction Through Apps' Functional and Technical Quality. In *Contemporary Issues in Entrepreneurship and Innovative Technology* (pp. 125–144). Springer Nature Switzerland. DOI: 10.1007/978-3-031-50927-8_8

Janssen, M., van der Voort, H., & Wahyudi, A. (2017). Factors influencing big data decision-making quality. *Journal of Business Research*, 70, 338–345. DOI: 10.1016/j.jbusres.2016.08.007

Jarmin, R. S., Klimek, S. D., & Miranda, J. (2009). The Role of Retail Chains: National, Regional, and Industry Results. In T. Dunne, J. Bradford Jensen & M.J Roberts (Eds), *Producer Dynamics: New Evidence from Micro Data* (p. 237-262). University of Chicago Press

Jasonos, M., & McCormick, R. (2017). *Technology Integration for Restaurants & Hospitality Industry in the Year 2025* [fi=Ylempi AMK-opinnäytetyö|sv=Högre YH-examensarbete|en=Master's thesis|]. Haaga-Helia ammattikorkeakoulu. https://www.theseus.fi/handle/10024/132779

Jaud, D. A., Braconnot, A. R., & Lunardo, R. (2023). Do stories (always) make food products taste better? The boundary effects of matching package type and product dimension. *Journal of Consumer Behaviour*, 22(5), 1224–1236. DOI: 10.1002/cb.2207

Jeon, G. (2022). Bisphenol a leaching from polycarbonate baby bottles into baby food, causes potential health issues. *Clinical and Experimental Pediatrics*, 65(9), 450–452. DOI: 10.3345/cep.2022.00661 PMID: 35879867

Jeon, H. M., Sung, H. J., & Kim, H. Y. (2020). Customers' acceptance intention of self-service technology of restaurant industry: Expanding UTAUT with perceived risk and innovativeness. *Service Business*, 14(4), 533–551. DOI: 10.1007/s11628-020-00425-6

Jeon, H. M., Yoo, S. R., & Kim, S. H. (2020). The relationships among experience, delight, and recollection for revisit intention in chocolate exposition. *Sustainability (Basel)*, 12(20), 8644. DOI: 10.3390/su12208644

Jiang, Z., & Benbasat, I. (2007). The effects of presentation formats and task complexity on online consumers' product understanding. *Management Information Systems Quarterly*, 31(3), 475–500. DOI: 10.2307/25148804

Jiao, H., Wong, I. A., & Lin, Z. C. J. (2024). Understanding customer multi-interactions, trust, social support and voluntary performance in smart restaurants. *Journal of Hospitality and Tourism Technology*. Advance online publication. DOI: 10.1108/JHTT-11-2023-0384

Jia, Y., Garg, A., & Shi, P. (2024). Research on Factors Influencing Hotel Consumers' Health: A Systematic Review and Ways Forward. *Sustainability (Basel)*, 16(5), 2099. DOI: 10.3390/su16052099

Jin, X., & Pan, X. (2023). Government attention, market competition and firm digital transformation. *Sustainability (Basel)*, 15(11), 9057. DOI: 10.3390/su15119057

Jiseon, A. (2021). Impact of cognitive aspects of food mobile application on customers' behaviour. *Current Issues in Tourism*. Advance online publication. DOI: 10.1080/13683500.2021.1890700

JO - Personality and social psychology review: an official journal of the Society for Personality and Social Psychology, Inc

Jobin, A., Ienca, M., & Vayena, E. (2019). The global landscape of AI ethics guidelines. *Nature Machine Intelligence*, 1(9), 389–399. DOI: 10.1038/s42256-019-0088-2

Johnson, V., Woolridge, R W., & Bell, J R. (2019, January 28). The Impact of Consumer Confusion on Mobile Self-Checkout Adoption. Taylor & Francis, 61(1), 76-86. https://doi.org/DOI: 10.1080/08874417.2019.1566802

Johnson, L. (2022). How does quality of mobile food delivery services influence customer loyalty? Gronroos's service quality perspective. *International Journal of Contemporary Hospitality Management*, 34(11), 4178–4205. DOI: 10.1108/IJCHM-08-2021-1039

Jones, K., & Albrecht, C. (2023). The role of Facebook in promoting local food businesses. *Journal of Retailing and Consumer Services*, 69, 102058.

Jo, Y. J., & Yoon, H. H. (2020). A Study on Relationship among Customer's Perceived Value, Trust, Flow, and Continuous Usage Intention Towards Coffee Branded Mobile Apps: Focus on Starbucks Siren Order. Korean. *Journal of Food and Cookery Science*, 36(03), 271–279. DOI: 10.9724/kfcs.2020.36.3.271

Joya, K., Ramli, N. N., Shamsudin, M. N., & Kamarulzaman, N. H. (2022). Consumers' willingness to pay for food safety attributes of tomato. *British Food Journal*, 124(3), 701–717. DOI: 10.1108/BFJ-02-2021-0164

Kabir, M. S. N., Reza, M. N., Chowdhury, M., Ali, M., Samsuzzaman, , Ali, M. R., Lee, K. Y., & Chung, S.-O. (2023). Technological trends and engineering issues on vertical farms: A review. *Horticulturae*, 9(11), 1229. DOI: 10.3390/horticulturae9111229

Kakani, V., Nguyen, V. H., Kumar, B. P., Kim, H., & Pasupuleti, V. R. (2020). A critical review on computer vision and artificial intelligence in the food industry. *Journal of Agriculture and Food Research*, 2, 100033. Advance online publication. DOI: 10.1016/j.jafr.2020.100033

Kalaivani, D., Jadhav, S., & Hedaoo, R. (2021). Impact of Varied Menu Nutrition Labelling Formats on Consumer Food Selections using FAFH. *Journal of Pharmaceutical Research International*, 33(43A), 199–207. DOI: 10.9734/jpri/2021/v33i43A32478

Kalinowska, A., & Żyliński, S. (2023). Promotional tactics of Polish fashion brands in social media on the example of Vesna and Marie Zélie. *Studia Medioznawcze*, 24(4), 36–49. DOI: 10.33077/uw.24511617.sm.2023.4.783

Kaman, G. S., Bozkurt, İ., Bölükbaş, R., Özhasar, Y., Demirci, B., & Yazicioğlu, İ. (2024). The strategy food waste in restaurants: A systematic literature review. *Trends in Food Science & Technology*, 151, 104625. DOI: 10.1016/j.tifs.2024.104625

Kamble, S. S., Gunasekaran, A., & Goh, M. (2020). Industry 4.0 and its implications for supply chain management: A systematic literature review. *International Journal of Production Economics*, 229, 107853. Advance online publication. DOI: 10.1016/j.ijpe.2020.107853

Kandasamy, S., Yoo, J., Yun, J., Kang, H., Seol, K., Kim, H., & Ham, J. (2021). Application of whey protein-based edible films and coatings in food industries: An updated overview. *Coatings*, 11(9), 1056. DOI: 10.3390/coatings11091056

Kang, J.-W. (2019). "The role of personalization on continuance intention in food service mobile apps: A privacy calculus perspective", *International Journal of Contemporary Hospitality Management*, 33(2), pp. 734-752. https://doi.org/. 9.DOI: 10.1108/IJCHM-12-2017-0783

Kang, J. (2012). Social media marketing: Strategies for engaging in Facebook, Twitter & other social media. *International Journal of Business and Information*, 7(2), 241–251.

Kansakar, P., Munir, A., & Shaban, N. (2018). Technology in Hospitality Industry: Prospects and Challenges. https://arxiv.org/pdf/1709.00105

Kanwal, M., Burki, U., Ali, R., & Dahlstrom, R. (2022). A systematic review of gender differences and similarities in online consumers' shopping behaviour. *Journal of Consumer Marketing*, 39(1), 29–43. DOI: 10.1108/JCM-01-2021-4356

Kanwar, R., Bakshi, I., & Singh, S. (2024). ANALYZING THE ROLE OF FOOD IN ENHANCING CUSTOMER DINING EXPERIENCE: AN EXPLORATORY STUDY ON HAVELI RESTAURANT IN HARYANA. *EPRA International Journal of Multidisciplinary Research (IJMR)*, 225–230. DOI: 10.36713/epra17341

Kaplan, A. M., & Haenlein, M. (2010). Users of the world, unite! The challenges and opportunities of social media. *Business Horizons*, 53(1), 59–68. DOI: 10.1016/j.bushor.2009.09.003

Kaplan, A., & Haenlein, M. (2020). Rulers of the world, unite! The challenges and opportunities of artificial intelligence. *Business Horizons*, 63(1), 37–50. DOI: 10.1016/j.bushor.2019.09.003

Kapoor, A. P., & Vij, M. (2018). Technology at the dinner table: Ordering food online through mobile apps. *Journal of Retailing and Consumer Services*, 43, 342–351. DOI: 10.1016/j.jretconser.2018.04.001

Karim, R. A., & Rabiul, M. K. (2024). The relationships of corporate sustainability, customer loyalty, and word of mouth: The mediating role of corporate image and customer satisfaction. *Journal of Quality Assurance in Hospitality & Tourism*, 25(3), 421–441. DOI: 10.1080/1528008X.2022.2135054

Kärkkäinen, T. (2015). Gearing Towards Omnichannel Grocery Retail Through Business Model Innovation.

Karthika, I., & Manojanaranjani, A. (2018). A Study on the various food ordering apps based on consumer preference. *World Wide Journal of Multidisciplinary Research and Development*, 4(11), 88–89.

Kasznik, D., & Łapniewska, Z. (2023). The end of plastic? The EU's directive on single-use plastics and its implementation in Poland. *Environmental Science & Policy*, 145, 151–163. DOI: 10.1016/j.envsci.2023.04.005

Katsikouli, P., Wilde, A. S., Dragoni, N., & Høgh-Jensen, H. (2021). On the benefits and challenges of blockchains for managing food supply chains. *Journal of the Science of Food and Agriculture*, 101(6), 2175–2181. DOI: 10.1002/jsfa.10883 PMID: 33063342

Kaufman, G. (2020). *Dunkin' Donuts and Charli D'Amelio's collaboration: A case study. Ad Age*. Retrieved from Ad Age.

Kaur, G., & Malhotra, N. (2023). Social media marketing strategies for promoting healthy eating habits. *Journal of Health Communication*, 28(3), 319–331.

Kaur, H., Paruthi, M., Islam, J., & Hollebeek, L. D. (2020). The role of brand community identification and reward on consumer brand engagement and brand loyalty in virtual brand communities. *Telematics and Informatics*, 46, 101321. DOI: 10.1016/j.tele.2019.101321

Kaushani, K. G., Rathnasinghe, N. L., Katuwawila, N., Jayasinghe, R. A., Nilmini, A. H. L. R., & Priyadarshana, G. (2022). Trends in smart packaging technologies for sustainable monitoring of food quality and safety. *International Journal of Research and Innovation in Applied Science, 7*(07), 07-30.

Kaushik, S., & Gokhale, N. (2021). Online Sensory Marketing: Developing Five- Dimensional Multi-Sensory Brand Experiences and its Effectiveness. *Revista GEINTEC*, 11(4), 5375–5391. DOI: 10.47059/revistageintec.v11i4.2567

Kaye, D. B. V., Zeng, J., & Wikstrom, P. (2022). *TikTok: Creativity and culture in short video*. John Wiley & Sons.

Kaye, L. (2020). *Digital marketing: Strategy and tactics*. Sage Publications.

Kayikci, Y., Subramanian, N., Dora, M., & Bhatia, M. S. (2020). Food supply chain in the era of Industry 4.0: Blockchain technology implementation opportunities and impediments from the perspective of people, process, performance, and technology. *Production Planning and Control*, •••, 1–14. DOI: 10.1080/09537287.2020.1810757

Kazandzhieva, V., & Filipova, E. (2019). Exploring consumer attitudes towards service robots in tourism. *Journal of Tourism Futures*, 5(3), 224–236.

Kehinde, B. A., Majid, I., Hussain, S., & Nanda, V. (2020). Innovations and future trends in product development and packaging technologies. In *Functional and preservative properties of phytochemicals* (pp. 377–409). Academic Press. DOI: 10.1016/B978-0-12-818593-3.00013-0

Keller, D. (2021). Amplification and its discontents: Why regulating the reach of online content is hard. *J. Free Speech L.*, 1, 227.

Kemper, J., & Rao, B. (2019). Do GDPR and blockchain align? Designing an access control model to comply with the General Data Protection Regulation. *Journal of Data Protection & Privacy*, 2(2), 142–158.

Kerpen, D. (2019). *Likeable social media: How to delight your customers, create an irresistible brand, and be amazing on Facebook, Twitter, LinkedIn, Instagram, Pinterest, and more*. McGraw-Hill Education.

Ketsripongsa, S., Thipkong, S., & Likitkijtham, S. (2018). Evolutionary machine learning for efficient food distribution: Case studies in seafood and milk products. *International Journal of Food Science & Technology*, 53(7), 1667–1675.

Ketsripongsa, U., Pitakaso, R., Sethanan, K., & Srivarapongse, T. (2018). An improved differential evolution algorithm for crop planning in the northeastern region of, ailand. *Mathematical & Computational Applications*, 23(3), 40. DOI: 10.3390/mca23030040

Keyes, C. L. M. (1998). Social Well-Being. *Social Psychology Quarterly*, 61(2), 121. DOI: 10.2307/2787065

Khan, P. W., Byun, Y. C., & Park, N. (2020). IoT-blockchain enabled optimized provenance system for food Industry 4.0 using advanced deep learning. *Sensors (Basel)*, 20(10), 2990. Advance online publication. DOI: 10.3390/s20102990 PMID: 32466209

Khan, S. K., Fatima, H., & Hussain, S. W. (2020). How Consumers' Skepticism is Derived from Deceptive Advertisements. *International Journal of Experiential Learning & Case Studies*, 5(2). Advance online publication. DOI: 10.22555/ijelcs.v5i2.106

Khlaif, Z. N., Sanmugam, M., & Ayyoub, A. (2022). Impact of technostress on continuance intentions to use mobile technology. *The Asia-Pacific Education Researcher*. Advance online publication. DOI: 10.1007/s40299-021-00638-x

Khrais, L. T. (2020). Role of artificial intelligence in shaping consumer demand in E-commerce. *Future Internet*, 12(12), 226. DOI: 10.3390/fi12120226

Kiliç, İ. (2022). Examination of thc rclationship between demographic information and science literacy in daily life. *American Educational Research Journal*, 10(2), 125–133. DOI: 10.30918/AERJ.102.22.024

Kim, H. J., Yang, K., & Lee, Y. E. (2018). Moderating effect of trust and commitment in customer satisfaction and customer loyalty on mobile grocery purchasing quality attributes.

Kim, D. J., & Mattila, A. S. (2019). *Hospitality and tourism marketing: Theories and applications*. Routledge.

Kim, E., & Park, S. (2022). Innovative AI Approaches for Restaurant Quality Assurance. *Journal of Culinary Science & Technology*, 14(2), 201–214.

Kimes, S. E. (2011). Customer Perceptions of Electronic Food Ordering. *Cornell Hospitality Report*, 6–15. Retrieved from https://scholarship.sha.cornell.edu/chrpubs/70/

Kimes, S. E. (2020). The rise of ghost kitchens: A new delivery model. *Cornell Hospitality Quarterly*, 61(2), 150–156. DOI: 10.1177/1938965519856922

Kimes, S. E. (2020). The role of predictive analytics in managing restaurant operations. *Cornell Hospitality Quarterly*, 61(1), 50–65. DOI: 10.1177/1938965519895387

Kim, H. (2013). Statistical notes for clinical researchers: Assessing normal distribution (2) using skewness and kurtosis. *Restorative Dentistry & Endodontics*, 38(1), 52. DOI: 10.5395/rde.2013.38.1.52 PMID: 23495371

Kim, H., & So, K. K. F. (2022). Two decades of customer experience research in hospitality and tourism: A bibliometric analysis and thematic content analysis. *International Journal of Hospitality Management*, 100, 103082. DOI: 10.1016/j.ijhm.2021.103082

Kim, H., & Yang, S. (2021). The role of service robots in hospitality: Insights from customers, employees, and managers. *Journal of Hospitality and Tourism Technology*, 12(4), 539–559.

Kim, J. (2021). *The BTS meal at McDonald's: A global influencer marketing success. Forbes*. Retrieved from Forbes.

Kim, J.-K., Yang, J.-J., & Lee, Y.-K. (2023). How Do Self-Service Kiosks Improve COVID-19 Pandemic Resilience in the Restaurant Industry? *Sustainability (Basel)*, 15(13), 10168. DOI: 10.3390/su151310168

Kim, M., & Qu, H. (2014). Travelers' behavioral intention toward hotel self-service kiosks usage. *International Journal of Contemporary Hospitality Management*, 26(2), 225–245. DOI: 10.1108/IJCHM-09-2012-0165

Kim, S. J., Jeong, Y., Park, S., Ryu, K., & Oh, G. (2018). A Survey of Drone use for Entertainment and AVR (Augmented and Virtual Reality). In Jung, T., & tom Dieck, M. (Eds.), *Augmented Reality and Virtual Reality. Progress in IS*. Springer., DOI: 10.1007/978-3-319-64027-3_23

Kim, S., Ham, S., Moon, H., Chua, B. L., & Han, H. (2019). Experience, brand prestige, perceived value (functional, hedonic, social, and financial), and loyalty among GROCERANT customers. *International Journal of Hospitality Management*, 77, 169–177. DOI: 10.1016/j.ijhm.2018.06.026

Kim, T., Wildey, L., Gleason, B., Bleser, J., Firestone, M., Bare, G., Bliss, J., Dewey-Mattia, D., Stueven, H., Brown, L., Dyjack, D., & Hedberg, C. (2022). Foodborne Outbreak Rates Associated with Restaurant Inspection Grading and Posting at the Point of Service: Evaluation Using National Foodborne Outbreak Surveillance Data. *Journal of Food Protection*, 85(7), 1000–1007. DOI: 10.4315/JFP-22-007 PMID: 35175331

Kim, Y., & Lee, J. (2019). The rise of social media in the food industry: Case study of influencer marketing. *Journal of Interactive Marketing*, 47, 23–32.

Kishore Austeen, X., Harish Kumar, V., Venkatesan, S., & Raghul, R. M. (2019). Design and implementation of aquaculture monitoring and controlling system using IoT. *International Research Journal of Engineering and Technology, 6*(3). https://www.irjet.net/archives/V6/i3/IRJET-V6I3899.pdf

Kittithammavong, V., Khanitchaidecha, W., & Thongsanit, P. (2023). Co2 emissions from plastic consumption behaviours in Thailand. *Sustainability (Basel)*, 15(16), 12135. DOI: 10.3390/su151612135

Kitz, R., Walker, T., Charlebois, S., & Music, J. (2021). Food packaging during the COVID-19 pandemic: Consumer perceptions. *International Journal of Consumer Studies*, 46(2), 434–448. DOI: 10.1111/ijcs.12691 PMID: 34230811

Klean. (2024). *The future of plastic recovery is Here*. Retrieved from https://www.klean.asia/

Klepek, M., & Bauerová, R. (2020). Why do retail customers hesitate for shopping grocery online? *Technological and Economic Development of Economy*, 26(6), 1444–1462. DOI: 10.3846/tede.2020.13970

Klouvidaki, M. I., Antonopoulos, N., Styliaras, G. D., & Kanavos, A. (2023). Virtual Restaurants: Customer Experience Keeps Their Businesses Alive. *Information (Basel)*, 14(7), 7. Advance online publication. DOI: 10.3390/info14070406

Koch, R. (2024). 'AI in the Food Industry is Transforming the Business', URL: https://www.clickworker.com/customer-blog/artificial-intelligence-food-industry/

Kolkur, S., Gandhi, M., Sakpal, R., & Madhwani, B. (2021, January 1). *Augmented Reality based Interactive Mobile Application for Restaurants. | Grenze International Journal of Engineering & Technology (GIJET) | EBSCOhost*. https://openurl.ebsco.com/contentitem/gcd:151423867?sid=ebsco:plink:crawler&id=ebsco:gcd:151423867

Kong, L., Chen, W., Luo, W., Chen, C., & Yang, Z. (2022). General Cutting Load Model for Workload Simulation in Spindle Reliability Test. *Machines (Basel)*, 10(2), 144. DOI: 10.3390/machines10020144

Konoplyannikova, M., Radkevych, L., Netreba, M., Bilan, M., Lorvi, I., & Nahorna, O. (2024). Digital marketing and communication strategies of agri-food enterprises on social media platforms. *Agronomy Research (Tartu)*, •••, 22.

Konur, S., Lan, Y., Thakker, D., & Mehdipour, A. (2023). Towards design and implementation of Industry 4.0 for food manufacturing. *Neural Computing & Applications*, 35(22), 23753–23765. DOI: 10.1007/s00521-021-05726-z

Kopalle, P. K., Gangwar, M., Kaplan, A., Ramachandran, D., Reinartz, W., & Rindfleisch, A. (2022). Examining artificial intelligence (AI) technologies in marketing via a global lens: Current trends and future research opportunities. *International Journal of Research in Marketing*, 39(2), 522–540. DOI: 10.1016/j.ijresmar.2021.11.002

Koshariya, A. K., Sharma, N., Satapathy, S. N., Thilagam, P., Akanksha, L. T., Laxman, T., Rai, S., & Singh, B. (2023). Safeguarding agriculture: A comprehensive review of plant protection strategies. *Int J Environ Clim Change*, 13(11), 272–281. DOI: 10.9734/ijecc/2023/v13i113168

Kotler, P., & Keller, K. L. (2016). *Marketing management* (15th ed.). Pearson.

Krishna, A. (2010). *An introduction to Sensory marketing*. Routledge.

Krishna, A. (2011). An integrative review of sensory marketing: Engaging the senses to affect perception, judgment and behavior. *Journal of Consumer Psychology*, 22(3), 332–351. DOI: 10.1016/j.jcps.2011.08.003

Krishna, A., & Morrin, M. (2008). Does Touch Affect Taste? The Perceptual Transfer of Product Container Haptic Cues. *The Journal of Consumer Research*, 34(6), 807–818. DOI: 10.1086/523286

Krishnamurthy, S. M., & Venkitachalam, K. (2022). The changing face of retailing, 1980–2020. *Journal of Strategy and Management*, (ahead-of-print).

Kroeber, A. R. (2020). *China's economy: What everyone needs to know*. Oxford University Press. DOI: 10.1093/wentk/9780190946470.001.0001

Kshetri, N. (2018). 1 Blockchain's roles in meeting key supply chain management objectives. *International Journal of Information Management*, 39, 80–89. DOI: 10.1016/j.ijinfomgt.2017.12.005

Kuijpers, D., Wintels, S., & Yamakawa, N. (2020). Reimagining food retail in Asia after [*McKinsey & Company.*]. *COVID*, •••, 19.

Kula, E., Greuter, E., Van Deursen, A., & Gousios, G. (2021). Factors affecting On-Time Delivery in Large-Scale Agile Software Development. *IEEE Transactions on Software Engineering*, 48(9), 3573–3592. DOI: 10.1109/TSE.2021.3101192

Kulshreshtha, K., & Sharma, R. (2022). AI in kitchen automation: Supply chain management and food quality. *Journal of Hospitality and Tourism Management*, 50(1), 153–165.

Kumar, A., Sikdar, P., Gupta, M., Singh, P., & Sinha, N. (2023). Drivers of satisfaction and usage continuance in e-grocery retailing: A collaborative design supported perspective. *Journal of Research in Interactive Marketing*, 17(2), 176–194. DOI: 10.1108/JRIM-02-2020-0035

Kumar, G. S., Kulkarni, M., & Rathi, N. (2022). Evolving food choices among the urban Indian middle-class: A qualitative study. *Frontiers in Nutrition*, 9, 844413. DOI: 10.3389/fnut.2022.844413 PMID: 35425799

Kumar, I., Rawat, J., Mohd, N., & Husain, S. (2021). Opportunities of Artificial Intelligence and Machine Learning in the Food Industry. *Journal of Food Quality*, 15(2), 301–315. DOI: 10.1155/2021/4535567

Kumar, R., & Sharma, A. (2024). Review of Pet Food Packaging in the US Market: Future Direction Towards Innovation and Sustainability. *Annual Research & Review in Biology*, 39(6), 16–30. DOI: 10.9734/arrb/2024/v39i62085

Kumar, S., & Shah, A. (2021). Revisiting food delivery apps during COVID-19 pandemic? Investigating the role of emotions. *Journal of Retailing and Consumer Services*, 62, 102595. Advance online publication. DOI: 10.1016/j.jretconser.2021.102595

Kurnia, S., & Schubert, P. TOWARD ACHIEVING CUSTOMER SATISFACTION IN ONLINE GROCERY SHOPPING. *Electronic Customer Relationship Management*, 177.

Kusumawati, A. (2020). How automation and AI reshape customer experience in the food service industry. *Journal of Service Research*, 23(2), 189–202. DOI: 10.1177/1094670520916415

Kwak, H., Lee, C., Park, H., & Moon, S. (2010). What is Twitter, a social network or a news media? *Proceedings of the 19th International Conference on World Wide Web (WWW '10)*, 591-600. DOI: 10.1145/1772690.1772751

Kwon, J., & Ahn, J. (2022). Role of customers' multidimensional perceived equity in the mobile food delivery industry. *Journal of Hospitality and Tourism Technology*, 13(5), 955–971. DOI: 10.1108/JHTT-08-2021-0223

Kwortnik, R. J., & Thompson, G. M. (2020). Unifying service marketing and operations management: A model of service experience. *Journal of Service Research*, 23(1), 28–44. DOI: 10.1177/1094670518805916

Kyrnis, N. (2024). *Application of artificial intelligence in the restaurant business. Restorannij i gotel'nyj konsal'ting*. Innovacii., DOI: 10.31866/2616-7468.7.1.2024.305960

Labroo, A. A., & Nielsen, J. H. (2010). Half the Thrill is in the Chase: Twisted Inferences from Embodied Cognitions and Brand Evaluation. *The Journal of Consumer Research*, 37(1), 143–158. DOI: 10.1086/649908

Labs, W. (2024). URL: https://www.foodengineeringmag.com/articles/99061-how-robots-help-processors-navigate-the-covid-19-pandemic

Lacap, J. P. G., Lugue, A., Bongon, C. D., Dimapilis, A., & Altar, F. (2024). Effects of Self-Order Kiosks Aesthetics on Revisit Intention: The Case of a Philippine Fast-Food Company. In *Consumer and Organizational Behavior in the Age of AI* (pp. 53–76). IGI Global. DOI: 10.4018/979-8-3693-8850-1.ch003

Lahane, S., Paliwal, V., & Kant, R. (2023). Evaluation and ranking of solutions to overcome the barriers of Industry 4.0 enabled sustainable food supply chain adoption. *Cleaner Logistics and Supply Chain*, 8, 100116. DOI: 10.1016/j.clscn.2023.100116

Lam, T. K., Heales, J., Hartley, N., & Hodkinson, C. (2020). Consumer trust in food safety requires information transparency. *AJIS. Australasian Journal of Information Systems*, 24, 24. DOI: 10.3127/ajis.v24i0.2219

Lassen, A., Beck, A., Leedo, E., Andersen, E., Christensen, T., Mejborn, H., Thorsen, A., & Tetens, I. (2014). Effectiveness of offering healthy labelled meals in improving the nutritional quality of lunch meals eaten in a worksite canteen. *Appetite*, 75, 128–134. DOI: 10.1016/j.appet.2013.12.005 PMID: 24373732

Latino, M. E., Corallo, A., Menegoli, M., & Nuzzo, B. (2021). Agriculture 4.0 as enabler of sustainable agri-food: A proposed taxonomy. *IEEE Transactions on Engineering Management*, 70(10), 3678–3696. DOI: 10.1109/TEM.2021.3101548

Lau, A. (2020). New technologies used in COVID-19 for business survival: Insights from the hotel sector in China. *Information Technology & Tourism*, 22(4), 497–504. DOI: 10.1007/s40558-020-00193-z

Law, R., & Buhalis, D. (2014). Analyzing the hotel online performance: Using online data to improve service quality. *International Journal of Contemporary Hospitality Management*, 26(7), 1062–1084.

Lawrence, M., & Friel, S. (Eds.), *Healthy and Sustainable Food Systems*. Routledge. DOI: 10.4324/9781351189033

Lazaro-Mojica, J., & Fernández, R I D. (2020, November 23). Review paper on the future of the food sector through education, capacity building, knowledge translation and open innovation. Elsevier BV, 38, 162-167. https://doi.org/DOI: 10.1016/j.cofs.2020.11.009

Lee, P. M., Chong, G., & Chan, C. M.L. (2017). Koufu: Fortune of an entrepreneurial Singapore hawker. *Asian Case Research Journal, 21*(1), 175-205. ResearchGate. https://doi.org/DOI: 10.1142/S0218927517500067

Lee, C., & Ahmed, G. (2021). Improving IoT privacy, data protection and security concerns. International Journal of Technology [IJTIM]. *Innovation and Management*, 1(1), 18–33. DOI: 10.54489/ijtim.v1i1.12

Lee, H., Park, J., & Kim, S. (2020). AI Implementation for Enhanced Food Safety Measures. *Food Science and Technology Journal*, 10(2), 115–126.

Lee, J., & Lim, H. (2023). Visual aesthetics and multisensory engagement in online food delivery services. *International Journal of Retail & Distribution Management*, 51(8), 975–990. DOI: 10.1108/IJRDM-09-2021-0451

Lee-Kwan, S., Pan, L., Maynard, L., McGuire, L., & Park, S. (2016). Factors Associated with Self-Reported Menu-Labeling Usage among US Adults. *Journal of the Academy of Nutrition and Dietetics*, 116(7), 1127–1135. DOI: 10.1016/j.jand.2015.12.015 PMID: 26875022

Lee, M., Yun, J. J., Pyka, A., Won, D., Kodama, F., Schiuma, G., Park, H., Jeon, J., Park, K., Jung, K., Yan, M.-R., Lee, S., & Zhao, X. (2018). How to respond to the fourth industrial revolution, or the second information technology revolution? Dynamic new combinations between technology, market, and society through open innovation. *Journal of Open Innovation*, 4(21), 1–24. DOI: 10.3390/joitmc4030021

Lee, R. C. (2012). A service-oriented analytics framework for Multi-Level marketing business. *Journal of Software Engineering and Applications*, 05(08), 527–535. DOI: 10.4236/jsea.2012.58061

Lee, S. M., & Lee, D. (2020). Untact: A new customer service strategy in the digital age. *Service Business*, 14(1), 1–22. DOI: 10.1007/s11628-019-00408-2

Lee, S. W. (2022). Regression analysis for continuous independent variables in medical research: Statistical standard and guideline of Life Cycle Committee. *Life Cycle*, 2, e3. Advance online publication. DOI: 10.54724/lc.2022.e3

Lee, Y.-K., Chang, C.-T., Lin, Y., & Cheng, Z.-H. (2014). The dark side of smartphone usage: Psychological traits, compulsive behavior and technostress. *Computers in Human Behavior*, 31, 373–383. DOI: 10.1016/j.chb.2013.10.047

Lei, L. I., Zhai, S.-X., & Bai, J.-F. (2021). The dynamic impact of income and income distribution on food consumption among adults in rural China. *Journal of Integrative Agriculture*, 20(1), 330–342. DOI: 10.1016/S2095-3119(20)63239-7

Lemon, K. N., & Verhoef, P. C. (2016). Understanding Customer Experience Throughout the Customer Journey. *Journal of Marketing*, 80(6), 69–96. DOI: 10.1509/jm.15.0420

Leon, C. (2021, December). The adoption of a mobile payment system: the user perspective. *Latin American Journal of Central Banking, 2*(4), 1-4. https://www.sciencedirect.com/science/article/pii/S2666143821000223#sec0001

Leppäniemi, M., Karjaluoto, H., & Saarijärvi, H. (2017). Customer perceived value, satisfaction, and loyalty: The role of willingness to share information. *International Review of Retail, Distribution and Consumer Research*, 27(2), 164–188. DOI: 10.1080/09593969.2016.1251482

Le, T. H., Arcodia, C., Novais, M. A., & Kralj, A. (2019). What we know and do not know about authenticity in dining experiences: A systematic literature review. *Tourism Management*, 74, 258–275. DOI: 10.1016/j.tourman.2019.02.012

Leung, X. Y. (2019). Are robots responsible? The impact of artificial intelligence on food service operations. *International Journal of Hospitality Management*, 82, 360–368. DOI: 10.1016/j.ijhm.2019.04.019

Leung, X. Y., & Wen, H. (2021). How emotions affect restaurant digital ordering experiences: A comparison of three ordering methods. *Journal of Hospitality and Tourism Technology*, 12(3), 439–453. DOI: 10.1108/JHTT-05-2020-0117

Leung, X., Torres, B., & Fan, A. (2021). Do kiosks outperform cashiers? An S-O-R framework of restaurant ordering experiences. *Journal of Hospitality and Tourism Technology*, 12(3), 580–592. DOI: 10.1108/JHTT-03-2020-0065

Lewis, K. O., Popov, V., & Fatima, S. S. (2024). From static web to metaverse: Reinventing medical education in the post-pandemic era. *Annals of Medicine*, 56(1), 2305694. DOI: 10.1080/07853890.2024.2305694 PMID: 38261592

Lezoche, M., Hernandez, J. E., Alemany Díaz, M. M., Panetto, H., & Kacprzyk, J. (2020). Agri-food I4.0: A survey of the supply chains and technologies for the future agriculture. *Computers in Industry*, 117, 103187. Advance online publication. DOI: 10.1016/j.compind.2020.103187

Li, D. (2020). *The impact of Chinese tourists' use of Weibo as their tourist destination selection to Thailand*.

Liang-Pholsena, A. (2020). *Artificial intelligence and the evolution of the hospitality industry*. University of Hawaii Press.

Liao, Y., Deschamps, F., Loures, E. F. R., & Ramos, L. F. P. (2017). Past, present and future of Industry 4.0: A systematic literature review and research agenda proposal. *International Journal of Production Research*, 55(12), 3609–3629. DOI: 10.1080/00207543.2017.1308576

Li, C. (2018). Consumer behavior in switching between membership cards and mobile applications: The case of Starbucks. *Computers in Human Behavior*, 84, 171–184. DOI: 10.1016/j.chb.2017.12.042

Li, C., Tang, J., & Wang, X. (2019). Predictive analytics in quick service restaurants: The case of McDonald's AI-powered drive-thru systems. *Computers & Industrial Engineering*, 137, 106037. DOI: 10.1016/j.cie.2019.106037

Liem, G. S., Koay, L. K., Pong, H. L., Poon, Z. Y., Gisca, A. P., Gupta, M., & Kee, D. M. H. (2023). AI-assisted Food Ordering and Delivery Management System for KFC: Insights from Malaysia, Indonesia and India. *Journal of The Community Development in Asia*, 6(3), 49–63. DOI: 10.32535/jcda.v6i3.2540

Li, H., Zhang, L., & Hsu, C. H. C. (2023). Research on user-generated photos in tourism and hospitality: A systematic review and way forward. *Tourism Management*, 96, 104714. DOI: 10.1016/j.tourman.2022.104714

Li, L., Yuan, L., & Tian, J. (2023). Influence of online E-commerce interaction on consumer satisfaction based on big data algorithm. *Heliyon*, 9(8), e18322. DOI: 10.1016/j.heliyon.2023.e18322 PMID: 37588603

Li, L., Zhang, J., & An, X. (2023). Using social media for efficient brand marketing: An evaluation of Chinese Universities using Bilibili. *Socio-Economic Planning Sciences*, 88, 101645. DOI: 10.1016/j.seps.2023.101645

Liljander, V., Gillberg, F., Gummerus, J., & Riel, A. V. (2006, May). Technology readiness and the evaluation and adoption of self-service technologies. *Journal of Retailing and Consumer Services*, 13(3), 177–191. https://www.sciencedirect.com.singaporetech.remotexs.co/science/article/pii/S096969890500055X?via%3Dihub. DOI: 10.1016/j.jretconser.2005.08.004

Lim, A. (2024, Feb 4). 'When good food goes to waste'. *The Star*. https://www.thestar.com.my/news/education/2024/02/04/when-good-food-goes-to-waste#:~:text=ACCORDING%20to%20the%20Solid%20Waste,going%20to%20waste%20every%20day

Lim, J. (2023). *Food courts*. NLB eResources. https://eresources.nlb.gov.sg/infopedia/articles/SIP_1636_2010-01-31.html

Li, M., Yin, D., Qiu, H., & Bai, B. (2022). Examining the effects of AI contactless services on customer psychological safety, perceived value, and hospitality service quality during the COVID-19 pandemic. *Journal of Hospitality Marketing & Management*, 31(1), 24–48. DOI: 10.1080/19368623.2021.1934932

Ling, E., Chua, B., & Han, H. (2023). In search of a reciprocal relationship in dessert cafés: Linking customer perceived innovativeness to value co-creation behavior. *Humanities & Social Sciences Communications*, 10(1), 897. Advance online publication. DOI: 10.1057/s41599-023-02353-y

Lin, J., Guia Julve, J., Xu, H., & Cui, Q. (2020). Food habits and tourist food consumption: An exploratory study on dining behaviours of Chinese outbound tourists in Spain. *Journal of Policy Research in Tourism, Leisure & Events*, 12(1), 82–99. DOI: 10.1080/19407963.2018.1506199

Lin, L., Zhang, X., Khan, M. A., Mehmood, M. A., & Khan, M. K. (2024). Eco-conscious consumption in the climate change era: Decoding the mediating role of food safety and environmental concerns between health literacy and take-out food consumption in China. *Sustainability (Basel)*, 16(11), 4357. DOI: 10.3390/su16114357

Lipschultz, J. H. (2020). *Social media communication: Concepts, practices, data, law and ethics*. Routledge. DOI: 10.4324/9780429202834

Lipsman, A., Mudd, G., Rich, M., & Bruich, S. (2021). The power of "like": How brands reach (and influence) fans through social media marketing. *Journal of Advertising Research*, 52(1), 40–52. DOI: 10.2501/JAR-52-1-040-052

Liu, Z., Du, J., & He, J. (2022). Marketing Dilemma and Countermeasures of Leisure Food Under Mobile Internet--A Case Study of Three Squirrels in E-Commerce Enterprises. *2022 2nd International Conference on Management Science and Software Engineering (ICMSSE 2022)*, 273–278.

Liu, C. F., & Lin, C. H. (2020). Online food shopping: A conceptual analysis for research propositions. *Frontiers in Psychology*, 11, 583768. DOI: 10.3389/fpsyg.2020.583768 PMID: 33041952

Liu, F., Xiao, B., Lim, E. T., & Tan, C. W. (2017). The art of appeal in electronic commerce: Understanding the impact of product and website quality on online purchases. *Internet Research*, 27(4), 752–771. DOI: 10.1108/IntR-09-2016-0280

Liu, G., & Chen, H. (2019). AI Solutions for Enhanced Restaurant Food Quality Testing. *International Journal of Gastronomy and Food Science*, 5(3), 275–288.

Liu, J., Vethaak, A., An, L., Liu, Q., Yue, Y., & Ding, J. (2021). An environmental dilemma for China during the COVID-19 pandemic is the explosion of disposable plastic waste. *Bulletin of Environmental Contamination and Toxicology*, 106(2), 237–240. DOI: 10.1007/s00128-021-03121-x PMID: 33515068

Liu, J., Xu, W., & Zhang, Y. (2021). The role of AI in transforming the food delivery sector: Evidence from Domino's Pizza. *Journal of Retailing and Consumer Services*, 60, 102507. DOI: 10.1016/j.jretconser.2021.102507

Liu, P. J., Bettman, J. R., Uhalde, A. R., & Ubel, P. A. (2015). 'How many calories are in my burrito?' Improving consumers' understanding of energy (calorie) range information. *Public Health Nutrition*, 18(1), 15–24. DOI: 10.1017/S1368980014000627 PMID: 24762709

Liu, R., Gao, Z., Snell, H. A., & Ma, H. (2020). Food safety concerns and consumer preferences for food safety attributes: Evidence from China. *Food Control*, 112, 107157. DOI: 10.1016/j.foodcont.2020.107157

Liu-Thompkins, Y. (2019). A decade of online advertising research: What we learned and what we need to know. *Journal of Advertising*, 48(1), 92–105. DOI: 10.1080/00913367.2018.1556138

Liu, X. (2021). *An analysis of digital marketing strategy in the era of social media in China*. Massachusetts Institute of Technology.

Liu, X., Xu, Y., Engel, B. A., Sun, S., Zhao, X., Wu, P., & Wang, Y. (2021). The impact of urbanization and aging on food security in developing countries: The view from Northwest China. *Journal of Cleaner Production*, 292, 126067. DOI: 10.1016/j.jclepro.2021.126067

Li, Y., Chen, C., & Wang, S. (2021). The role of technology in enhancing service quality in fast-casual restaurants: A case study of Starbucks. *Journal of Retailing and Consumer Services*, 63, 102662. DOI: 10.1016/j.jretconser.2021.102662

Li, Y., Hu, C., Huang, C., & Duan, L. (2017). The concept of smart tourism in the context of tourism information services. *Tourism Management*, 58, 293–300. DOI: 10.1016/j.tourman.2016.03.014

Li, Y., Li, X., & Cai, J. (2021). How attachment affects user stickiness on live streaming platforms: A socio-technical approach perspective. *Journal of Retailing and Consumer Services*, 60, 102478. DOI: 10.1016/j.jretconser.2021.102478

Li, Y., & Xie, Y. (2020). Is a picture worth a thousand words? An empirical study of image content and social media engagement. *JMR, Journal of Marketing Research*, 57(1), 1–19. DOI: 10.1177/0022243719881113

Llanera, P. (2023). *Enhancing Restaurant Visibility: Standardised Handbook for Food Presentation on Social Media*.

Lopez, A., & Garza, R. (2021). Do sensory reviews make more sense? The mediation of objective perception in online review helpfulness. *Journal of Research in Interactive Marketing*, 16(3), 438–456. DOI: 10.1108/JRIM-04-2021-0121

Lopez, M., & Gonzalez, A. (2023). The influence of social media on food tourism: A case study of Instagram foodies. *Tourism Management*, 96, 104684.

López-Morales, J. A., Martínez, J. A., & Skarmeta, A. F. (2020). Digital Transformation of Agriculture through the Use of an Interoperable Platform. *Sensors (Basel)*, 20(4), 1153. DOI: 10.3390/s20041153 PMID: 32093147

Lorenzo, J. M., Domínguez, R., Pateiro, M., & Munekata, P. E. S. (Eds.). (2022). *Methods to assess the quality of meat products*. Springer., DOI: 10.1007/978-1-0716-2002-1

Lu, J., Jia, X., Lev, B., Zhang, C., Gao, Y., Zhao, M., & He, Y. (2021). How to understand "salable fake goods" and "unsalable quality goods"? An insight from the view of quality responsibility and consumers' brand loyalty. *Technology in Society*, 67, 101793. DOI: 10.1016/j.techsoc.2021.101793

Lukanova, G., & Ilieva, G. (2019). Robots, artificial intelligence, and service automation in hotels. In S. Ivanov & C. Webster (Eds.), *Robots, artificial intelligence, and service automation in travel, tourism and hospitality* (pp. 157-183). Emerald Publishing. DOI: 10.1108/978-1-78756-687-320191009

Lu, L., Cai, R., & Gursoy, D. (2021). Developing and testing a customer-centric technology readiness index (TRI) in the context of service robots. *International Journal of Hospitality Management*, 94, 102854.

Lu, L., Zhang, P., & Zhang, T. C. (2021). Leveraging "human-likeness" of robotic service at restaurants. *International Journal of Hospitality Management*, 94, 102823. Advance online publication. DOI: 10.1016/j.ijhm.2020.102823

Luo, X., Tong, S., Fang, Z., & Qu, Z. (2019). Frontiers: Machines vs. humans: The impact of AI chatbots on consumer patronage. *Marketing Science*, 38(6), 937–947.

Luqman, A., Nugrahapraja, H., Wahyuono, R., Islami, I., Haekal, M., Fardiansyah, Y., Putri, B. Q., Amalludin, F. I., Rofiqa, E. A., Götz, F., & Wibowo, A. (2021). Microplastic contamination in human stools, foods, and drinking water is associated with the Indonesian coastal population. *Environments (Basel, Switzerland)*, 8(12), 138. DOI: 10.3390/environments8120138

Lu, Y. (2017). Industry 4.0: A survey on technologies, applications and open research issues. *Journal of Industrial Information Integration*, 6(4), 1–10. DOI: 10.1016/j.jii.2017.04.005

Lu, Z., & Nam, I. (2021). Research on the influence of new media technology on internet short video content production under artificial intelligence background. *Complexity*, 2021(1), 8875700. DOI: 10.1155/2021/8875700

Lv, J., Wang, Z., Huang, Y., Wang, T., & Wang, Y. (2020). How can e-commerce businesses implement discount strategies through social media? *Sustainability (Basel)*, 12(18), 7459. DOI: 10.3390/su12187459

Lyu, X., Jia, F., & Zhao, B. (2023). Impact of big data and cloud-driven learning technologies in healthy and smart cities on marketing automation. *Soft Computing*, 27(7), 4209–4222. DOI: 10.1007/s00500-022-07031-w

Mabhaudhi, T., Nhamo, L., Chibarabada, T. P., Mabaya, G., Mpandeli, S., Liphadzi, S., Senzanje, A., Naidoo, D., Modi, A. T., & Chivenge, P. P. (2021). Assessing progress towards sustainable development goals through nexus planning. *Water (Basel)*, 13(9), 1321. DOI: 10.3390/w13091321

Macready, A. L., Hieke, S., Klimczuk-Kochańska, M., Szumiał, S., Vranken, L., & Grunert, K. G. (2020). Consumer trust in the food value chain and its impact on consumer confidence: A model for assessing consumer trust and evidence from a 5-country study in Europe. *Food Policy*, 92, 101880. DOI: 10.1016/j.foodpol.2020.101880

Madhu, S., Soundararajan, V., & Parayitam, S. (2022). Online promotions and hedonic motives as moderators in the relationship between e-Impulsive Buying tendency and customer satisfaction: Evidence from India. *Journal of Internet Commerce*, 22(3), 395–431. DOI: 10.1080/15332861.2022.2088035

Madzharov, A. V., Block, L. G., & Morrin, M. (2015). The Cool Scent of Power: Effects of Ambient Scent on Consumer Preferences and Choice Behavior. *Journal of Marketing*, 79(1), 83–96. DOI: 10.1509/jm.13.0263

Ma, E., Bao, Y., Huang, L., Wang, D., & Kim, M. (2023). When a Robot Makes Your Dinner: A Comparative Analysis of Product Level and Customer Experience Between the U.S. and Chinese Robotic Restaurants. *Cornell Hospitality Quarterly*, 64(2), 184–211. DOI: 10.1177/19389655211052286

Maggioni, I. (2016). What drives customer loyalty in grocery retail? Exploring shoppers' perceptions through associative networks. *Journal of Retailing and Consumer Services*, 33, 120–126. DOI: 10.1016/j.jretconser.2016.08.012

Magrey, B. S., & Chauhan, A., & Ramneet. (2023). Enhancing Dining Experiences: Virtual Food Menu with Aroma Dispenser Integration. *2023 Global Conference on Information Technologies and Communications (GCITC)*, 1–5. DOI: 10.1109/GCITC60406.2023.10426287

Mahadev Madgule, N. (2023). Vinayaka, Yeshwant M. Sonkhaskar, Dhiren Ramanbhai Patel, R. Karthikeyan, P. Selvakumar,(2023). Mechanical properties and microstructure of activated TIG welded similar joints of Inconel alloys by desirability approaches. *Materials Today: Proceedings*, 77, 528–533. DOI: 10.1016/j.matpr.2022.12.250

Mahmoud, A., Attia, M. A., & Wahba, D. (2024). The Impact of Customers' Nutritional Awareness on Food Habits, Behaviors, and Choices in Fast Food Restaurants. *Minia Journal of Tourism and Hospitality Research MJTHR*, 18(1), 109–133. DOI: 10.21608/mjthr.2024.296274.1161

Majeed, M. U., Aslam, S., Murtaza, S. A., Attila, S., & Molnár, E. (2022). Green marketing approaches and their impact on green purchase intentions: Mediating role of green brand image and consumer beliefs towards the environment. *Sustainability (Basel)*, 14(18), 11703. DOI: 10.3390/su141811703

Majeed, M., Asare, C., Fatawu, A., & Abubakari, A. (2022). An analysis of the effects of customer satisfaction and engagement on social media on repurchase intention in the hospitality industry. *Cogent Business & Management*, 9(1), 2028331. Advance online publication. DOI: 10.1080/23311975.2022.2028331

Malik, M., Gahlawat, V. K., Mor, R. S., Agnihotri, S., Panghal, A., Rahul, K., & Emanuel, N. (2023). Artificial Intelligence and Data Science in Food Processing Industry. In *Digital Transformation and Industry 4.0 for Sustainable Supply Chain Performance* (pp. 231–244). Springer International Publishing. DOI: 10.1007/978-3-031-19711-6_11

Ma, M., Shi, G., & Li, F. (2019). Privacy-Oriented Blockchain-Based Distributed Key Management Architecture for Hierarchical Access Control in the IoT Scenario. *IEEE Access : Practical Innovations, Open Solutions*, 7, 34045–34059. DOI: 10.1109/ACCESS.2019.2904042

Manavalan, E., & Jayakrishna, K. (2019). A review of Internet of Things (IoT) embedded sustainable supply chain for industry 4.0 requirements. *Computers & Industrial Engineering*, 127, 925–953. DOI: 10.1016/j.cie.2018.11.030

Mandracchia, F., Tarro, L., Llauradó, E., Valls, R. M., & Solà, R. (2022). The "Healthy Meals" web app for the assessment of nutritional content and food allergens in restaurant meals: Development, evaluation and validation. *Digital Health*, 8, 205520762210816. DOI: 10.1177/20552076221081690 PMID: 35251681

Manhas, P. S., Sharma, P., & Quintela, J. A. (2024). Product Innovation and Customer Experience: Catalysts for Enhancing Satisfaction in Quick Service Restaurants. *Tourism and Hospitality*, 5(3), 559–576. DOI: 10.3390/tourhosp5030034

Manikandan, M. K. M. (2020). Store brand and perceived risk on private label brand attitude. *Journal of Indian Business Research*, 12(1), 133–150. DOI: 10.1108/JIBR-09-2019-0280

Manyika, J., Chui, M., Bisson, P., Woetzel, J., Dobbs, R., Bughin, J., & Aharon, D. (2015). *The internet of things: mapping the value beyond the hype*. McKinsey Global Institute. https://www.mckinsey.com/~/media/mckinsey/industries/technology%20media%20and%20teleco mmunications/high%20tech/our%20insights/the%20internet%20of%20things%20the%20value%20 of%20digitizing%20the%20physical%20world/unlocking_the_potential_of_the_internet_of_things_executive_summary.pdf

Manzoor, M. H., & Hasan, O. (2021). A Comparative Study on the Characteristics of Mobile Applications for the Restaurant Industry. *2021 International Conference on Computer Science and Engineering (IC2SE), 1*, 1–5. DOI: 10.1109/IC2SE52832.2021.9791944

Ma, P., Lau, C. P., Yu, N., Li, A., & Sheng, J. (2022). Application of deep learning for image-based Chinese market food nutrients estimation. *Food Chemistry*, 373, 130994. Advance online publication. DOI: 10.1016/j.foodchem.2021.130994 PMID: 34731793

Maria Correia Loureiro, S., & Miranda, J., F., & Breazeale, M. (. (2014). Who needs delight? The greater impact of value, trust and satisfaction in utilitarian, frequent-use retail. *Journal of Service Management*, 25(1), 101–124. DOI: 10.1108/JOSM-06-2012-0106

Marin-Garcia, A., Gil-Saura, I., & Ruiz-Molina, M. E. (2022). Do innovation and sustainability influence customer satisfaction in retail? A question of gender. *Economic research-. Ekonomska Istrazivanja*, 35(1), 546–563. DOI: 10.1080/1331677X.2021.1924217

Marin, L. (2021). Sharing (mis) information on social networking sites. An exploration of the norms for distributing content authored by others. *Ethics and Information Technology*, 23(3), 363–372. DOI: 10.1007/s10676-021-09578-y

Marques, C., Correia, E., Dinis, L., & Vilela, A. (2022). An overview of sensory characterization techniques: From classical descriptive analysis to the emergence of novel profiling methods. *Foods*, 11(3), 255. DOI: 10.3390/foods11030255 PMID: 35159407

Marr, B. (2018). How Domino's uses AI and data analytics to succeed. Forbes. Retrieved from https://www.forbes.com/sites/bernardmarr/2018/05/21/how-dominos-uses-ai-and-data-analytics-to-succeed/

Marra, F. (2023). Combining computer aided food engineering and electro-heating applications as contribution to food processing sustainability. *Frontiers in Sustainability*, 4, 1170467. DOI: 10.3389/frsus.2023.1170467

Marr, B. (2019). Robots on the menu: How delivery robots, AI, and automation are affecting the food industry. *Forbes*.

Marr, B. (2021). The 4th Industrial Revolution: How AI, Big Data, and the Internet of Things are Changing Business. *Forbes*.

Martin, F. (2019, March 8). *What robots mean for the future of the hospitality industry*. Bauer Business Focus. https://www.houstonpublicmedia.org/articles/shows/bauer-business-focus/2019/03/08/324596/what-robots-mean-for-the-future-of-the-hospitality-industry/

Martinelli, E., & Balboni, B. (2012). Retail service quality is a key activator of grocery store loyalty. *Service Industries Journal*, 32(14), 2233–2247. DOI: 10.1080/02642069.2011.582499

Maslow, A. H. (1943). A theory of human motivation. *Psychological Review*, 50(4), 370–396. DOI: 10.1037/h0054346

Mason, R. (2019). Developing a profitable online grocery logistics business: Exploring innovations in ordering, fulfilment, and distribution at Ocado. In *Contemporary Operations and Logistics* (pp. 365–383). Palgrave Macmillan. DOI: 10.1007/978-3-030-14493-7_19

Matin, A., Khoshtaria, T., & Todua, N. (2022). The impact of social media influencers on brand awareness, image and trust in their sponsored content: An empirical study from Georgian social media users. *International Journal of Marketing, Communication and New Media, 10*(18).

Matyushok, V., Vera Krasavina, V., Berezin, A., & Sendra García, J. (2021). The global economy in technological transformation conditions: A review of modern trends. *Ekonomska Istrazivanja*, 34(1), 1471–1497. DOI: 10.1080/1331677X.2020.1844030

Ma, Y. J., Gam, H. J., & Banning, J. (2017). Perceived ease of use and usefulness of sustainability labels on apparel products: Application of the technology acceptance model. *Fashion and Textiles*, 4(1), 1–20. DOI: 10.1186/s40691-017-0093-1

Mboga, J. (2017). Ethical sourcing to ensure sustainability in the food and beverage industry and eliciting millennial perspectives. *European Journal of Economic and Financial Research*.

McCarthy, R., & Sweeney, E. (2021). AI and analytics in food service: How restaurants are leveraging technology for efficiency. *Journal of Foodservice Business Research*, 24(1), 72–90. DOI: 10.1080/15378020.2020.1865050

McClure, C., & Seock, Y.-K. (2020). The role of involvement: Investigating the effect of brand's social media pages on consumer purchase intention. *Journal of Retailing and Consumer Services*, 53, 101975. DOI: 10.1016/j.jretconser.2019.101975

Meißner, M., Pfeiffer, J., Peukert, C., Dietrich, H., & Pfeiffer, T. (2020). How virtual reality affects consumer choice. *Journal of Business Research*, 117, 219–231. DOI: 10.1016/j.jbusres.2020.06.004

Melewar, T., Foroudi, P., & Jin, Z. (2020). Corporate branding, identity, image and reputation: Current and future trends, developments and challenges. *Journal of Business Research*, 117, 672–674. DOI: 10.1016/j.jbusres.2020.06.030

Mell, P., & Grance, T. (2011). The NIST Definition of Cloud Computing. https://csrc.nist.gov/pubs/sp/800/145/final

Melo, M., Gonçalves, G., Monteiro, P., Coelho, H., Vasconcelos-Raposo, J., & Bessa, M. (2020). Do multisensory stimuli benefit the virtual reality experience? A systematic review. *IEEE Transactions on Visualization and Computer Graphics*, 28(2), 1428–1442. DOI: 10.1109/TVCG.2020.3010088 PMID: 32746276

MENGXI, Z. (n.d.). *Marketing strategies for new media in the internet Era–DouYin short video as an example*.

Menon, S., & Jain, K. (2024). Blockchain Technology for Transparency in Agri-Food Supply Chain: Use Cases, Limitations, and Future Directions. *IEEE Transactions on Engineering Management*, 71, 106–120. DOI: 10.1109/TEM.2021.3110903

Merhi, M., Hone, K., & Tarhini, A. (2019). A cross-cultural study of the intention to use mobile banking between Lebanese and British consumers: Extending UTAUT2 with security, privacy and trust. *Technology in Society*, 59, 101151. DOI: 10.1016/j.techsoc.2019.101151

Merican, F., Osman, S., Zainudin, N., Jusoh, Z., & Puteh, F. (2022). Exploring consumer single-use plastic reduction behaviour: A conceptual framework. *Malaysian Journal of Society and Space*, 18(1). Advance online publication. DOI: 10.17576/geo-2022-1801-03

Mesías, F. J., Martín, A., & Hernández, A. (2021). Consumers' growing appetite for natural foods: Perceptions towards the use of natural preservatives in fresh fruit. *Food Research International*, 150, 110749. DOI: 10.1016/j.foodres.2021.110749 PMID: 34865767

Miah, J. H., Griffiths, A., McNeill, R., Halvorson, S., Schenker, U., Espinoza-Orias, N., Morse, S., Yang, A., & Sadhukhan, J. (2018). A framework for increasing the availability of life cycle inventory data based on the role of multinational companies. *The International Journal of Life Cycle Assessment*, 23(9), 1744–1760. DOI: 10.1007/s11367-017-1391-y PMID: 30956413

Micossi, S. (2015). The monetary policy of the European Central Bank (2002-2015). *CEPS Special Report, 109*.

Mieras, E., Gaasbeek, A., & Kan, D. (2019). How to Seize the Opportunities of New Technologies in Life Cycle Analysis Data Collection: A Case Study of the Dutch Dairy Farming Sector. *Challenges*, 10(1), 8. DOI: 10.3390/challe10010008

Mihalic, T., & Buhalis, D. (2013). Information communication technology (ICT) as a new competitive advantage factor—Case of small transitional hotel sector. *Economic and Business Review for Central and South-Eastern Europe*, 15(1), 33–56. DOI: 10.2139/ssrn.2178728

Milesi, E. (n.d.). *Italian food internationalisation process: the case of Beretta and Senfter in China*.

Misra,N.N., Dixit,Y., Al-Mallahi, A., Bhullar, M. S., Upadhyay, R. and Martynenko, A.(2020). IoT, Big Data, and Artificial Intelligence in Agriculture and Food Industry. IEEE Internet of Things Journal, vol. 9, no. 9, pp. 6305-6324, 1 May1, 2022, .DOI: 10.1109/JIOT.2020.2998584

Mitchell, A. (2019). The rise of live-streamed cooking shows: Engaging customers in real-time. *Food Industry Journal*, 4(2), 123–135.

Mittendorf, C., Berente, N., & Holten, R. (2019). Trust in sharing encounters among millennials. *Information Systems Journal*, 29(5), 1083–1119. DOI: 10.1111/isj.12237

Mohamad, M., Tasnim, R., & Ya'kob, S. A. (2023). Continued use of food delivery applications (fdas) post COVID-19 in Malaysia: Barriers and growth. *Environment-Behaviour Proceedings Journal*, 8(SI15), 19–24. DOI: 10.21834/e-bpj.v8iSI15.5095

Mohammad, T., Yusop, A. S., & Azam, N. A. A. (n.d.). *FACTORS AFFECTING URBAN CONSUMERS'PURCHASE DECISIONS FOR READY-TO-EAT FOODS: A STUDY IN PULAU PINANG, MALAYSIA*.

Mohammad, A. A., & AbouElezz, M. (2020). A Holistic Model for Sustainable Restaurant Operations using the Business Model Canvas Approach. *Journal of Association of Arab Universities for Tourism and Hospitality*, 19(3), 207–227. DOI: 10.21608/jaauth.2021.54916.1104

Mohammed, A., Potdar, V., Quaddus, M., & Hui, W. (2023). Blockchain Adoption in Food Supply Chains: A Systematic Literature Review on Enablers, Benefits, and Barriers. *IEEE Access : Practical Innovations, Open Solutions*, 11, 14236–14255. DOI: 10.1109/ACCESS.2023.3236666

Mohdhar, A., & Shaalan, K. (2021). The future of e commerce systems: 2030 and beyond. *Recent Advances in Technology Acceptance Models and Theories*, 311–330.

Mok, W. K., Tan, Y. X., & Chen, W. N. (2020). Technology innovations for food security in Singapore: A case study of future food systems for an increasingly natural resource-scarce world. *Trends in Food Science & Technology*, 102, 155–168. DOI: 10.1016/j.tifs.2020.06.013 PMID: 32834499

Mokyr, J. (2020). *The Industrial Revolution: A Very Short Introduction*. University Press.

Moldenhauer, L., & Londt, C. (2019). Leadership, artificial intelligence and the need to redefine future skills development. *Journal of Leadership, Accountability and Ethics*, 16(1), 54–60.

Molejon, M. G., & Comendador, B. E. V. (2020). Augmented Reality Ordering System With Data Analytics To Support Decision Making In The Restaurant Chains. *Innovatus*, 3(1), 18–28.

Møller Jensen, J. (2011). Consumer loyalty on the grocery product market: An empirical application of Dick and Basu's framework. *Journal of Consumer Marketing*, 28(5), 333–343. DOI: 10.1108/07363761111149983

Monteiro, C. M., Santos, C., & Castro, P. M. L. (2023). Extensive green roofs: Different time approaches to runoff coefficient determination. *Water (Basel)*, 15(10), 1852. DOI: 10.3390/w15101852

Monty, R. C. da S. (2018). Creative Economy: How the interface of Uber Eats and iFood could change your menu. *Brazilian Journal of Operations & Production Management*, 15(3), 413–419. DOI: 10.14488/BJOPM.2018.v15.n3.a8

Moragues-Faus, A., & Battersby, J. (2021). Urban food policies for a sustainable and just future: Concpets and tools for renewed agenda. *Food Policy*, 103, 102124. DOI: 10.1016/j.foodpol.2021.102124

Moran, G., Muzellec, L., & Johnson, D. (2020). Message content features and social media engagement: Evidence from the media industry. *Journal of Product and Brand Management*, 29(5), 533–545. DOI: 10.1108/JPBM-09-2018-2014

Moreno, P., & Tejada, P. (2019). Reviewing the progress of information and communication technology in the restaurant industry. *Journal of Hospitality and Tourism Technology*, 10(4), 673–688. DOI: 10.1108/JHTT-07-2018-0072

Morgan, J., Levin, K., Song, J., & Osorino, J. (2015). Driving Transformative Change: The Role of the Private Sector in Advancing Short-term and Long-term Signals in the Paris Climate Agreement. In *Policy File*. World Resources Institute. https://www.wri.org/research/driving-transformative-change-roleprivate-sector-advancing-short-term-and-long-term

Morrone, D., Raimo, N., Tarulli, A., & Vitolla, F. (2021). Digitalisation in the hospitality industry: Motivations, effects and role of Covid-19. *International Journal of Digital Culture and Electronic Tourism*, 3(3-4), 257–270. DOI: 10.1504/IJDCET.2021.116475

Mortimer, G., Fazal e Hasan, S., Andrews, L., & Martin, J. (2016). Online grocery shopping: The impact of shopping frequency on perceived risk. *International Review of Retail, Distribution and Consumer Research*, 26(2), 202–223. DOI: 10.1080/09593969.2015.1130737

Mosseri, A. (2018). Bringing people closer together. *Facebook Newsroom*. Retrieved from https://about.fb.com/news/2018/01/news-feed-fyi-bringing-people-closer-together/

Motyl, B., Baronio, G., Uberti, S., Speranza, D., & Filippi, S. (2017). How will change the future engineers' skills in the Industry 4.0 framework? A questionnaire survey. *Procedia Manufacturing*, 11, 1501-1509. https://doi.org/. 282DOI: 10.1016/j.promfg.2017.07

Mougayar, W., & Buterin, V. (2016). *The business blockchain: promise, practice, and application of the next Internet technology*. John Wiley & Sons. http://cds.cern.ch/record/2222158

Mozeik, C. M., & Shoemaker, S. (2009). Customer adoption of technology: Exploring AI's role in restaurant loyalty programs. *Journal of Hospitality Marketing & Management*, 18(3), 311–330.

Mróz, B. (2021). Consumer shopping behaviours on social media platforms: Trends, challenges, business implications. In *Disruptive Platforms* (pp. 113–129). Routledge. DOI: 10.4324/9781003207481-7

Mukhopadhyay, B. (2016). Understanding cashless payments in India. *Financial Innovation*. https://doi .org/*households ready to engage with smart home technology?* EBSCO Host. https://web.p.ebscohost .com.singaporetech.remotexs.co/ehost/pdfviewer/pdfviewer?vid=0&sid=08ecdee6-cd4c-4955-a170 -3a9f1a5d68d7%40redisDOI: 10.1186/s40854-016-0047-4

Mulcahy, R., & Riedel, A. (2021). "Going on a sensory adventure, a touchy subject?": Investigating haptic technology and consumer adventure orientation. *Journal of Service Theory and Practice*, 32(1), 5–29. DOI: 10.1108/JSTP-11-2020-0244

Mulyadi, B., & Masatip, A. (2020). The generation Z characteristics and hotel choices. *Tourism and Leisure, 9*.

Mulyanto, G., Kusumaningrum, H. D., & Wulandari, N. (2023). Food safety knowledge and awareness among stakeholders of the online-food-delivery system in Depok City Indonesia. *Food Research*, 7(5), 29–41. DOI: 10.26656/fr.2017.7(5).881

Munaro, A. C., Barcelos, R. H., Maffezzolli, E. C. F., Rodrigues, J. P. S., & Paraíso, E. C. (2021). To engage or not engage? The features of video content on YouTube affecting digital consumer engagement. *Journal of Consumer Behaviour*, 20(5), 1336–1352. DOI: 10.1002/cb.1939

Munson, J., Tiropanis, T., & Lowe, M. (2017). Online grocery shopping: Identifying change in consumption practices. In *Internet Science: 4th International Conference, INSCI 2017, Thessaloniki, Greece, November 22-24, 2017* [Springer International Publishing.]. *Proceedings*, 4, 192–211.

Muntinga, D. G., Moorman, M., & Smit, E. G. (2019). Introducing COBRAs: Exploring motivations for brand-related social media use. *International Journal of Advertising*, 38(3), 450–473.

Murphy, J., & Gretzel, U. (2019). Robots in restaurants: The impact on customer experience. *Journal of Hospitality and Tourism Technology*, 10(1), 54–68.

Murphy, J., Gretzel, U., & Pesonen, J. (2019). Marketing robot services in hospitality and tourism: The role of anthropomorphism. *Journal of Travel & Tourism Marketing*, 36(7), 784–795. DOI: 10.1080/10548408.2019.1571983

Murray, S., & Caraher, M. (2019). Food Retail and Distribution: A focus on supermarkets. In

Murugeah, M. K. (2024). *Enhancing efficiency and personalization in food and beverage service through AI: Future trends and challenges. International Journal for Multidimensional Research Perspective.* IJMRP., DOI: 10.61877/ijmrp.v2i7.162

Musetsho, K. D., Mwendera, E., Madzivhandila, T., Makungo, R., Volenzo, T. E., Mamphweli, N. S., & Nephawe, K. A. (2024). Assessing and mapping water-energy-food nexus smart innovations and practices in Vhembe District Municipality, Limpopo Province, South Africa. *Frontiers in Water*, 6, 1253921. DOI: 10.3389/frwa.2024.1253921

Musicus, A. A., Moran, A. J., Lawman, H. G., & Roberto, C. A. (2019). Online Randomized Controlled Trials of Restaurant Sodium Warning Labels. *American Journal of Preventive Medicine*, 57(6), e181–e193. DOI: 10.1016/j.amepre.2019.06.024 PMID: 31753271

Mustafa, A. M., Azimli, A., & Jaf, R. S. (2022). The role of resource consumption accounting in achieving competitive prices and sustainable profitability. *Energies*, 15(11), 4155. DOI: 10.3390/en15114155

MyGovernment. (2019, July 12). *National Policy on Industry 4.0- Industry4WRD*. Prime Minister's Office of Malaysia Official Website. https://www.pmo.gov.my/2019/07/national-policy-on-industry-4-0-industry4wrd/

Naini, N. F., Santoso, N. S., Andriani, T. S., Claudia, U. G., & Nurfadillah, N. (2022). The effect of product quality, service quality, customer satisfaction on customer loyalty. *Journal of Consumer Sciences*, 7(1), 34–50. DOI: 10.29244/jcs.7.1.34-50

Nair, S. S., Trafiałek, J., & Kolanowski, W. (2023). Edible packaging: A technological update for the sustainable future of the food industry. *Applied Sciences (Basel, Switzerland)*, 13(14), 8234. DOI: 10.3390/app13148234

Nam, J., Kim, S., & Jung, Y. (2023, March 26). Elderly Users' Emotional and Behavioral Responses to Self-Service Technology in Fast-Food Restaurants. *Behavioral Sciences (Basel, Switzerland)*, 13(4), 284–284. DOI: 10.3390/bs13040284 PMID: 37102799

Nam, K., Dutt, C. S., Chathoth, P., Daghfous, A., & Khan, M. S. (2020). The adoption of artificial intelligence and robotics in the hotel industry: Prospects and challenges. *Electronic Markets*. Advance online publication. DOI: 10.1007/s12525-020-00442-3

Nangpiire, C., Dawdi, A. A., Shahadu, F. Z., Majeed, M., & Salifu, Z. N. (2024). The Effects of Sustainable Hospitality Supply Chain on Customer Satisfaction and Customer Repurchase Intentions. *Journal of Law and Sustainable Development*, 12(1), e2605–e2605. DOI: 10.55908/sdgs.v12i1.2605

Na, T., Lee, S., & Yang, J. Y. (2021, July 10). Moderating Effect of Gender on the Relationship between Technology Readiness Index and Consumers' Continuous Use Intention of Self-Service Restaurant Kiosks. *Information (Basel)*, 12(7), 280–280. DOI: 10.3390/info12070280

Na, T., Yang, J. Y., & Lee, S. (2021, July 1). Determinants of Behavioral Intention of the Use of Self-Order Kiosks in Fast-Food Restaurants: Focus on the Moderating Effect of Difference Age. *SAGE Open*, 11(3), 21582440211031907. Advance online publication. DOI: 10.1177/21582440211031907

National Restaurant Association (NRA). (2021). *Restaurant industry facts at a glance*. Retrieved from NRA.

Naumov, N., & Petrov, P. (2019). AI in tourism: Enhancing service quality and customer satisfaction. *Journal of Tourism Futures*, 5(2), 99–109.

Naveed, S., & Murtaza, U. U. R. (2023). Role of marketing Ethics for clients' satisfaction. *Journal of Social Sciences Review*, 3(2), 987–994. DOI: 10.54183/jssr.v3i2.337

Ncube, L., Ude, A., Ogunmuyiwa, E., Zulkifli, R., & Nongwe, I. (2021). An overview of plastic waste generation and management in food packaging industries. *Recycling*, 6(1), 12. DOI: 10.3390/recycling6010012

Nebolisa, C., Abiagom, T., & Ijomah, I. (2024). *Enhancing customer experience through AI-driven language processing in service interactions*. Open Access Research Journal of Engineering and Technology., DOI: 10.53022/oarjet.2024.7.1.0027

Negassa, B., Anbese, A. T., Worku, G., Areba, A. S., Seboka, B. T., Debela, B. G., Kanno, G. G., & Soboksa, N. E. (2023). Food hygiene practices and associated factors among street food vendors in urban areas of Gedeo Zone, southern Ethiopia. *Environmental Health Insights*, 17, 117863022311685. DOI: 10.1177/11786302231168531 PMID: 37122687

Ngobo, P. V. (2017). The trajectory of customer loyalty: An empirical test of Dick and Basu's loyalty framework. *Journal of the Academy of Marketing Science*, 45(2), 229–250. DOI: 10.1007/s11747-016-0493-6

Nguyen, T., Huang, E., & Nguyen, D. M. (2023). Food delivery app continuance: A dual model and segmentation approach. *International Journal of Retail & Distribution Management*, 51(5), 569–589. DOI: 10.1108/IJRDM-06-2022-0217

Nguyen, T., & Tran, L. (2023). Social media engagement and consumer loyalty in the food sector: A mediation analysis. *Journal of Business Research*, 148, 280–293.

Nicolescu, L., & Tudorache, M. T. (2022). Human-computer interaction in customer service: The experience with AI chatbots—a systematic literature review. *Electronics (Basel)*, 11(10), 1579. DOI: 10.3390/electronics11101579

Niedenthal et al. (2005) SP - 184,EP - 211,T1 - Embodiment in Attitudes, Social Perception, and Emotion,VL - 9, DO - DOI: 10.1207/s15327957pspr0903_1

Nielsen, J. (2020). *10 usability heuristics for user interface design*. Nielsen Norman Group. https://www.nngroup.com/articles/ten-usability-heuristics/

Nielsen. (2012). Global trust in advertising and brand messages. *Nielsen Insights*. Retrieved from Nielsen.

Nielsen. (2018). The Nielsen global survey of e-commerce. Retrieved from Nielsen.

Nielsen. (2019). The rise of visual content in digital marketing. *Nielsen Insights*. Retrieved from Nielsen.

Nikolicic, S., Kilibarda, M., Maslaric, M., Mircetic, D., & Bojic, S. (2021). Reducing food waste in the retail supply chains by improving efficiency of logistics operations. *Sustainability (Basel)*, 13(12), 6511. DOI: 10.3390/su13126511

Niszczota, P., Rybicka, I., & Kamini, N. (2023). The credibility of dietary advice formulated by ChatGPT: Robo-diets for people with food allergies. *Nutrition (Burbank, Los Angeles County, Calif.)*, 112, 112076. Advance online publication. DOI: 10.1016/j.nut.2023.112076 PMID: 37269717

Niven, P., Morley, B., Dixon, H., Martin, J., Jones, A., Petersen, K., & Wakefield, M. (2019). Effects of health star labelling on the healthiness of adults' fast food meal selections: An experimental study. *Appetite*, 136, 146–153. DOI: 10.1016/j.appet.2019.01.018 PMID: 30684644

Nozawa, C., Togawa, T., Vel, C., & Motoki, K. (2022). Consumer Responses to the Use of Artificial Intelligence in Luxury and Non-Luxury Restaurants. *Food Quality and Preference*, 36(4), 567–581. DOI: 10.1016/j.foodqual.2021.104436

Nozawa, T., & Ishikawa, H. (2022). The impact of AI on luxury dining experiences. *Journal of Hospitality & Tourism Research (Washington, D.C.)*, 46(3), 436–454.

Nugroho, M. A., & Fajar, A. M. (2017). Effects of technology readiness towards acceptance of mandatory web-based attendance system. *Procedia Computer Science*, 124, 319–328. https://www.researchgate.net/publication/322074997_Effects_of_Technology_Readiness_Towards_Acceptance_of_Mandatory_Web-Based_Attendance_System. DOI: 10.1016/j.procs.2017.12.161

Nuong, M. D., & Ari Ragavan, N. (2023). Digital future of the hospitality industry and hospitality education globally: Review of related literature. *Asia-Pacific Journal of Futures in Education and Society*, 2(2), 71–100. DOI: 10.58946/apjfes-2.2.P5

O'Brien, E., & Kelly, D. (2023). The impact of social media on food safety communication during the COVID-19 pandemic. *Food Control*, 144, 108650.

O'Neill, S. (2015, 4 February) *In Japan, humanoid robots may soon run a hotel.* http:// www.tnooz.com/article/japan-hotel-run-humanoid- robots/

Ogutu, M., Akor, J., Mulindwa, M., Heshima, O., & Nsengimana, C. (2023). Implementing circular economy and sustainability policies in Rwanda: Experiences of Rwandan manufacturers with the plastic ban policy. *Frontiers in Sustainability*, 4, 1092107. Advance online publication. DOI: 10.3389/frsus.2023.1092107

Ojo, O. O., Shah, S., Coutroubis, A., Jimenez, M. T., & Munoz Ocana, Y. (2018). Potential impact of Industry 4.0 in sustainable food supply chain environment. In *Proceedings of the 2018 IEEE International Conference on Technology Management, Operations and Decisions (ICTMOD)* (pp. 172–177). IEEE. https://doi.org/DOI: 10.1109/ITMC.2018.8691223

Okumus, B., Ali, F., Bilgihan, A., & Ozturk, A. (2018). Psychological factors influencing customers' acceptance of smartphone diet apps when ordering food at restaurants. *International Journal of Hospitality Management*, 72, 67–77. DOI: 10.1016/j.ijhm.2018.01.001

Olavarria-Key, N., Ding, A., Legendre, T. S., & Min, J. (2021). Communication of food waste messages: The effects of communication modality, presentation order, and mindfulness on food waste reduction intention. *International Journal of Hospitality Management*, 96, 102962. DOI: 10.1016/j.ijhm.2021.102962

Oliveira, W., Azeredo, H., Neri-Numa, I., & Pastore, G. (2021). Food packaging wastes amid the covid-19 pandemic: Trends and challenges. *Trends in Food Science & Technology*, 116, 1195–1199. DOI: 10.1016/j.tifs.2021.05.027 PMID: 34092920

Olsson, J. (2021). Exploring unattended delivery services in e-grocery retail: A consumer-centric perspective on last-mile logistics.

Ong, D., Chiu, S., Andrews, E., & Nadarajan, G. (2023). One needs to be reminded and motivated: Mediating role of digital nudging for food waste reduction. *Journal of Social Marketing*, 13(3), 449–471. DOI: 10.1108/JSOCM-02-2023-0025

Ong, H. T., Samsudin, H., & Soto-Valdez, H. (2022). Migration of endocrine-disrupting chemicals into food from plastic packaging materials: An overview of chemical risk assessment, techniques to monitor migration and international regulations. *Critical Reviews in Food Science and Nutrition*, 62(4), 957–979. DOI: 10.1080/10408398.2020.1830747 PMID: 33081493

Onofrei, G., Filieri, R., & Kennedy, L. (2022). Social media interactions, purchase intention, and behavioural engagement: The mediating role of source and content factors. *Journal of Business Research*, 142, 100–112. DOI: 10.1016/j.jbusres.2021.12.031

Onyeaka, H., Tamasiga, P., Nwauzoma, U. M., Miri, T., Juliet, U. C., Nwaiwu, O., & Akinsemolu, A. A. (2023). Using artificial intelligence to tackle food waste and enhance the circular economy: Maximising resource efficiency and Minimising environmental impact: A review. *Sustainability (Basel)*, 15(13), 10482. DOI: 10.3390/su151310482

Orel, F. D., & Kara, A. (2014). Supermarket self-checkout service quality, customer satisfaction, and loyalty: Empirical evidence from an emerging market. *Journal of Retailing and Consumer Services*, 21(2), 118–129. DOI: 10.1016/j.jretconser.2013.07.002

Oriekhoe, O. I., Adisa, O., & Ilugbusi, B. S. (2024). Climate change and food supply chain economics: A comprehensive analysis of impacts, adaptations, and sustainability. *International Journal of Applied Research in Social Sciences*, 6(3), 267–278. DOI: 10.51594/ijarss.v6i3.885

Oronsky, C., & Chathoth, P. K. (2007). Dynamics of restaurant technology adoption. *International Journal of Hospitality Management*, 26(4), 723–740.

Osei, B. A., Ragavanm, N. A., & Mensah, H. K. (2020). Prospects of the fourth industrial revolution for the hospitality industry: A literature review. *Journal of Hospitality and Tourism Technology*, 11(3), 479–494. DOI: 10.1108/JHTT-08-2019-0107

Osei, B. A., Ragavan, N. A., Mensah, H. K., & Kandappan, B. (2020). Hospitality revolution 4.0: A literature review on a unified typology of IR 4.0 technologies for the tourism and hospitality industry in the era of COVID-19. *Asia-Pacific Journal of Innovation in Hospitality and Tourism*, 9(1), 25–45.

Ouyang, H., Li, B., McCarthy, M., Miao, S., Kilcawley, K., Fenelon, M., Kelly, A., & Sheehan, J. J. (2021). Understanding preferences for and consumer behavior toward cheese among a cohort of young, educated, internationally mobile Chinese consumers. *Journal of Dairy Science*, 104(12), 12415–12426. DOI: 10.3168/jds.2021-20598 PMID: 34482973

Pacific Coast Food Waste Management. (2022). Case Study: Using Artificial Intelligence to Reduce Food Waste in Grocery Retail. Progress on the Path to Cut Food Waste in Half by 2030. Pacific Coast Food Waste Management. https://pacificcoastcollaborative.org/wp-content/uploads/2022/12/PCFWC-Case-Study_AI_Final.pdf

Pai, S. and Mayya, S. (2022). A study on consumer preferences with reference to online food delivery amenities. *International Journal of Management Technology and Social Sciences*, 144-166. DOI: 10.47992/IJMTS.2581.6012.0214

Palalic, R., Ramadani, V., Mariam Gilani, S., Gërguri-Rashiti, S., & Dana, L. (2021). Social media and consumer buying behavior decision: What entrepreneurs should know? *Management Decision*, 59(6), 1249–1270. DOI: 10.1108/MD-10-2019-1461

Paley, N. (2021). *The manager's guide to competitive marketing strategies*. Routledge. DOI: 10.4324/9780203736463

Palinkas, L. A., Horwitz, S. M., Green, C. A., Wisdom, J. P., Duan, N., & Hoagwood, K. (2013). Purposeful sampling for qualitative data collection and analysis in mixed method implementation research. *Administration and Policy in Mental Health*, 42(5), 533–544. DOI: 10.1007/s10488-013-0528-y PMID: 24193818

Palisidis, G., Giazitzi, K., Karathanos, V., & Boskou, G. (2016). Nutritional application software for restaurants: The tool of customer satisfaction and behaviour. *International Journal of Electronic Customer Relationship Management*, 10(2–4), 198–215. DOI: 10.1504/IJECRM.2016.082197

Pallant, J. (2020). SPSS Survival Manual. In Routledge eBooks. https://doi.org/DOI: 10.4324/9781003117452

Pallarés, N., Berrada, H., Ferrer, E., Zhou, J., Wang, M., Barba, F. J., & Brnčić, M. (2021). Ultrasound processing: A sustainable alternative. In *Sustainable Production Technology in Food* (pp. 155–164). Academic Press. DOI: 10.1016/B978-0-12-821233-2.00006-X

Paluch, S., & Wirtz, J. (2020). Artificial intelligence and robots in the service encounter. *Journal of Service Management Research*, 4(1), 3–21. DOI: 10.15358/2511-8676-2020-1-3

Pandey, S. (2023). AI-Lead Supply Chain Optimization in Food Industry. *Journal of Biology, 12*(1), 001-007.

Pang, J., & Hammond, D. (2013). Efficacy and Consumer Preferences for Different Approaches to Calorie Labeling on Menus. *Journal of Nutrition Education and Behavior*, 45(6), 669–675. DOI: 10.1016/j.jneb.2013.06.005 PMID: 23928179

Pantano, E., & Servidio, R. (2012). Modeling innovative points of sales through virtual and immersive technologies. *Journal of Retailing and Consumer Services*, 19(3), 279–286. DOI: 10.1016/j.jretconser.2012.02.002

Pantelidis, I. S. (2010). Electronic Meal Experience: A content analysis of online restaurant comments. *Cornell Hospitality Quarterly*, 51(4), 483–491. DOI: 10.1177/1938965510378574

Pantoja, F., & Borges, A. (2021). Background music tempo effects on food evaluations and purchase intentions. *Journal of Retailing and Consumer Services*, 63, 102730. DOI: 10.1016/j.jretconser.2021.102730

Papagiannis, H. (2020, March 18). How AR and VR can be used for virtual travel and tourism in a time of self-isolation and closed borders.

Papagiannis, H. (2017). *Augmented human: How technology is shaping the new reality*. O'Reilly Media.

Papleontiou-Louca, E. (2007). The concept and instruction of metacognition. *An international journal of teachers' professional development, 7*(1), 9-30. https://doi.org/DOI: 10.1080/13664530300200184

Parasuraman, A. (2000). Technology Readiness Index (Tri): A multiple-item scale to measure readiness to embrace new technologies. *Journal of Service Research*, 2(4), 307–320. https://journals.sagepub.com .singaporetech.remotexs.co/doi/epdf/10.1177/109467050024001. DOI: 10.1177/109467050024001

Parasuraman, A., & Colby, C. (2014). An updated and streamlined technology readiness index. *Journal of Service Research*, 18(1), 59–74. DOI: 10.1177/1094670514539730

Parasuraman, A., & Colby, C. L. (2001). *Techno-ready marketing: How and why customers adopt new technologies*. The Free Press.

Park, D. H., Lee, J., & Han, I. (2007). The effect of on-line consumer reviews on consumer purchasing intention: The moderating role of involvement. *International Journal of Electronic Commerce*, 11(4), 125–148. DOI: 10.2753/JEC1086-4415110405

Park, H., Jiang, S., Lee, O.-K. D., & Chang, Y. (2024). Exploring the Attractiveness of Service Robots in the Hospitality Industry: Analysis of Online Reviews. *Information Systems Frontiers*, 26(1), 41–61. DOI: 10.1007/s10796-021-10207-8

Park, M., Нааман, M., & Berger, J. (2021). A Data-Driven Study of view duration on YouTube. *Proceedings of the International AAAI Conference on Web and Social Media, 10*(1), 651–654. https://doi .org/DOI: 10.1609/icwsm.v10i1.14781

Parviainen, P., Tihinen, M., Kääriäinen, J., & Teppola, S. (2017). Tackling the digitalization challenge: How to benefit from digitalization in practice. *International Journal of Information Systems and Project Management*, 5(1), 63–77. DOI: 10.12821/ijispm050104

Patel, D., & Shah, R. (2022). Enhancing Consumer Satisfaction through AI powered Food Quality Measures. *Journal of Quality Assurance in Hospitality & Tourism*, 12(1), 57–68.

Patel, K., Patel, S., Scholar, P., & Salazar, C. (2016). *Internet of Things-IOT: Definition*. Characteristics, Architecture, Enabling Technologies, Application & Future Challenges.

Patel, N., & Shah, R. (2023). Social media and the promotion of plant-based diets: A case study of vegan influencers. *Appetite*, 181, 106381.

Paulo, D. A. (2017). *In Singapore, the race to dethrone cash as king of payments, with lessons from China | moni*. Moni. https://www.monigroup.com/tc/node/97

Paulraj, M. S., Nuzhat, S., & Hussain, C. M. (2021). *Source reduction and waste minimization*. Elsevier.

Paul, S. K., Karuppiah, K., Sankaranarayanan, B., & Ali, S. M. (2023). Barriers for Sustainable Supply Chain Management and Their Overcoming Strategies in Context of the Indian Automobile Industry. In *Data Analytics for Supply Chain Networks* (pp. 129–165). Springer International Publishing. DOI: 10.1007/978-3-031-29823-3_5

Pellissier, H. (2012). Recent developments in asymmetric organocatalytic domino reactions. *Advanced Synthesis & Catalysis*, 354(2–3), 237–294. DOI: 10.1002/adsc.201100714

Pellissier, R. (2012). The use of technology in the food service industry: A case study of Domino's Pizza. *Journal of Foodservice Business Research*, 15(2), 99–112. DOI: 10.1080/15378020.2012.685054

Peng, J., Peng, Z., Lei, S., & Xie, L. (2024). Family-customer happiness and its impact on customer citizenship behavior: A study of parent–child consumption in robot restaurants. *Tourism Management Perspectives*, 53, 101273. Advance online publication. DOI: 10.1016/j.tmp.2024.101273

Peraković, D., Periša, M., & Zorić, P. (2020). Challenges and Issues of ICT in Industry 4.0. In Ivanov, V., Trojanowska, J., Machado, J., Liaposhchenko, O., Zajac, J., Pavlenko, I., Edl, M., & Perakovic, D. (Eds.), *Advances in Design, Simulation and Manufacturing* (pp. 259–269). Springer International Publishing. DOI: 10.1007/978-3-030-22365-6_26

Pereira, D., Bozzato, A., Dario, P., & Ciuti, G. (2022, July). Towards Foodservice Robotics: A Taxonomy of Actions of Foodservice Workers and a Critical Review of Supportive Technology. *IEEE Transactions on Automation Science and Engineering*, 19(3), 1820–1858. DOI: 10.1109/TASE.2021.3129077

Peremutter, S. M. J. (2023, April 17). 10 of the worst food safety scandals in recent history. *Xtalk*. https://xtalks.com/10-of-the-worst-food-safety-scandals-in-recent-history-3435/

Peschel, A. O., & Aschemann-Witzel, J. (2020). Sell more for less or less for more? The role of transparency in consumer response to upcycled food products. *Journal of Cleaner Production*, 273, 122884. DOI: 10.1016/j.jclepro.2020.122884

Peters, K., Chen, Y., Kaplan, A. M., Ognibeni, B., & Pauwels, K. (2013). Social media metrics — A framework and guidelines for managing social media. *Journal of Interactive Marketing*, 27(4), 281–298. DOI: 10.1016/j.intmar.2013.09.007

Petit, O., Velasco, C., & Spence, C. (2019). Digital sensory marketing: Integrating new technologies into multisensory online experience. *Journal of Interactive Marketing*, 45(1), 42–61. DOI: 10.1016/j.intmar.2018.07.004

Phelan, S. (2011). Case study research: Design and methods. *Evaluation and Research in Education*, 24(3), 221–222. DOI: 10.1080/09500790.2011.582317

Pickering, C., & Byrne, J. (2014). The benefits of publishing systematic quantitative literature reviews for PhD candidates and other early-career researchers. *Higher Education Research & Development*, 33(3), 534–548. DOI: 10.1080/07294360.2013.841651

Pietrosanto, A., Scarfato, P., Maio, L., Nobile, M., & Incarnato, L. (2020). Evaluation of the suitability of poly(lactide)/poly(butylene-adipate-co-terephthalate) blown films for chilled and frozen food packaging applications. *Polymers*, 12(4), 804. DOI: 10.3390/polym12040804 PMID: 32260170

Pileliene, L., & Zikiene, K. (2017). Customer loyalty to a grocery retailer: differences between urban and rural areas of Lithuania. *Research for rural development, 2*, 203-209.

Pincheira Caro, M. R., Ali, M. S., Vecchio, M., & Giaffreda, R. (2018). *Blockchain-based traceability in Agri-Food supply chain management: A practical implementation.* DOI: 10.1109/IOT-TUSCANY.2018.8373021

Pine, B. J., & Gilmore, J. H. (1999). *The experience economy: Work is theatre & every business a stage*. Harvard Business School Press.

Pine, B. J., & Gilmore, J. H. (2013). The experience economy: past, present and future. In Sundbo, J., & Sørensen, F. (Eds.), *Handbook on the Experience Economy* (pp. 21–44). Edward Elgar. DOI: 10.4337/9781781004227.00007

Polman, C. H., Reingold, S. C., Banwell, B., Clanet, M., Cohen, J. A., Filippi, M., Fujihara, K., Havrdova, E., Hutchinson, M., Kappos, L., Lublin, F. D., Montalban, X., O'Connor, P., Sandberg-Wollheim, M., Thompson, A. J., Waubant, E., Weinshenker, B., & Wolinsky, J. S. (2011). Diagnostic criteria for multiple sclerosis: 2010 Revisions to the McDonald criteria. *Annals of Neurology*, 69(2), 292–302. DOI: 10.1002/ana.22366 PMID: 21387374

Popescu, P., Popa, E., Miteluţ, A., & Popa, M. (2020). Development of recyclable and biodegradable food packaging materials – opportunities and risks. *Current Trends in Natural Sciences*, 9(17), 142–146. DOI: 10.47068/ctns.2020.v9i17.016

Pour, M. J., Rafiei, K., Khani, M., & Sabrirazm, A. (2021). Gamification and customer experience: The mediating role of brand engagement in online grocery retailing. *Nankai Business Review International.*

Poushter, J. (2019). The future of retail: Virtual and augmented reality. *Journal of Retailing and Consumer Services*, 48, 26–34.

Prasad, C. J., & Raghu, Y. (2020). Determinant Attributes of Online Grocery Shopping in India - An Empirical Analysis. *International Journal of Advanced Science and Technology*, 29(7), 10754–10764.

Prathibanandhi, K., Janani, R., Shruthi, M., Sivaprasad, R., Yaashuwanth, C., & Malini, V. (2022). Augmented Reality-Based Restaurants. *2022 International Conference on Power, Energy, Control and Transmission Systems (ICPECTS)*, 1–4. DOI: 10.1109/ICPECTS56089.2022.10047608

Priananda, I., Stevani, M., Sutanto, T. I., & Mariani, M. (2020, March). Grassroots economy towards cashless society: An empirical analysis Of micro-merchant's readiness in continuing the usage of cashless payment system. *International Journal of Scientific & Technology Research*, 9(3). https://reader.elsevier.com/reader/sd/pii/S0160791X21000294?token=4D1C0461504512047F3532BE345138CF51B709BF769AD7FD759A2B73AA1BBF361C4111C97FF6D958CED786437100BDEA&originRegion=eu-west-1&originCreation=20230313043349

Primasiwi, C., Irawan, M. I., & Ambarwati, R. (2021). Key Performance Indicators for Influencer Marketing on Instagram. *2nd International Conference on Business and Management of Technology (Iconbmt 2020)*, 154–163. DOI: 10.2991/aebmr.k.210510.027

Priyadarshi, R., Purohit, S., Roy, S., Ghosh, T., Rhim, J., & Han, S. (2022). Antiviral biodegradable food packaging and edible coating materials in the COVID-19 era: A mini-review. *Coatings*, 12(5), 577. DOI: 10.3390/coatings12050577

Prowse, R., Lee, K., Chen, E., Zuo, F., Hammond, D., & Hobin, E. (2020). Testing the efficacy of and parents' preferences for nutrition labels on children's menus from a full-service chain restaurant: Results of an online experiment. *Public Health Nutrition*, 23(10), 1820–1831. DOI: 10.1017/S1368980019004488 PMID: 32308190

Pulizzi, J. (2014). *Epic content marketing: How to tell a different story, break through the clutter, and win more customers by marketing less*. McGraw-Hill Education.

Purwandoko, P. B., Seminar, K. B., Sutrisno, , & Sugiyanta, . (2018). Framework for Design of Traceability System on Organic Rice Certification. *IOP Conference Series. Earth and Environmental Science*, 147(1), 12044. DOI: 10.1088/1755-1315/147/1/012044

Puvaneswary, S. (2024). Malaysia to propel smart hotel innovations. TTG Asia. https://www.ttgasia.com/2024/07/15/malaysia-to-propel-smart-hotel-innovations

Qayyum, A. (2022). Adoption of mobile food ordering apps for O2O food delivery services during the COVID-19 outbreak. *British Food Journal*, 124(11), 3368–3395. DOI: 10.1108/BFJ-09-2020-0781

Qian, J., Dai, B., Wang, B., Zha, Y., & Song, Q. (2022). Traceability in food processing: Problems, methods, and performance evaluations—A review. *Critical Reviews in Food Science and Nutrition*, 62(3), 679–692. DOI: 10.1080/10408398.2020.1825925 PMID: 33016094

Qin, Z., & Xu, W. (2023). Social media marketing for food brands: The role of consumer-generated content. *Journal of Brand Management*, 30(1), 84–97.

Quek, R. Y. C., Jen, G. H., & Henry, C. J. (2019). Energy density of ethnic cuisines in Singaporean hawker centres: A comparative study of Chinese, Malay and Indian foods. *Malaysian Journal of Nutrition*, 25(1), 171–184. DOI: 10.31246/mjn-2018-0113.

Quintana-García, C., Benavides-Chicón, C. G., & Marchante-Lara, M. (2021). Does a green supply chain improve corporate reputation? Empirical evidence from European manufacturing sectors. *Industrial Marketing Management*, 92, 344–353. DOI: 10.1016/j.indmarman.2019.12.011

Qu, Y., Cieślik, A., Fang, S., & Qing, Y. (2023). The role of online interaction in user stickiness of social commerce: The shopping value perspective. *Digital Business*, 3(2), 100061. DOI: 10.1016/j.digbus.2023.100061

Rahaman, J., & Batcha, M. S. (2023). How is industry 4.0 changing food technology? A scientometric profile. *Journal of Data Science, Informetrics, and Citation Studies*, 2(1), 25–31. DOI: 10.5530/jcitation.2.1.4

Rahman, O., Fung, B. C. M., & Chen, Z. (2020). Young Chinese consumers' choice between product-related and sustainable cues—The Effects of Gender Differences and Consumer Innovativeness. *Sustainability (Basel)*, 12(9), 3818. DOI: 10.3390/su12093818

Raj, M., Sundararajan, A., & You, C. (2020). COVID-19 and Digital Resilience: Evidence from Uber Eats. SSRN *Electronic Journal.* DOI: 10.2139/ssrn.3625638

Rajeh Hanaysha, J., Sharma, A., & M. Momani, A. (2021). An Exploration of Social Media Marketing Features and Brand Loyalty in the Fast-Food Industry. Journal of Content Community and Communication.

Rakshit, S., Islam, N., Mondal, S., & Paul, T. (2022). An integrated social network marketing metric for business-to-business SMEs. *Journal of Business Research*, 150, 73–88. DOI: 10.1016/j.jbusres.2022.06.006

Ramakrishnan, T., Mohan Gift, M. D., Chitradevi, S., Jegan, R., Hency Jose, P. S., Nagaraja, H. N., & Hailegiorgis, S. M. (2022). Study of numerous resins used in polymer matrix composite materials. *Advances in Materials Science and Engineering*, 2022(1), 1088926.

Ramakrishna, S., Ngowi, A., De Jager, H., & Awuzie, B. O. (2020). Emerging Industrial Revolution: Symbiosis of Industry 4.0 and Circular Economy: The Role of Universities. *Science, Technology & Society*, 25(3), 505–525. DOI: 10.1177/0971721820912918

Ramanathan, U., & Tey, Y. (2021). Predictive analytics for inventory management in foodservice: A case study of Domino's Pizza. *British Food Journal*, 123(8), 2784–2797. DOI: 10.1108/BFJ-11-2020-1029

Ramundo, L., Taisch, M., & Terzi, S. (2016). *State of the art of technology in the food sector value chain towards the IoT*. DOI: 10.1109/RTSI.2016.7740612

Rane, N. (2023). Enhancing customer loyalty through Artificial Intelligence (AI), Internet of Things (IoT), and Big Data technologies: improving customer satisfaction, engagement, relationship, and experience. *Internet of Things (IoT), and Big Data Technologies: Improving Customer Satisfaction, Engagement, Relationship, and Experience (October 13, 2023).*

Rantala, J., Salminen, K., Raisamo, R., & Surakka, V. (2013). Touch gestures in communicating emotional intention via vibrotactile stimulation. *International Journal of Human-Computer Studies*, 71(6), 679–690. DOI: 10.1016/j.ijhcs.2013.02.004

Rao, S., & Maheshwari, V. (2023). The impact of social media on food choices and health outcomes. *Journal of Public Health Policy*, 44(2), 245–259.

Rastegar, N., Flaherty, J., Liang, L J., & Choi, H C. (2021, March 1). The adoption of self-service kiosks in quick-service restaurants. Varna University of Management, 27, 2709-2709. https://doi.org/DOI: 10.54055/ejtr.v27i.2139

Ratilla, M., Karolyova, D., Haider, L., Dohnalova, Z., & Horak, M. (2022). NUDGING HEALTHY RESTAURANT SELECTION IN AN ONLINE FOOD DELIVERY PLATFORM: THE EFFECT OF AVAILABILITY AND PRIMING. *Transformations in Business & Economics*, 21(3C), 395–411.

Ravandi, B., & Jovanovic, N. (2019). Impact of plate size on food waste: Agent-based simulation of food consumption. *Resources, Conservation and Recycling*, 149, 550–565. DOI: 10.1016/j.resconrec.2019.05.033

Ray, E., & Merle, P. (2021). Disgusting Face, Disease-ridden Place?: Emoji Influence on the Interpretation of Restaurant Inspection Reports. *Health Communication*, 36(14), 1867–1878. DOI: 10.1080/10410236.2020.1802867 PMID: 32806958

Ray, P., Duraipandian, R., Kiranmai, G., Rao, R., & Jose, M. J. (2021). An Exploratory Study of Risks and Food Insecurity in the Agri Supply Chain. *Shanlax International Journal of Management*, 8(S1-Feb, no. S1), 1–12. DOI: 10.34293/management.v8iS1-Feb.3752

Reddy, G., & Dam, R. M. v. (2020) Food, culture, and identity in multicultural societies: Insights from Singapore. *Appetite, 149*. ScienceDirect. https://doi.org/DOI: 10.1016/j.appet.2020.104633

Reddy, M. S., & Krishna, S. M. (2019). Influential role of retail service quality in food and grocery retailing: A comparative study between traditional and multi-channel retailing. *Int J Management and Business Research*, 9(2), 68–73.

Reddy, S. R. B. (2022). Enhancing Customer Experience through AI-Powered Marketing Automation: Strategies and Best Practices for Industry 4.0. *Journal of Artificial Intelligence Research*, 2(1), 36–46.

Régnier, P. (2023). Innovation, appropriate technologies and entrepreneurship for global sustainability development: A review until the early twenty-first century. *The Journal of Entrepreneurship*, 32(2, suppl), S12–S26. DOI: 10.1177/09713557231201115

Reinholdsson, T., Hedesström, M., Ejelöv, E., Hansla, A., Bergquist, M., Svenfelt, A., & Nilsson, A. (2023). Nudging green food: The effects of a hedonic cue, menu position, a warm-glow cue, and a descriptive norm. *Journal of Consumer Behaviour*, 22(3), 557–568. DOI: 10.1002/cb.2129

Reis, J., Amorim, M., Melao, N., Cohen, Y., & Rodrigues, M. (2020). *Digitalization: A Literature Review and Research Agenda.*, DOI: 10.1007/978-3-030-43616-2_47

Rejab, A., Keohj, J. G., Zailani, S., Treiblmaier, H., & Rjeab, K. (2020). Blockchain technology in the food industry: A review of potentials, challenges and future research directions. *Logistics (Basel)*, 4(4), 27. Advance online publication. DOI: 10.3390/logistics4040027

Rejeb, A., Keogh, J. G., & Treiblmaier, H. (2019). Leveraging the Internet of Things and Blockchain Technology in Supply Chain Management. *Future Internet*, 11(7), 161. DOI: 10.3390/fi11070161

Rejeb, A., Suhaiza, Z., Rejeb, K., Seuring, S., & Treiblmaier, H. (2022). The Internet of Things and the circular economy: A systematic literature review and research agenda. *Journal of Cleaner Production*, 350(131439), 131439. DOI: 10.1016/j.jclepro.2022.131439

Rennings, K. (2000). Redefining innovation — Eco-innovation research and the contribution from ecological economics. *Ecological Economics*, 32(2), 319–332. DOI: 10.1016/S0921-8009(99)00112-3

Restrepo, B. J. (2017). Calorie Labeling in Chain Restaurants and Body Weight: Evidence from New York. *Health Economics*, 26(10), 1191–1209. DOI: 10.1002/hec.3389 PMID: 27451966

Rha, J., Nam, Y., Yoon, J., & Lee, B. (2023). Korean consumers' use and concerns about food delivery service. *Nutrition Research and Practice*, 17(3), 583. DOI: 10.4162/nrp.2023.17.3.583 PMID: 37266118

Riaz, H., Ahmed, H., & Akhtar, S. (2019). *The Role of Social Media Marketing on Building Brand Equity (An Insight of Fast Food Industry of Pakistan)*. New Media and Mass Communication. DOI: 10.22161/ijels.4.2.30

Riccioli, F., Moruzzo, R., Zhang, Z., Zhao, J., Tang, Y., Tinacci, L., Boncinelli, F., De Martino, D., & Guidi, A. (2020). Willingness to pay in main cities of Zheijiang provice (China) for quality and safety in food market. *Food Control*, 108, 106831. DOI: 10.1016/j.foodcont.2019.106831

Ricky, M. Y. (2014). Mobile Food Ordering Application using Android OS Platform. *EPJ Web of Conferences*, 68, 00041. DOI: 10.1051/epjconf/20146800041

Rifin, A., Harianto, , Feryanto, , & Herawati, . (2022). Strengthening Supply Chain for Post COVID-19 Food Security: An Exploratory Research Review. *Sustainability Science and Resources*, 3, 85–107. DOI: 10.55168/ssr2809-6029.2022.3005

Rinalducci, S. N. (2023). Industry 1.0 to 4.0 – Brief History of the Industrial Revolution. *Sustainability Success*. https://sustainability-success.com/industry-1-0-to-4-0-2-3-revolution

Rita, P., Eiriz, V., & Conde, B. (2023). The role of information for the customer journey in mobile food ordering apps. *Journal of Services Marketing*, 37(5), 574–591. DOI: 10.1108/JSM-11-2021-0407

Rivera, S., & Walker, T. (2023). Social media campaigns and their effectiveness in the organic food market. *Journal of Agricultural and Food Marketing*, 15(2), 197–210.

Riza, A.F. & Wijayanti, D.M. (2018). The Triangle of Sensory Marketing Model: Does it Stimulate Brand Experience and Loyalty? *Jurnal Bisnis dan Manajemen, 8* (1), 57–66. http://dx.doi.org/DOI: 10.15408/ess.v8i1.6058

Robbins, T. (2024). Future of AI in hospitality: A managerial perspective. *Journal of Hospitality and Tourism Technology*. Advance online publication. DOI: 10.1108/JHTT-12-2023-0145

Roberto, C. A., Haynos, A. F., Schwartz, M. B., Brownell, K. D., & White, M. A. (2013). Calorie estimation accuracy and menu labeling perceptions among individuals with and without binge eating and/or purging disorders. *Eating and Weight Disorders*, 18(3), 255–261. DOI: 10.1007/s40519-013-0035-x PMID: 23760909

Robotics, M. (2021). *Moley Robotic Kitchen: The future of cooking*. Moley Robotics.

Rohit, A. K., & Mueller, F. (2019). Human-Food Interaction. *Foundations and Trends in Human–Computer Interaction*, 12(4), 238–415. DOI: 10.1561/1100000074

Roman, J. (2024). The hidden health crisis: microplastics and their medical consequences. *Journal of Education Health and Sport*, p. 72, 51690. DOI: 10.12775/JEHS.2024.72.51690

Romanov, A., & Barinova, N. (2024). Digital transformation of the food service industry: AI's role in supply chain and inventory management. *Service Science*. Advance online publication. DOI: 10.1287/serv.2024.0034

Rosário, A. T., & Dias, J. C. (2022). Industry 4.0 and marketing: Towards an integrated future research agenda. *Journal of Sensor and Actuator Networks*, 11(3), 30. DOI: 10.3390/jsan11030030

Rowley, J. (2008). Understanding digital content marketing. *Journal of Marketing Management*, 24(5-6), 517–540. DOI: 10.1362/026725708X325977

Ruangkanjanases, A., Sirisrisakulchai, P., Sonata, N., & Simamora, B. H. (2021). Predicting consumer intention to adopt online grocery shopping: A comparative study between millennials in Thailand and Indonesia. *International Journal of Electronic Commerce Studies*, 12(2), 193–208. DOI: 10.7903/ijecs.1894

Rudd, R. E., Anderson, J. E., Oppenheimer, S., & Nath, C. (2023). Health Literacy: An Update of Medical and Public Health Literature. In J. Comings, B. Garner, & C. Smith, Review of Adult Learning and Literacy, Volume 7 (1st ed., pp. 175–204). Routledge. DOI: 10.4324/9781003417996-6

Ruiz-Mafe, C., Bigné-Alcañiz, E., & Currás-Pérez, R. (2020). The effect of emotions, eWOM quality and online review sequence on consumer intention to follow advice obtained from digital services. *Journal of Service Management*, 31(3), 465–487. DOI: 10.1108/JOSM-11-2018-0349

Ruiz-Molina, M. E., Gómez-Borja, M. Á., & Mollá-Descals, A. (2021). Can offline–online congruence explain online loyalty in electronic commerce? *International Journal of Retail & Distribution Management*, 49(9), 1271–1294. DOI: 10.1108/IJRDM-02-2020-0060

Rust, R. T., Rand, W., Huang, M.-H., Stephen, A. T., Brooks, G., & Chabuk, T. (2021). Real-time brand reputation tracking using social media. *Journal of Marketing*, 85(4), 21–43. DOI: 10.1177/0022242921995173

Saadat, S., Pandya, H., Dey, A., & Rawtani, D. (2022). Food forensics: Techniques for authenticity determination of food products. *Forensic Science International*, 333, 111243. Advance online publication. DOI: 10.1016/j.forsciint.2022.111243 PMID: 35240505

Sachdeva, I., & Goel, S. (2015). Retail store environment and customer experience: A paradigm. *Journal of Fashion Marketing and Management*, 19(3), 290–298. DOI: 10.1108/JFMM-03-2015-0021

Sadilek, A., Kautz, H., DiPrete, L., Labus, B., Portman, E., Teitel, J., & Silenzio, V. (2017). Deploying nEmesis: Preventing Foodborne Illness by Data Mining Social Media. *AI Magazine*, 38(1), 37–48. DOI: 10.1609/aimag.v38i1.2711

Safeer, A. A., Abrar, M., Liu, H., & Yuanqiong, H. (2022). Effects of perceived brand localness and perceived brand globalness on consumer behavioral intentions in emerging markets. *Management Decision*, 60(9), 2482–2502. DOI: 10.1108/MD-10-2021-1296

Saghiri, S., Aktas, E., & Mohammadipour, M. (2023). Grocery omnichannel perishable inventories: performance measures and influencing factors. *International Journal of Operations & Production Management*, (ahead-of-print).

Sağkaya Güngör, A., & Ozansoy Çadırcı, T. (2022). Understanding digital consumer: A review, synthesis, and future research agenda. *International Journal of Consumer Studies*, 46(5), 1829–1858. DOI: 10.1111/ijcs.12809

Saha, J., Saha, A., Chatterjee, A., Agrawal, S., Saha, A., Kar, A., & Saha, H. (2018). *Advanced IOT based combined remote health monitoring, home automation and alarm system*. DOI: 10.1109/CCWC.2018.8301659

Sahi, A. M., Khalid, H., Abbas, A. F., & Khatib, S. F. (2021, December). The evolving research of customer adoption of digital payment: Learning from content and statistical analysis of the literature. *Journal of Open Innovation*, 7(4), 230. DOI: 10.3390/joitmc7040230

Sahoo, M., Vishwakarma, S., Panigrahi, C., & Kumar, J. (2021). Nanotechnology: Current applications and future scope in food. *Food Frontiers*, 2(1), 3–22. DOI: 10.1002/fft2.58

Saito, K., & Yoshida, M. (2023). The influence of social media on dietary behaviors and food preferences among adolescents. *Journal of Adolescence*, 97, 32–45.

Sajid, & Haddara. (2016) NFC mobile payments: Are we ready for them? *016 SAI Computing Conference (SAI)*, 960–967. https://doi.org/DOI: 10.1109/SAI.2016.7556096

Sakina, F., & Yafiz, M. (2023). Using customer satisfaction as a mediating variable to boost service quality and build trust in repeat business. *JURNAL MANAJEMEN BISNIS*, 10(1), 44–56. DOI: 10.33096/jmb.v10i1.468

Saleem, M., Khan, M. M., Ahmed, M. E., Shah, S. N., & Surti, S. R. (2018). Online grocery shopping and consumer perception: a case of Karachi market in Pakistan. *Journal of Internet and e-Business studies, 2018*, 1-13.

Salim, P. (2022). Immersive Technology Study As A Science Innovation to Enhance Modern Dining Experience.

Samonte, W. G. A. (2024). Event industry green practices and management strategies towards client satisfaction in Panay Island: Basis of a sustainability framework. *International Journal of Research Studies in Management*, 12(10), 219–235. DOI: 10.5861/ijrsm.2024.1246

Samsudin, A., Izzuddin, M., Kamarudin, W., Manap, M., & Ngah, H. (2022). Consumers' motivational factors on the use of online food-delivery apps in Malaysia. *International Journal of Academic Research in Business & Social Sciences*, 12(11). Advance online publication. DOI: 10.6007/IJARBSS/v12-i11/15617

Sander, B. (2021). Democratic disruption in the age of social media: Between marketized and structural conceptions of human rights law. *European Journal of International Law*, 32(1), 159–193. DOI: 10.1093/ejil/chab022

Sangeetha, J., Mundaragi, A., Thangadurai, D., Maxim, S. S., Pandhari, R. M., & Alabhai, J. M. (2019). Nanobiotechnology for agricultural productivity, food security and environmental sustainability. *Nanotechnology for Agriculture: Crop Production & Protection*, 1-23.

Santana, S., Brach, C., Harris, L., Ochiai, E., Blakey, C., Bevington, F., Kleinman, D., & Pronk, N. (2021). Updating Health Literacy for Healthy People 2030: Defining Its Importance for a New Decade in Public Health. *Journal of Public Health Management and Practice*, 27(Supplement 6), S258–S264. DOI: 10.1097/PHH.0000000000001324 PMID: 33729194

Santos, Z. R., Cheung, C. M. K., Coelho, P. S., & Rita, P. (2022). Consumer engagement in social media brand communities: A literature review. *International Journal of Information Management*, 63, 102457. DOI: 10.1016/j.ijinfomgt.2021.102457

Saphores, J. D., & Xu, L. (2021). E-shopping changes and the state of E-grocery shopping in the Evidence by national travel and time-use surveys. *Research in Transportation Economics*, 87, 100864. DOI: 10.1016/j.retrec.2020.100864

Sardjono, W., & Perdana, W. (2019). Green information technology readiness model using factor analysis method in Indonesia. *Social Economics and Ecology International Journal (Seeij)*, 3(2), 13–21. DOI: 10.21512/seeij.v3i2.6216

Sarmah, B., Kamboj, S., & Rahman, Z. (2017). Co-creation in hotel service innovation using smart phone apps: An empirical study. *International Journal of Contemporary Hospitality Management*, 29(10), 2647–2667. DOI: 10.1108/IJCHM-12-2015-0681

Sarmiento, C. V., & El Hanandeh, A. (2018). Customers' perceptions and expectations of environmentally sustainable restaurant and the development of green index: The case of the Gold Coast, Australia. *Sustainable Production and Consumption*, 15, 16–24. DOI: 10.1016/j.spc.2018.04.001

Saulais, L., Corcuff, R., & Boonefaes, E. (2023). Natural and healthy? Consumers knowledge, understanding and preferences regarding naturalness and healthiness of processed foods. *International Journal of Gastronomy and Food Science*, 31, 100662. DOI: 10.1016/j.ijgfs.2023.100662

Schawbel, D. (2019, November, 15). *How artificial intelligence is redefining the role of manager*. World Economic Forum. https://www.weforum.org/agenda/2019/11/how-artificial-intelligence-is-redefining-the-role-of-manager/

Scherer, R., Siddiq, F., & Tondeur, J. (2019). The technology acceptance model (TAM): A meta-analytic structural equation modeling approach to explaining teachers' adoption of digital technology in education. *Computers & Education*, 128, 13–35. DOI: 10.1016/j.compedu.2018.09.009

Schermerhorn, J. R., Bachrach, D. G., & Cohn, M. A. (2020). Management: A global, innovative, and entrepreneurial perspective. *Journal of Business Research*, 118, 116–126. DOI: 10.1016/j.jbusres.2020.06.046

Schifferstein, H. N., Kudrowitz, B., & Breuer, C. (2020). Food Perception and Aesthetics Linking sensory science to culinary practice. *Journal of Culinary Science & Technology*, 20(4), 293–335. DOI: 10.1080/15428052.2020.1824833

Schiffman, L. G., & Wisenblit, J. (2019). *Consumer behavior* (12th ed.). Pearson.

Schirmer, A. (2022). *Payment methods in China: How China became a mobile-first nation*. Daxueconsulting. https://daxueconsulting.com/payment-methods-in-china/

Schiro, J. L., Shan, L. C., Tatlow-Golden, M., Li, C., & Wall, P. (2020). # Healthy: Smart digital food safety and nutrition communication strategies—a critical commentary. *NPJ Science of Food*, 4(1), 14. DOI: 10.1038/s41538-020-00074-z PMID: 33083546

Schlussel, H., & Frosh, P. (2023). The taste of video: Facebook videos as multi-sensory experiences. *Convergence (London)*, 29(4), 980–996. DOI: 10.1177/13548565231179958

Schnack, A., Wright, M. J., & Holdershaw, J. L. (2020). An exploratory investigation of shopper behaviour in an immersive virtual reality store. *Journal of Consumer Behaviour*, 19(2), 182–195. DOI: 10.1002/cb.1803

Schober, P., Boer, C., & Schwarte, L. A. (2018). Correlation Coefficients: Appropriate use and interpretation. *Anesthesia and Analgesia*, 126(5), 1763–1768. DOI: 10.1213/ANE.0000000000002864 PMID: 29481436

Scholten, H., Verdouw, C. N., Beulens, A., & van der Vorst, J. G. A. J. (2016). 2 - Defining and Analyzing Traceability Systems in Food Supply Chains. In Espiñeira, M., & Santaclara, F. J. (Eds.), *Advances in Food Traceability Techniques and Technologies* (pp. 9–33). Woodhead Publishing., DOI: 10.1016/B978-0-08-100310-7.00002-8

Schwab, K. (2016). *The Fourth Industrial Revolution*. Penguin Random House.

Scott, D. M. (2015). *The new rules of marketing & PR: How to use social media, online video, mobile applications, blogs, news releases, and viral marketing to reach buyers directly* (5th ed.). Wiley. DOI: 10.1002/9781119172499.ch02

Seadon, J. K. (2010). Sustainable waste management systems. *Journal of Cleaner Production*, 18(16-17), 1639–1651. DOI: 10.1016/j.jclepro.2010.07.009

Seal, P. P. (2023). Robots in the hotel kitchen. *In Advances in environmental engineering and green technologies book series* (pp. 89–97). DOI: 10.4018/978-1-6684-9094-5.ch006

Seal, P. P. (2023). Robots in the Hotel Kitchen: The Future Chef. In Impactful Technologies Transforming the Food Industry (pp. 89-97). IGI Global.

Sebatjane, M. (2022). The impact of preservation technology investments on lot-sizing and shipment strategies in a three-echelon food supply chain involving growing and deteriorating items. *Operations Research Perspectives*, 9, 100241. DOI: 10.1016/j.orp.2022.100241

Secondi, L., Principato, L., & Mattia, G. (2019). Can digital solutions help in the minimization of out-of-home waste? An analysis from the client and business perspective. *British Food Journal*, 122(5), 1341–1359. DOI: 10.1108/BFJ-03-2019-0205

Seetharam, A., Kumar, T., Gupta, H., & Karia, D. (2023). A Web-based AR Solution for Restaurant Menus to Reduce Food Waste. *2023 Global Conference on Information Technologies and Communications (GCITC)*, 1–9. DOI: 10.1109/GCITC60406.2023.10426326

Selvakumar, P. (2024). Emerging Engineering Technologies: Design, Development, and Industrial Applications of IoT-Based Aquaculture Monitoring System. In El Kacimi, Y., & Alaoui, K. (Eds.), *Emerging Engineering Technologies and Industrial Applications* (pp. 332–341). IGI Global., DOI: 10.4018/979-8-3693-1335-0.ch016

Selvakumar, P., Mariappan, P., Shunmugam, S., Paul, R., & Jabez, S. (2024). Removal of chemicals from effluent using photobioreactor technology to improve environmental and health impacts. *Zeitschrift für Physikalische Chemie*, 2024(7), 1295–1302. Advance online publication. DOI: 10.1515/zpch-2023-0450

Selvakumar, P., Muthusamy, S., Satishkumar, D., Vigneshkumar, P., Selvamurugan, C., & Satheesh Kumar, P. (2024). AI-Powered Tools. In Satishkumar, D., & Sivaraja, M. (Eds.), *Using Real-Time Data and AI for Thrust Manufacturing* (pp. 20–42). IGI Global., DOI: 10.4018/979-8-3693-2615-2.ch002

Selvakumar, P., Palanisamy, S. K., Cinthaikinian, S., Palanisamy, V., Mariappan, R., & Selvakumar, P. K. (2024). Biosensors and its diverse applications in healthcare systems. *Zeitschrift für Physikalische Chemie*, 2024. Advance online publication. DOI: 10.1515/zpch-2023-0406

Seo, K. H. (2020, October 22). A Study on the Application of Kiosk Service as the Workplace Flexibility: The Determinants of Expanded Technology Adoption and Trust of Quick Service Restaurant Customers. *Sustainability (Basel)*, 12(21), 8790–8790. DOI: 10.3390/su12218790

Serhan, H., & Yannou-Lebris, G. (2021). The engineering of food with sustainable development goals: Policies, curriculums, business models, and practices. *International Journal of Sustainable Engineering*, 14(1), 12–25. DOI: 10.1080/19397038.2020.1722765

Shaalan, A., Agag, G., & Tourky, M. (2022). Harnessing Customer Mindset Metrics to Boost Consumer Spending: A Cross-Country study on routes to economic and business growth. *British Journal of Management*, 34(1), 442–465. DOI: 10.1111/1467-8551.12596

Shaer, N. E. (2019). Evaluating food court operation in shopping malls to enhance customer satisfaction for different market segments. *International Journal of Heritage Tourism and Hospitality, 13*(1), 152-172. ResearchGate. https://doi.org/DOI: 10.21608/ijhth.2019.35112

Shah, A. M., & Ali, M. (2020). Customers perceived value and dining choice through mobile apps in Indonesia. *Asia Pacific Journal of Marketing and Logistics*, 33(1), 1–28. DOI: 10.1108/APJML-03-2019-0167

Shahbaznezhad, H., Dolan, R., & Rashidirad, M. (2021). The role of social media content format and platform in users' engagement behavior. *Journal of Interactive Marketing*, 53(1), 47–65. DOI: 10.1016/j.intmar.2020.05.001

Shahhosseini, M., & Khalili Nasr, A. (2024). What attributes affect customer satisfaction in green restaurants? An aspect-based sentiment analysis approach. *Journal of Travel & Tourism Marketing*, 41(4), 472–490. DOI: 10.1080/10548408.2024.2306358

Shahid, S., Paul, J., Gilal, F. G., & Ansari, S. (2022). The role of sensory marketing and brand experience in building emotional attachment and brand loyalty in luxury retail stores. *Psychology and Marketing*, 39(7), 1398–1412. DOI: 10.1002/mar.21661

Shahriari, E., Torres, I. M., Zúñiga, M. Á., & Alfayez, N. (2019). Picture this: The role of mental imagery in induction of food craving – a theoretical framework based on the elaborated intrusion theory. *Journal of Consumer Marketing*, 37(1), 31–42. DOI: 10.1108/JCM-02-2018-2553

Shahril, Z., Zulkafly, H A., Ismail, N S., & Sharif, N U N M. (2021, January 28). Customer Satisfaction Towards Self-Service Kiosks for Quick Service Restaurants (QSRs) in Klang Valley., 11(13). https://doi.org/DOI: 10.6007/IJARBSS/v11-i13/8502

Shah, Z. Q. (2020). Development of Usability Framework for Projection Mapping to increase Food Dining Experience. *International Journal of Advanced Trends in Computer Science and Engineering*, 9(3), 3150–3156. DOI: 10.30534/ijatcse/2020/102932020

Shao, Z., Zhang, L., Chen, K., & Zhang, C. (2020). Examining user satisfaction and stickiness in social networking sites from a technology affordance lens: Uncovering the moderating effect of user experience. *Industrial Management & Data Systems*, 120(7), 1331–1360. DOI: 10.1108/IMDS-11-2019-0614

Sharma, D. (2023). "Consumers 'Attitude towards Using Food Delivery Apps" published by IGI Global publications. Published 29 August 2023, Pages 75-88. DOI: . Copyright © 2023, IGI Global.DOI: 10.4018/978-1-6684-9094-5.ch005

Sharma, A. P. (2021). Consumers' purchase behaviour and green marketing: A synthesis, review and agenda. *International Journal of Consumer Studies*, 45(6), 1217–1238. DOI: 10.1111/ijcs.12722

Sharma, A., Mittal, K., Kumar, S., Sharma, U., & Upadhyay, P. (2022). Impact of Artificial Intelligence and Machine Learning in the Food Industry: A Survey. In *Artificial Intelligence Applications in Agriculture and Food Quality Improvement* (pp. 190–215). IGI Global. DOI: 10.4018/978-1-6684-5141-0.ch011

Sharma, A., Zanotti, P., & Musunur, L. P. (2020). Drive through robotics: Robotic automation for last mile distribution of food and essentials during pandemics. *IEEE Access : Practical Innovations, Open Solutions*, 8, 127190–127219. DOI: 10.1109/ACCESS.2020.3007064 PMID: 34786277

Sharma, P., Nair, V., & Jyotishi, A. (2014, October). Patterns of online grocery shopping in India: an empirical study. In *Proceedings of the 2014 International Conference on Interdisciplinary Advances in Applied Computing* (pp. 1-5). DOI: 10.1145/2660859.2660939

Sharma, S., Gahlawat, V. K., Rahul, K., Mor, R. S., & Malik, M. (2021). Sustainable innovations in the food industry through artificial intelligence and big data analytics. *Logistics (Basel)*, 5(4), 66. DOI: 10.3390/logistics5040066

Sharma, S., & Patil, S. V. (2015). Key indicators of rice production and consumption, correlation between them and supplydemand prediction. *International Journal of Productivity and Performance Management*, 64(8), 1113–1137. DOI: 10.1108/IJPPM-06-2014-0088

Sharma, S., Singh, G., & Prasad, B. (2023). Portion perception and waste awareness: Investigating the effects of Augmented Reality menus on over-ordering intentions in various dining settings. *Current Issues in Tourism*, 0(0), 1–16. DOI: 10.1080/13683500.2023.2273913

Sharma, T., & Singh, A. (2021). Understanding the implications of AI on restaurant customer service. *Journal of Retailing and Consumer Services*, 59, 102–211.

Shen, B., & Chen, C. (2020). Quality management in outsourced global fashion supply chains: An exploratory case study. *Production Planning and Control*, 31(9), 757–769. DOI: 10.1080/09537287.2019.1683774

Shepherd, M., Turner, J. A., Small, B., & Wheeler, D. (2020). Priorities for science to overcome hurdles thwarting the full promise of the 'digital agriculture' revolution. *Journal of the Science of Food and Agriculture*, 100(14), 5080–5087. DOI: 10.1002/jsfa.9346 PMID: 30191570

Shereni, N. C., Saarinen, J., & Rogerson, C. M. (2022). Sustainability consciousness in the hospitality sector in Zimbabwe. In *Southern African Perspectives on Sustainable Tourism Management: Tourism and Changing Localities* (pp. 15–29). Springer International Publishing. DOI: 10.1007/978-3-030-99435-8_2

Shimmura, T., Ichikari, R., Okuma, T., Ito, H., Okada, K., & Nonaka, T. (2020). Service robot introduction to a restaurant enhances both labor productivity and service quality. *Procedia CIRP*, 88, 589–594. DOI: 10.1016/j.procir.2020.05.103

Shirazi, F., & Hajli, N. (2021). IT-enabled sustainable innovation and the global digital divides. *Sustainability (Basel)*, 13(17), 9711. DOI: 10.3390/su13179711

Shiyab, W., Ferguson, C., Rolls, K., & Halcomb, E. (2023). Solutions to address low response rates in online surveys. *European Journal of Cardiovascular Nursing*, 22(4), 441–444. DOI: 10.1093/eurjcn/zvad030 PMID: 36827086

Shukla, K. A., Sofian, A. D. A. B. A., Singh, A., Chen, W. H., Show, P. L., & Chan, Y. J. (2024). Food waste management and sustainable waste to energy: Current efforts, anaerobic digestion, incinerator and hydrothermal carbonization with a focus in Malaysia. *Journal of Cleaner Production*, 448, 141457. DOI: 10.1016/j.jclepro.2024.141457

Shumakova, E. V. (2021). Impact of Digitalization in Hotel Industry Development. Proceeding of the International Science and Technology Conference "FarEastCon 2020". Smart Innovation, Systems and Technologies, vol 227. Springer, Singapore. https://doi.org/DOI: 10.1007/978-981-16-0953-4_57

Silva, A., Prata, J., Duarte, A., Barceló, D., & Rocha-Santos, T. (2021). An urgent call to think globally and act locally on landfill disposable plastics under and after covid-19 pandemic: Pollution prevention and technological (bio) remediation solutions. *Chemical Engineering Journal*, 426, 131201. DOI: 10.1016/j.cej.2021.131201 PMID: 35791349

Silva, E. G., Cardoso, S., Bettencourt, A. F., & Ribeiro, I. A. (2022). Latest trends in sustainable polymeric food packaging films. *Foods*, 12(1), 168. DOI: 10.3390/foods12010168 PMID: 36613384

Silva, G., Dias, Á., & Rodrigues, M. (2022). Continuity of use of food delivery apps: An integrated approach to the health belief model and the technology readiness and acceptance model. *Journal of Open Innovation*, 8(3), 114. DOI: 10.3390/joitmc8030114

Silva, S. C., Duarte, P. A. O., & Almeida, S. R. (2020). How companies evaluate the ROI of social media marketing programmes: Insights from B2B and B2C. *Journal of Business and Industrial Marketing*, 35(12), 2097–2110. DOI: 10.1108/JBIM-06-2019-0291

Silvestri, B. (2020). The future of fashion: How the quest for digitization and the use of artificial intelligence and extended reality will reshape the fashion industry after COVID-19. *ZoneModa Journal*, 10(2), 61–73.

Sima, V., Gheorghe, I. G., Subić, J., & Nancu, D. (2020). Influences of the industry 4.0 revolution on the human capital development and consumer behavior: A systematic review. *Sustainability (Basel)*, 12(10), 4035. DOI: 10.3390/su12104035

Simmons, W. K., Martin, A., & Barsalou, L. W. (2005). Pictures of Appetizing Foods Activate Gustatory Cortices for Taste and Reward. *Cerebral Cortex (New York, N.Y.)*, 15(10), 1602–1608. DOI: 10.1093/cercor/bhi038 PMID: 15703257

Singapore. (2010). *National nutrition survey*. Singapore: Health Promotion Board of Singapore Smart Nation and Digital Government Office. (2018). *Smart nation: The way forward executive summary 1. What is smart nation? A smart nation is a Singapore where people will be mor*. Smart Nation Singapore. https://www.smartnation.gov.sg/files/publications/smart-nation-strategy-nov2018.pdf

Singh, D., & Tilak, G. (2020). Implementation of education model 4.0: Developing industrial 4.0 skills in graduates engineers for improving employability skills. *Humanities & Social Science Reviews*, 8(2), 601–613. DOI: 10.18510/hssr.2020.8268

Singh, H. L., Khaturia, S., & Chahar, M. (2021). Energy efficiency. In *Introduction to AI Techniques for Renewable Energy System* (pp. 185–200). CRC Press. DOI: 10.1201/9781003104445-12

Singh, R., & Rosengren, S. (2020). Why do online grocery shoppers switch? An empirical investigation of drivers of switching in online grocery. *Journal of Retailing and Consumer Services*, 53, 101962. DOI: 10.1016/j.jretconser.2019.101962

Singh, V., Archana, T., Singh, A., & Tyagi, P. K. (2024). Utilizing Technology for Food Waste Management in the Hospitality Industry Hotels and Restaurants. In *Sustainable Disposal Methods of Food Wastes in Hospitality Operations* (pp. 287–295). IGI Global. DOI: 10.4018/979-8-3693-2181-2.ch019

Singh, V., Realyvasquez, J., Simcox, T., Rozell, J. C., Schwarzkopf, R., & Davidovitch, R. I. (2021). Robotics versus navigation versus conventional total hip arthroplasty: Does the use of technology yield superior outcomes? *The Journal of Arthroplasty*, 36(8), 2801–2807. DOI: 10.1016/j.arth.2021.02.074 PMID: 33773864

Sin, L. (2022). Will you continue to use food delivery services during the transition to the endemic phase of the COVID-19 pandemic? *International Journal of Tourism and Hospitality in Asia Pacific*, 5(3), 26–37. DOI: 10.32535/ijthap.v5i3.1877

Si, R. (2021). *China livestreaming e-commerce industry insights*. Springer. DOI: 10.1007/978-981-16-5344-5

Skare, M., & Soriano, D. R. (2021). How globalization is changing digital technology adoption: An international perspective. *Journal of Innovation & Knowledge*, 6(4), 222–233. DOI: 10.1016/j.jik.2021.04.001

Slobodan, I., Luka, P., & Ivana, G. (2015). Impact of technological development on business efficiency in the food and beverage department. *UTMS Journal of Economics (Skopje)*, 6(2), 321–330.

Smith, A. N. (2018). The role of influencers in promoting food and beverage brands. *JMR, Journal of Marketing Research*, 55(3), 345–362. DOI: 10.1177/0022243717750083

Smith, A., & Anderson, M. (2018). *Social media use in 2018*. Pew Research Center.

Smith, K. T. (2011). Digital marketing strategies that Millennials find appealing, motivating, or just annoying. *Journal of Strategic Marketing*, 19(6), 489–499. DOI: 10.1080/0965254X.2011.581383

Smith, M. (2021). The power of live Q&A sessions for brands: Building trust and engagement. *Marketing Today*, 3(5), 67–72.

Smith, T., & Johnson, L. (2020). AI Integration in Restaurant Quality Management. *Journal of Food Service Technology*, 18(4), 531–544.

Sniderman, B., Mahto, M., & Cotteleer, M. J. (2016). *Industry 4.0 and manufacturing ecosystems* - Exploring the world of connected enterprises. Deloitte. https://www2.deloitte.com/content/dam/Deloitte/de/Documents/consumer[REMOVED HYPERLINK FIELD]industrial-products/Deloitte-Industry-4-0-and-manufacturing-ecosystems.pdf

Sobaih, A. E. E. (2023). Saudi Zero Food Waste Certification: A Novel Approach for FoodWaste Management in Saudi Arabia. *Agronomy (Basel)*, 13(6), 1654. DOI: 10.3390/agronomy13061654

Sobhani, Z., Ye, L., Tang, Y., Wu, L., Zhang, X., Naidu, R., & Fang, C. (2020). Microplastics generated when opening plastic packaging. *Scientific Reports*, 10(1), 4841. Advance online publication. DOI: 10.1038/s41598-020-61146-4 PMID: 32193409

Sobika, K. A., & Raj, S. V. (2021). A study on predicting customer willingness to order food online during COVID-19 pandemic using machine learning algorithms. 2021 4th International Conference on Computing and Communications Technologies (ICCCT), 27, 236–241. https://doi.org/DOI: 10.1109/ICCCT53315.2021.9711904

Sodano, M. (2020). *Do shopping lists help in saving time during online grocery shopping? A qualitative study among Italian consumers* (Doctoral dissertation).

Sohu.com. (2024). *2023 Guide to China's Social Media Platforms (WeChat, Jieyin, Xiaohongshu, Shutterstock, Meibiao, Weibo, B Station)*. https://www.sohu.com/a/682966128_121123886

Solnet, D., Baum, T., Robinson, R. N. S., & Lockstone-Binney, L. (2015). What about the workers? Roles and Skills for employees in hotels of the future. *Journal of Vacation Marketing*, •••, 1–15. DOI: 10.1177/1356766715617403

Solomon, M. R. (2018). *Consumer behavior: Buying, having, and being* (12th ed.). Pearson.

Song, S., Zhao, Y. C., Yao, X., Ba, Z., & Zhu, Q. (2021). Short video apps as a health information source: An investigation of affordances, user experience and users' intention to continue the use of TikTok. *Internet Research*, 31(6), 2120–2142. DOI: 10.1108/INTR-10-2020-0593

Soni, G., Hussain, S., & Kareem, S. (2022). Environment Friendly Practices Adopted in Hotels and their Impact on Customer Satisfaction: A Critical Review of the Literature and Research Implications for the Hospitality Industry. *Atna Journal of Tourism Studies*, 17(1), 115–142. DOI: 10.12727/ajts.27.5

Sousa, R. D., Bragança, L., da Silva, M. V., & Oliveira, R. S. (2024). Challenges and solutions for sustainable food systems: The potential of home hydroponics. *Sustainability (Basel)*, 16(2), 817. DOI: 10.3390/su16020817

Spanish government. (2022). Proyecto de Ley de prevención de las pérdidas y el desperdicio alimentario. https://www.mapa.gob.es/es/prensa/anteproyectoleydesperdicio_tcm30-620834.pdf

Spence, C. (2023). Robots in gastronomy: Psychological and financial considerations. *International Journal of Gastronomy and Food Science*, 32, 100707. Advance online publication. DOI: 10.1016/j.ijgfs.2023.100707

Spooren, N. (2021). Effects of sensory language on the experience of food. *2021 Master Scriptie Communicatie*. https://theses.ubn.ru.nl/server/api/core/bitstreams/41885a5e- 1bf5-4cdf-a7da-7ee355c5b0d5/ content value, cognitive value, and purchase intention. *Psychology & Marketing, 37*(8), 1031– 1056. https://doi.org/DOI: 10.1002/mar.21338

Spotts, H. E., Weinberger, M. G., Assaf, A. G., & Weinberger, M. F. (2022). The role of paid media, earned media, and sales promotions in driving marcom sales performance in consumer services. *Journal of Business Research*, 152, 387–397. DOI: 10.1016/j.jbusres.2022.07.047

Spyce. (2022). How Spyce reimagined fast food with robotics. *Spyce Company Profile.*

Stackla. (2019). Consumer content report: Influence in the digital age. *Stackla*. Retrieved from Stackla.

Stankov, U., Filimonau, V., & Slivar, I. (2018). Calm ICT design in hotels: A critical review of applications and implications. *International Journal of Hospitality Management*. Advance online publication. DOI: 10.1016/j.ijhm.2018.10.012

Stankov, U., & Gretzel, U. (2020). Tourism 4.0 technologies and tourist experiences: A human-centered design perspective. *Information Technology & Tourism*, 22(3), 477–488. DOI: 10.1007/s40558-020-00186-y

Starbucks. (2021). How Starbucks uses Instagram Stories for customer engagement. Retrieved from Starbucks Stories.

Starbucks. (2021). Starbucks' Instagram strategy: How to use user-generated content. *Starbucks Stories*. Retrieved from Starbucks.

Starbucks. (2021). The visual strategy behind Starbucks' Instagram. *Starbucks Stories*. Retrieved from Starbucks.

Statista. (n.d.). Online food delivery - Worldwide | Statista market forecast. https://www.statista.com/outlook/emo/online-food-delivery/worldwide

Steenmans, K., Taylor, P., & Steenmans, I. (2021). Blockchain technology for governance of plastic waste management: Where are we? *Social Sciences (Basel, Switzerland)*, 10(11), 434. DOI: 10.3390/socsci10110434

Steuer, J. (1992). Defining virtual reality: Dimensions determining telepresence. *Journal of Communication*, 42(4), 73–93. DOI: 10.1111/j.1460-2466.1992.tb00812.x

Stone, M., Desai, K. K., & McKinnon, A. C. (2020). Data-driven decision-making in the restaurant industry: An empirical study. *Journal of Hospitality and Tourism Management*, 43, 223–230. DOI: 10.1016/j.jhtm.2020.03.003

Strategies for Optimizing Self-Serve Kiosk Performance and Revenues. (2023, September 8). https://www.kioskmarketplace.com/resources/strategies-for-optimizing-self-serve-kiosk-performance-and-revenues/

Stuber, J. M., Lakerveld, J., Kievitsbosch, L. W., Mackenbach, J. D., & Beulens, J. W. J. (2022). Nudging customers towards healthier food and beverage purchases in a real-life online supermarket: A multi-arm randomized controlled trial. *BMC Medicine*, 20(1), 10. Advance online publication. DOI: 10.1186/s12916-021-02205-z PMID: 35034635

Styliaras, G. D. (2021). Augmented Reality in Food Promotion and Analysis: Review and Potentials. *Digital*, 1(4), 4. Advance online publication. DOI: 10.3390/digital1040016

Success Robotics, A. K. (2024). Robot Waiters in Restaurants to Discover in Malaysia. https://aksuccessrobotics.com.my/

Sudirjo, N. F., Ratnawati, N. R., Hadiyati, N. R., Sutaguna, N. I. N. T., & Yusuf, N. M. (2023). THE INFLUENCE OF ONLINE CUSTOMER REVIEWS AND E-SERVICE QUALITY ON BUYING DECISIONS IN ELECTRONIC COMMERCE. *Journal of Management and Creative Business*, 1(2), 156–181. DOI: 10.30640/jmcbus.v1i2.941

Suganda, U. K., & Oktavia, P. (n.d.). The Effect of Experiential Marketing and Service Quality on Customer Loyalty of Domino's Pizza in Cirebon City.

Suherlan, S., & Okombo, M. O. (2023). Technological Innovation in Marketing and its Effect on Consumer Behaviour. [TACIT]. *Technology and Society Perspectives*, 1(2), 94–103. DOI: 10.61100/tacit.v1i2.57

Sullivan, V. S., Smeltzer, M. E., Cox, G. R., & MacKenzie-Shalders, K. L. (2021). Consumer expectation and responses to environmental sustainability initiatives and their impact in foodservice operations: A systematic review. *Journal of Human Nutrition and Dietetics*, 34(6), 994–1013. DOI: 10.1111/jhn.12897 PMID: 34050994

Sultana, A., Billah, M. M., Ahmed, M. M., Aftab, R. S., Kaosar, M., & Uddin, M. S. (2024). Applications of IoT-Enabled Smart Model: A Model for Enhancing Food Service Operation in Developing Countries. [JAETS]. *Journal of Applied Engineering and Technological Science*, 5(2), 1123–1141. DOI: 10.37385/jaets.v5i2.4937

Sundar, S. S. (2020). Rise of the machines: Promises and perils of artificial intelligence. *Journal of Consumer Psychology*, 30(4), 742–760.

Sureeyatanapas, P., & Damapong, K. (2023). Performance assessment and comparison of online food delivery service providers based upon the aggregated perspectives of restaurant operators. *Expert Systems with Applications*, 236, 121262. DOI: 10.1016/j.eswa.2023.121262

Sutaguna, N. I. N. T. (2023). Hanan Catering's Instagram promotions, pricing, and menu variety influence consumer purchasing decisions in Bandung. *International Journal of Economics and Management Research*, 2(1), 76–87. DOI: 10.55606/ijemr.v2i1.67

Su, Y. (2022). Accurate Marketing Algorithm of Network Video Based on User Big Data Analysis. *Mathematical Problems in Engineering*, 2022(1), 3317234. DOI: 10.1155/2022/3317234

Su, Y., Ghaderi, H., & Dia, H. (2024). The role of traffic simulation in shaping effective and sustainable innovative urban delivery interventions. *EURO Journal on Transportation and Logistics*, 13, 100130. DOI: 10.1016/j.ejtl.2024.100130

Szocs, C., Kim, Y., Lim, M., Mera, C. A., & Biswas, D. (2023). The store of the future: Engaging customers through sensory elements, personalized atmospherics, and interpersonal interaction. *Journal of Retailing*, 99(4), 605–620. DOI: 10.1016/j.jretai.2023.11.005

Taherdoost, H. (2022). What are Different Research Approaches? Comprehensive Review of Qualitative, Quantitative, and Mixed Method Research, Their Applications, Types, and Limitations. *Journal of Management Science & Engineering Research*, 5(1), 53–63. DOI: 10.30564/jmser.v5i1.4538

Tallapally, S. (2021). Modern Restaurants Using QR Code with Android.

Tan, S. B. (2015). *Keeping Char Kway Teow cheap—At what price? "Hawker centres are a great social leveller in Singapore, a place where people.* Lee Kuan Yew School of Public Policy. https://lkyspp.nus.edu.sg/docs/default-source/case-studies/hawker-centre-case-study.pdf

Tan, T A. (2017, June 5). An Empirical Study to Evaluate the Impact of Demographic Variables to Complaint Behavior of Customers in a Dine-In Restaurant Industry. IGI Global, 4(2), 19-32. https://doi.org/DOI: 10.4018/IJAIE.2017070102

Tang, J., & Li, Q. (2023). Social media strategies for promoting traditional cuisines: A case study of Chinese food brands. *Journal of Foodservice Business Research*, 26(3), 255–270.

Tan, J., Tiwari, S., & Ramakrishna, S. (2021). Single-use plastics in the food services industry: Can it be sustainable? *Materials Circular Economy*, 3(1), 7. Advance online publication. DOI: 10.1007/s42824-021-00019-1

Tan, Z., Sadiq, B., Bashir, T., Mahmood, H., & Rasool, Y. (2022). Investigating the impact of green marketing components on purchase intention: The mediating role of brand image and brand trust. *Sustainability (Basel)*, 14(10), 5939. DOI: 10.3390/su14105939

Tarmazi, S., Ismail, W., Azmin, N., & Bakar, A. (2021). Consumer purchase intention toward online food delivery service: The implication for future research. [MJSSH]. *Malaysian Journal of Social Sciences and Humanities*, 6(9), 347–354. DOI: 10.47405/mjssh.v6i9.972

Tavakol, M., & Dennick, R. (2011). Making sense of Cronbach's alpha. *International Journal of Medical Education*, 2, 53–55. DOI: 10.5116/ijme.4dfb.8dfd PMID: 28029643

Tavill, G. (2020). Industry challenges and approaches to food waste. *Physiology & Behavior*, 223, 112993. DOI: 10.1016/j.physbeh.2020.112993 PMID: 32502525

Taylor, S., Colonna, A., Jung, J., Gutierrez, J., & Zhao, Y. (2024). Consumer perception and acceptance of edible packaging for various food products. *Journal of Food Science*, 89(4), 2423–2437. DOI: 10.1111/1750-3841.16992 PMID: 38433384

Tendur, S. T., Hutabarat, V. V., & Tumbelaka, S. S. (2021). Price perception, service quality and customer satisfaction (Empirical study on cafes at Tondano City). *International Journal of Tourism and Hospitality in Asia Pasific*, 4(3), 19–31. DOI: 10.32535/ijthap.v4i3.1196

Teoh, B. (2023). Intellectual capital and business model innovation: Boosting brand equity through SME food outlets' entrepreneurial efforts. *Journal of Advanced Research in Applied Sciences and Engineering Technology*, 34(2), 210–221. DOI: 10.37934/araset.34.2.210221

Teo, T. S. H., Srivastava, S. C., & Jiang, L. (2008). Trust and Electronic Government Success: An Empirical study. *Journal of Management Information Systems*, 25(3), 99–132. DOI: 10.2753/MIS0742-1222250303

Terefe, N. S. (2022). Recent developments in fermentation technology: toward the next revolution in food production. *Food engineering innovations across the food supply chain*, 89-106.

Tetrault, A., Nyback, M., Fagerström, L., & Vaartio-Rajalin, H. (2023). "A perfect storm" or missed care? Focus group interviews with dementia care professionals on Advance Care Planning. *BMC Geriatrics*, 23(1), 313. Advance online publication. DOI: 10.1186/s12877-023-04033-7 PMID: 37210508

Thakuria, T., & Baruah, L. D. (2023). Microplastic: Its effect on human health. *Asian Journal of Microbiology, Biotechnology & Environmental Sciences : AJMBES*, 25(04), 782–786. DOI: 10.53550/AJMBES.2023.v25i04.033

Thakur, R., Maiti, J., & Mukherjee, A. (2021). Virtual restaurants: The evolution of cloud kitchens in the hospitality industry. *International Journal of Hospitality Management*, 97, 102984. DOI: 10.1016/j.ijhm.2021.102984

The Sustainable Development Goals Report. (2024). United Nations publication issued by the Department of Economic and Social Affairs (DESA). New York.

The World Health Organization. (1946). Constitution of the World Health Organization. *American Journal of Public Health and the Nation's Health*, 36(11), 1315–1323. DOI: 10.2105/AJPH.36.11.1315 PMID: 18016450

Thirupathi, M., Kolur, V. B., & Sriram, V., KM, D. N., ShanmugaPriya, B., & Kala, P. S. (2022). *A Meta-Appraisal on UTAUT Model towards Accessibility and Adaptability of Digital Mobile Wallet Usage in India.* Paper presented at the 2022 International Conference on Innovative Computing, Intelligent Communication and Smart Electrical Systems (ICSES).

Thiruvengadam, M., Rajakumar, G., & Chung, I. M. (2018). Nanotechnology: current uses and future applications in the food industry. *3 Biotech, 8*, 1-13.

Thoene, M., Dzika, E., Gonkowski, S., & Wojtkiewicz, J. (2020). Bisphenol in food causes hormonal and obesogenic effects comparable to or worse than bisphenol A: A literature review. *Nutrients*, 12(2), 532. DOI: 10.3390/nu12020532 PMID: 32092919

Thoughtworks (2024), URL: https://www.thoughtworks.com/en-in/clients/mackmyra

Tian, F. (2016). An agri-food supply chain traceability system for China based on RFID & blockchain technology. *2016 13th International Conference on Service Systems and Service Management (ICSSSM)*, 1–6. DOI: 10.1109/ICSSSM.2016.7538424

Tian, J., Bryksa, B. C., & Yada, R. Y. (2016). Feeding the world into the future–food and nutrition security: The role of food science and technology. *Frontiers in Life Science*, 9(3), 155–166. DOI: 10.1080/21553769.2016.1174958

Tichoniuk, M., Biegańska, M., & Cierpiszewski, R. (2021). Intelligent Packaging: Sustainable food processing and engineering challenges. In *Sustainable food processing and engineering challenges* (pp. 279-313). Academic Press.

TikTok. (2020). *How TikTok drives food trends and engages audiences. TikTok for Business*. Retrieved from TikTok.

TikTok. (2020). *The #ChipotleLidFlip challenge: How Chipotle engages with TikTok's Gen Z audience*. Retrieved from TikTok Business.

Tipmontian, J., Alcover, J. C., & Rajmohan, M. (2020, January). Impact of blockchain adoption for safe food supply chain management through system dynamics approach from management perspectives in Thailand. In *Proceedings* (Vol. 39, No. 1, p. 14). MDPI.

Toha, M., & Supriyanto, S. (2023). Factors Influencing the Consumer Research Process: Market Target, Purchasing Behavior and Market Demand (Literature Review of Consumer Behavior). *Danadyaksa: Post Modern Economy Journal*, 1(1), 1–17. DOI: 10.69965/danadyaksa.v1i1.5

Torkayesh, A. E., Rajaeifar, M. A., Rostom, M., Malmir, B., Yazdani, M., Suh, S., & Heidrich, O. (2022). Integrating life cycle assessment and multi criteria decision making for sustainable waste management: Key issues and recommendations for future studies. *Renewable & Sustainable Energy Reviews*, 168, 112819. DOI: 10.1016/j.rser.2022.112819

Torrico, D. D., Han, Y., Sharma, C., Fuentes, S., Viejo, C. G., & Dunshea, F. R. (2020). Effects of context and virtual reality environments on the wine tasting experience, acceptability, and emotional responses of consumers. *Foods*, 9(2), 191. Advance online publication. DOI: 10.3390/foods9020191 PMID: 32075018

Tourism Malaysia. (2018). *Annual Report 2018*. www.tourism.gov.my/

Toussaint, B., Barbara, R., Angers-Loustau, A., Gilliland, D., Kestens, V., Petrillo, M., & Eede, G. (2019). Review of micro- and nanoplastic contamination in the food chain. *Food Additives & Contaminants. Part A, Chemistry, Analysis, Control, Exposure & Risk Assessment*, 36(5), 639–673. DOI: 10.1080/19440049.2019.1583381 PMID: 30985273

Tracey, R., Hoang, L., Subelet, F., & Elisseev, V. (2020). AI-driven holistic approach to energy efficient HPC. In *High Performance Computing: ISC High Performance 2020 International Workshops, Frankfurt, Germany, June 21–25, 2020, Revised Selected Papers 35* (pp. 267-279). Springer International Publishing. DOI: 10.1007/978-3-030-59851-8_17

Treiblmaier, H. (2018). The impact of the blockchain on the supply chain: A theory-based research framework and a call for action. *Supply Chain Management*, 23(6), 545–559. DOI: 10.1108/SCM-01-2018-0029

Trivedi, J., & Jauhari, V. (2020). AI in the kitchen: Transforming the restaurant industry. *Journal of Hospitality and Tourism Technology*, 11(3), 349–363.

Truong, V. A., Lang, B., & Conroy, D. M. (2022). When food governance matters to consumer food choice: Consumer perception of and preference for food quality certifications. *Appetite*, 168(105688), 105688. DOI: 10.1016/j.appet.2021.105688 PMID: 34509543

Tseng, Y. F., & Wu, Y. (2020). The AI revolution in restaurants: A customer service perspective. *Journal of Hospitality and Tourism Technology*, 11(3), 336–348.

Tsou, H., & Hsu, H. (2017, January 1). Self-Service Technology Investment, Electronic Customer Relationship Management Practices, and Service Innovation Capability: An Extended Abstract. *Springer International Publishing*, 477-481, 477–481. Advance online publication. DOI: 10.1007/978-3-319-47331-4_92

Tuncer, A. D., Mavuş, R., Gökçe, C., Koşan, M., & Aktaş, M. (2019). Efficient energy systems models for sustainable food processing. *Turkish Journal of Agriculture-Food Science and Technology*, 7(8), 1138–1145. DOI: 10.24925/turjaf.v7i8.1138-1145.2439

Tung, V. W. S., & Au, N. (2018). Exploring customer experiences with robotics in hospitality. *International Journal of Contemporary Hospitality Management*, 30(7), 2680–2697. DOI: 10.1108/IJCHM-06-2017-0322

Tuomi, A., & Ascenção, M. P. (2023). Intelligent automation in hospitality: Exploring the relative automatability of frontline food service tasks. *Journal of Hospitality and Tourism Insights*, 6(1), 151–173. DOI: 10.1108/JHTI-07-2021-0175

Tuomi, A., & Tussyadiah, I. (2020). The transformative role of digital technology in hospitality and tourism: A review of current trends and research. *Journal of Hospitality and Tourism Technology*, 11(4), 643–663.

Tussyadiah, I., Wang, D., & Jia, C. (2016). Exploring the persuasive power of virtual reality imagery for destination marketing. *Tourism Management*, Retrieved from https://ira.lib.polyu.edu.hk/handle/10397/63584

Tuten, T. L. (2023). *Social media marketing*. Sage publications limited.

Tuten, T. L., & Solomon, M. R. (2018). *Social media marketing*. Sage Publications.

Udayalakshmi, C., & Sridevi, J. (2023). *Service Quality Models: A Review with Respect to Fast Food Restaurants*. BOHR International Journal of Social Sciences.

Uddin, S., & Karim, M. (2023). The role of social media in promoting food sustainability: A consumer perspective. *Journal of Sustainable Marketing*, 4(1), 45–59.

United Nations Environment Programme. (2021). Food Waste Index Report 2021. Nairobi.

Urdea, A.-M., Constantin, C. P., & Purcaru, I.-M. (2021). Implementing experiential marketing in the digital age for a more sustainable customer relationship. *Sustainability (Basel)*, 13(4), 1865. DOI: 10.3390/su13041865

Utami, H.N., Wiyono, S.N., Ishmah, H.A., & Hayuni, H.Z. (2024). Building Brand Awareness Through Product Quality and Social Media Marketing For Food Service Business Development. Journal of Law and Sustainable Development.

Utami, A. F., Ekaputra, I. A., Japutra, A., & Van Doorn, S. (2022). The role of interactivity on customer engagement in mobile e-commerce applications. *International Journal of Market Research*, 64(2), 269–291. DOI: 10.1177/14707853211027483

Vakulenko, Y., Oghazi, P., & Hellström, D. (2019, July 26). Innovative framework for self-service kiosks: Integrating customer value knowledge. Elsevier BV, 4(4), 262-268. https://doi.org/DOI: 10.1016/j.jik.2019.06.001

Valdez, P. (2020). "Apple defect detection using deep learning based object detection for better post harvest handling," https://arxiv.org/abs/2005.06089

Valencia-Payan, C., Grass-Ramírez, J. F., Ramirez-Gonzalez, G., & Corrales, J. C. (2022). A Smart Contract for Coffee Transport and Storage With Data Validation. *IEEE Access : Practical Innovations, Open Solutions*, 10, 37857–37869. DOI: 10.1109/ACCESS.2022.3165087

Van Den Bogaert, L., & Geerts, D. (2020). User-Defined Mid-Air Haptic Sensations for Interacting with an AR Menu Environment. *Lecture Notes in Computer Science*, 12272, 25–32. DOI: 10.1007/978-3-030-58147-3_3

Van Doorn, J., & Verhoef, P. C. (2019). The impact of service delivery AI on frontline employee roles. *Journal of Service Research*, 22(4), 409–424.

Van Hoboken, J., & Fathaigh, R. Ó. (2021). Smartphone platforms as privacy regulators. *Computer Law & Security Report*, 41, 105557. DOI: 10.1016/j.clsr.2021.105557

Vandna, & Kumar, K. (2023). Understanding the challenges and opportunities for sustainable practices in online food delivery platforms. *International Journal of Advanced Research in Management and Social Sciences, 12*(12), 19-36. https://doi.org/DOI: 10.4236/ijarmss.44586.33695

Varese, E., Cesarani, M. C., Kabaja, B., Sołtysik, M., & Wojnarowska, M. (2024). Online food delivery habits and its environmental impact during the COVID-19 pandemic: An Italian and Polish study. *British Food Journal*, 126(1), 191–204. DOI: 10.1108/BFJ-12-2022-1120

Vasanthraj, A., Kaur, A., Potdar, V., & Agrawal, H. (2023). Kaur, V. Potdar and H. Agrawal, H. (2023) Industry 4.0 Adoption in Food Supply Chain to Improve Visibility and Operational Efficiency—A Content Analysis. *IEEE Access : Practical Innovations, Open Solutions*, 11, 7392273958. DOI: 10.1109/ACCESS.2023.3295780

Vasić, N., Kilibarda, M., & Kaurin, T. (2019). The influence of online shopping determinants on customer satisfaction in the Serbian market. *Journal of Theoretical and Applied Electronic Commerce Research*, 14(2), 70–89. DOI: 10.4067/S0718-18762019000200107

Vasquez, M., & Romero, P. (2023). Social media marketing in the food industry: A cross-cultural analysis. *Journal of International Consumer Marketing*, 35(2), 115–129.

Vazquez Melendez, E. I., Bergey, P., & Smith, B. (2024). Blockchain technology for supply chain provenance: Increasing supply chain efficiency and consumer trust. *Supply Chain Management*, 29(4), 706–730. DOI: 10.1108/SCM-08-2023-0383

Vecchio, P. D., Mele, G., Ndou, V., & Secundo, G. (2018). Creating value from social big data: Implications for smart tourism destinations. *Information Processing & Management*, 54(5), 847–860. DOI: 10.1016/j.ipm.2017.10.006

Vedantam, P., Kashyap, S., Sanil, P., Fathima, T., & Jha, V. (2021). *Food Magic: An Augmented Reality RestaurantApplication. 23*(9).

Venkatakrishnan, J., Alagiriswamy, R., & Parayitam, S. (2023). Web design and trust as moderators in the relationship between e-service quality, customer satisfaction and customer loyalty. *The TQM Journal*, 35(8), 2455–2484. DOI: 10.1108/TQM-10-2022-0298

Venkatesh, N., Morris, N., Davis, N., & Davis, N. (2003). User acceptance of information Technology: Toward a unified view. *Management Information Systems Quarterly*, 27(3), 425. DOI: 10.2307/30036540

Venkatesh, V., Thong, J., & Xu, X. (2016). Unified Theory of Acceptance and Use of Technology: A Synthesis and the Road ahead. *Journal of the Association for Information Systems*, 17(5), 328–376. DOI: 10.17705/1jais.00428

Verma, P., & Pant, M. K. (2021). The effect of price verification, product display, and assortment satisfaction upon overall satisfaction, online patronage intention, and customer loyalty. *Journal of Food Products Marketing*, 27(6), 291–318. DOI: 10.1080/10454446.2021.1994078

Vermesan, O., & Friess, P. (2013). Internet of Things: Converging Technologies for Smart Environments and Integrated Ecosystems. In *River Publishers Series in Communications* (1st ed.). Routledge., DOI: 10.1201/9781003338659

Vermesan, O., & Friess, P. (2014). *Internet of Things - From Research and Innovation to Market Deployment* (1st ed.). Routledge., DOI: 10.1201/9781003338628

Vernier, C., Loeillet, D., Thomopoulos, R., & Macombe, C. (2021). Adoption of ICTs in Agri-food logistics: Potential and limitations for supply chain sustainability. *Sustainability (Basel)*, 13(12), 6702. Advance online publication. DOI: 10.3390/su13126702

Verstraeten, J., Van Kerckhove, A., Lei, J., & Zhao, Y. (2020). *More Eggs in the Same Basket: How Shopping Online Reduces Variety Seeking in Purchases*. ACR North American Advances.

Verzijl, D., Rouwmaat, E., Dervojeda, K., Probst, L., & Frideres, L. (2015). Traceability across the Value Chain - Standards, processes and traceability. In *European Commission*. https://single-market[REMOVED HYPERLINK FIELD]economy.ec.europa.eu/system/files/2017-07/42-tvc-standards-processes-and-traceability_en_0.pdf

Vijayakumar, G., Rajkumar, M., Rajiv Chandar, N., Selvakumar, P., & Duraisamy, R. (2024). Muniyandi Rajkumar, Rajiv Chandar N, Selvakumar P and Ramesh Duraisamy, (2024). Environmentally friendly TDS removal from waste water by electrochemical ion exchange batch-type recirculation (EIR) technique. *Environmental Science. Water Research & Technology*, 10(4), 826–835. DOI: 10.1039/D3EW00793F

Vitsentzatou, E., Tsoulfas, G. T., & Mihiotis, A. N. (2022). The digital transformation of the marketing mix in the food and beverage service supply chain: A Grey DEMATEL approach. *Sustainability (Basel)*, 14(22), 15228. DOI: 10.3390/su142215228

Vlachos, P. A., Theotokis, A., Pramatari, K., & Vrechopoulos, A. (2010). Consumer-retailer emotional attachment: Some antecedents and the moderating role of attachment anxiety. *European Journal of Marketing*, 44(9/10), 1478–1499. DOI: 10.1108/03090561011062934

Voigt, P., & Von dem Bussche, A. (2017). *The EU General Data Protection Regulation (GDPR): A practical guide*. Springer International Publishing. DOI: 10.1007/978-3-319-57959-7

Voipio, V., Vilko, J., Elfvengren, K., & Korpela, J. (2023). The future of work: Skills and knowledge perspective on service automation in the foodservice industry. *Technology Analysis and Strategic Management*, •••, 1–15. DOI: 10.1080/09537325.2023.2165440

Wagner, L., Pinto, C., & Amorim, P. (2021). On the value of subscription models for online grocery retail. *European Journal of Operational Research*, 294(3), 874–894. DOI: 10.1016/j.ejor.2020.05.011

Wahl, C. (2019). Uber eats the world. *New Labor Forum*, 28(2), 87–90. DOI: 10.1177/1095796019836750

Walczuch, R., Lemmink, J., & Streukens, S. (2007). The effect of service employees' technology readiness on technology acceptance. *Information & Management*, 44(2), 206–215. DOI: 10.1016/j.im.2006.12.005

Walker, T., McGuinty, E., Charlebois, S., & Music, J. (2021). Single-use plastic packaging in the Canadian food industry: Consumer behaviour and perceptions. *Humanities & Social Sciences Communications*, 8(1), 80. Advance online publication. DOI: 10.1057/s41599-021-00747-4

Wamba, S. F., Gunasekaran, A., Akter, S., Ren, S. J. F., Dubey, R., & Childe, S. J. (2017). Big data analytics and firm performance: Effects of dynamic capabilities. *Journal of Business Research*, 70, 356–365. DOI: 10.1016/j.jbusres.2016.08.009

Wang, P., Mi, X., Liao, X., Wang, X., Yuan, K., Qian, F., & Beyah, R. (2018, January 1). Game of Missuggestions: Semantic Analysis of Search-Autocomplete Manipulations. https://doi.org/DOI: 10.14722/ndss.2018.23036

Wang, B., Shen, C., Cai, Y., Dai, L., Gai, S., & Liu, D. (2023). Consumer culture in traditional food market: The influence of Chinese consumers to the cultural construction of Chinese barbecue. *Food Control*, 143, 109311. DOI: 10.1016/j.foodcont.2022.109311

Wang, C., & Zhang, H. (2020). Customer satisfaction with AI in restaurant service: A qualitative analysis. *Journal of Hospitality and Tourism Insights*, 3(4), 387–402.

Wang, E., An, N., Gao, Z., Kiprop, E., & Geng, X. (2020). Consumer food stockpiling behavior and willingness to pay for food reserves in COVID-19. *Food Security*, 12(4), 739–747. DOI: 10.1007/s12571-020-01092-1 PMID: 32837661

Wang, H., & Chen, X. (2023). Social media and consumer trust in food brands: An exploratory study. *The Journal of Consumer Affairs*, 57(1), 39–54.

Wang, H., Lan, Y., Kong, F., & Weng, L. (2020). Fresh agricultural products cold chain location selection in context of big data. *Journal of Physics: Conference Series*, 1631(1), 012122. Advance online publication. DOI: 10.1088/1742-6596/1631/1/012122

Wang, Q., & Li, Z. (2021). Improving Food Safety with AI and ML Technologies. *Journal of Restaurant Management*, 27(1), 92–104.

Wang, X. V., & Wang, L. (2021). A literature survey of the robotic technologies during the COVID-19 pandemic. *Journal of Manufacturing Systems*, 60, 823–836. DOI: 10.1016/j.jmsy.2021.02.005 PMID: 33612914

Wang, X., Li, X. R., Zhen, F., & Zhang, J. (2016). How smart is your tourist attraction?: Measuring tourist preferences of smart tourism attractions via a FCEM-AHP and IPA approach. *Tourism Management*, 54, 309–320. DOI: 10.1016/j.tourman.2015.12.003

Wang, Y., Xu, Y., & Li, X. (2020). AI and big data analytics in food supply chain management: A systematic literature review. *International Journal of Production Economics*, 218, 282–294. DOI: 10.1016/j.ijpe.2019.05.023

Wan, X., Wang, W., Liu, J., & Tong, T. (2014). Estimating the sample mean and standard deviation from the sample size, median, range and/or interquartile range. *BMC Medical Research Methodology*, 14(1), 135. Advance online publication. DOI: 10.1186/1471-2288-14-135 PMID: 25524443

Weaver, D. B., & Moyle, B. D. (2019). Tourist stupidity' as a basic characteristic of 'smart tourism': Challenges for destination planning and management. *Tourism Recreation Research*, 44(3), 387–391. DOI: 10.1080/02508281.2019.1637611

Weber, P., Ludwig, T., Brodesser, S., & Grönewald, L. (2021). "It's a Kind of Art!": Understanding Food Influencers as Influential Content Creators. *Proceedings of the 2021 CHI Conference on Human Factors in Computing Systems*, 1–14.

Webster, C., & Ivanov, S. (2020). Robotics, Artificial Intelligence, and the Evolving Nature of Work. In George, B., & Paul, J. (Eds.), *Digital Transformation in Business and Society*. Palgrave Macmillan., DOI: 10.1007/978-3-030-08277-2_8

Webster, K. T. (2023). *Handbook of price impact modeling*. Chapman and Hall/CRC. DOI: 10.1201/9781003316923

Weerasooriya, R. R., Liyanage, L. P. K., Rathnappriya, R. H. K., Bandara, W. B. M. A. C., Perera, T. A. N. T., Gunarathna, M. H. J. P., & Jayasinghe, G. Y. (2021). Industrial water conservation by water footprint and sustainable development goals: A review. *Environment, Development and Sustainability*, 23(9), 12661–12709. DOI: 10.1007/s10668-020-01184-0

Wei, W. (2023). Re-feminizing Beauty in the Multimodal Storytelling Practices of Chinese Social Media Influencers on Xiaohongshu (RED). *International Conference on Human-Computer Interaction*, 400–419. DOI: 10.1007/978-3-031-48044-7_29

Wei, W., Zhang, L., Rathjens, B., & McGinley, S. (2022). Electronic Consumer-to-Consumer Interaction (eCCI) Post a Service Failure: The Psychological Power of Need for Approval. *Journal of Hospitality & Tourism Research (Washington, D.C.)*. Advance online publication. DOI: 10.1177/10963480221141649

Wei, Y., & Simay, A. E. (2023). AI Adoption in the Chinese Food and Beverage Industry: An Exploratory Study. *FIRM Journal of Management Studies*, 8(2), 145–160. DOI: 10.33021/firm.v8i2.4412

Wen, J., Kozak, M., Yang, S., & Liu, F. (2021). COVID-19: Potential effects on Chinese citizens' lifestyle and travel. *Tourism Review*, 76(1), 74–87. DOI: 10.1108/TR-03-2020-0110

Werme, J., Van Der Sluis, S., Posthuma, D., & De Leeuw, C. A. (2022). An integrated framework for local genetic correlation analysis. *Nature Genetics*, 54(3), 274–282. DOI: 10.1038/s41588-022-01017-y PMID: 35288712

Williams, J., & Nguyen, M. (2024). The role of social media in promoting food safety awareness. *Food Control*, 148, 108872.

Winnberg, A., & Mårtensson, F. (2021). What does it take to make you stay? A study on customers' willingness to stay with the same grocery retailer while moving from offline to online.

Wirtz, B. W., Weyerer, J. C., & Geyer, C. (2018). Artificial intelligence and the public sector—Applications and challenges. *International Journal of Public Administration*, 42(7), 596–615. DOI: 10.1080/01900692.2018.1498103

Wirtz, J., Patterson, P., Kunz, W. H., Gruber, T., Lu, V. N., Paluch, S., & Martins, A. (2018). Brave new world: Service robots in the frontline. *Journal of Service Management*, 29(5), 907–931. DOI: 10.1108/JOSM-04-2018-0119

Wong, I. A., Huang, J., Lin, Z., & Jiao, H. (2022). Smart dining, smart restaurant, and smart service quality (SSQ). *International Journal of Contemporary Hospitality Management*, 34(6), 2272–2297. DOI: 10.1108/IJCHM-10-2021-1207

Wong, I. K. A., Huang, J., Lin, Z., & Jiao, H. (2022). Smart Dining, Smart Restaurant, and Smart Service Quality (SSQ). *International Journal of Hospitality Management*, 20(4), 982–997.

Wongprapinkul, B., & Vassanadumrongdee, S. (2022). A systems thinking approach towards reducing single-use plastics in Thailand's food delivery business: s*ustainability, 14*(15), 9173.

Wongsansukcharoen, J. (2022). Effect of community relationship management, relationship marketing orientation, customer engagement, and brand trust on brand loyalty: The case of a commercial bank in Thailand. *Journal ofRetailing and Consumer Services*, 64, 102826. DOI: 10.1016/j.jretconser.2021.102826

Woods, S. (2016). #Sponsored: The emergence of influencer marketing. *Thesis*. University of Tennessee. Retrieved from UTK Scholar.

Wu, S. (2023). Influencing factors of mobile shortvideo APP users' willingness to continue using. *Proceedings of the 2nd International Conference on Bigdata Blockchain and Economy Management, ICBBEM 2023, May 19–21, 2023, Hangzhou, China.*

Wulf, A. J., & Seizov, O. (2024). "Please understand we cannot provide further information": Evaluating content and transparency of GDPR-mandated AI disclosures. *AI & Society*, 39(1), 235–256. DOI: 10.1007/s00146-022-01424-z

Xiang, Z., Du, Q., Ma, Y., & Fan, W. (2017). A comparative analysis of major online review platforms: Implications for social media analytics in hospitality and tourism. *Tourism Management*, 58, 51–65. DOI: 10.1016/j.tourman.2016.10.001

Xie, J., Xu, Y., & Li, H. (2020). Environmental impact of express food delivery in China: The role of personal consumption choice. *Environment, Development and Sustainability*, 23(6), 8234–8251. DOI: 10.1007/s10668-020-00961-1 PMID: 32874127

Xing, Y., Li, M., & Liao, Y. (2022). Trust, price sensitivity and consumers' organic food purchasing behaviour in China. *Food Science and Technology (Campinas)*, 42, e42422. DOI: 10.1590/fst.42422

Xin, X., Wu, J., Huang, L., Shang, S., & Chen, P. (2022). Effect of multi-channel integration on customer purchase intention. *Journal of Computer Information Systems*, 62(5), 1036–1047. DOI: 10.1080/08874417.2021.1965052

XU, C. (2023). *The determinants of creator performance on creative content platforms: Evidence from Xiaohongshu and Bilibili.*

Xu, C., Park, J., & Lee, J. C. (2022). The effect of shopping channel (online vs offline) on consumer decision process and firm's marketing strategy. *Internet Research*, 32(3), 971–987. DOI: 10.1108/INTR-11-2020-0660

Xu, L., & Huang, J. (2023). Social media influence on consumer attitudes toward food packaging sustainability. *Journal of Environmental Psychology*, 86, 101848.

Xu, M., David, J. M., & Kim, S. H. (2018). The fourth industrial revolution: Opportunities and Challenges. *International Journal of Financial Research*, 9(2), 90–95. DOI: 10.5430/ijfr.v9n2p90

Xu, W. (2023). Bilibili video streaming platform: Community culture identity vs. commercial culture. In *Cases on Social Justice in China and Perspectives on Chinese Brands* (pp. 237–250). IGI Global. DOI: 10.4018/978-1-6684-4955-4.ch017

Xu, Y. (2014). Understanding CSR from the perspective of Chinese diners: The case of McDonald's. *International Journal of Contemporary Hospitality Management*, 26(6), 1002–1020. DOI: 10.1108/IJCHM-01-2013-0051

Yadav, S. (2020). AI in the hotel industry: Adoption and application of artificial intelligence in hotel industry. *Hospitality & Travel Connaisseur Magazine*, 30–32.

Yadav, S. J. (2024b). Voices From Within: Exploring Indian Perspectives on Sex Tourism. In *Examining Tourist Behaviors and Community Involvement in Destination Rejuvenation* (pp. 263–272). IGI Global. https://www.igi-global.com/chapter/voices-from-within/348915

Yadav, S. (2021). Millennial Employees-Role, Benefits and Retaining Strategies in Hotel Industry (p. 64). DOI: 10.6084/m9.figshare.13719949.v1

Yadav, S. J. (2024a). Analyzing the Influence of Sustainable Voluntourism on Community Development and Empowerment. In *Special Interest Trends for Sustainable Tourism* (pp. 152–165). IGI Global., https://www.igi-global.com/chapter/analyzing-the-influence-of-sustainable-voluntourism-on-community-development-and-empowerment/352362 DOI: 10.4018/979-8-3693-5903-7.ch009

Yaiprasert, C., & Hidayanto, A. N. (2024). AI-powered in the digital age: Ensemble innovation personalizes the food recommendations. *Journal of Open Innovation*, 10(2), 100261. DOI: 10.1016/j.joitmc.2024.100261

Yang, J., & Zhao, L. (2021). AI-enabled Tools for Real-time Quality Monitoring in Restaurants. *International Journal of Hospitality & Tourism Administration*, 17(4), 421–434.

Yang, L., Weng, T., & He, H. (2012). Online ordering systems and consumer acceptance - using box lunch order systems as a case study. *International Journal of Business and Management*, 7(18). Advance online publication. DOI: 10.5539/ijbm.v7n18p26

Yang, M., Lee, C., & Lee, H. (2020). Exploring the impact of AI-based personalized recommendations on customer decision-making in the quick-service restaurant industry. *Journal of Hospitality and Tourism Technology*, 11(4), 525–542. DOI: 10.1108/JHTT-01-2020-0005

Yang, Q., Hayat, N., Al Mamun, A., Makhbul, Z. K. M., & Zainol, N. R. (2022). Sustainable customer retention through social media marketing activities using hybrid SEM-neural network approach. *PLoS One*, 17(3), e0264899. DOI: 10.1371/journal.pone.0264899 PMID: 35245323

Yang, S., & Park, H. (2023). Social media marketing effectiveness in the dairy industry: A case study of consumer engagement. *Journal of Dairy Science*, 106(6), 3789–3802.

Yang, X., & Fang, Y. (2021). Application of artificial intelligence in personalized menu recommendations: An empirical study. *International Journal of Contemporary Hospitality Management*, 33(2), 724–741.

Yan, M. R., Hsieh, S., & Ricacho, N. (2022). Innovative food packaging, food quality and safety, and consumer perspectives. *Processes (Basel, Switzerland)*, 10(4), 747. DOI: 10.3390/pr10040747

Yaqi, Z., Lee, J.-Y., & Liu, S. (2021). Research on the Uses and Gratifications of Tiktok (Douyin short video). *International Journal of Contents*, 17(1), 37–53.

Yen, C. H., & Teng, H. Y. (2015). A holistic perspective on service robots: The role of human-robot interaction in hospitality. *International Journal of Hospitality Management*, 46, 131–142. DOI: 10.1016/j.ijhm.2014.09.002

Yıldız, B., & Savelsbergh, M. (2019). Providing high-quality solutions for the meal delivery routing problem. *Transportation Science*, 53(5), 1372–1388. DOI: 10.1287/trsc.2018.0887

Yim, M. Y. C., Chu, S. C., & Sauer, P. L. (2017). Is augmented reality technology an effective tool for e-commerce? An interactivity and vividness perspective. *Journal of Interactive Marketing, 39*, 89–103. https://doi.org/. intmar.2017.04.001DOI: 10.1016/j

Yoo, Y., & Kim, S. (2021). AI adoption in hospitality: A stakeholder perspective. *Journal of Hospitality and Tourism Technology*, 12(1), 36–54.

Youhasan, P., Chen, Y., Lyndon, M., & Henning, M. (2020). Development and validation of a measurement scale to assess nursing students' readiness for the flipped classroom in Sri Lanka. *Journal of Educational Evaluation for Health Professions*, pp. 17, 41. DOI: 10.3352/jeehp.2020.17.41

Yousefi, H., Su, H. M., Imani, S. M., Alkhaldi, K. M., Filipe, C. D., & Didar, T. F. (2019). Intelligent food packaging: A review of smart sensing technologies for monitoring food quality. *ACS Sensors*, 4(4), 808–821. DOI: 10.1021/acssensors.9b00440 PMID: 30864438

YouTube. (2021). *Food channels to follow for cooking inspiration. YouTube Creator Blog*. Retrieved from YouTube.

Yu, Y., & Sen, Z. (2023). Research on Immersive Dining Space Design Based on New Media Digital Technology. *Proceedings of the 2nd International Conference on Information, Control and Automation, ICICA 2022, December 2-4, 2022, Chongqing, China*. Proceedings of the 2nd International Conference on Information, Control and Automation, ICICA 2022, December 2-4, 2022, Chongqing, China, Chongqing, People's Republic of China. DOI: 10.4108/eai.2-12-2022.2327948

Yuan, Y., Xu, C., & Fang, F. (2022). Discussion on Stock Price Trend of Chinese Dairy Industry. *2022 7th International Conference on Social Sciences and Economic Development (ICSSED 2022)*, 886–889.

Yuan, Y.-H., & Wu, C. K. (2008). Relationships Among Experiential Marketing, Experiential Value, and Customer Satisfaction. *Journal of Hospitality & Tourism Research (Washington, D.C.)*, 32(3), 387–410. DOI: 10.1177/1096348008317392

Yuen, K. F., & Wang, X. (2022). AI-enabled customer service: Trends and challenges in the hospitality industry. *Tourism Management*, 88, 104399. DOI: 10.1016/j.tourman.2021.104399

Yung, R., Khoo-Lattimore, C., & Potter, L. E. (2020). Virtual reality and tourism marketing: Conceptualizing a framework on presence, emotion, and intention. *Current Issues in Tourism*, 24(11), 1505–1525. DOI: 10.1080/13683500.2020.1820454

Yu, Z., Jung, D., Park, S., Hu, Y., Huang, K., Rasco, B. A., Wang, S., Ronholm, J., Lu, X., & Chen, J. (2022). Smart traceability for food safety. *Critical Reviews in Food Science and Nutrition*, 62(4), 905–916. DOI: 10.1080/10408398.2020.1830262 PMID: 33030032

Zadeike, D., & Degutyte, R. (2023). Recent advances in acoustic technology in food processing. *Foods*, 12(18), 3365. DOI: 10.3390/foods12183365 PMID: 37761074

Zarifis, A., & Fu, S. (2023). Re-Evaluating trust and privacy concerns when purchasing a mobile app: Re-Calibrating for the increasing role of artificial intelligence. *Digital*, 3(4), 286–299. DOI: 10.3390/digital3040018

Zarrella, D. (2019). *The social media marketing book*. O'Reilly Media.

Zbucki, Ł. (2024). *Mechanical grinding of spices in grinders with polymeric burrs and transfer of microplastics to food*. Health Problems of Civilization., DOI: 10.5114/hpc.2024.135399

Zeng, L., Li, R. Y. M., Mao, Y., Chen, H., & Zeng, H. (2022). A comparative study on LinkedIn and Sina Weibo users' perceptions of the carbon-neutral city. *Frontiers in Environmental Science*, 10, 962367. DOI: 10.3389/fenvs.2022.962367

Zha, D., Foroudi, P., Jin, Z., & Melewar, T. C. (2022). Making sense of sensory brand experience: Constructing an integrative framework for future research. *International Journal of Management Reviews*, 24(1), 130–167. DOI: 10.1111/ijmr.12270

Zhang, A., Zhong, R. Y., Farooque, M., Kang, K., & Venkatesh, V. G. (2020). Blockchain-based life cycle assessment: An implementation framework and system architecture. *Resources, Conservation and Recycling*, 152, 104512. DOI: 10.1016/j.resconrec.2019.104512

Zhang, D., Yang, W., & Appelbaum, D. (2019). The challenges of implementing AI-based systems: Data quality and trust issues. *Journal of Information Systems*, 33(2), 95–112. DOI: 10.2308/isys-52336

Zhang, H., Gupta, S., Sun, W., & Zou, Y. (2020). How social-media-enabled co-creation between customers and the firm drives business value? The perspective of organizational learning and social Capital. *Information & Management*, 57(3), 103200. DOI: 10.1016/j.im.2019.103200

Zhang, J. Z., & Chang, C.-W. (2021). Consumer dynamics: Theories, methods, and emerging directions. *Journal of the Academy of Marketing Science*, 49(1), 166–196. DOI: 10.1007/s11747-020-00720-8

Zhang, J., Du, Q., Yang, Y., Zhang, J., Han, R., & Wang, J. (2023). Research progress and future trends of low temperature plasma application in food industry: A review. *Molecules (Basel, Switzerland)*, 28(12), 4714. DOI: 10.3390/molecules28124714 PMID: 37375267

Zhang, M., Hu, H., & Zhao, X. (2020). Developing product recall capability through supply chain quality management. *International Journal of Production Economics*, 229, 107795. DOI: 10.1016/j.ijpe.2020.107795

Zhang, S., Hu, Z., Li, X., & Ren, A. (2022). The impact of service principal (service robot vs. Human staff) on service quality: The mediating role of service principal attribute. *Journal of Hospitality and Tourism Management*, 52, 170–183. DOI: 10.1016/j.jhtm.2022.06.014

Zhang, S., Zhou, L., & Zhao, Y. (2020). How to Present Calorie Information on the Electronic Menu to Help People Order More Healthily. In Kurosu, M. (Ed.), *Human-Computer Interaction. Human Values and Quality of Life* (Vol. 12183, pp. 200–212). Springer International Publishing., DOI: 10.1007/978-3-030-49065-2_15

Zhang, W. (2024). Influence of Live Commerce on Consumer Purchase Intention: Based on Internet-famous Food Research. *International Journal of Global Economics and Management*, 3(2), 486–514. DOI: 10.62051/ijgem.v3n2.56

Zhang, W., Chen, Z., Huang, J., & Wan, X. (2019). The influence of placing orientation on searching for food in a virtual restaurant. *Food Quality and Preference*, 78, 103728. DOI: 10.1016/j.foodqual.2019.103728

Zhang, X., Jiang, L., & Zhao, J. (2020). Redesigning store layout to improve customer flow during peak hours. *Journal of Consumer Marketing*, 37(6), 641–651. DOI: 10.1108/JCM-12-2019-4185

Zhang, Y., Diao, X., Chen, K. Z., Robinson, S., & Fan, S. (2020). Impact of COVID-19 on China's macroeconomy and agri-food system–an economy-wide multiplier model analysis. *China Agricultural Economic Review*, 12(3), 387–407. DOI: 10.1108/CAER-04-2020-0063

Zhao, Y. D. (2020). Machine learning based identification of food desert effect in urbun development, Ph.D. thesis, Cleveland State University, Cleveland, OH, USA.

Zhao, H., Chang, J., Havlík, P., van Dijk, M., Valin, H., Janssens, C., Ma, L., Bai, Z., Herrero, M., Smith, P., & Obersteiner, M. (2021). China's future food demand and its implications for trade and environment. *Nature Sustainability*, 4(12), 1042–1051. DOI: 10.1038/s41893-021-00784-6

Zhao, J., Butt, R. S., Murad, M., Mirza, F., & Saleh Al-Faryan, M. A. (2022). Untying the influence of advertisements on consumers buying behavior and brand loyalty through brand awareness: The moderating role of perceived quality. *Frontiers in Psychology*, 12, 803348. DOI: 10.3389/fpsyg.2021.803348 PMID: 35153925

Zhao, J., & Lin, M. (2023). The impact of social media marketing on consumer purchase intentions in the food industry: A meta-analysis. *JMR, Journal of Marketing Research*, 60(3), 411–428.

Zhao, T., Feng, A., Jin, S., Shi, Y., Hou, B., & Yan, Y. (2020). Research progress on artificial intelligence human sensor. In Peng, Y., & Dong, X. (Eds.), *Proceedings of 2018 International Conference on Optoelectronics and Measurement* (Vol. 567, pp. 403-412). Springer. https://doi.org/DOI: 10.1007/978-981-13-8595-7_35

Zhao, X., Lu, L., & Han, Y. (2023). Impact of AI technologies on the performance of food service businesses: Evidence from Domino's Pizza. *Service Business*, 17(2), 265–287. DOI: 10.1007/s11628-023-00507-2

Zheng, C. (2023). Research on the flow experience and social influences of users of short online videos. A case study of DouYin. *Scientific Reports*, 13(1), 3312. DOI: 10.1038/s41598-023-30525-y PMID: 36849531

Zheng, M., Zhang, S., Zhang, Y., & Hu, B. (2021). Construct food safety traceability system for people's health under the Internet of Things and big data. *IEEE Access : Practical Innovations, Open Solutions*, 9, 70571–70583. DOI: 10.1109/ACCESS.2021.3078536

Zheng, Q., Chen, J., Zhang, R., & Wang, H. H. (2020). What factors affect Chinese consumers' online grocery shopping? Product attributes, e-vendor characteristics and consumer perceptions. *China Agricultural Economic Review*, 12(2), 193–213. DOI: 10.1108/CAER-09-2018-0201

Zheng, T., & Davis, M. A. (2021). AI in hospitality: Customer perceptions of AI-driven service interactions. *Journal of Hospitality and Tourism Insights*, 4(3), 261–279.

Zhong, R. Y., Xu, X., Klotz, E., & Newman, S. T. (2017). Intelligent manufacturing in the context of Industry 4.0: A review. *Engineering (Beijing)*, 3(5), 616–630. DOI: 10.1016/J.ENG.2017.05.015

Zhong, S., Wang, M., Zhu, Y., Chen, Z., & Huang, X. (2022). Urban expansion and the urban–rural income gap: Empirical evidence from China. *Cities (London, England)*, 129, 103831. DOI: 10.1016/j.cities.2022.103831

Zhou, Y., Shan, Y., Guan, D., Liang, X., Cai, Y., Liu, J., Xie, W., Xue, J., Ma, Z., & Yang, Z. (2020). Sharing tableware reduces waste generation, emissions and water consumption in China's takeaway packaging waste dilemma. *Nature Food*, 1(9), 552–561. DOI: 10.1038/s43016-020-00145-0 PMID: 37128017

Zhu, D. H. (2022). Effects of robot restaurants' food quality, service quality and high-tech atmosphere perception on customers' behavioral intentions. *Journal of Hospitality and Tourism Technology*, 13(4), 699–714. DOI: 10.1108/JHTT-01-2021-0022

Zickafoose, A., Lu, P., & Baker, M. (2022). Forecasting food innovations with a Delphi Study. *Foods*, 11(22), 3723. DOI: 10.3390/foods11223723 PMID: 36429315

Zong, S., Dowpiset, K., & Nuangjamnong, C. (2023). Understanding Payment Transaction Behavior of Social Media Users: An Empirical Study on WeChat. *The BSSS Conference*. DOI: 10.2139/ssrn.4433487

Zulham, Z. (2023). A Critical Review Of Indonesian Online Consumer Protection Online Shopping, False Advertising, And Legal Protection For Indonesian E-Commerce Customers. *Journal of Law and Sustainable Development*, 11(5), 1–15. DOI: 10.55908/sdgs.v11i5.740

About the Contributors

Anshul Garg is associated as a Senior Lecturer with the School of Hospitality, Tourism and Events at Taylor's University, Malaysia. He is a food and beverage expert, a well-recognized hospitality trainer in the region and a seasoned researcher. His research interests include self-service technologies in the hospitality and restaurant industry, service quality, service clues, hospitality service, hospitality education, human resource management, and food waste management. He is also skilled in MS Office, Quantitative Research, SPSS, AMOS, and Structural Equation Modeling. To date, he has authored 17 journal articles, nine book chapters and one book in various SCOPUS and Web of Science-indexed journals and highly recognised publishers (Emerald, CABI, IGI-Global). He also served as a plenary speaker and keynote at various international conferences and is an active editorial board member of various journals and is an international advisory board member for numerous international conferences.

***

Mohd Aliff Abdul Majid is a senior lecturer at the Faculty of Hotel and Tourism Management, Universiti Teknologi MARA, Malaysia. He completed his PhD in Foodservice Business Management from Universiti Putra Malaysia in 2019. He authored various publications in foodservice management, hospitality research and food security.

Radhika Arora is Associate Professor in Presidency Business School, Bangalore.

Kandappan Balasubramanian (Dr Kandy) is an Associate Professor from the School of Hospitality, Tourism and Events - Faculty of Social Sciences and Leisure Management (FSLM), Taylor's University, Malaysia who has embraced technology as part of his teaching and learning pedagogy and continuously empowers to innovate himself with the latest developments of technology in order to meet the changing needs of today's learners. He has taken the mandate and made it as personal aspiration on, striving to broaden his ability in the area of technology integration in the classroom. Dr Kandappan received the title of ADE (Apple Distinguished Educator), a global community of educators on leaders recognized for doing amazing things with Apple technology in and out of the classroom. His key roles as Cluster Leader of Teaching and Learning in the school also includes his contribution in various projects such as Education 4.0, MOOC, e-learning initiatives and student-centered learning. He also leads the Management Grand Prix, a management hospitality simulation competition organized for the Malaysian hoteliers in collaboration with Malaysian Association of Hotels (MAH). Dr. Kandappan won the EMAS (Exemplary Meritorious Academic Staff) award for his transformation of training restaurant from traditional to digital, Bronze medal in IUCEL 2018 & 2017, Silver medal in IIUCEL 2016 & NUCEL 2015 for his innovation in teaching and learning practices. Kandy shares his learning experiences through a series of training sessions for staff as a contribution to the overall development of the academic world. He has also presented and published research papers in International and National level conferences. He is also actively publishing his research and innovation in SSCI and SCOPUS-Indexed journals. His recent research projects at Taylor's university include service innovation, augmented and virtual reality, artificial intelligence (AI) in the hospitality/restaurant industry, and higher education. He also contributed to the university as a resource person, panelist, and moderators in International conference, panel discussion and forum. Last year he received "Best Paper Award" for his research towards the integration of augmented reality into dining space and "Gold Medal" for his teaching innovation in the International University E-Learning Carnival (IUCEL) 2019 in Sarawak, Malaysia. In recent years, he is getting recognized as trainer cum keynote speaker in the Philippines, Indonesia, India, and Malaysia for his current research in Industrial Revolution 4.0, Service innovation in Hospitality 4.0, and Teaching Innovation towards transformation in the education and industry sector.

Sumanta Bhattacharya from Salkia, Howrah, West Bengal is an Expert commissioner member IUCN Environmental, economics and social policy, Individual Policy Analyst (ADB) . He is among the top 2% world scientist (AD Index), Special civilian member Ministry of Defence, (USI) Member at Ministry of Culture (AS) . Member of Ministry of Defence { [Defence and strategic analysis] IDSA }, Member of World Economic Forum, littérateur at National Economic Research Bureau, Member of Ministry of Personnel, Pension and Public grievance (IIPA) He completed his B.Tech, M.Tech in Textile Technology along with that he has MA in Development studies, M.Sc in Environmental Science, LLB, MA in security and defence law from NALSAR, MA in Economics, MBA, Post Graduate Diploma in Environment and Sustainable Development, DIA&D, DS&DS, MPI(Oxford University) . Being a research scholar he has 216 research papers published in International and Scopus index journal, Wiley, Springer, Hindawi in various sectors like law, economic, Development studies, Textiles, Climate Change, SDGs, Public policy, Nanotechnology, Biotechnology, cancer, environment studies, 57 Book chapters published, Edited 2 books, wrote 1 book, 80 patents International and National, 4 copyrights, attended 93 International and National conference and presented papers and won 25 awards for his excellent in education, policy making and innovation which includes Best Water Management Solution Award 2022, Young Researcher Award 2020, Bravo International Book of Records, Mahatma Gandhi Ratna Award 2020, Sustainable Technology Award 2022, Global Change Maker Award 2020, Best Water Management Solution Award at the Rural & Urban Development Summit & Awards 2022, New Delhi, The Progress Global Awards 2023 for Excellence in Research, GIS -Person of the year – Water Conservation, Green India award, 2023, Global Legend Award 2023 by GSIL Educational Society . He is also a member of various International and National organization which includes IEI, IICHE, Asiatic Society, IIPA, IDSA, YOUNGO, IUCN, USI and many more .

Noelah Mae Borbon Currently, the research coordinator and tourism faculty at the National University, Philippines, Lipa Campus. Recently just passed the Licensed examination for Professional teachers and has been serving the academe for 12 years, formerly connected to the College of International Tourism and Hospitality Management and Graduate School of Lyceum of the Philippines University Batangas, and formerly the Deputy Director in the Center for Research and Innovation and Manager of International Research Journal in the same university. She also taught tourism courses and research at Batangas State University, Malvar, FAITH Colleges and at ManipalNxt University, Malaysia. The founder of CollabWritive Publishing House and founding president of United Tourism and Hospitality

Professionals and appointed as the National Coordinator for the Private Sector for the Network of Professional Researchers and Educators. She is also an Associate Editor in the Consortia Academia Group of Journals and International Scholars Society of Research Activities, Scientific and Technical Committee & Editorial Review Board Member in the World Academy of Science, Engineering, and Technology. She has published 10 books, and more than 50 research with 162 citations, an h-index of 6, and an i10-index of 3 based on the Google Scholar data. She have handled 40 Masters and PhD Students and more than 50 groups in the undergraduate program, which most of her advisee have already presented in national and international research conference and published their research in a refereed journal.

Venkatesh Ganapathy is a research scholar in School of Management, Presidency University, Bangalore.

Karthik K is an Assistant Professor Sr. Grade 1 in the Department of Analytics at the School of Computer Science and Engineering, Vellore Institute of Technology (VIT). He gained his doctoral degree from National Institute of Technology Karnataka, Surathkal under the supervision of Dr. Sowmya Kamath S. He has also worked as research fellow for a funded project titled "A Framework for Deep Learning based Analytics for Intelligent Healthcare Applications" by SERB, Department of Science and Technology, Govt. of India. His research interest includes computer vision, machine learning, deep learning, data mining and analytics. With a strong background in analytics, Dr. Karthik contributes to the advancement of the department through his expertise and dedication to teaching and research. As a valued member of the VIT faculty, he is committed to fostering a learning environment that promotes innovation and excellence in the field of computer science and engineering.

Sanjeev Kumar is Professor at School of Hotel Management and Tourism, Lovely Professional University, Phagwara

Afnan Mahusain is a dynamic and visionary lecturer at Taylor's University, specialising in Food & Beverage and Room Division for the School of Hospitality, Tourism, & Events. With a Master's in International Hospitality Management from the University of Birmingham and a PhD in Hospitality & Tourism, Afnan blends practical industry insights with theoretical expertise. His hands-on experience managing a 3-star hotel has honed his skills in cost cutting, budgeting, and strategic planning. His passion for leadership, career growth, human capital management, and innovative teaching strategies shines through his transformative contributions to hotel operations and academic endeavors. Afnan is dedicated to sculpting future leaders in hospitality, driven by creativity and a commitment to advancing hospitality education through innovation and excellence.

Pavitira Manogaran is a senior lecturer at Faculty of Hospitality, Tourism and Wellness, Universiti Malaysia Kelantan. She holds a Ph.D. in Business Information Technology and an MBA from Universiti Sains Malaysia. Her professional journey includes background in sales, marketing, client engagement, customer service and front office operations. Pavitira's research focuses on areas such as business information technology, smart cities, digital identities, tourism and hospitality, and sustainability practices, fields in which she is dedicated to fostering innovative, sustainable solutions. Her work is characterized by a vision to reshape the convergence of technology and business, driving intelligent growth across sectors.

Vishakini Manogaran is a Master's in Business Administration at the Graduate School of Business, Universiti Sains Malaysia, and is strongly committed to advancing ethical practices in accountancy, audit, and sustainability. Her research interests align seamlessly with her extensive experience in audit and tax roles at esteemed firms, where she honed her skills in audit planning, financial analysis, and regulatory compliance for PLCs, MNCs, and SMEs. Known for her expertise in risk assessment, report preparation, and mentoring, Vishakini is equally focused on sustainability within the financial and audit sectors, driven to foster responsible practices that uphold today's global standards. Her professional and academic pursuits reflect a clear dedication to impactful, forward-thinking contributions in her field.

Sree Kala Nair has more than 10 years of experience in the industry within the field of Human Resources Management, Marketing and Operations Management holding managerial positions. Likewise, her teaching career started as a Montessori kindergarten teacher and progressed up to PhD level, lecturing over a span of 19 years. While teaching in the Universities, she was involved in lecturing, doing research, training for public and private organizations, supervising students, presenting papers at conferences and moderating sessions at conferences. Dr.Sree Nair has a BA (Sociology) degree from University of Iowa, USA, a Masters Degree in Psychology from University Kebangsaan Malaysia and a Doctorate in Business Administration degree from University of South Australia, Australia. Dr. Sree Nair had carried out research in the areas pertaining to Sexual Harassment, Stress management, Attitude towards changes, Risk Management in Healthcare Industry, Risk Management in Hospitality Industry, Food Safety and Tourism and presented at various conferences and at seminars. She is also actively involved in various NGOs doing community and charity work especially among depressed individuals and underprivileged women to ensure humanity still strives forever and not forgotten and has been volunteering at Befrienders for 9 years. Recently, she pursued her 2nd Masters in Counseling and has been giving training in Stress management, Work Life Balance, Being Positive and Self Care.

P. Selvakumar is currently an Associate Professor in the Department of Science and Humanities at Nehru Institute of Technology, Coimbatore, Tamil Nadu, India. Since 2023, he has served as the Department IQAC Coordinator at the institute. Prior to joining Nehru Institute of Technology, Dr. Selvakumar held positions as an Assistant Professor in the Department of Science and Humanities at Info Institute of Engineering and Dr. N.G.P Institute of Technology, both located in Coimbatore, Tamil Nadu, India, spanning from 2011 to 2023. Dr. Selvakumar's academic and research interests lie primarily in the field of phytochemistry. He has made significant contributions to his field, with an impressive record that includes 30 journal publications, 12 patents, and 20 conference papers. Additionally, he has organized 5 seminars and conferences, further demonstrating his commitment to academic and scientific exchange. Throughout his career, Dr. Selvakumar has been recognized for his dedication and excellence in teaching, having been honored with several awards, including the Best Teacher Awards. He holds a prominent position in the academic community, contributing actively to research.

Senthilmurugan Paramasivam is Assistant professor and researcher working with Christ (Deemed to be Univeristy) as assistant professor.

Roop Raj is working as Associate Professor in Economics. Raj has done his 10th and 12th education from Jawahar Navodaya Vidyalaya Jhajjar, Haryana, after which he hasobtained BA Economics Hons, MA Economics, UGC-NET-JRF Economics, M.Phil Economics and PhD Economics degree. Raj has published 42 research papers in international journals, most of which have been published by foreign publishers like Springer, Elsevier, Wiley, Emerald etc. Most of the research papers are Scopus, web of Science, SCI indexed and UGC-Care listed. Raj has also registered 16 patents till now, out of which 6 are design patents and 10 are utility patents.

Mohammed Ruqaimi Bin Remeli is a lecturer at the Faculty of Hospitality, Tourism & Wellness, Universiti Malaysia Kelantan. With a Master in Gastronomy (2012) and a Bachelor of Science (Hons) in Culinary Arts Management with a Minor in Foodservice Management (2010), both from Universiti Teknologi MARA, he has a strong academic foundation in the culinary and food service fields. Currently pursuing a PhD with a focus on food safety, Mr. Ruqaimi is passionate about improving food safety practices through academic research and practical applications. As part of the academic staff, Mr. Ruqaimi teaches various courses, including Introduction to Hospitality Industry, Hospitality Product Development, Restaurant and Food Service Management, Food and Beverage Management, and Occupational Safety & Health. Additionally, he served as the Hospitality Program Coordinator in 2017, contributing to the administrative management of the program. Despite the challenges of balancing academic and professional responsibilities, Mr. Ruqaimi remains committed to advancing knowledge in the field and contributing to the education of future hospitality professionals.

Wella Gem Samonte A graduate of Bachelor of Science in Hotel and Restaurant Management with masters in Hospitality Management and a doctor of Philosophy in International Hospitality and Tourism Management. An Assistant Professor III in Aklan State University-Ibajay Campus, BSHM Program, Philippines. A research enthusiast and active in extension programs in the university. with specialization in event management, housekeeping, strategic and quality management with a heart for sustainability efforts. A regional Director for Western Visayas of United Tourism and Hospitality Professionals in the Philippines.

Azlina Samsudin is a dedicated academician at the Faculty of Hotel and Tourism Management, Universiti Teknologi MARA (UiTM) Terengganu, with over 10 years of teaching experience. She earned her Master's degree in Hospitality Management from Universiti Teknologi MARA Shah Alam, Selangor, in 2010. In 2023, she was appointed as the Program Coordinator in the Faculty of Hotel and Tourism Management at UiTM Terengganu. Her research interests span various aspects of hospitality management and food and beverage service. Azlina is committed to advancing the field of hospitality management through her research and academic contributions.

Pamarthi Styanarayana B.A., LL.M.,(CONSTITUTIONAL LAW), working as an Assistant Professor of Political Department of Law, School of Law, Vel Tech University since December 2021. She has done her Ph.D research on "Right to Privacy and Freedom of Press Contemporary Issues" in PG and Research Department of Law, Aachrya Nagarjuna University,Guntur, Andhra Pradesh, waiting for award. He has completed his Bachelor Degree (B.A LL.B,.) in Law (2013) and Master of Law (LL.M) in CONSTITUTIONAL LAW (2015) at Veeravalli College of Law, Rajahmandry under the affiliation of Andhra University. He has secured University 60%of marks in LL.M in his Post-Graduation (constitutional law).He has totally published 02 papers, all papers in International Journals (2 UGC approved Journals) he participated International conference participated has presented 5 in National / International conferences. He has attended 5 Faculty Development / Short Term Training Programs, 3 workshops and participated in 2 National / International conferences. His specialization in teaching is Constitutional law as well as special skills in Evidence act and in Indian Penal Code.

Manisha Saxena, an accomplished academic professional with over 15 years of teaching experience and currently serving as an Assistant Professor, School of Business and Management at Christ University, Bannerghatta Campus, Bengaluru, is a distinguished expert in organizational behavior, strategic HRM, and human resource development. Holding a Ph.D. in Business Administration from Aligarh Muslim University in the area of Human Resource Management and backed by a Master's in Business Administration, she has a proven track record in guiding project work, orchestrating outbound training activities, and leading impactful team-building initiatives. Driven by a commitment to scholarly contributions, she has published research papers in reputable journals, including the Jindal Journal of Business Research. Complemented by certifications in UGC-NET, PGDHRM from Symbiosis Institute of Business Management, and GNIIT from NIIT, her expertise is continually honed through participation in workshops, seminars, and webinars, showcasing an unwavering commitment to continuous learning and professional development.

Deepa Sharma has done Ph.D., MBA in Human Resource Management, currently working as Assistant Professor at MMIM, Maharishi Markandeshwar (Deemed to be University), NAAC Accredited Grade 'A++' University, Mullana, Ambala (Haryana). She has more than 7 years of experience in academics. She has written 45+ research papers for various Scopus and UGC listed referred National & International Journals. And has published two book chapters out of which 1 book chapter is published in Taylor & Francis and has earned 45 citations and an h-index of 4 credentials that may be verified on various research platforms like Google Scholar, SSRN, LinkedIn, and Research gate and 5 papers appear in the Scopus preview. She has actively participated in national and international conferences.

Vipin Singh is highly experienced professional with a Ph.D. in Hotel Management, a master's degree in Tourism. His academic journey, spanning over 12 years, reflects a strong commitment to both the hospitality industry and academia. Currently, I hold the esteemed position of Assistant Professor at Vellore Institute of Technology University in Vellore. He has published more than 20 research paper and 05 book chapters in reputed journals including scopus & emerald publication. My career is characterized by an unwavering dedication to education and the development of future hospitality professionals. I am enthusiastic about embracing learning opportunities and staying updated with industry trends and academic advancements. My core expertise revolves around training and education in the realm of Hospitality Academics, where I am deeply committed to fostering the growth and excellence of the next generation of professionals in the field.

Viji S. is a distinguished academic with a Ph.D. in Management from G.R. Damodaran Academy of Management, Coimbatore. With extensive teaching experience, Dr. Viji has made significant contributions to the field of management education, focusing on developing future leaders and professionals. She expertise spans various aspects of management, and they are committed to fostering a deep understanding of business principles and practices among their students. Dr. Viji's dedication to education and research has earned them a respected position in the academic community.

Chithambar Vankadari is Professor and Area Chair (Marketing) at Presidency University, Bangalore.

Shazia Waheed is a Research Scholar at School of Hotel Management and Tourism, Lovely Professional University, Phagwara Punjab.

Suraj Yadav is an accomplished professional with a background in Hospitality, holding a bachelor's degree from Pune University and a Master in Hotel Management & Tourism from Madurai Kamaraj University, Madurai. Currently serving as an Assistant Professor and Training & Placement Officer at D Y Patil School of Hospitality in Kolhapur, Maharashtra, India, he brings extensive expertise to the field. Suraj is also dedicated to furthering his academic pursuits and is actively pursuing a Ph.D. at D Y Patil Agricultural & Technical University in Kolhapur. His commitment to education and training has made a significant impact in the realm of hospitality.

Jia Yanan received her Bachelor's degree in Nursing from Heilongjiang University of Traditional Chinese Medicine, China in 2013 and her Master's degree in Tourism Administration from Nankai University, China in 2022, where she was awarded the university's outstanding thesis. She is now pursuing her Doctor of Philosophy (PhD) in Hospitality and Tourism at the School of Hospitality, Tourism and Events, Taylor's University, Malaysia. She has consistently focused on research related to the health of hotel consumers and tourists, with results published in reputable journals.

Index

A

B

C

D

E

F

G

T

U

V

Z

www.ingramcontent.com/pod-product-compliance
Lightning Source LLC
LaVergne TN
LVHW080406011026
849161LV00009B/2358
* 9 7 9 8 3 6 9 3 7 6 8 3 6 *